Graphis Inc. is committed to presenting exceptional work in international Design, Advertising, Illustration & Photography.

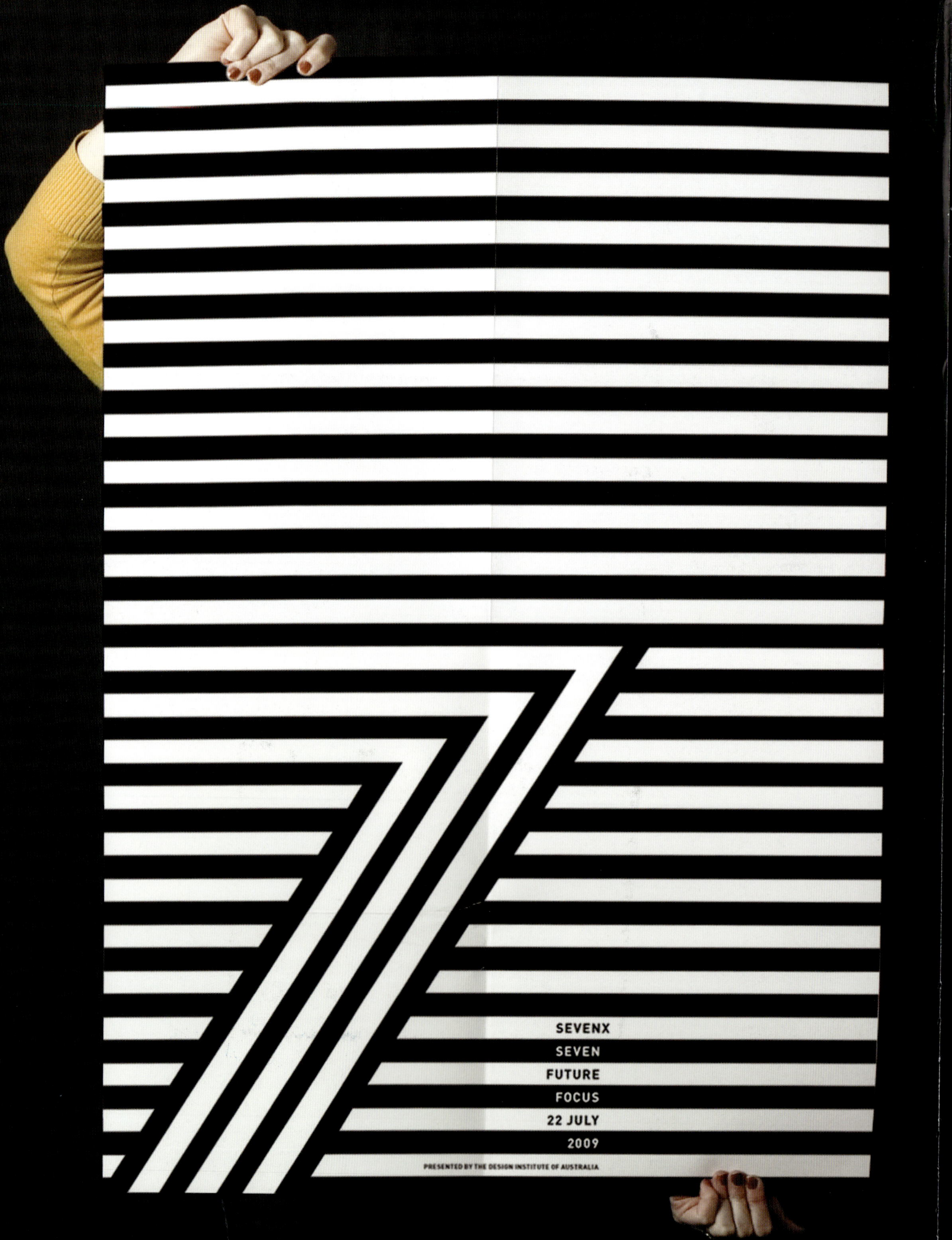
SEVENX
SEVEN
FUTURE
FOCUS
22 JULY
2009
PRESENTED BY THE DESIGN INSTITUTE OF AUSTRALIA

Published by Graphis | Publisher & Creative Director: B. Martin Pedersen | Designer: Jimin Nam | Editors: Annemarie McNamara & Roger DeGennaro | Production: Linh Truong | Executive Assistant: Sara Allen

Remarks: We extend our heartfelt thanks to contributors throughout the world who have made it possible to publish a wide and international spectrum of the best work in this field. Entry instructions for all Graphis Books may be requested from: Graphis Inc., 307 Fifth Avenue, Tenth Floor, New York, New York 10016, or visit our website at www.graphis.com.

Anmerkungen: Unser Dank gilt den Einsendern aus aller Welt, die es uns ermöglicht haben, ein breites, internationales. Spektrum der besten Arbeiten zu veröffentlichen. Teilnahmebedingungen für die Graphis-Bücher sind erhältlich bei: Graphis, Inc., 307 Fifth Avenue, Tenth Floor, New York, New York 10016. Besuchen Sie uns im, www.graphis.com.

Remerciements: Nous remercions les participants du monde entier qui ont rendu possible la publication de cet ouvrage offrant un panorama complet des meilleurs travaux. Les modalités d'inscription peuvent être obtenues auprès de: Graphis, Inc., 307 Fifth Avenue, Tenth Floor, NY, NY 10016. Rendez-nous visite sur notre site web: www.graphis.com.

 ISBN: 978-1-932026-78-8. Printed in China.

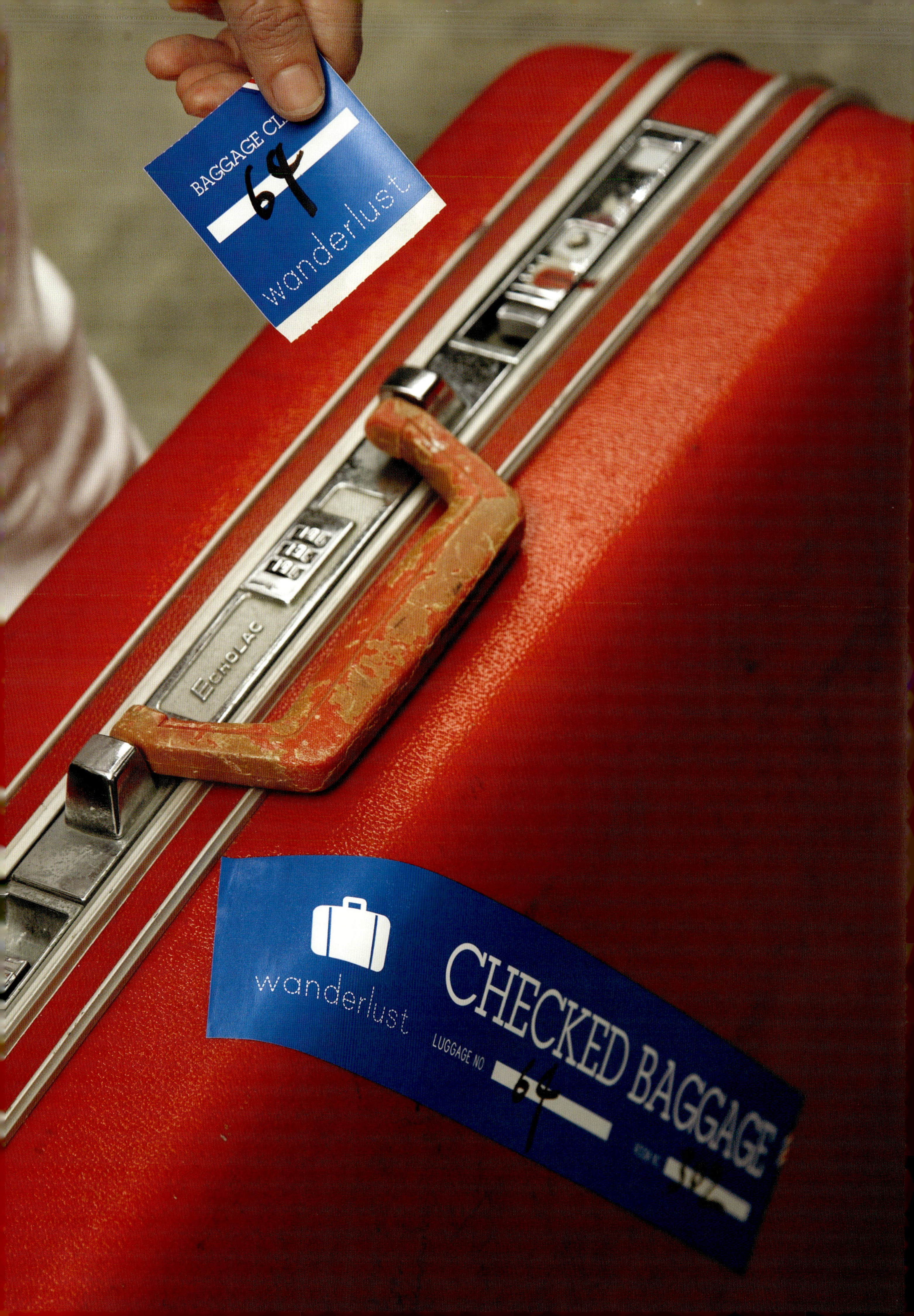
64
wanderlust
ECHOLAC
wanderlust
CHECKED BAGGAGE
LUGGAGE NO
64

Contents

The eight branding successes presented here are from a variety of international industries: a textile company, a wine producer, an ad agency, three eateries, and a literary venue, among others, emerged through the final selection.

DJ Stout and Stu Taylor, of Pentagram's Austin office, designed a promotional campaign for 2011's Texas Book Festival, which celebrated the newest books by some of the world's best authors while raising money for Texas libraries.

By combining traditional German elements and then flipping some on their head, WAX created a sophisticated yet playful identity that worked equally well for an upscale restaurant and a raucous beer hall located upstairs and downstairs in the same establishment.

After a long history in the commercial textiles industry, Guilford of Maine went through three ownership changes and three different market-facing names. Peopledesign developed a clear, new direction for the company that carved out a specific niche for the Guilford brand that eventually helped launch a newly refocused business.

An industry leader in organic practices for over twenty years, Bonterra wines was facing increased competition in the marketplace. Cue designed a roadshow, a new brand expression, and new packaging to help Bonterra receive the credit it has earned.

Firewood Inc. created a brand identity for their ad company that reflected the company's basic values of comfort and familiarity, while simultaneously invoking the spirit of creativity and innovation that makes Firewood stand out in the marketplace.

There are lessons here. Lessons of devoted commitment to the client, dedication to quality, and a continued focus on the project's financial success. B.Martin Pedersen

Previous spread: Seven X Seven by Landor Associates | *Opposite page:* Wunderlust Hotel Tag by Foreign Policy Design Group | *Following spread:* AIGA Design Journeys by TODA

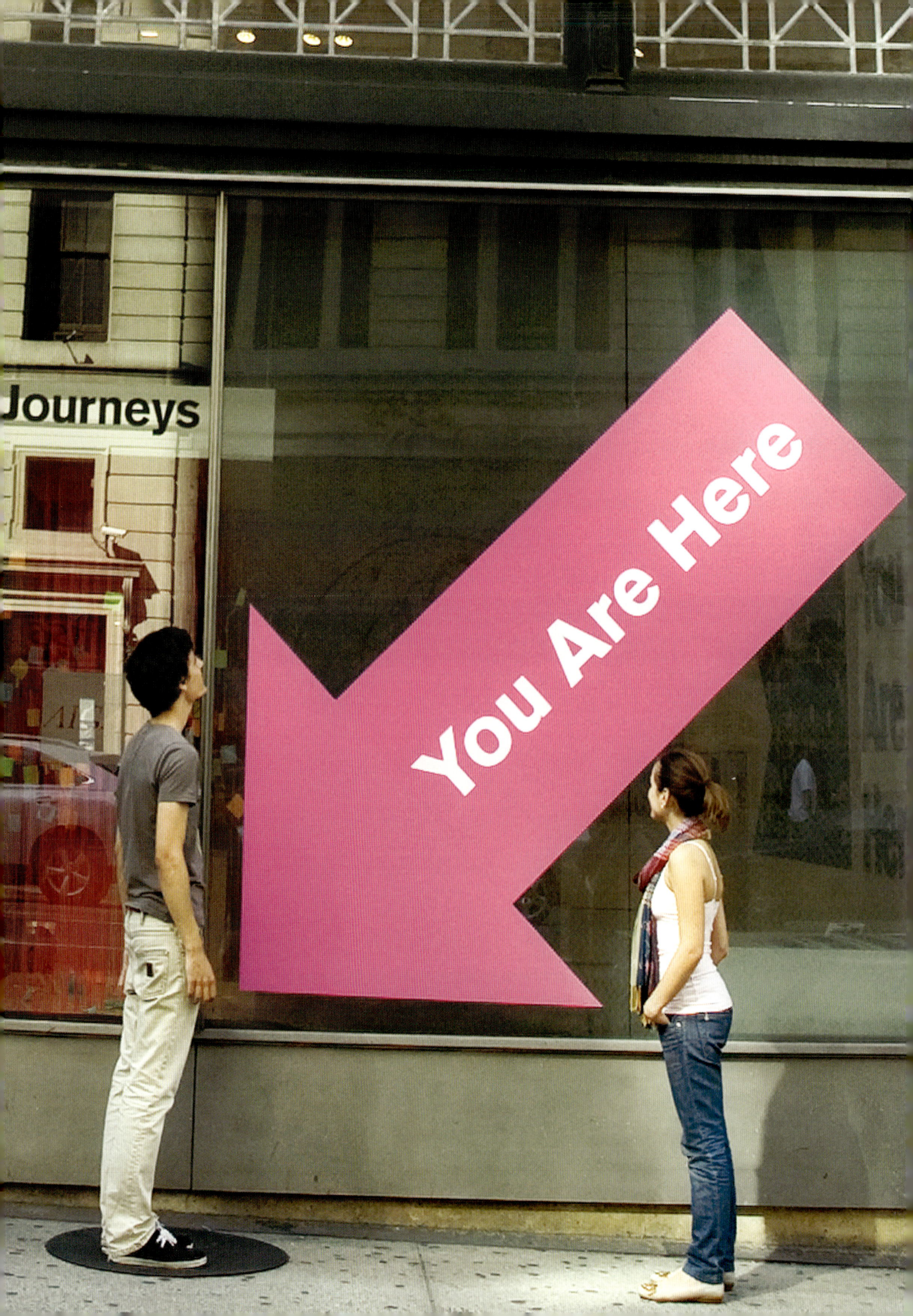
Journeys
You Are Here

GraphisPlatinum&GoldAwardWinners

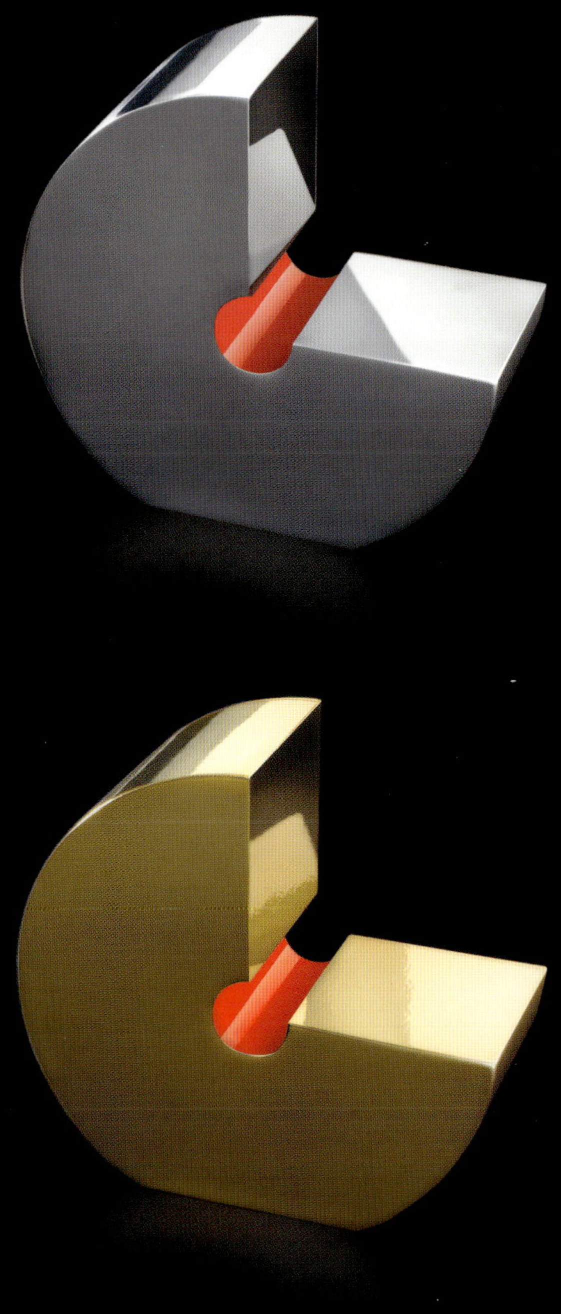

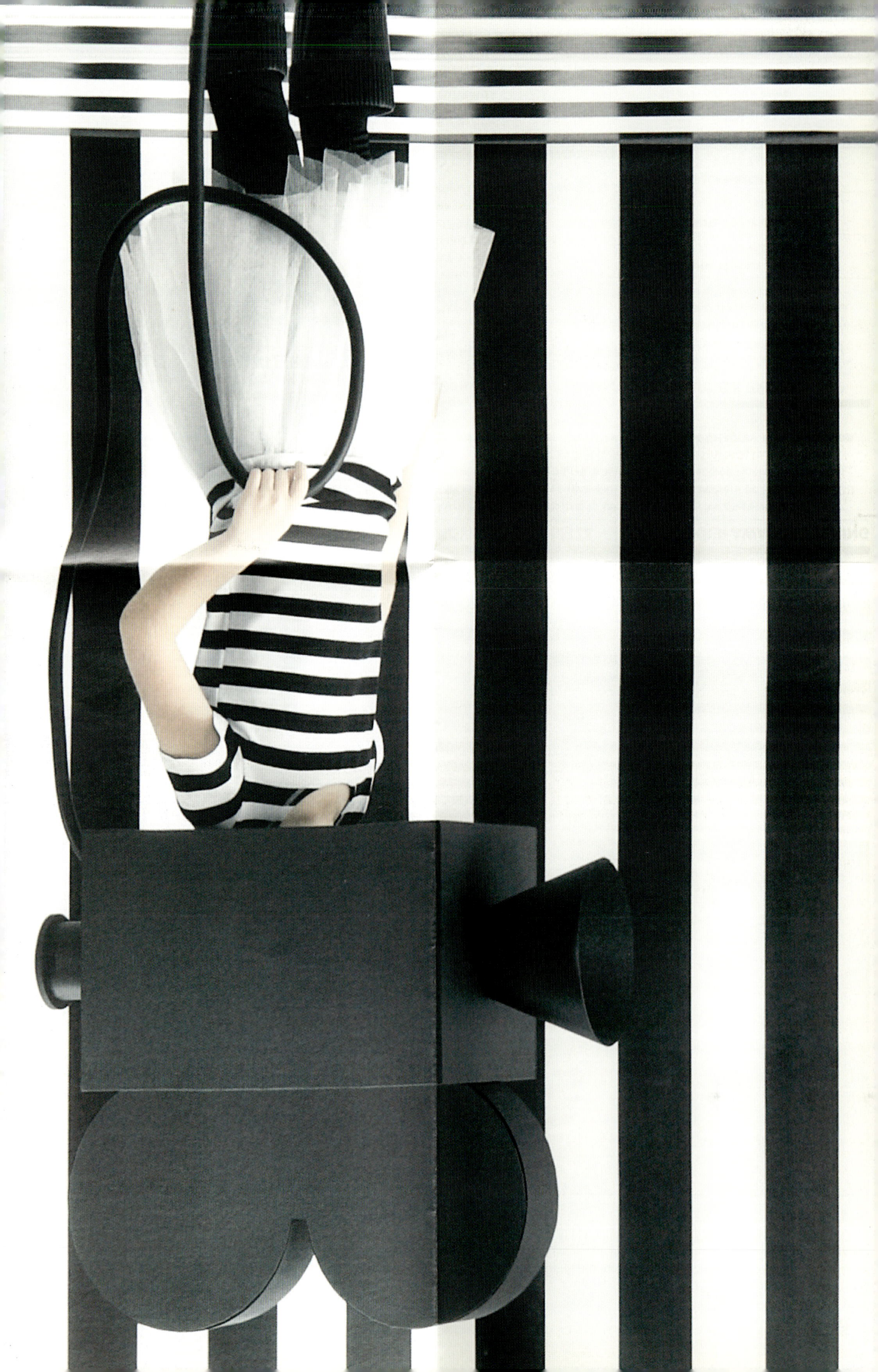

8 Branding Case Studies:

Opposite Page: Auckland Museum - I AM Campaign by Alt Group

Pentagram & Texas Book Festival

Partner DJ Stout and designer Stu Taylor in Pentagram's Austin office have designed a multi-faceted promotional campaign for 2011's Texas Book Festival. The 16th edition of the annual event celebrates the newest books by some of the best and brightest authors in the world, and raises money for Texas libraries. Founded by Laura Bush in 1995, the festival has featured literary luminaries like Frank McCourt, Robert Caro, Barack Obama, and R.L. Stine. 2011's festival featured over 200 authors, including Jim Lehrer, Molly Shannon, Chuck Palahniuk, and Susan Orlean.

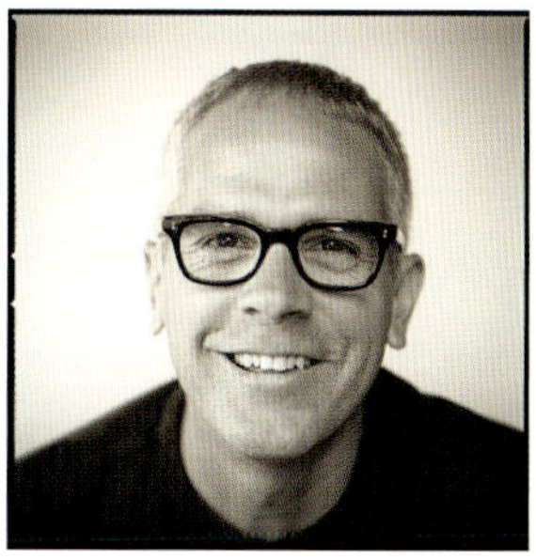

DJ Stout, Photo by Kenny Braun

Texas Book Festival 2011

BENEFITING LITERATURE, LIBRARIES, AND LITERACY

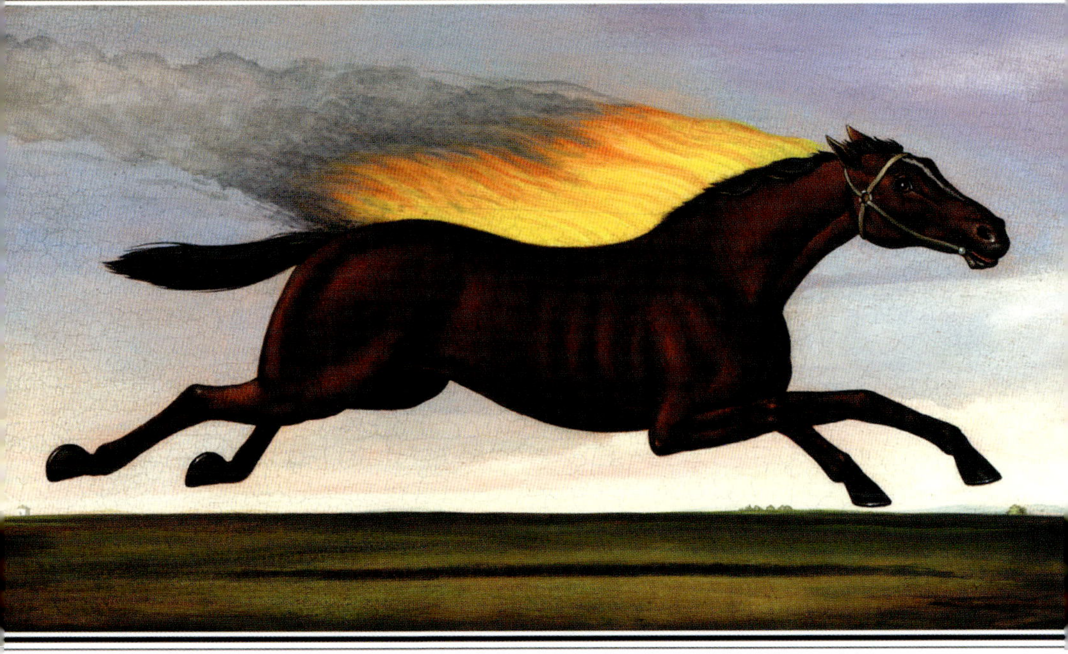

First Edition Literary Gala

FOUR SEASONS HOTEL IN AUSTIN, TEXAS

FRIDAY OCTOBER 21ST

Q&A with Pentagram

Pentagram Austin designed all the marketing and collateral materials for the Texas Book Festival back in 2001, which featured the work of fine art photographer Kate Breakey. For this year's edition of the literary festival, Taylor and Stout designed a consistent, branded campaign consisting of a variety of posters, advertising, multi-page newspaper inserts, banners, e-mail, t-shirts, and bookmarks featuring the work of illustrator extraordinaire Marc Burckhardt.

Stout, a longtime champion of illustration and illustrators, says this about the long overdue selection. "Over the years the book festival has featured painters, photographers, collagists, and other Texas-based fine artists, but never an illustrator. This has been a glaring oversight. Illustrators have been an integral part of books and bookmaking throughout the history of literature. N.C. Wyeth is one of my all-time favorite artists and his work was primarily created for books and book covers."

Burckhardt, who lives in Austin, has illustrated scores of books and book covers over the years, and his work is frequently published in magazines such as *Rolling Stone*, *Time*, *Texas Monthly*, and *The New York Times*. A recent children's book he illustrated, *When Bob Met Woody: The Story of the Young Bob Dylan,* was featured in the book festival. Burckhardt is also the recipient of the 2011 Hamilton King Award, a lifetime achievement award given by the Society of Illustrators. The Hamilton King Award is one of the highest honors that can be bestowed on an illustrator in his lifetime.

"After I proposed the idea of featuring Marc's work in the book festival's promotional materials, it dawned on me that the campaign should look very literary to complement his wonderful illustrations, like a classic set of book plates," says Stout. "Much of Marc's work is influenced by classical painting and historical art genres, and even includes the distinctive cracked paint of old oil paintings you find in museums." Taylor and Stout created the bookplate feeling with a restrained combination of white space, Scotch rules, and a beautiful roman typeface designed by Jonathan Hoefler. The white space and classic typographic styling make the promotional materials distinctive. The ads stand out amongst the overly colorful and frenetic advertising usually found in newspapers and magazines.

The primary image for the promotional materials features a painting Burckhardt made of a horse on fire running across a flat Texas landscape. The illustration of the burning horse references the devastating wildfires that destroyed thousands of acres, burned down hundreds of houses and miles of fencing, and killed scores of horses and cows out in the Marfa and Fort Davis area of West Texas last spring. Then another wildfire erupted in the heavily wooded area south of Austin in September that seriously threatened the city. "There was some concern that the painting of the burning horse was too relevant and too close to home, given the unforeseen events," says Stout. "But in my opinion the painting functions the way all great art does. It comments on current events in an emotional visual language, the way that the best illustrations in books have throughout time."

"It's the first time in the 16-year history of the Texas Book Festival that an illustrator has been the featured artist for the campaign, and Burckhardt was DJ Stout's choice."

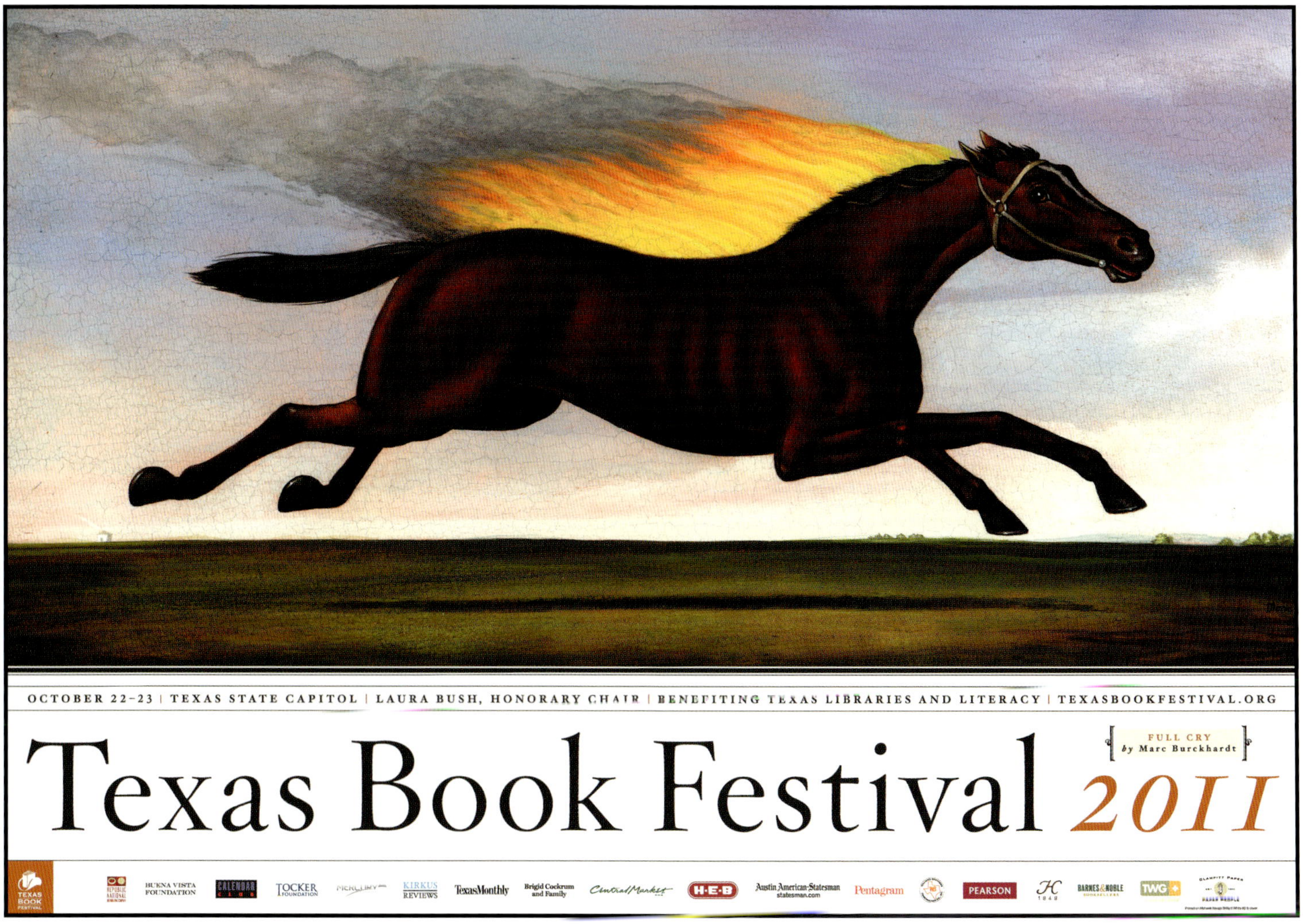

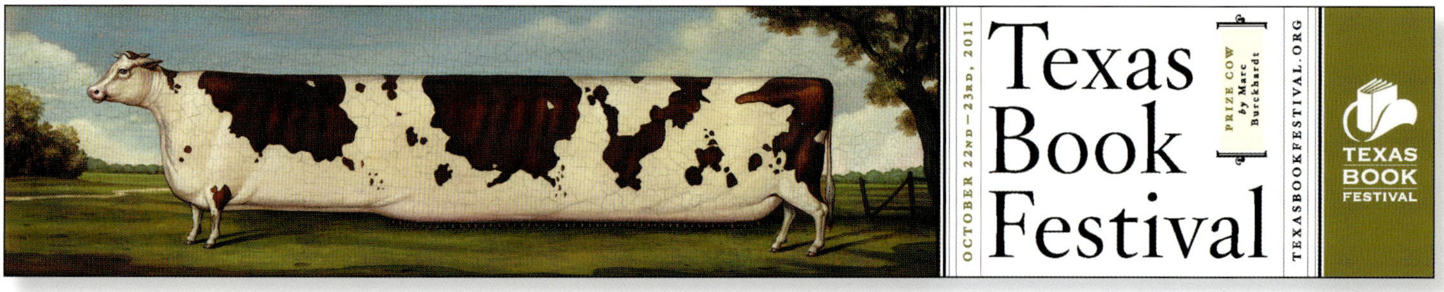

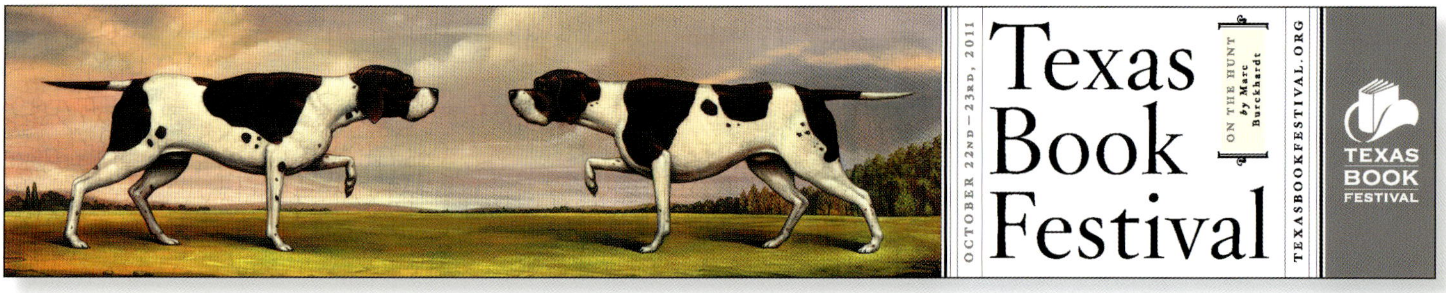

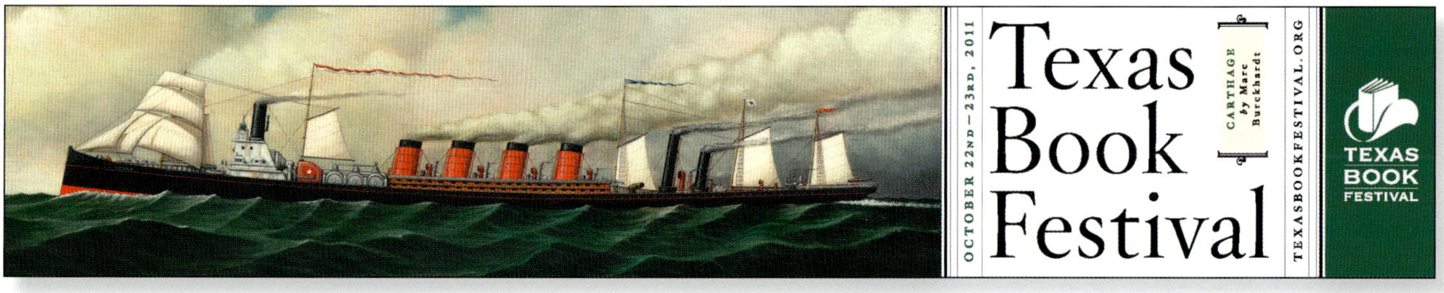

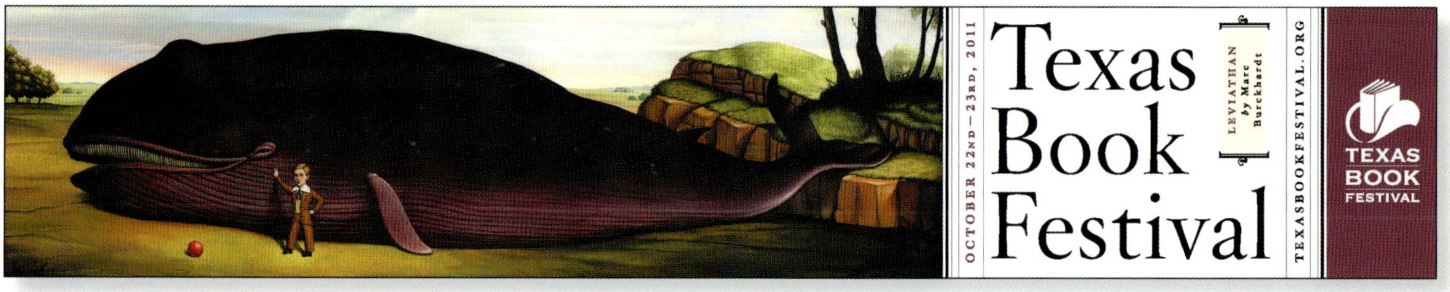

Designers: DJ Stout, Stu Taylor | **Design Firm:** Pentagram | **Art Director:** DJ Stout | **Illustrator:** Marc Burckhardt | **Client:** Texas Book Festival

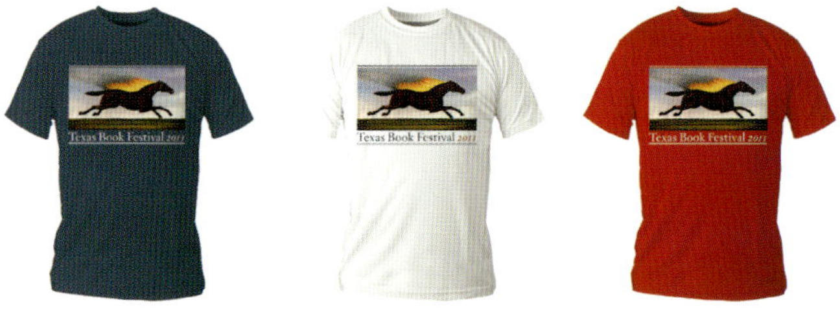

WAX & Wurst

When it came to branding Wurst, the initial challenge lay in creating an identity that worked for two unique spaces within the same establishment—an upscale restaurant upstairs and a raucous beer hall downstairs.

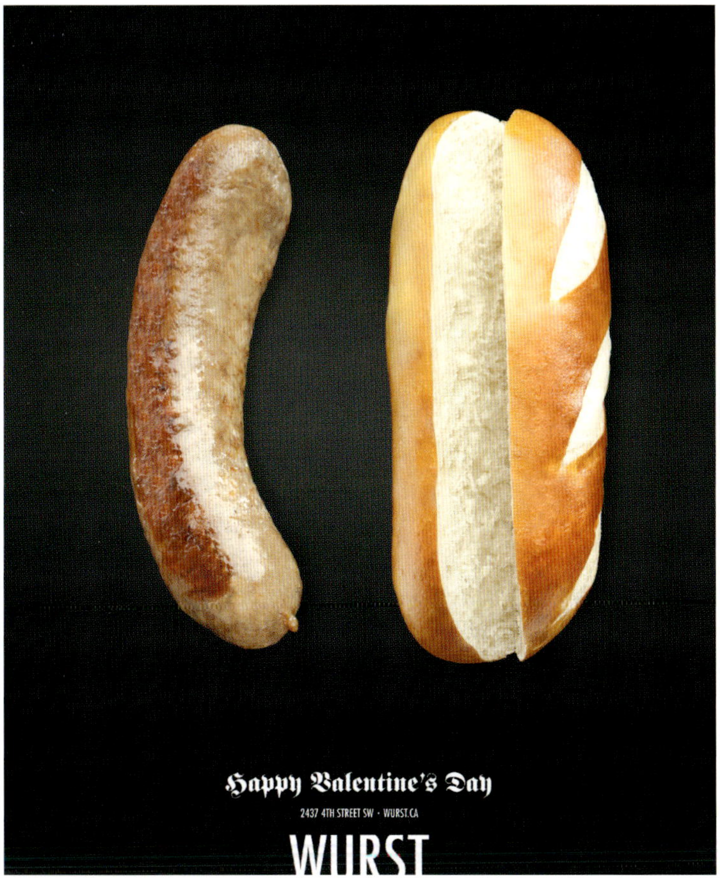

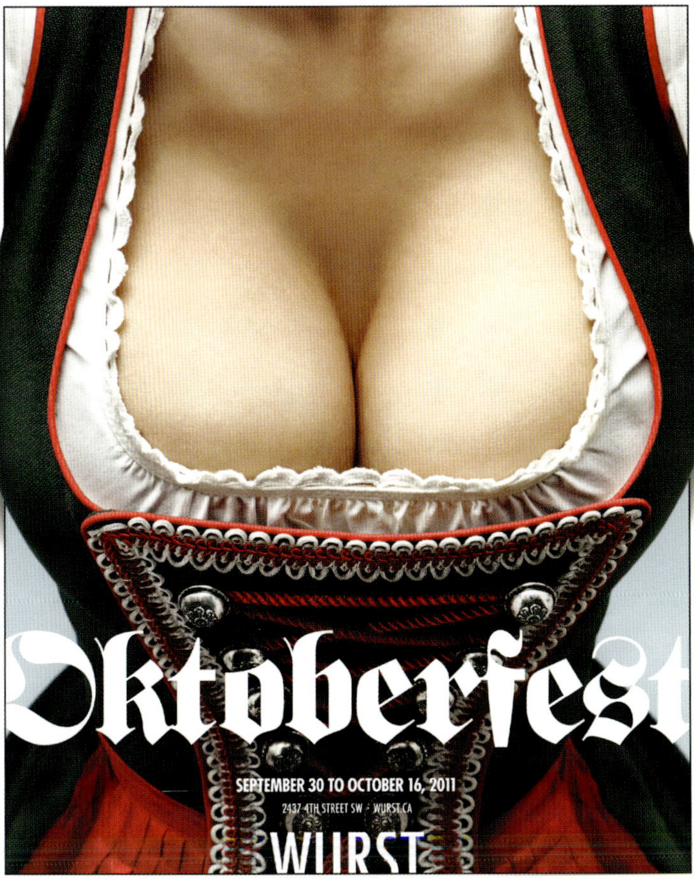

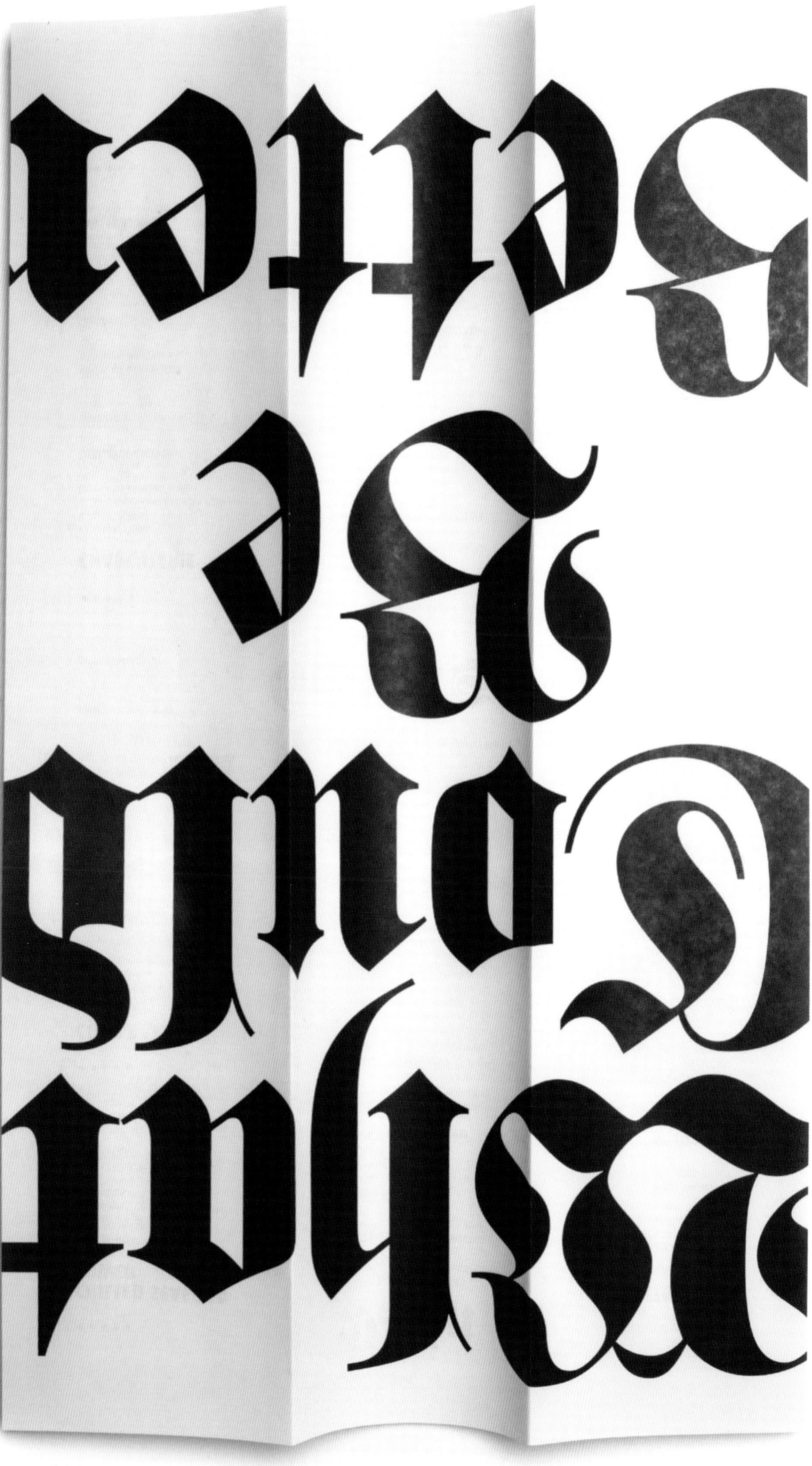

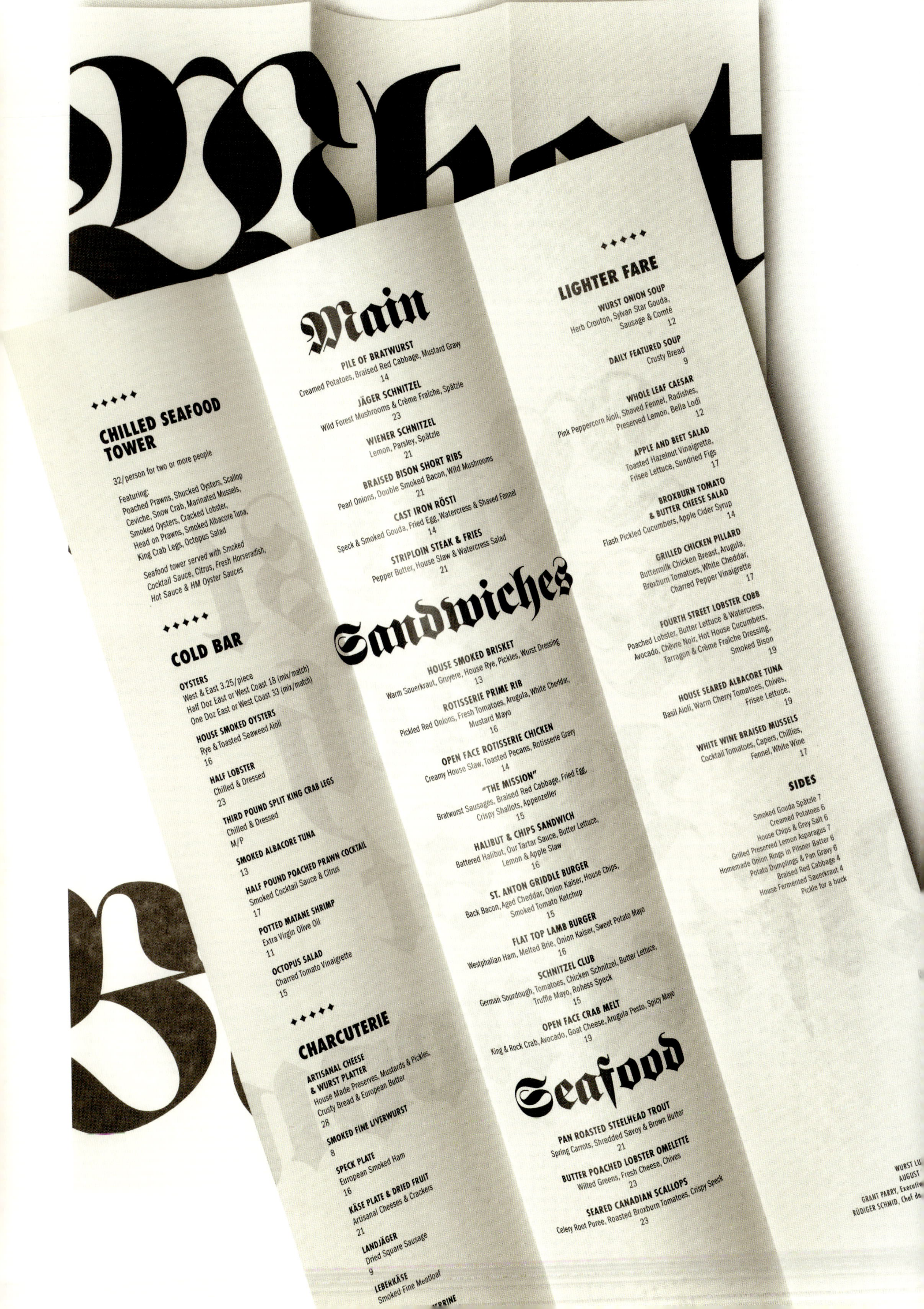
Main
PILE OF BRATWURST
Creamed Potatoes, Braised Red Cabbage, Mustard Gravy
14
JÄGER SCHNITZEL
Wild Forest Mushrooms & Crème Fraîche, Spätzle
23
WIENER SCHNITZEL
Lemon, Parsley, Spätzle
21
BRAISED BISON SHORT RIBS
Pearl Onions, Double Smoked Bacon, Wild Mushrooms
21
CAST IRON RÖSTI
Speck & Smoked Gouda, Fried Egg, Watercress & Shaved Fennel
14
STRIPLOIN STEAK & FRIES
Pepper Butter, House Slaw & Watercress Salad
21
CHILLED SEAFOOD TOWER
32/person for two or more people
Featuring:
Poached Prawns, Shucked Oysters, Scallop Ceviche, Snow Crab, Marinated Mussels, Smoked Oysters, Cracked Lobster, Head on Prawns, Smoked Albacore Tuna, King Crab Legs, Octopus Salad
Seafood tower served with Smoked Cocktail Sauce, Citrus, Fresh Horseradish, Hot Sauce & HM Oyster Sauces
COLD BAR
OYSTERS
West & East 3.25/piece
Half Doz East or West Coast 18 (mix/match)
One Doz East or West Coast 33 (mix/match)
HOUSE SMOKED OYSTERS
Rye & Toasted Seaweed Aioli
16
HALF LOBSTER
Chilled & Dressed
23
THIRD POUND SPLIT KING CRAB LEGS
Chilled & Dressed
M/P
SMOKED ALBACORE TUNA
13
HALF POUND POACHED PRAWN COCKTAIL
Smoked Cocktail Sauce & Citrus
17
POTTED MATANE SHRIMP
Extra Virgin Olive Oil
11
OCTOPUS SALAD
Charred Tomato Vinaigrette
15
CHARCUTERIE
ARTISANAL CHEESE & WURST PLATTER
House Made Preserves, Mustards & Pickles, Crusty Bread & European Butter
28
SMOKED FINE LIVERWURST
8
SPECK PLATE
European Smoked Ham
16
KÄSE PLATE & DRIED FRUIT
Artisanal Cheeses & Crackers
21
LANDJÄGER
Dried Square Sausage
9
LEBERKÄSE
Smoked Fine Meatloaf
Sandwiches
HOUSE SMOKED BRISKET
Warm Sauerkraut, Gruyere, House Rye, Pickles, Wurst Dressing
13
ROTISSERIE PRIME RIB
Pickled Red Onions, Fresh Tomatoes, Arugula, White Cheddar, Mustard Mayo
16
OPEN FACE ROTISSERIE CHICKEN
Creamy House Slaw, Toasted Pecans, Rotisserie Gravy
14
"THE MISSION"
Bratwurst Sausages, Braised Red Cabbage, Fried Egg, Crispy Shallots, Appenzeller
15
HALIBUT & CHIPS SANDWICH
Battered Halibut, Our Tartar Sauce, Butter Lettuce, Lemon & Apple Slaw
16
ST. ANTON GRIDDLE BURGER
Back Bacon, Aged Cheddar, Onion Kaiser, House Chips, Smoked Tomato Ketchup
15
FLAT TOP LAMB BURGER
Westphalian Ham, Melted Brie, Onion Kaiser, Sweet Potato Mayo
16
SCHNITZEL CLUB
German Sourdough, Tomatoes, Chicken Schnitzel, Butter Lettuce, Truffle Mayo, Rohess Speck
15
OPEN FACE CRAB MELT
King & Rock Crab, Avocado, Goat Cheese, Arugula Pesto, Spicy Mayo
19
Seafood
PAN ROASTED STEELHEAD TROUT
Spring Carrots, Shredded Savoy & Brown Butter
21
BUTTER POACHED LOBSTER OMELETTE
Wilted Greens, Fresh Cheese, Chives
23
SEARED CANADIAN SCALLOPS
Celery Root Puree, Roasted Broxburn Tomatoes, Crispy Speck
23
LIGHTER FARE
WURST ONION SOUP
Herb Crouton, Sylvan Star Gouda, Sausage & Comté
12
DAILY FEATURED SOUP
Crusty Bread
9
WHOLE LEAF CAESAR
Pink Peppercorn Aioli, Shaved Fennel, Radishes, Preserved Lemon, Bella Lodi
12
APPLE AND BEET SALAD
Toasted Hazelnut Vinaigrette, Frisee Lettuce, Sundried Figs
17
BROXBURN TOMATO & BUTTER CHEESE SALAD
Flash Pickled Cucumbers, Apple Cider Syrup
14
GRILLED CHICKEN PILLARD
Buttermilk Chicken Breast, Arugula, Broxburn Tomatoes, White Cheddar, Charred Pepper Vinaigrette
17
FOURTH STREET LOBSTER COBB
Poached Lobster, Butter Lettuce & Watercress, Avocado, Chèvre Noir, Hot House Cucumbers, Tarragon & Crème Fraîche Dressing, Smoked Bison
19
HOUSE SEARED ALBACORE TUNA
Basil Aioli, Warm Cherry Tomatoes, Chives, Frisee Lettuce,
19
WHITE WINE BRAISED MUSSELS
Cocktail Tomatoes, Capers, Chillies, Fennel, White Wine
17
SIDES
Smoked Gouda Spätzle 7
Creamed Potatoes 6
House Chips & Grey Salt 6
Grilled Preserved Lemon Asparagus 7
Homemade Onion Rings in Pilsner Batter 6
Potato Dumplings & Pan Gravy 6
Braised Red Cabbage 4
House Fermented Sauerkraut 4
Pickle for a buck

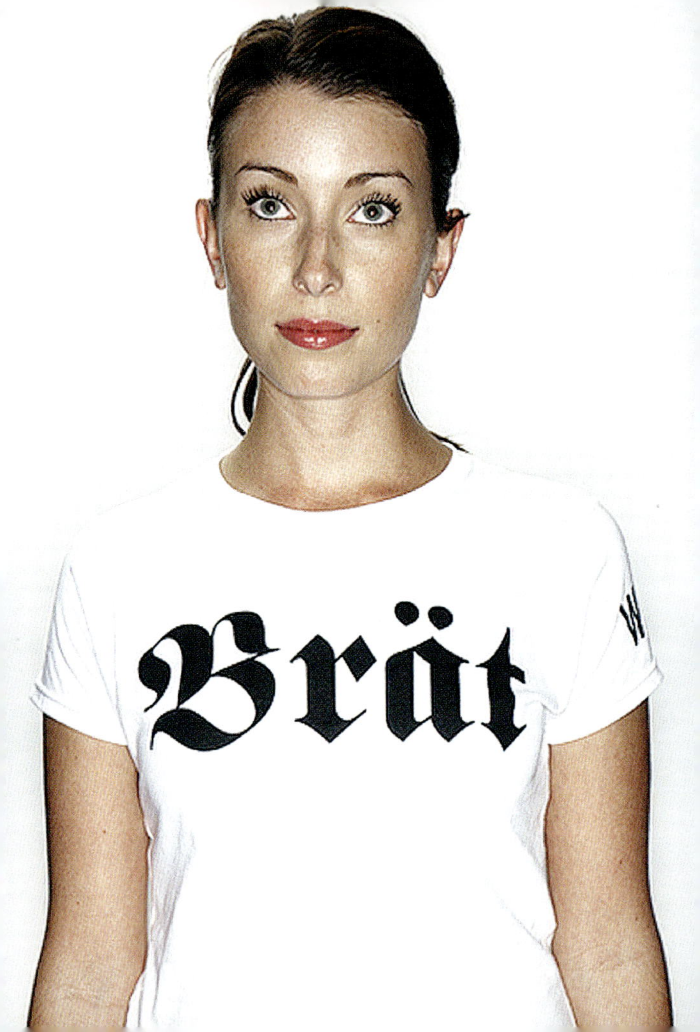
Brät

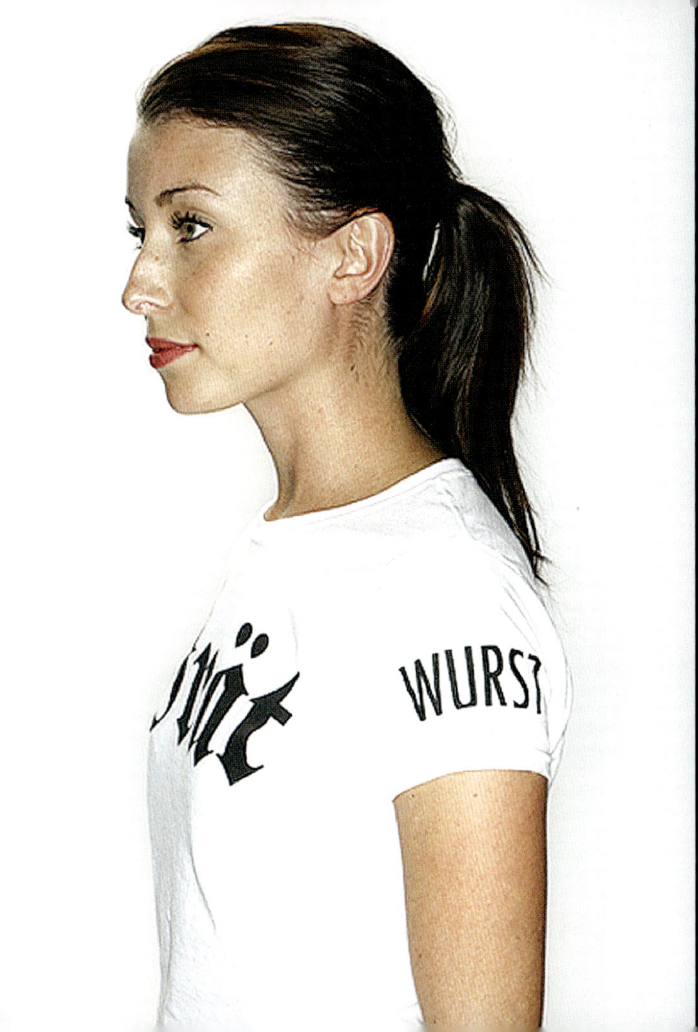
WURST

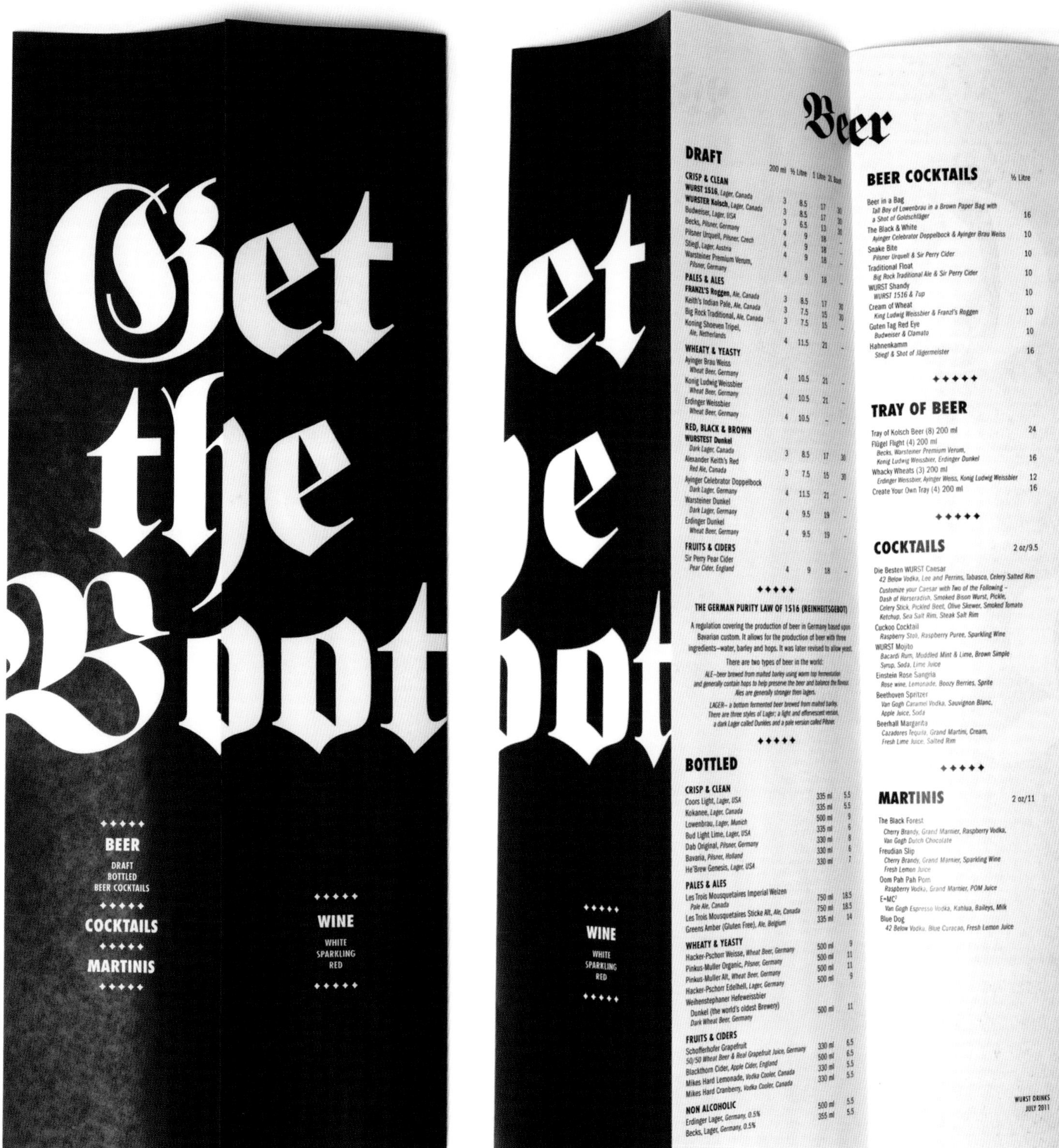
Get the Boot
BEER
DRAFT
BOTTLED
BEER COCKTAILS
COCKTAILS
MARTINIS
WINE
WHITE
SPARKLING
RED
Beer
DRAFT
BOTTLED
THE GERMAN PURITY LAW OF 1516 (REINHEITSGEBOT)
BEER COCKTAILS
TRAY OF BEER
COCKTAILS
MARTINIS
WURST DRINKS
JULY 2011

Q&A with WAX

Our Approach We combined traditional German elements and flipped many of them on their head, giving WURST a sophisticated, yet playful feel. We chose the restaurant/beer hall's name because sausage is featured so heavily on the menu, and because it sounds like worst, and who in their right mind would name their restaurant something like that? The logo leans on classic German imagery with a modern twist, featuring a two-headed eagle holding a bratwurst and stein, one side refined and one side tipsy. Two typefaces were used for the coasters, menu, and signage: Futura and Fette Fraktur. Both are German: a modern and sleek sans serif balanced by a traditional blackletter font.

Results The identity was well received by both the client and the general public. WURST just celebrated its first birthday and is lined up out the door every weekend.

Designer: Theresa Kwan | **Design Firm:** WAX | **Art Director:** Brad Connell | **Creative Directors:** Monique Gamache, Joe Hospodarec

Illustrator: James Steinberg | **Writers:** Tim Anderson, Shayne McBride, Max May | **Client:** WURST

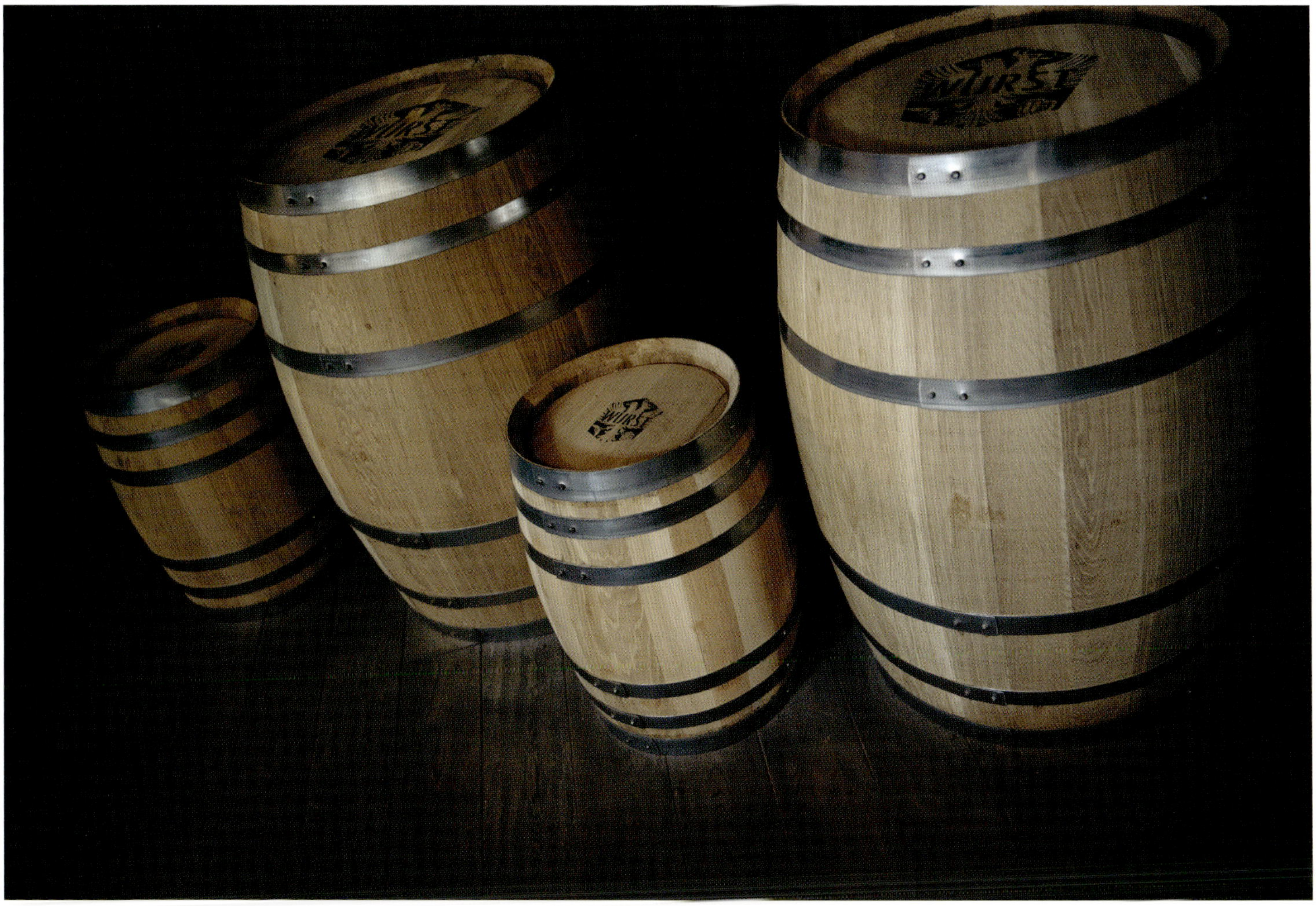

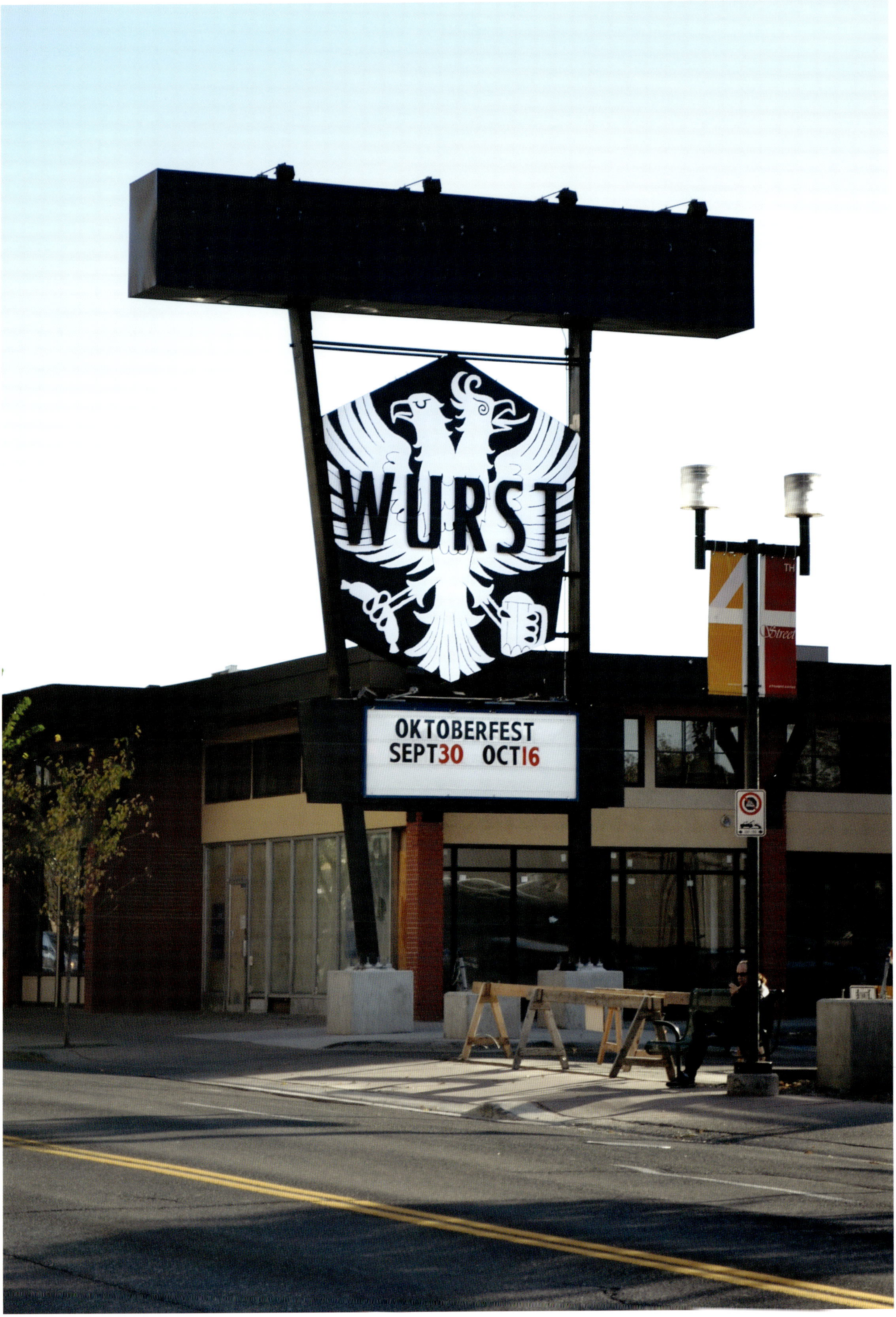
WURST
OKTOBERFEST
SEPT30 OCT16
4
TH
Street

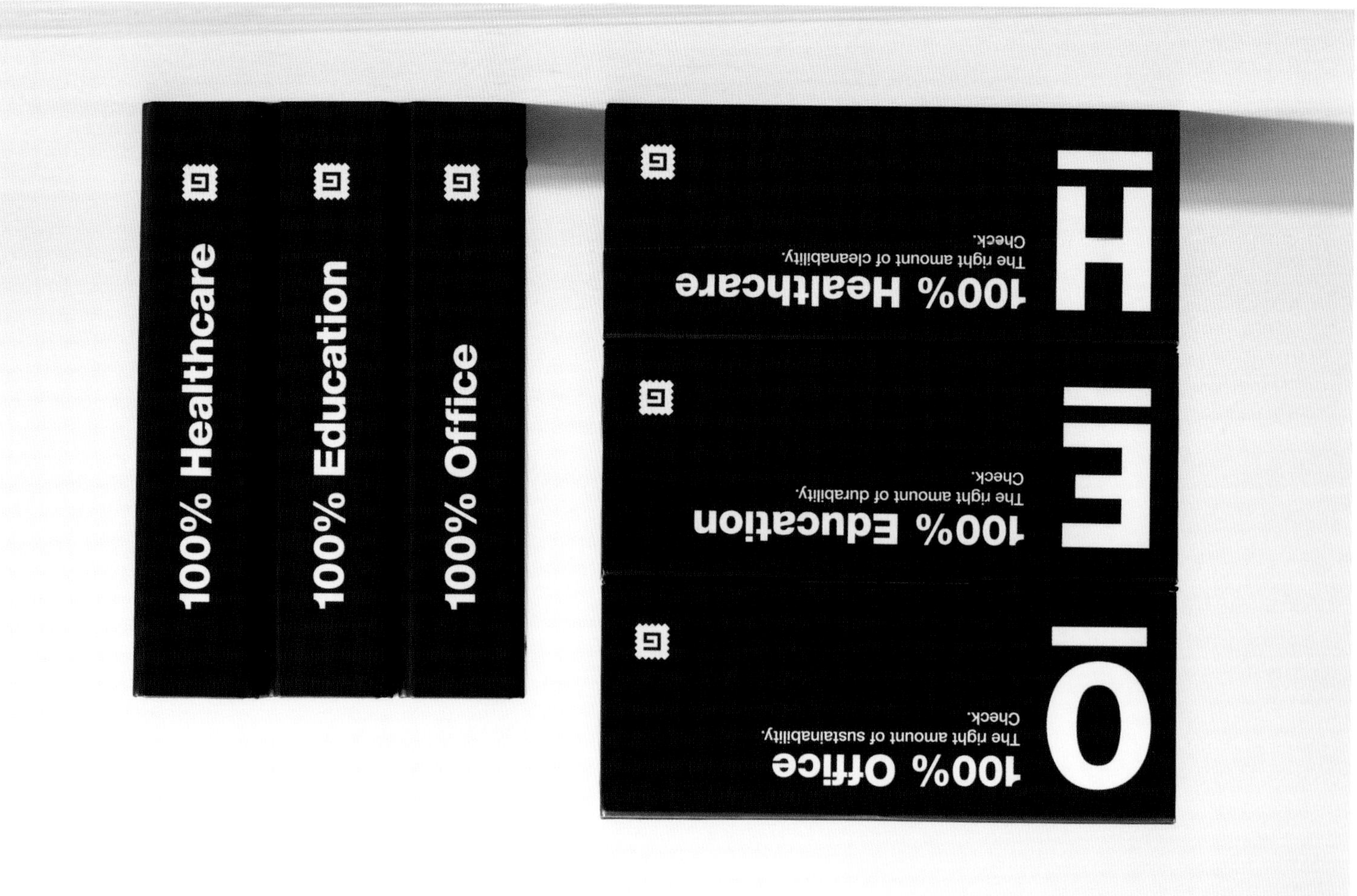
100% Healthcare
100% Education
100% Office
100% Healthcare
The right amount of cleanability.
Check.
100% Education
The right amount of durability.
Check.
100% Office
The right amount of sustainability.
Check.

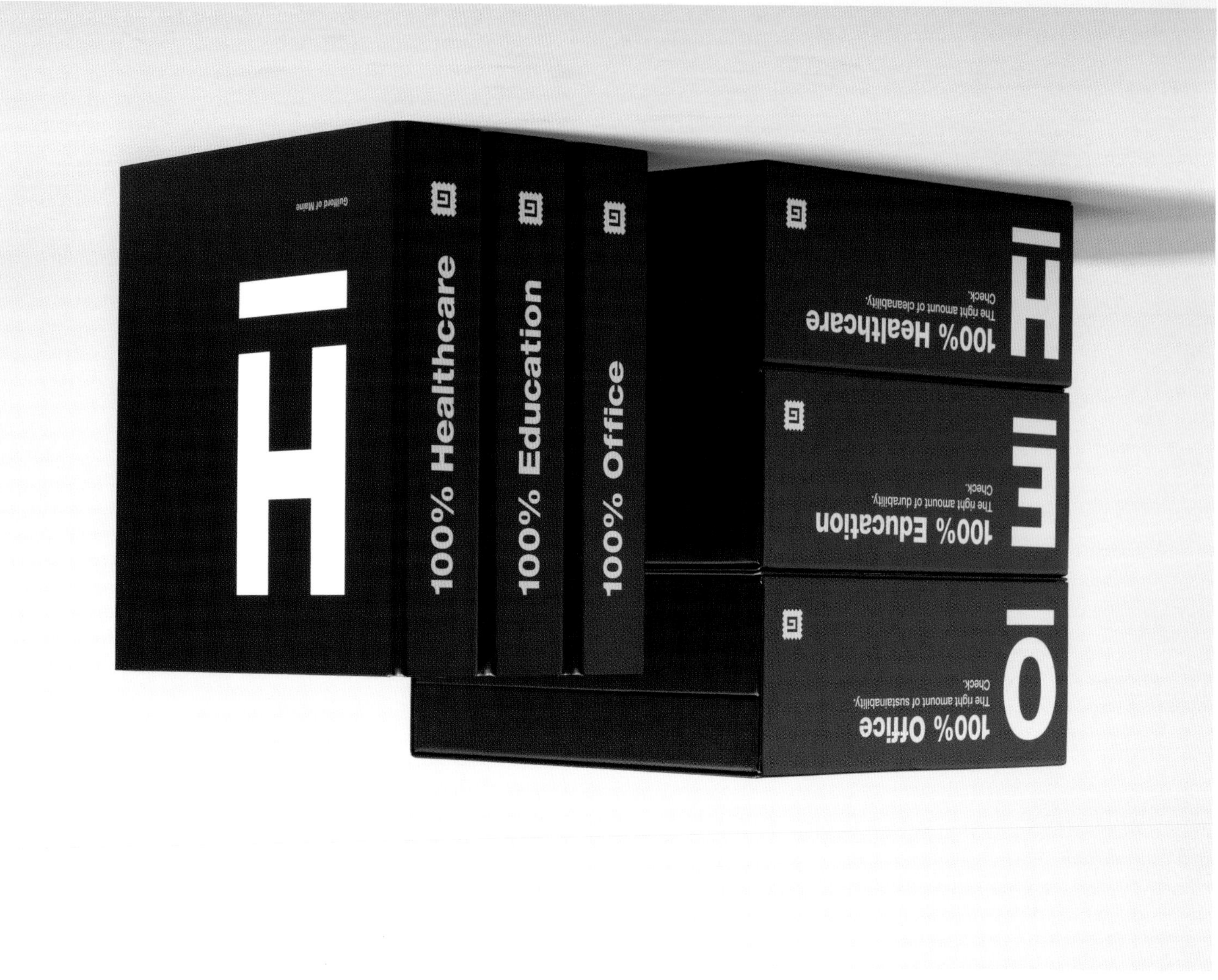
Guilford of Maine
100% Healthcare
100% Education
100% Office
100% Healthcare
The right amount of cleanability.
Check.
100% Education
The right amount of durability.
Check.
100% Office
The right amount of sustainability.
Check.

Guilford of Maine & Peopledesign

True Textiles, is a really smart, successful, careful manufacturer, supplier, and marketer of textiles. Despite being a top provider to Herman Miller, Haworth, HON, Maharam, Momentum, and other huge furniture companies, changes in their ownership–they were acquired, then spun off (puns are not beneath us) from flooring leader Interface–made for brand confusion in the marketplace. Were they True, or Guilford of Maine (True's open line fabrics brand), or were they still Interface (True's former parent company)? Our early conversations with True Textiles could easily devolve into a helpless Who's-on-First? hunt for clarity. True leadership engaged Peopledesign to help find a clear new direction for their brand. We began with customer research to sort out markets and their needs, along with brand measures of the key players in each market. We brought the findings in and together established a new strategic path, leading with the strong performance attributes of the Guilford of Maine brand.

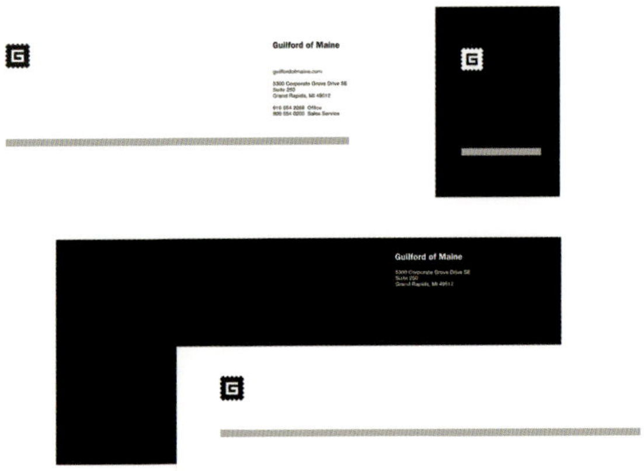

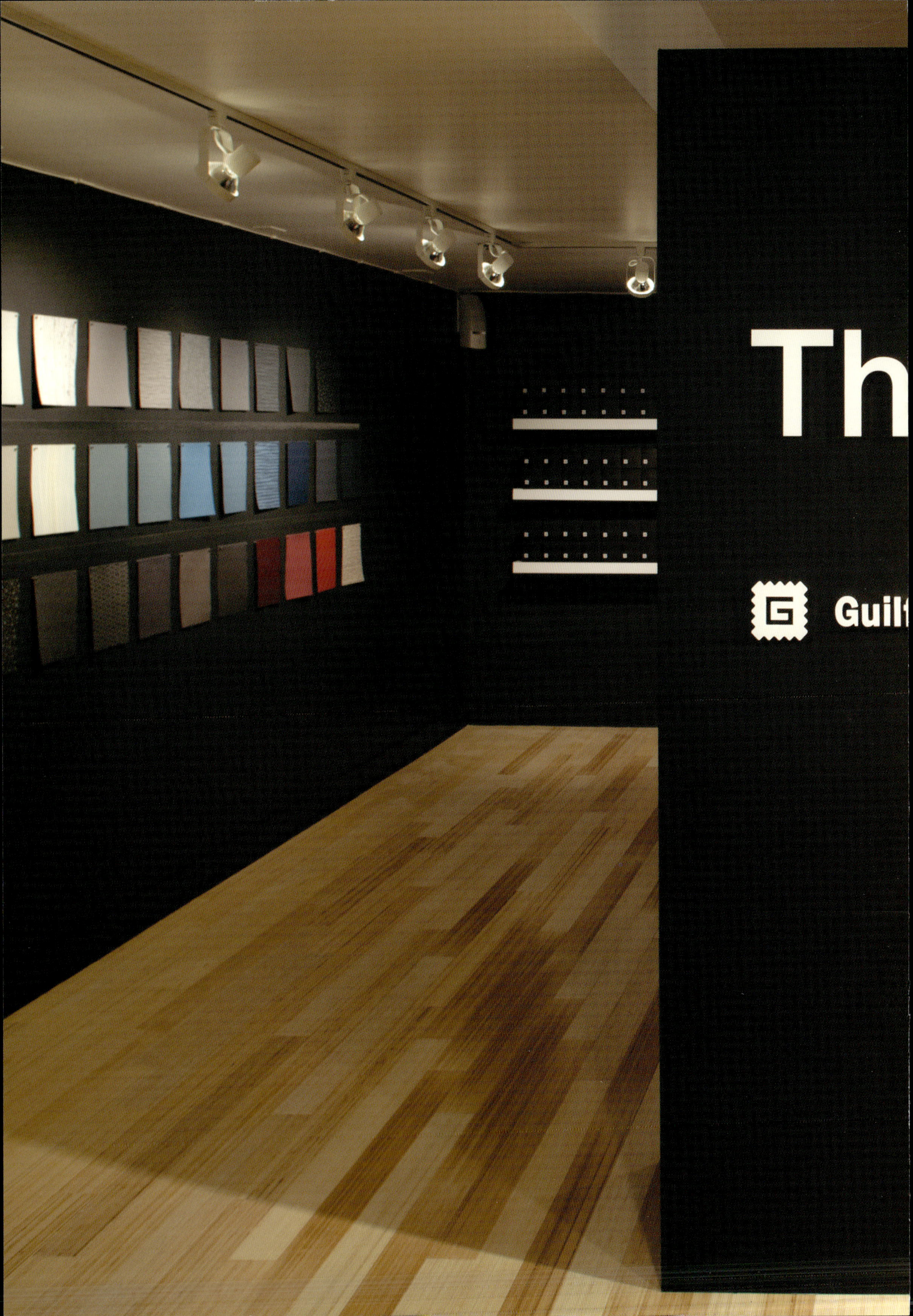
Th
Guilf

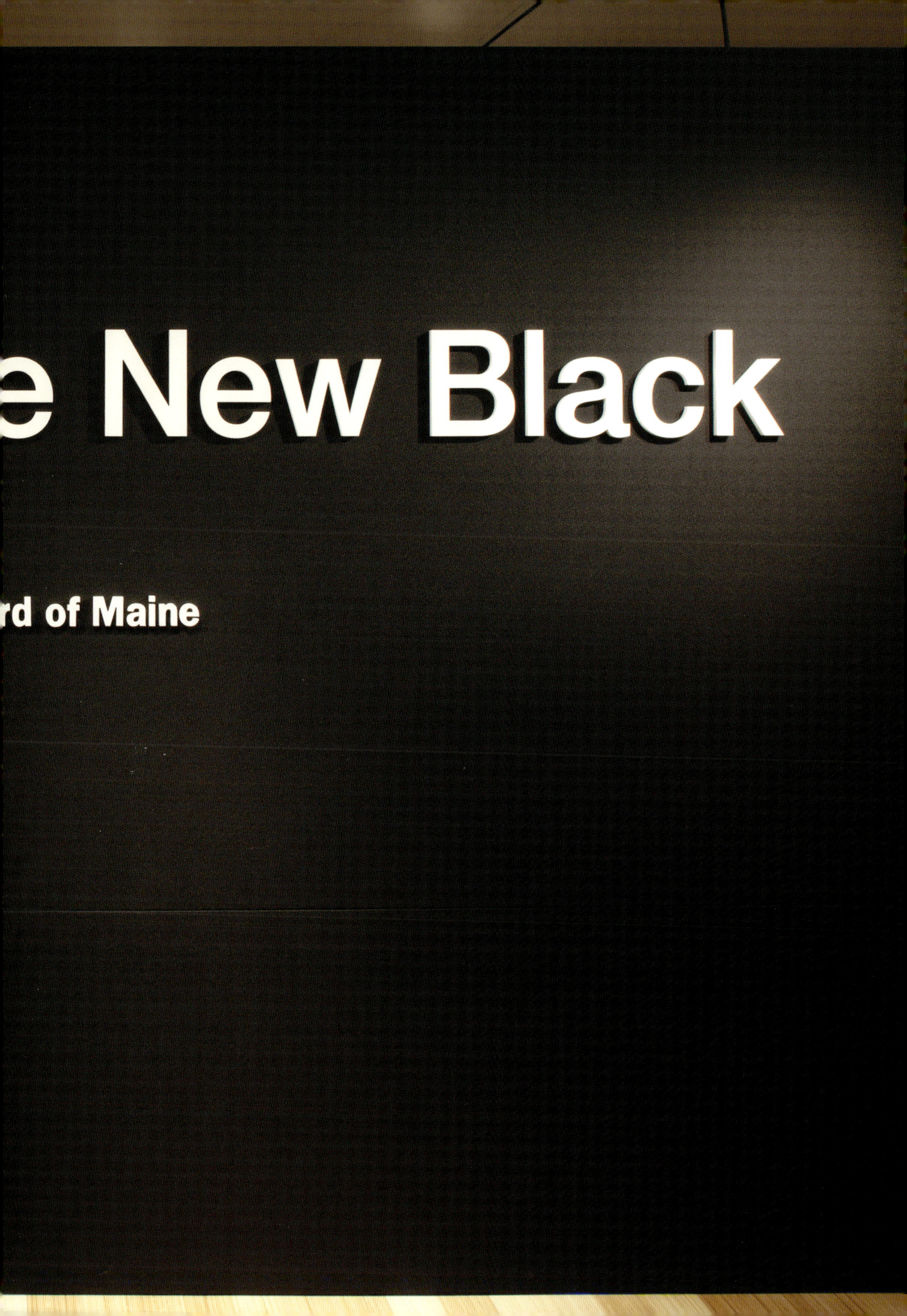
e New Black
rd of Maine

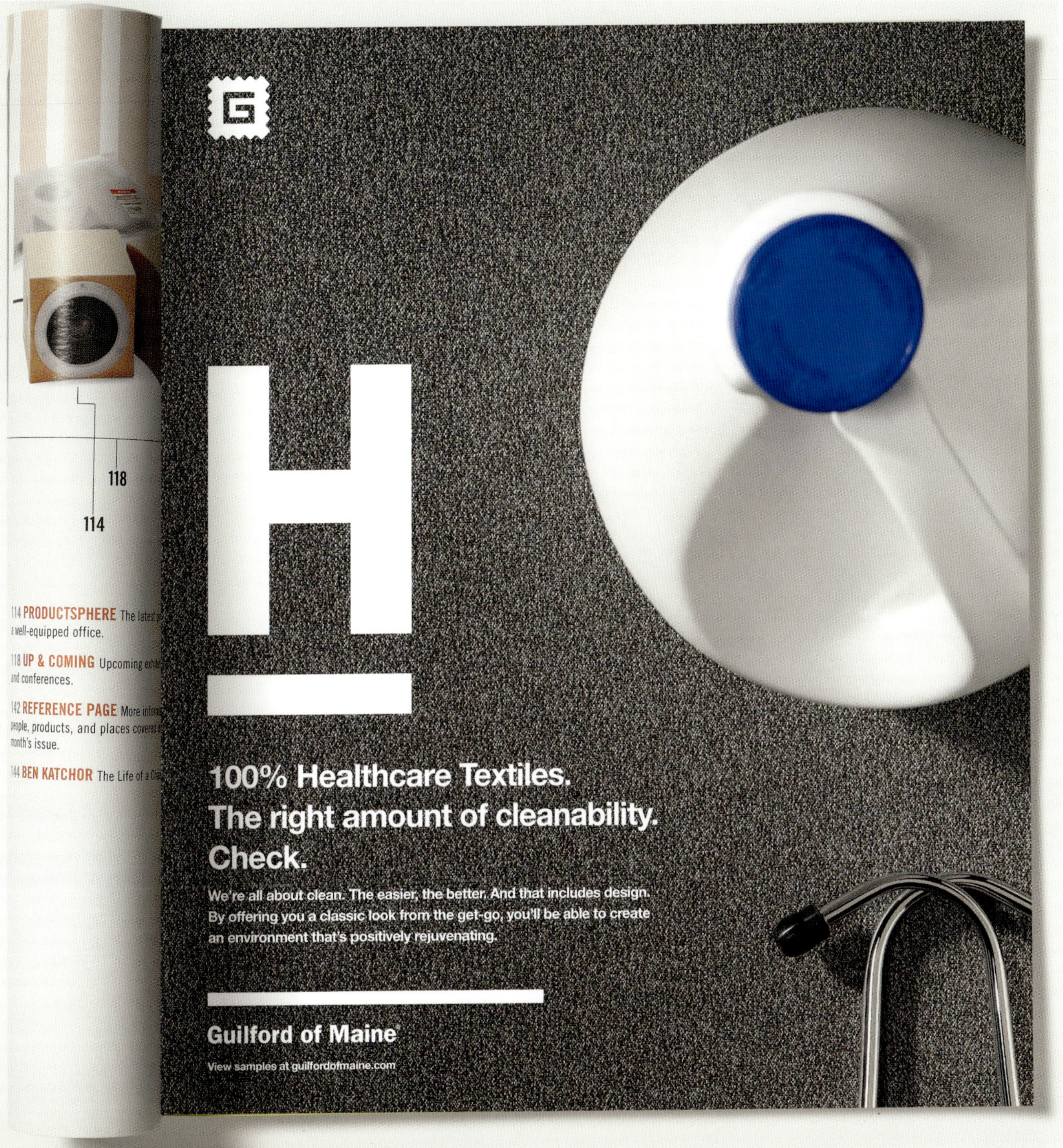
H
100% Healthcare Textiles.
The right amount of cleanability.
Check.
We're all about clean. The easier, the better. And that includes design. By offering you a classic look from the get-go, you'll be able to create an environment that's positively rejuvenating.
Guilford of Maine
View samples at guilfordofmaine.com
118
114
114 PRODUCTSPHERE The latest
a well-equipped office.
118 UP & COMING Upcoming
and conferences.
142 REFERENCE PAGE More
people, products, and places covered
month's issue.
144 BEN KATCHOR The Life of a

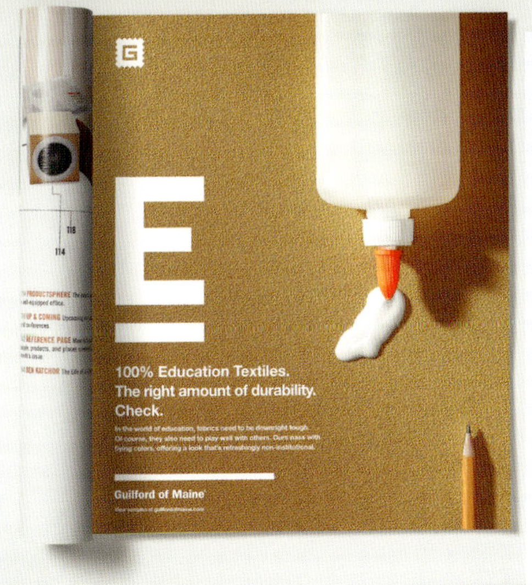
E
100% Education Textiles.
The right amount of durability.
Check.
Guilford of Maine

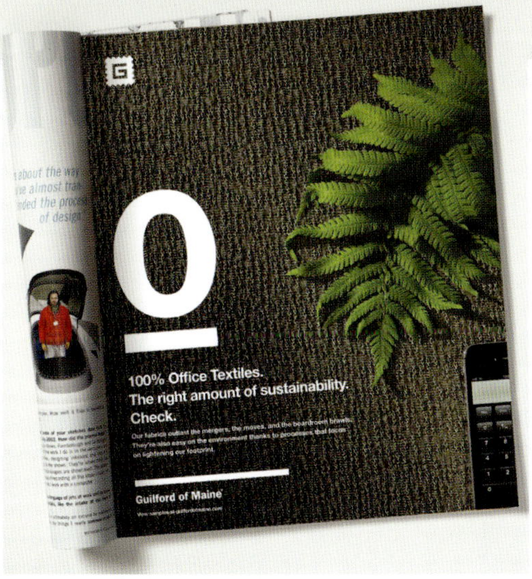
O
100% Office Textiles.
The right amount of sustainability.
Check.
Guilford of Maine

Industrial Setting Over a recent 12-year period in the long history of the commercial textile brand Guilford of Maine, the company went through three ownership changes and three different market-facing names (Guilford of Maine, Interface Textiles, and True Textiles). Elsewhere in the industry, other textile marketers were enjoying a higher profile, but not all of them were manufacturers (mills) like Guilford, which added to the confusion.

Challenge Guilford was struggling with a basic question: Who are we? Their leadership had been contemplating a shift in emphasis toward True Textiles, their OEM brand, focusing on manufacturers and leading with a sustainability message. With manufacturers increasingly commodity-driven and the lack of meaningful market differentiation that could be achieved with sustainability, however, we recommended a clear, new direction for Guilford.

Strategy While conducting interviews with architects and interior designers to better understand the needs of this market, we implemented a bridge strategy for NeoCon 2010. Building on the established brand equity of Guilford of Maine rather than True, we signaled a forthcoming change and produced an award-winning showroom experience. Upon completion of our research, we identified "performance" as a key motivator driving A&D decisions, and the lack of a clear market leader in this space. Emphasizing the strong performance attributes of Guilford of Maine products, and focusing on A&D and, specifically, the Office, Education, and Healthcare markets they serve, we carved out a specific niche Guilford could own and defend.

Results This new strategic brand positioning not only led to a new identity program (communication materials, identity, print, web, showroom, and sample center), but also an entire overhaul of Guilford's product offer. Our business design recommendations evolved internal sales training and helped launch the newly refocused business.

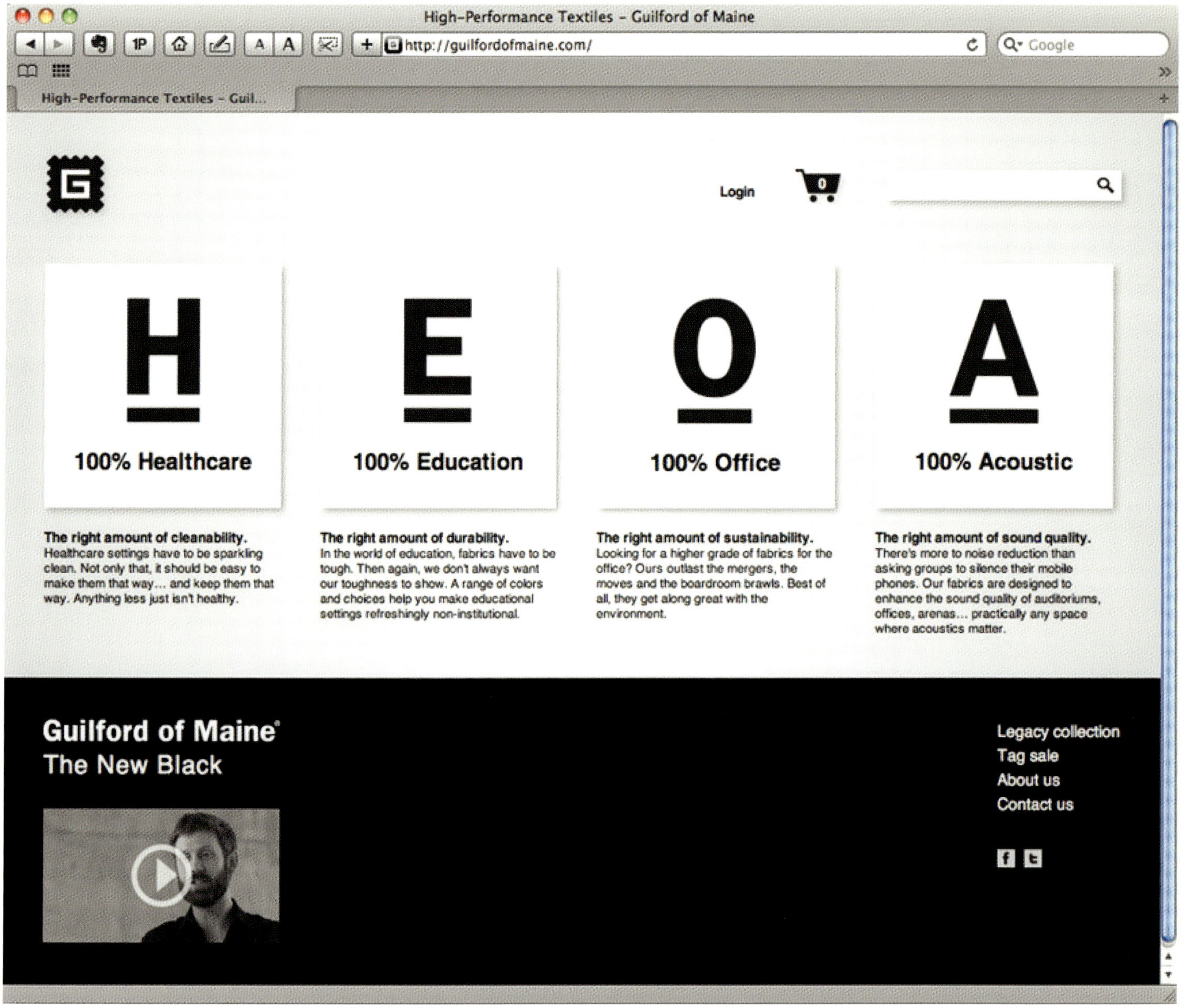

Designer: Peopledesign | Design Firm: Peopledesign | Client: Guilford of Maine

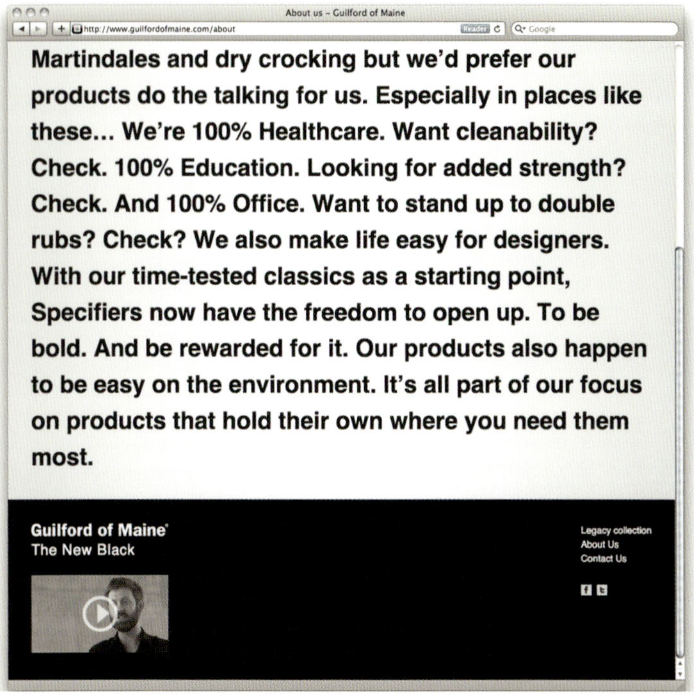
About us - Guilford of Maine
http://www.guilfordofmaine.com/about
Martindales and dry crocking but we'd prefer our products do the talking for us. Especially in places like these... We're 100% Healthcare. Want cleanability? Check. 100% Education. Looking for added strength? Check. And 100% Office. Want to stand up to double rubs? Check? We also make life easy for designers. With our time-tested classics as a starting point, Specifiers now have the freedom to open up. To be bold. And be rewarded for it. Our products also happen to be easy on the environment. It's all part of our focus on products that hold their own where you need them most.
Guilford of Maine
The New Black
Legacy collection
About Us
Contact Us

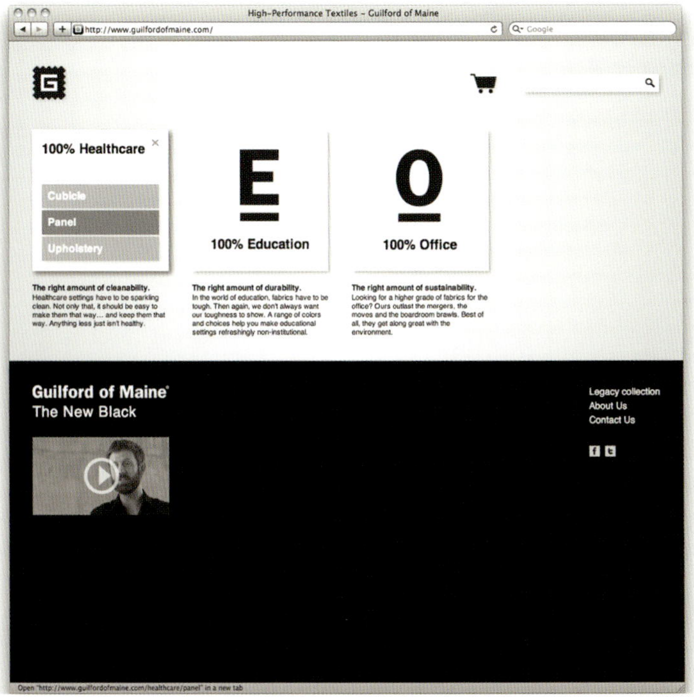
High-Performance Textiles - Guilford of Maine
http://www.guilfordofmaine.com/
100% Healthcare
Cubicle
Panel
Upholstery
100% Education
100% Office
Guilford of Maine
The New Black
Legacy collection
About Us
Contact Us

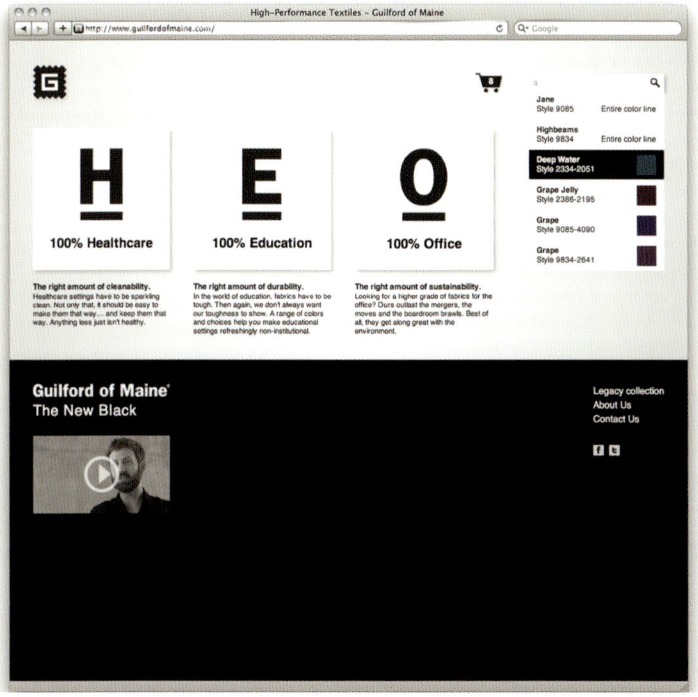
High-Performance Textiles - Guilford of Maine
http://www.guilfordofmaine.com/
100% Healthcare
100% Education
100% Office
Guilford of Maine
The New Black
Legacy collection
About Us
Contact Us

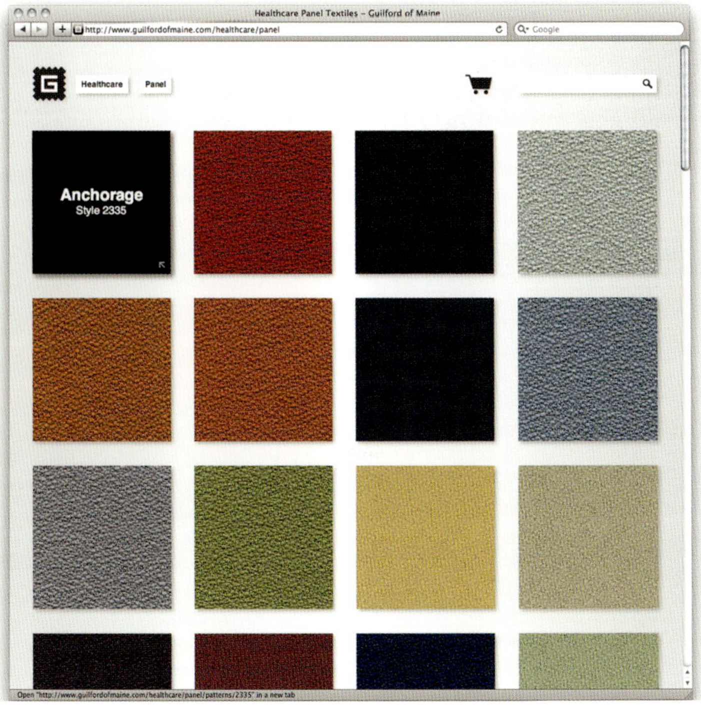
Healthcare Panel Textiles - Guilford of Maine
http://www.guilfordofmaine.com/healthcare/panel
Healthcare
Panel
Anchorage
Style 2335

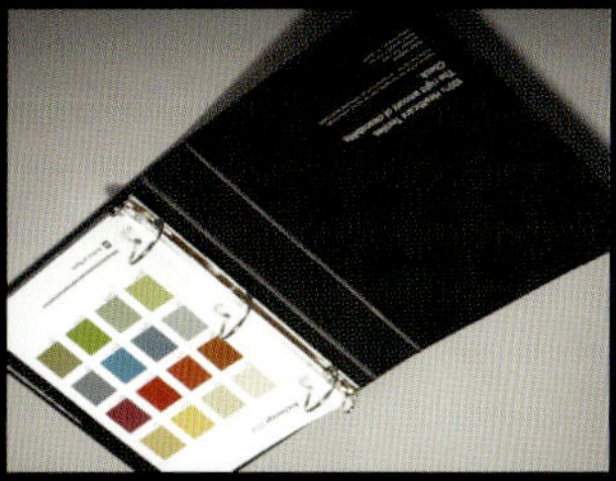

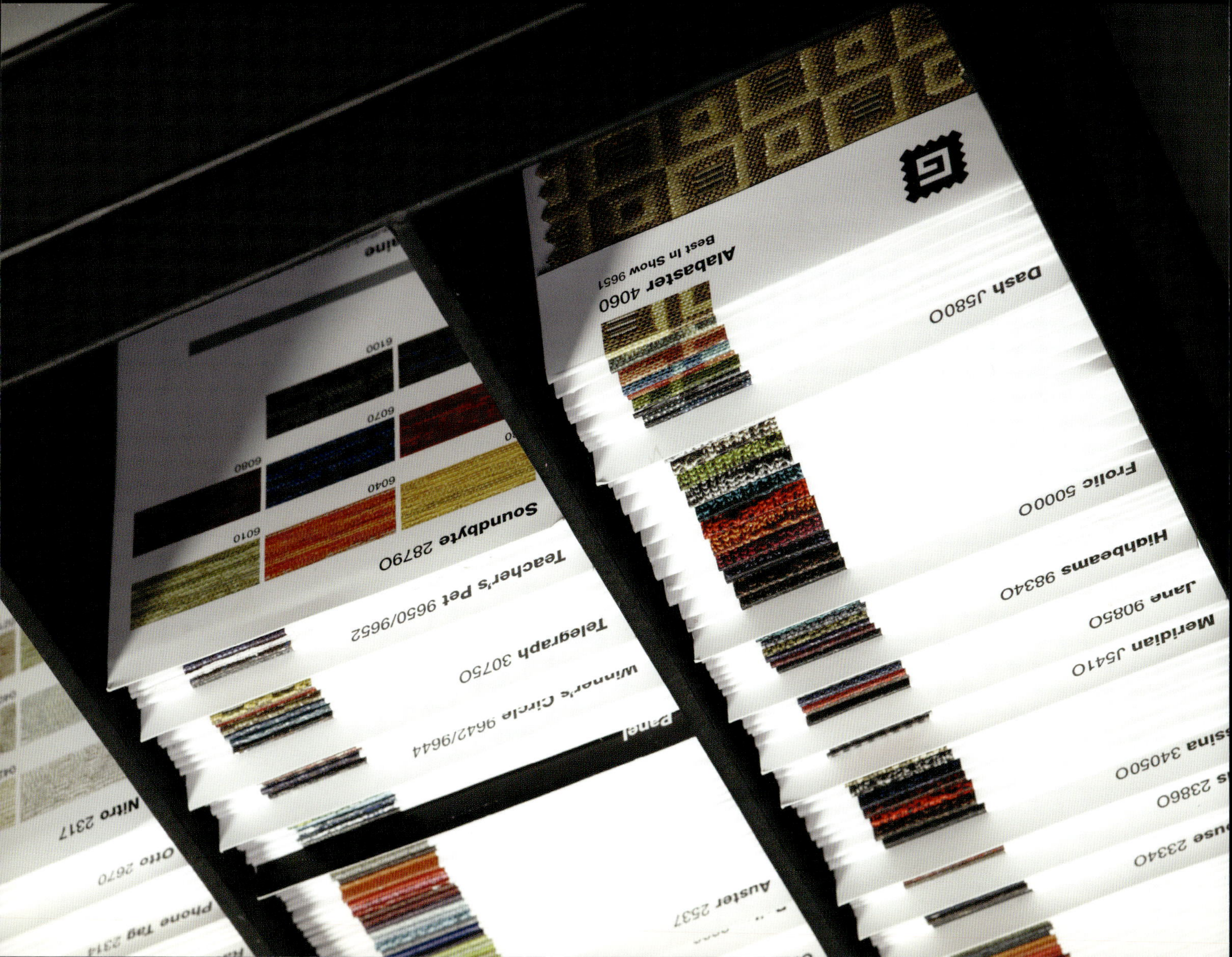
Alabaster 4060
Best In Show 9651
Dash J580O
Frolic 5000O
Highbeams 9834O
Jane 9085O
Meridian J541O
Soundbyte 2879O
Teacher's Pet 9650/9652
Telegraph 3075O
Winner's Circle 9642/9644
Nitro 2317
Otto 2670
Auster 2537

Cue & Bonterra

Bonterra produces award-winning wines made from organically grown grapes in Mendocino County, California. The vineyard has been an industry leader in organic practices for over twenty years, but Bonterra's brand essence—"organic grapes make better wine"— had yet to be leveraged. With new organic brands entering the market, it became even more important for the brand to tell its story. Cue designed the Bonterra Roadshow to highlight Bonterra's leading role in the organic wine industry. The roadshow includes a multimedia presentation on Bonterra's organic practices and a wine tasting featuring several award-winning varietals. Then, we created a new brand expression to tell the story of the ranch and help Bonterra receive the credit it has earned. Finally, we brought that expression to the shelf with new packaging for all Bonterra varietals.

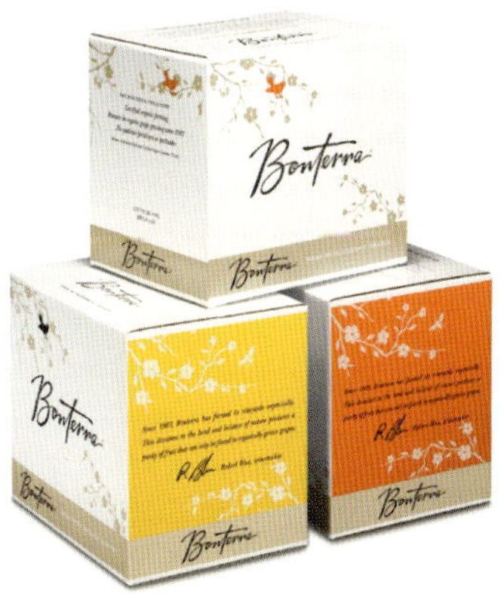

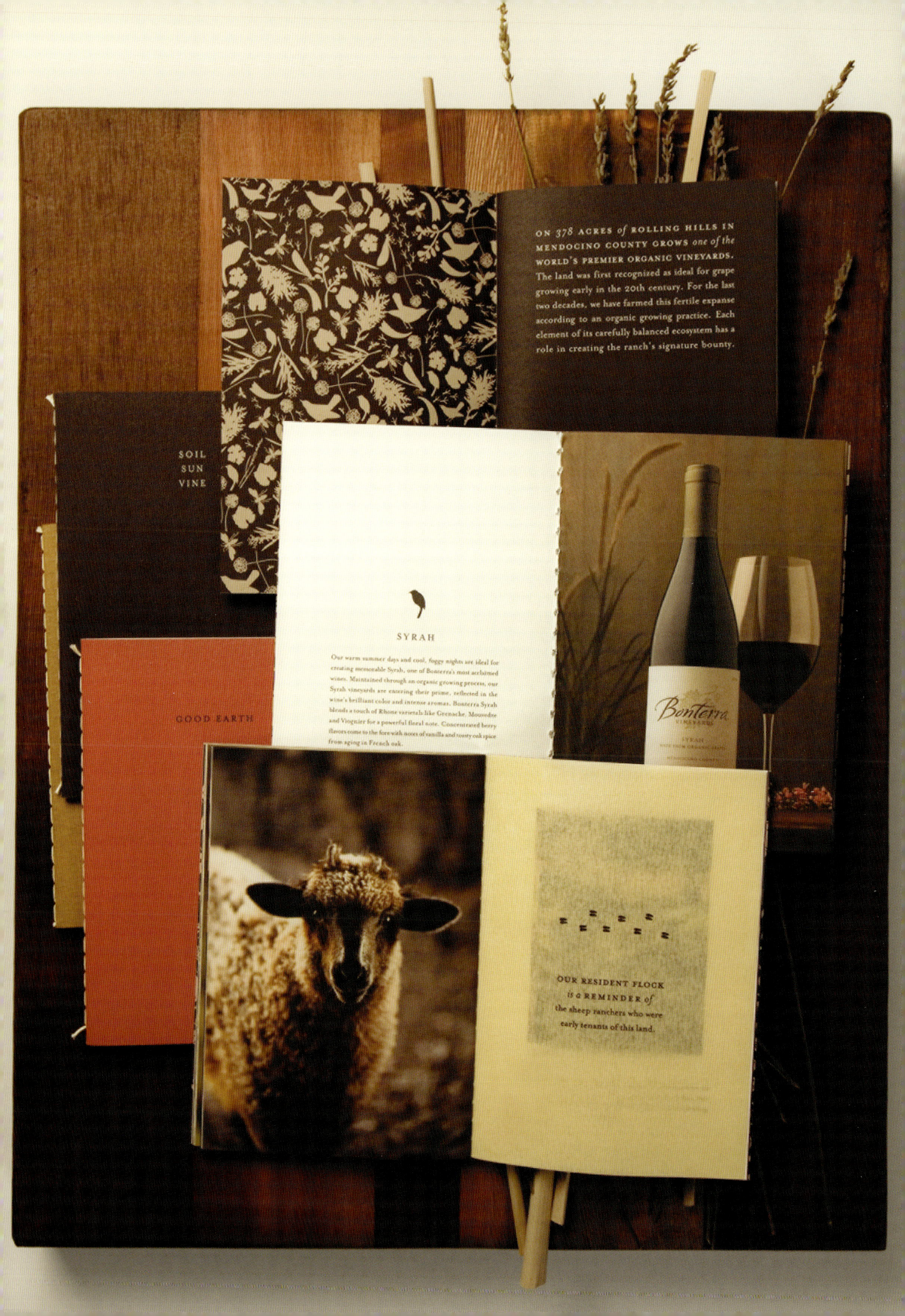
ON 378 ACRES of ROLLING HILLS IN MENDOCINO COUNTY GROWS one of the WORLD'S PREMIER ORGANIC VINEYARDS. The land was first recognized as ideal for grape growing early in the 20th century. For the last two decades, we have farmed this fertile expanse according to an organic growing practice. Each element of its carefully balanced ecosystem has a role in creating the ranch's signature bounty.
SOIL
SUN
VINE
SYRAH
Our warm summer days and cool, foggy nights are ideal for creating memorable Syrah, one of Bonterra's most acclaimed wines. Maintained through an organic growing process, our Syrah vineyards are entering their prime, reflected in the wine's brilliant color and intense aromas. Bonterra Syrah blends a touch of Rhone varietals like Grenache, Mourvedre and Viognier for a powerful floral note. Concentrated berry flavors come to the fore with notes of vanilla and toasty oak spice from aging in French oak.
GOOD EARTH
Bonterra
VINEYARDS
SYRAH
OUR RESIDENT FLOCK
is a REMINDER of
the sheep ranchers who were
early tenants of this land.

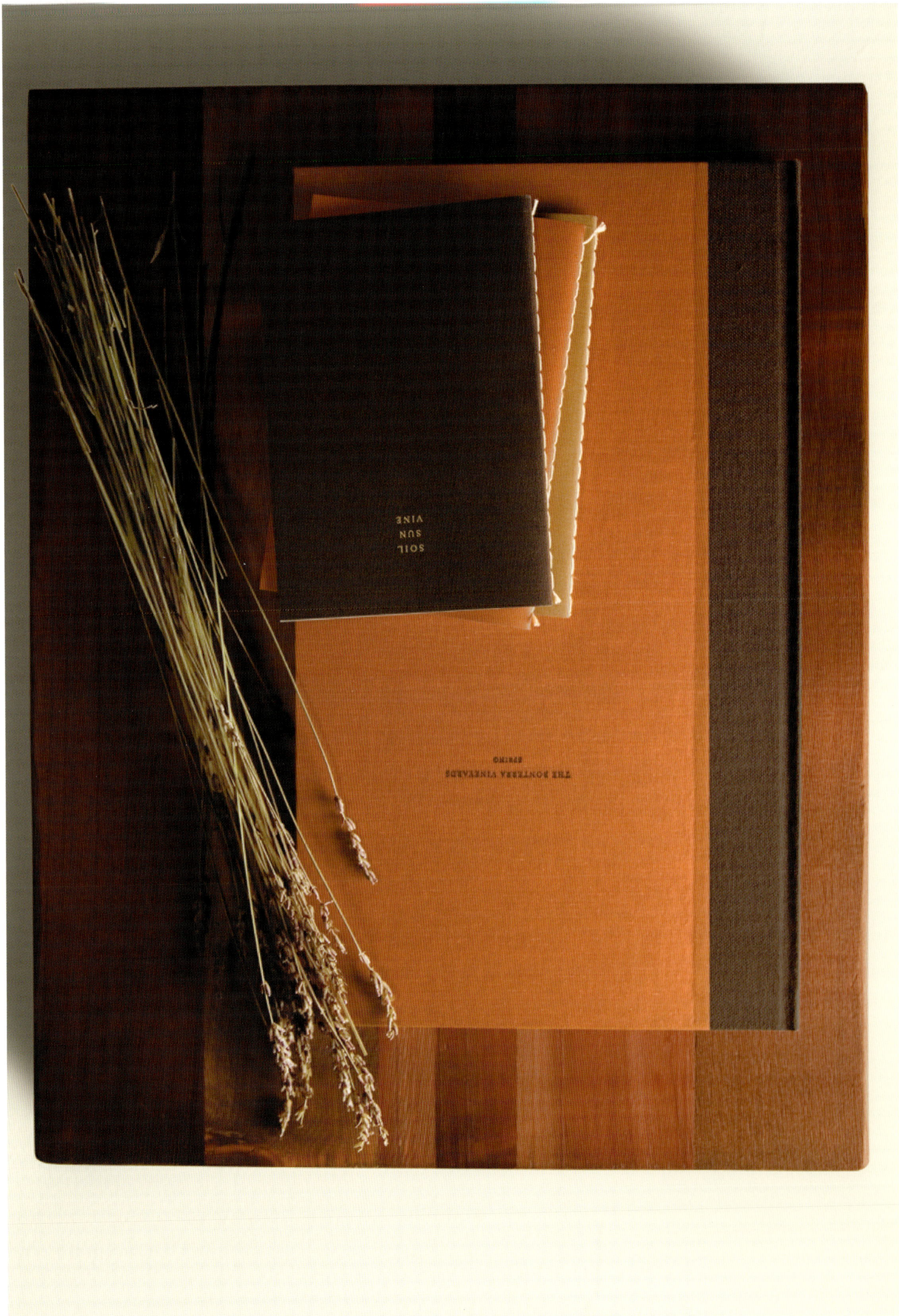
SOIL
SUN
VINE
THE BONTERRA VINEYARDS
SPRING

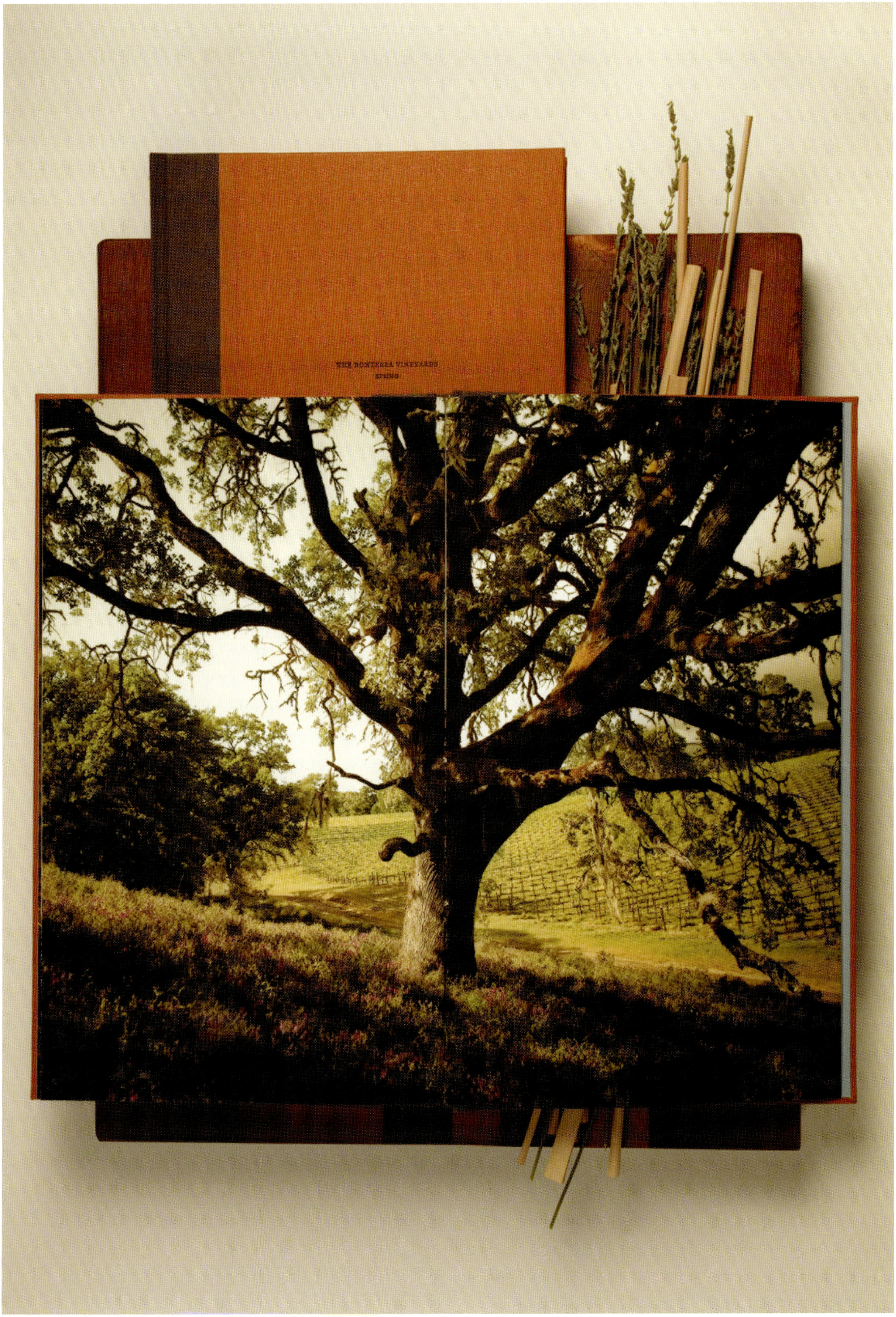
THE BONTERRA VINEYARDS
SPRING

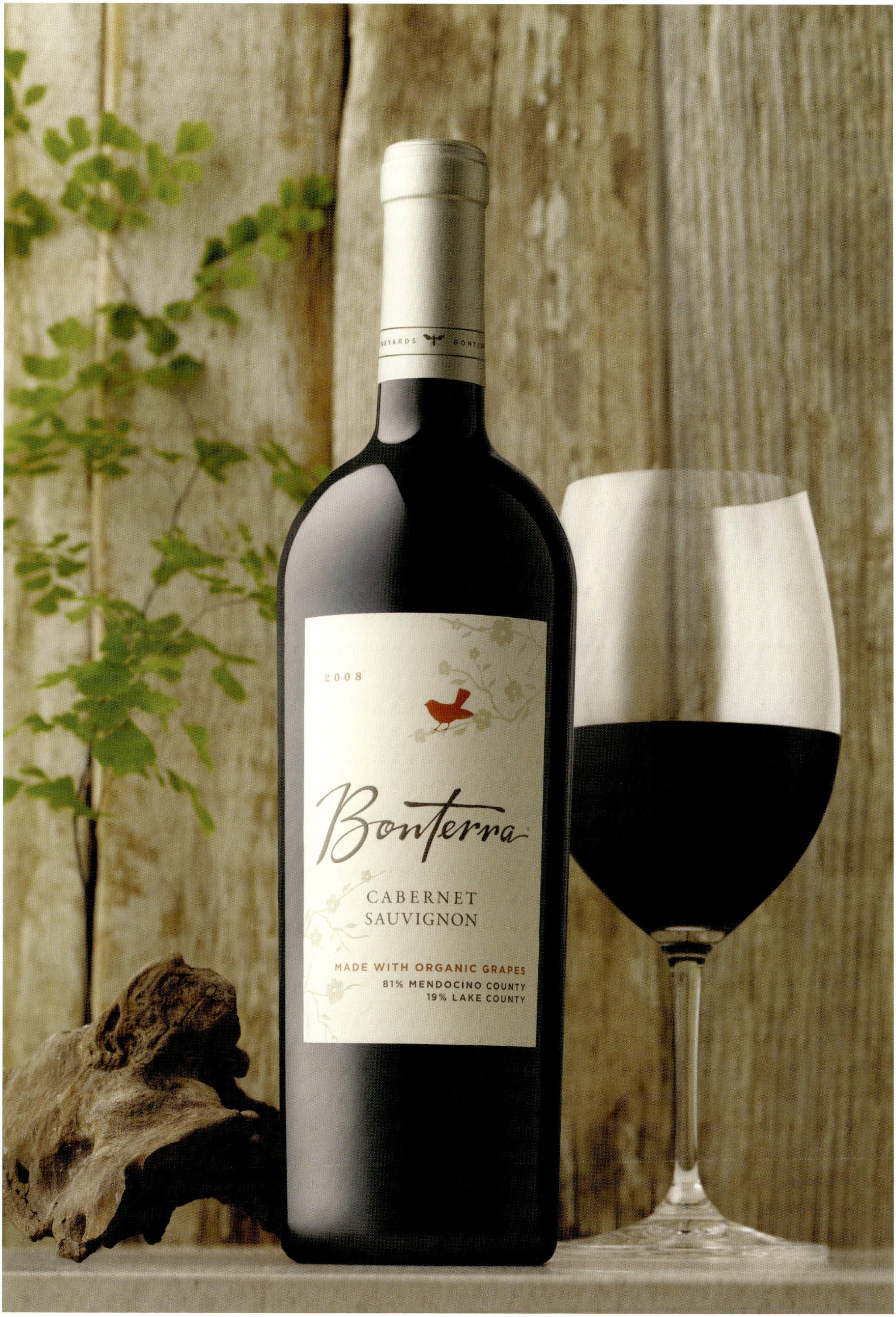
2008
Bonterra
CABERNET
SAUVIGNON
MADE WITH ORGANIC GRAPES
81% MENDOCINO COUNTY
19% LAKE COUNTY

Q&A with Cue

Approach We explored three ways to tell the story based on brand characteristics. Our solution focused on the theme of relationships: soil, sun, and vine; farmer and wine maker; people, nature, and enjoyment of life. Through the filter of these relationships, people are invited to experience the Bonterra brand in new ways, creating their own definitions of what "better" means. "Better" is an overarching theme that positions Bonterra as a better way to enjoy wine, a better way to farm the land, a better way to live. We set out to create a visual language that could supplement and surround the brand expression with an eye toward a future evolution. Juxtapositions of imagery, iconography, and language create a palette of ingredients that express Bonterra in a way that invites consumers to participate on an emotional level and consider what is important to them.

Results The look, feel, and voice provided the tools the brand needed to tell a rich, authentic story. The Roadshow informed distributors and retailers across the country, thereby creating valuable "brand ambassadors." The brand now gets credit for its leadership in organic farming and sustainable practices. Bonterra has a story, a differentiating point of view, and tools to communicate it—from primary package to point of sale and advertising. Packaging tested well with consumers who felt it delivered a premium expression without resorting to category clichés or novelty execution.

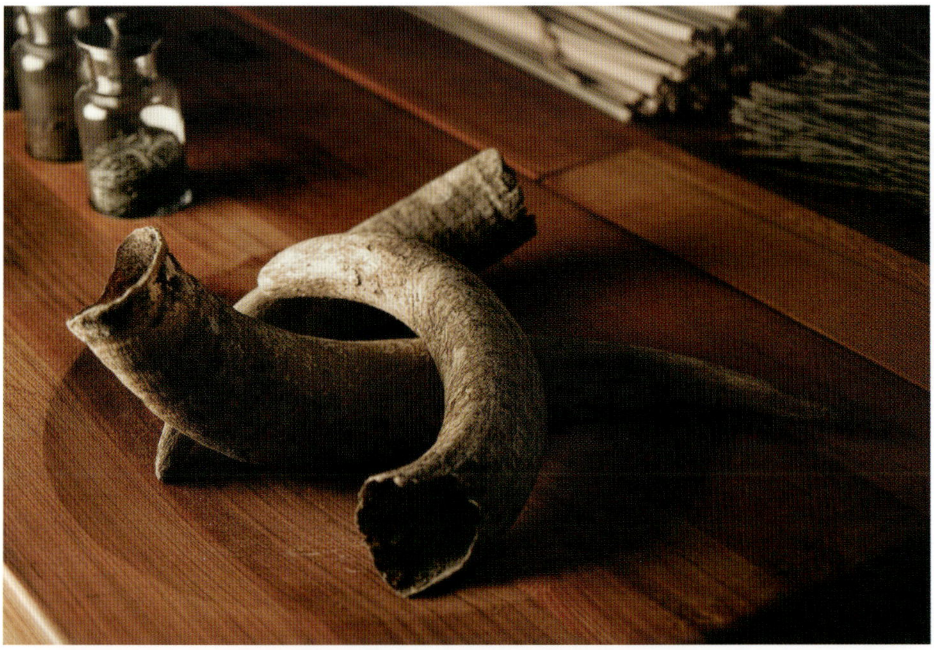

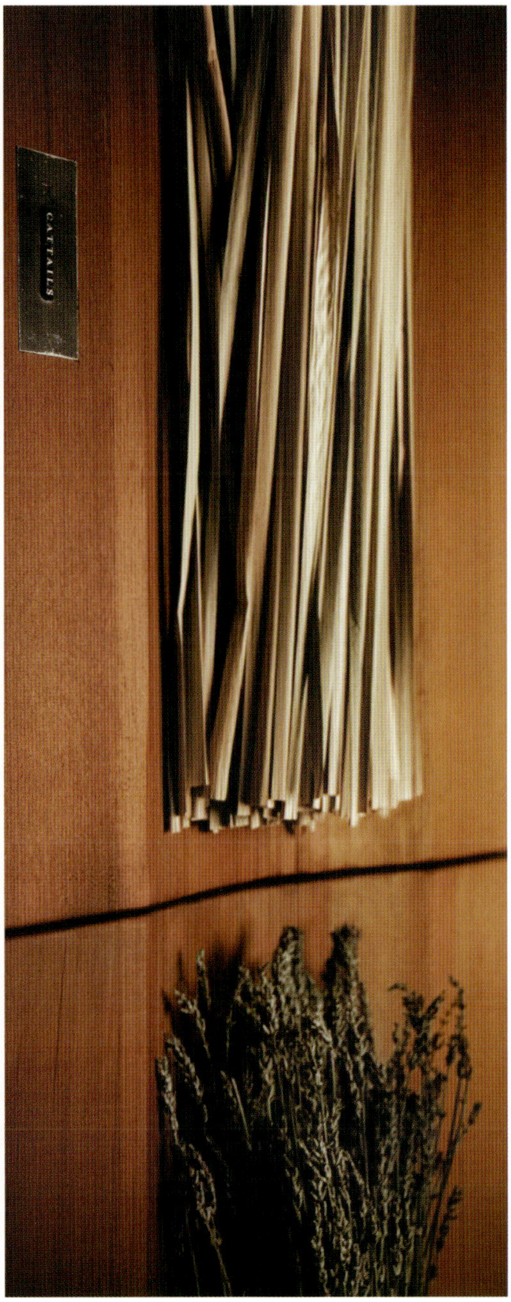

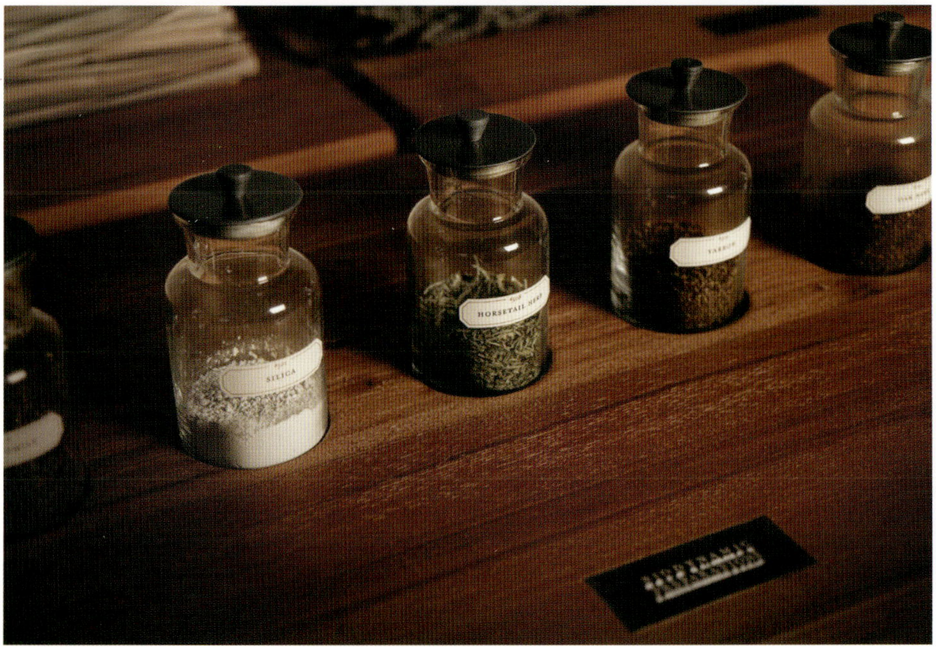

Designers: Kate Arends, Paul Sieka | **Design Firm:** Cue | **Creative Director:** Alan Colvin
Photographers: Graham Brown, Andy Anderson | **Producer:** Chris Thomas | **Printer:** Franklin Press | **Client:** Brown-Forman

> "Those who experience our roadshow presentation walk away more emotionally connected to Bonterra, which is exactly what we set out to do."

Don Freytag, *Foundation Wines, Brown-Forman Corp.*

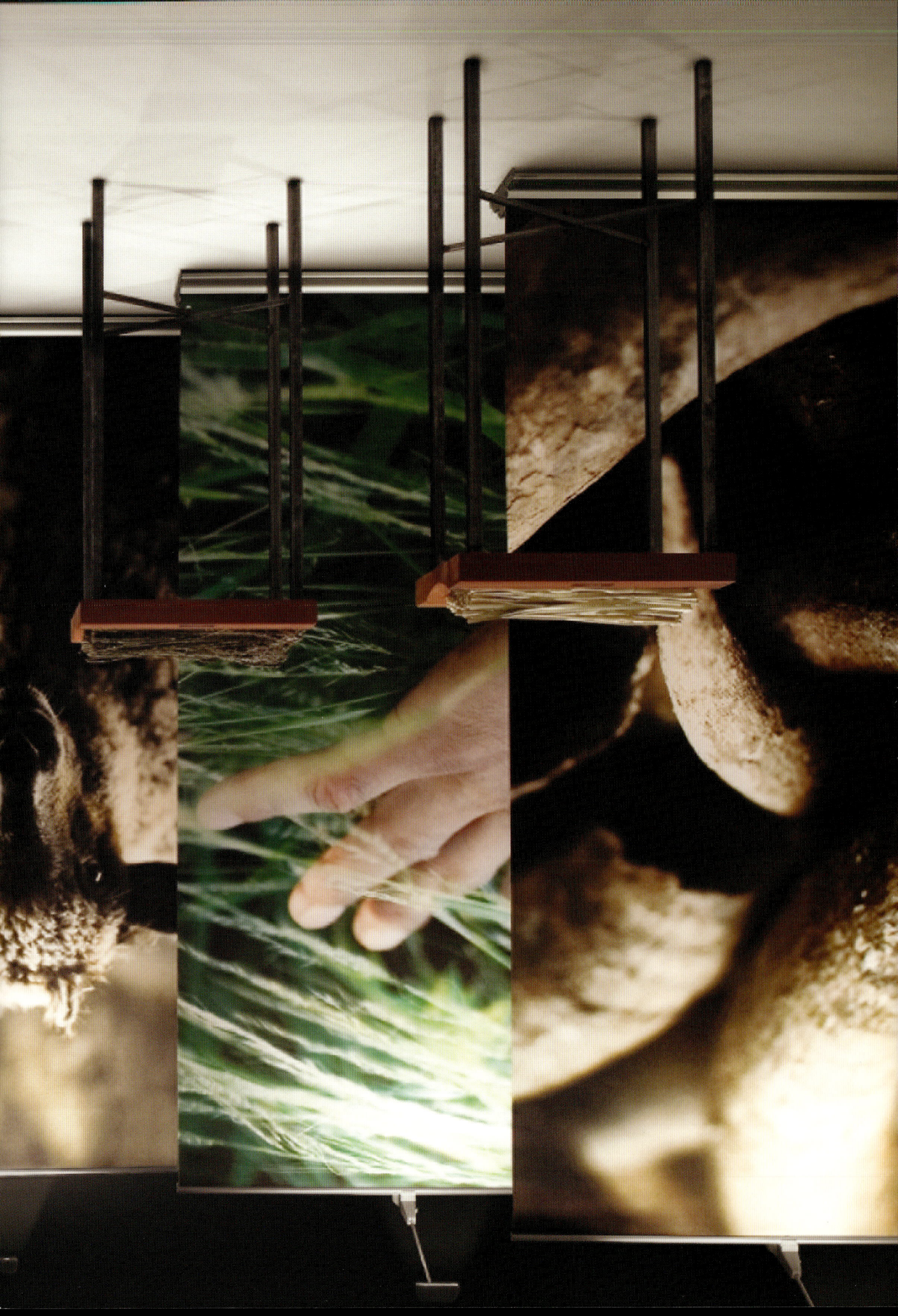

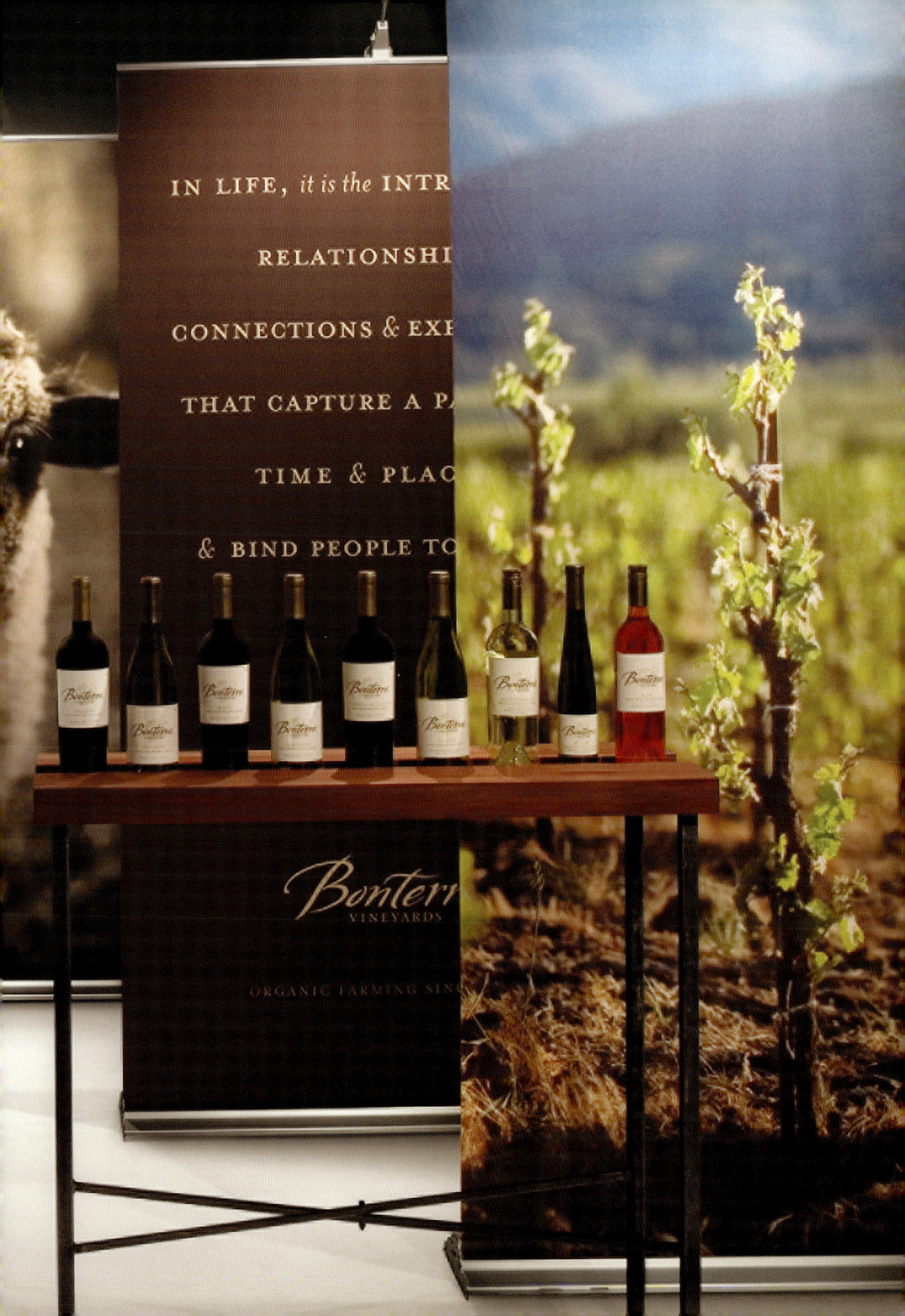
IN LIFE, it is the INTR
RELATIONSHI
CONNECTIONS & EXP
THAT CAPTURE A PA
TIME & PLAC
& BIND PEOPLE TO
Bonterr
VINEYARDS
ORGANIC FARMING SIN

Firewood & Firewood Inc.

In 2002, at the tail-end of the dotcom implosion and in the wake of the Great Holding Company Agency Buy-up Frenzy, the three Firewood partners yearned for a chance to get back to basics. Basics to us meant: create a vibrant agency workplace with a family atmosphere, but keep it small (no more than twenty-five employees, with respect for work/life balance); make sure the partners kept their hands dirty (as opposed to walking around "managing" all day); and focus on doing great work. We needed to create a brand that reflected those values and points-of-view, and stood out among the seemingly countless digital identities in the marketplace at that time. We sought to foster a brand that would immediately convey a sense of warmth, comfort, and grounded familiarity—while simultaneously invoking the spirits of creativity and innovation.

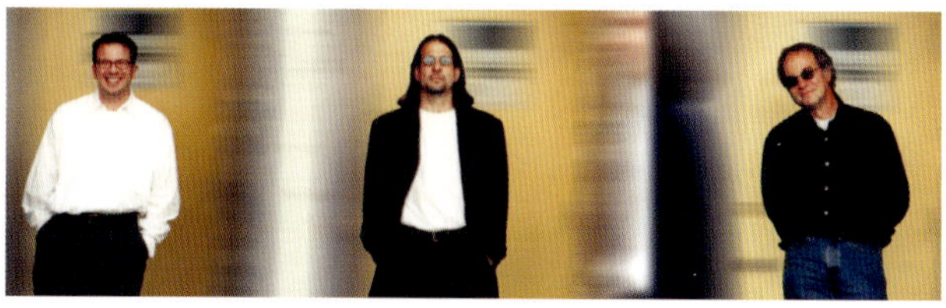

firewood

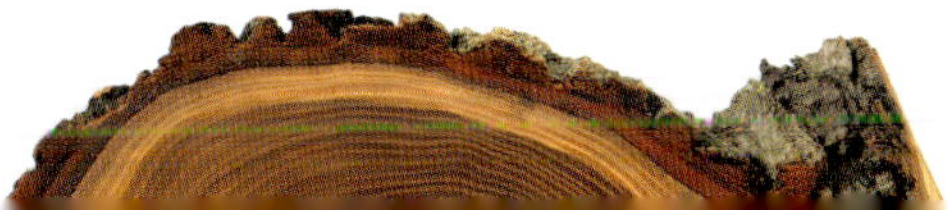

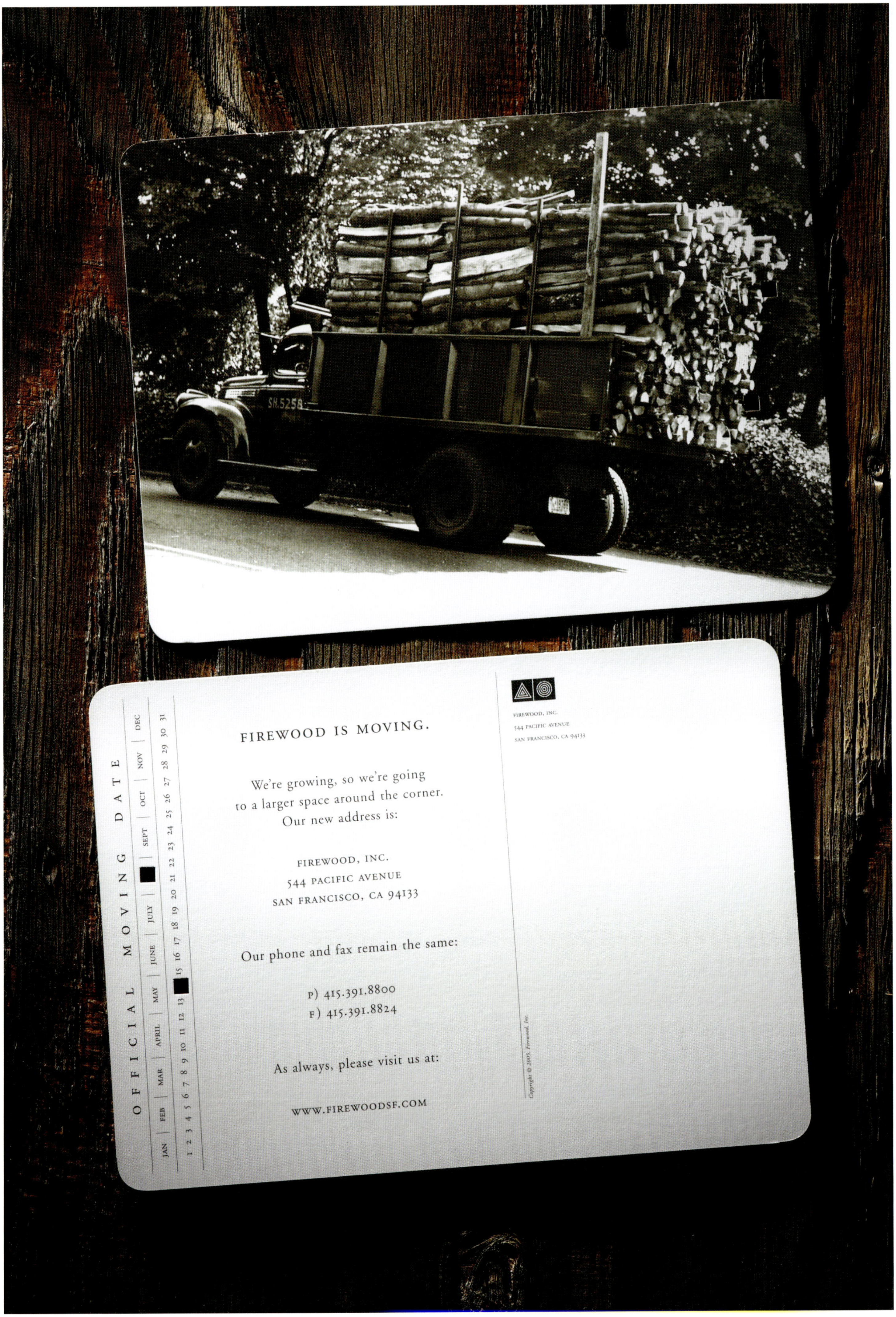
SH.5258
OFFICIAL MOVING DATE
JAN | FEB | MAR | APRIL | MAY | JUNE | JULY | SEPT | OCT | NOV | DEC
1 2 3 4 5 6 7 8 9 10 11 12 13 15 16 17 18 19 20 21 22 23 24 25 26 27 28 29 30 31
FIREWOOD IS MOVING.
We're growing, so we're going
to a larger space around the corner.
Our new address is:
FIREWOOD, INC.
544 PACIFIC AVENUE
SAN FRANCISCO, CA 94133
Our phone and fax remain the same:
P) 415.391.8800
F) 415.391.8824
As always, please visit us at:
WWW.FIREWOODSF.COM
Copyright © 2005, Firewood, Inc.
FIREWOOD, INC.
544 PACIFIC AVENUE
SAN FRANCISCO, CA 94133

Q&A with Firewood Inc.

Approach We tackled the dirty work first by defining our offering, our core beliefs, our brand "essence," our unique differences in the marketplace, and our vision of what kind of agency we wanted to be. We also spent some time articulating the type of clients we wanted to have. We did the due diligence of performing a series of traditional positioning and messaging exercises (you know, the type of thing we'd do for a real, paying client). As brand builders, we treated the challenge of building our own brand as a grand experiment as to what's possible. Not so much in a "sky's the limit" sort of way, but more in terms of how hard we could push the creative edges while working within a thoughtful set of established criteria. For starters, we wanted an emotionally-based brand nomenclature that would suggest (and allow us to tap into) a rich, associated visual vocabulary. We also wanted a brand that would be inclusive rather than exclusive in its ability to absorb many influences/elements from many different sources and environments. And lastly, we wanted an earthy yet contemporary brand that made every physical encounter with it an unexpected and tactile experience. With that foundation, we moved on to naming: brainstorming individually at first, then reviewing collectively, and finally battle-testing against our established criteria. So what to call it? Firewood. As our oldest source of fuel (bringing warmth to the hearth and food to the table—all while hopefully keeping the wolves at bay) it's a word that conjures up a world of positive yet visceral experiences and memories, touching heavily upon all five senses. And along with the notion of "firewood" comes an amazing and varied world of visual associations, ranging from the Famous Artist School's "Draw the Lumberjack," to U.S. Forest Service signage, to "flame socks" (that served as post-new-business-meeting gifts to potential clients). After naming, we moved on quickly to identity, with website and collateral following in short order. As we executed, we strove to ensure that the Firewood brand could grow organically, taking form in different ways that suited our business and aesthetic goals over time. Thus, the core elements—the icon-based logomark along with the logotype—could be used in any number of situations and placements, and not limited to a classic "lockup."

Results As for results, the success of one's own brand is a difficult thing to measure quantitatively. We can say with confidence that, almost to a person, we were asked, "How did you come up with the name?" when meeting prospective clients or doing a new business pitch—and those conversations allowed us to show the human side of our agency, which might easily have been subsumed by the business at hand.

And our letter-pressed business cards and annual mailings/invitations were almost universally met with comments such as, "Every year I look forward to receiving your New Year's Card!" or, "How do you guys keep coming up with something so fresh and unique within such a simple framework?!" (The sense of touch was critical in creating a tactile Firewood experience, with consistent use of letterpress printing, along with toothy stocks and chipboard to help in solidifying our earthy-yet-sophisticated brand.) Finally, given our financial and professional successes over the course of the eight years of the agency's existence, we all agree that Firewood was the most interesting, exciting, unique, and financially rewarding brand the three of us have ever been associated with. So far, anyway.

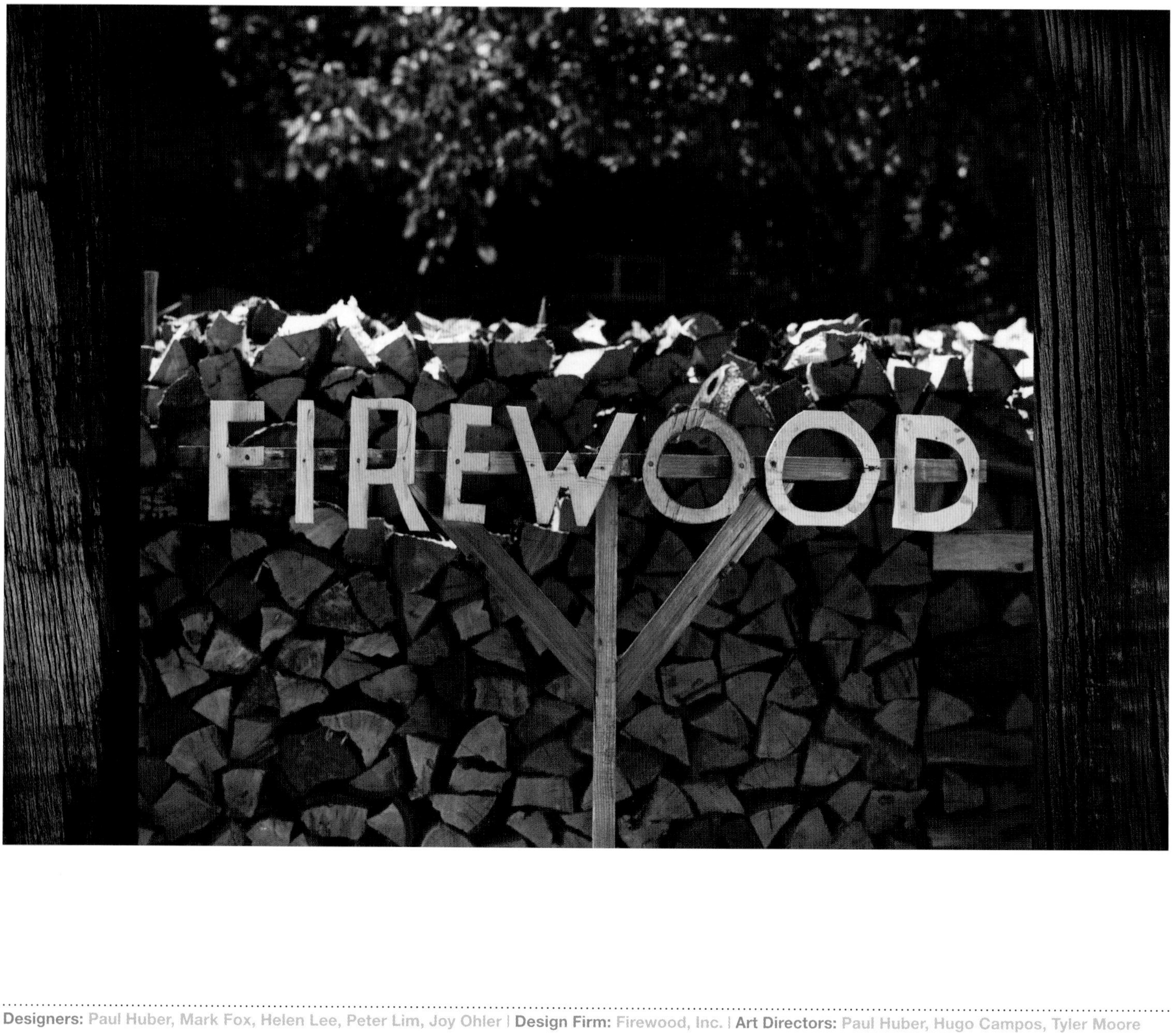

Designers: Paul Huber, Mark Fox, Helen Lee, Peter Lim, Joy Ohler | **Design Firm:** Firewood, Inc. | **Art Directors:** Paul Huber, Hugo Campos, Tyler Moore
Creative Directors: Paul Huber, John Parsons, Bradley Hazelrigg | **Writer:** John Parsons | **Client:** Firewood, Inc

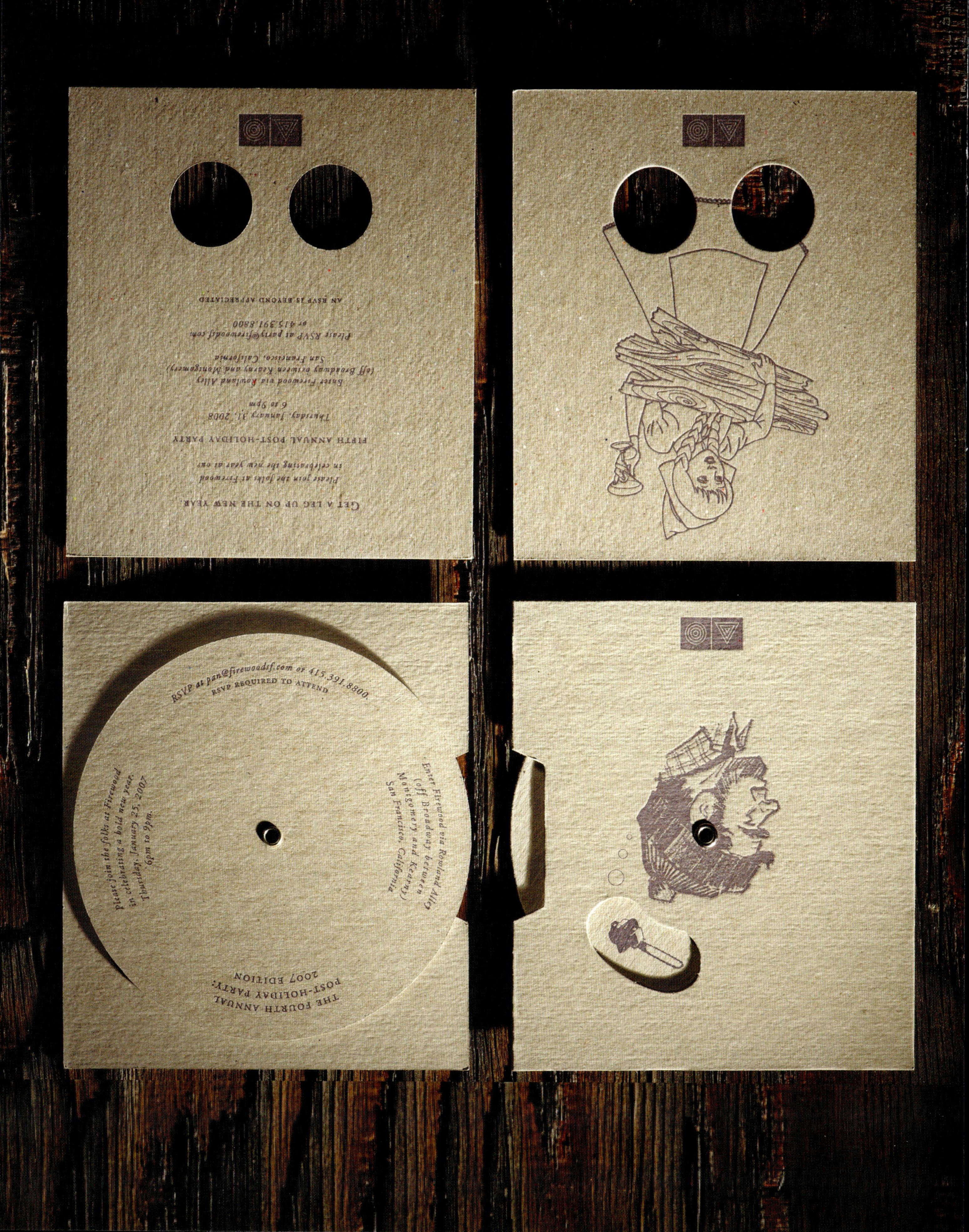
Get a leg up on the new year
Please join the folks at Firewood
in celebrating the new year at our
Fifth Annual Post-Holiday Party
Thursday, January 31, 2008
6 to 9pm
Enter Firewood via Rowland Alley
(off Broadway between Kearny and Montgomery)
San Francisco, California
Please RSVP at party@firewoodsf.com
or 415.391.8800
An RSVP is beyond appreciated
RSVP at pan@firewoodsf.com or 415.391.8800.
RSVP required to attend.
Enter Firewood via Rowland Alley
(off Broadway between
Montgomery and Kearny)
San Francisco, California
The Fourth Annual
Post-Holiday Party:
2007 Edition
Please join the folks at Firewood
in celebrating a bold new year.
Thursday, January 25, 2007
6pm to 9pm.

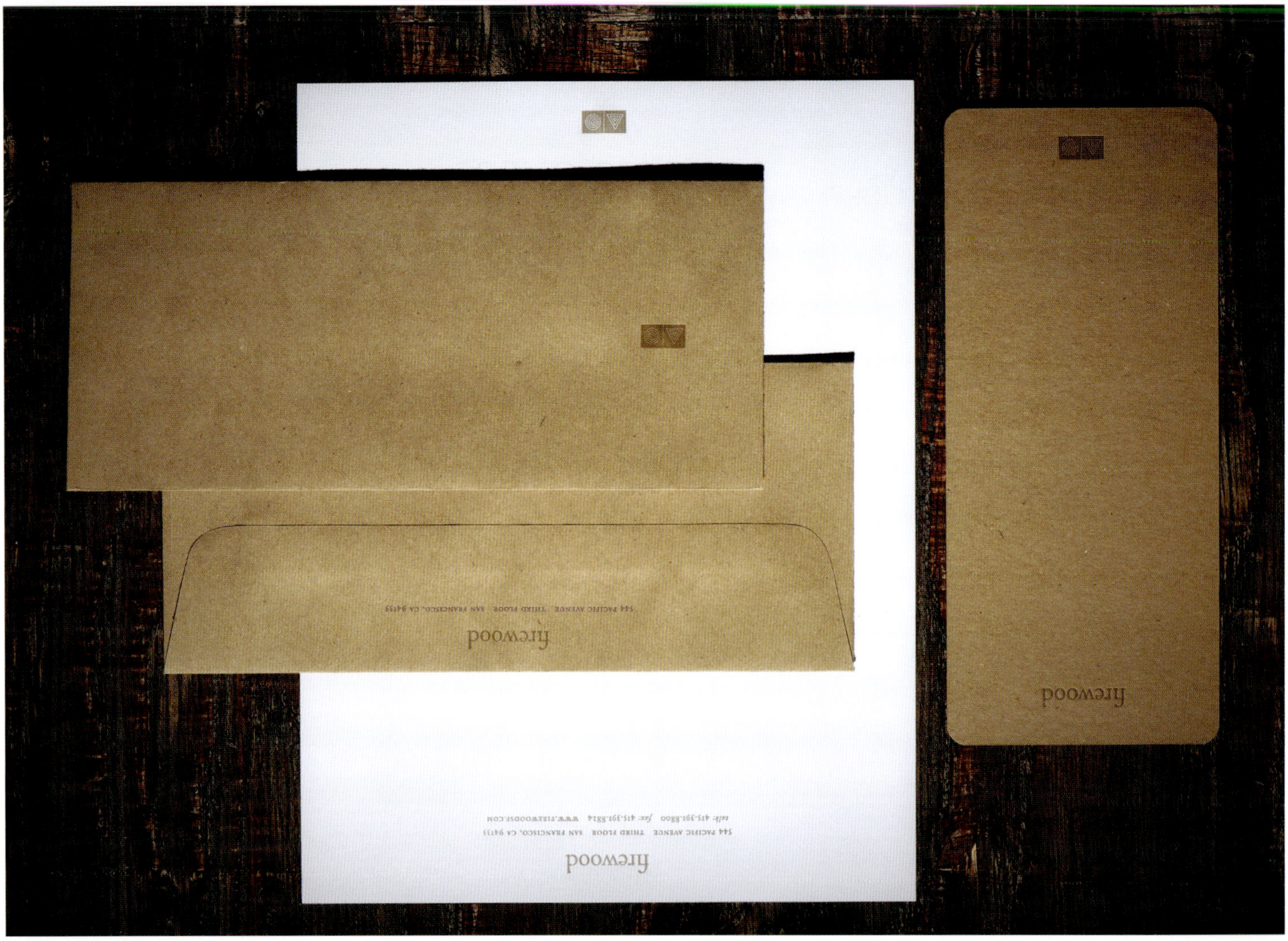
firewood
firewood
firewood

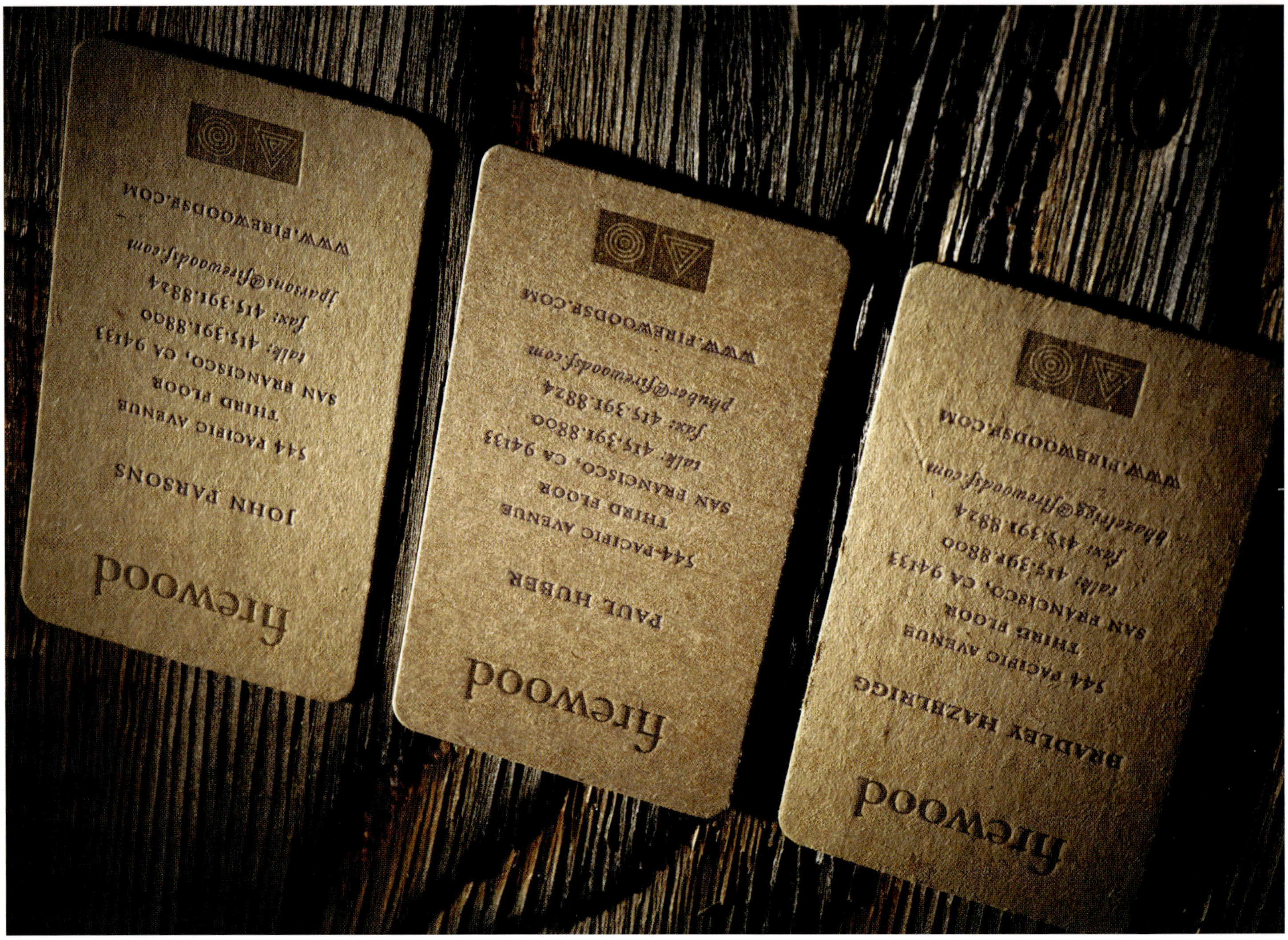
firewood
JOHN PARSONS
544 PACIFIC AVENUE
THIRD FLOOR
SAN FRANCISCO, CA 94133
talk: 415.391.8800
fax: 415.391.8824
jparsons@firewoodsf.com
WWW.FIREWOODSF.COM
firewood
PAUL HUBER
544 PACIFIC AVENUE
THIRD FLOOR
SAN FRANCISCO, CA 94133
talk: 415.391.8800
fax: 415.391.8824
phuber@firewoodsf.com
WWW.FIREWOODSF.COM
firewood
BRADLEY HAZELRIGG
544 PACIFIC AVENUE
THIRD FLOOR
SAN FRANCISCO, CA 94133
talk: 415.391.8800
fax: 415.391.8824
bhazelrigg@firewoodsf.com
WWW.FIREWOODSF.COM

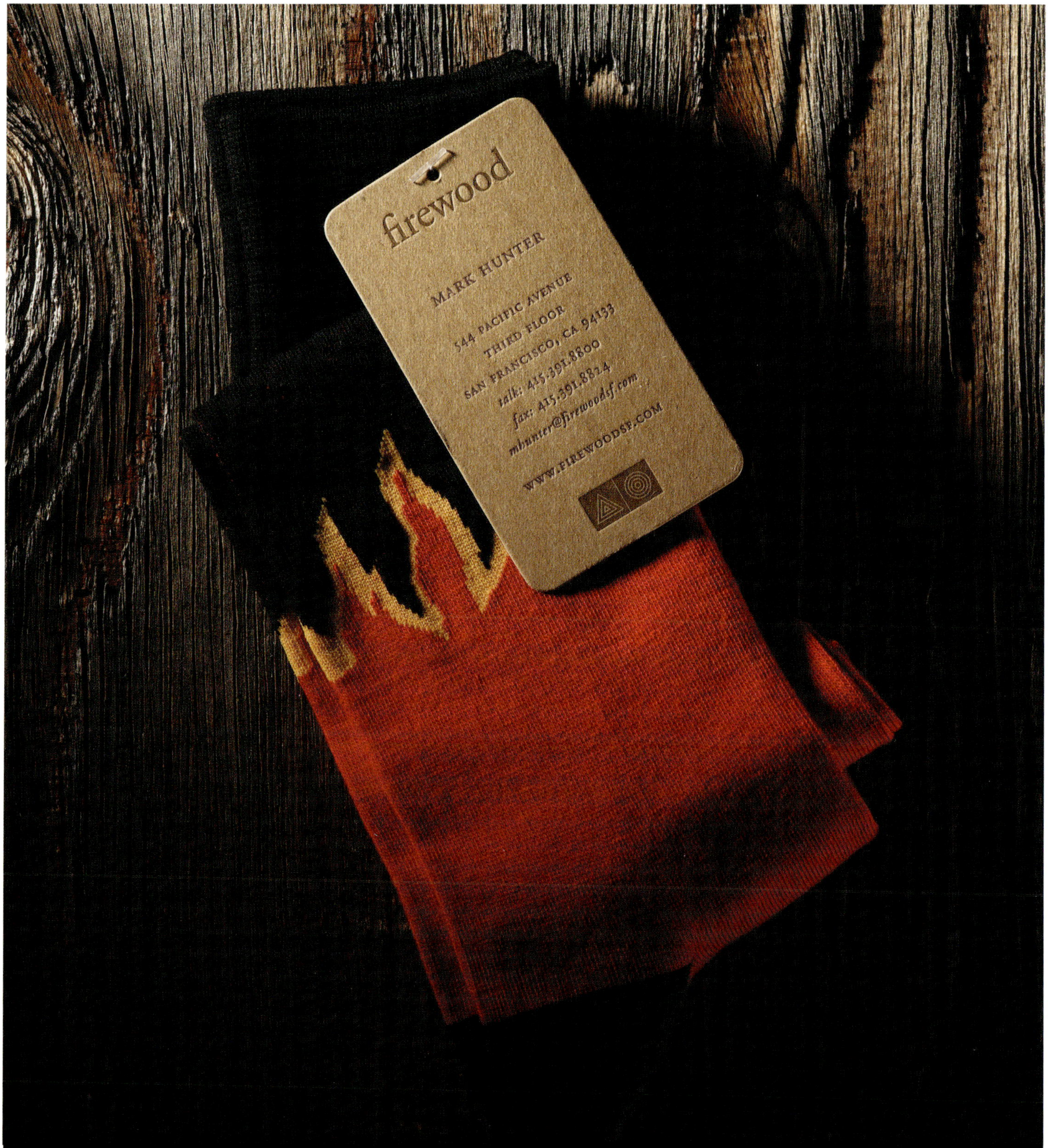
firewood
MARK HUNTER
544 PACIFIC AVENUE
THIRD FLOOR
SAN FRANCISCO, CA 94133
talk: 415.391.8800
fax: 415.391.8824
mhunter@firewoodsf.com
WWW.FIREWOODSF.COM

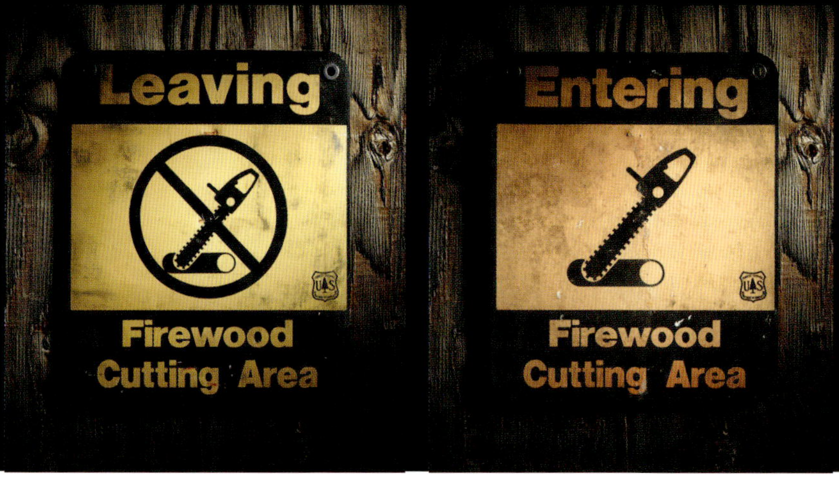
Leaving
Firewood
Cutting Area
Entering
Firewood
Cutting Area

The General Design Co. & Graffiato Identity System

Graffiato is an Italian-inspired restaurant by Mike Isabella, a Top Chef All Stars *runner-up, who became a television celebrity loved and loathed for his tough-talking persona. Mike approached us very early on while he was developing the restaurant concept. We talked him through the evolution of the concept, as well as several name changes. By the time we were ready to start translating the brand into a visual identity system, we had months and months of processing and digesting the key attributes and personality traits of not only the restaurant, but more importantly, of Mike. The project involved developing a broad visual identity system that included logo design, business cards, menus, signage, interior graphics, and a variety of ephemera such as coasters, to-go bags, and toothpicks.*

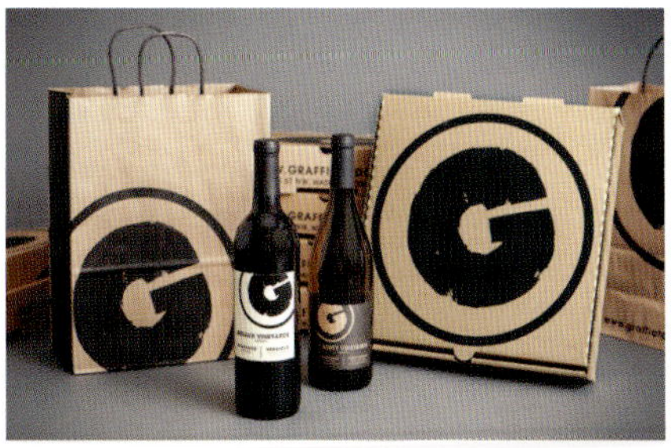

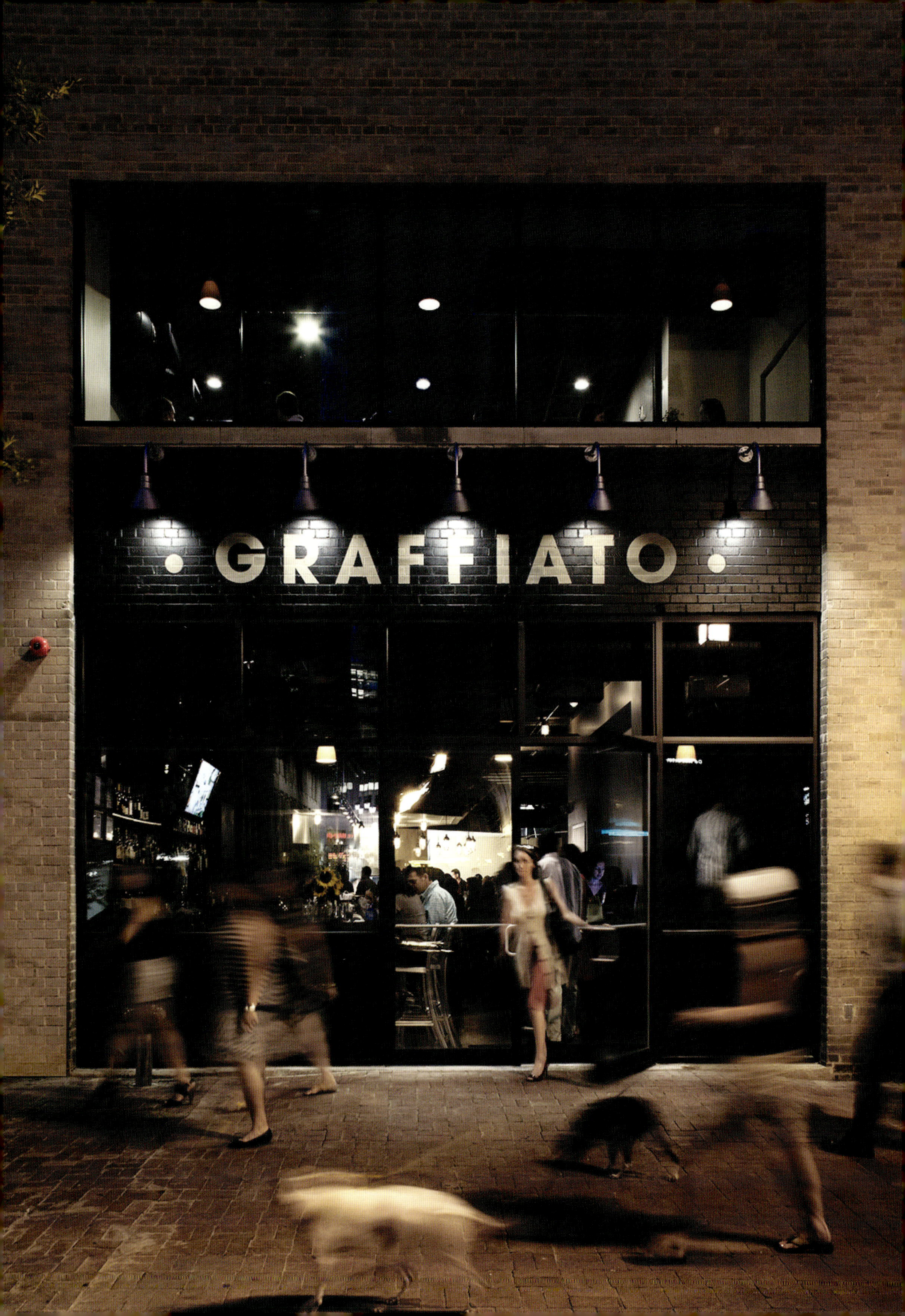
GRAFFIATO

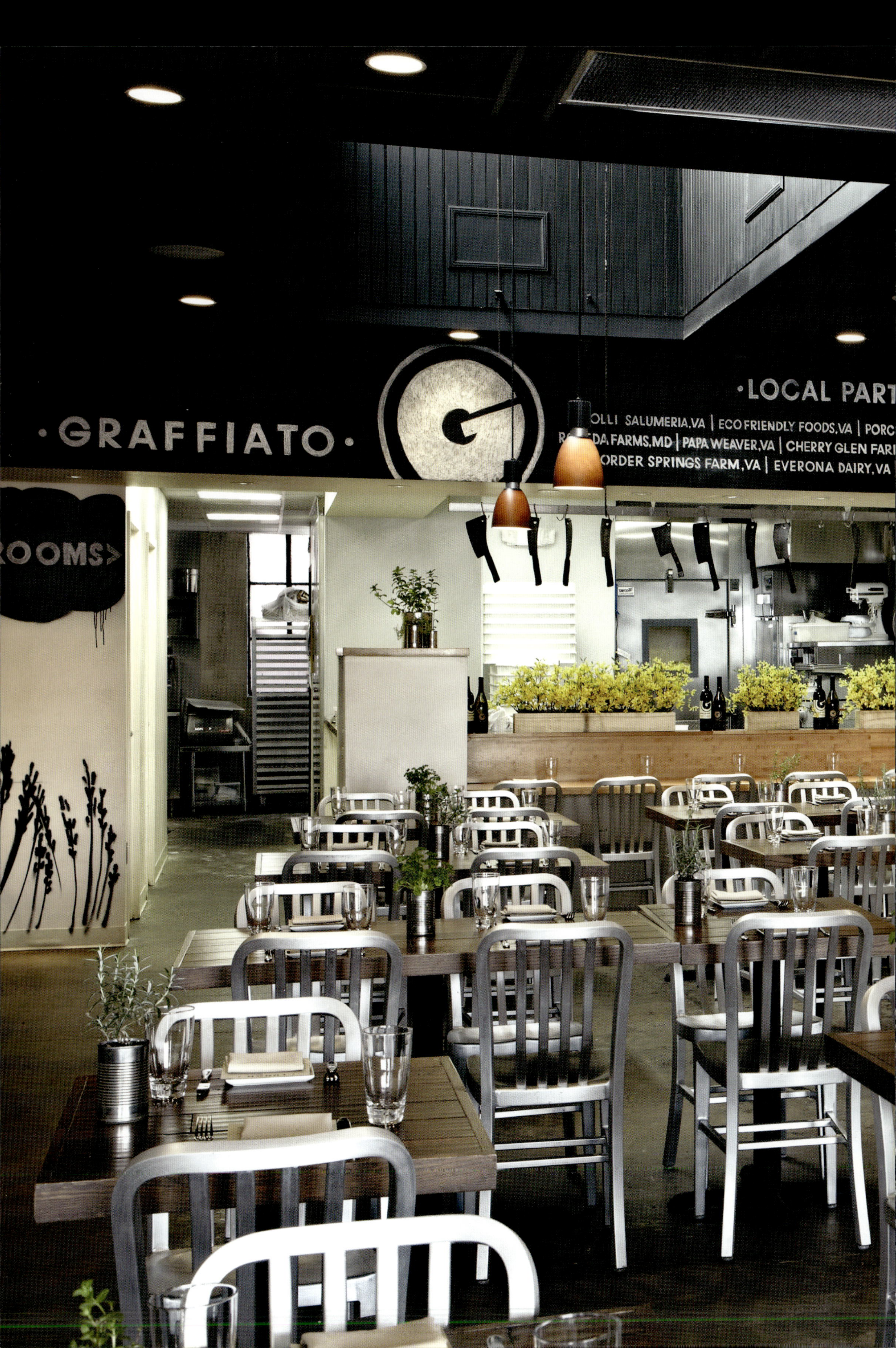
·GRAFFIATO·
ROOMS>
·LOCAL PART
OLLI SALUMERIA,VA | ECO FRIENDLY FOODS,VA | PORC
DA FARMS,MD | PAPA WEAVER,VA | CHERRY GLEN FAR
ORDER SPRINGS FARM,VA | EVERONA DAIRY,VA

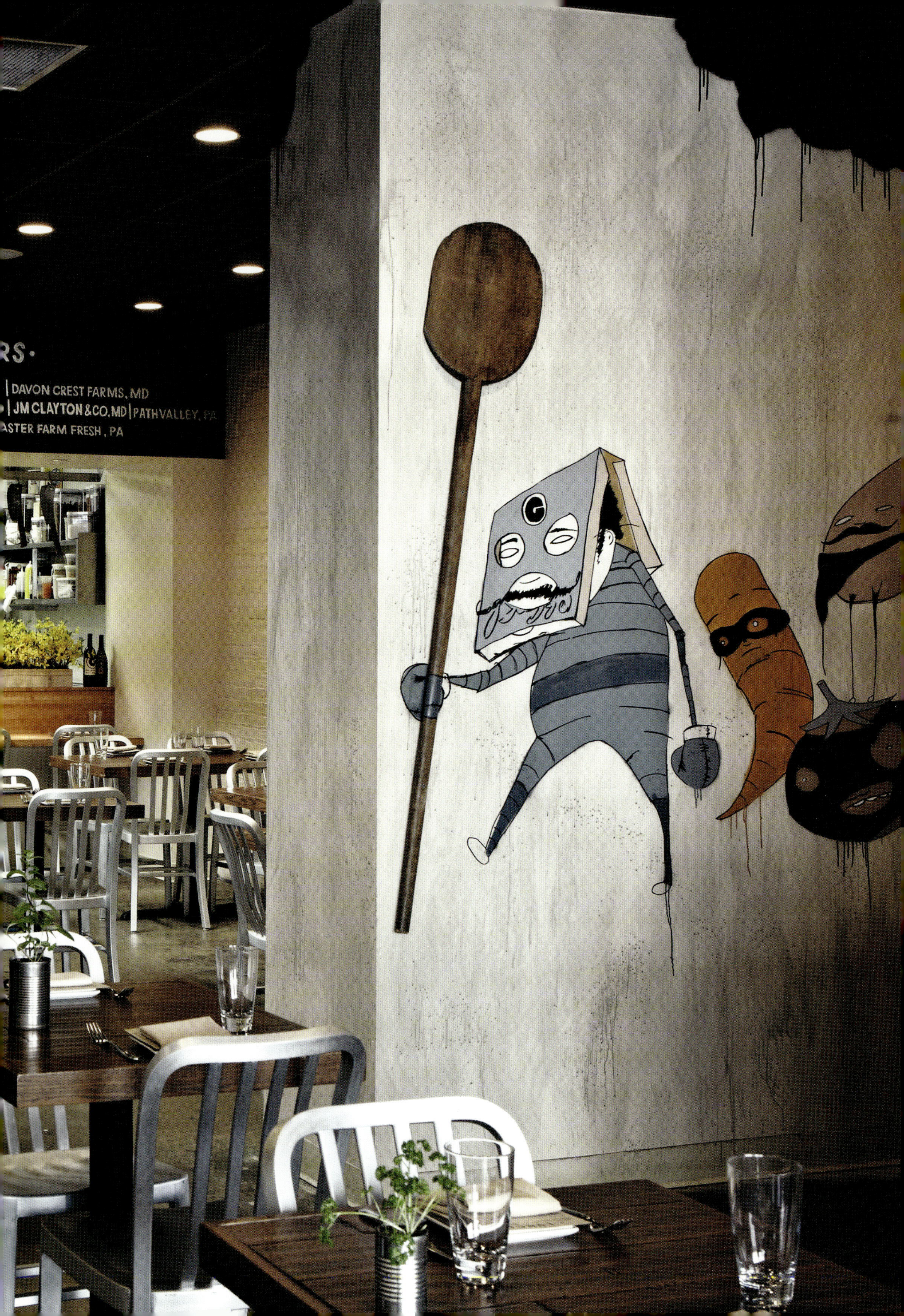
RS·
| DAVON CREST FARMS, MD
| JM CLAYTON & CO, MD | PATHVALLEY, PA
ASTER FARM FRESH, PA

Q&A with The General Design Co.

Our Approach It was important to develop a brand that was able to hold up to the big, bold personality of a chef quickly on his way to becoming a household name and food celebrity. With a background in some of the country's top restaurants serving Mediterranean and Latin small plates, Graffiato was Mike's opportunity to focus on the food he grew up eating in his Italian-American grandmother's kitchen. When asked what region of Italy his food focuses on, Mike's response is New Jersey. He is loud, covered in tattoos, and quick to smile. It was important to him to create a space that reflected his personality—raw, with high-energy—while serving food with unique twists and bold flavors.

The creative process involved a variety of concepts that ranged from focusing on his loud and tattooed persona to more emphasis on his Italian roots. Because the name is Graffiato, which is graffiti in Italian and means "to scratch," we wanted to avoid the obvious route of using graffiti. In the end, the most successful direction was one that focused on his philosophy on cooking: simple dishes with bold flavors. We created a bold, graphic G that could be stamped on a variety of collateral, representing the impact that Mike Isabella and Graffiato are making on Washington, D.C.'s exploding restaurant scene. The simplicity of the visual identity system and interior space allowed for whimsical murals depicting a shepherd herding pizza peels and mischievous veggie bandits. The art on the walls, along with the chalkboard lists of local partners, all speak to the restaurant's mission of highlighting locally sourced, high-quality ingredients.

Results The feedback and reception to the branding and design has been overwhelmingly positive—from comments about how easy it is for diners to find interesting information on the website, to how engaging and delightful the interior art and graphics are. As for the chef himself, his reaction to the finished project was to run out and get a custom-made scooter with the G logo embedded in the floor bed.

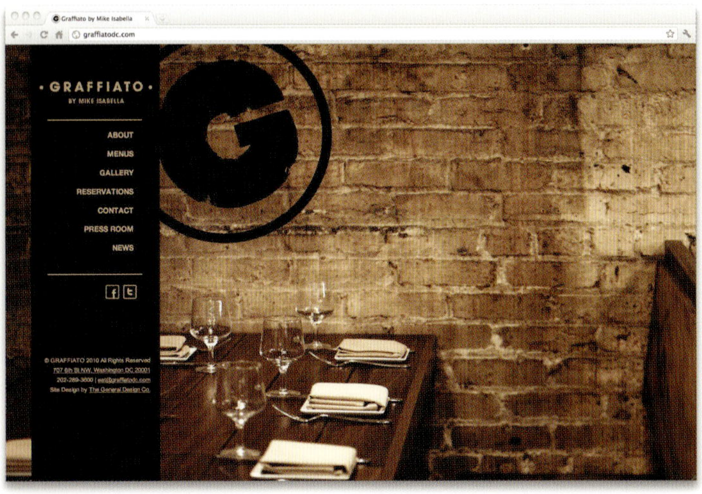

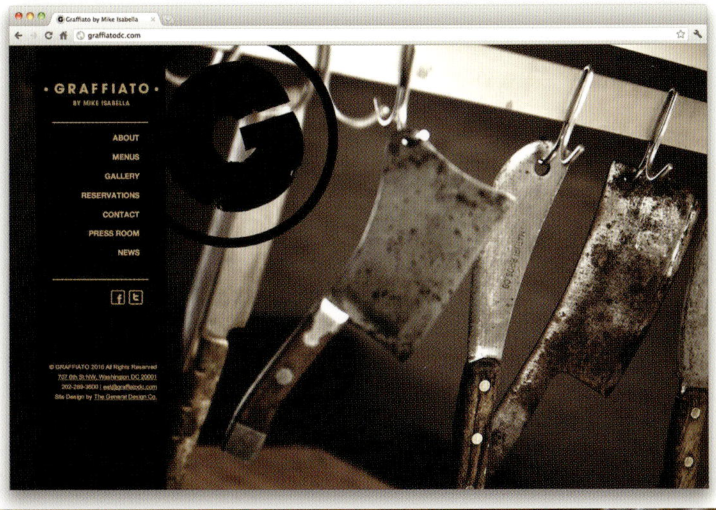

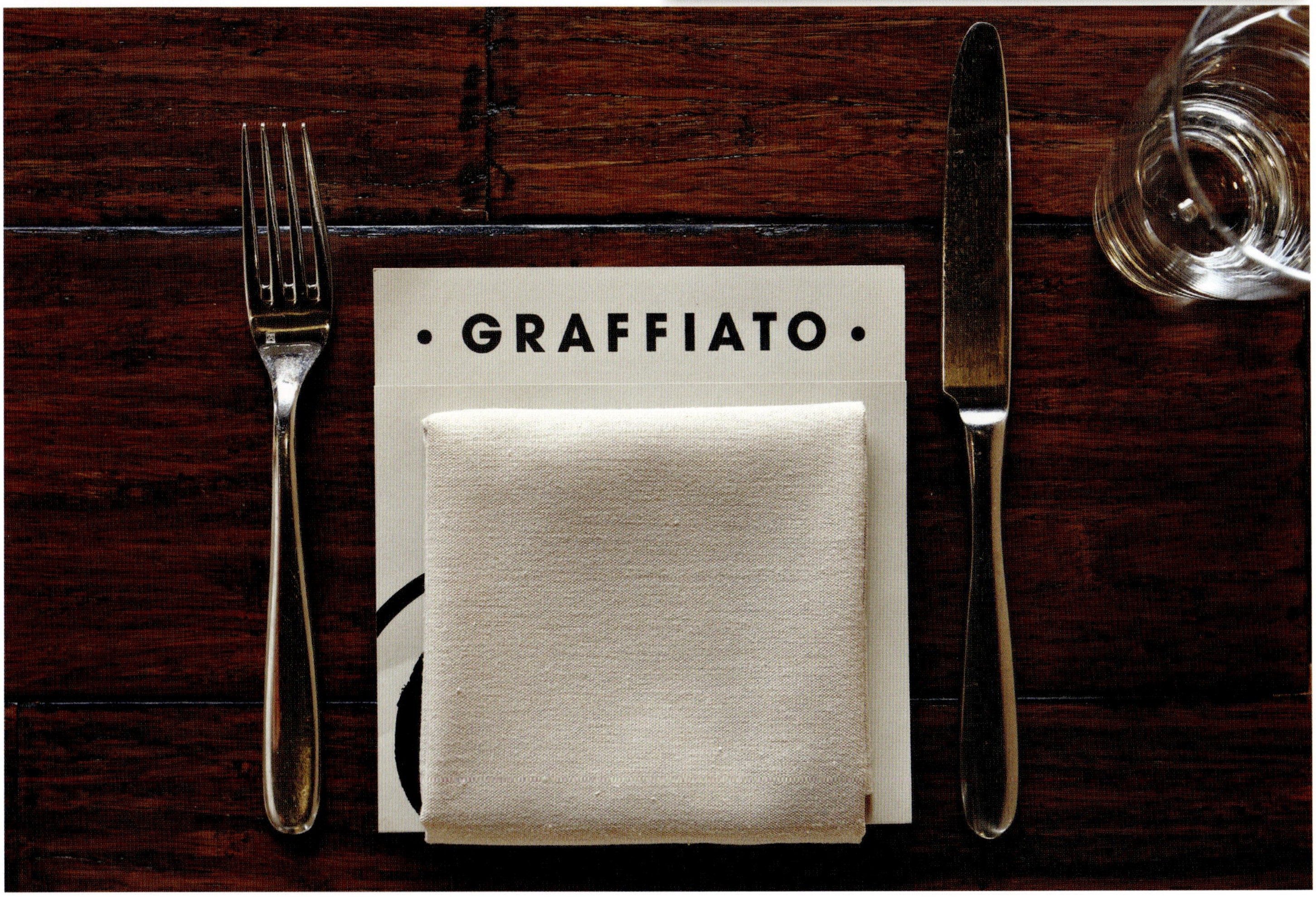

Designer: Kaleena Porter | **Design Firm:** The General Design Co. | **Art Director:** Soung Wiser | **Creative Directors:** Soung Wiser, Scott Livingston

Client: Graffiato by Mike Isabella

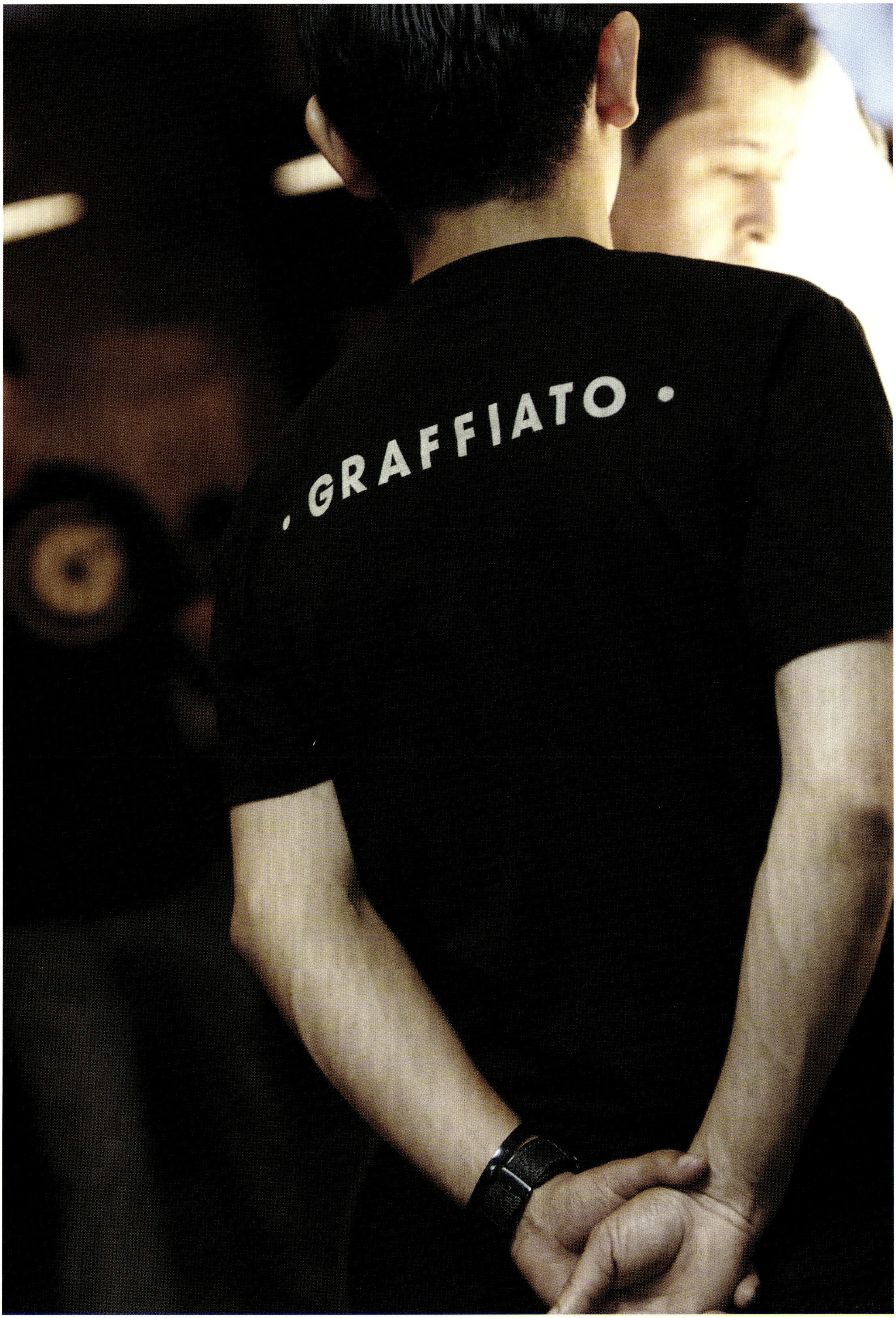
GRAFFIATO

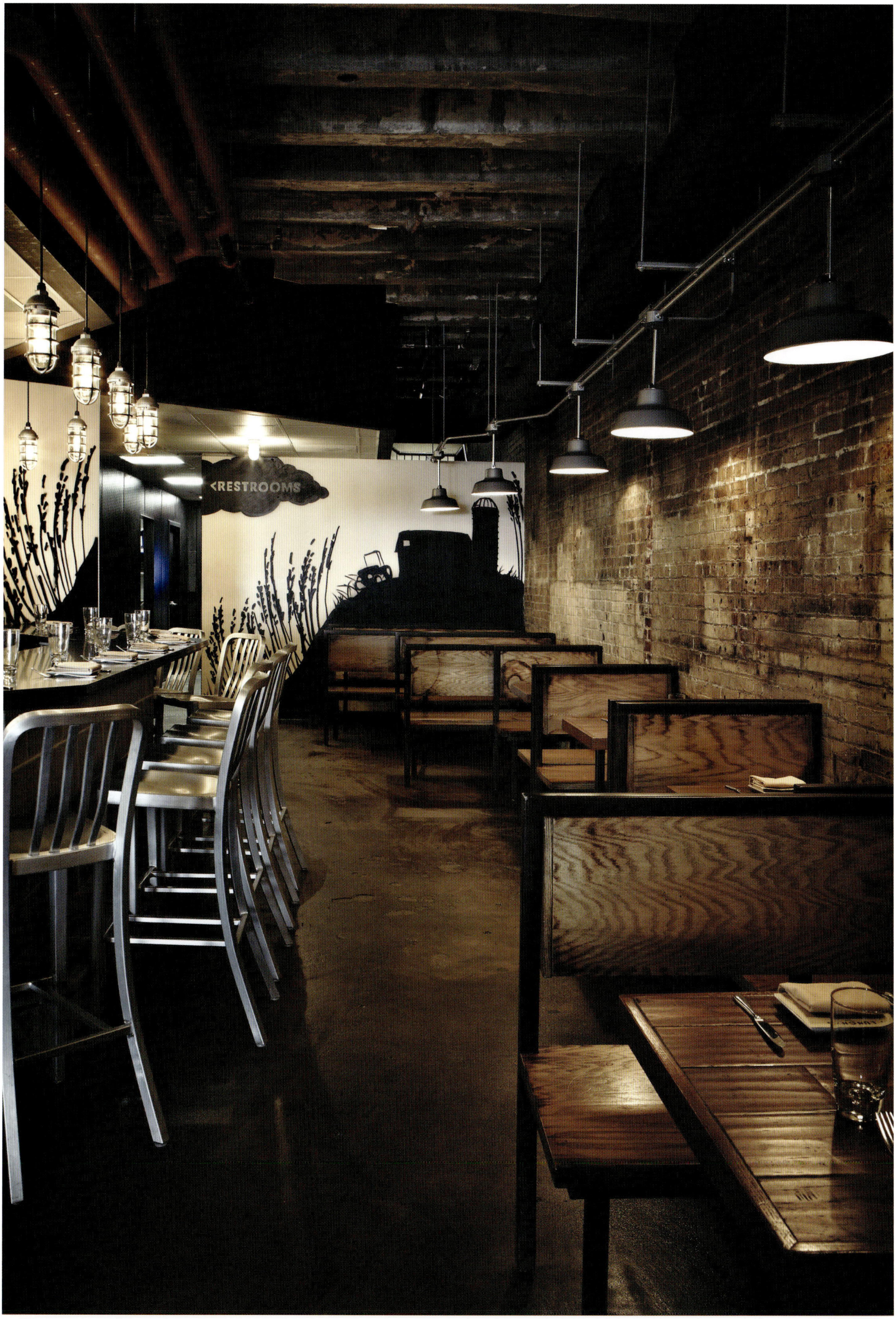
<RESTROOMS

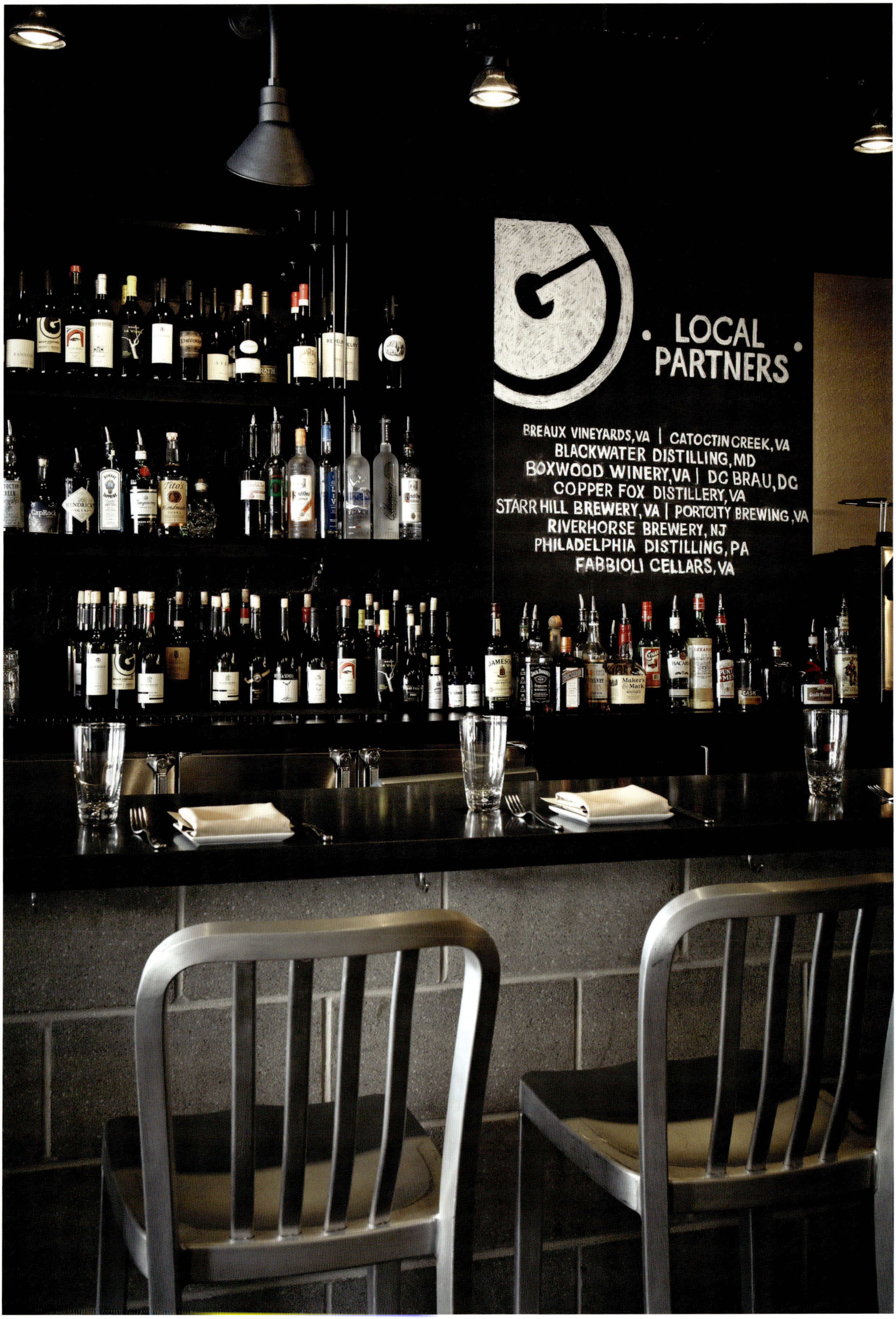
LOCAL PARTNERS
BREAUX VINEYARDS, VA | CATOCTIN CREEK, VA
BLACKWATER DISTILLING, MD
BOXWOOD WINERY, VA | DC BRAU, DC
COPPER FOX DISTILLERY, VA
STARR HILL BREWERY, VA | PORTCITY BREWING, VA
RIVERHORSE BREWERY, NJ
PHILADELPHIA DISTILLING, PA
FABBIOLI CELLARS, VA

Institute IGH d.d. has grown into a leading and dominant civil engineering consulting company in Central and Eastern Europe. Logo IGH is a layered project that shows the company's services: planning, supervision, and building facilities, including a wide range of roads, bridges, and large objects in civil engineering and building construction. The specificity of the solution is a square grid on the letter H, which aligns with the Croatian visual code IGH. The implementation of the logo is significant in 2D and 3D. In the 3D version, there are two versions of cross sections: a square and a circle. The new IGH logo has strengthened its brand position in the European and World markets. The logo's application through various features with a default program of visual identity creates a complete impression of a very strong project and construction company.

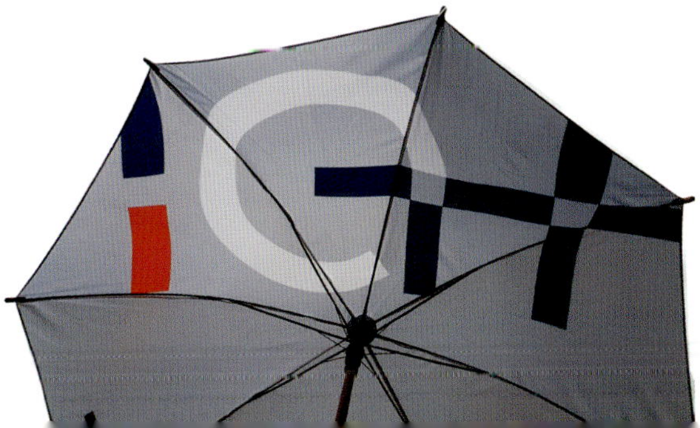

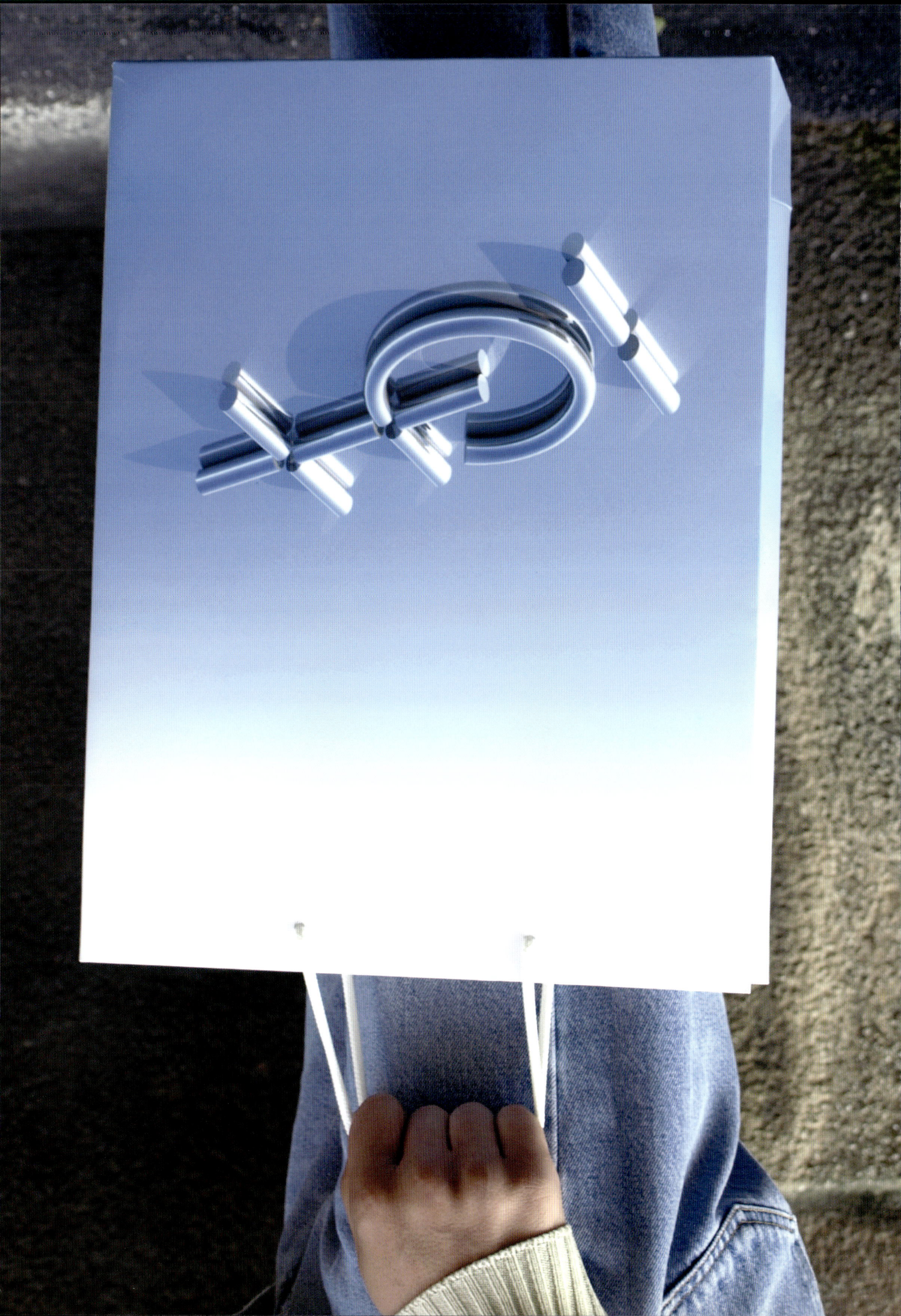

Q&A with Studio International

Assignment The project's main goal was to create a unique, modern, and recognizable corporate identity for a big architectural and building corporation. Their existing visual identity was quite unrecognizable—only one green color. The formation of the Republic of Croatia as an independent state created need for a new logo. The expanding business in surrounding countries, and the increasing number of companies under unique logo, all needed to be encircled by a visual identity that would be unique, but different in its implementation.

Our Approach The main idea was to create a complete and unique visual-identity project representing a very diverse corporation that, within its system, has several companies whose main activity is planning and building big public structures and services. The corporation name, IGH, is derived from the initial letters of its full name—*Institut Graditeljstva Hrvatske* (the Croatian Engineering Institute). Logo IGH was designed under a network diagram as a project for performance in construction, high and low construction, and road and bridge building, which is the corporation's specialty. The network diagram is squared, so it represents Croatian national identity as well. Red, silver-gray (white), and blue are the colors of the Croatian flag. The corporation has companies not only in Croatia, but also in other surrounding countries. To visually communicate their corporate identity, the logo in 3D has the appearance of construction and building in metal and glass. Logo applications are easily implemented in either 2D and 3D. The large number of applications allows for diversity on one side, and integrity on the other.

Results IGH has strengthened its appearance in the market and achieved the image of a modern, ambitious, and effective corporation, even outside of its region (it implements construction projects globally). Its bridges and airport projects win international awards, which the corporation's visual identity confirms with its unique design. The fact that the design is globally successful means a lot to the corporation. The new visual identity improves the corporation's public appearance, and assists with getting new jobs and further development.

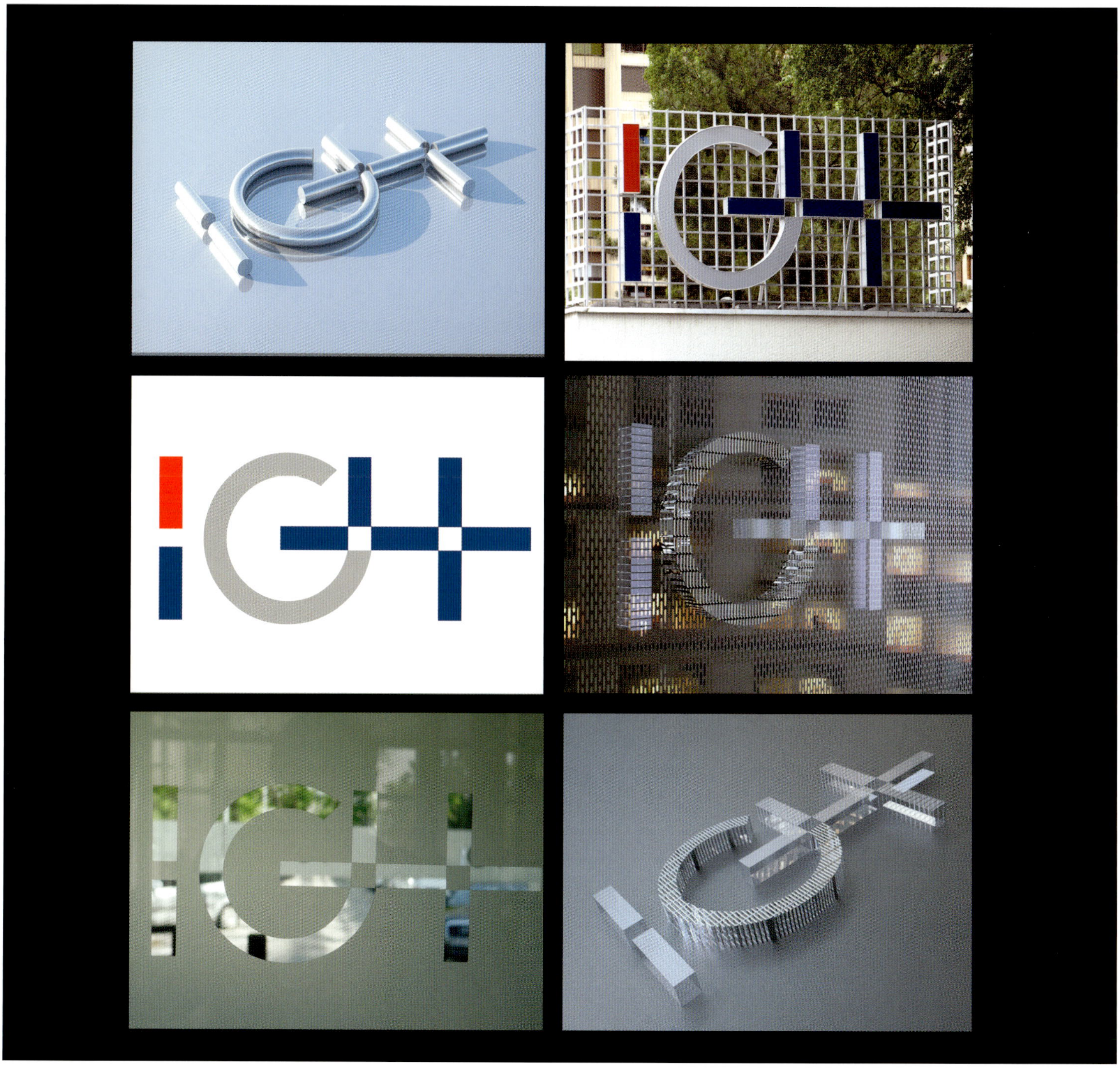

Designer: Boris Ljubicic | **Design Firm:** STUDIO INTERNATIONAL | **Art Director:** Boris Ljubicic | **Creative Director:** Boris Ljubicic
Illustrator: Igor Ljubicic | **Client:** IGH (Croatian Engineering Institute)

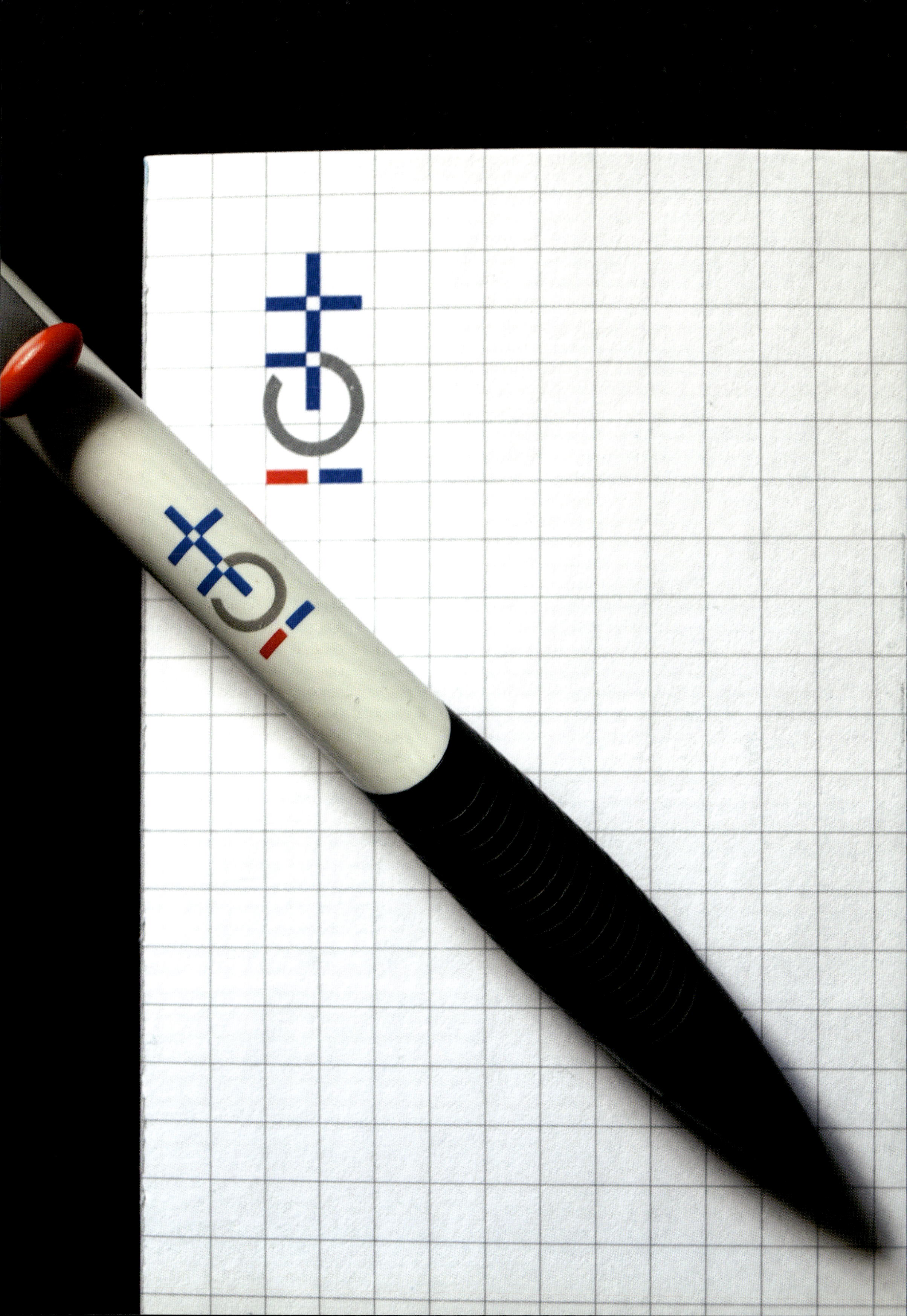

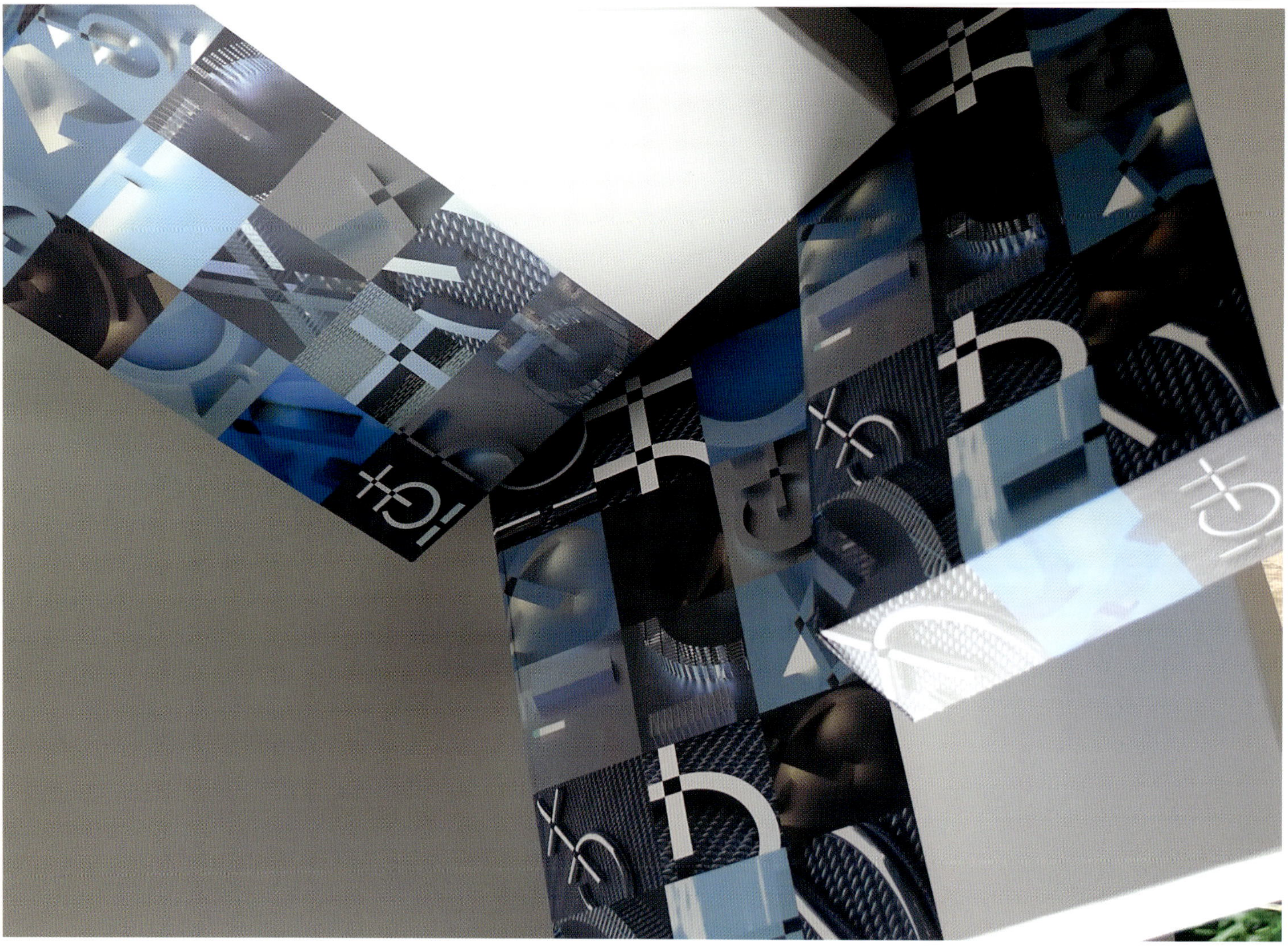

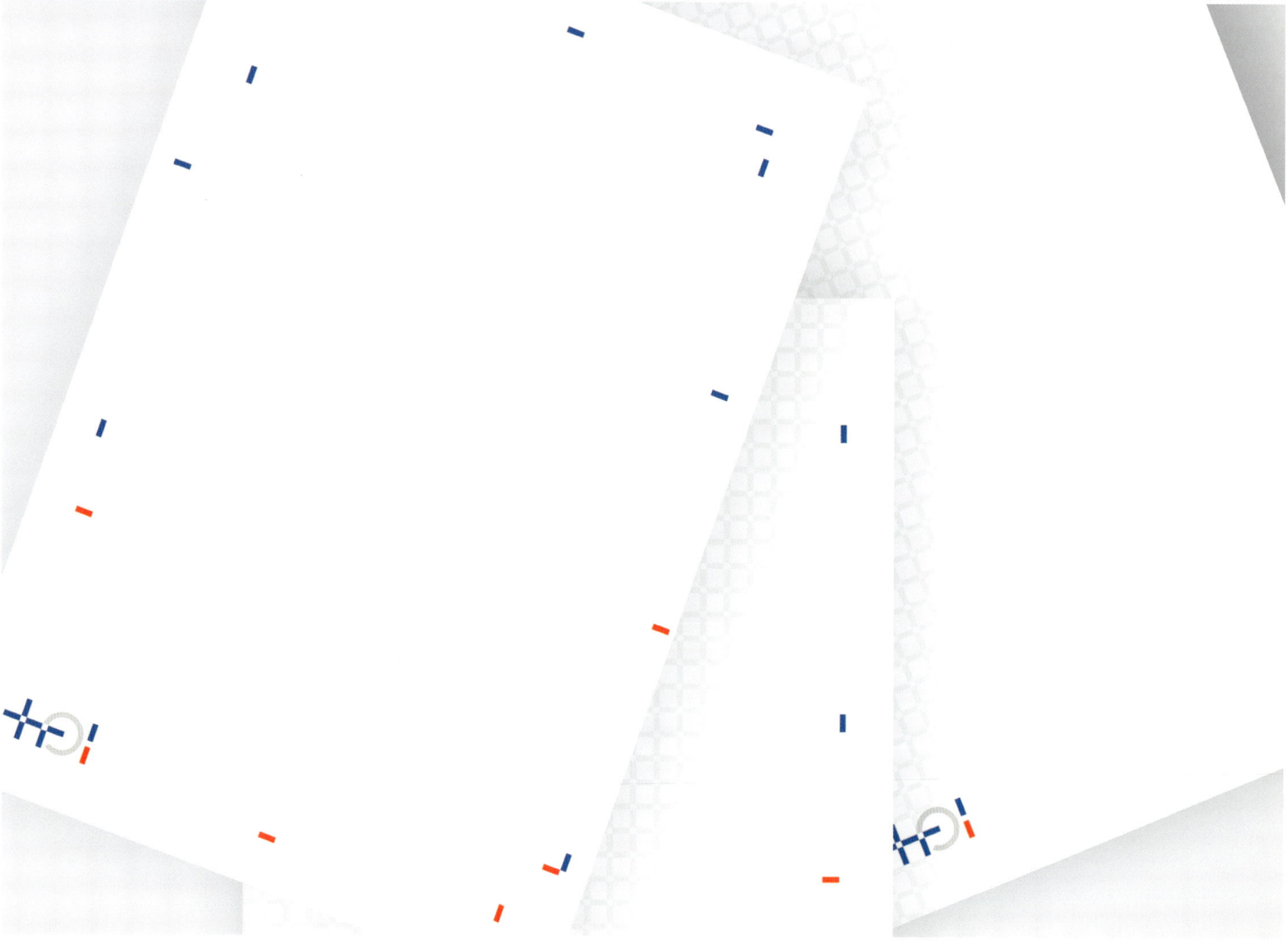

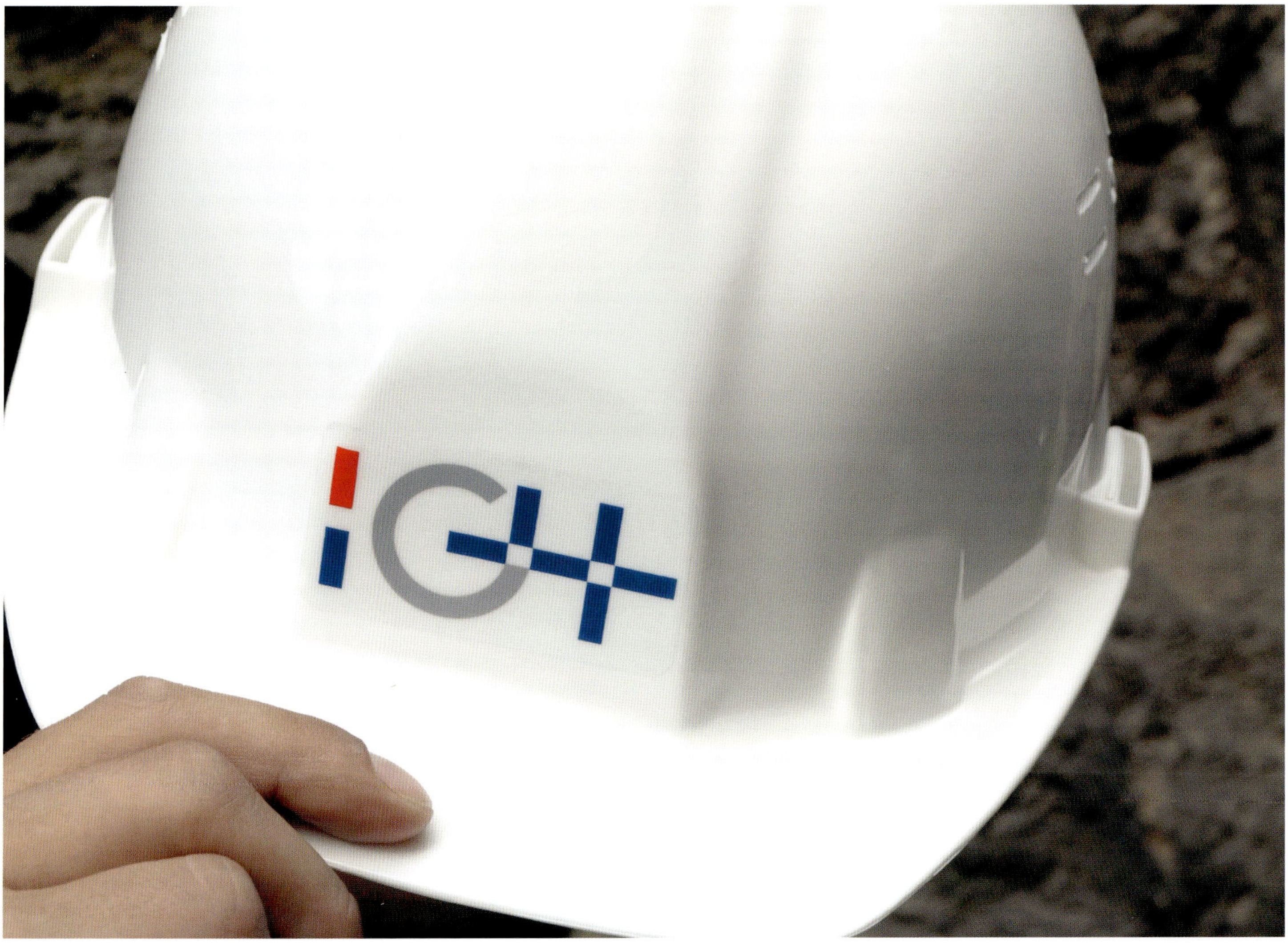
IGH

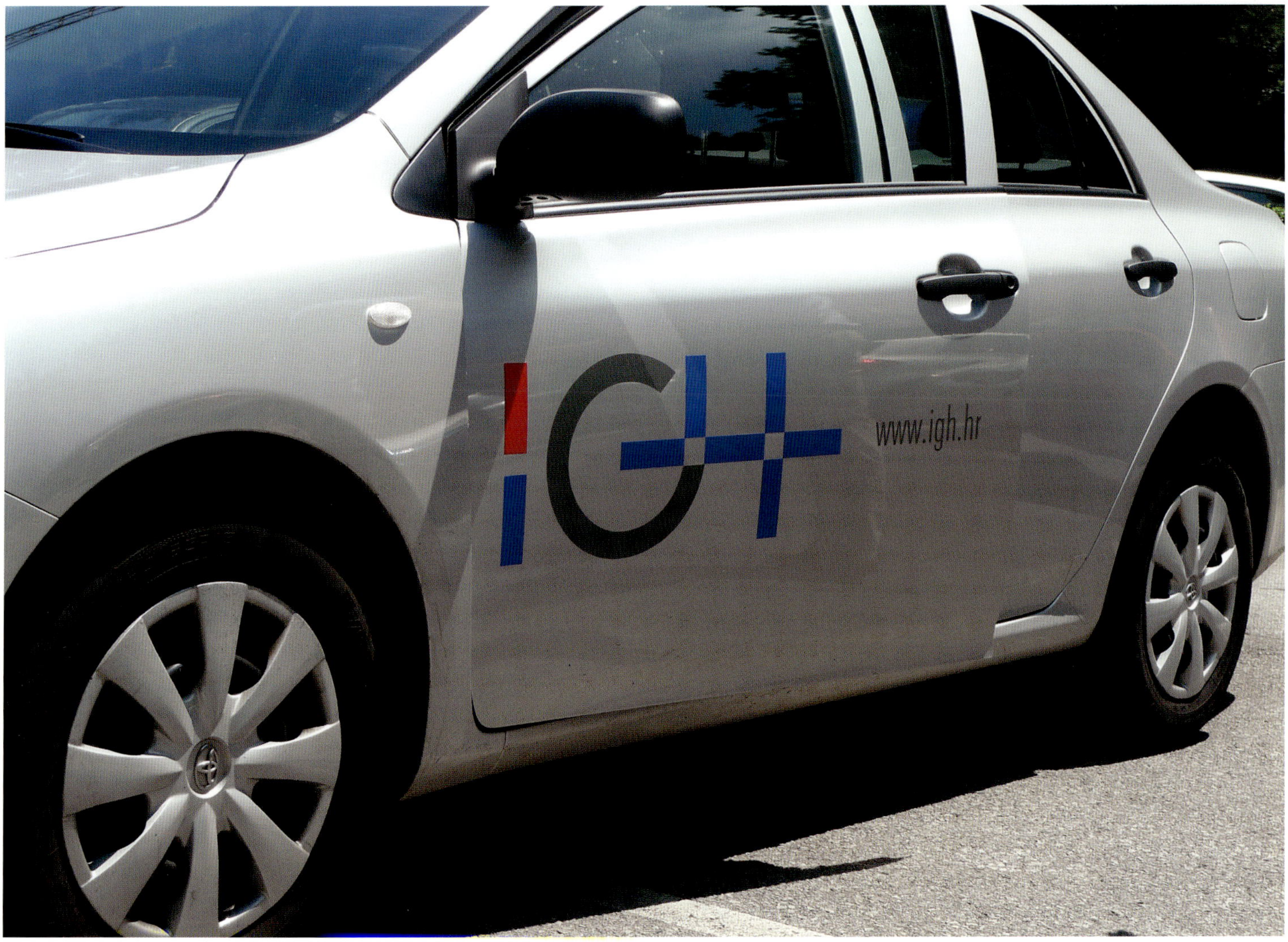
IGH
www.igh.hr

Alt Group & Box Café Identity

Box Café is located at the entry of a performing arts center (the Aotea Centre) and functions as an information center, ticketing office, and venue. The identity was implemented throughout signage, wayfinding, uniform, collateral, and campaign. Box's location is a strategic one–it is part of a performing arts center located on a popular inner-city square; however, there is extensive competition in the area. Box needed a distinctive identity to create an enhanced visual presence that could offer a different kind of experience. It needed to serve as a friendly interface between the public square and the performing arts center. In order to perform well as a multi-functional space, it was essential that careful attention was paid to an internal wayfinding system that could direct customers to which service they required, whether it be café service or ticketing.

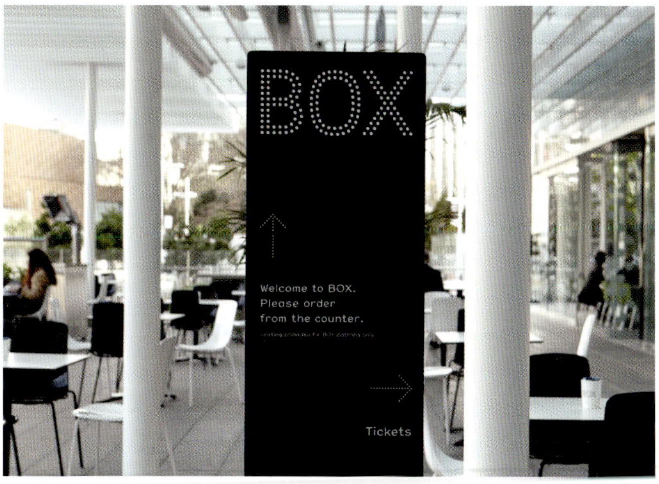

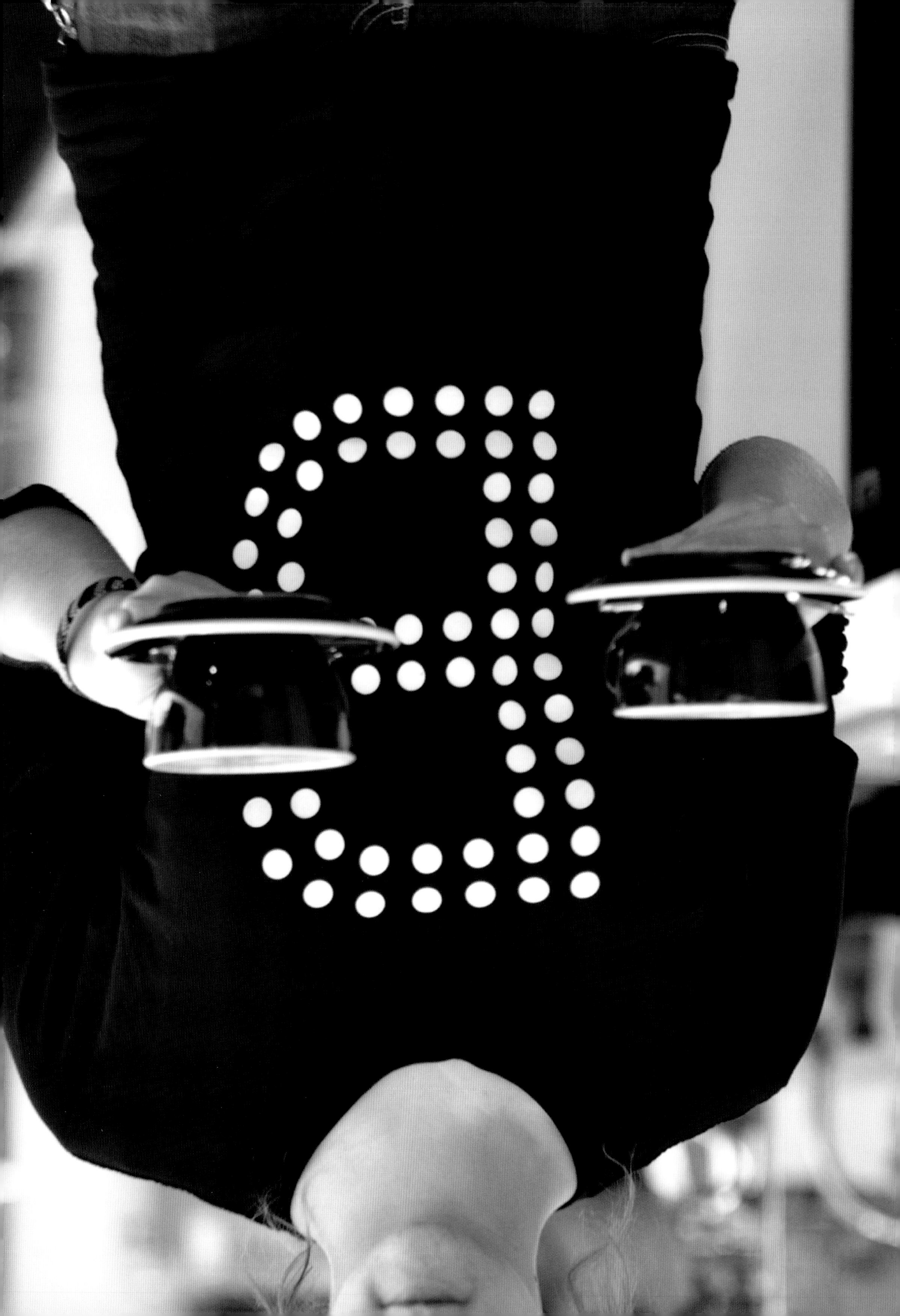

Q&A with Alt Group

Project Description Box Café is a key element of the Aotea Square refurbishment project. It is located at the entry of Aotea Centre, functioning as an information center, ticketing office, and venue. Both the name and visual identity needed to communicate the offering simply. The name says what it does—it is a café, a ticket office, a bar, a lunch destination, as well as a space for private events. The logomark is built from of a series of dots that reference the design vernacular of theater lighting—Vegas, Broadway, or the West End. It also visually references dot matrix printers, commonly found in ticket offices, as well as the configurations of dots produced by punches used to perforate cardboard admission tickets.

Project Challenges Box Café is part of a performing arts center located on a popular inner-city square. While its location is strategic, there is extensive competition in the area. Box needed an enhanced visual presence that would distinguish it from the competition.

In order to perform well as a multi-functional space, careful attention was paid to an internal wayfinding system that could direct customers to whichever service they required, whether it be café service or ticketing.

Effectiveness An oversized logomark application on the café's glass walls invites customers and patrons from across the square and serves as a friendly interface between the public square and the performing arts center. The Aotea Square refurbishment project (of which Box Café was a key element) was awarded the Public Sector Project of the Year Award from the Project Management Institute of New Zealand. The mark lends itself to a range of executions and finishes, whether printed, die-cut, embossed, recessed, or floated. This was extended into a broader visual language and series of icons, and a pattern language that communicates the offering in a pictorial sense. The identity was implemented throughout signage, wayfinding, uniform, collateral, and campaign.

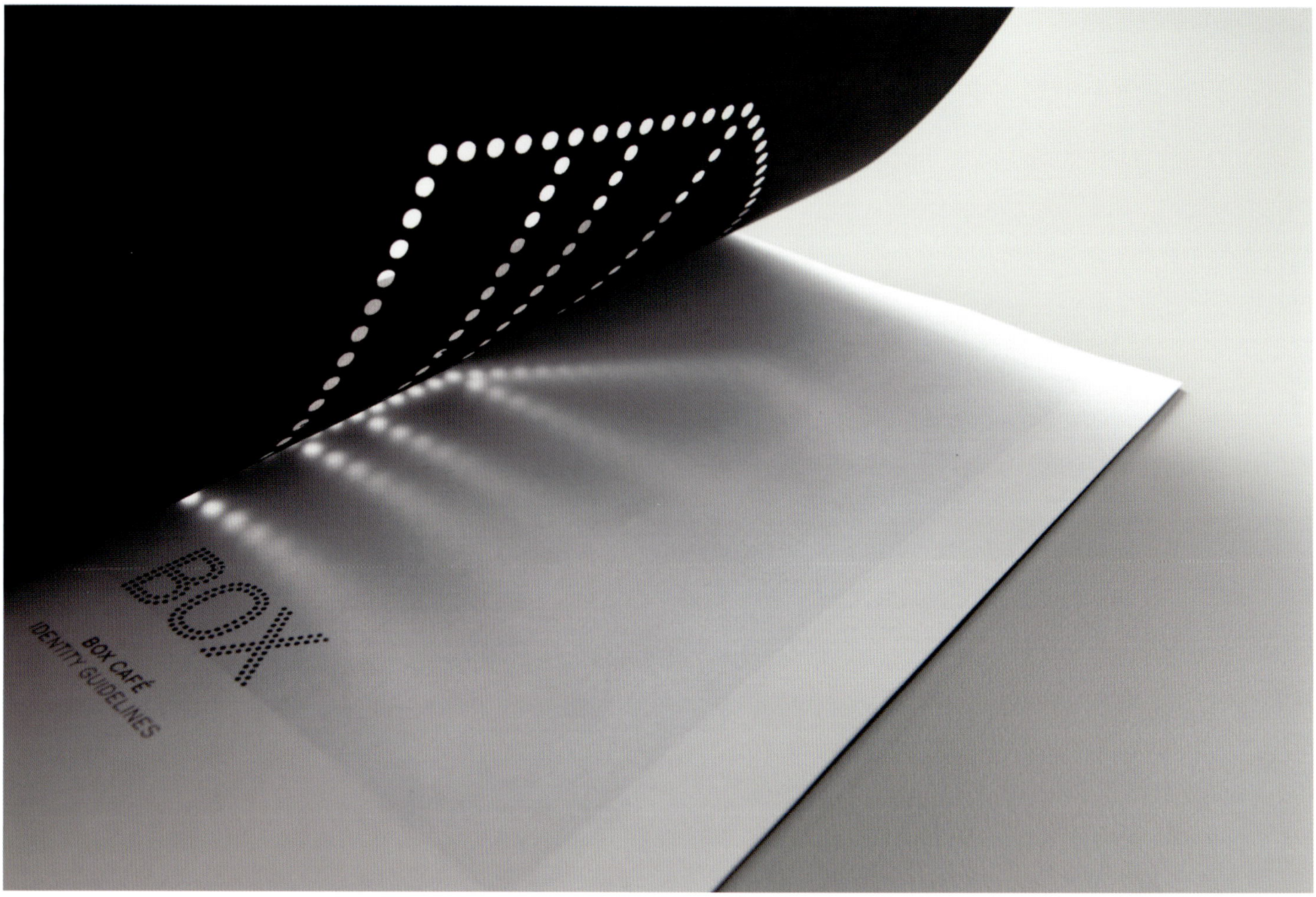

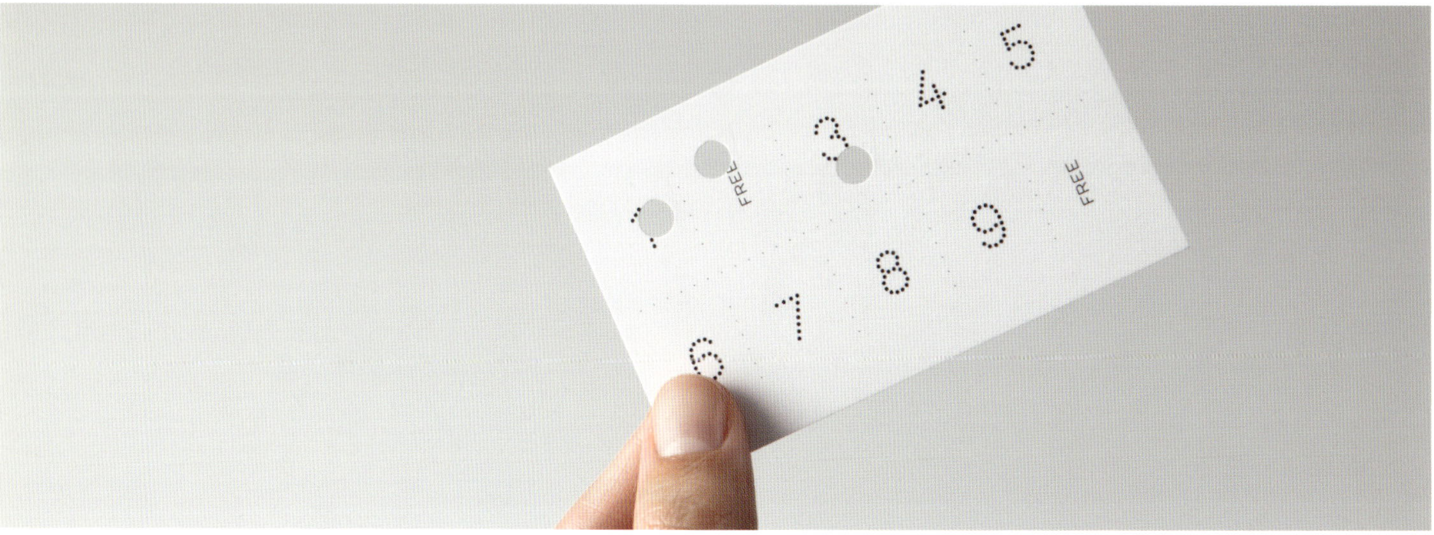

Designers: Toby Curnow, Janson Chau | **Design Firm:** Alt Group | **Creative Director:** Dean Poole

Writers: Dean Poole, Ben Corban | **Client:** The Edge

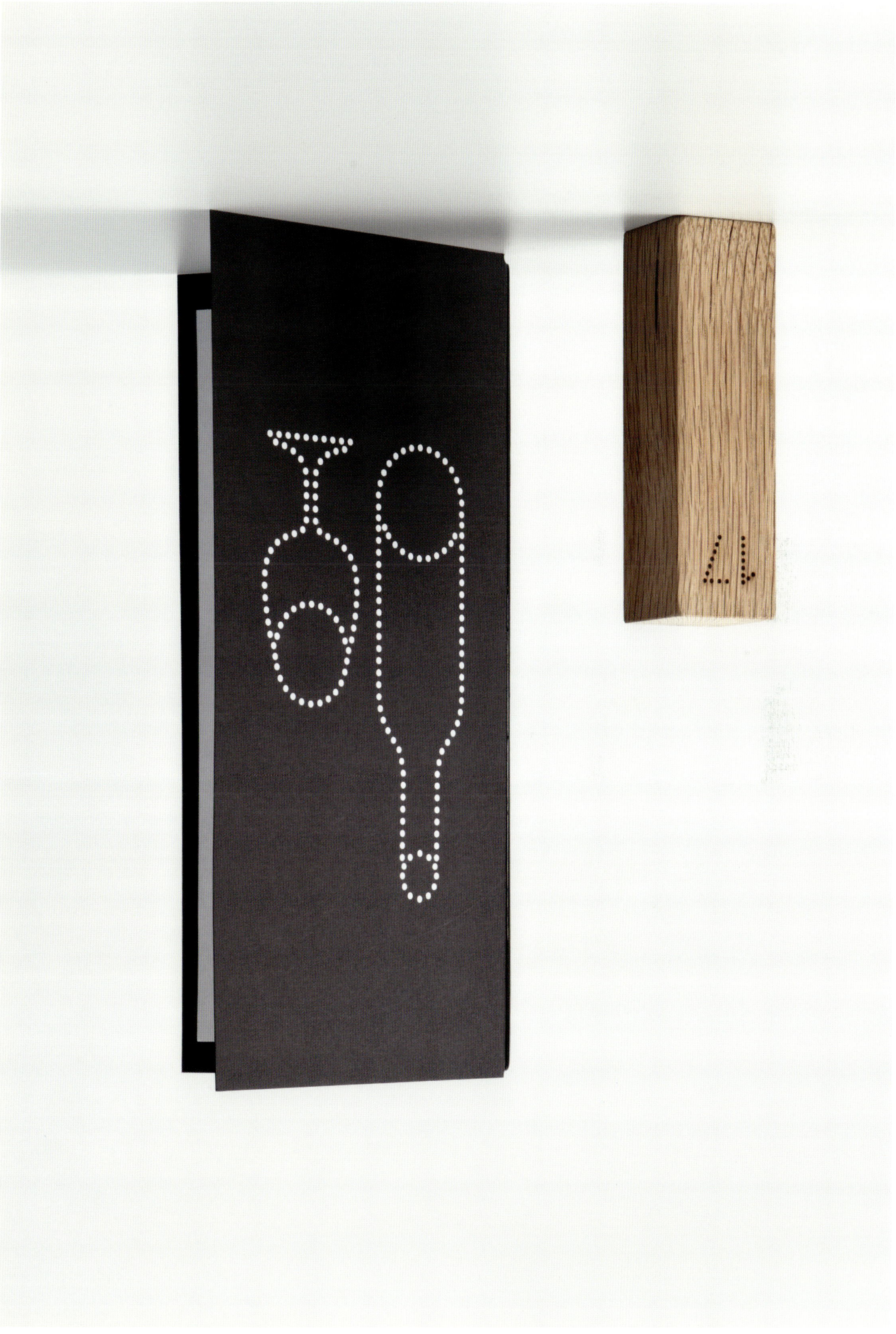

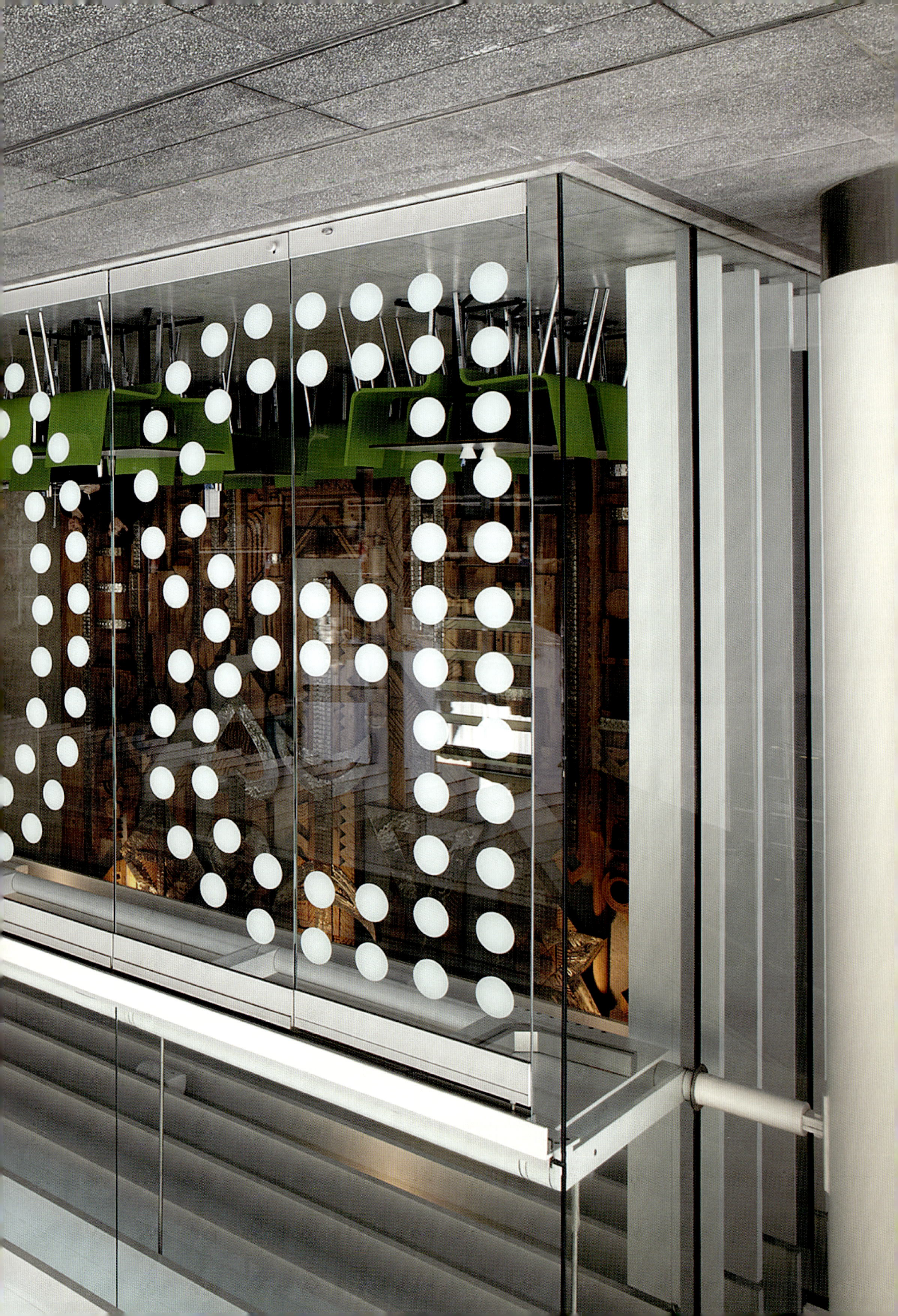

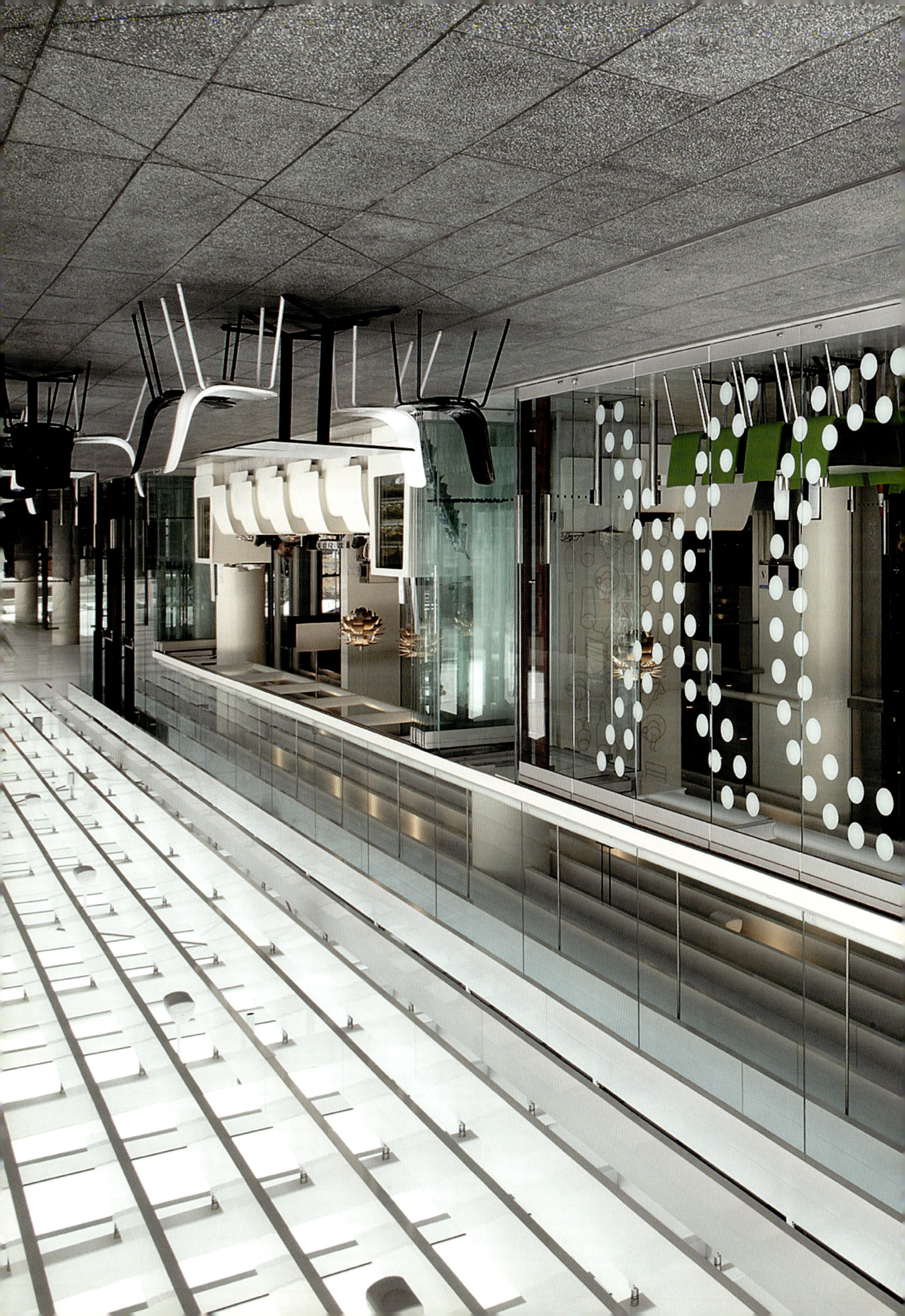

Assignment: Global rebranding. A new brand identity and profound change in the retail network: three years to surprise the world.

Results: "Results were beyond expectations."—Xavier Duchemin, Marketing and Communication Director

Designers: Alice Genaud, Johanna Roca | **Design Firm:** Landor Associates France | **Writer:** Pierre Nabhan | **Client:** Citroën

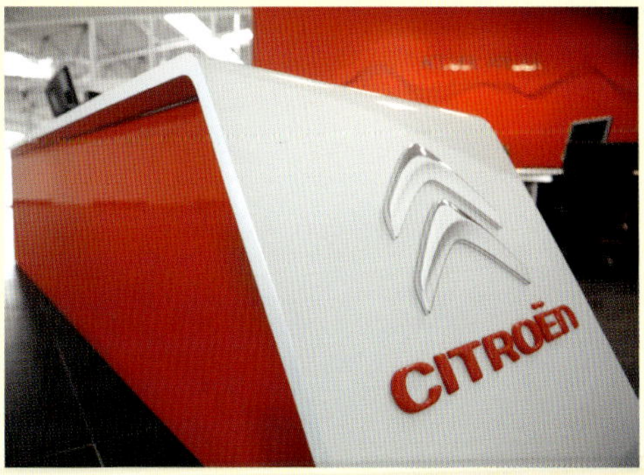

Landor Associates France(this spread)|Citroën|Automotive**64**

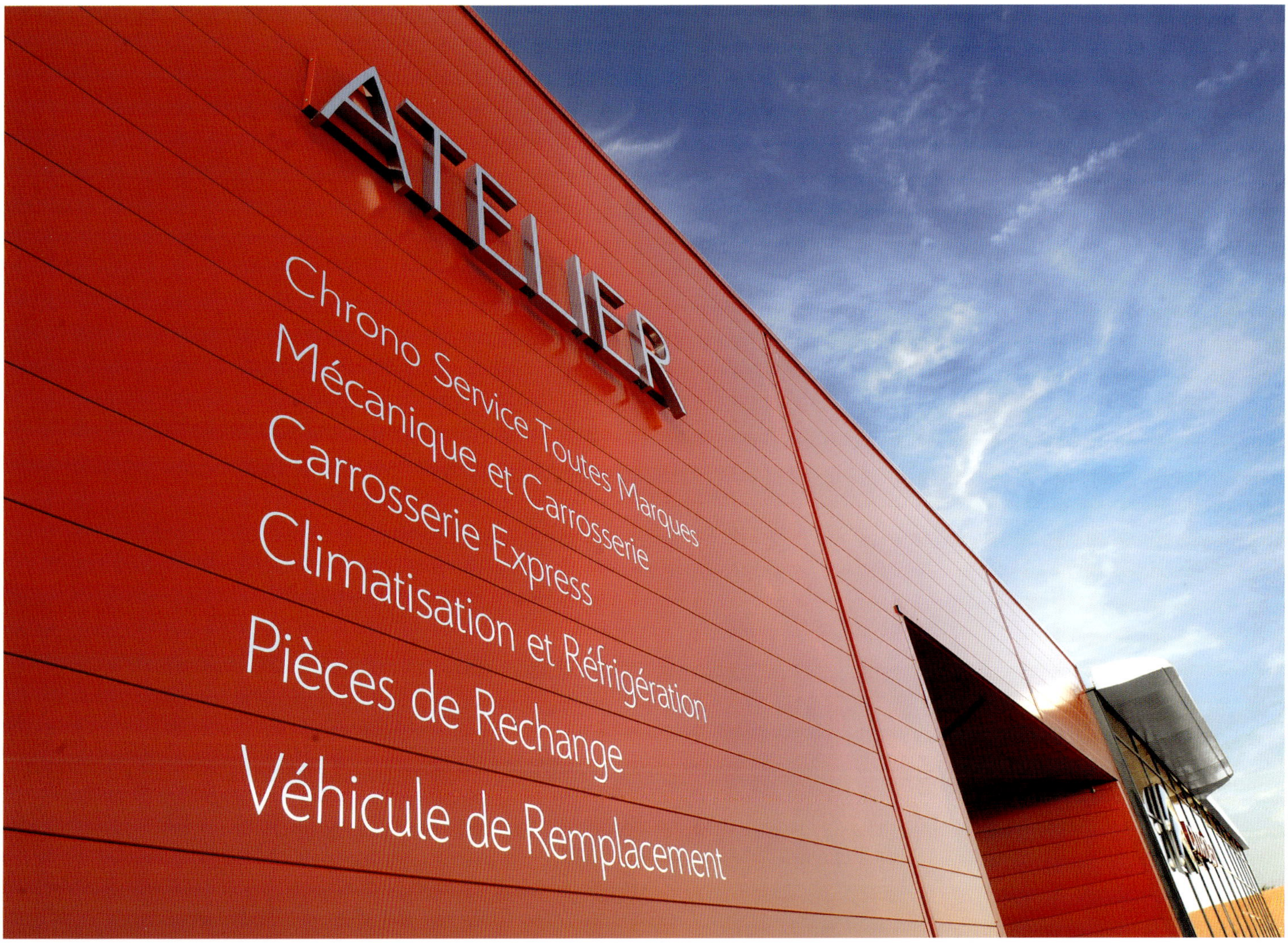
ATELIER
Chrono Service Toutes Marques
Mécanique et Carrosserie
Carrosserie Express
Climatisation et Réfrigération
Pièces de Rechange
Véhicule de Remplacement

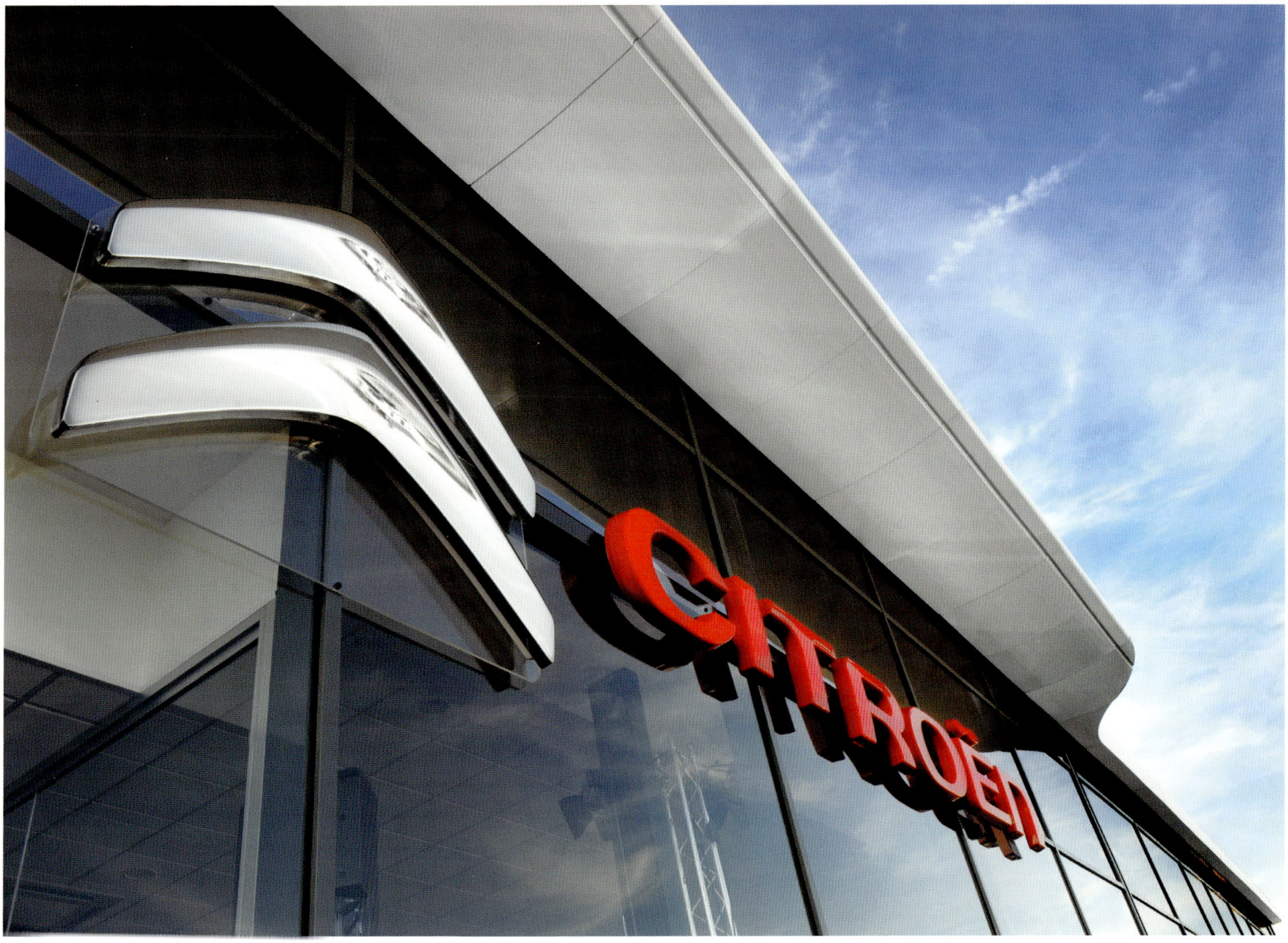
CITROËN

Assignment: Our brief was to express a new brand positioning for the VB label, with its associated values, and to create a visual system that would unify various brand divisions, such as high-fashion dresses, denim, eye wear, or bags, now and in the future.

Approach: First in line was the development of the logotype. Our sense was that the immediate recognition of the brand comes from the association of Victoria and Beckham—the two words separately carried a host of alternative connotations. So we tried removing the break between the two words. In the process, we discovered an interesting rhythm to the word, with Victoria's last A providing a subtle division between the name and surname, while at the same time providing a unifying bridge, a harmonious center point. The noted repetition of the triangular characters—V, A, and M – was suitably striking and hinted at a graphic solution that was at once unique and subtle. Expressed through light letterforms and the deliberate wide spacing of characters, the outcome provided an elegant, confident, and stylized reflection on the brand's evolved positioning. We also managed to convince the client to eliminate the secondary symbol/monogram composed of DVB letters. This reinforced confidence in the purity of the brand logotype. Undeniably, there is an immediate, almost instinctive experience attached to clothing: we feel somehow urged to feel, to touch the fabric before anything as reflective as trying anything on takes place. We therefore decided to extend this sensual experience into the packaging and paraphernalia realms, experimenting with printing processes such as die cutting, foil blocking, thermographic print, etc. Ultimately, we developed an individual texture for each division, to be embossed on paper surfaces and supported by a unique color.

Designer: Sasha Vidakovic | **Design Firm:** SVIDesign | **Art Director:** Sasha Vidakovic | **Creative Director:** Sasha Vidakovic
Typographer: Sasha Vidakovic | **Client:** 19 Entertainment

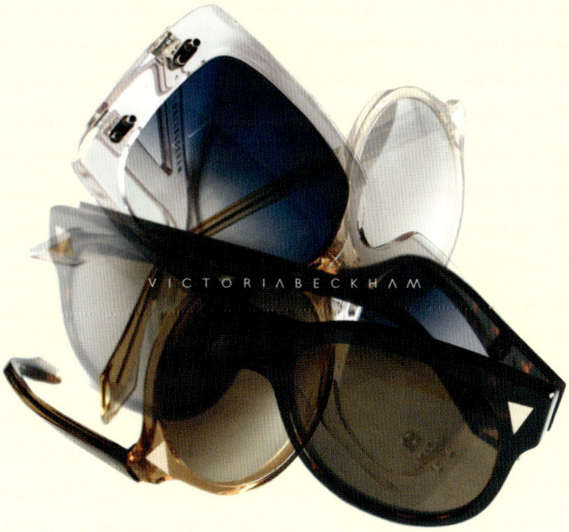

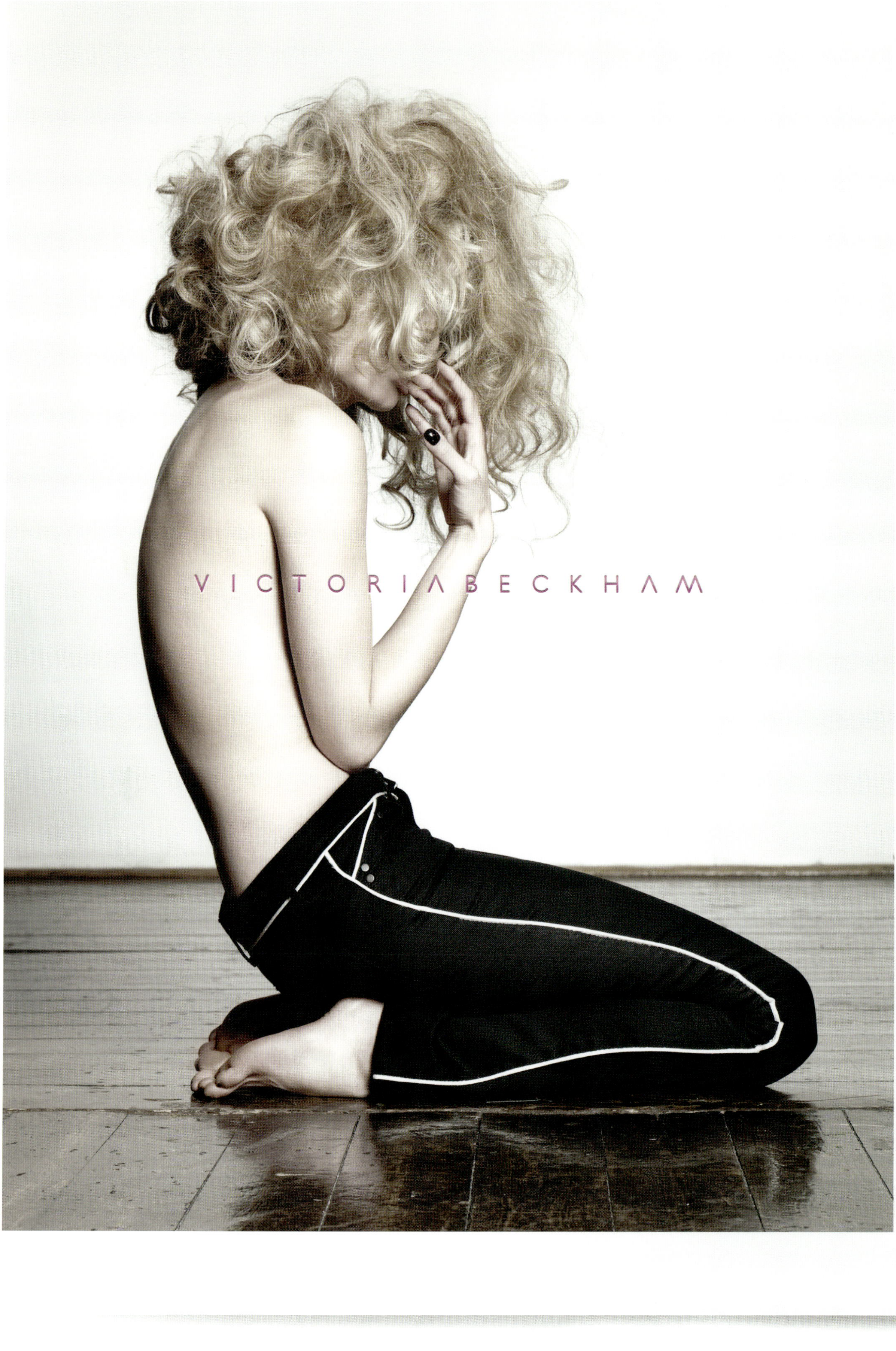

SVIDesign (this spread) | 19Entertainment | Beauty&Fashion

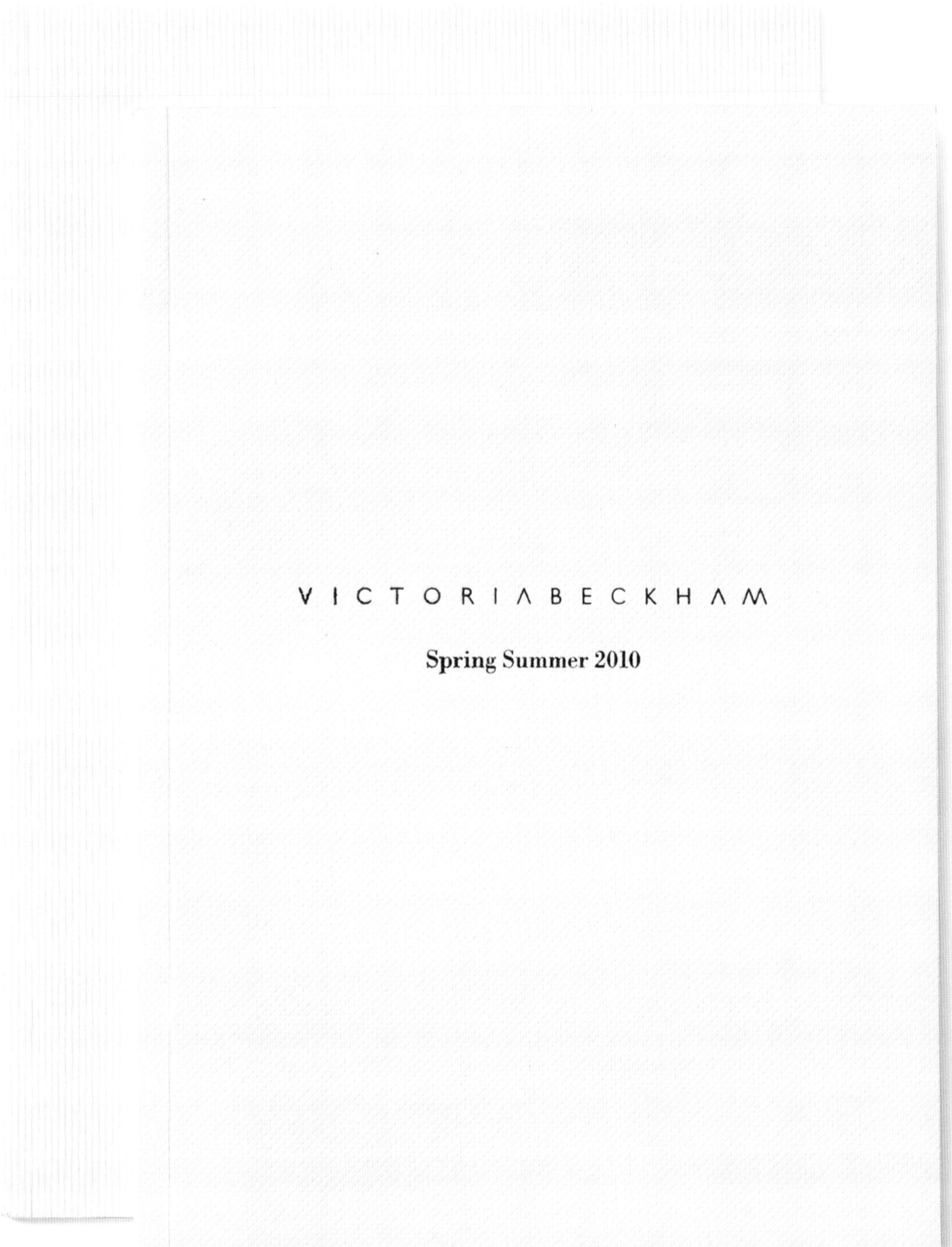
VICTORIABECKHAM
Spring Summer 2010

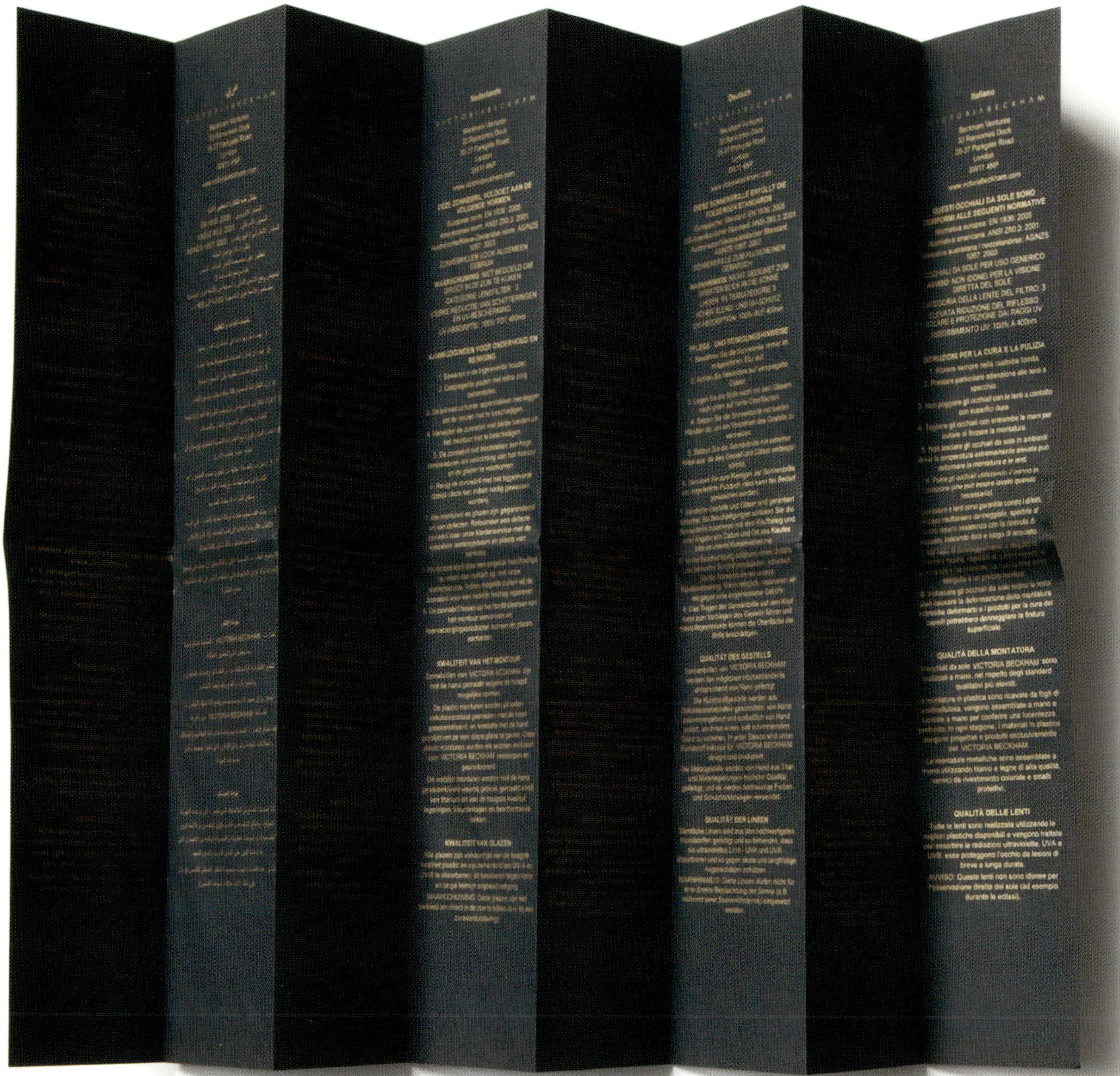

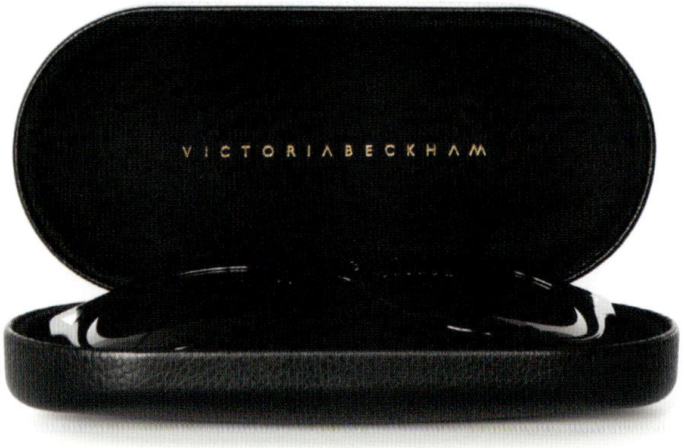
VICTORIABECKHAM

Assignment: The image had not kept pace with the innovation, so the challenge was to reposition AWI as the creators of the worlds most desirable luxury fabric.

Approach: We created a dynamic logo for AWI that reflects the innovative nature of the organization and that has the ability to move and grow. To create the visual style, we took rolls of wool to the Australian outback, and on location created garments inspired by colors and shapes of its dramatic landscapes. These images formed the basis of the communications material and, coupled with handcrafted typography, gave AWI a tool to engage fashion houses around the world.

Designer: Sam Pemberton | **Design Firm:** Landor Sydney | **Creative Director:** Nichola Dearn
Writer: John Mathews | **Photographer:** Georges Antoni | **Client:** AWI

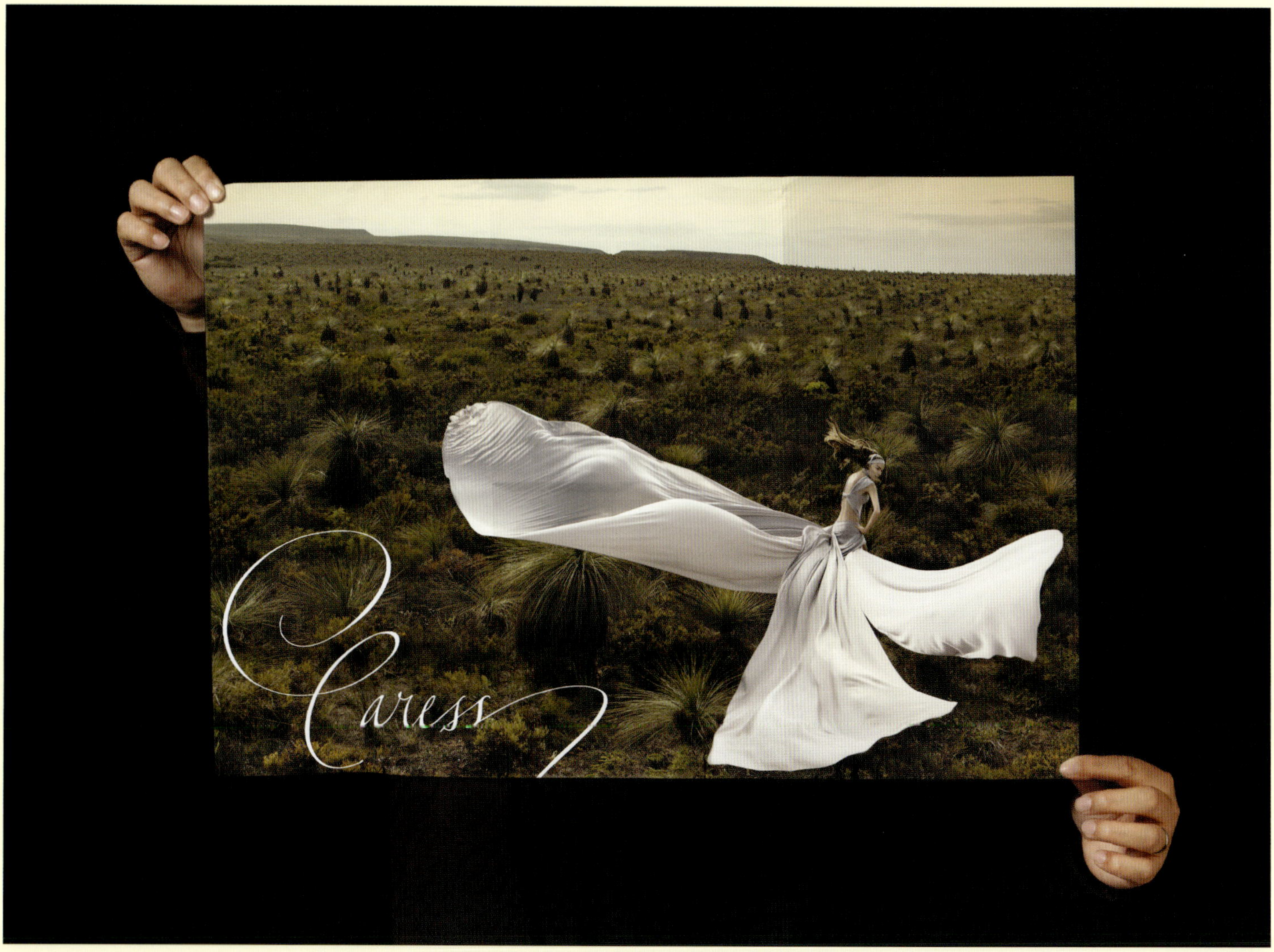

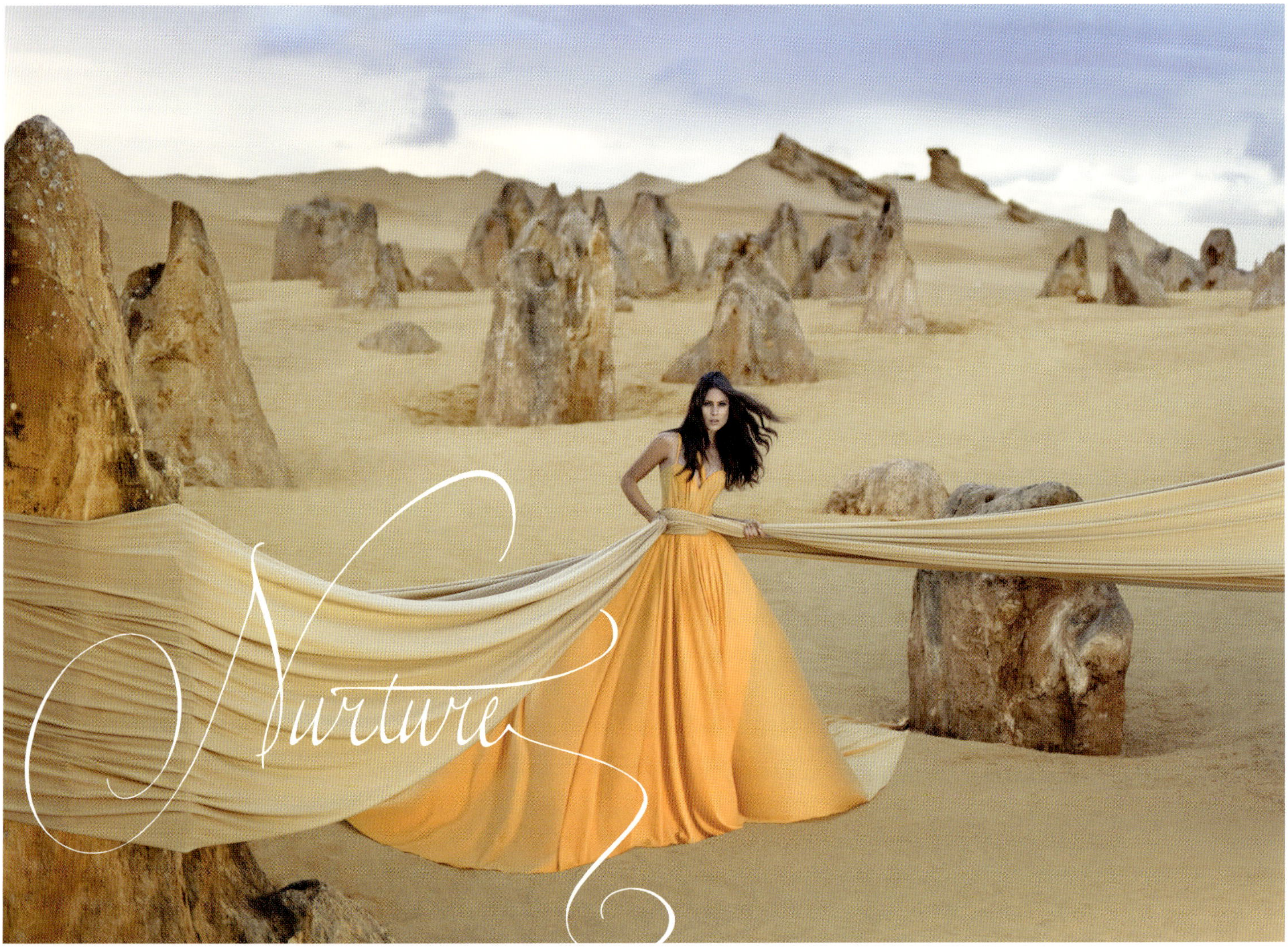

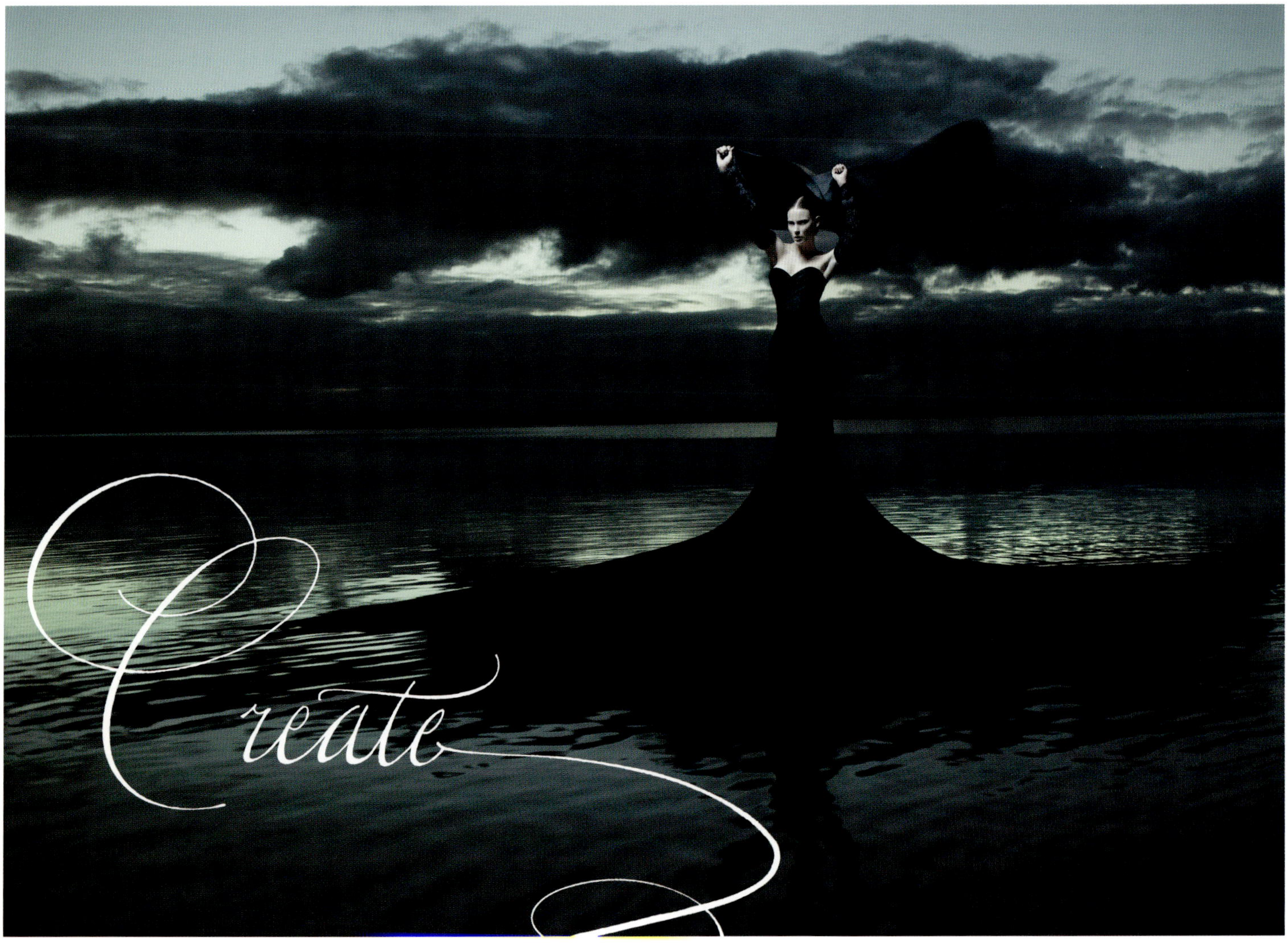

Landor Sydney (this spread)

Assignment: Biko is a boutique Toronto jewellery company founded by designer Corrine Anestopoulos in 2004. Back in her university days, Corrine began designing friendship bracelets, which her friends hoarded on a daily basis. When she completed her Bachelor of Design program in 2005, Corrine dived into jewellery-making full time, creating her own boutique jewellery company. Biko immediately developed a strong cult following, but needed some professional design assistance to help to take her business to the next level, since the original company brand ID was designed by Corrine herself. Corrine approached The White Room with a mission: to make her brand image reflect the sophistication of her fashion-forward jewellery, and enable her to take her business to new heights by making her brand attractive to high-end indie boutiques in Toronto and New York.

Approach: After meeting with this young and talented designer, and researching her desired market, we knew that one logo alone would not be sufficient to identify the brand across the jewellery itself, its coveted velvet jewellery cases and bags, and other retail packaging. With jewellery, a large part of the pride of purchase is in the accoutrements. Next, The White Room Creative Directors thoroughly researched the world of fashion and celebrity, fashion magazines, and boutique jewellery lines. Before going to the drawing board, we also listened to all of our client's concerns regarding reproduction and legibility of a logo when engraved on the many metals used in forging her craft. We also studied her entire product line to ensure any logos or word marks created would be practicable. With all the results of our research and client collaboration in mind, The White Room created a new twofold visual identity and tag line, comprised of both a word mark and a prestigious crest. The word mark encapsulates the classic and timeless jewellery pieces, and works well when engraved on even the smallest size of jewellery tag. The crest adds a touch of high-end glamour and campy authority to the line, and is versatile in numerous keepsake and packaging applications—bestowing the purchaser with label-boasting iconic pride. The tagline "Modern Nostalgia" summarizes the brand perfectly in two words. Biko draws inspiration from memories of the past and translates these ideas into wearable, contemporary pieces. To reinforce the feeling of nostalgia, we chose cream stock and a prominent, timeless black color for Biko's stationery range, and black velvet with a modern take on the laurel crest, in classic white. The touch of metallic throughout her brand extension line reflects back on the nature of her products, and the Biko word mark has a look of timeless luxe, engraved in a variety of metal tags to match the piece. The White Room also produced Biko's first look book, Golden Haze. The booklet captured the essence of the boutique bijoux brand, with images shot at a local underground bar. The vibe and energy of the look book further reflects the youthful aesthetic of the brand.

Results: "The rebranding of my business by The White Room has opened up so many new and exciting doors for the business. I have seen a 50% increase in sales and brand recognition, huge press coverage, sales representation internationally, and a move to a larger studio as a result. Customers love the logo and packaging, and my website hits and e-sales have increased by 80%. I couldn't be prouder to show off my brand identity!"—Corrine Anestopoulos, Designer & Founder.

Designer: Karolina Loboda | **Design Firm:** The White Room Inc. | **Art Director:** Karolina Loboda
Creative Directors: Karolina Loboda, Neil Rodman | **Photographer:** Angela Lewis | **Client:** Corrine Anestopoulos

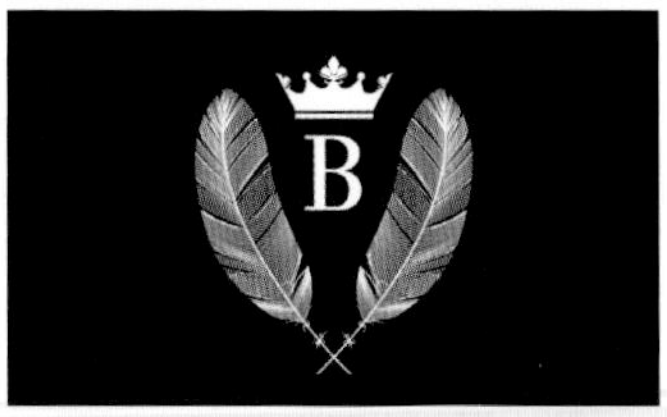

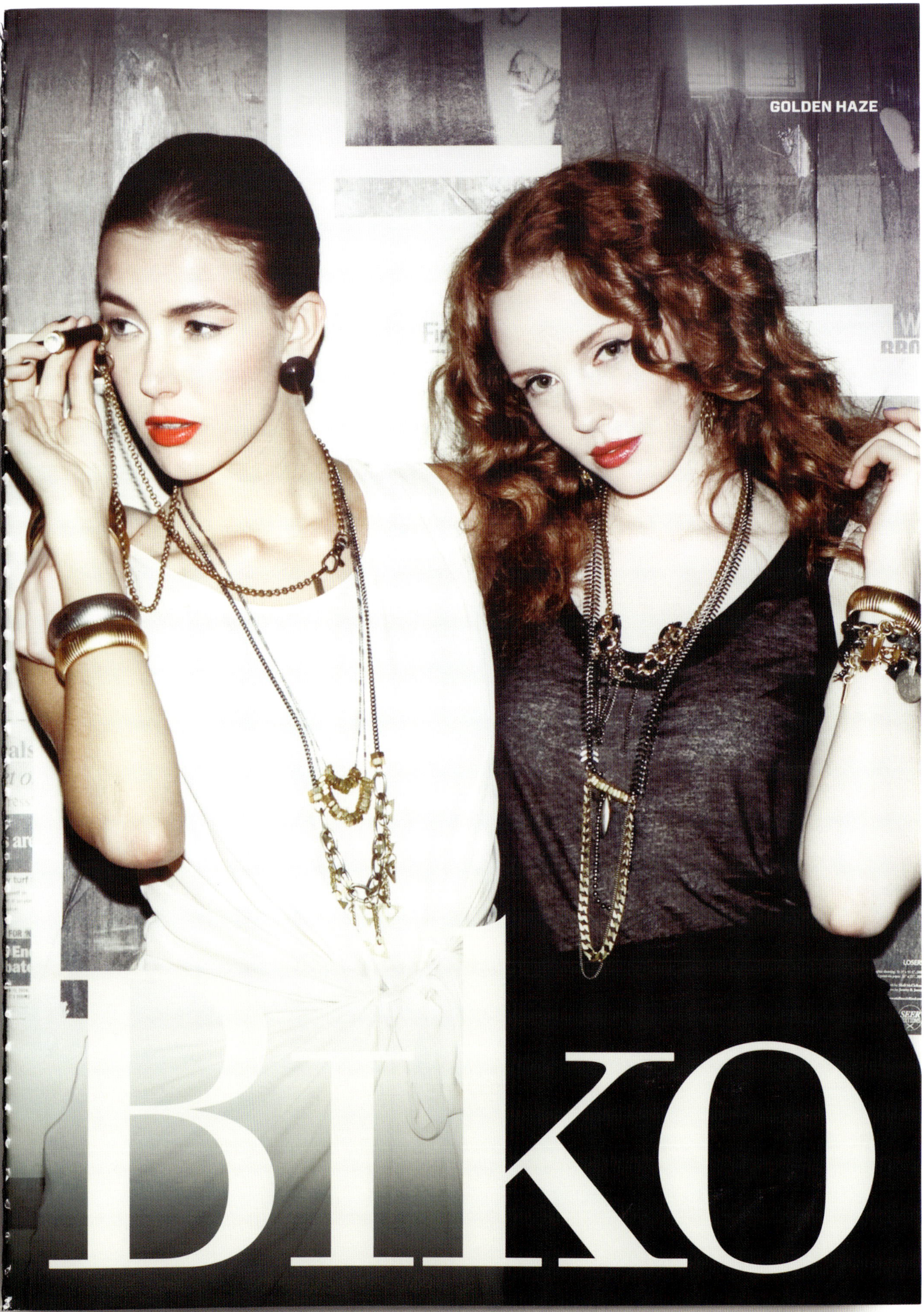
GOLDEN HAZE
Biko

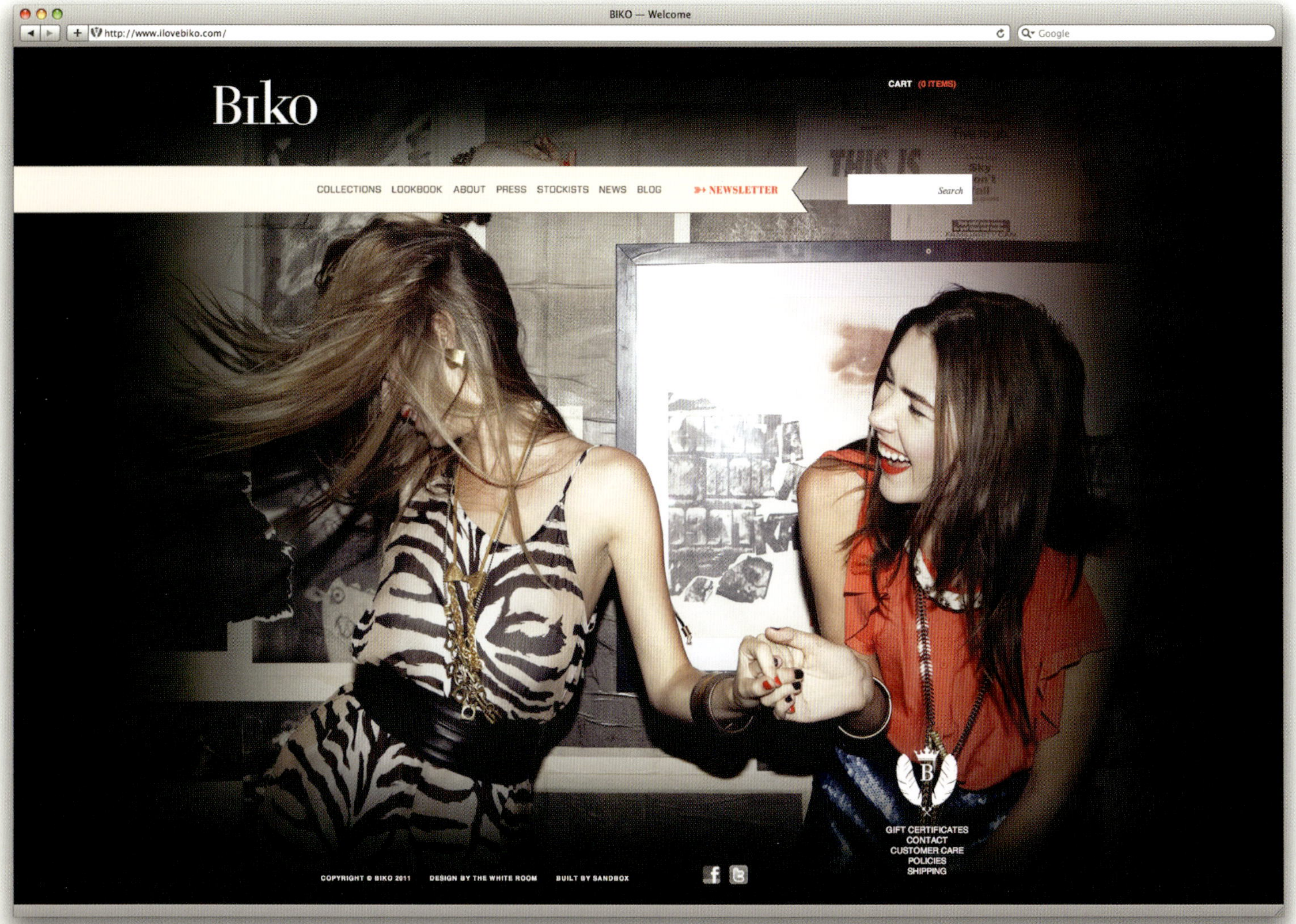
BIKO — Welcome
http://www.ilovebiko.com/
Google
Biko
CART (0 ITEMS)
COLLECTIONS LOOKBOOK ABOUT PRESS STOCKISTS NEWS BLOG
NEWSLETTER
Search
GIFT CERTIFICATES
CONTACT
CUSTOMER CARE
POLICIES
SHIPPING
COPYRIGHT © BIKO 2011
DESIGN BY THE WHITE ROOM
BUILT BY SANDBOX

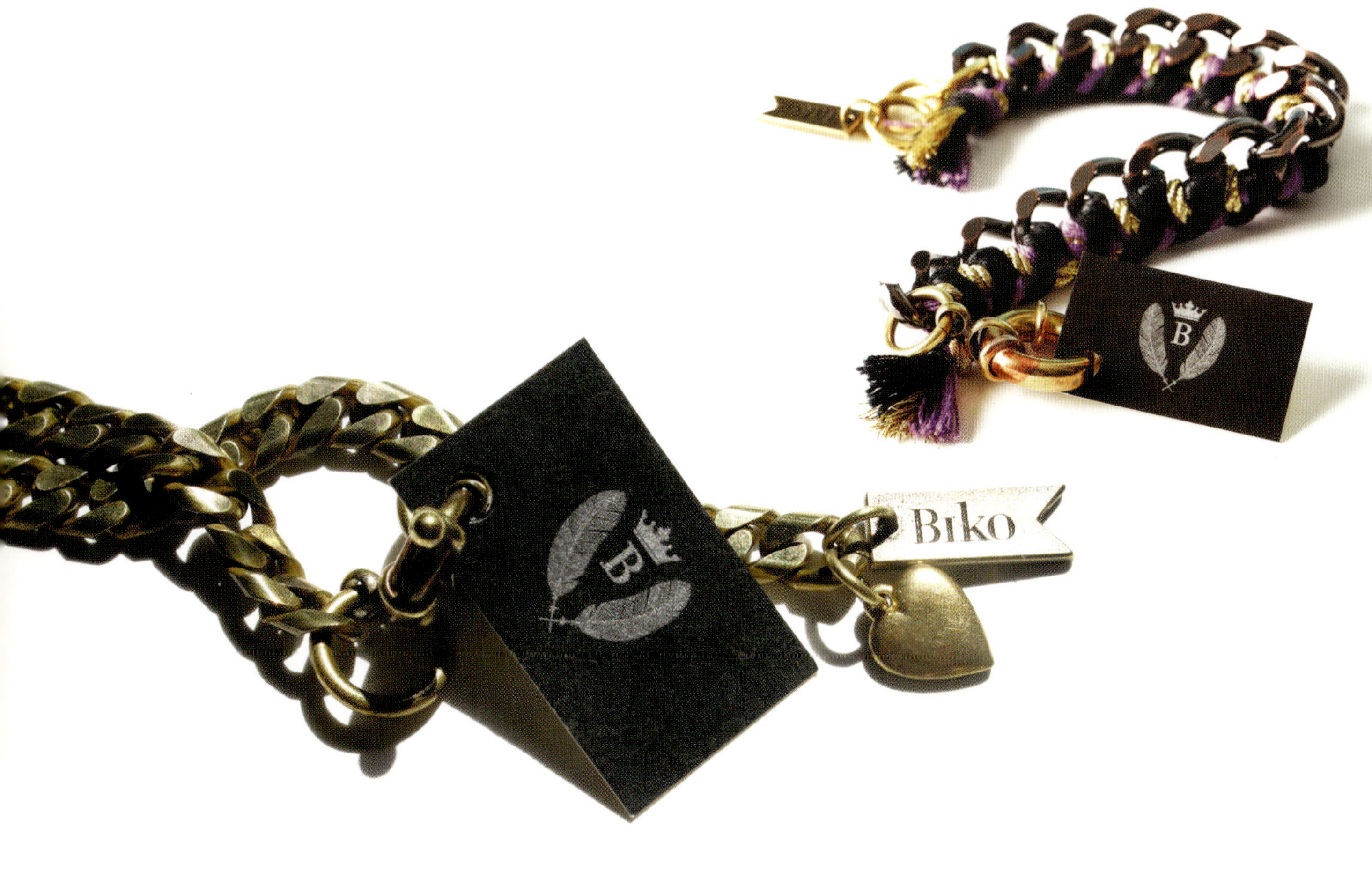
Biko

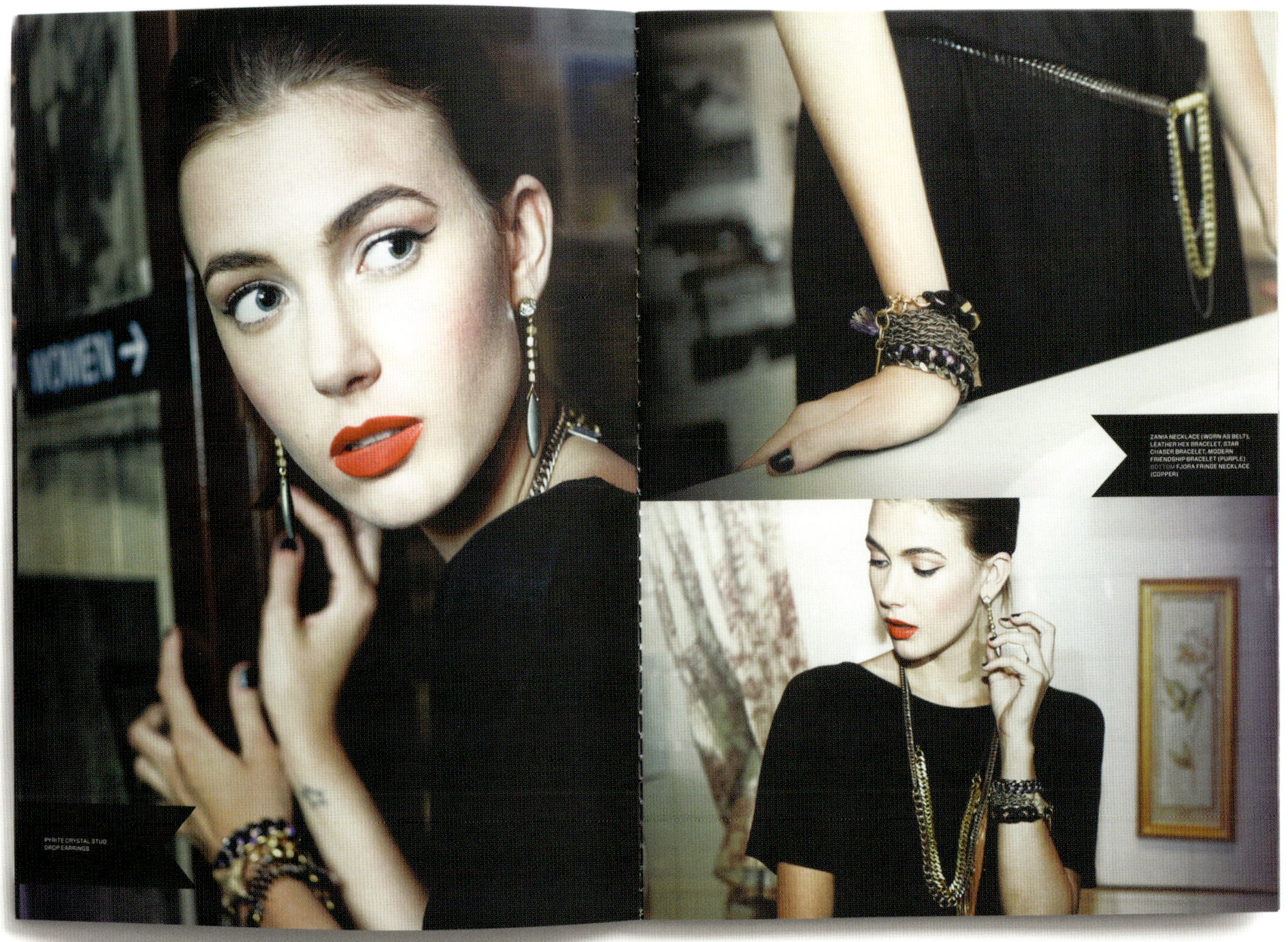
WOMEN →
PYRITE CRYSTAL STUD DROP EARRINGS
ZANIA NECKLACE (WORN AS BELT), LEATHER HEX BRACELET, STAR CHASER BRACELET, MODERN FRIENDSHIP BRACELET (PURPLE) BOTTOM FJORA FRINGE NECKLACE (COPPER)

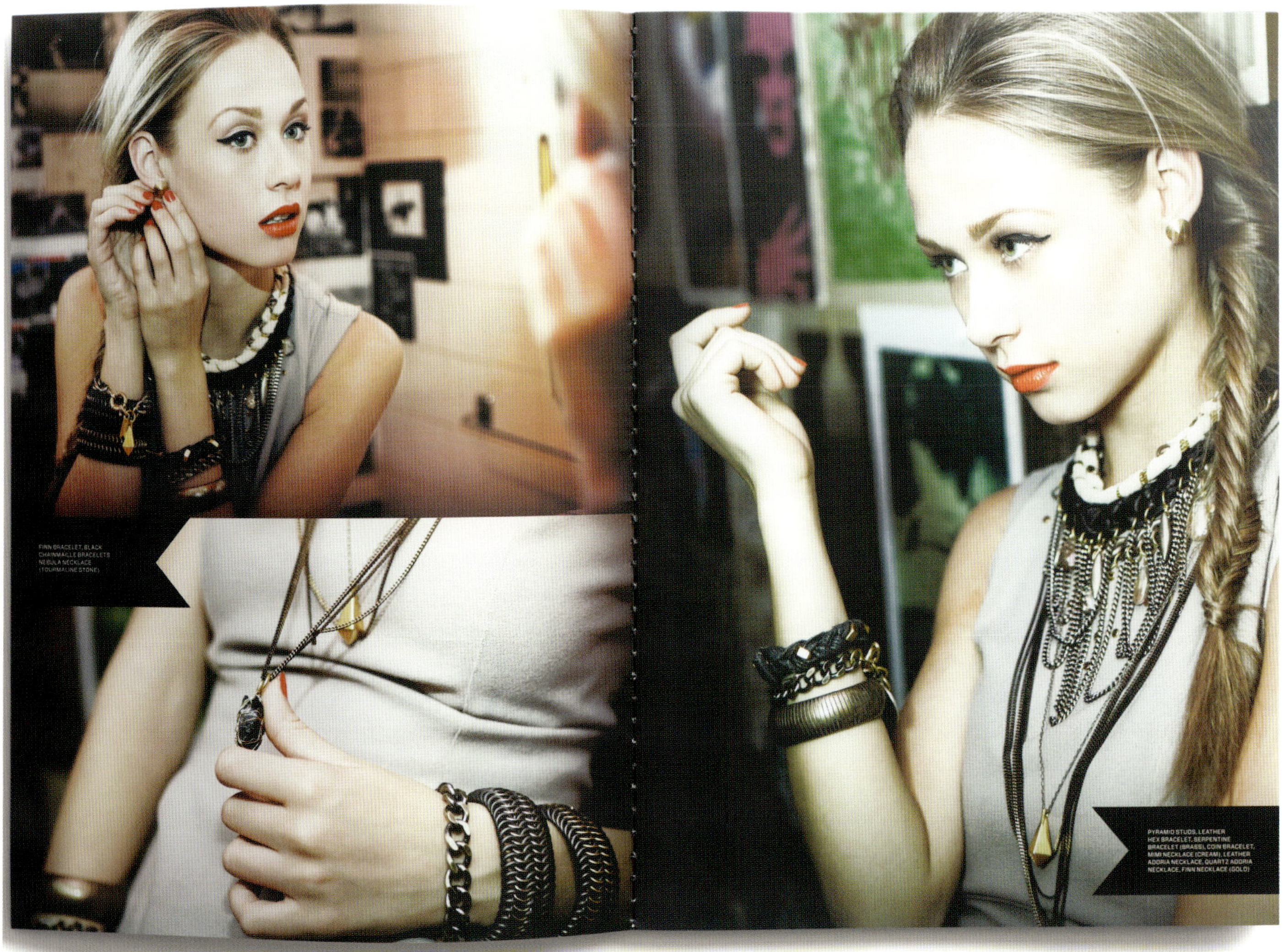
FINN BRACELET, BLACK CHAINMAILLE BRACELETS NEBULA NECKLACE (TOURMALINE STONE)
PYRAMID STUDS, LEATHER HEX BRACELET, SERPENTINE BRACELET (BRASS), COIN BRACELET, MIMI NECKLACE (CREAM), LEATHER ADORIA NECKLACE, QUARTZ ADORIA NECKLACE, FINN NECKLACE (GOLD)

Assignment: Bite Beauty is a line of lip products made from food-grade and entirely natural ingredients. Bite is the first ever lipstick line to contain red wine resveratrol, delivering a micro-dose of antioxidants with every application. Resveratrol is the health-boosting component found in red wine whose powerful antioxidant effects assist the body in the fight against free radicals.

Approach: The brand is a new venture by Susanne Lang Fragrance (SLF), with whom Concrete had previously rebranded the company's fragrance line, as well as launching the Sula Beauty brand. Concrete worked closely with SLF in developing the new line's strategic positioning, brand story, and brand identity. Contrary to competitive brands that emphasize the natural aspect of their products, Concrete felt that performance, color, and fashion would be stronger drivers for this market segment. While beauty consumers are becoming increasing aware of the harmful effects of certain ingredients, the desire for strong fashionable colors and wearability are still very strong determining purchasing factors.

Designers: Ryan Crouchman, Leticia Luna, Brittany Tessier | **Design Firm:** Concrete Design Communications
Creative Directors: Diti Katona, John Pylypczak | **Client:** Susanne Lang Fragrance

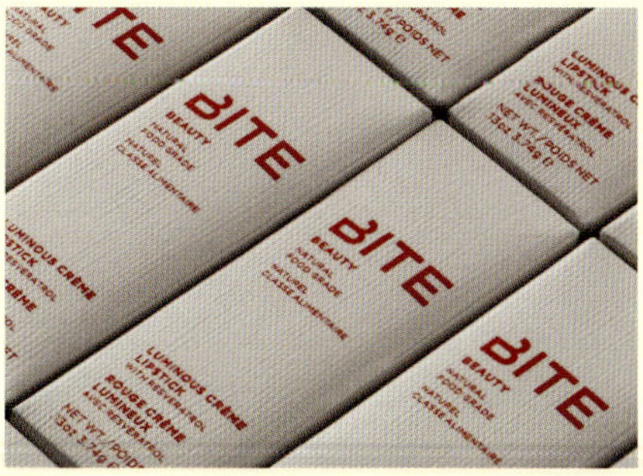

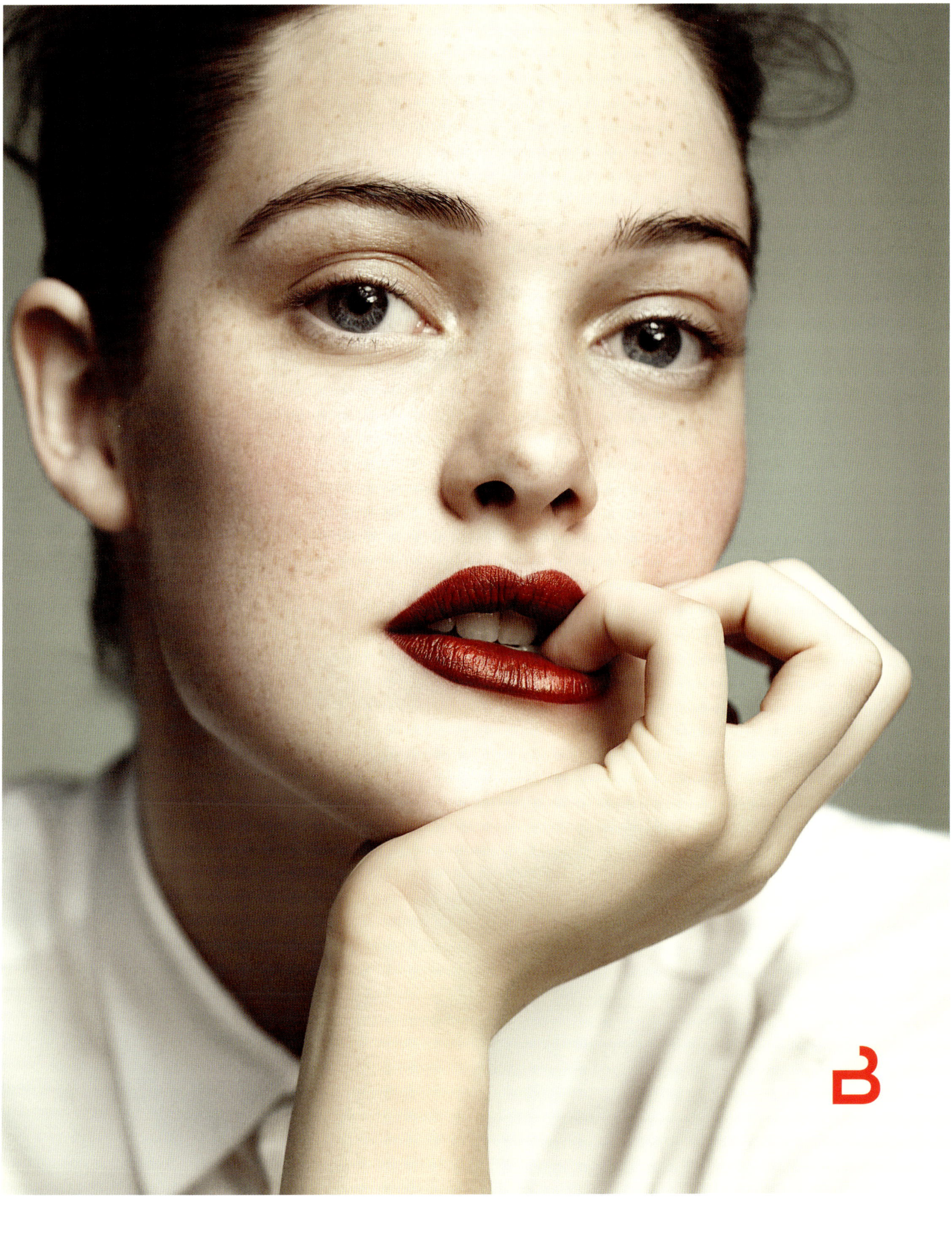

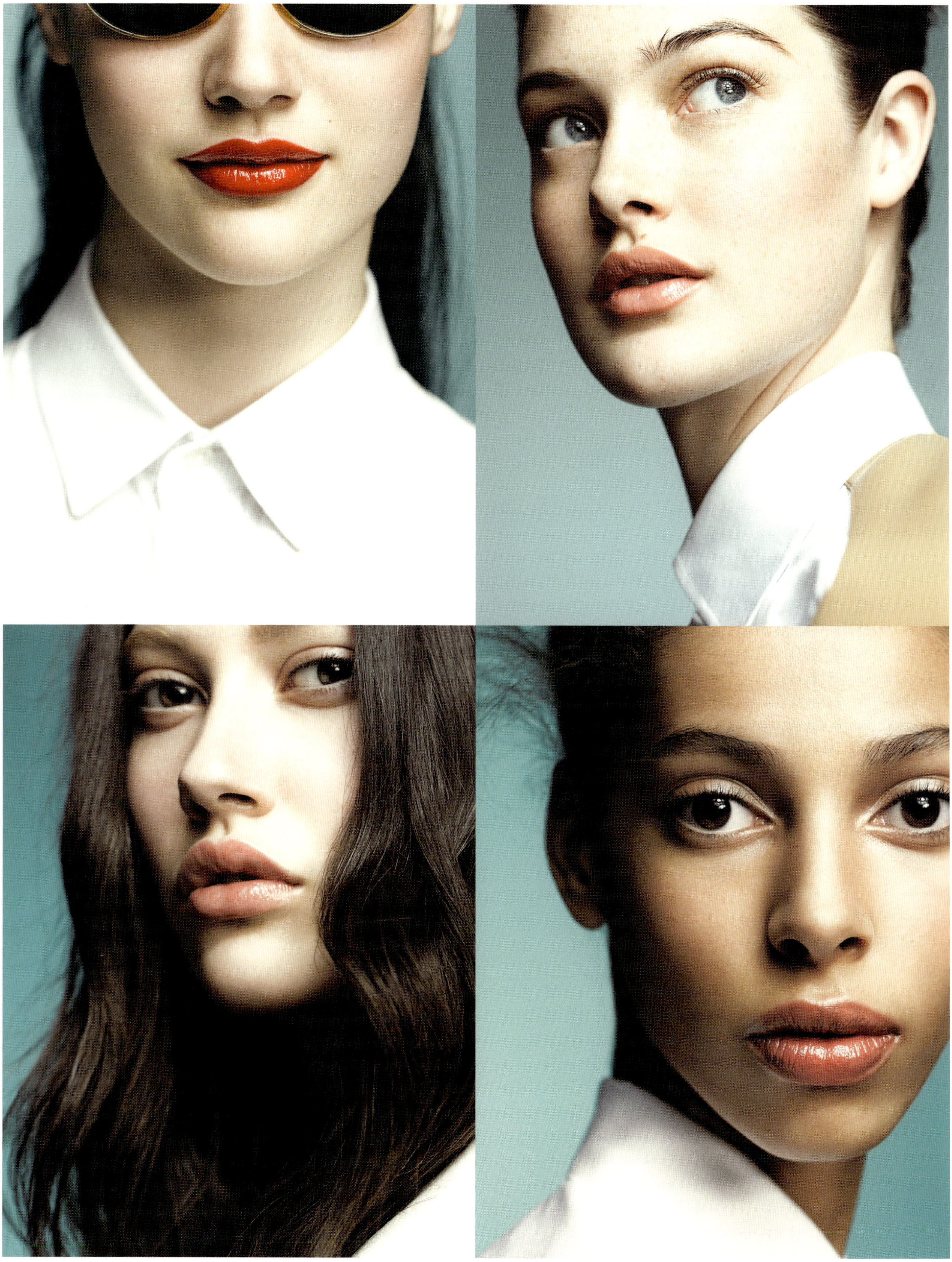

BITE

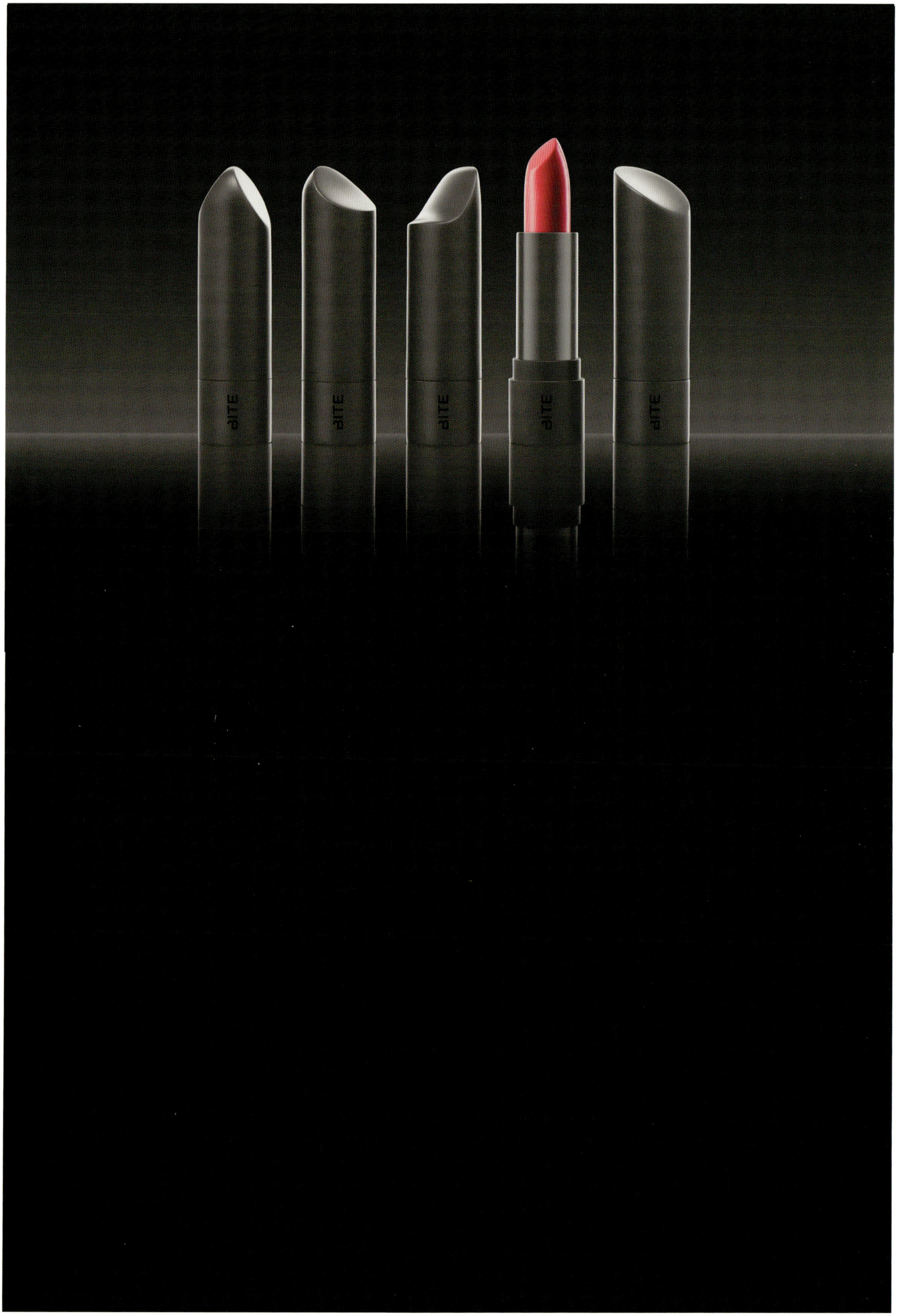
BITE
BITE
BITE
BITE
BITE

Assignment: Dr. Nicholas Perricone has been called the guru dermatologist to the stars, having enjoyed extensive media coverage on Oprah, PBS, and Larry King, and in Vanity Fair, Vogue, and The New York Times. He is also the creator of Perricone MD, a wide range of products including topical anti-inflammatory formulations to reverse and prevent damage to skin, as well as dietary supplements that are scientifically designed to promote healthy, youthful skin.

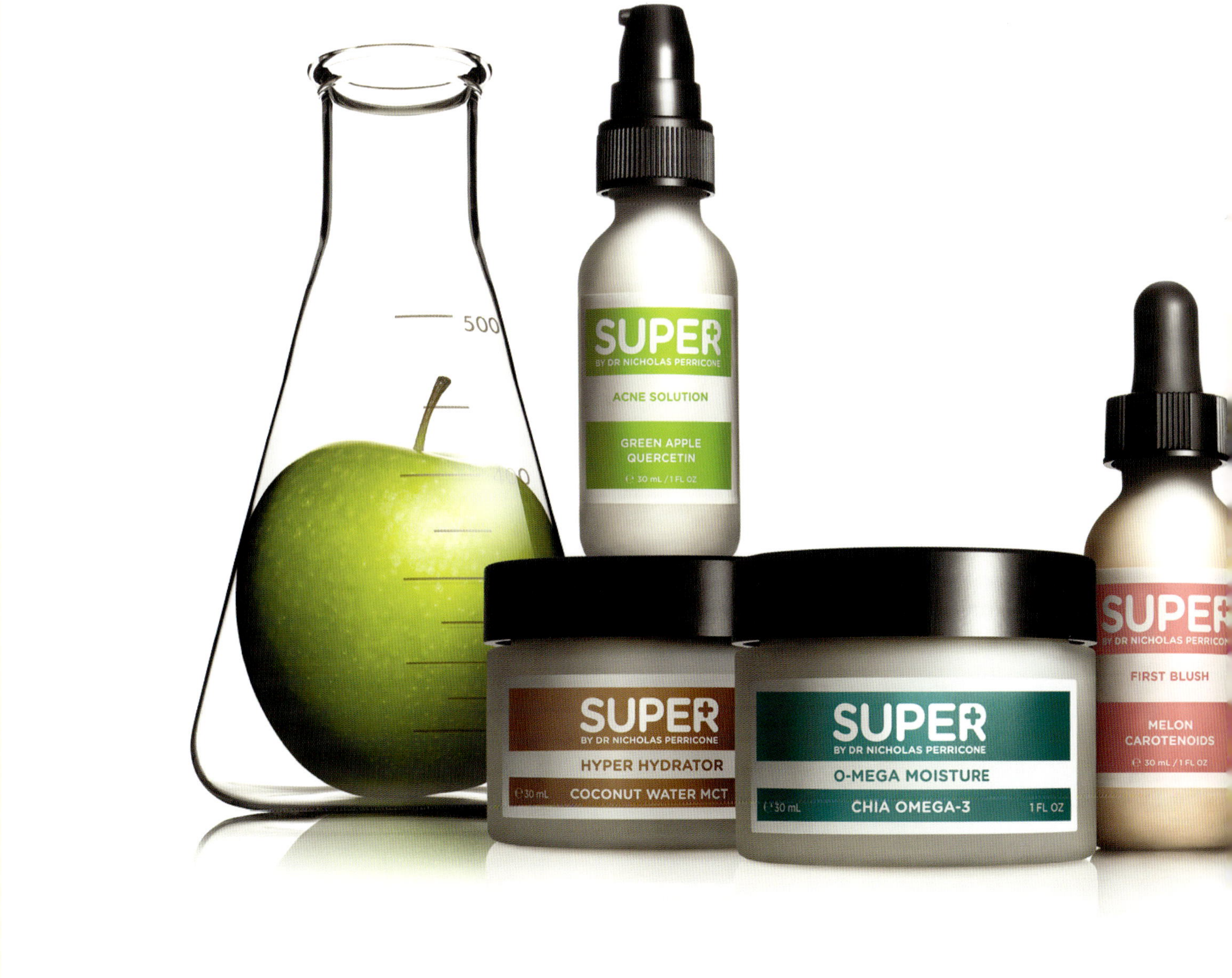

Approach: The Concrete rebrand of the Perricone MD skin care line has enjoyed great success. However, the market had become saturated with doctor brands and the company was looking for ways of reaching new customers. Working closely with company management, Concrete developed a skin care brand concept based on the nutritional ingredients of "superfooods." In fact it was Dr. Nicholas Perricone himself who coined the term in his books written a decade earlier, a word used to describe foods that contain significant amounts of antioxidants. The visual approach crystallized once Concrete developed the name: SUPER by Dr. Nicolas Perricone. Super obviously referred to the superfood science of the product, but it also suggested a voice for the brand. We now had a super product for super model legs. You could be a super woman and super sexy.

Designer: Ty Whittington | **Design Firm:** Concrete Design Communications
Creative Directors: Diti Katona, John Pylypczak | **Client:** Dr. Nicholas Perricone

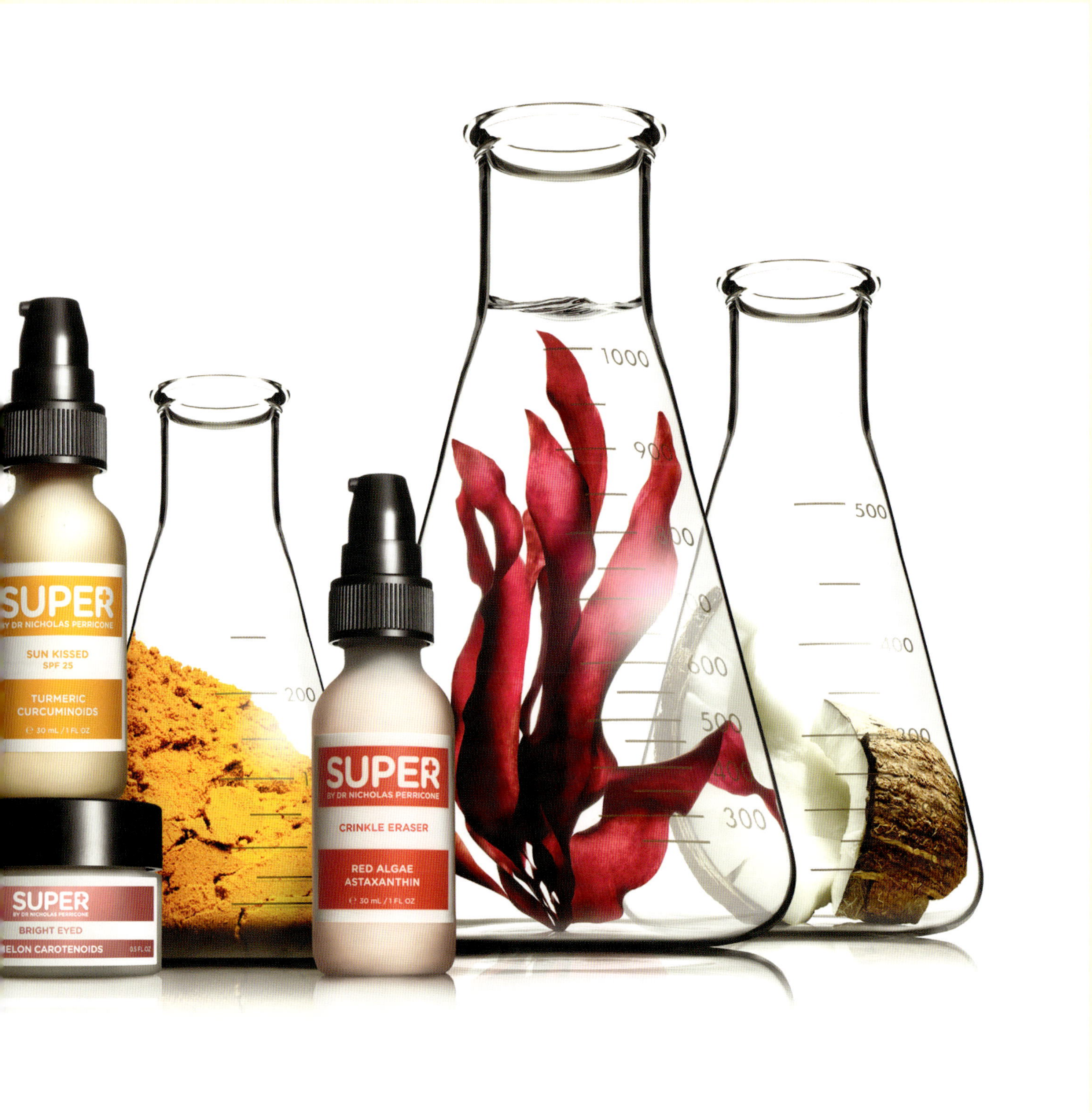

Assignment: Hörst is a men's clothing brand that has been distributed in different boutiques across Canada for the last fifteen years. The high-end collection contains mainly suits, coats, shirts, accessories, and dress clothes. Hörst offers the modern man an authentic way of being. Its philosophy rests on the German values of impeccably tailored cuts and quality craftsmanship, producing a confident and inspiring style. Despite this solid philosophy, Hörst had been suffering from a poorly defined brand positioning for some time. Consumers considered it too expensive for what they saw as a mid-range line; the brand simply wasn't well known or respected enough to be considered high end. Lg2boutique's mandate was to completely restyle the Hörst's brand platform. Strategic research and the perceptual axes of the competitive field helped identify an important opportunity: among large international players, such as Hugo Boss, Versace, Strellson, Paul Smith, and Ermenegildo Zegna, seduction proved to be the most ignored perceptual axis. This insight held great potential and offered the brand a credible positioning with which to enter the high-end market. A shopping devotee, Hörst's target is constantly on the lookout for that little elegant or eccentric something to reaffirm his style. He is a mature man who maintains a somewhat mysterious air. Seduction, in his view, is a game. With a slight penchant for the extravagant, he is the embodiment of the modern-day dandy. He takes great pleasure from his lifestyle, never slavishly bowing to the dictates of fashion. Going to the barber, learning music, or taking the train for business are all things he makes time for. His entire person is seductive, rising above the everyday. He is authentic.

Approach: Hörst's brand identity positions the company as an authentic brand that combines romanticism and elegance. The photos present a modern-day dandy—elegant and mysterious with a touch of the extravagant about him. All graphic elements also celebrate both the brand's rich German heritage and the modernness of its style.

Results: A new branding that gained worldwide attention. Our modern dandy has been posted all over the web, which is something we are very proud of, as is the client!

Designer: Serge Côté | **Design Firm:** lg2boutique | **Art Director:** Serge Côté | **Creative Director:** Claude Auchu
Writers: François Sauvé, Pierre Lussier | **Client:** Jean-Sébastien Octeau (Ango Mode)

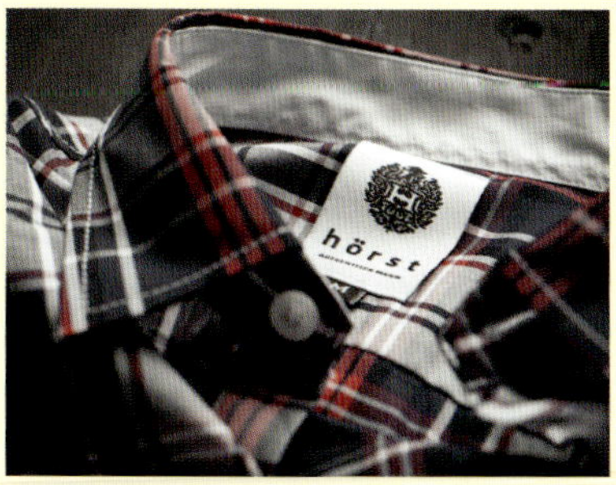

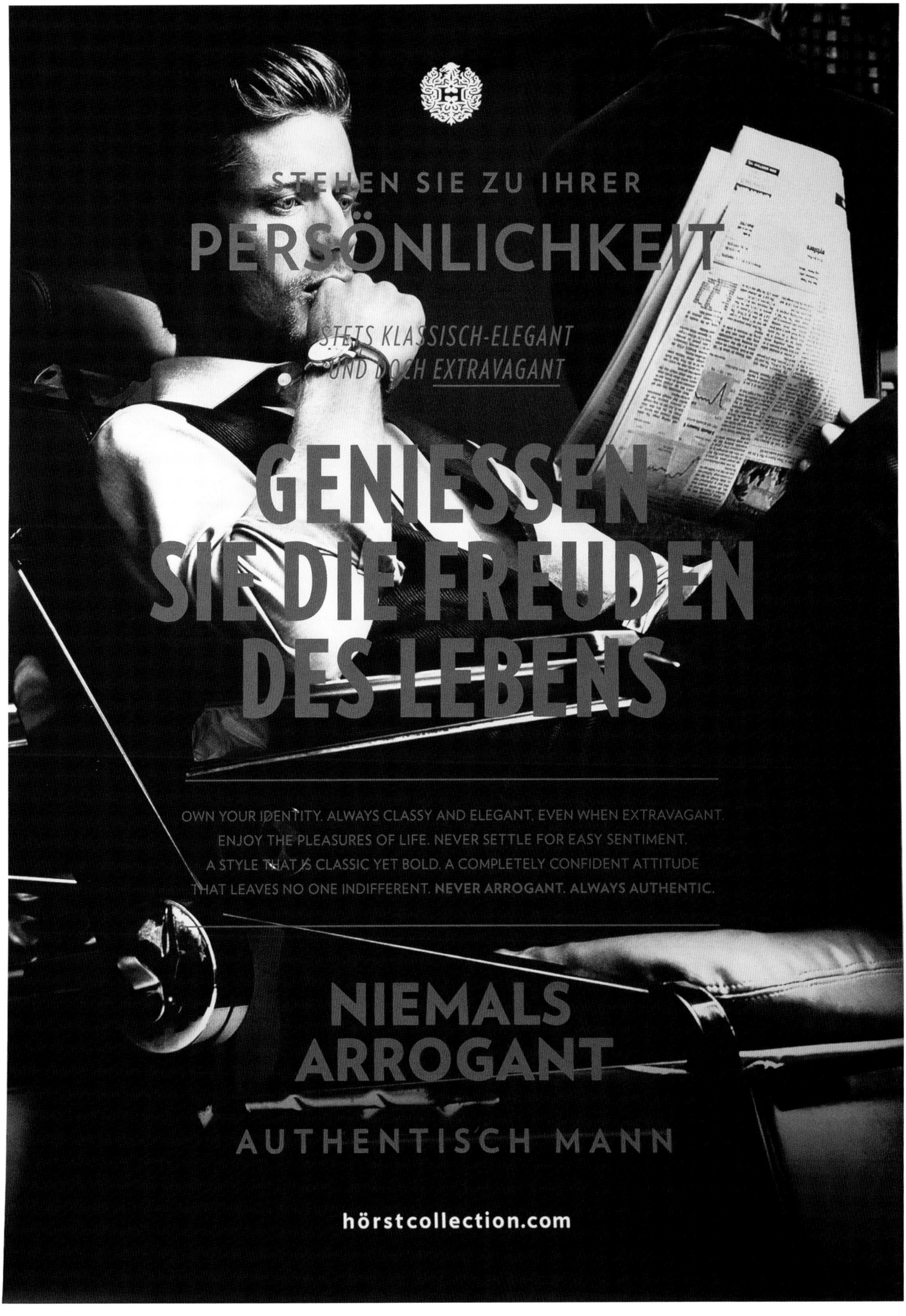
STEHEN SIE ZU IHRER
PERSÖNLICHKEIT
STETS KLASSISCH-ELEGANT
UND DOCH EXTRAVAGANT
GENIESSEN
SIE DIE FREUDEN
DES LEBENS
OWN YOUR IDENTITY. ALWAYS CLASSY AND ELEGANT, EVEN WHEN EXTRAVAGANT.
ENJOY THE PLEASURES OF LIFE. NEVER SETTLE FOR EASY SENTIMENT.
A STYLE THAT IS CLASSIC YET BOLD. A COMPLETELY CONFIDENT ATTITUDE
THAT LEAVES NO ONE INDIFFERENT. NEVER ARROGANT. ALWAYS AUTHENTIC.
NIEMALS
ARROGANT
AUTHENTISCH MANN
hörstcollection.com

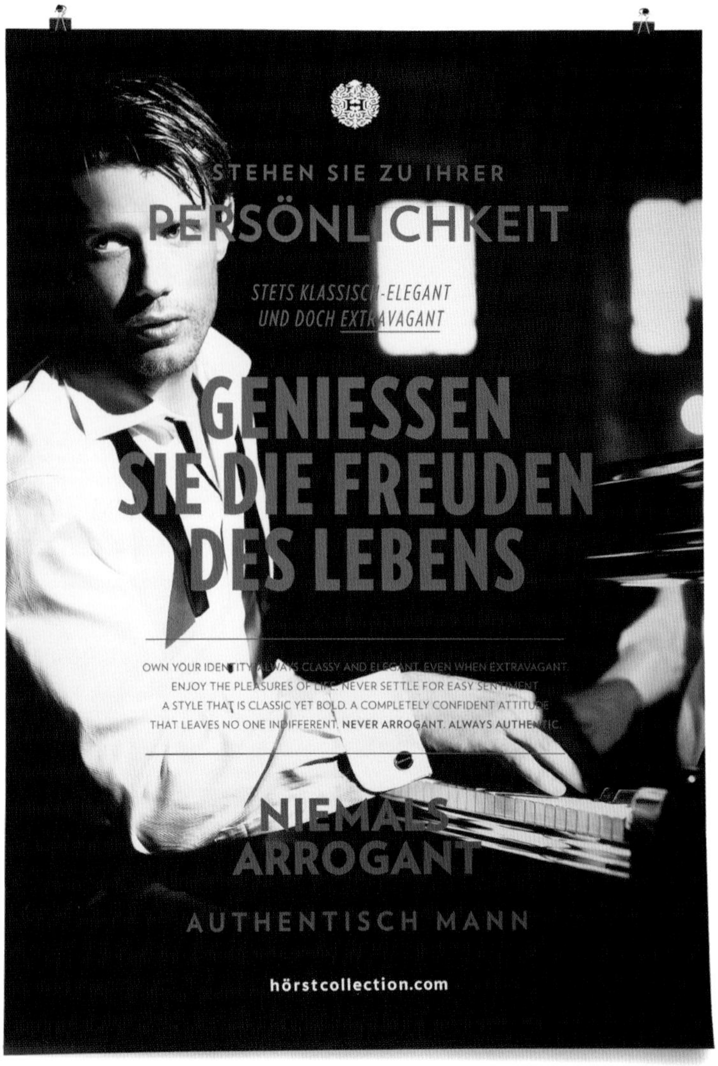
STEHEN SIE ZU IHRER
PERSÖNLICHKEIT
STETS KLASSISCH-ELEGANT
UND DOCH EXTRAVAGANT
GENIESSEN
SIE DIE FREUDEN
DES LEBENS
OWN YOUR IDENTITY. ALWAYS CLASSY AND ELEGANT, EVEN WHEN EXTRAVAGANT.
ENJOY THE PLEASURES OF LIFE. NEVER SETTLE FOR EASY SENTIMENT.
A STYLE THAT IS CLASSIC YET BOLD. A COMPLETELY CONFIDENT ATTITUDE
THAT LEAVES NO ONE INDIFFERENT. NEVER ARROGANT. ALWAYS AUTHENTIC.
NIEMALS
ARROGANT
AUTHENTISCH MANN
hörstcollection.com

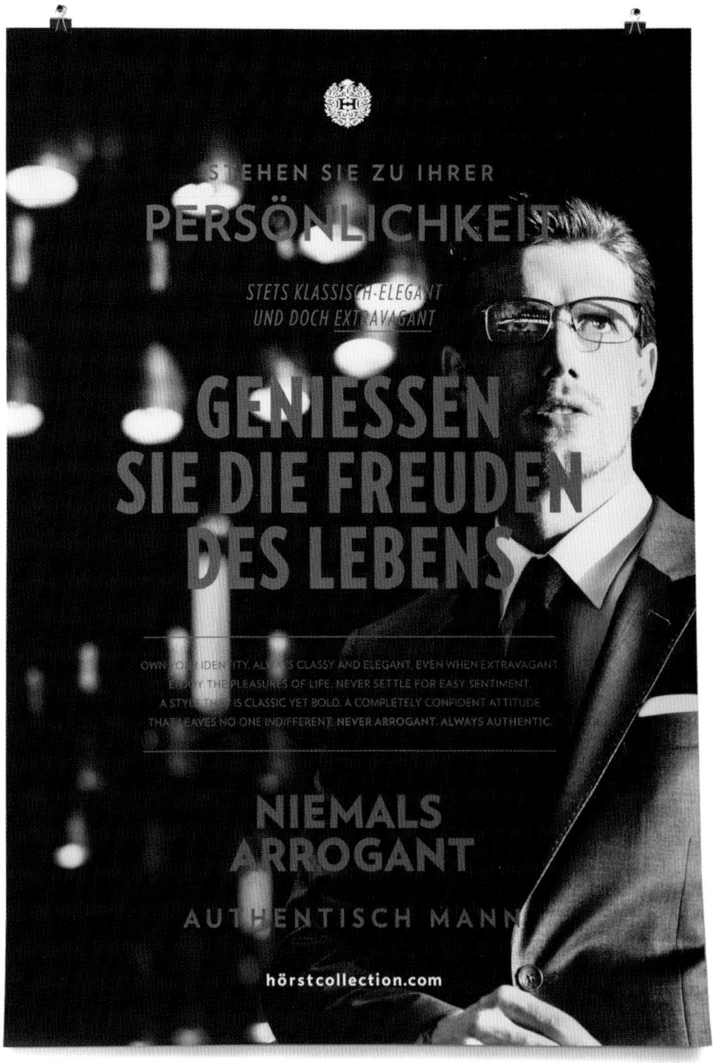
STEHEN SIE ZU IHRER
PERSÖNLICHKEIT
STETS KLASSISCH-ELEGANT
UND DOCH EXTRAVAGANT
GENIESSEN
SIE DIE FREUDEN
DES LEBENS
OWN YOUR IDENTITY. ALWAYS CLASSY AND ELEGANT, EVEN WHEN EXTRAVAGANT.
ENJOY THE PLEASURES OF LIFE. NEVER SETTLE FOR EASY SENTIMENT.
A STYLE THAT IS CLASSIC YET BOLD. A COMPLETELY CONFIDENT ATTITUDE
THAT LEAVES NO ONE INDIFFERENT. NEVER ARROGANT. ALWAYS AUTHENTIC.
NIEMALS
ARROGANT
AUTHENTISCH MANN
hörstcollection.com

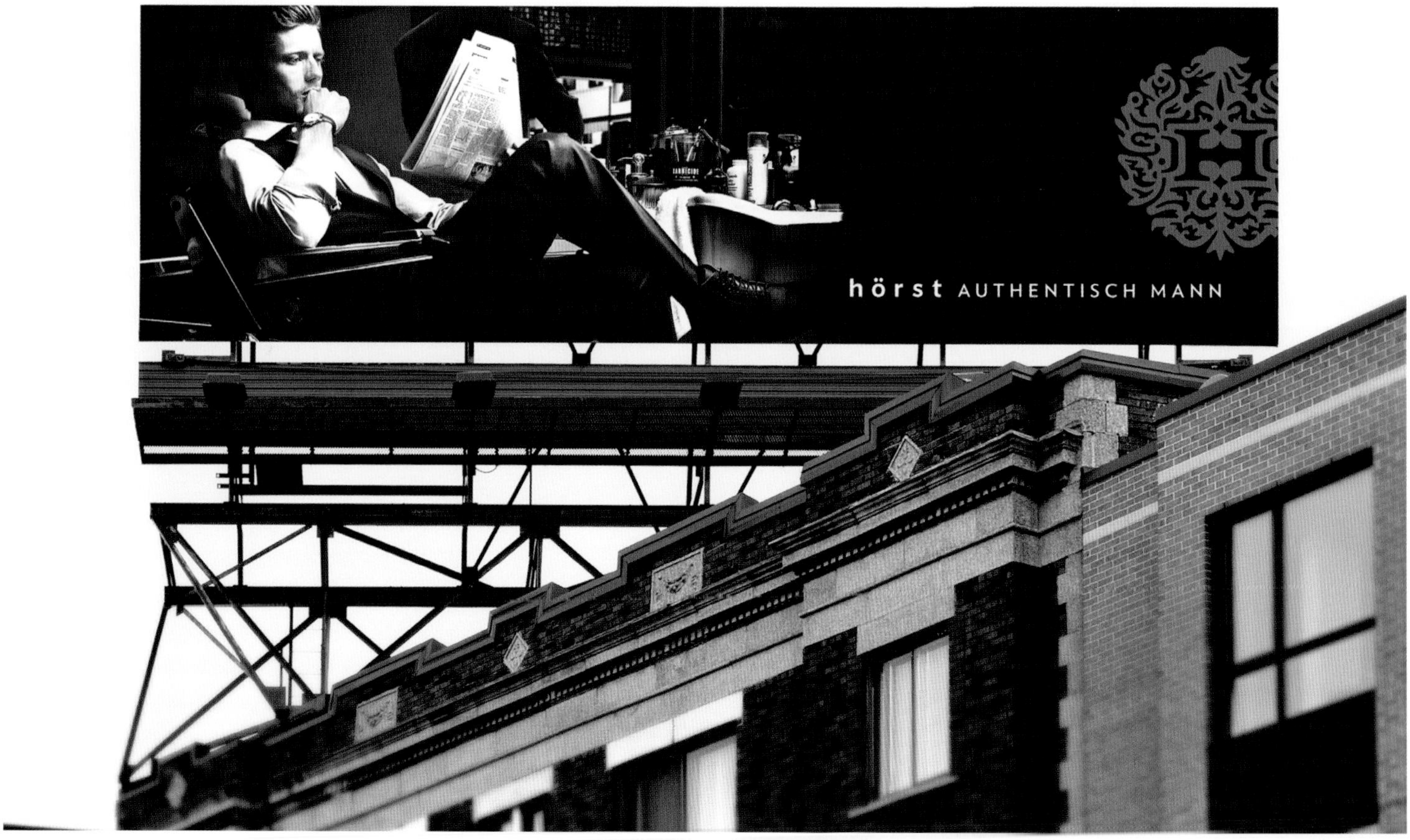
hörst AUTHENTISCH MANN

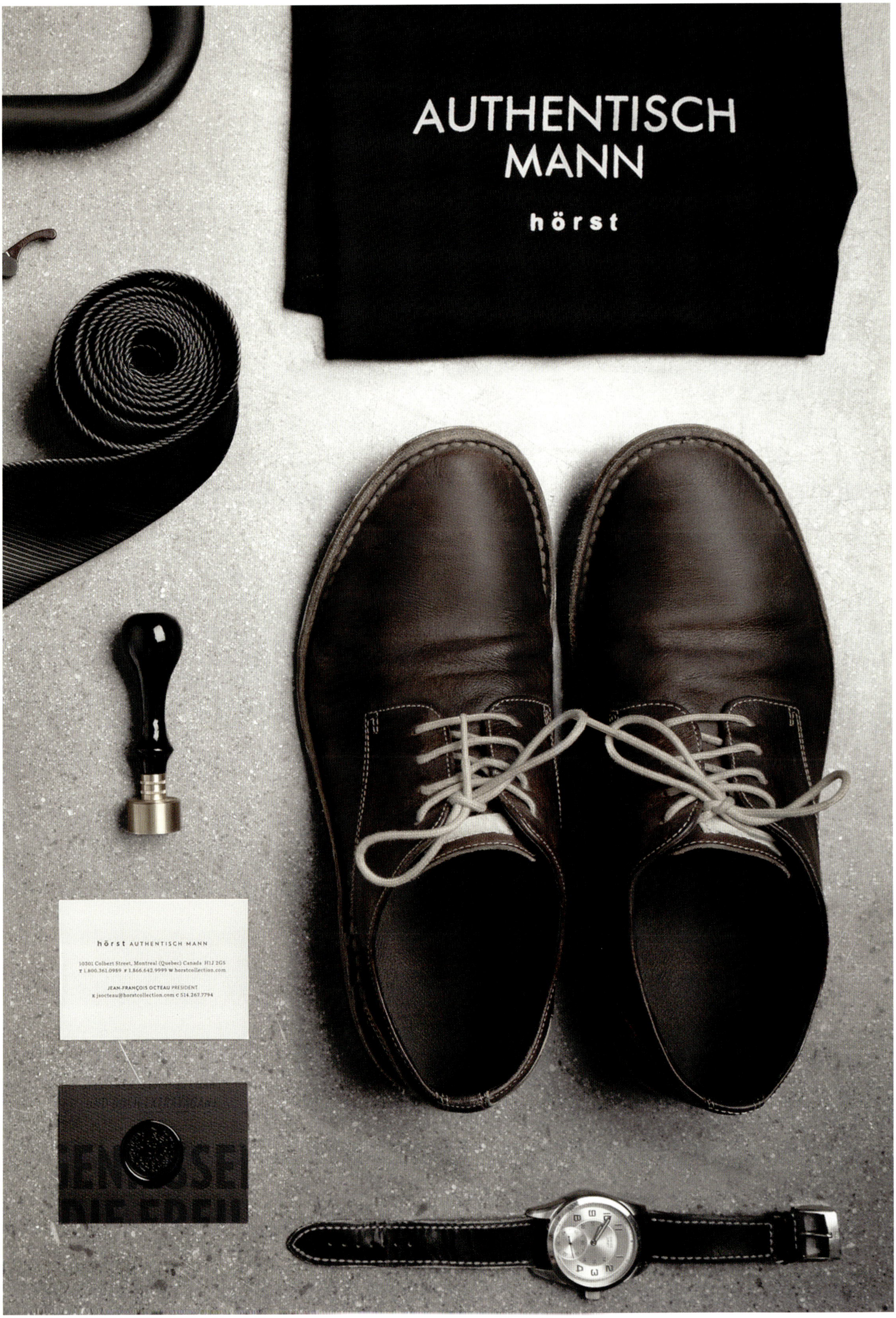
AUTHENTISCH
MANN
hörst
hörst AUTHENTISCH MANN
10301 Colbert Street, Montreal (Quebec) Canada H1J 2G5
T 1.800.361.0989 F 1.866.642.9999 W horstcollection.com
JEAN-FRANÇOIS OCTEAU PRESIDENT
E jocteau@horstcollection.com C 514.267.7794

Assignment: Bounded by Greenwich Street, Houston Street, Sixth Avenue, and Canal Street, Hudson Square is home to more than 30,000 people working in advertising, design, media, and communication businesses. Functioning as the Business Improvement District (BID) for this lower Manhattan neighborhood, Hudson Square Connection is the primary catalyst in an effort to transform this area into an attractive, lively, 24-7 neighborhood and major creative business hub. It aims to build a long-term vision for a connected community in a happening new Manhattan neighborhood. Hudson Square Connection commissioned Poulin + Morris to develop a new graphic identity and branding program, which includes a logotype, business stationery, event banners, promotional posters, and an annual report. The solution for the new logotype relies upon form, vibrant color, and distinctive sans serif typography. It is a composite of multiple colored squares, evoking the movement, diversity, and innovation of the BID, and complements the essence and character of the organization and the neighborhood itself. The collective goal of Hudson Square Connection's new graphic identity and branding program is to capture the spirit that thrives in the commercial spaces and to bring that energy into the public realm.

Designers: Douglas Morris, Andy Schoonmaker | **Design Firm:** Poulin + Morris Inc. | **Art Director:** Douglas Morris
Client: Hudson Square Connection Business Improvement District

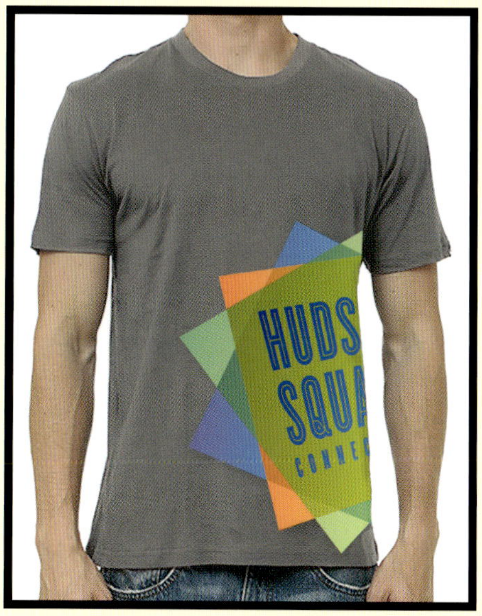

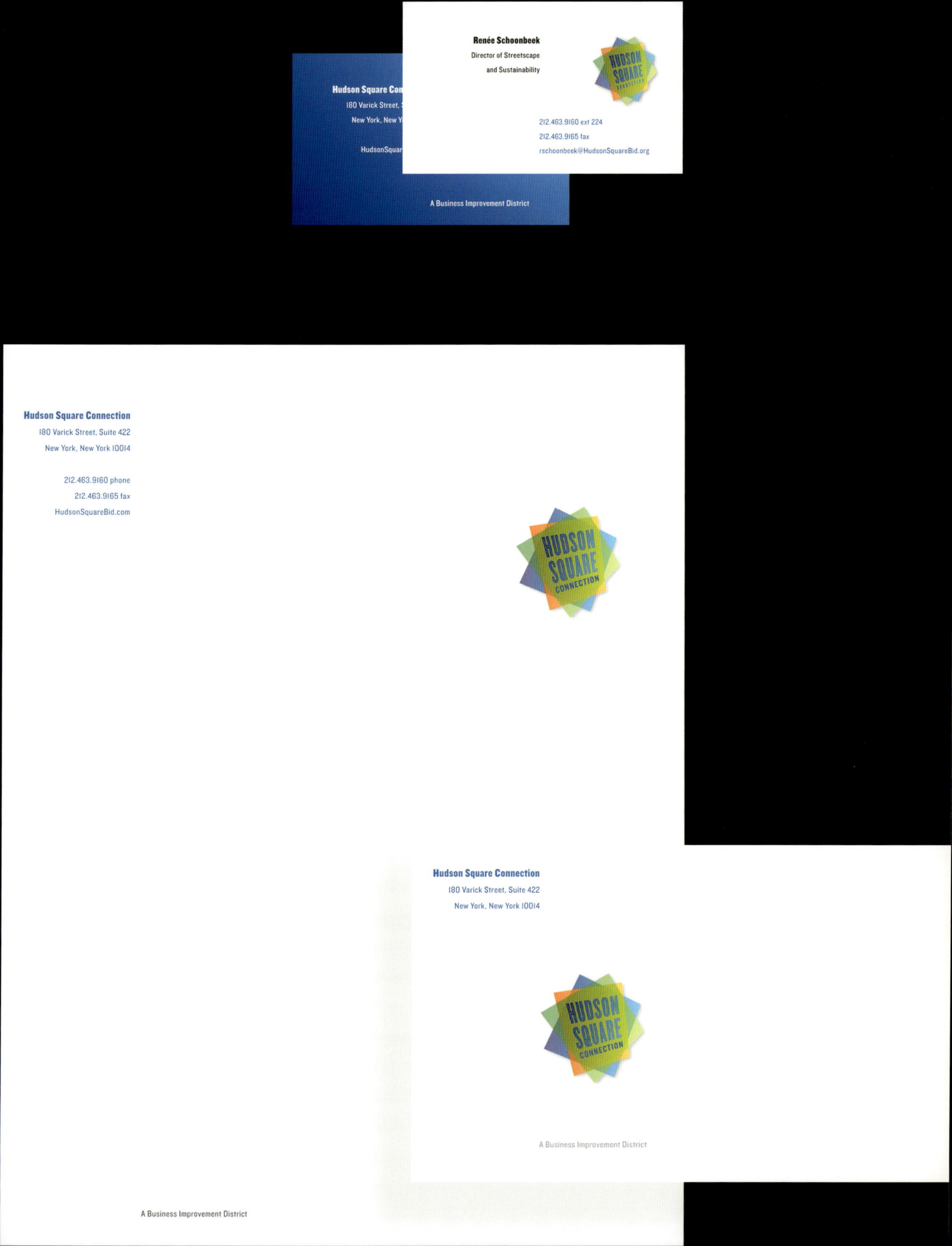
Renée Schoonbeek
Director of Streetscape
and Sustainability
212.463.9160 ext 224
212.463.9165 fax
rschoonbeek@HudsonSquareBid.org
Hudson Square Con
180 Varick Street,
New York, New Y
HudsonSquar
A Business Improvement District
Hudson Square Connection
180 Varick Street, Suite 422
New York, New York 10014
212.463.9160 phone
212.463.9165 fax
HudsonSquareBid.com
HUDSON SQUARE CONNECTION
A Business Improvement District
Hudson Square Connection
180 Varick Street, Suite 422
New York, New York 10014
HUDSON SQUARE CONNECTION
A Business Improvement District

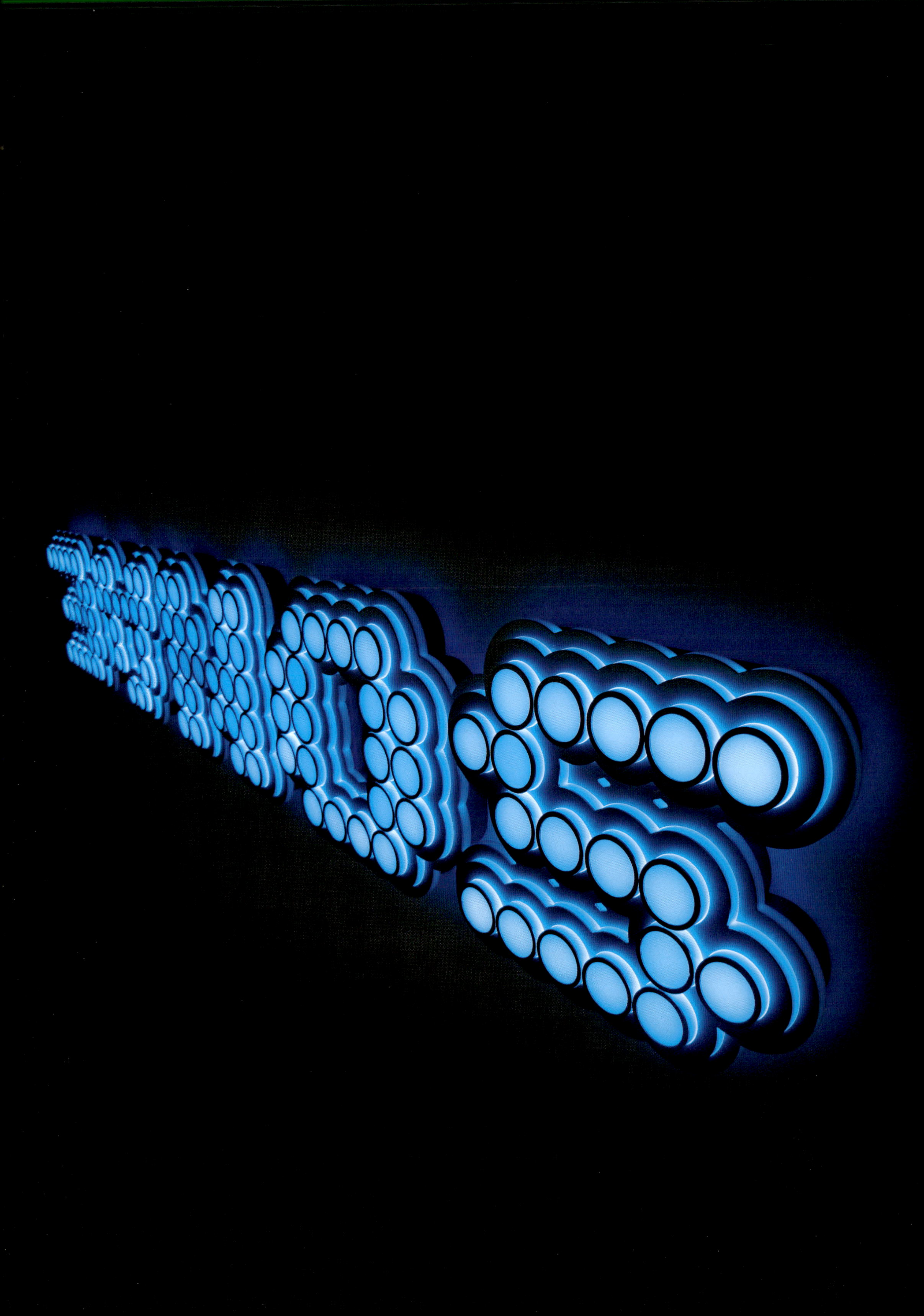

Assignment: Sonae has always been ahead of its time. After fifty years of existence, this multinational retail company with over 43,000 employees worldwide has implemented profound, organizational, and structural changes. The company wanted to communicate these changes in a dynamic and unifying manner. In order to give these changes substance, and to make them visually tangible, a new identity system had to be created. The new system had to be able to interpret and reflect the company's wide diversity, be consistent with the brand's attributes, and be adaptable to different levels of representation, in particular via new media and new technologies.

Approach: The circle has been a common element throughout Sonae's history, expressing the company's stability and solidity, and serving as a visual foundation for the brand. A word mark brand was proposed, delivering not just a single idea, but rather an immense multiplicity of ideas and points of contact organized in a unified way. The Expanding Circles concept was the point of departure for the new Sonae brand.
The approach creates a new model to establish a set of brand guidelines, which explore shape, movement, and interactivity.
It is a multidimensional brand, built up at three levels: a multicolored brand; a metamorphic brand; and a dynamic, changeable, and synergetic system that is constantly evolving. In order to achieve and manage this ambitious goal, Sonae has set up a technical mainframe for the project SONAE BRAND GENERATOR, which will ensure the durability, strength, and technical quality of an infinite number of applications. Sonae's new identity challenges the static concept of a brand, a challenge based on the belief that a personal touch and creativity have a fundamental role to play. And as vector representation is limited, the brand also takes on an infinite number of thematic representations that are originally nonvector in origin.

Results: The Sonae brand lives off inspiration. Creativity in its use is fundamental so that its essence can be respected. This is a dynamic brand, in constant development. Every day it is built by the imagination of those who work it, and the perception of those who receive it. It is a brand in constant mutation, apt to adapt to the different demands of its public presence and to adequately represent the immense visual universe that comprises Sonae. It is a brand with a complex personality, but is highly flexible. It is multi-chromatic because it can assume any color. It is multidimensional, in the sense that it plays with concepts of depth and tri-dimensionality. It is a result of its three-tiered independent layers, which provoke perception alterations when they are manipulated. It is metamorphosis, because it allows for different artistic expressions in its creative use. Over the last two years, the new brand has generated a level of enthusiasm that is unparalleled in the history of the company, and has thus achieved the objective of signalling the need to focus on the future and stimulate change.

Design Firm: Ivity Brand Corp. | **Client:** Sonae

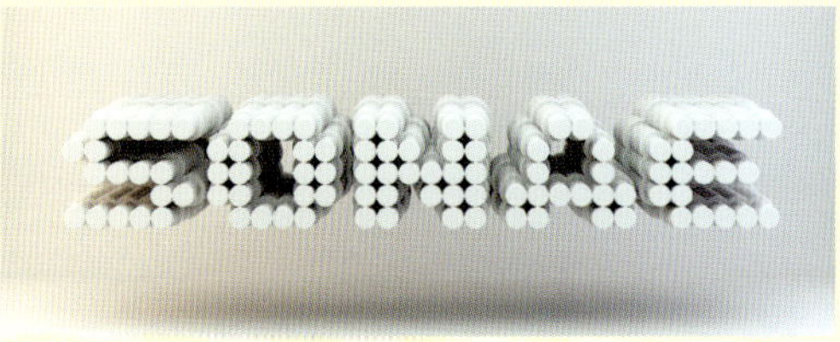
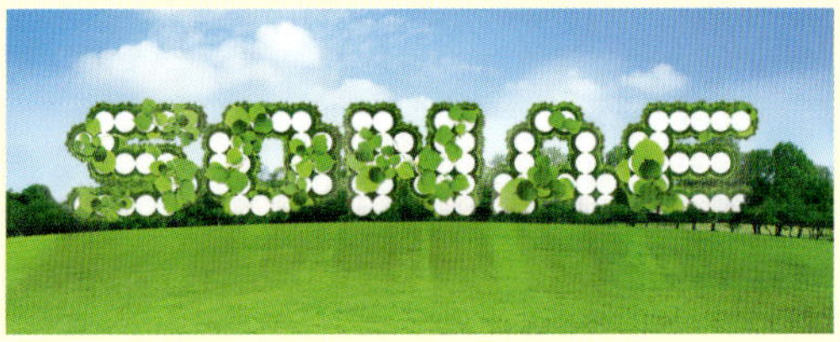

IvityBrandCorp.(this spread)|Sonae|Corporate**89**

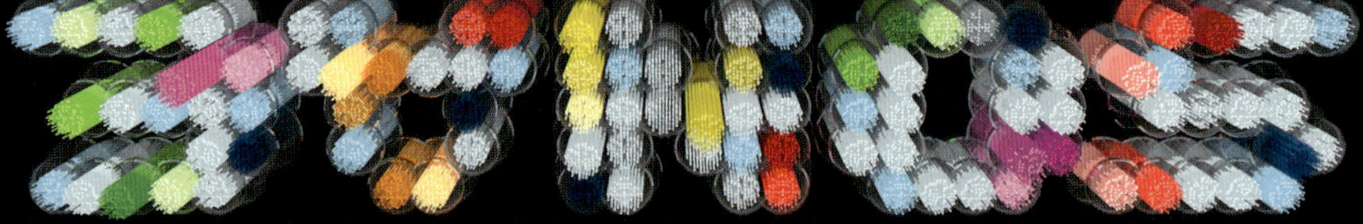

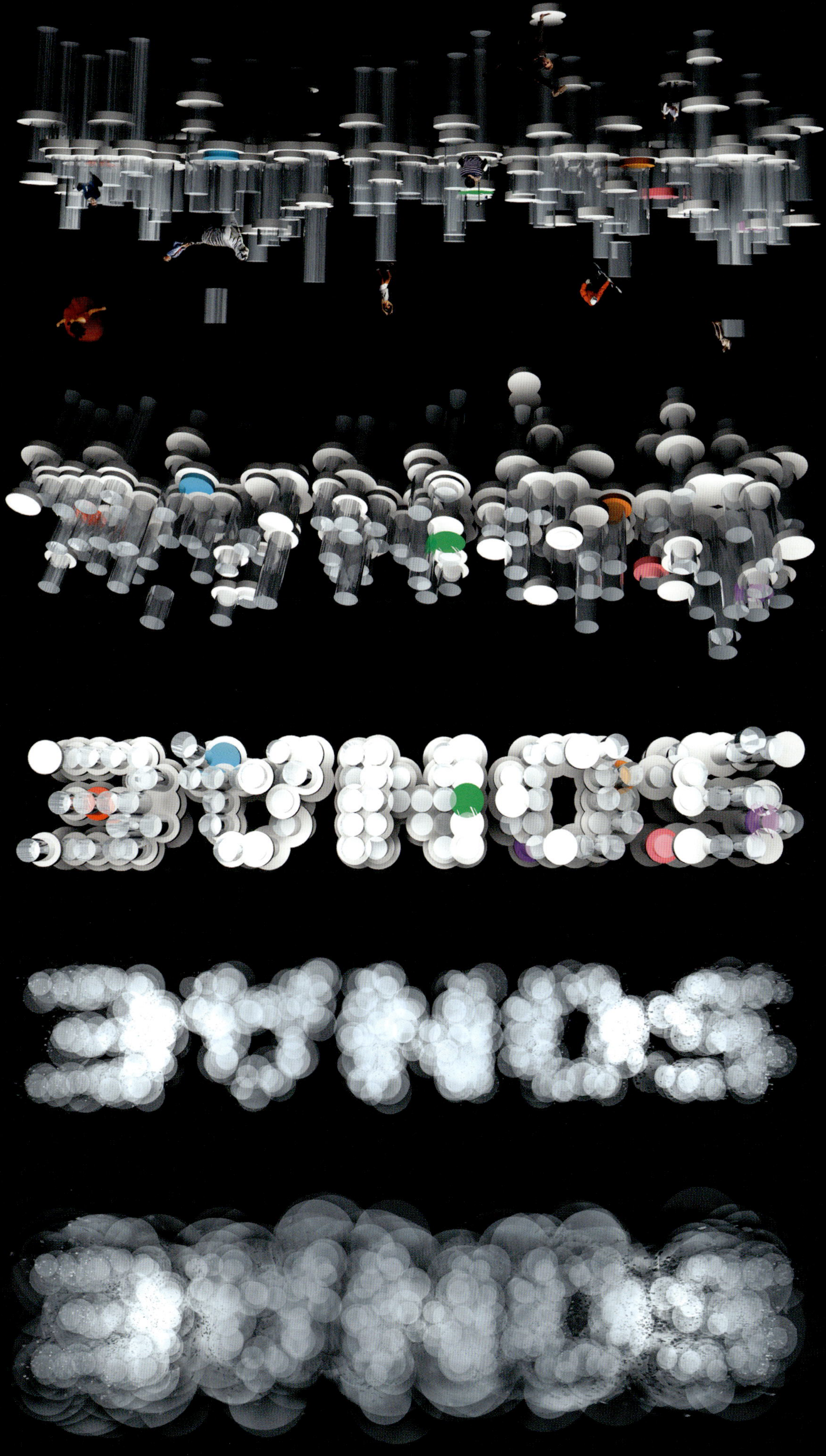

Assignment:

Company Introduction: Off-Site Records Management, established in 1988 and located in Santa Clara, California, provides a complete range of records storage, destruction, imaging, and digital storage solutions to help customers manage their company's information throughout the records' life cycle. Off-Site specializes in creating a customized solution to meet its customer's needs for both hard copy and electronic records, providing customers with the ability to select the combination of services required.

Market Overview: As a result of Off-Site's Silicon Valley location, the company's primary market consists of large technology firms, accounting and law firms, and healthcare organizations with voluminous records and the need for security and privacy. Secondary markets include small- and medium-sized businesses of many types that need to keep records to comply with a range of legal standards, including privacy and security laws.

Competitive Background: Despite experiencing steady growth from its inception, Off-Site was facing increasing competition from national records management chains in the Bay Area, including Iron Mountain and Cor-O-Van. After a careful review of competition within the document storage industry, we determined that while a number of competing firms in the Silicon Valley region offered individual document storage, scanning, and destruction services, few firms in this market provided a complete range of document storage solutions. Customers would sometimes need to engage different companies to store their records or shred their documents, providing a market opportunity for a firm to that could be the single source for these services. We saw an opportunity for Off-Site to be the firm that had the expertise to manage the region's large scale Silicon Valley technology accounts, while offering the personalized service and competitive pricing valued by mid-size businesses.

Coordinating the Marketing Effort: Off-Site sought to coordinate its marketing efforts to present a more professional image with a unified and cohesive branding program encompassing its logo, tagline, symbol system, stationery, document storage box, vehicle graphics, exterior signage, and website, all driven by a comprehensive brand strategy.

Attracting a Larger Client Base: Off-Site wanted to build upon and expand its existing client base of Silicon Valley technology firms, accounting and law firms, and healthcare organizations to more effectively compete with the large national records storage chains, while still offering the personalized service that distinguished the company.

Educating and Building Awareness: Off-Site's customer research indicated that a significant number of current and prospective customers were not aware of the wide range of services that Off-Site provided. In addition, many current and prospective customers did not realize their legal responsibilities regarding the responsible handling of their clients' confidential information and the importance of engaging a professional records management company.

Positioning as a Complete Resource: Based upon our research findings of customers needing to engage several different firms to meet their records management needs, we saw an opportunity for Off-Site to appeal to customers as a comprehensive and complete resource for all records storage solutions a client might need, including document storage, scanning, and destruction services.

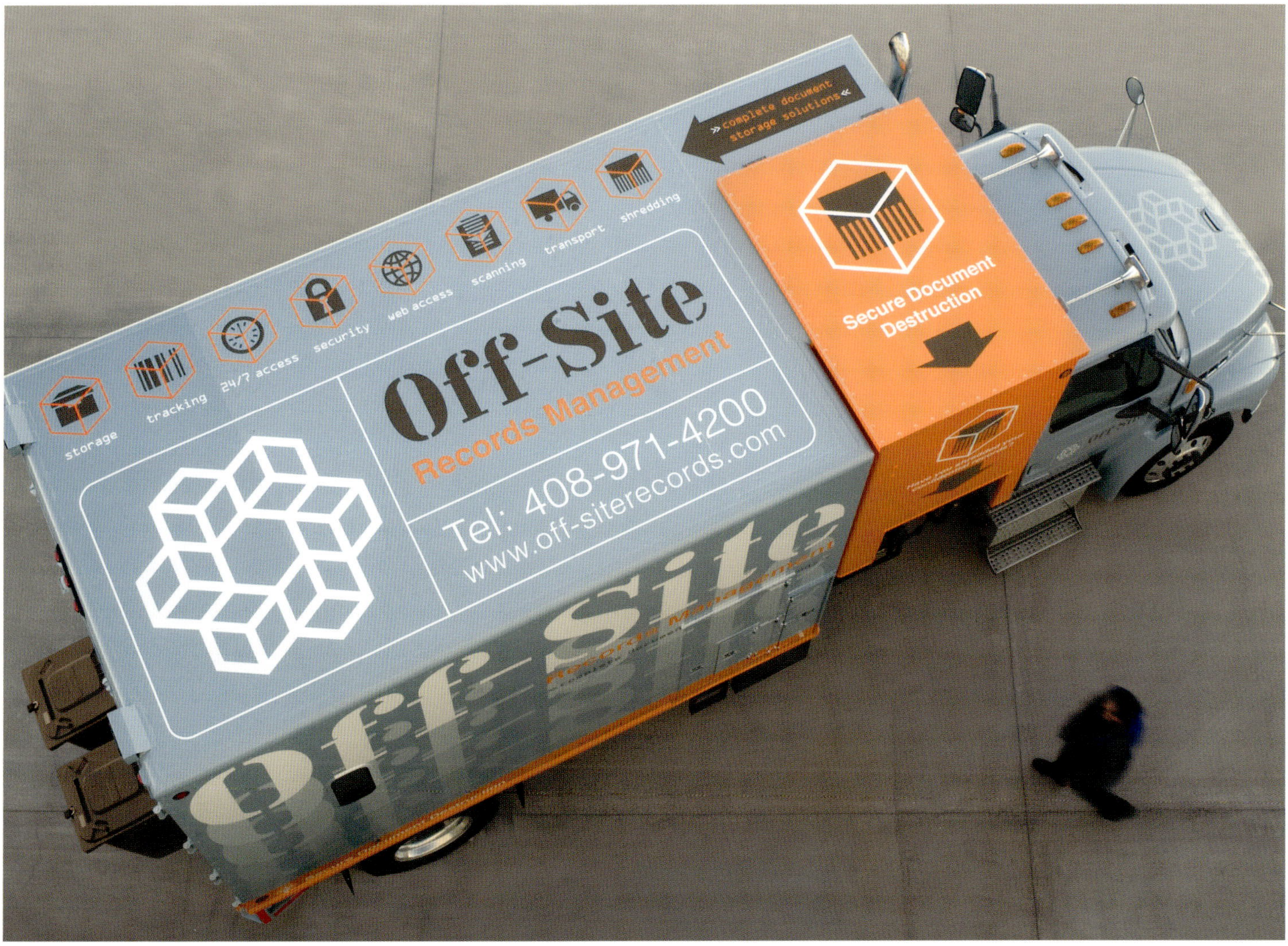
» complete document storage solutions «
Secure Document Destruction
storage
tracking
24/7 access
security
web access
scanning
transport
shredding
Off-Site
Records Management
Tel: 408-971-4200
www.off-siterecords.com

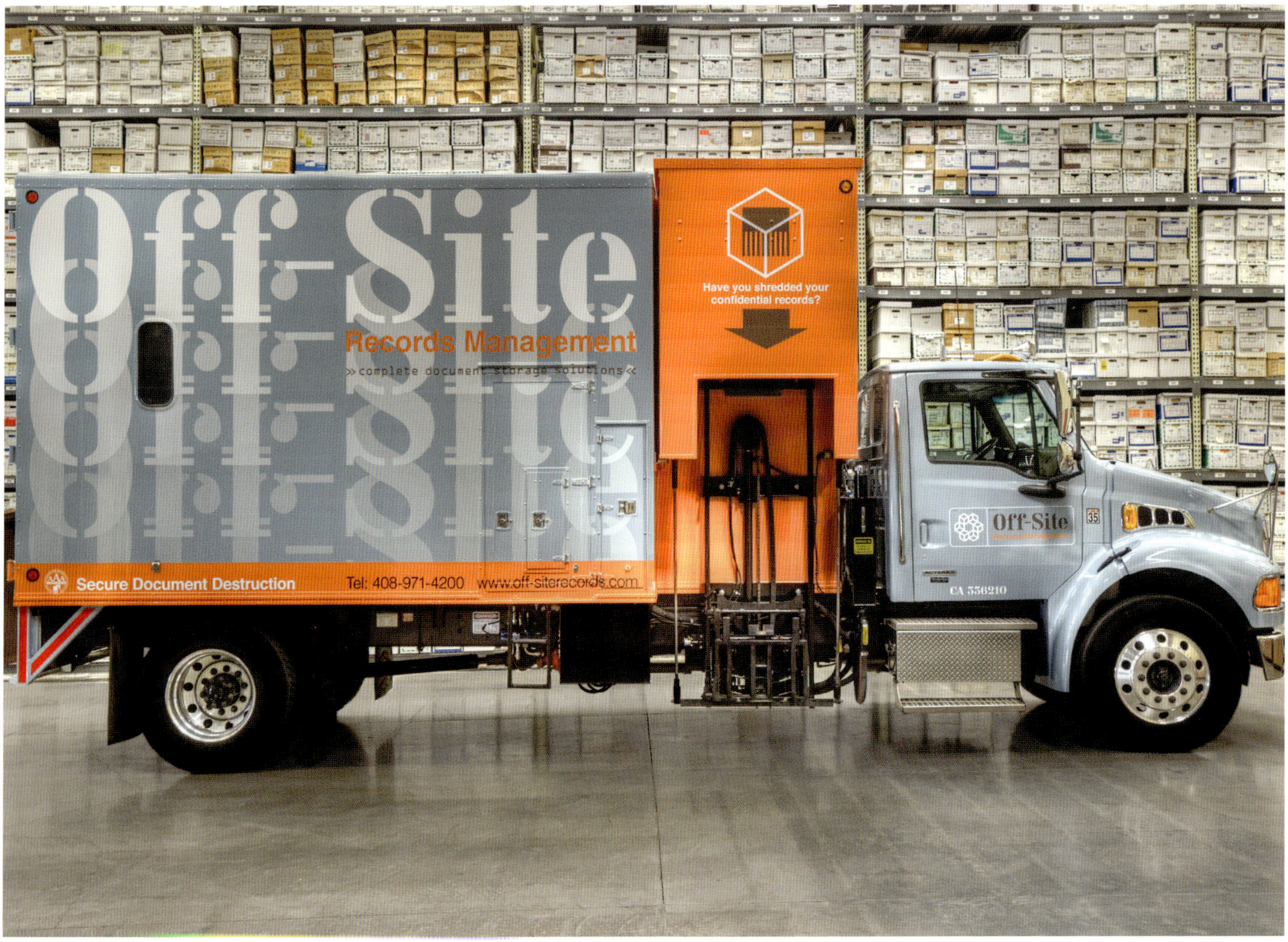
Off-Site
Records Management
» complete document storage solutions «
Have you shredded your confidential records?
Secure Document Destruction
Tel: 408-971-4200
www.off-siterecords.com
Off-Site
CA 556210

Approach:

Our design strategy was to create name recognition for Off-Site, communicate its commitment to providing complete document storage solutions, and extend the company brand. The logo, tagline, service symbols, and typographic pattern are used in a strategic manner to create a flexible, cohesive, and comprehensive program.

Logo, Tagline, Symbols, and Pattern

The logo's dimensional boxes suggest space and storage, while forming a circle to represent the access, retrieval, and linking of information throughout the records management life cycle. Our "complete document storage solutions" tagline enables Off-Site to stand out from its competition as the single point of contact for all records storage services. To support this positioning, we developed service symbols that visually depict the full range of services offered. These symbols appear on all branding applications, enabling the audience to consistently associate Off-Site with a complete range of services. We combined Off-Site's uniquely descriptive name with gradation to create a proprietary typographic pattern. Used on the storage boxes and vehicles, the stacking pattern creates a metaphor for customers moving their documents off-site.

Stationery and Presentation Folder

The letterhead and envelope flap use a file folder motif, displaying the company's complete document storage solutions in a vertical column. The back of the letterhead uses a pattern of interconnected logos to form a giant logo. The business card resembles an information tag, complete with punched hole and ball chain, and displays Off-Site's complete range of services on the back. On the presentation folder the logo becomes a dimensional flap, revealing the company's document service solutions available to customers inside.

Document Storage Box

Off-Site's descriptive name is used to create a continuous pattern when stacked and a metaphor for customers moving their documents off-site. As these storage boxes remain in customers' offices for months at a time, we transformed these utilitarian objects into moving billboards for the company. On the bottom, the logo's six-sided shape outlines the box assembly in six simple steps.

Shred and Delivery Trucks

The truck graphics showcase the symbol on one side and company name on the other, combining Off-Site's descriptive name with gradation as a metaphor for customers moving their documents off-site. The shredder mechanism is highlighted in orange. The top functions as a moving billboard to display the firm's complete range of services. On the delivery truck, an orange band strategically positioned at eye-level displays Off-Site's service symbols. The truck's roll-up door encourages new customers to imagine the arrival of their documents.

Exterior Signage

The Off-Site monument sign signals the entrance to the facility. The dimensional logo provides different views from all angles, representing the company's multi-dimensional approach to servicing its customers. The forty-foot windows display icons representing the firm's complete range of document storage solutions. The super-graphic loading dock signage enables customers to identify the appropriate door at a distance. The logo is used as a decorative pattern on the roll-up doors to enhance the building's appearance and extend the brand.

Website

The Off-Site logo creates a unique navigational interface as a metaphor for the information life cycle and a representation of the company's complete document storage solutions. An image of each service category dissolves into the logo in a continuous sequence. Secondary pages use symbolic icons as navigational buttons, revealing bright orange pull-down menus for easy navigation. The sidebar features a video of the shred truck in operation and engaging factoids. Informational flow charts with orange headers use a hexagonal grid to explain the simple steps customers can take to safeguard their documents.

Results: Client Response

Off-Site President Beth Seibert felt the branding program clearly exceeded her expectations. After the program roll-out, Off-Site experienced a 30% increase in new business inquiries as customers began to embrace Off-Site's comprehensive services and move more of their records to the company. Most importantly, Off-Site's customers began to perceive the company as a valuable partner for their businesses. Off-Site was better able to compete with national chains for coveted Silicon Valley accounts and to establish itself as one of the Bay Area's leading document storage firms.

Strategic Results

The branding program identified a successful strategy for Off-Site to effectively compete with larger national chains by offering complete document storage solutions as expressed in our tagline. The logo created a proprietary and recognizable brand, distinguished the firm from competition, and clearly communicated the records management life cycle. Every brand application uses Off-Site's proprietary service symbols to align with the project's intent and positioning. The truck graphics have provided visibility for Off-Site, transforming their fleet into moving billboards for the company's services and extending the company brand throughout the Bay Area.

Employee Buy-In

After the vehicle graphics rollout, our client noticed that her drivers demonstrated a greater sense of pride and purpose in their work, and better understood their role as ambassadors for Off-Site, as in many cases the customer's interaction with the driver provides the only face-to-face contact they may have with Off-Site.

Value Through Design

We transformed utilitarian items, such as Off-Site's document storage boxes and its shred truck, into compelling three-dimensional brand extensions and rewarding customer experiences. After learning that Off-Site's document storage boxes reside in customers' offices for months

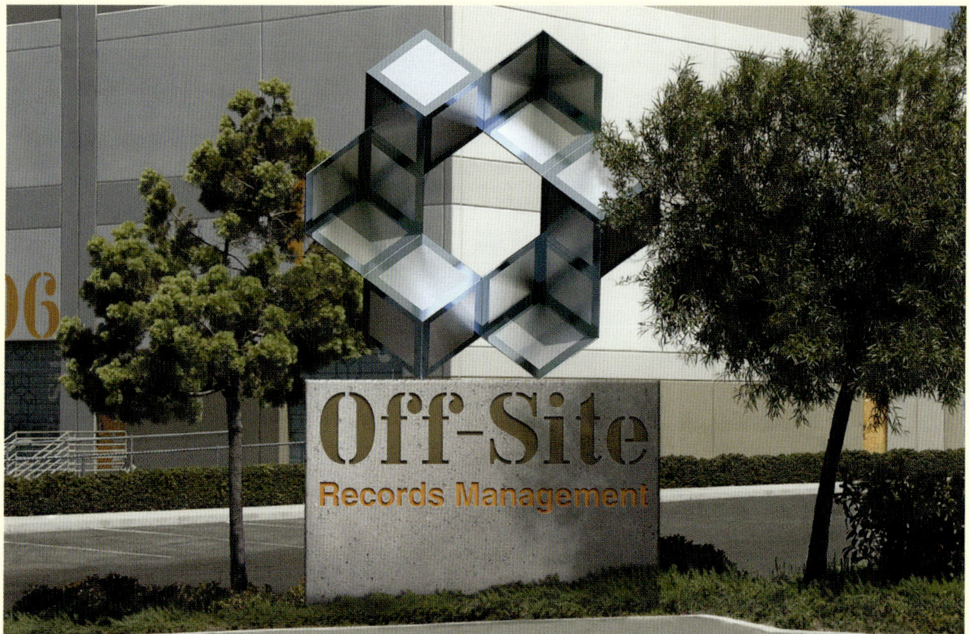

before being delivered to Off-Site's warehouse, we elevated these boxes to vehicles of brand recognition. Upon examination of Off-Site's curbside shredding procedure, we found that many customers have a legal responsibility to witness the operator shred their confidential documents, thus providing an opportunity to reimagine Off-Site's shred truck as an ambassador of the brand.

Flexibility and Scalability

The branding program has proven to be extremely flexible and scalable, from the intricate logo pattern on the stationery to the super-graphic 20-foot-high loading dock doors. The Off-Site typographic pattern is used in many different ways throughout the program. The branding program has translated exceedingly well across the multiple platforms of print, vehicles, signage, and web. The website was successful in achieving Off-Site's goal of utilizing technology to generate new leads.

Client Value

The branding program's value-driven approach enabled Off-Site to allocate its limited funds to derive a high value for its investment. The design strategy and implementation helped change how customers think about Off-Site, enabling it to be perceived as a much larger player in the region. Our careful consideration of Off-Site's market resulted in a program that clearly resonates with its target audience, enabling Off-Site to receive many accolades for their boxes, trucks, and website. The branding program also enabled Off-Site to gain recognition from industry organizations like the National Association for Information Destruction (NAID) as exemplary of the profession's best practices.

Client Quote

"We have been very pleased with the success of our branding program in educating prospects about our services and inspiring them to contact us. We are able to compete against larger competitors because our wide range of services are clearly demonstrated through text, photographs, diagrams, and video. We have received so many compliments on the design and content of the program."

—Beth Seibert, President, Off-Site Records Management

Designers: Earl Gee, Fani Chung | **Design Firm:** Gee + Chung Design | **Art Director:** Earl Gee | **Creative Director:** Earl Gee
Illustrator: Earl Gee | **Client:** Off-Site Records Management

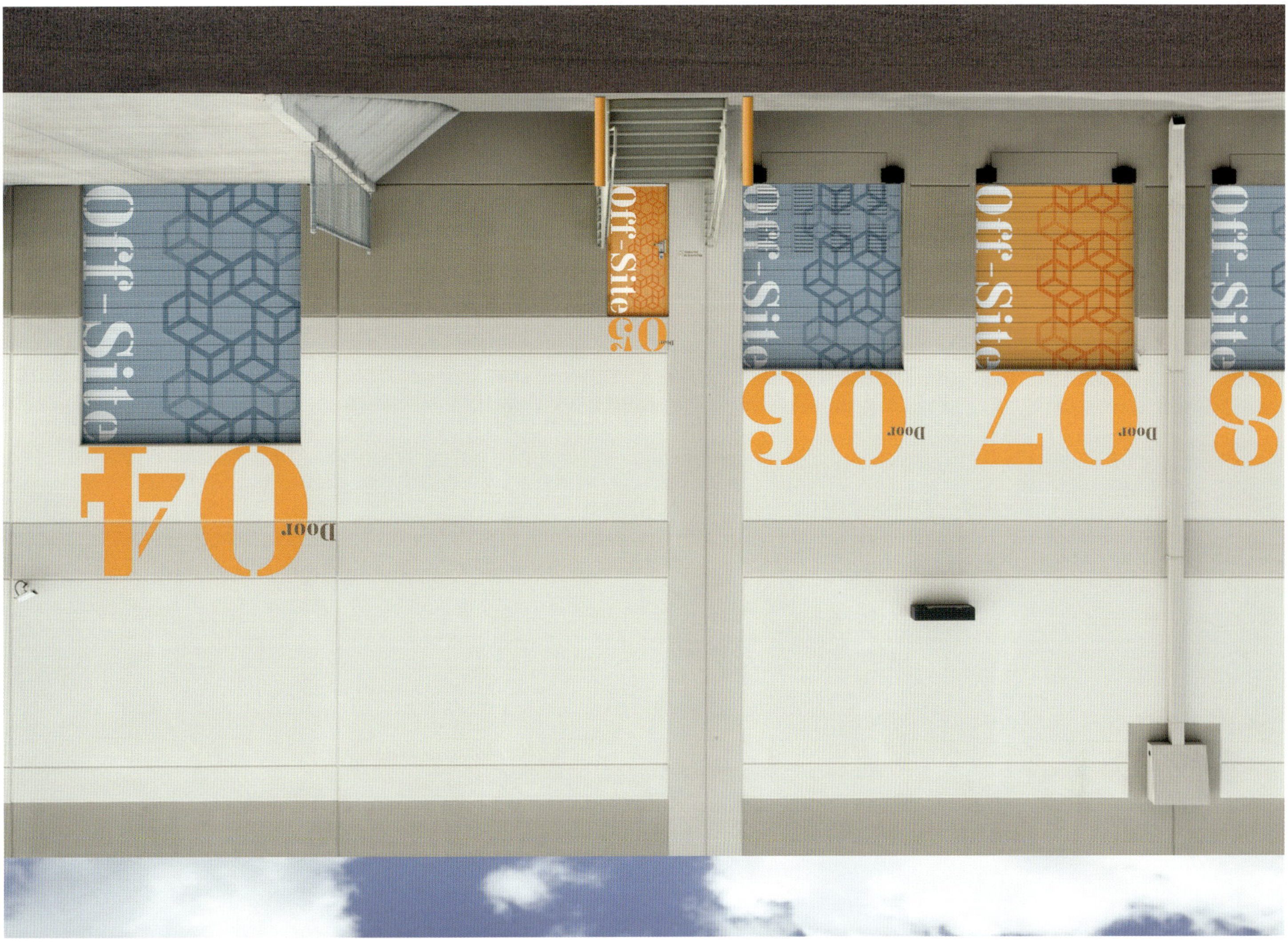
Off-Site
Door 04
Off-Site
Door 05
Off-Site
Door 06
Off-Site
Door 07
Off-Site

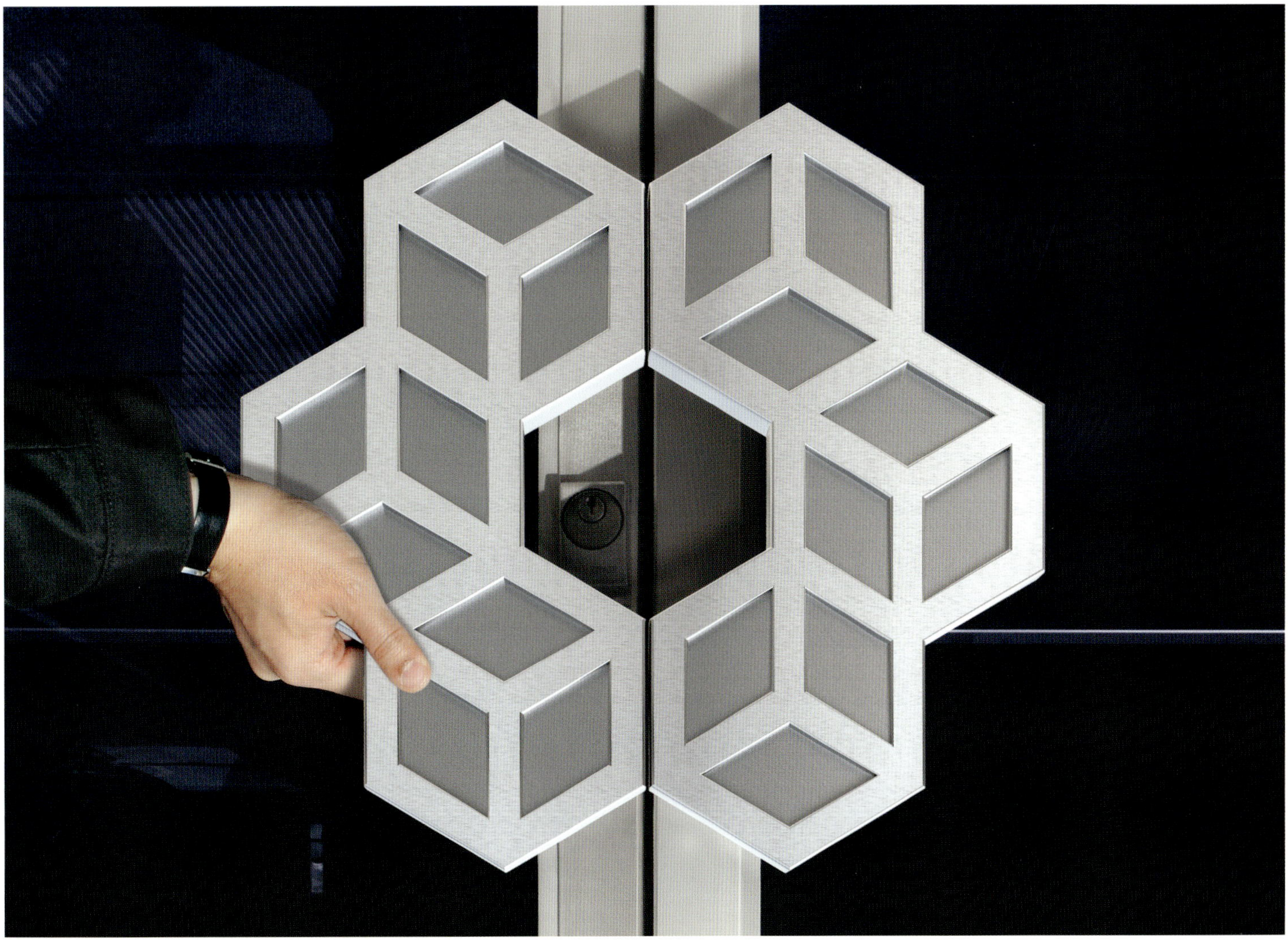

Assignment: We were involved in the branding plan for the company name change. TableMark, the new name of the company, is a foodstuffs company, one of the most famous major corporations in the frozen food industry in Japan. General consumers buy the corporation's products directly, and therefore the brand design is very important to convey its corporate values.

Approach: We avoided using a table as an element of the design, although the new company's name includes *table*. We adopted as a main motif a tablecloth, symbolic of the time and space around a table, using tablecloths of various materials and printed patterns from all over the world. We wanted the newly constructed design to express the happiness and pleasure of food. The motion logo is also a very important item—a simple and comprehensive design to communicate with general consumers.

Results: By the motion logo of a soft tablecloth flown in commercial film, and by a lot of quality commodities, the name TableMark extended nationwide in Japan. Around the world, people eat various foods in different environments, but a table with a delicious supper always lies at the heart. A sumptuous dinner table provides for family gathering, talking, and smiling faces—a visual expression of the company's value equation of "happiness and food."

Designer: Toshihiro Onimaru | **Design Firm:** Graphics & Designing Inc. | **Art Director:** Atsushi Takeuchi
Creative Director: Toshihiro Onimaru | **Client:** TableMark Co., Ltd.

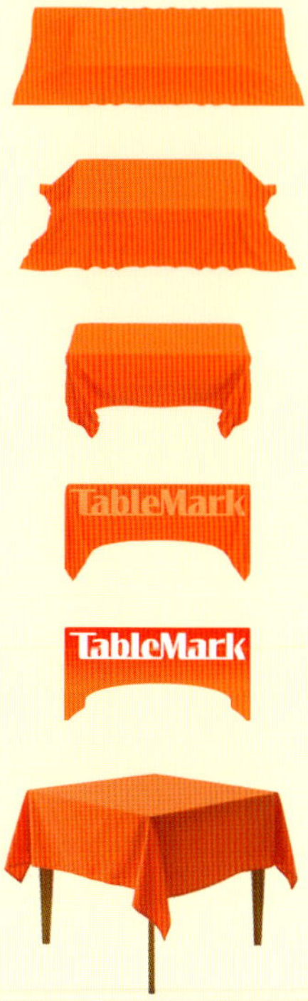

Graphics & Designing Inc.(this spread)|TableMarkCo.,Ltd|Corporate98

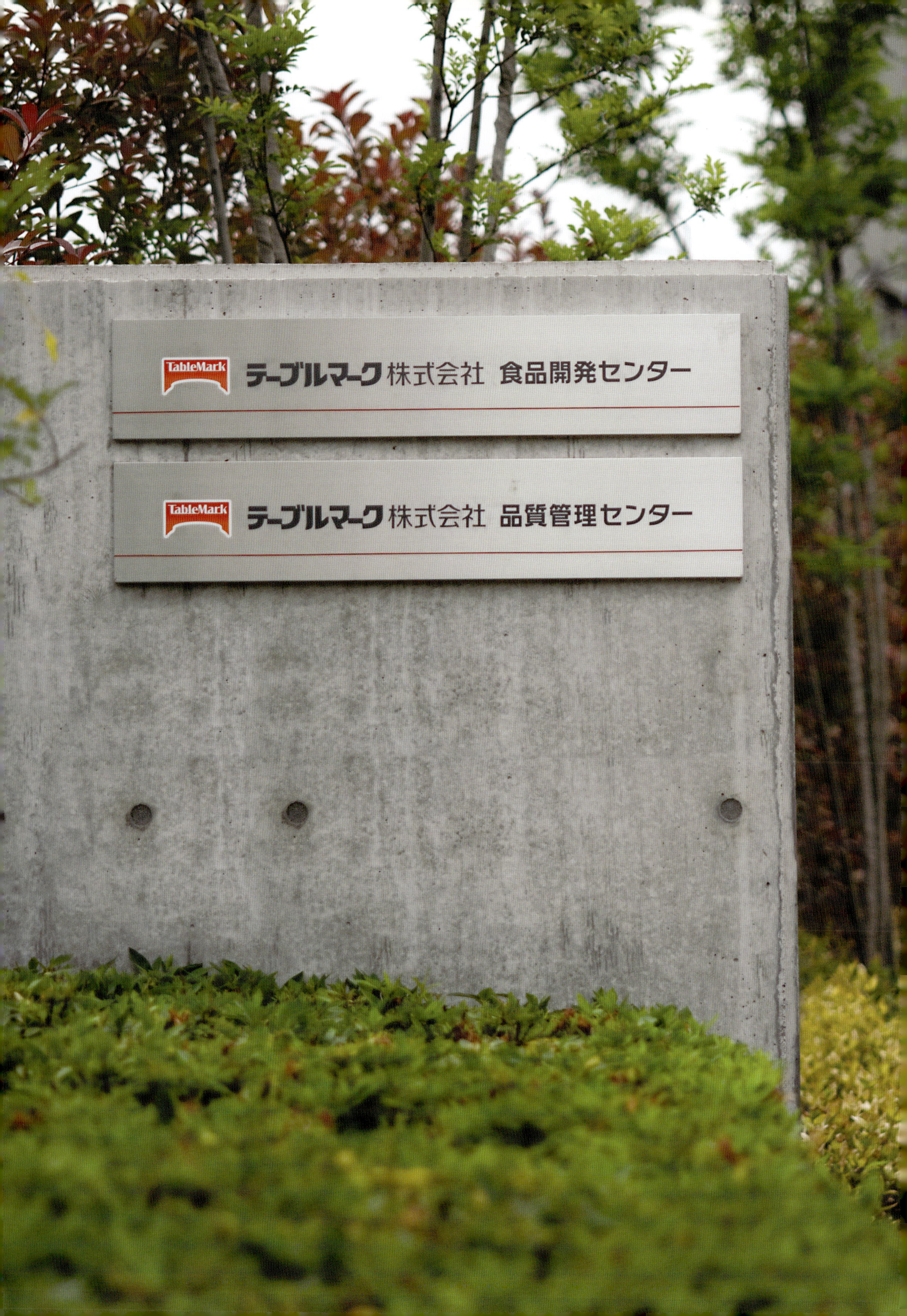
TableMark
テーブルマーク株式会社 食品開発センター
TableMark
テーブルマーク株式会社 品質管理センター

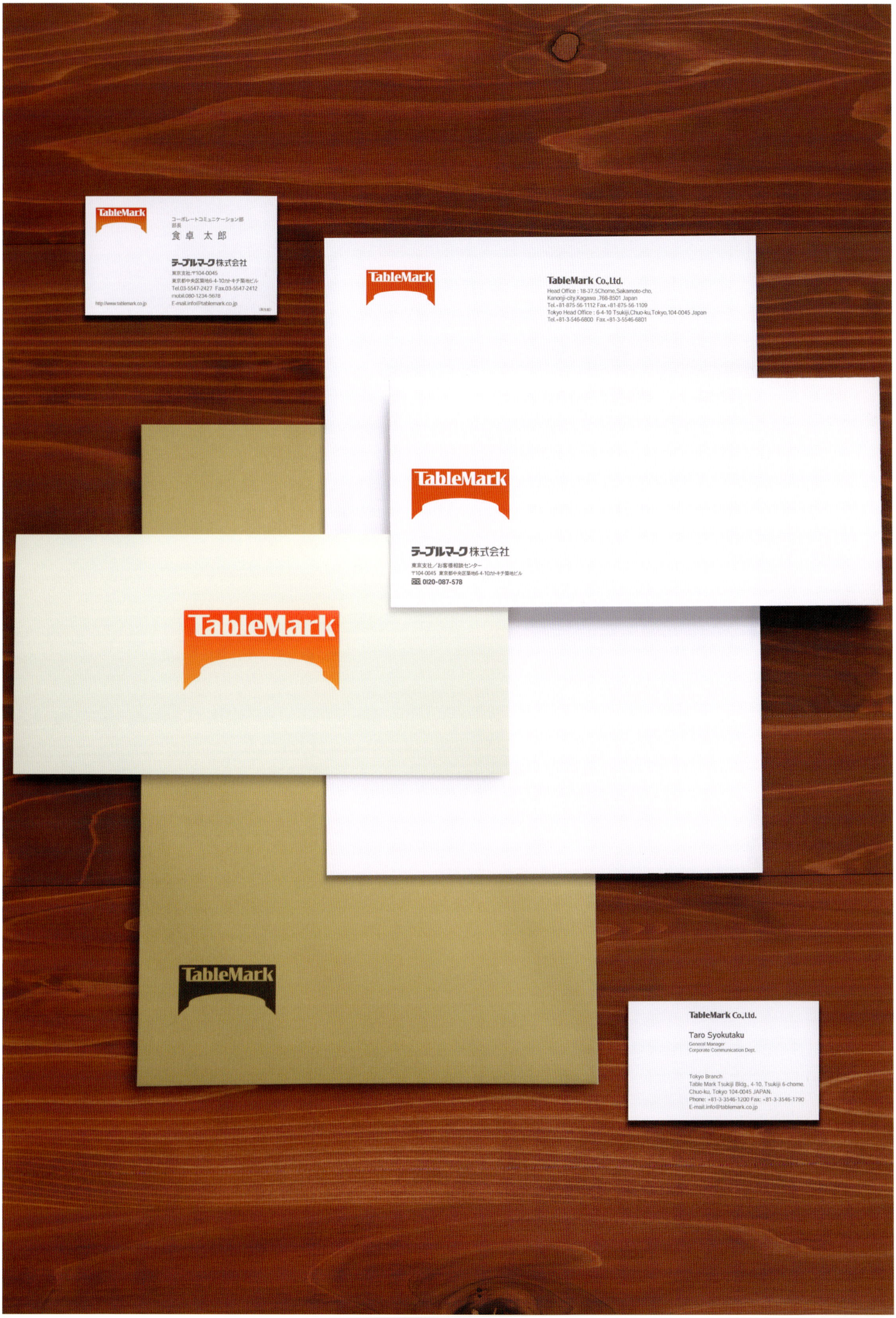
コーポレートコミュニケーション部
部長
食卓 太郎
テーブルマーク株式会社
東京支社:〒104-0045
東京都中央区築地6-4-10カトキチ築地ビル
Tel.03-5547-2427 Fax.03-5547-2412
mobil.080-1234-5678
E-mail.info@tablemark.co.jp
http://www.tablemark.co.jp
TableMark Co.,Ltd.
Head Office : 18-37,5Chome,Sakamoto-cho,
Kanonji-city,Kagawa ,768-8501 Japan
Tel.+81-875-56-1112 Fax.+81-875-56-1109
Tokyo Head Office : 6-4-10 Tsukiji,Chuo-ku,Tokyo,104-0045 Japan
Tel.+81-3-546-6800 Fax.+81-3-5546-6801
テーブルマーク株式会社
東京支社／お客様相談センター
〒104-0045 東京都中央区築地6-4-10カトキチ築地ビル
0120-087-578
TableMark Co.,Ltd.
Taro Syokutaku
General Manager
Corporate Communication Dept.
Tokyo Branch
Table Mark Tsukiji Bldg., 4-10, Tsukiji 6-chome,
Chuo-ku, Tokyo 104-0045 JAPAN.
Phone: +81-3-3546-1200 Fax: +81-3-3546-1790
E-mail.info@tablemark.co.jp

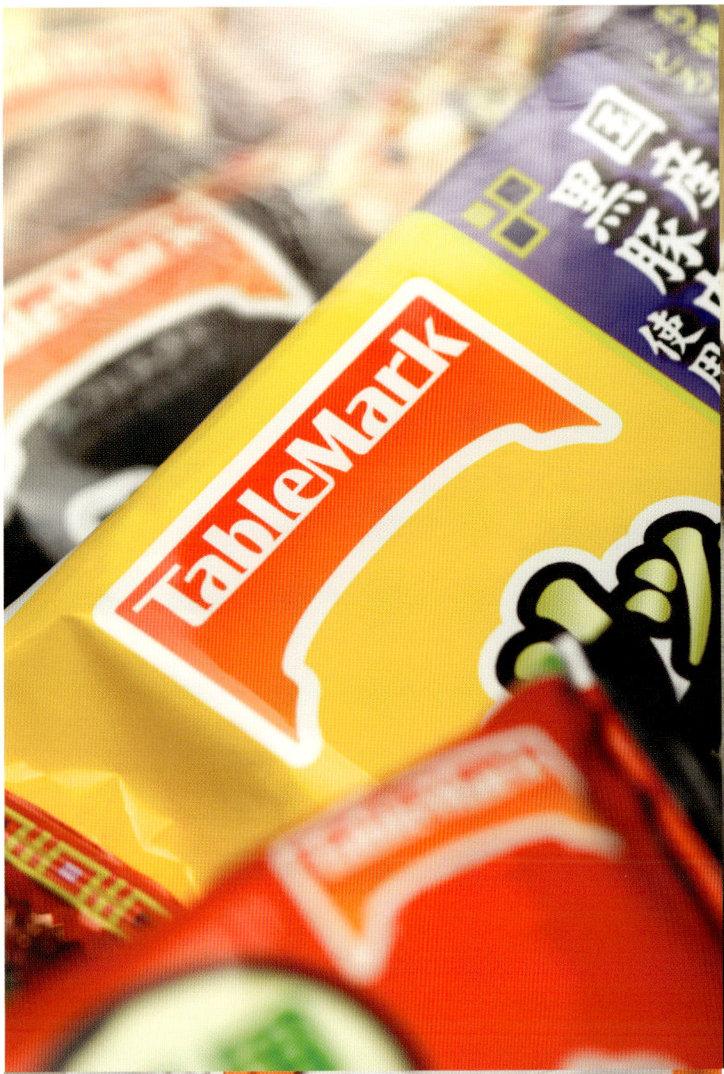
TableMark
黒豚

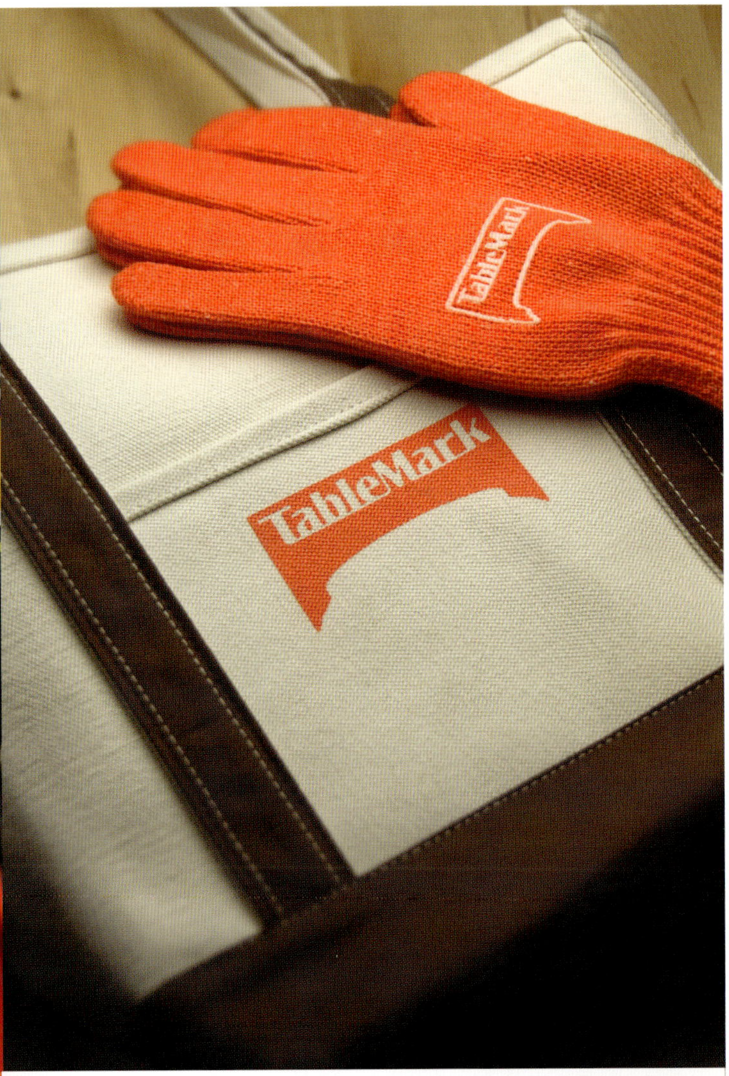
TableMark
TableMark

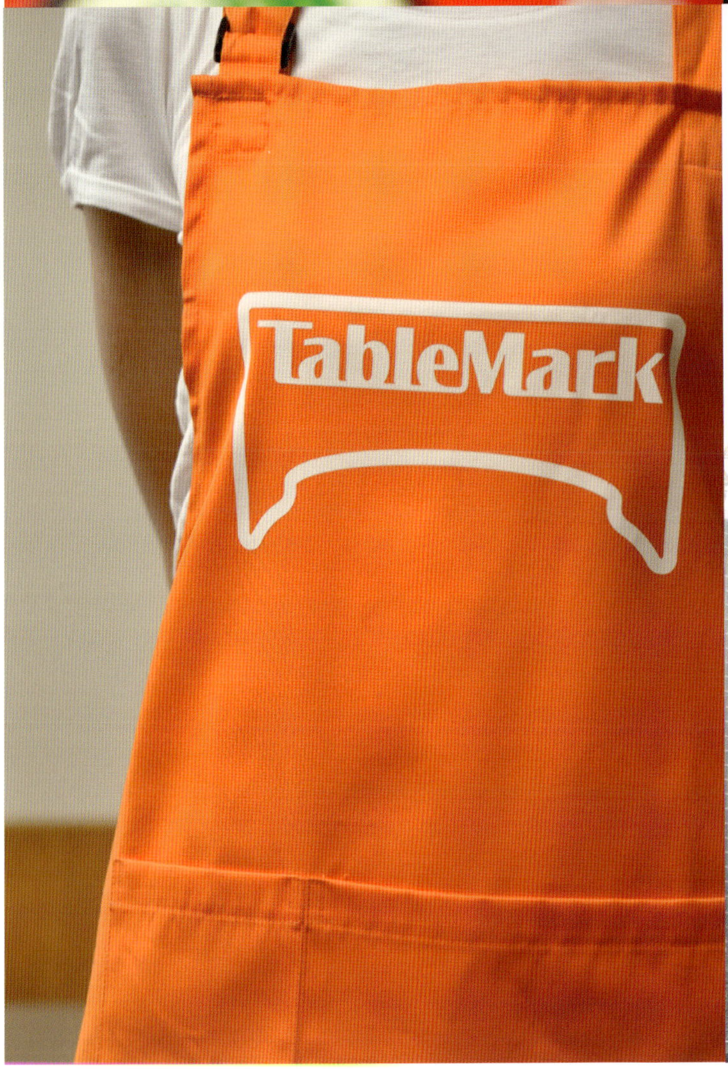
TableMark

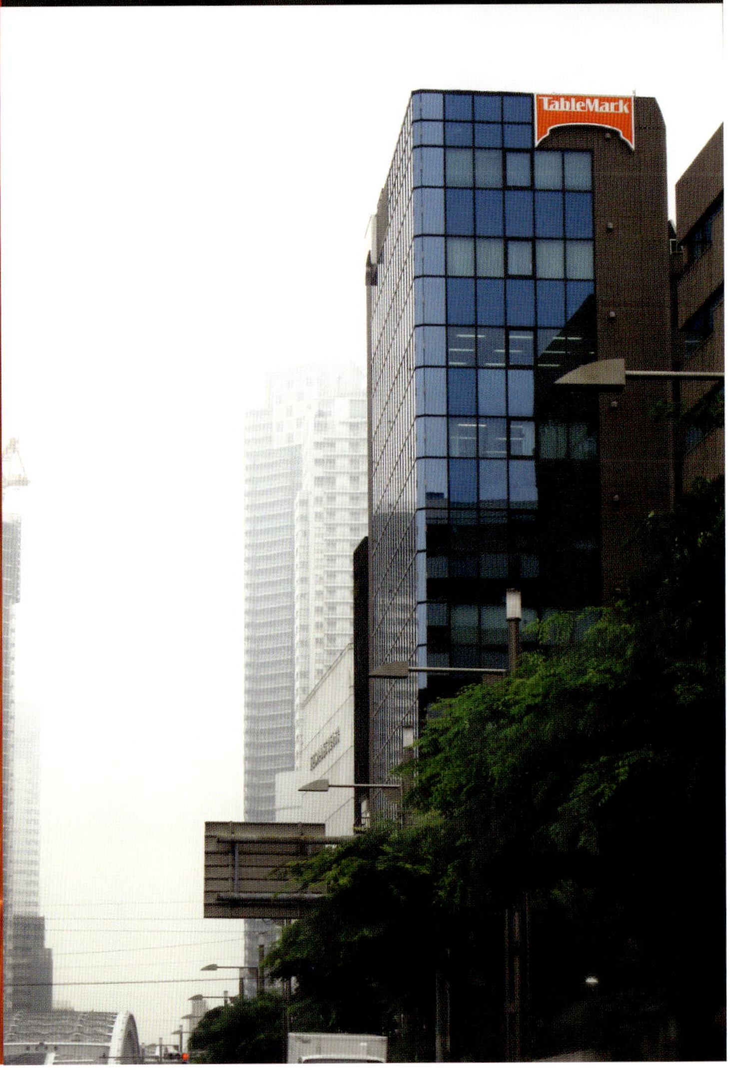
TableMark

Assignment: Shepherd is an agency that values the role creativity plays in all successful marketing, regardless of client category or marketing vehicle. After streamlining the name from the Robin Shepherd Group to founder Robin Shepherd's last name, "Shepherd," we wanted to create a strong, forward-thinking brand that would not be constrained by the conventional rules of branding.

Approach: Execution and technique aside, the act of branding traditionally calls for designing a brand mark, establishing the color palette and type family, and then stamping everything out with unwavering consistency. We believe branding can have more depth than that, and if you're not careful, that *consistent* can quickly turn into *boring*. In order to make the new brand stretch the boundaries of what branding means to most people, and to stand as an example of what it could grow into in the future, we set out to create an identity that would be consistent, but flexible and expandable too. We wanted personalized branding that could be customized without being bastardized. The key to achieving that was the egg. The agency identity has always included a painted robin's egg, going back to 1984, when Robin Shepherd founded the agency. Through the years, the robin's egg has served both as a nice play on Robin's name, and as a symbol for creativity and the potential every idea holds. In creating the new brand, we did establish a consistent type system and design architecture. But we then gave every employee the chance to create their own egg, something that would represent their interests, personality, or passion. The only rule was that their egg design had to be contained within the egg shape. We then incorporated each design into the overall brand identity architecture.

Results: At this point, our branding system includes a few self-portraits, sporting equipment, illustrations, money, and even a green egg in honor of Dr. Seuss. And, in a sign of admiration for old school Shepherd ideals, more than one employee still uses the original robin's egg in their card. The branding system can be customized to appeal to prospects in multiple categories, and is now ownable by each of our employees. It regularly receives compliments from our existing clients and prospects, particularly in larger group meetings when the classic flurry of business card swapping begins. We've even had clients remark that they wish they had eggs of their own.

Designer: Shepherd | **Design Firm:** Shepherd | **Art Director:** Shepherd | **Creative Directors:** Robin Shepherd, Tom Schifanella | **Client:** Shepherd

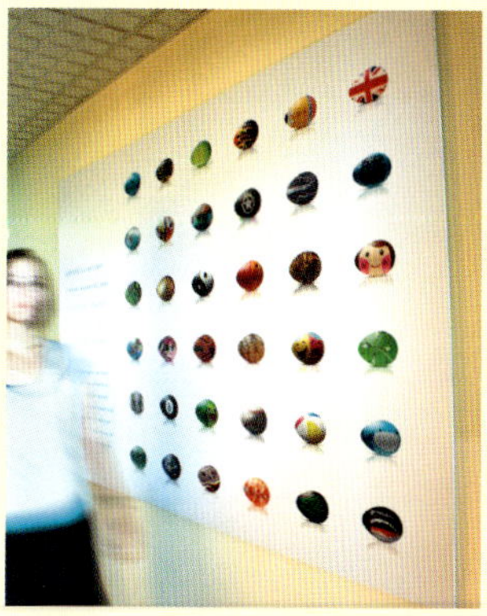

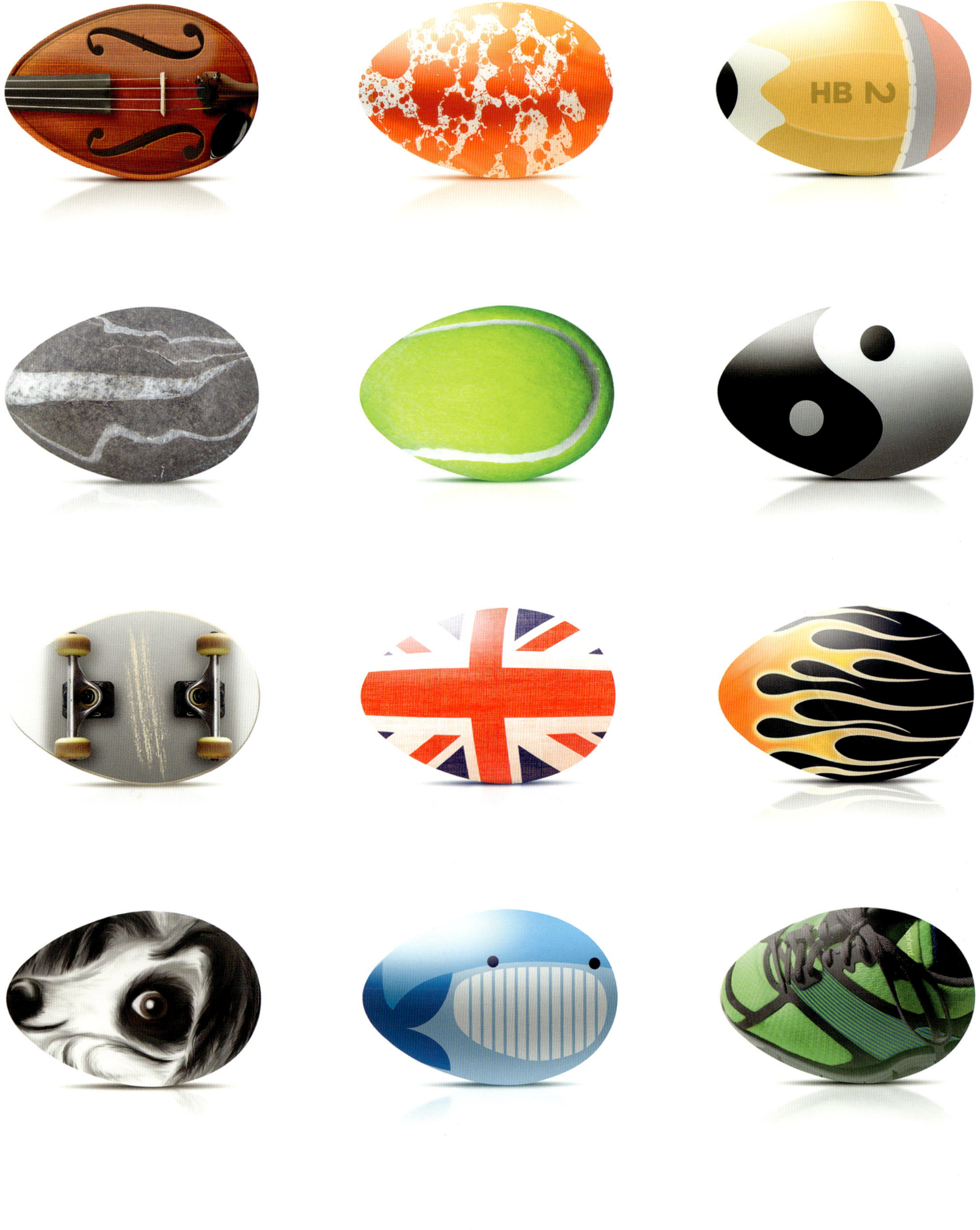

Shepherd (this spread) | Shepherd | Corporate

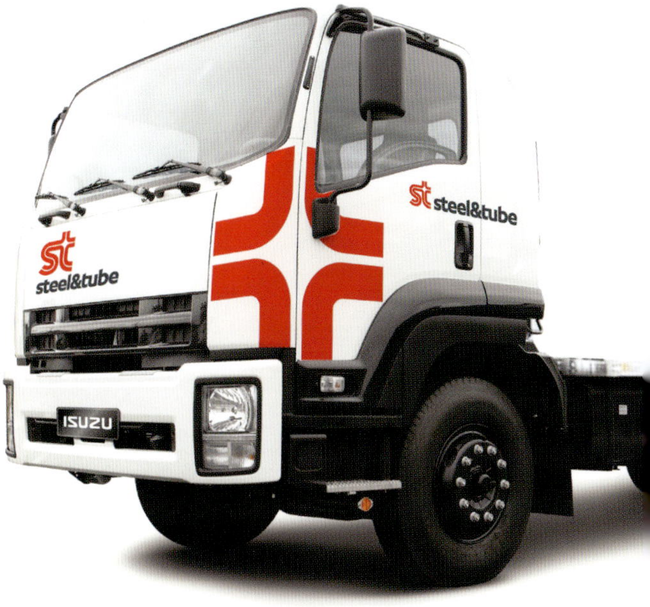
steel&tube
steel&tube
ISUZU

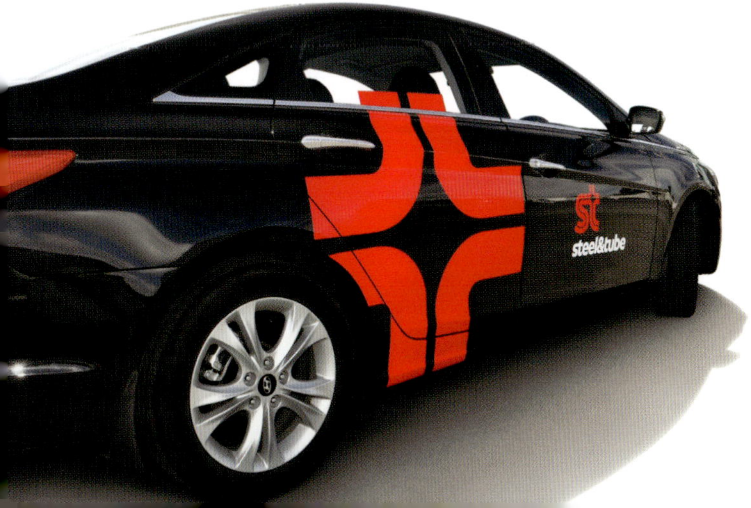
steel&tube

Assignment: In short, Steel and Tube needed to differentiate themselves in what is the intensely price-competitive and commodity-driven steel provider industry. They were looking to deliver greater value to the market in order to drive profitable growth that would appeal to investors.

Approach: A "Stronger in Everyway" graphically strong identifier was created that was directly formed from elements of the core mark. Four directional arrows that converge onto the center of the "t" represents strong outcomes from every way or different parts of the organization. This convergence positions Steel & Tube as one company, a cohesive unit with many different facets. The center of the "t" or convergence point also represents the highlight or sheen of light reflected on steel. An extension of this idea of strong outcomes from every way through the development of these directional arrows was used as a platform that was applied throughout communications.

Results: Steel & Tube currently has within their market sector the biggest turnover, broadest product range, largest nationwide reach, the most expertise within their people, a solid yield, and strong customer relationships. In the near future, they are working toward a "one company" consolidated structure delivering increased efficiency, and upskilled staff offering a new direction with new market opportunities. The "Stronger in Everyway" brand positioning was developed to herald a confidence that catapulted Steel & Tube to market leader within their industry sector.

Designer: Greg Dyne | **Design Firm:** DNA Design | **Creative Directors:** Grenville Main, Phil Dunstan-Brown
Account Director: Josh Burt | **Insight Strategy:** Sherryn Macdonald | **Clients:** Andy Millard, Steel & Tube

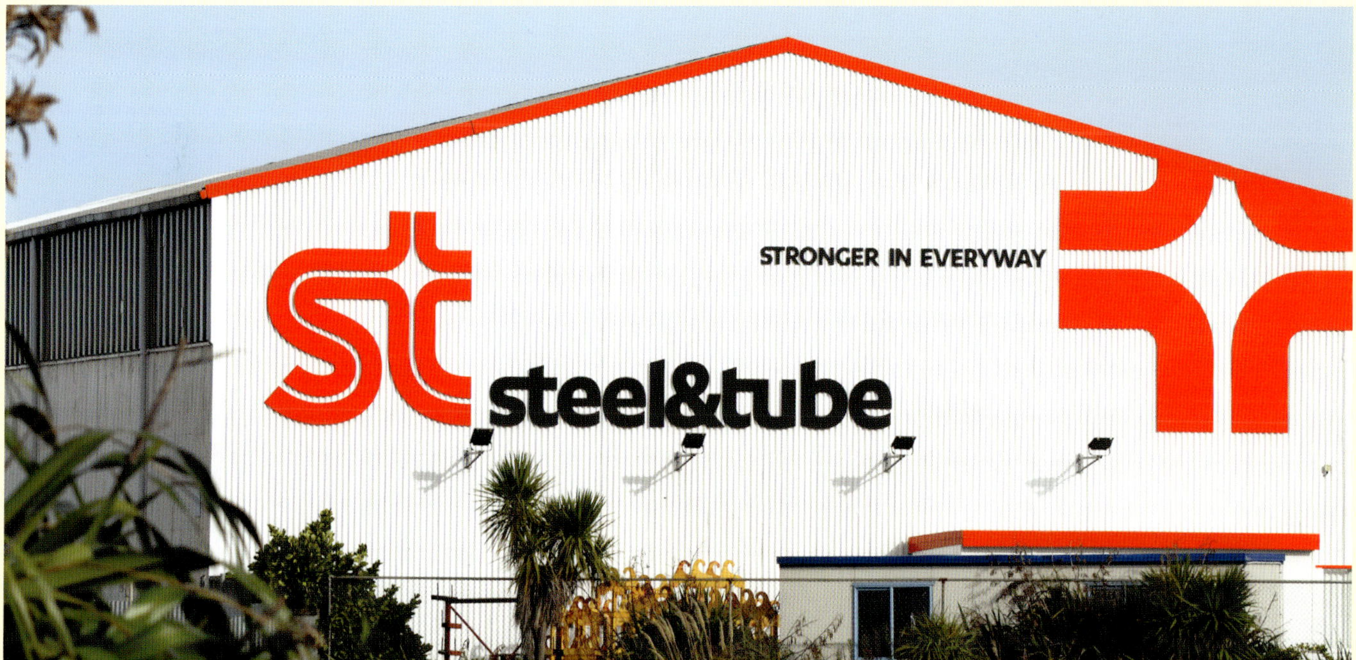

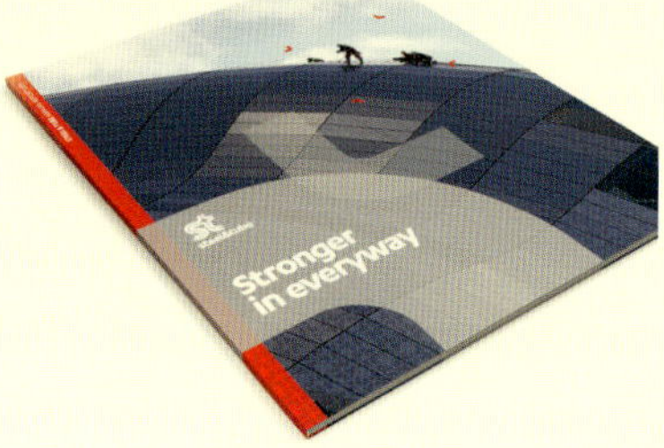

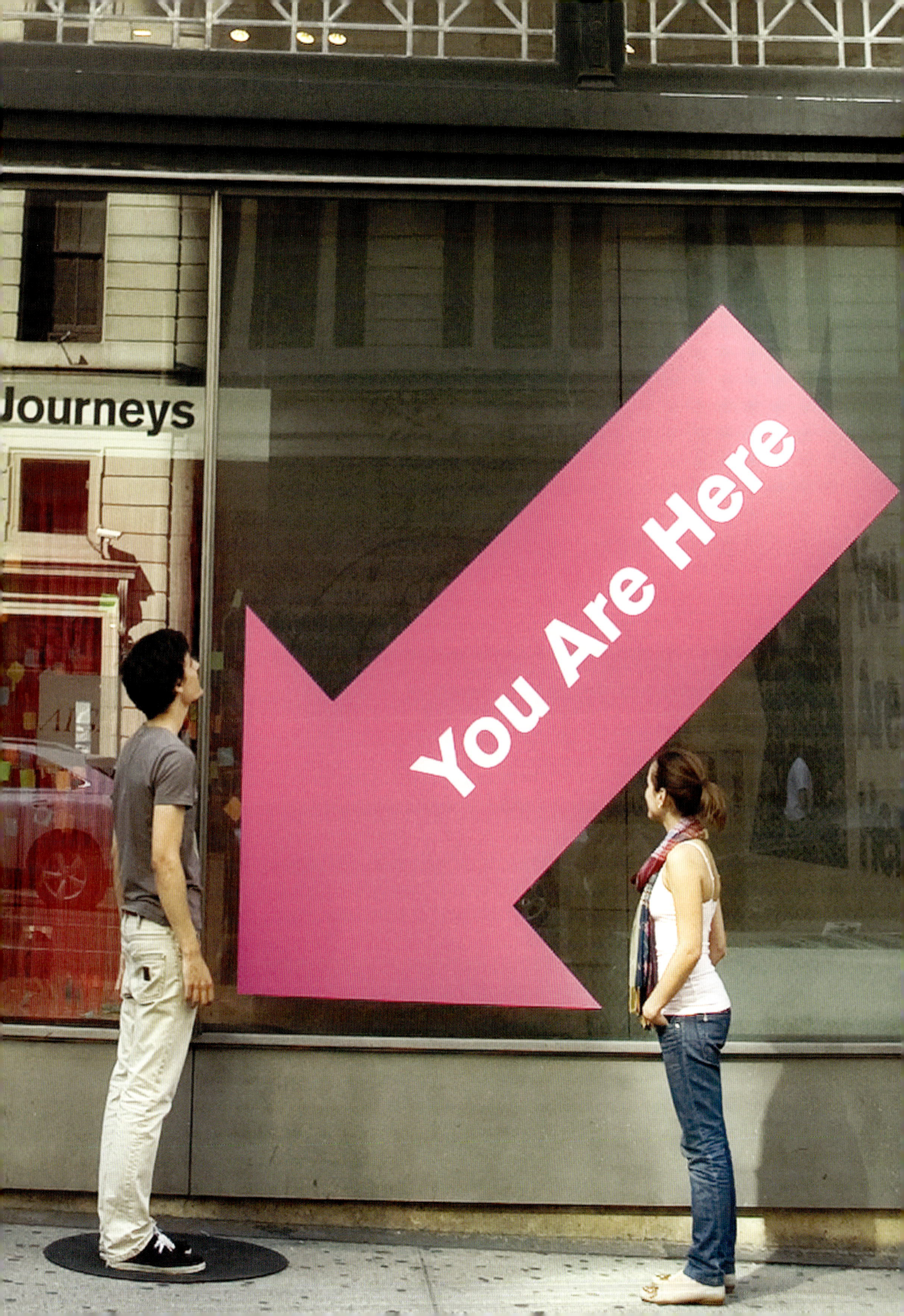
Journeys
You Are Here

Assignment: The exhibit sought to create an awareness of the need for greater diversity in the graphic design profession. This was done by inviting visitors to explore their own journey and diversity, presenting the work of twenty-five diverse and important designers, and educating the community on the benefits of increased diversity within the design industry. TODA wanted to not only educate viewers of the exhibit, but to also create an ongoing story that everyone could add to by creating an interactive space that highlighted every person's diversity regardless of statistics or demographics.

Approach: In designing this exhibit at the AIGA Gallery, *Design Journeys: You Are Here,* TODA engaged in a process that would allow for a thorough, inspiring, and interactive experience for visitors. The exhibition examines the role of diversity in design by featuring twenty-five successful design professionals with an emphasis on inclusiveness. Among the installations were a suspended world map made of bright pink string, a larger-than-life magnetic arrow, and a fill-in-the-blank questionnaire. Each station called visitors to interact and think about the questions: "Where did you come from?" "Why are you here?" and "Where are you going?" The large-scale mural was designed by Alfalfa Studio for visitors to color in.

Results: The results were strong as seen in the success of the opening night. Throughout its entire run, the exhibit received positive responses, spurring thoughtful discussions and personal reflections on how our own journeys are diverse. Throughout the life of the exhibit, visitors to the gallery could continue to add content and interact with the exhibit, adding their own stories to the larger community.

Designers: Melissa Showalter, Marco de Mel, Yelena Avanesova | **Design Firm:** TODA, The Office of Design and Architecture
Creative Directors: Marcos Chavez, Rafael Esquer, Pablo Medina | **Architects:** Esti Sanz; Installation: Lisa Hein | **Client:** AIGA

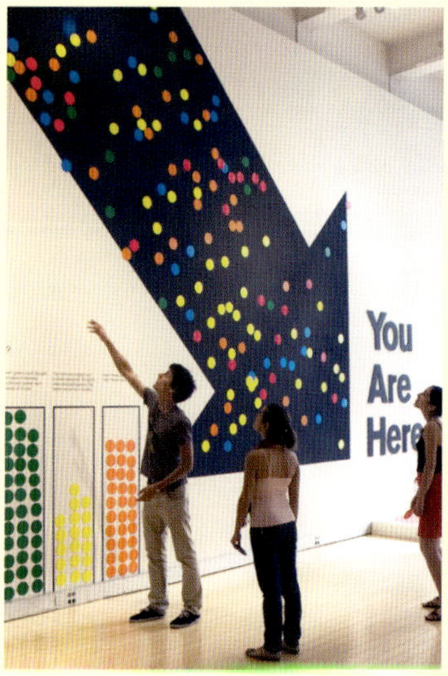

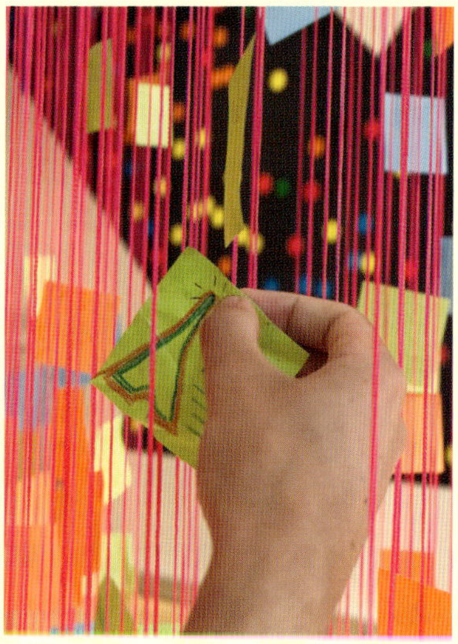

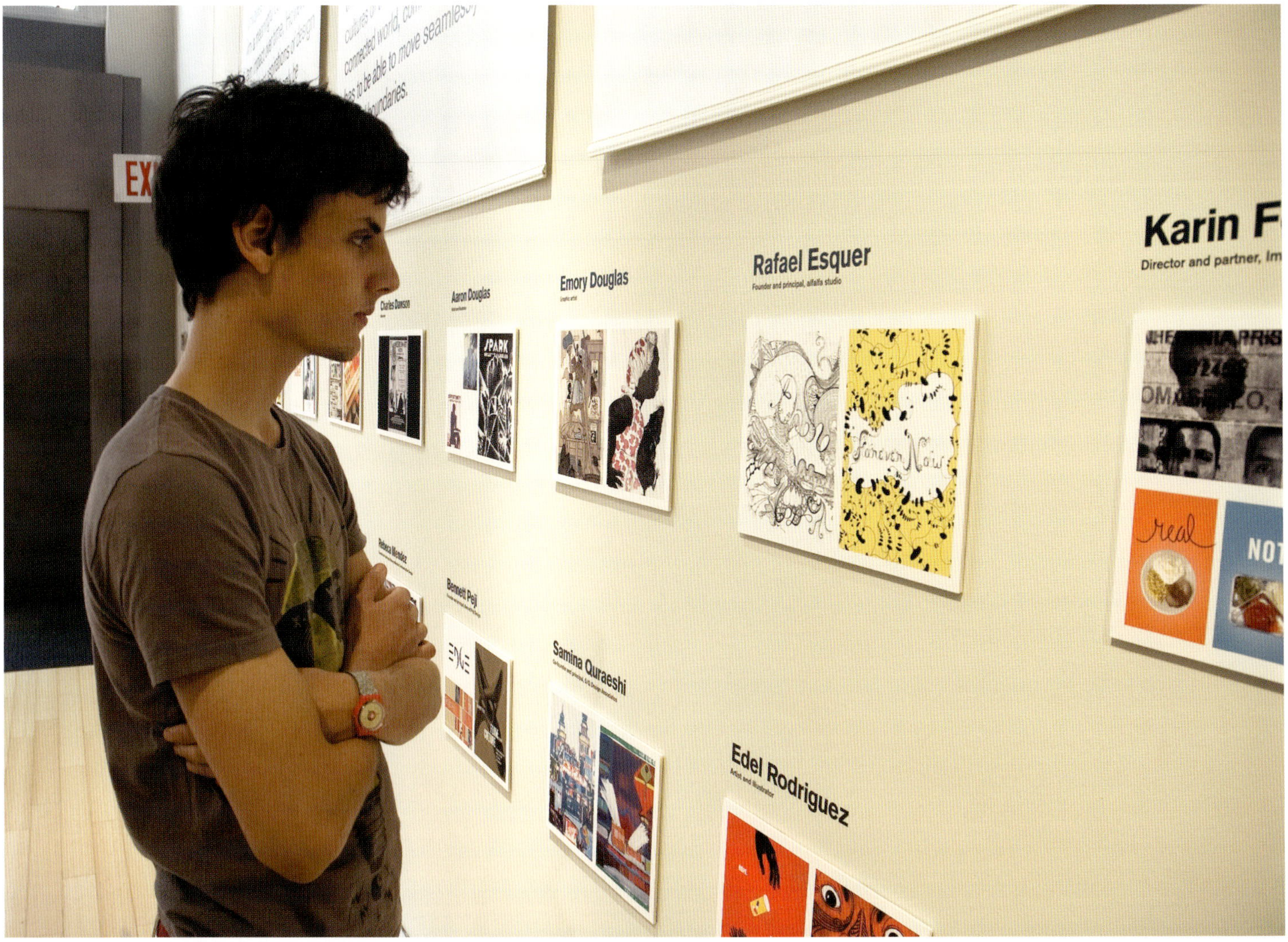
Karin F
Director and partner, Im
Rafael Esquer
Founder and principal, alfalfa studio
Emory Douglas
Aaron Douglas
Charles Dawson
Bennett Peji
Samina Quraeshi
Edel Rodriguez
Artist and illustrator

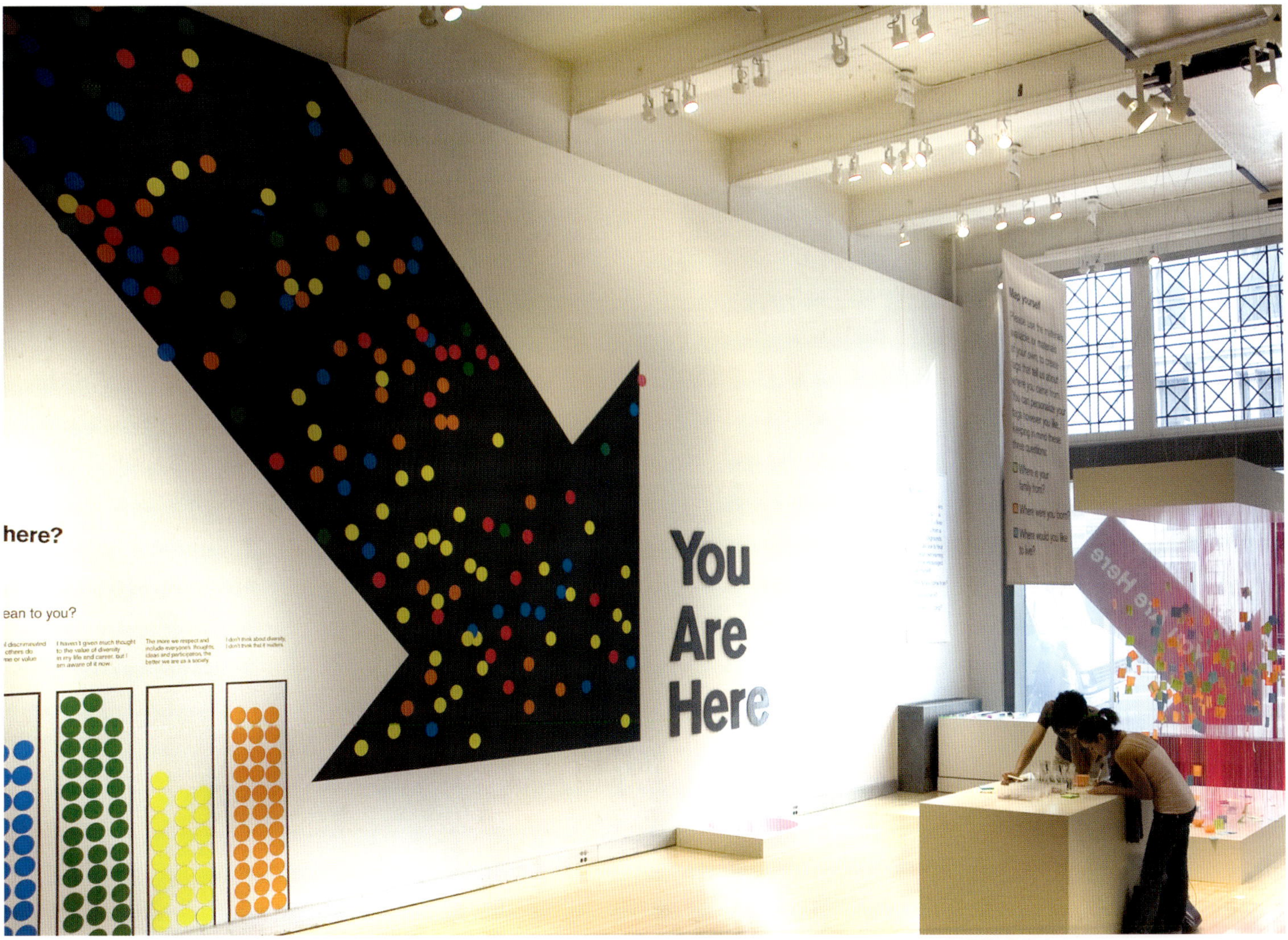
You
Are
Here
here?
ean to you?

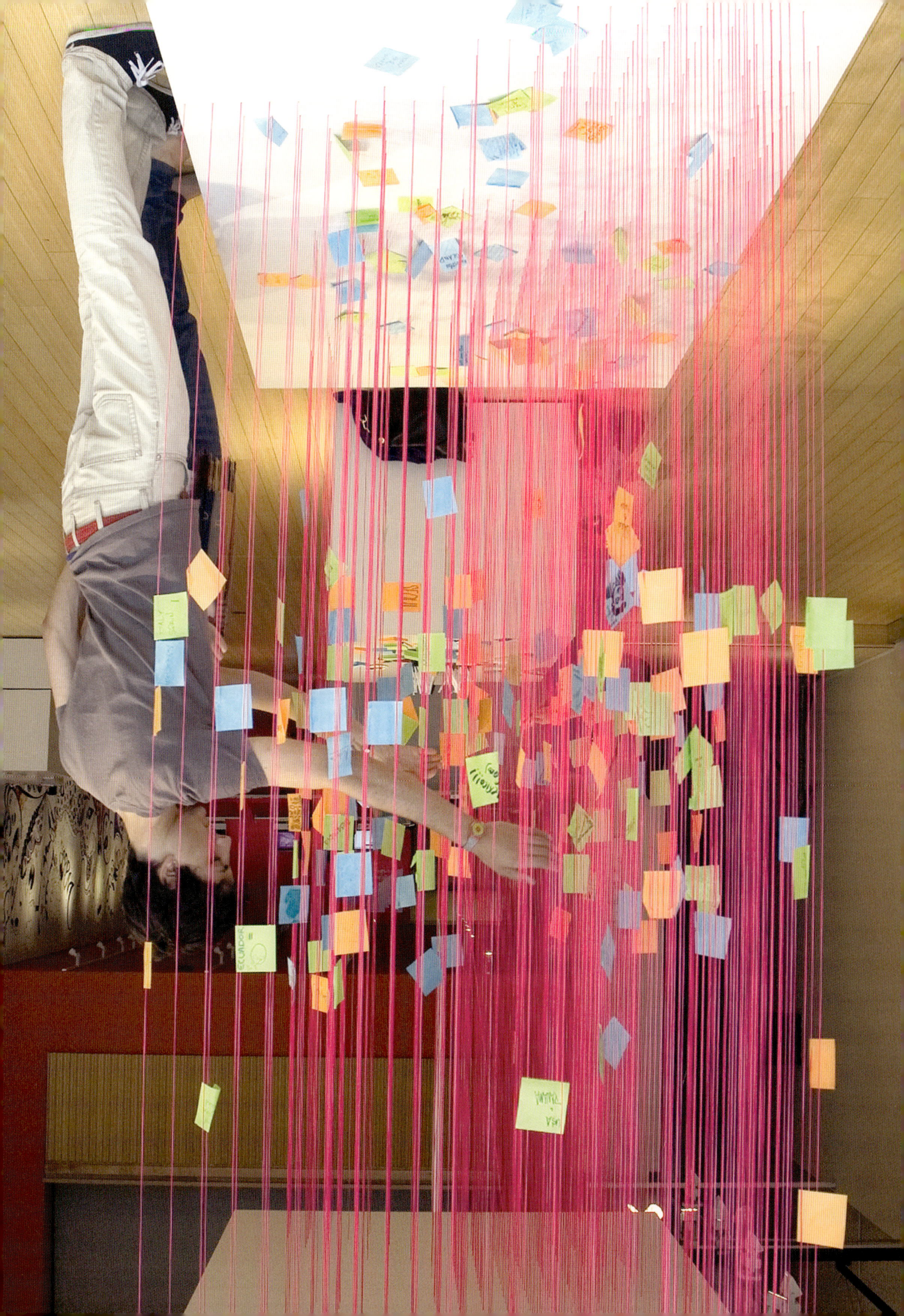

Berta Medina

['berta me'ðina]

english teacher

Assignment: Berta Medina is an English teacher whose aim was to convey the purity of the English language. She needed a graphic identity that "speaks and teaches" English.

Approach: The logo and stationery should be as illustrative as a dictionary or a grammar book, Berta's favorite tools.

Results: The result was very successful; with very few elements Berta Medina could be recognized and remembered.

Designer: Alvaro Perez | **Design Firms:** El Paso, Galeria de Comunicacion | **Art Director:** Alvaro Perez
Creative Directors: Alvaro Perez, Curra Media | **Client:** Berta Medina

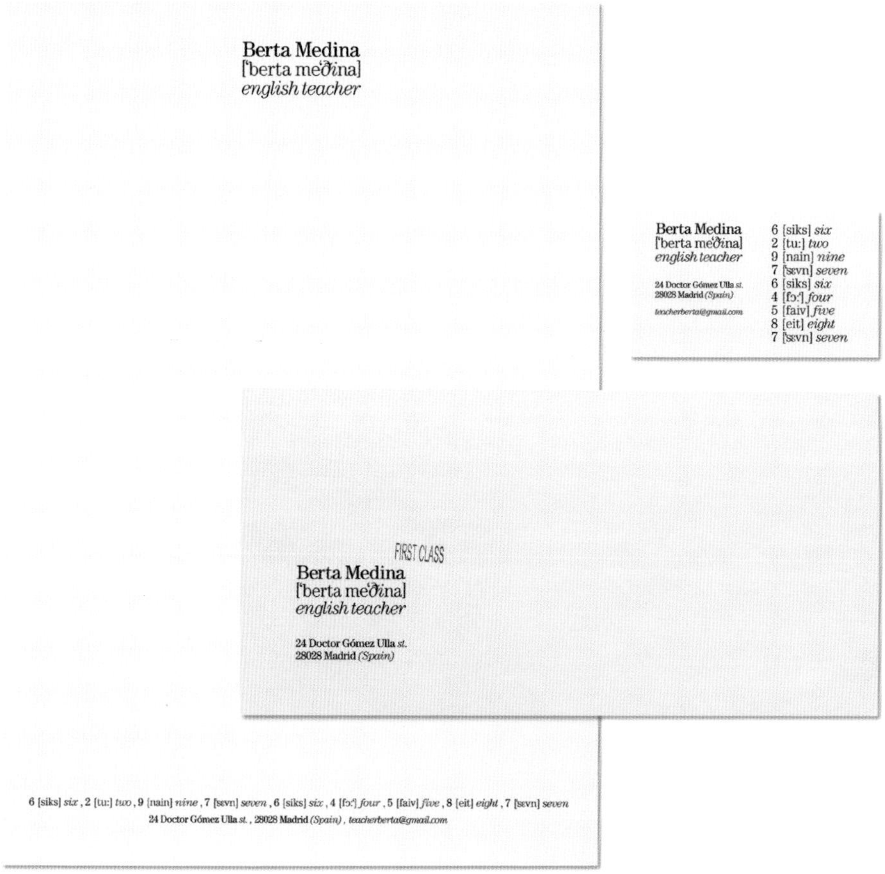

Assignment: Executive Leadership Development is the same type of course the world over, or is it? Our client does it quite differently; they take different leadership philosophies from around the world and throw people into a leadership course with a totally new dimension. Neo Leaders' courses are immersive, kinesthetic, and absorbing. They could be in Queenstown, New Zealand, using the environment, adrenalin, and fear, or in the Australian Outback, based on ancient aboriginal tribal philosophies, or out of China, using Confucianist ideas and principles. It was our task to create a brand and identity that communicated this point of difference, yet made it easy to see the intrinsic value for stakeholders sponsoring course participants.

Approach: We had to start from the top—with a naming exercise, to create a brand that reflected leadership, renewal, and growth—but do this through alternative means. Through the process one seemed to stand out: Neo. The name seemed to wrap all the requirements up, suggesting renewal and growth, while demonstrating leadership in a fresh way. The brand identity had to work to support the idea behind this new "experiential/educational" concept. It also had to support the nuances of the freshly developed name. The solution was to draw out a visual element that suggested energy and renewal, something that didn't stop moving. The logo is expressed in these ever-changing whirls of energy. No one application of it would be the same. The whirl device and the word mark would always have a dynamic relationship.

The application really became a place to add layers of expression, both graphically and through a communication "spirit." A tone and manner was created to help support the principles of the business.

Results: Neo is on an exciting development program. An international network is falling into place. Things are picking up pace. The first courses were held in late 2011.

Designer: Phil Dunstan-Brown | **Design Firm:** DNA Design | **Creative Director:** Phil Dunstan-Brown
Account Director: Josh Burt | **Clients:** Ben Ponne, Neo Leaders

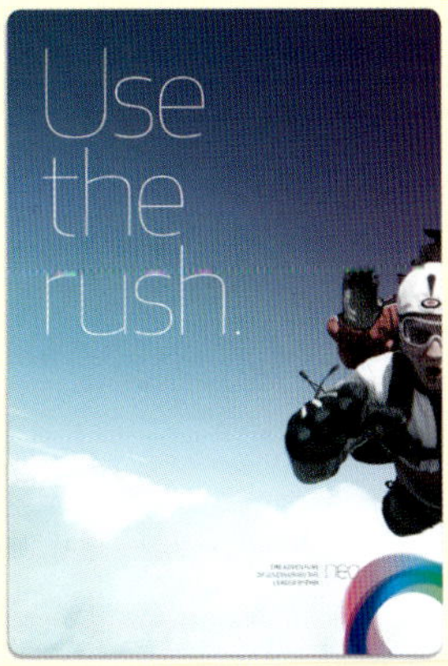

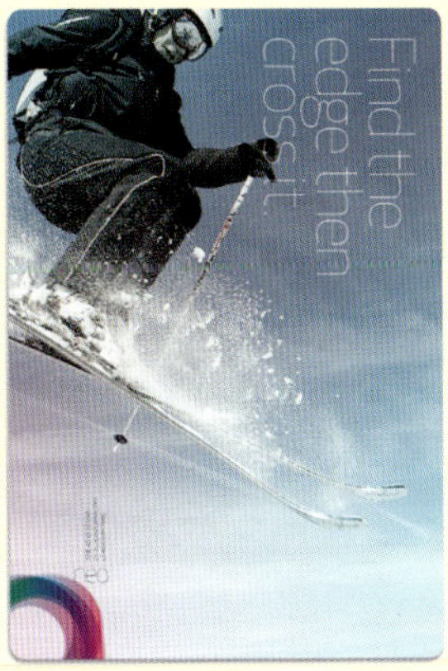

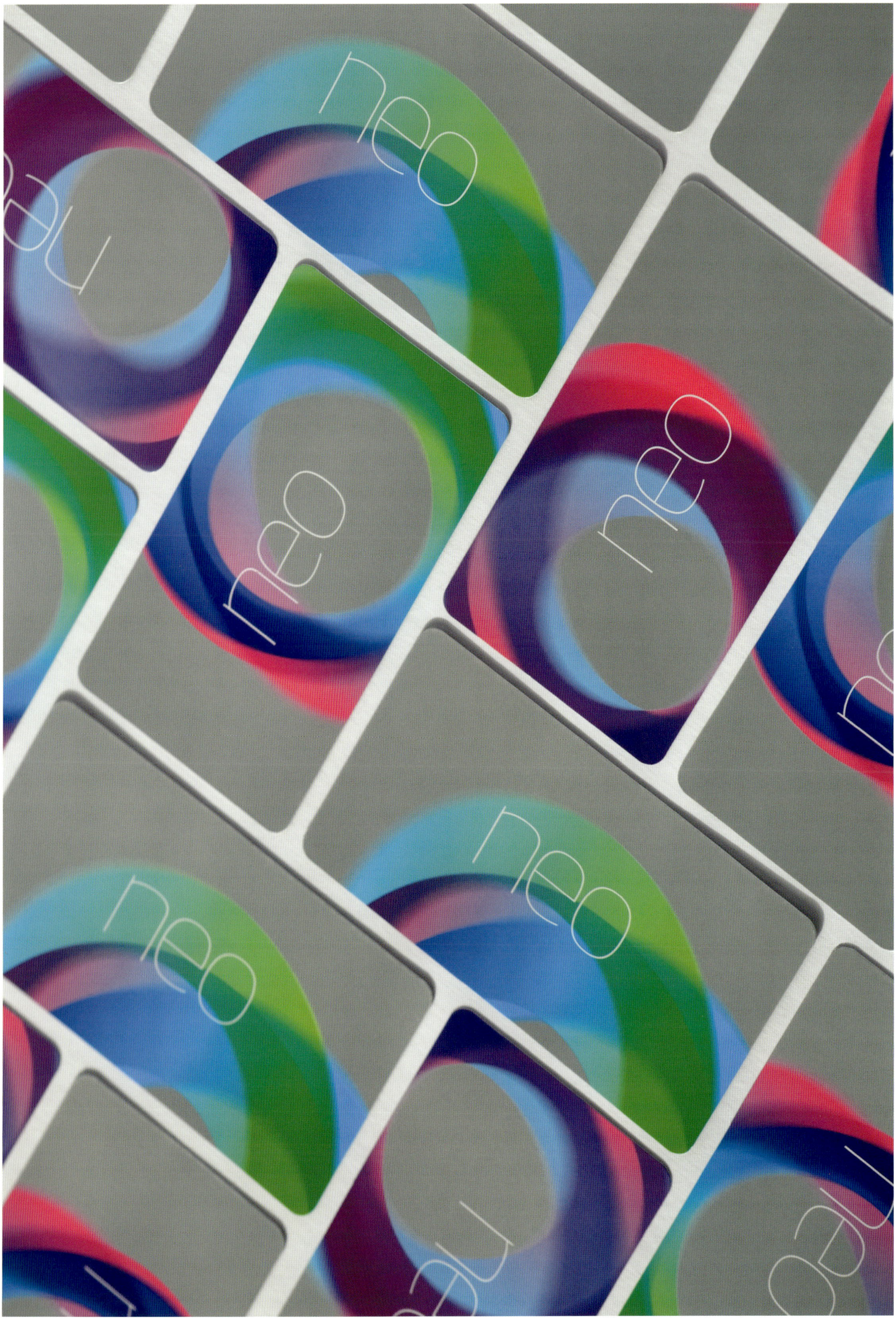
neo
neo
neo
neo
neo

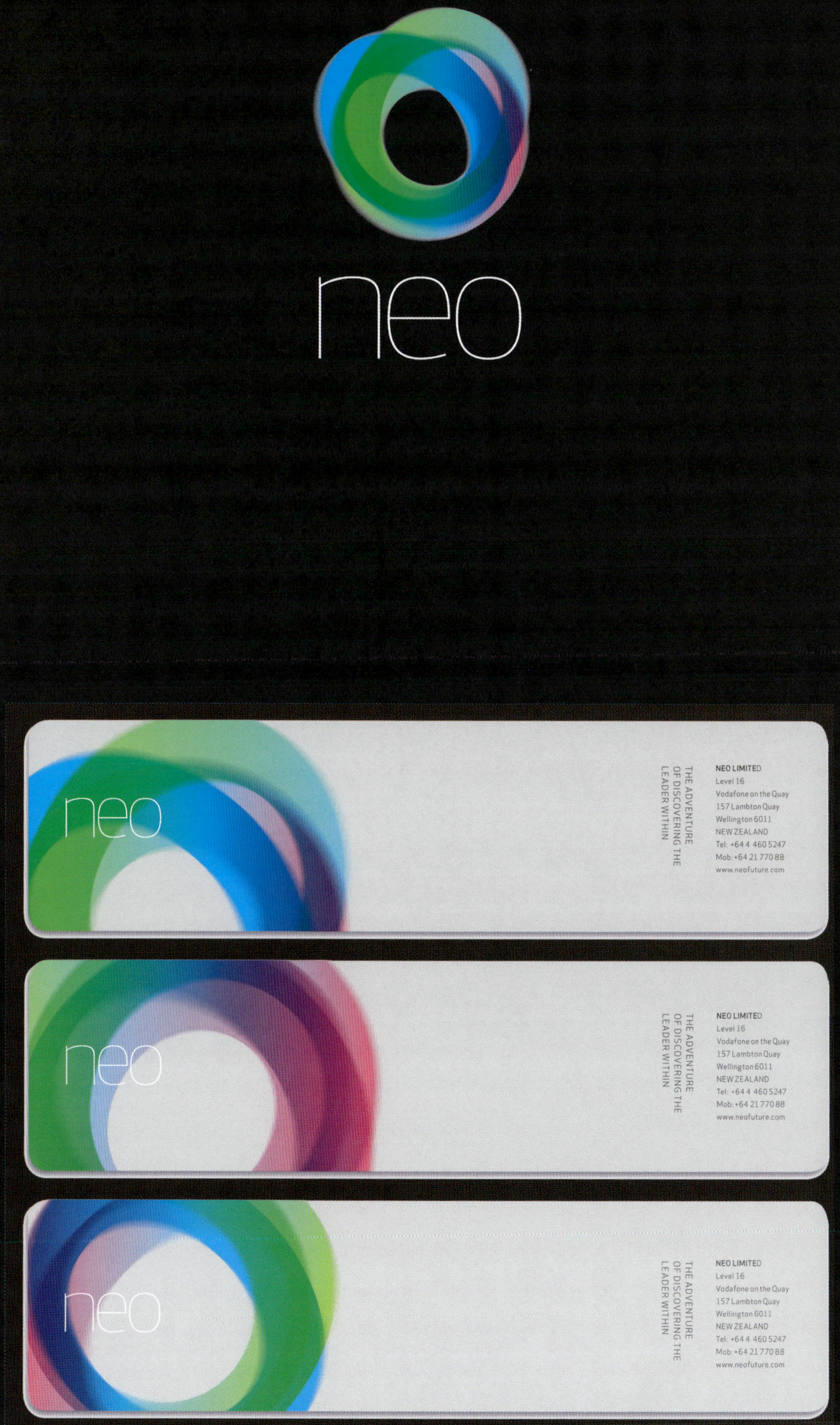
neo
neo
THE ADVENTURE OF DISCOVERING THE LEADER WITHIN
NEO LIMITED
Level 16
Vodafone on the Quay
157 Lambton Quay
Wellington 6011
NEW ZEALAND
Tel: +64 4 460 5247
Mob: +64 21 770 88
www.neofuture.com

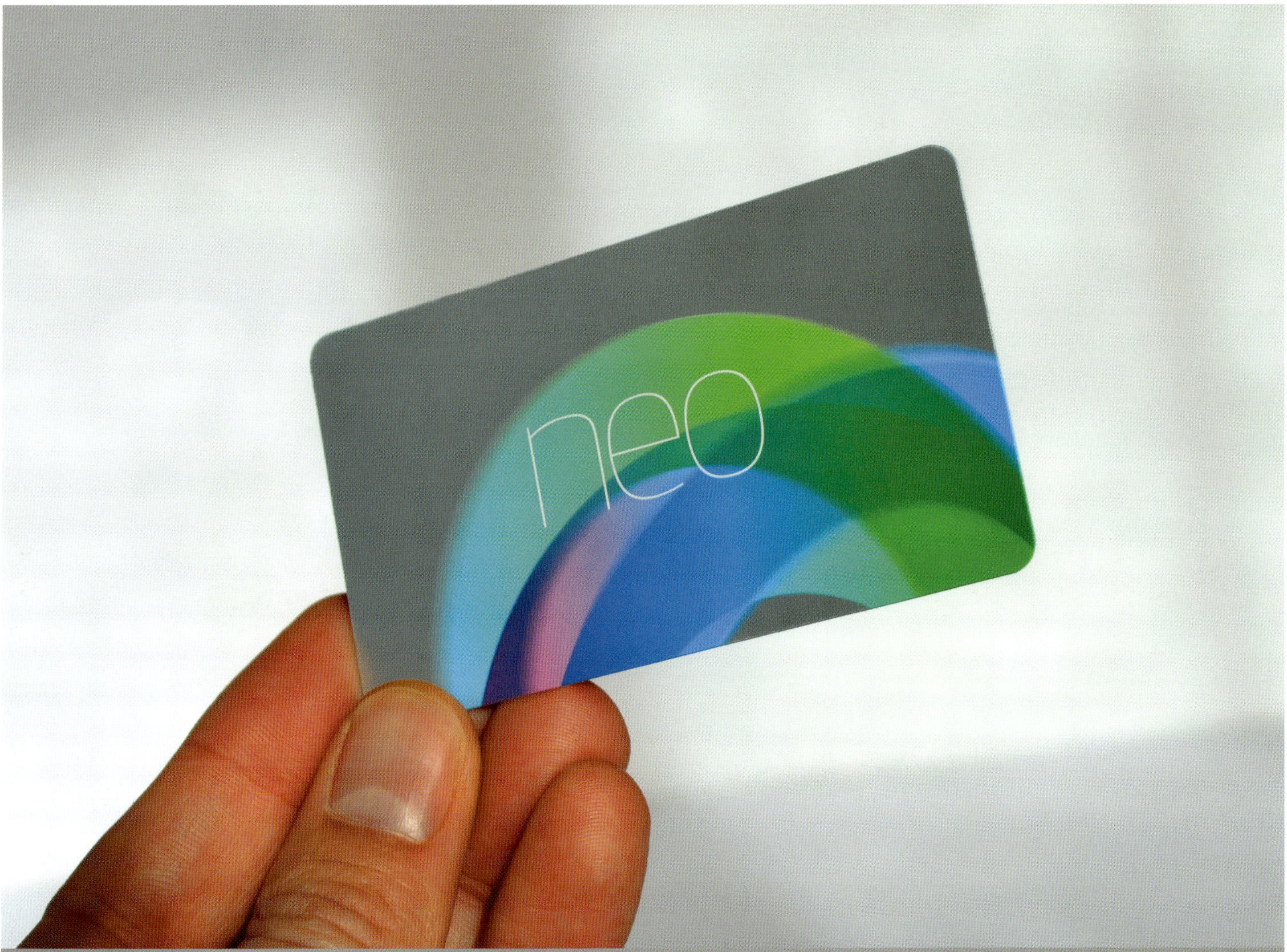

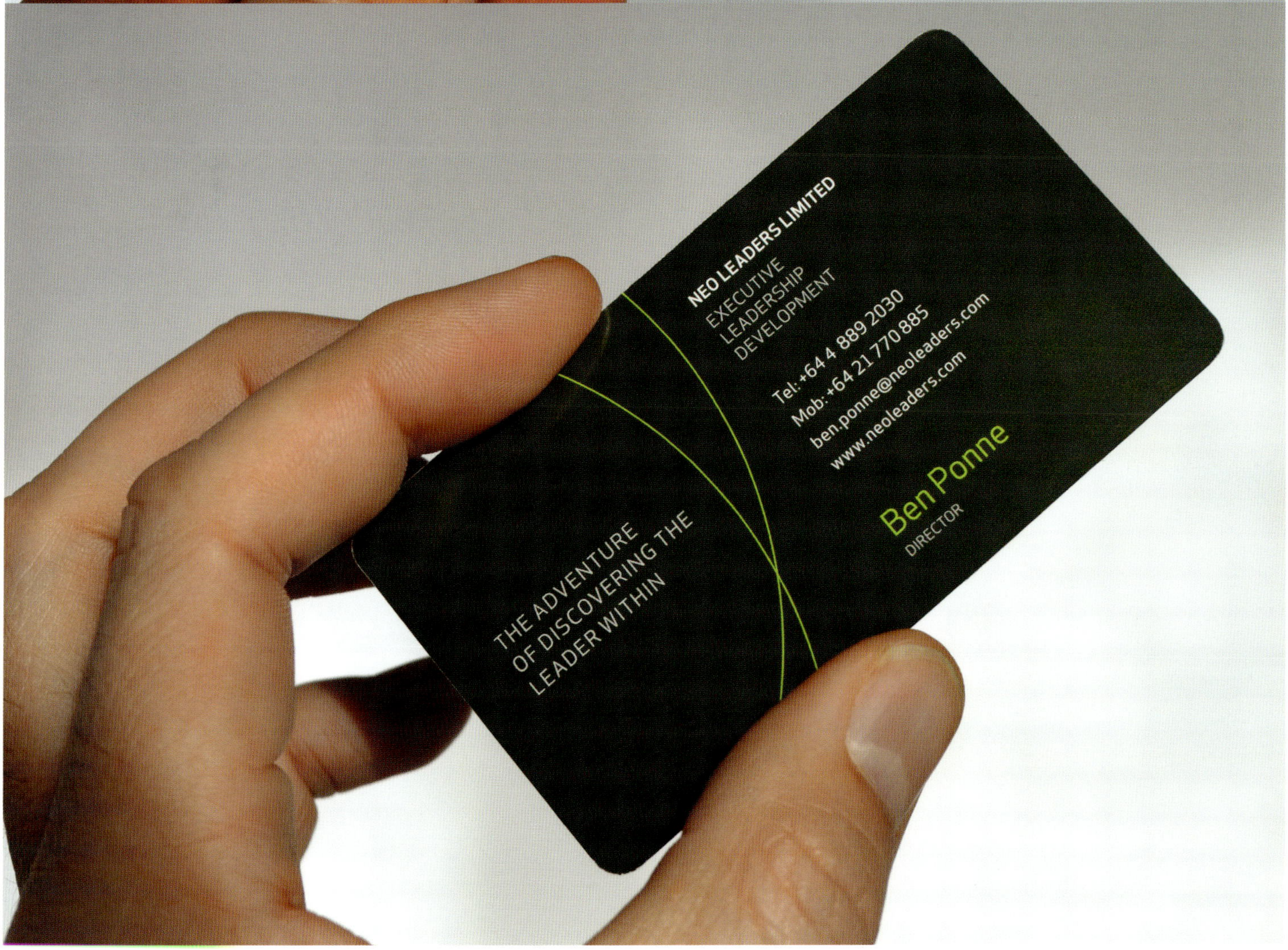

DNA Design (this spread) | Ben Ponne, Neo Leaders | Education

Assignment: Seven industry leaders multiplied by seven future trends: Seven x Seven. “Future Focus” was the fourth in the Design Institute of Australia’s iconic lecture series, held during the Melbourne Design Festival in 2009. Luminaries from seven design disciplines presented their top seven future industry trends and predictions at a fast-paced, highly visual event to an audience of creatives from all design sectors and the general public.

Approach: The initial idea was built around the idea that the numeral 7 could be created through the use of seven lines of positive and negative space. This was to reflect the idea of looking beyond the obvious to see more than is immediately visible, just as the speakers had to do with their insights. This thinking was then carried through the communications with the strong graphic language of stripes used as the core visual asset, disrupted and intersected by diagonal lines, changing the general order of things, yet also revealing the number seven.

Results: The event identity and collateral design were to used to create awareness, and more importantly put bums on seats. As a sold out event, it not only achieved its goal and reflected the calibre of speakers, but more importantly, it positioned the Design Institute of Australia as a leading organization that helped spread awareness of good design to the public.

Designer: Malin Holmstrom | **Design Firm:** Landor Associates | **Art Director:** Jason Little
Creative Director: Jason Little | **Client:** DIA Design Institute of Australia

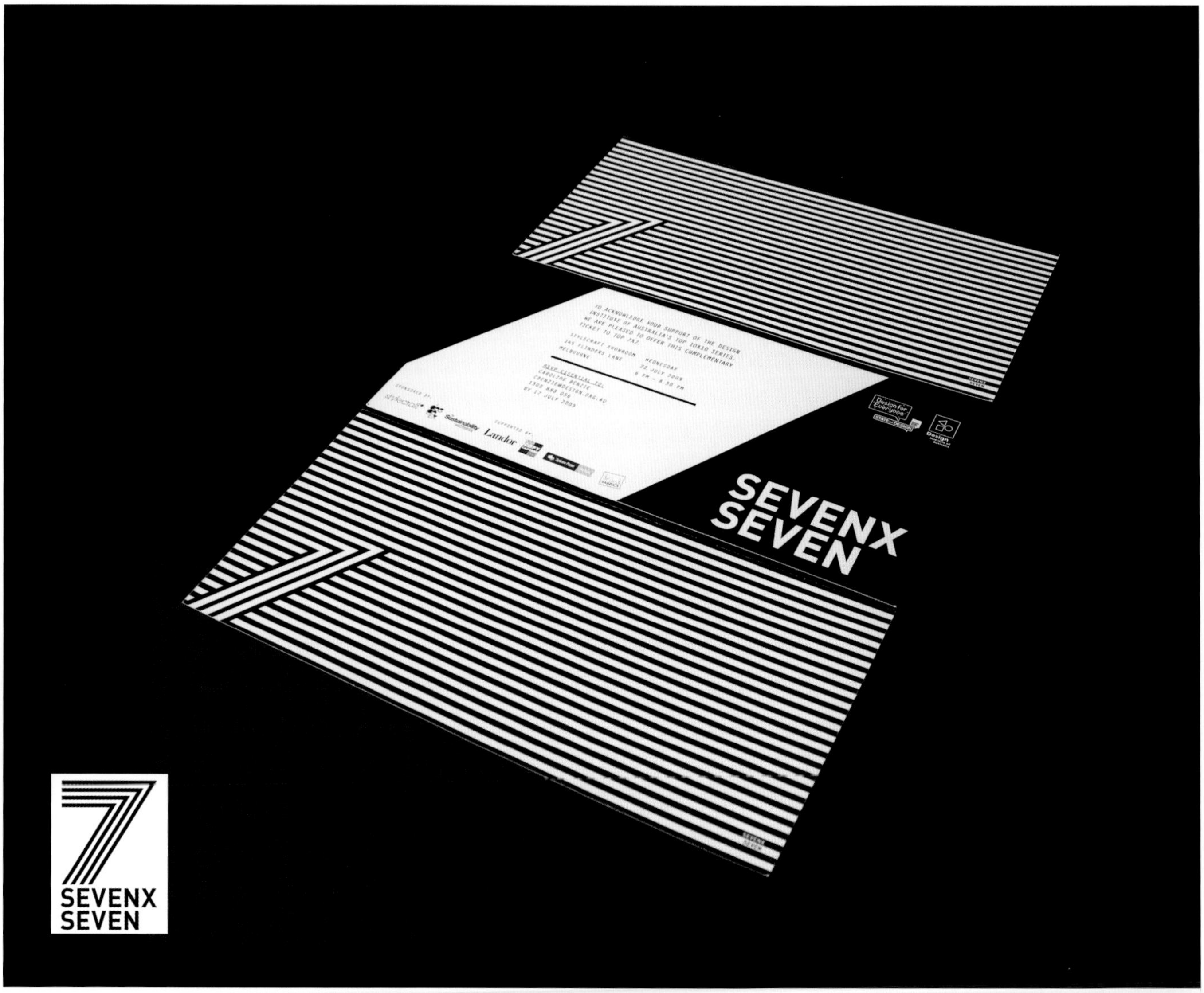

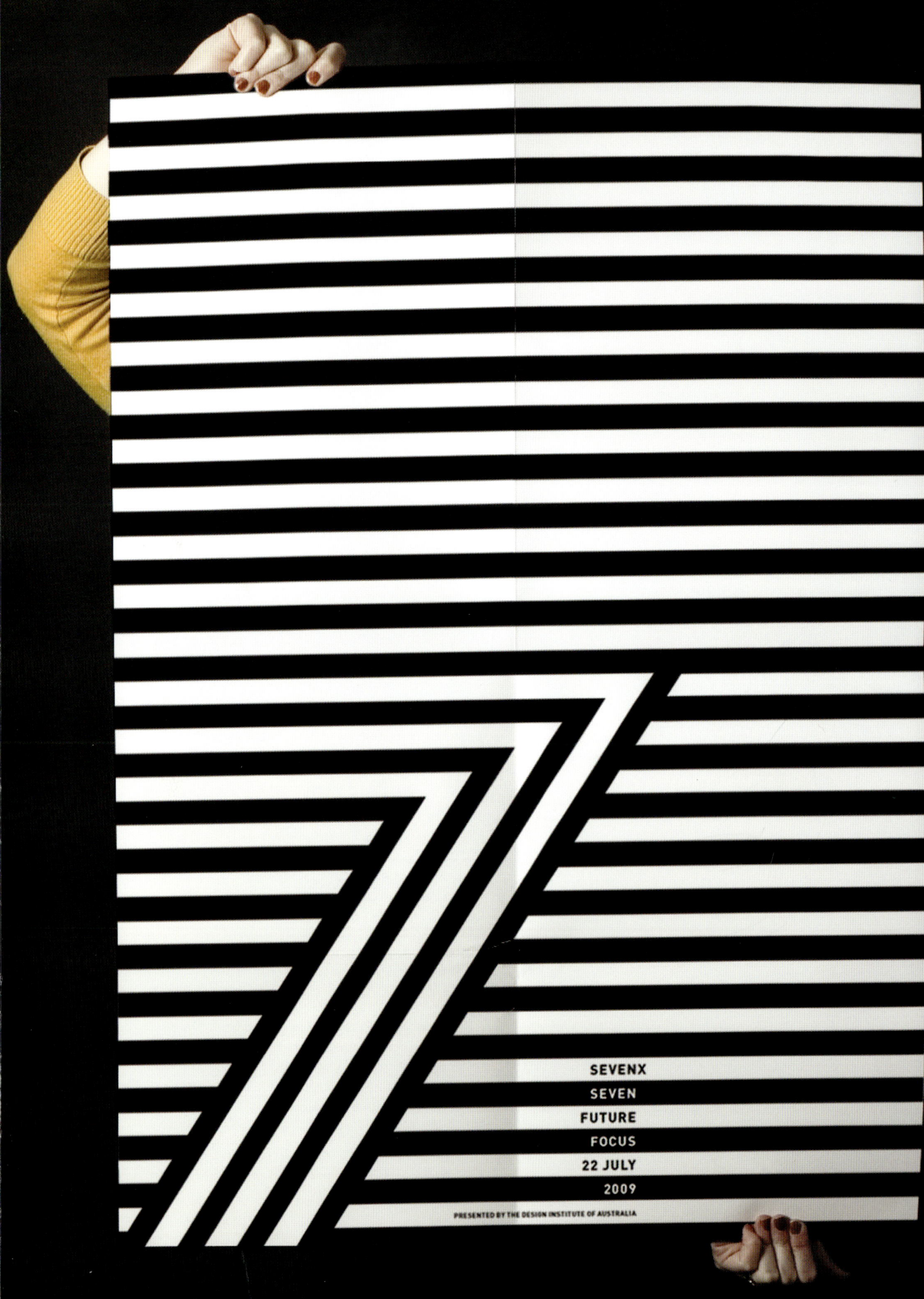
SEVENX
SEVEN
FUTURE
FOCUS
22 JULY
2009
PRESENTED BY THE DESIGN INSTITUTE OF AUSTRALIA

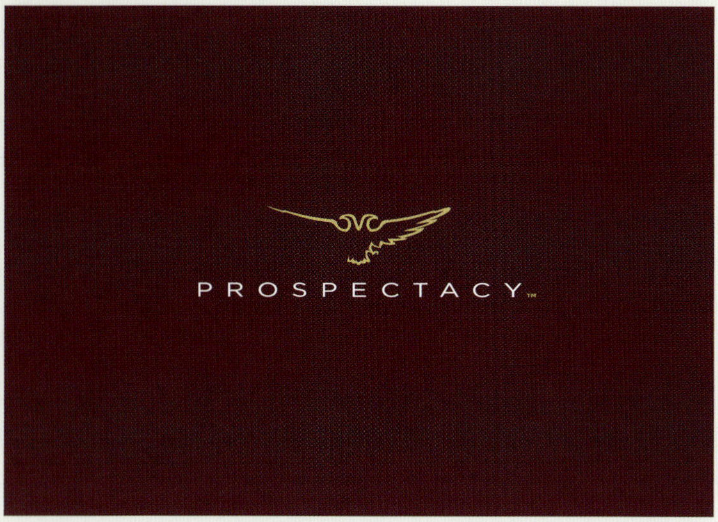
PROSPECTACY™
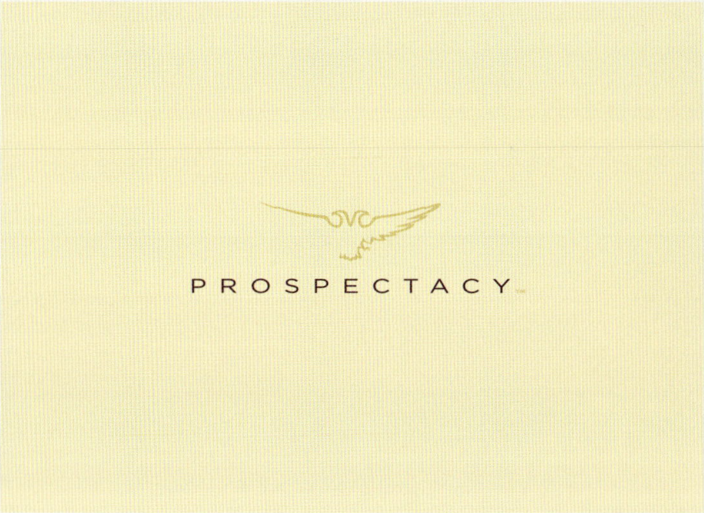
PROSPECTACY™
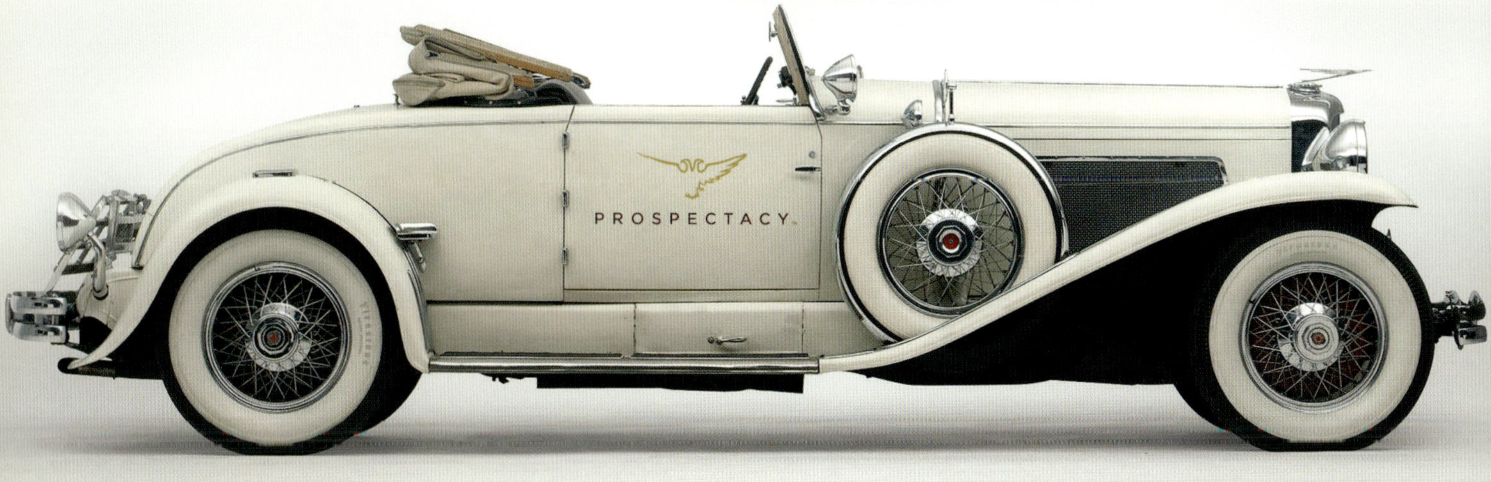
PROSPECTACY

Assignment: Established in Cyprus, Prospectacy offers insightful solutions, expert advice, and results in the global business sector—all delivered with unmatched client service. Raising corporate statutory compliance standards, fulfilling accounting obligations, dealing with tax compliance issues, performing payroll functions, and offering related services—accurately, objectively, and with integrity—are the core values of the Prospectacy brand.

The client approached us needing a new brand identity that would help the brand stand out among the competition. As most of the client's business was with Russian companies, he wanted to incorporate the two-headed eagle symbol, which is featured in both the Russian coat of arms and on the Cypriot national guard emblem. The challenge was to find a fresh and different angle on the symbol.

Approach: Since the client had very specific requirements about the new symbol, we focused on finding a way to make our eagle stand out from all the symbols incorporating the same mark. Through research we collected hundreds of such symbols that had one thing in common, they were highly stylized depictions. A logical way forward was to seek a rendering that would present the eagle in a more natural pose. That's how the solution came to be. After numerous revisions, and with help from the client, we were able to create the final outlined shape, which was elegant and understated—the antithesis of the way most two-headed eagles are drawn; but it was also proud and memorable, the best way to depict the brand.

Designers: Kostadin Kostadinov, Alex Veresovich | **Design Firm:** Higher | **Creative Director:** Victor Novak
Photographer: Alex Veresovich | **Client:** Prospectacy

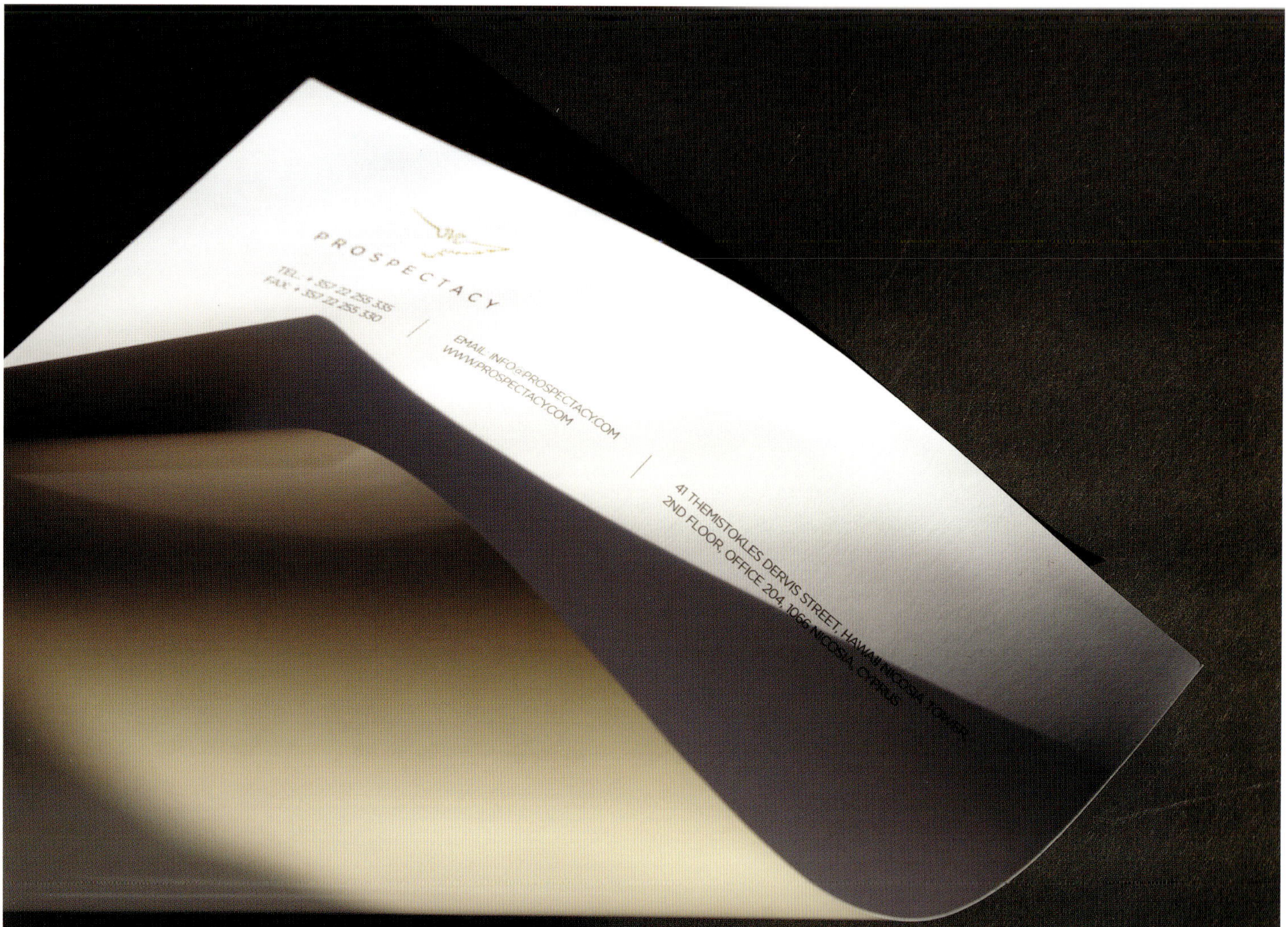
PROSPECTACY
TEL: + 357 22 255 335
FAX: + 357 22 255 330
EMAIL: INFO@PROSPECTACY.COM
WWW.PROSPECTACY.COM
41 THEMISTOKLES DERVIS STREET, HAWAII NICOSIA TOWER
2ND FLOOR, OFFICE 204, 1066 NICOSIA, CYPRUS

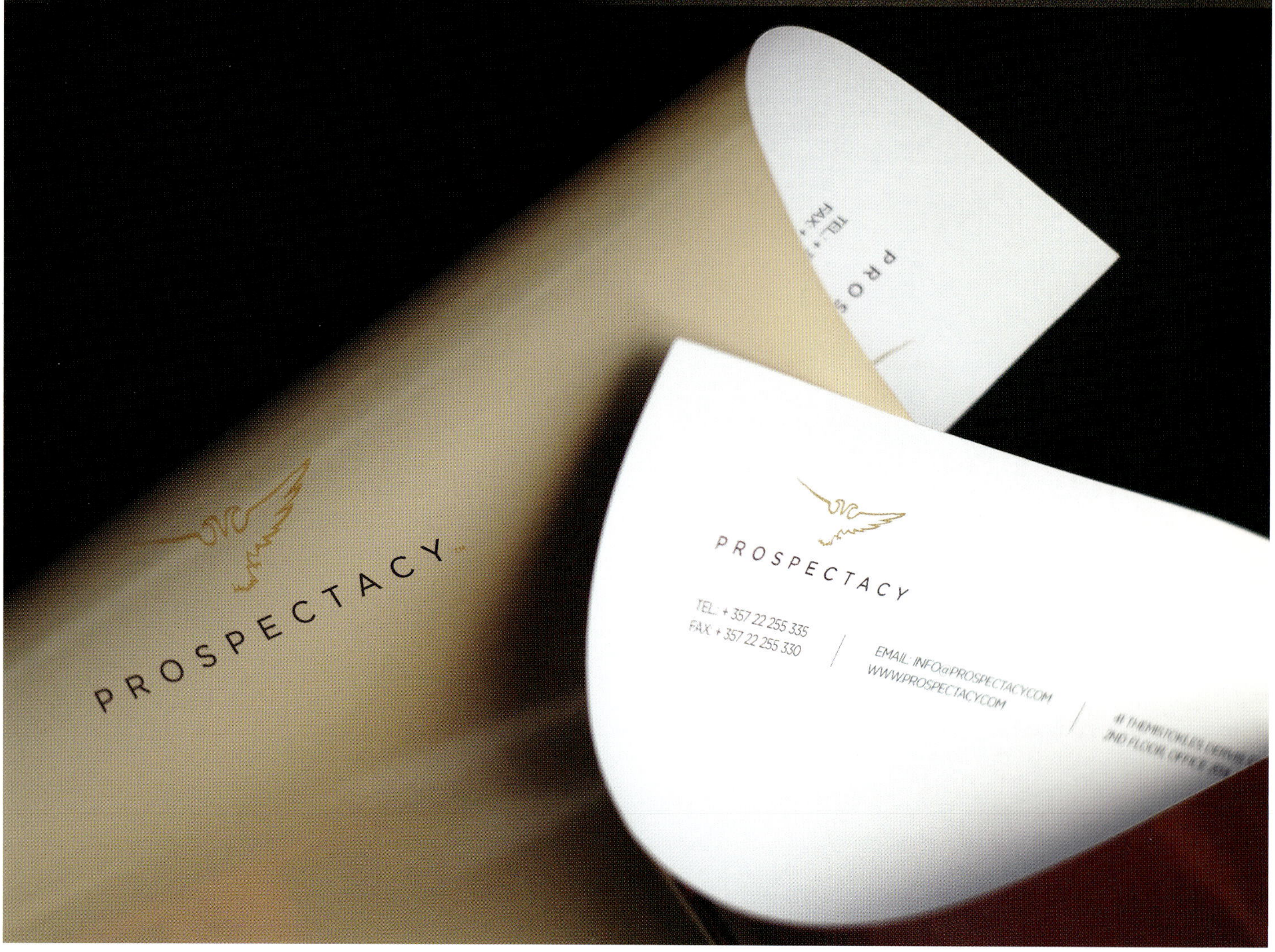
PROSPECTACY
PROSPECTACY
TEL: + 357 22 255 335
FAX: + 357 22 255 330
EMAIL: INFO@PROSPECTACY.COM
WWW.PROSPECTACY.COM

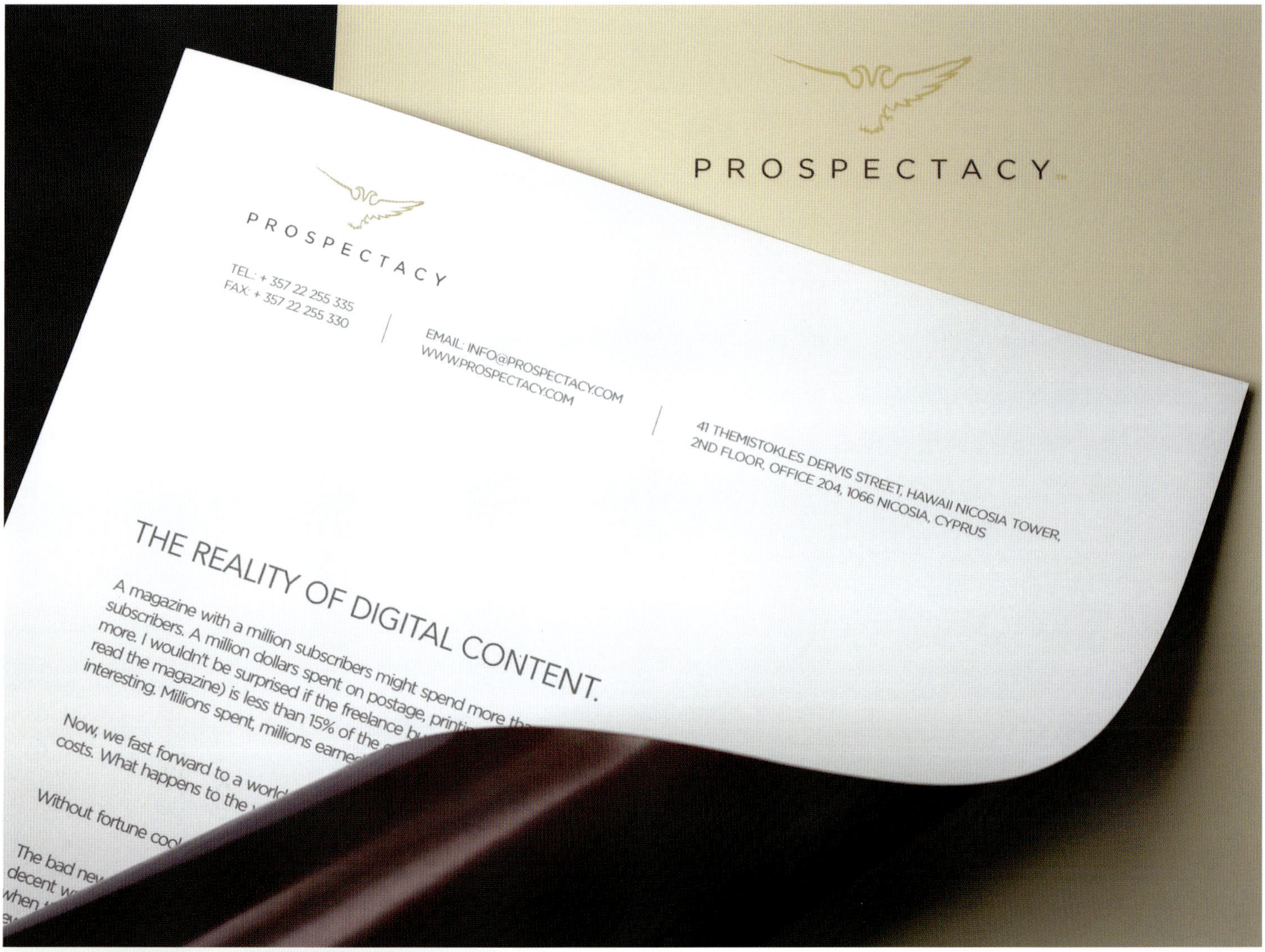
PROSPECTACY
PROSPECTACY
TEL: + 357 22 255 335
FAX: + 357 22 255 330
EMAIL: INFO@PROSPECTACY.COM
WWW.PROSPECTACY.COM
41 THEMISTOKLES DERVIS STREET, HAWAII NICOSIA TOWER,
2ND FLOOR, OFFICE 204, 1066 NICOSIA, CYPRUS
THE REALITY OF DIGITAL CONTENT.

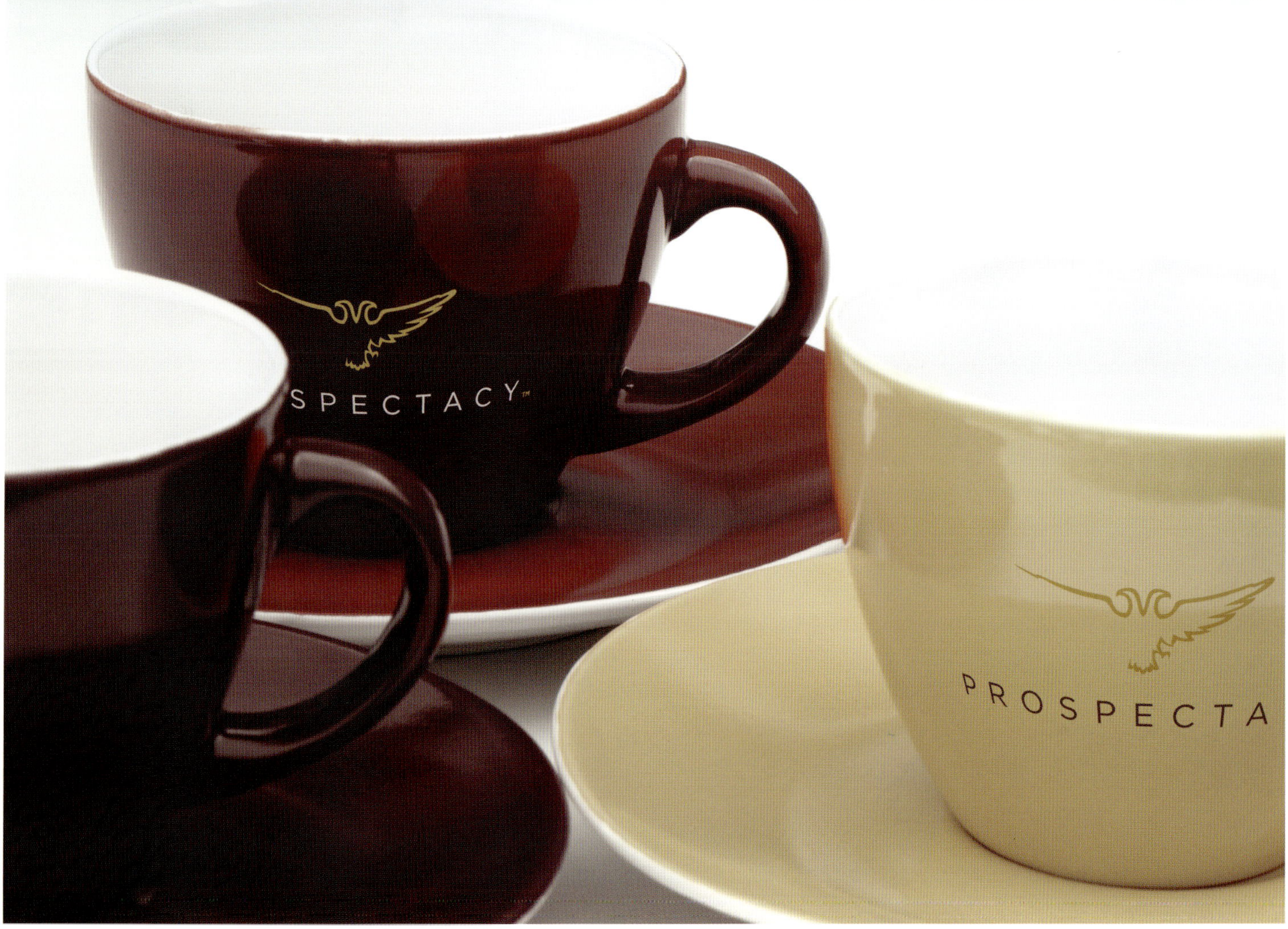
SPECTACY
PROSPECTA

Assignment: The assignment was the further development of the existing corporate design in consideration of the realignment of the bank and the newly defined positioning attributes. The objective was to take a moderate step in the direction of being a dynamic, innovative bank company, while maintaining the positive image and canon of values of an exclusive and independent private bank. The new appearance of the Sal. Oppenheim Bank is designed to combine the exclusivity and character of a private bank with the strength and performance of a major international bank.

Approach: The task was to create a premium, attention-grabbing corporate design to communicate the sophisticated self-conception of Sal. Oppenheim. With its classic, representative character, the corporate design communicates consciously lived values, tradition, innovation, and exclusiveness in an unintrusive way.

Designer: Bernd Vollmöller | **Design Firm:** Simon & Goetz Design GmbH & Co. KG | **Art Director:** Bernd Vollmöller
Creative Director: Bernd Vollmöller | **Client:** Sal. Oppenheim jr. & Cie.

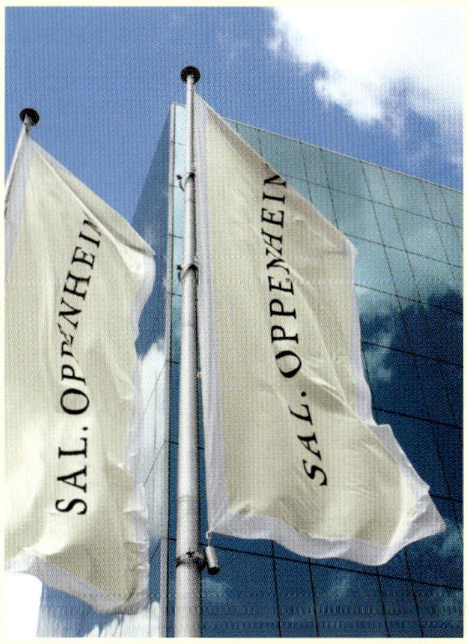

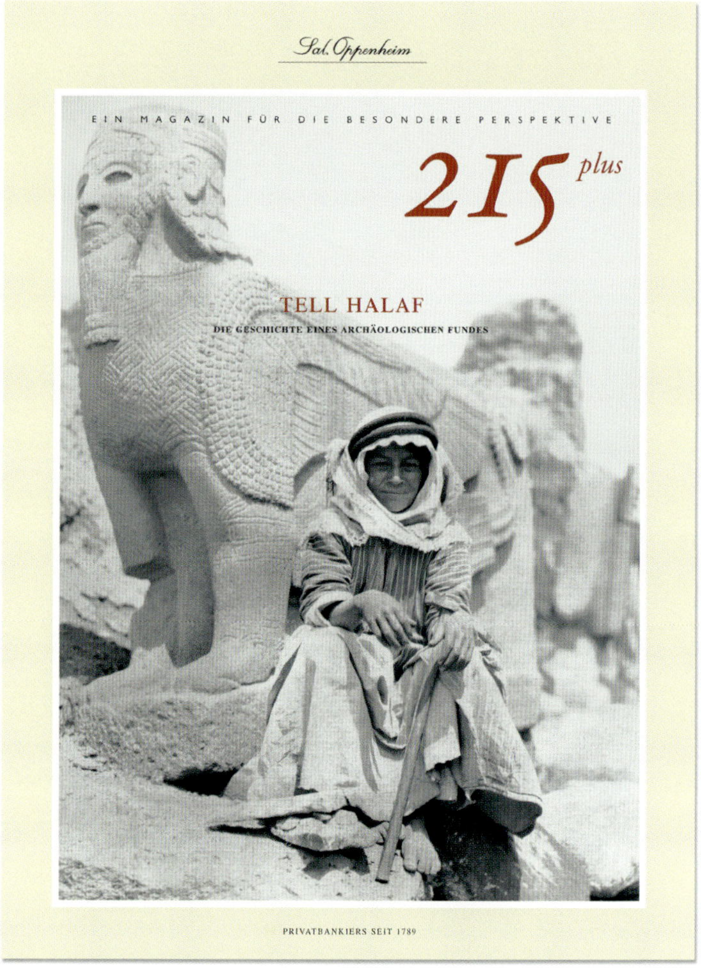
Sal. Oppenheim
EIN MAGAZIN FÜR DIE BESONDERE PERSPEKTIVE
215 plus
TELL HALAF
DIE GESCHICHTE EINES ARCHÄOLOGISCHEN FUNDES
PRIVATBANKIERS SEIT 1789

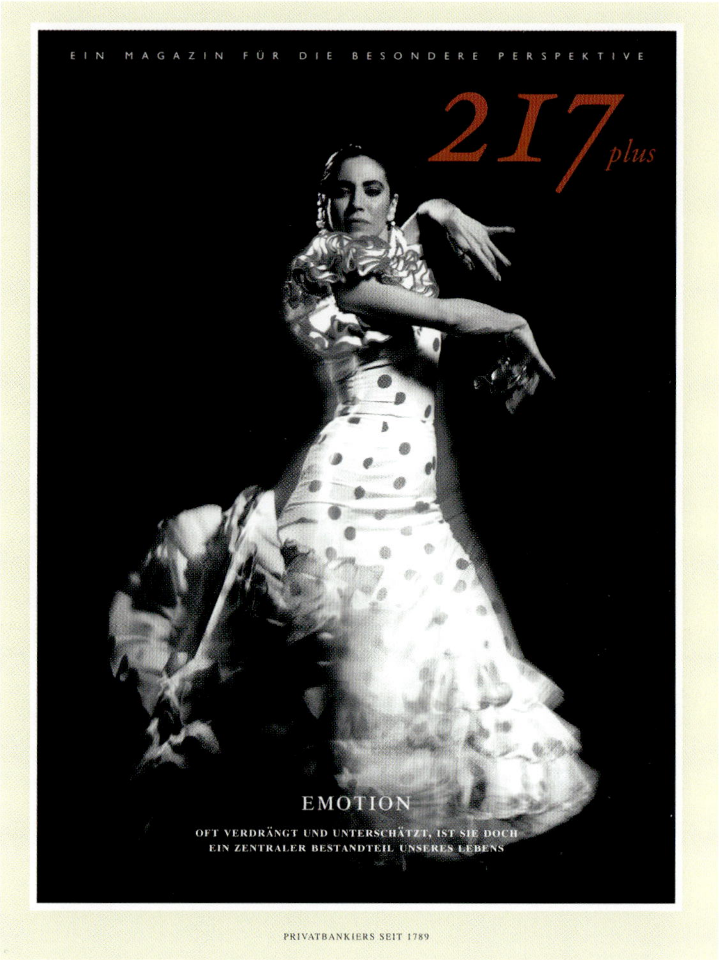
EIN MAGAZIN FÜR DIE BESONDERE PERSPEKTIVE
217 plus
EMOTION
OFT VERDRÄNGT UND UNTERSCHÄTZT, IST SIE DOCH
EIN ZENTRALER BESTANDTEIL UNSERES LEBENS
PRIVATBANKIERS SEIT 1789

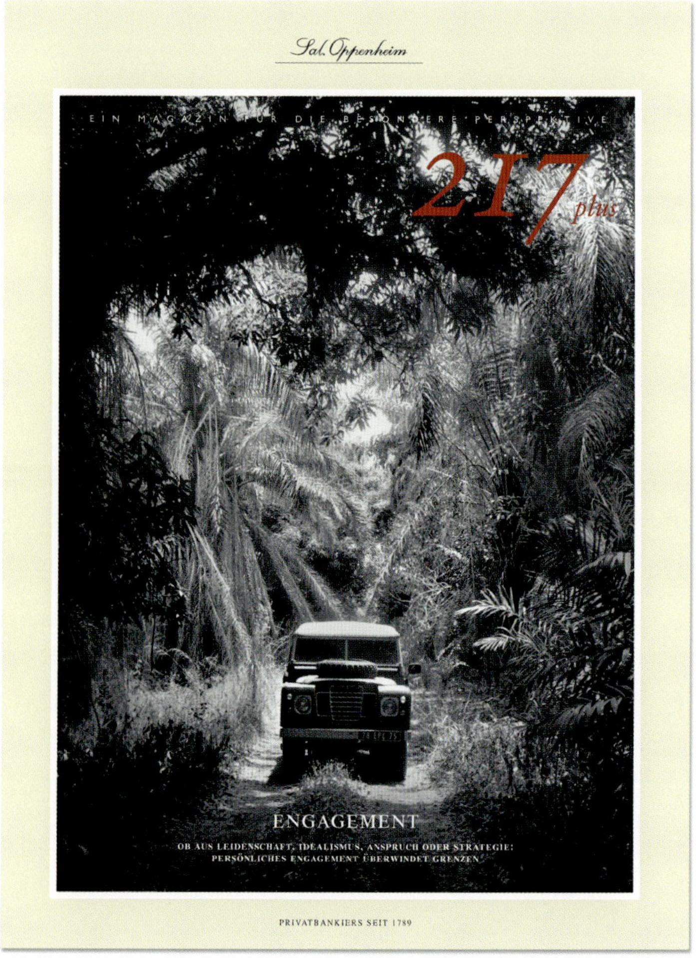
Sal. Oppenheim
EIN MAGAZIN FÜR DIE BESONDERE PERSPEKTIVE
217 plus
ENGAGEMENT
OB AUS LEIDENSCHAFT, IDEALISMUS, ANSPRUCH ODER STRATEGIE:
PERSÖNLICHES ENGAGEMENT ÜBERWINDET GRENZEN
PRIVATBANKIERS SEIT 1789

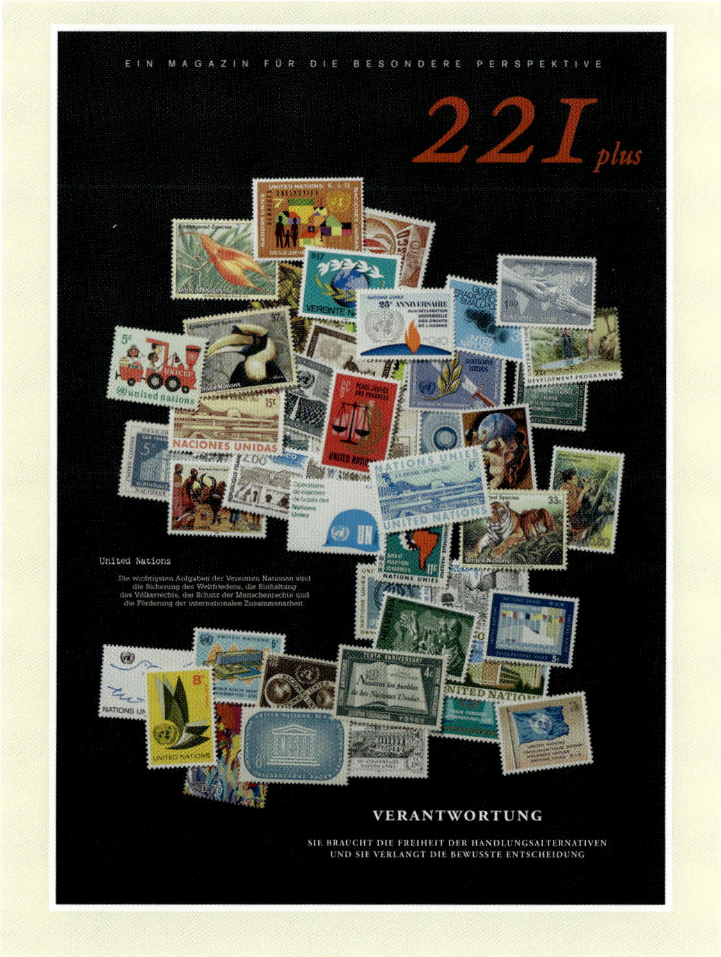
EIN MAGAZIN FÜR DIE BESONDERE PERSPEKTIVE
221 plus
United Nations
Die wichtigsten Aufgaben der Vereinten Nationen sind die Sicherung des Weltfriedens, die Einhaltung des Völkerrechts, der Schutz der Menschenrechte und die Förderung der internationalen Zusammenarbeit.
VERANTWORTUNG
SIE BRAUCHT DIE FREIHEIT DER HANDLUNGSALTERNATIVEN
UND SIE VERLANGT DIE BEWUSSTE ENTSCHEIDUNG

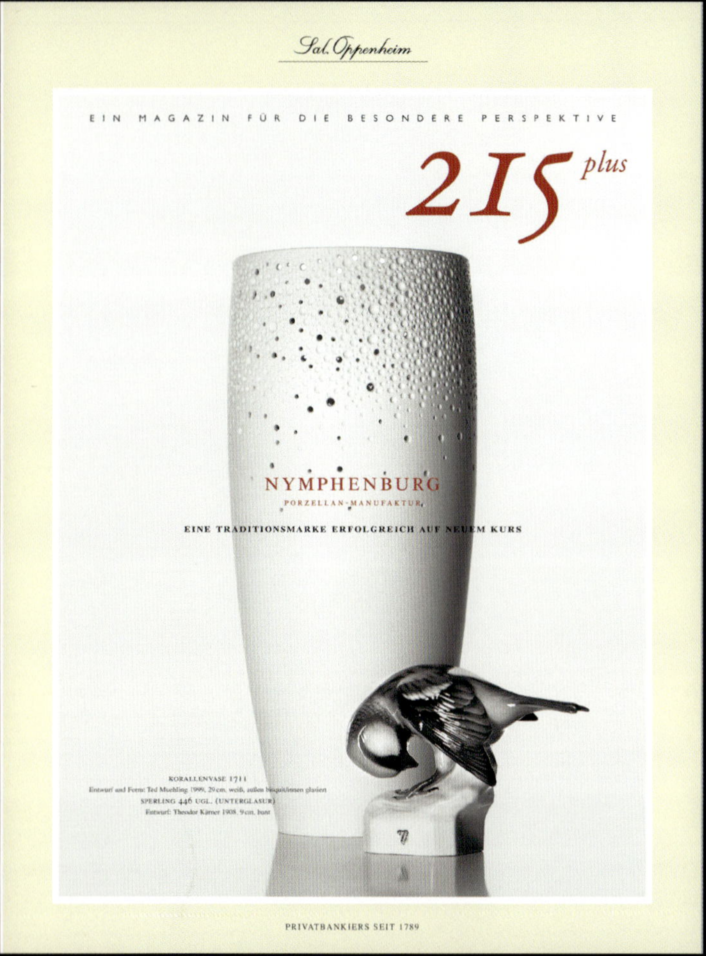
Sal. Oppenheim
EIN MAGAZIN FÜR DIE BESONDERE PERSPEKTIVE
215 plus
NYMPHENBURG
PORZELLAN-MANUFAKTUR
EINE TRADITIONSMARKE ERFOLGREICH AUF NEUEM KURS
KORALLENVASE 1711
SPERLING 446 UGL. (UNTERGLASUR)
PRIVATBANKIERS SEIT 1789

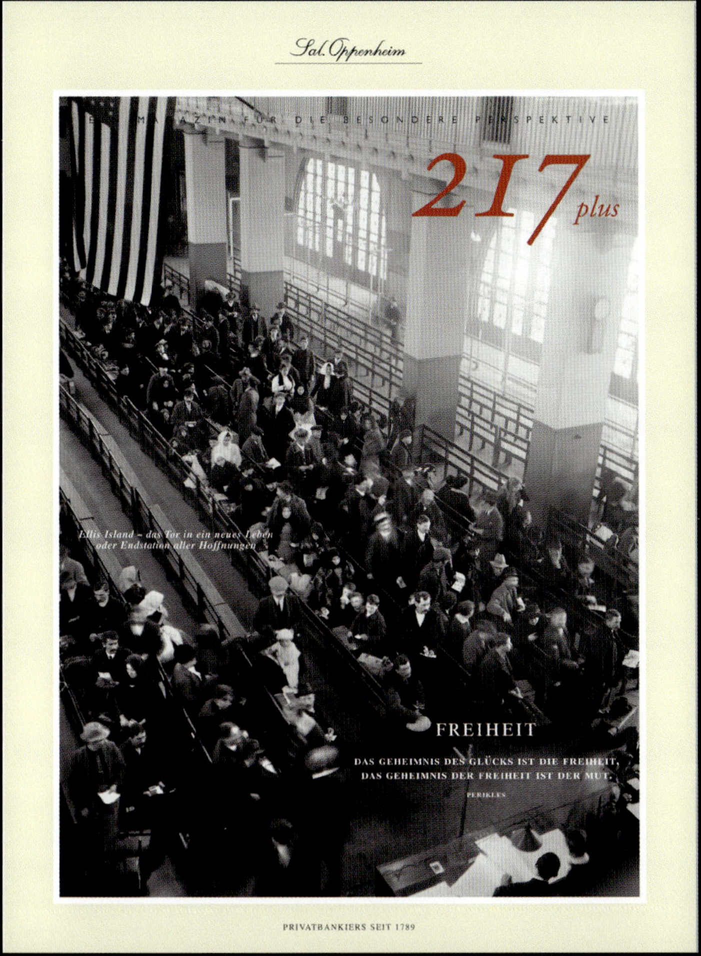
Sal. Oppenheim
EIN MAGAZIN FÜR DIE BESONDERE PERSPEKTIVE
217 plus
Ellis Island – das Tor in ein neues Leben
oder Endstation aller Hoffnungen
FREIHEIT
DAS GEHEIMNIS DES GLÜCKS IST DIE FREIHEIT,
DAS GEHEIMNIS DER FREIHEIT IST DER MUT.
PERIKLES
PRIVATBANKIERS SEIT 1789

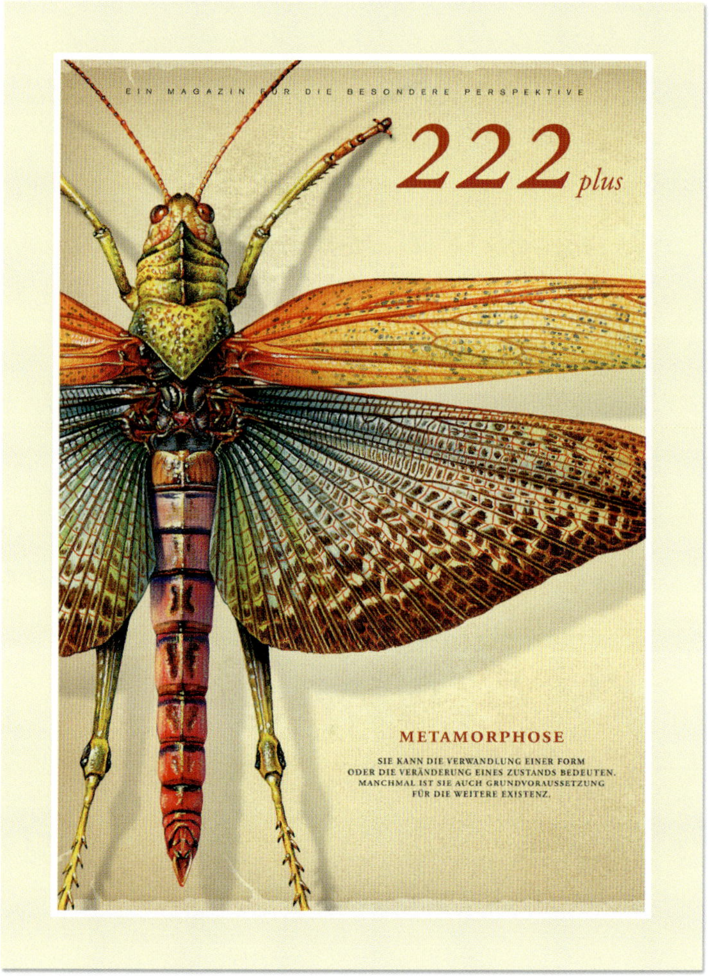
EIN MAGAZIN FÜR DIE BESONDERE PERSPEKTIVE
222 plus
METAMORPHOSE
SIE KANN DIE VERWANDLUNG EINER FORM ODER DIE VERÄNDERUNG EINES ZUSTANDS BEDEUTEN. MANCHMAL IST SIE AUCH GRUNDVORAUSSETZUNG FÜR DIE WEITERE EXISTENZ.

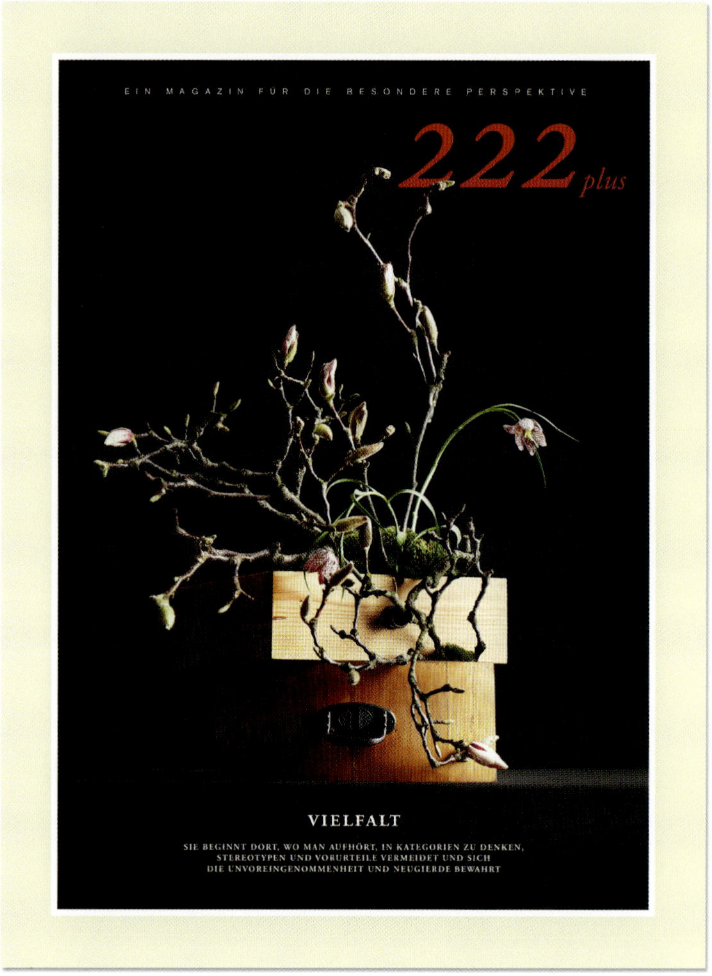
EIN MAGAZIN FÜR DIE BESONDERE PERSPEKTIVE
222 plus
VIELFALT
SIE BEGINNT DORT, WO MAN AUFHÖRT, IN KATEGORIEN ZU DENKEN, STEREOTYPEN UND VORURTEILE VERMEIDET UND SICH DIE UNVOREINGENOMMENHEIT UND NEUGIERDE BEWAHRT

Assignment: This family-owned creamery, located in the hills of western Sonoma County, is an award-winning pioneer in the production of sheep and cow milk aged farmstead cheeses and yogurt. Our objective was to create a memorable branding program that projected the values and personal character of the owners and employees, and the unique artisanal quality of the products.

Approach: Over the years our branding and packaging design firm has used storytelling in a very effective fashion. Storytelling can elicit emotional responses from consumers, which generally compel them to notice the product, if not pick it up for inspection. We proposed to the client the use of a distinctive storybook illustration of great warmth and homespun quality, paired with traditional type fonts. Our approach had the advantage not only of reflecting the values of a country farm, but also of keeping the reproduction to an affordable three colors—easily reproducible using flexography on a variety of structures and stocks. We went in the opposite direction from the competition, creating a friendly and approachable brand that stood out from the crowd of look-alike products.

Results: Since the brand and packaging were introduced, Bellwether Farms has grown to be the leading producer of sheep milk artisanal cheeses and yogurt in the country. It is sold from coast-to-coast and is featured in natural products stores and fine restaurants nationwide. The client's reaction to the branding wasn't so much to say that it was what they wanted, but to say instead that it fit naturally, like a comfortable old coat they had always loved.

Designer: Mark Oliver | **Design Firm:** Mark Oliver, Inc.| **Art Director:** Patty Driskel | **Creative Director:** Mark Oliver
Writers: Mark Oliver, Liam Callahan | **Illustrator:** Sudi McCollum | **Photographer:** Alan Campbell | **Client:** Bellwether Farms

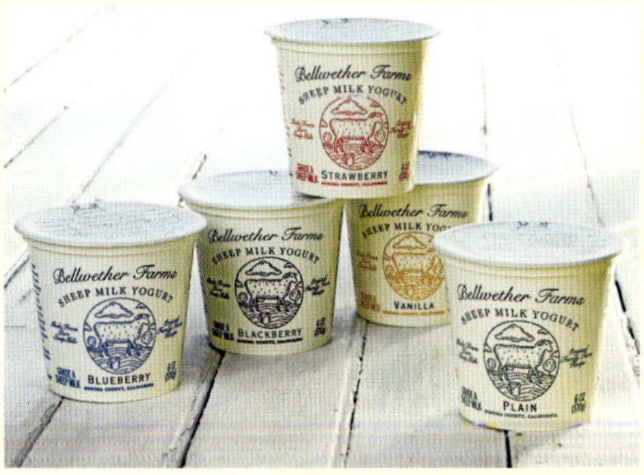

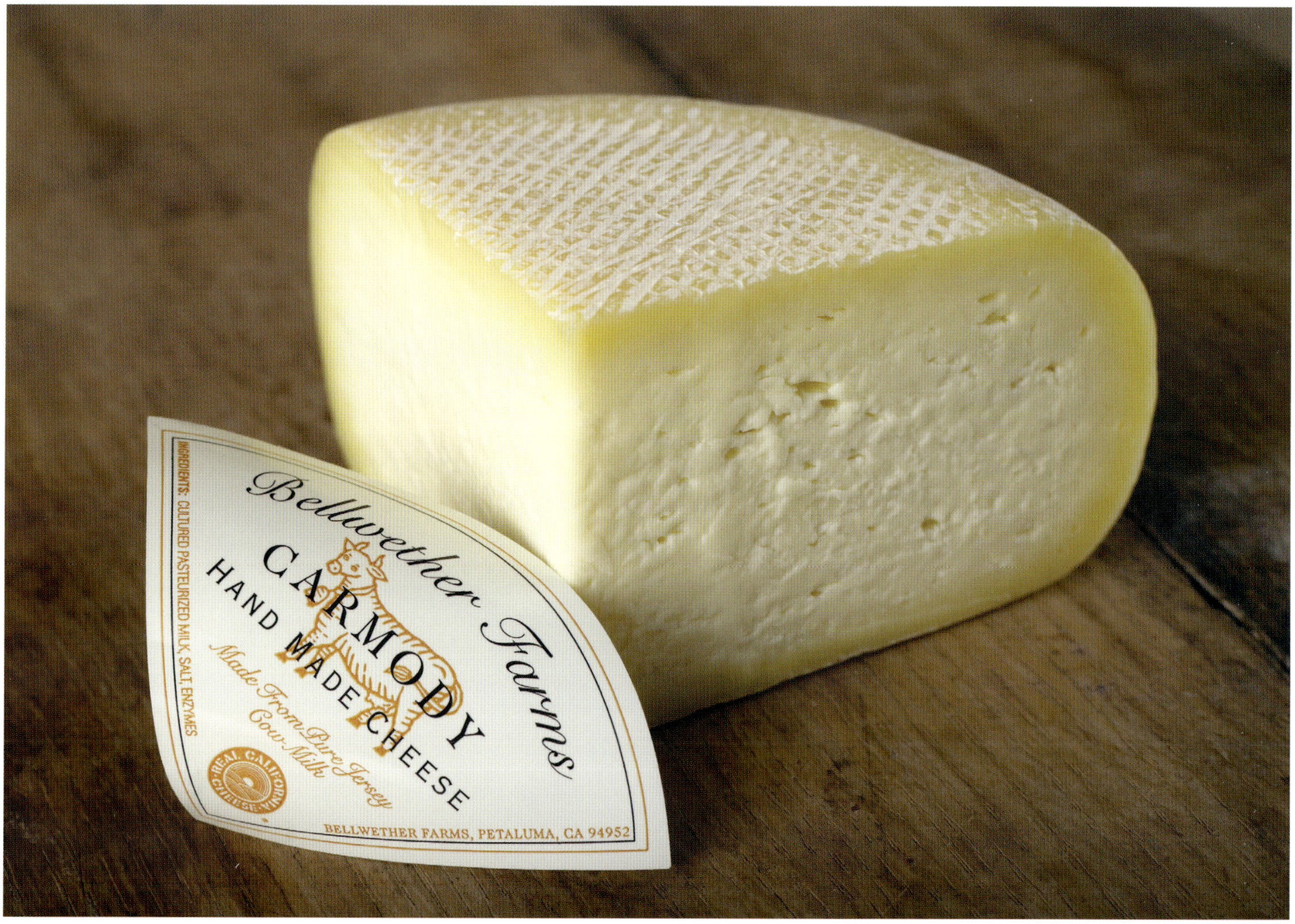
Bellwether Farms
CARMODY
HAND MADE CHEESE
Made From Pure Jersey Cow Milk
INGREDIENTS: CULTURED PASTEURIZED MILK, SALT, ENZYMES
BELLWETHER FARMS, PETALUMA, CA 94952

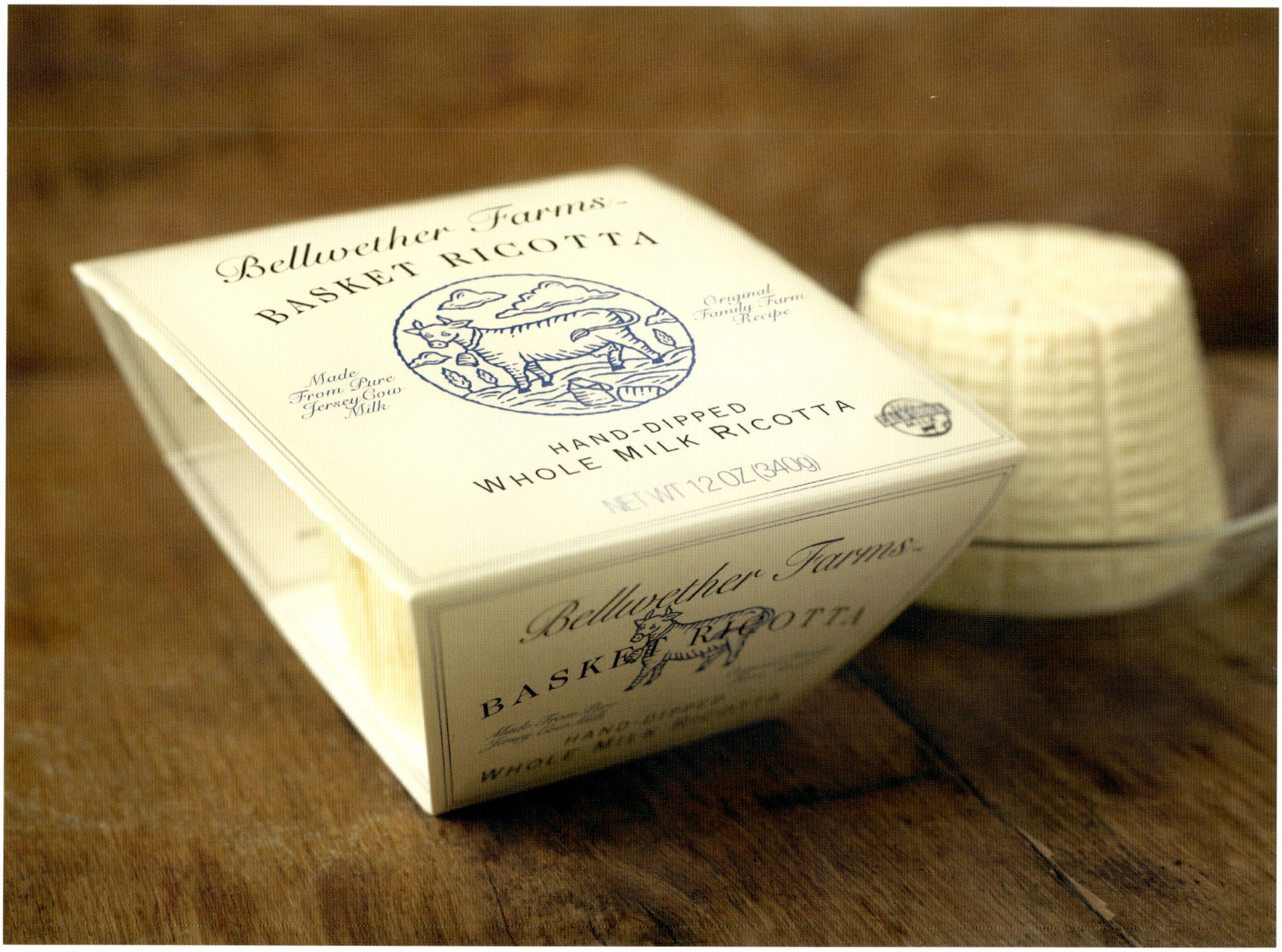
Bellwether Farms
BASKET RICOTTA
Original Family Farm Recipe
Made From Pure Jersey Cow Milk
HAND-DIPPED
WHOLE MILK RICOTTA
NET WT 12 OZ (340g)

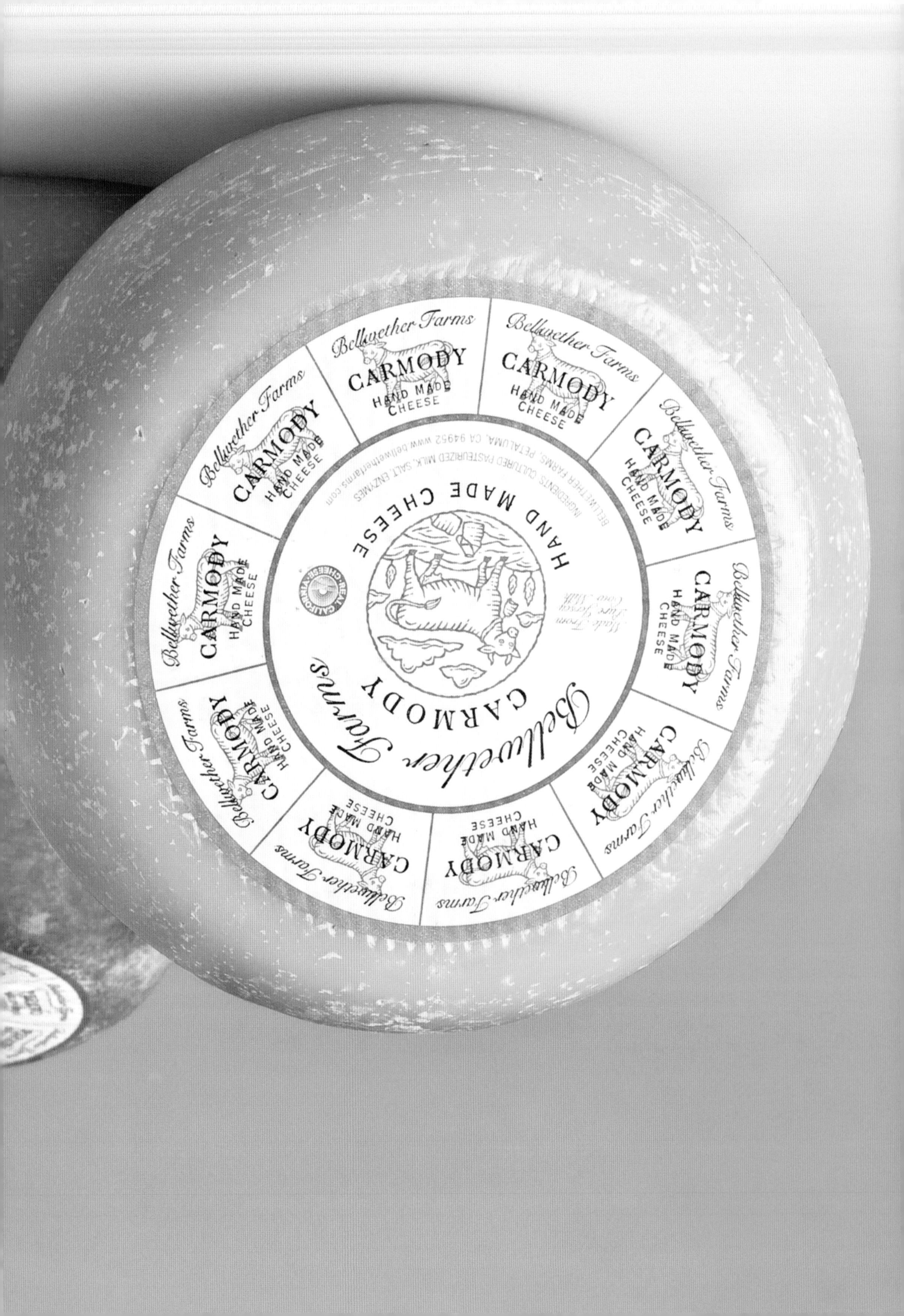
Bellwether Farms
CARMODY
HAND MADE CHEESE
BELLWETHER FARMS, PETALUMA, CA 94952 www.bellwetherfarms.com
INGREDIENTS: CULTURED PASTEURIZED MILK, SALT, ENZYMES

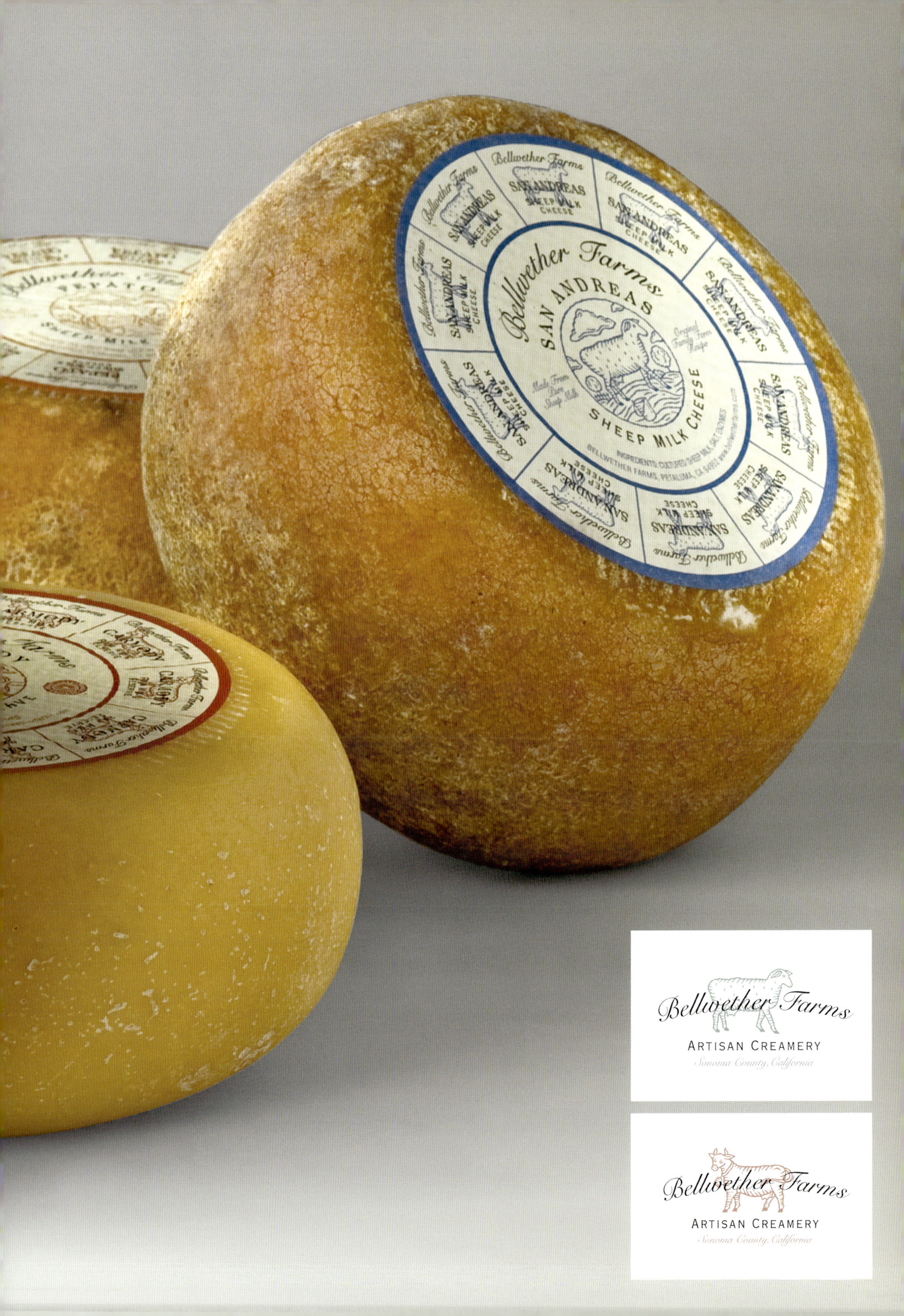
Bellwether Farms
SAN ANDREAS
SHEEP MILK CHEESE
Bellwether Farms
ARTISAN CREAMERY
Sonoma County, California
Bellwether Farms
ARTISAN CREAMERY
Sonoma County, California

Assignment: The brief was to create a new brand for snacks. After conducting a market research and a category audit, we discovered that in Romania, in a market full of products that address particularly young people between 15 and 25 years of age, there are no products that look and speak the language of youth! Precisely for that consumer, the need arises for "X," X snacks.

Approach: It's the small break you need when you're working; it's the friends that accompany you when you're alone and watching TV, or out drinking a beer; it's the little snack when you are a bit hungry, the appetite satisfaction of chewing, the antidote to boredom, the concentration aid ... this is the "X"!

The "X" symbol says: "I have been in front of my computer for quite some time now. I sure need a short break. I'm going to move the mouse toward the X button to close the software I'm using, then I'm going to my X." Based on the "X" symbol used for closing computer software, we created the X Snacks symbol.

Results: The client was convinced from the first sketches. The reaction of the distributors was unexpected; they loved the brand and the packaging at first sight.

Designer: Irinel Ionescu | **Design Firm:** AMPRO DESIGN CONSULTANTS | **Art Director:** Oliwer Iovanovici
Creative Director: Irinel Ionescu | **Writer:** Irinel Ionescu | **Illustrator:** Alin Patru | **Artwork Production:** Danubiu Birzu | **Client:** Engelmi SRL

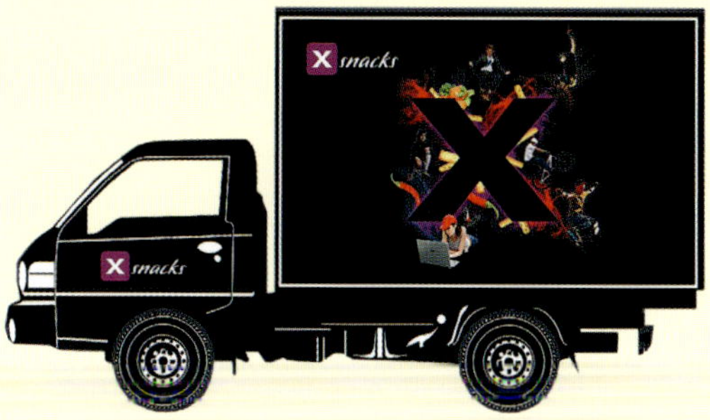

AMPRO DESIGN CONSULTATNS(this spread)|EngelmiSRL|Food&Beverage130

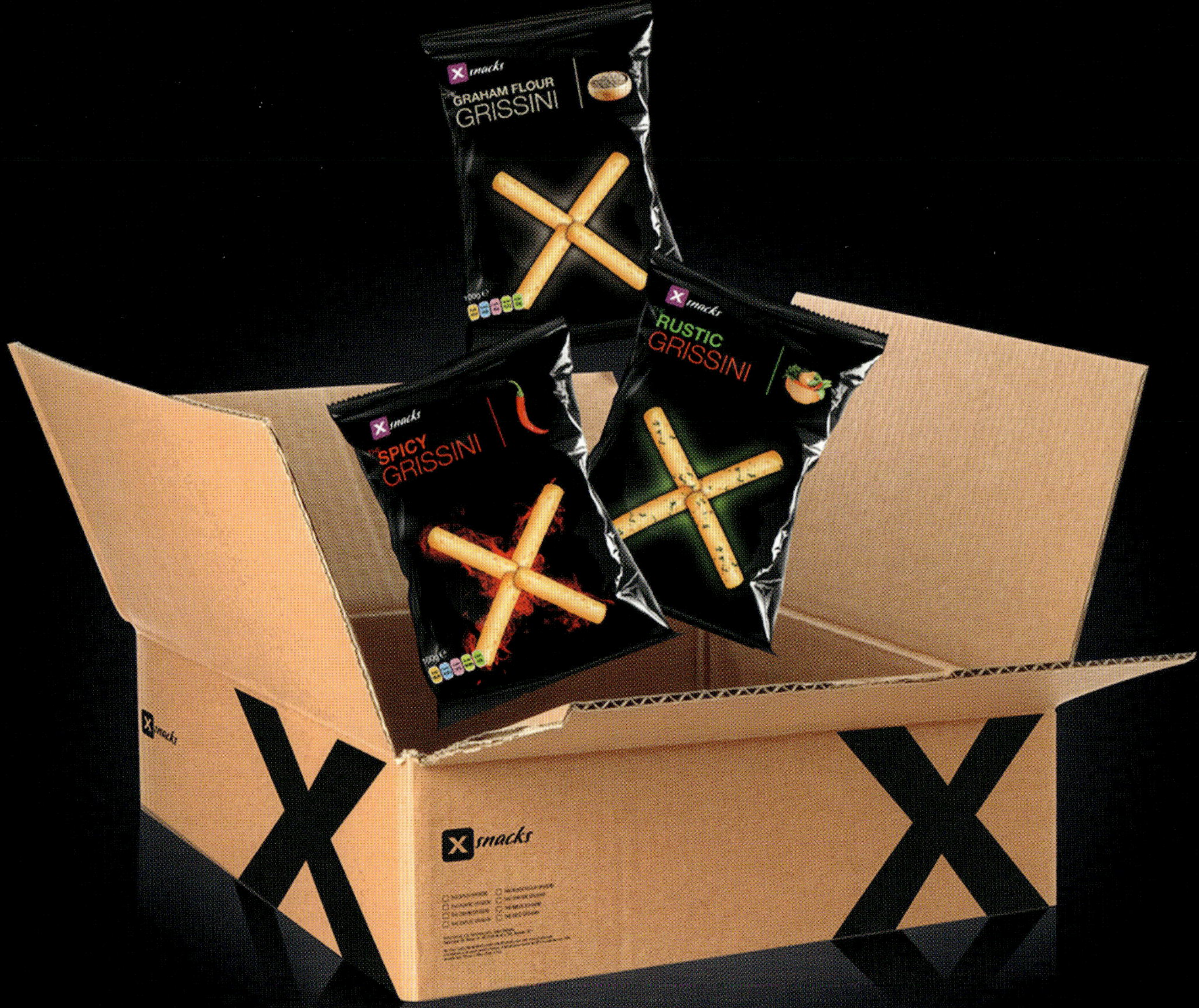
snacks
GRAHAM FLOUR
GRISSINI
SPICY
GRISSINI
RUSTIC
GRISSINI
snacks

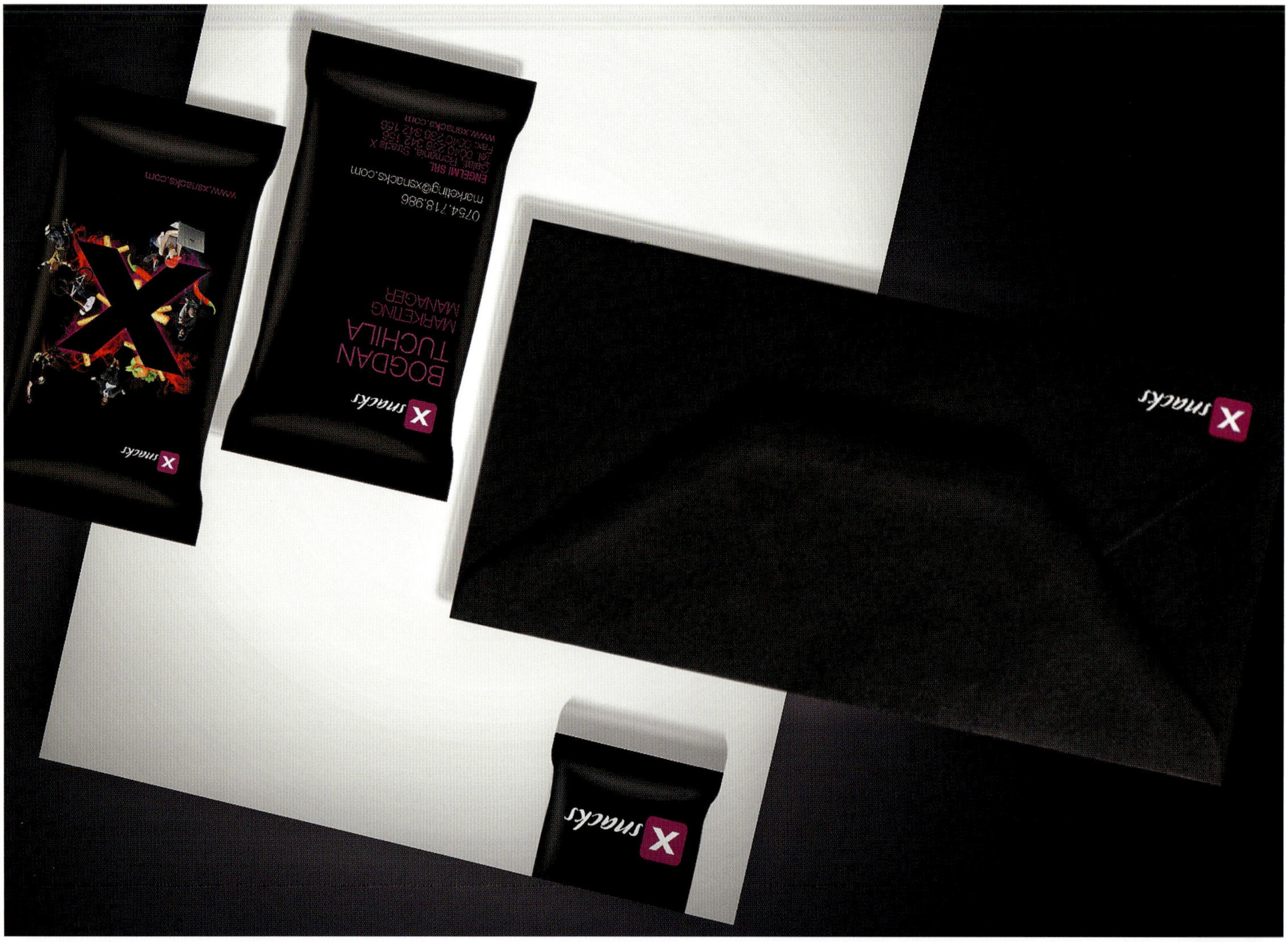
x snacks
BOGDAN
TUCHILA
MARKETING
MANAGER
0754.718.986
marketing@xsnacks.com
www.xsnacks.com

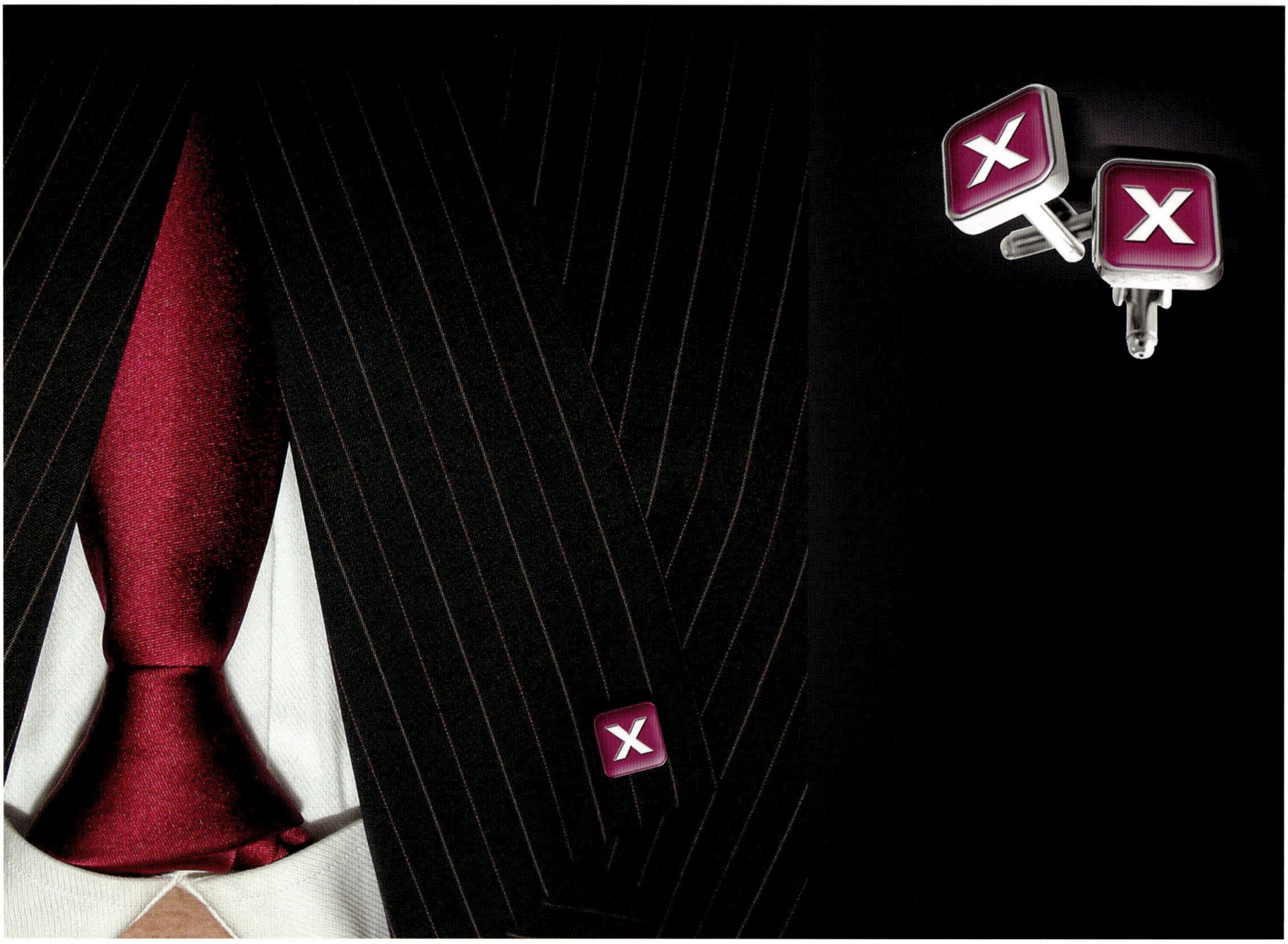

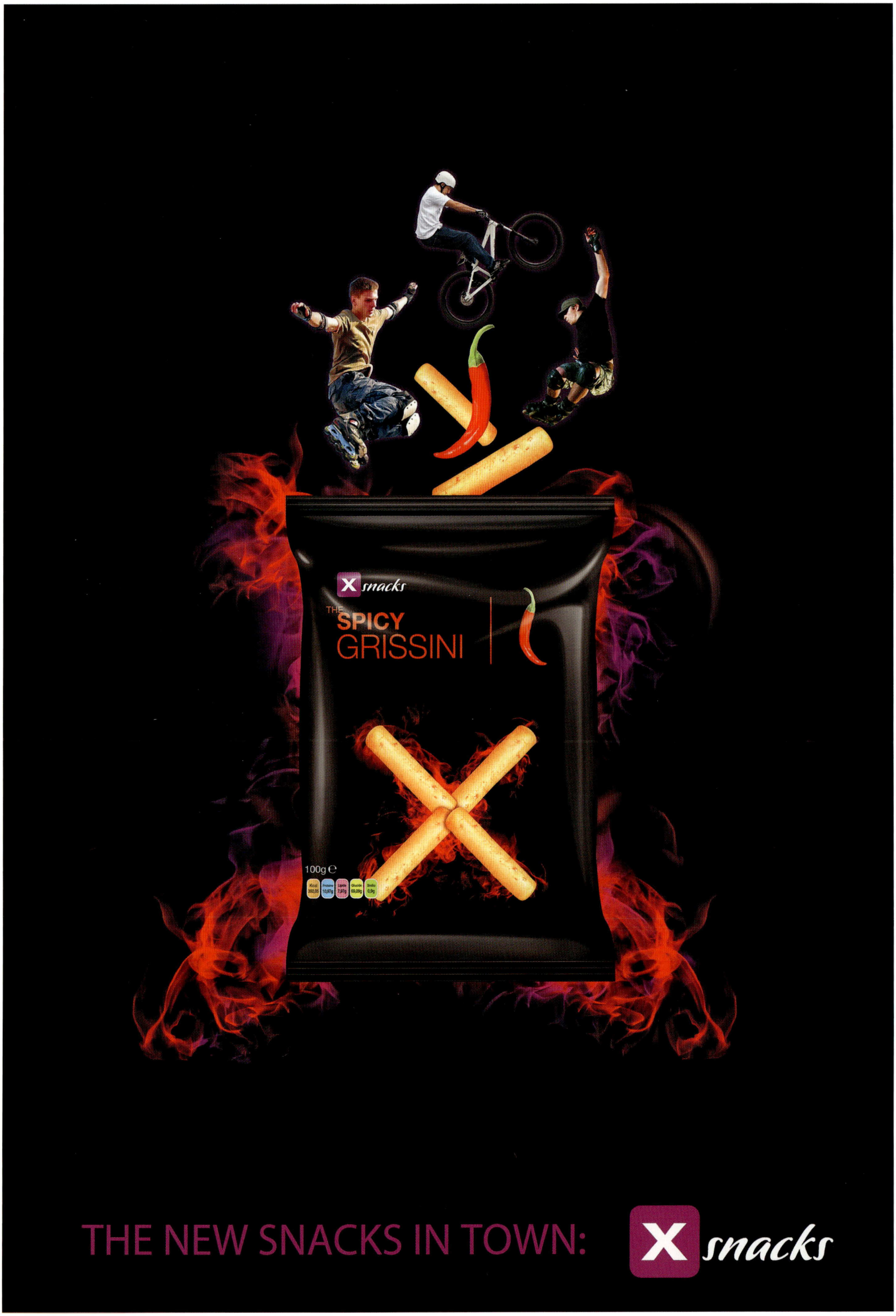
X snacks
THE SPICY GRISSINI
100g e
THE NEW SNACKS IN TOWN:
X snacks

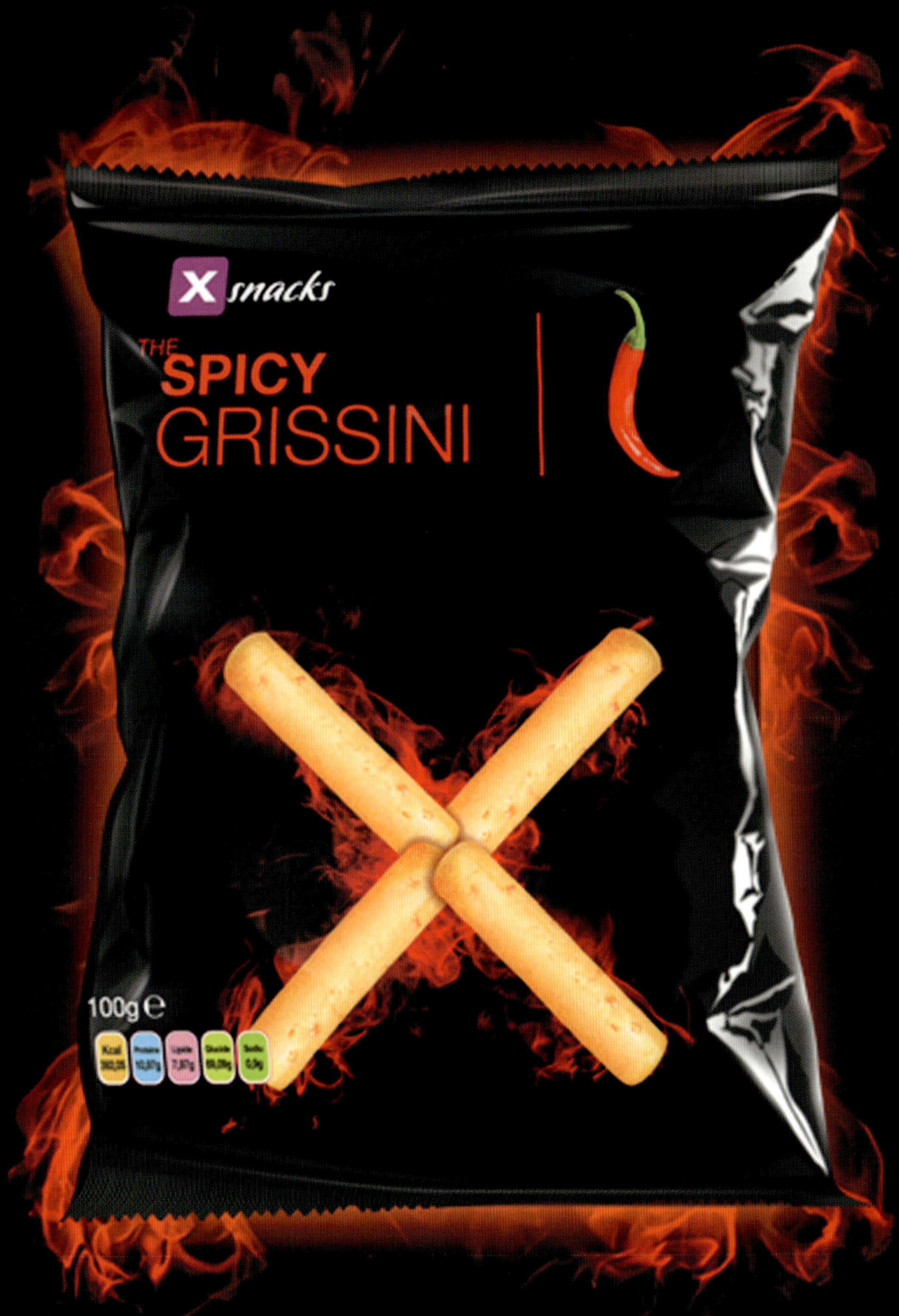
X snacks
THE SPICY GRISSINI
100g ℮

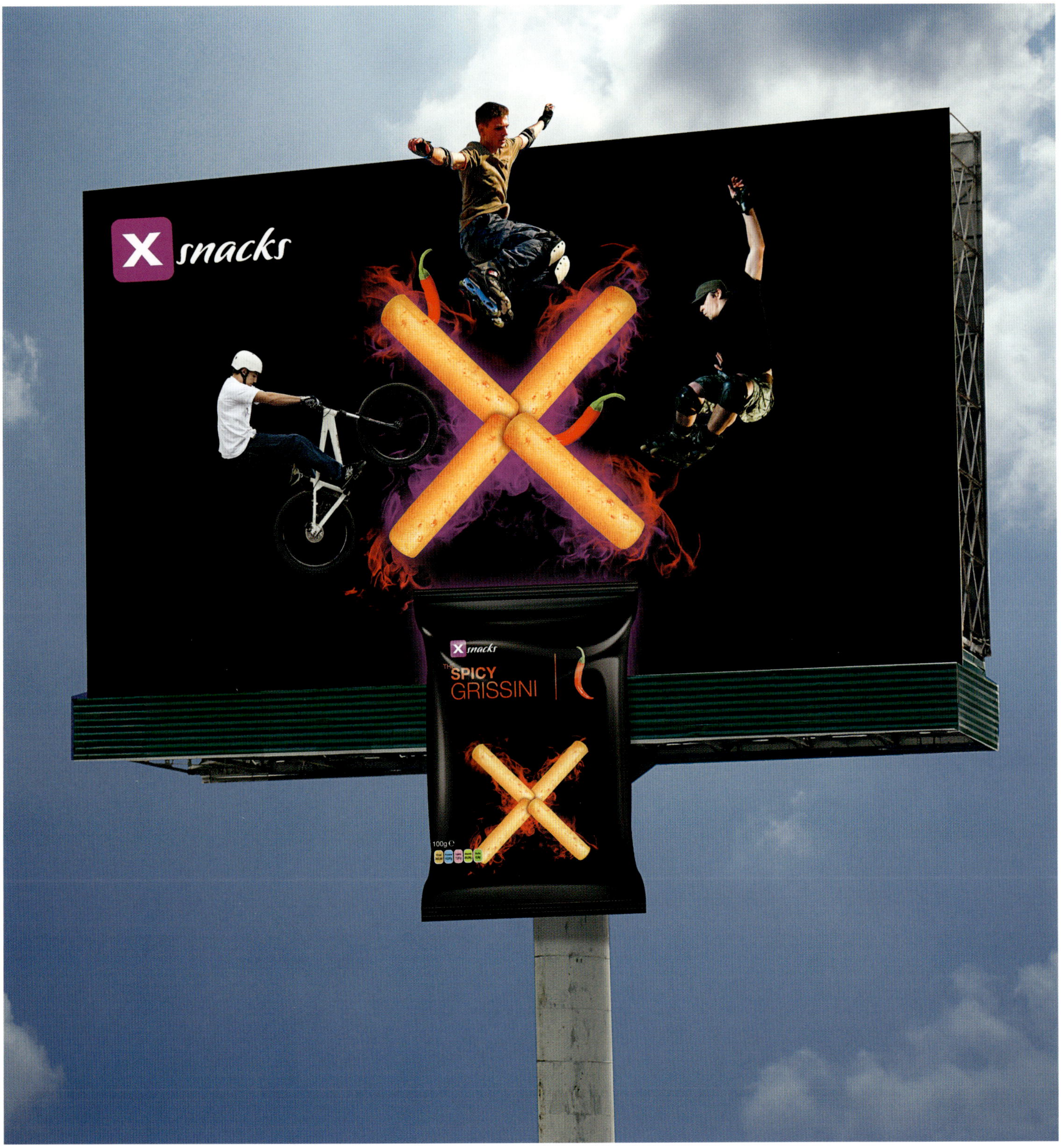
X snacks
X snacks
THE SPICY GRISSINI
100g

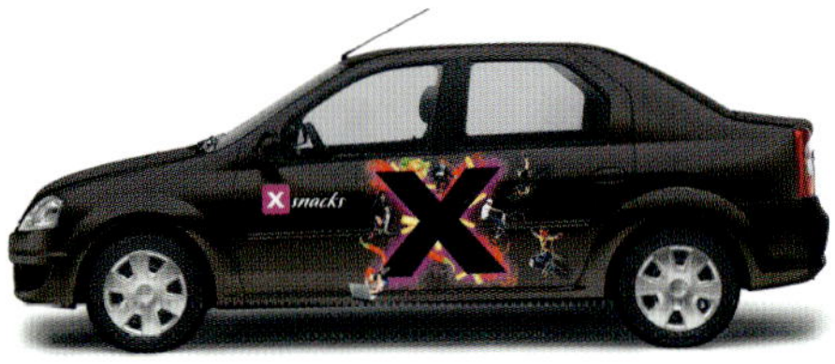
X snacks

Assignment: A little-known liqueur with Italian roots and strong taste appeal, Tuaca was often overlooked on the shelf, lacking an understandable persona. Instead, the brand relied on bartenders and word of mouth to validate its credibility. Described as easy to love and easy to share, Tuaca is a bridge to new friends and adventure—but the old design was anything but adventurous. There was an opportunity for Tuaca to create a new, higher energy persona for a premium spirit that invites consumers to step beyond the familiar. The redesign is bold, without abandoning the brand's heritage credentials.

Approach: The new design sheds the old without throwing away elements of its rich heritage and story. Italian design sensibilities inspire a look that is bold, timeless, and inviting. Tuaca is a liqueur with a taste that's highly mixable and right for almost any occasion. New branding makes it appealing to an audience that's open to trying new things in new ways. Consumed primarily as a shot, the product is exceptionally flexible—it can be consumed straight or mixed, cold or warm, sweet or sour. The new design is inspired by that variety and created to deliver a dynamic, inviting persona. To be relevant, brands need to get noticed, speak in a consistent voice, and engage in interesting ways. More and more, brands are activated at the local level. To provide tools and communicate with the field, we created the Tuaca Brand Activation Guide. It provides branding elements and programs packaged in a cool, Tuaca way.

Results: The new brand identity and package are more visible, compelling, and energetic. The package more accurately represents the product's taste profile. The extended identity system encourages more interesting activation with a "kit of parts" that can be used in a variety of ways. Qualitative research has validated the new identity and label design for the brand. Consumers recognize the product as more premium and relevant, and it has grown through a reinvigorated promotional effort.

Designer: Kate Arends | **Design Firm:** Cue | **Creative Director:** Alan Colvin | **Producer:** Chris Thomas
Photographer: Bruton Stroube | **Printer:** Franklin Press | **Client:** Brown-Forman

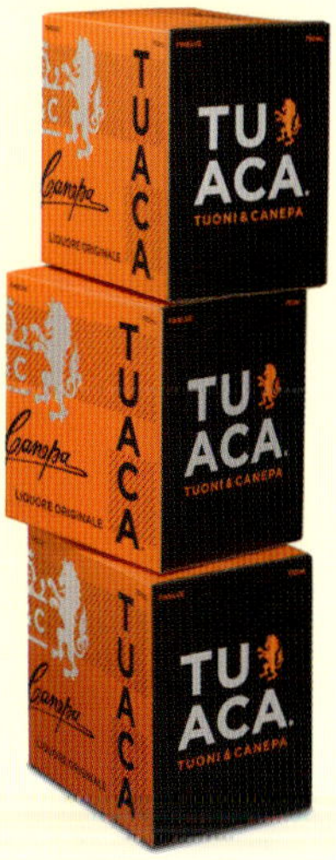

Cue (this spread) | Brown-Forman | Food&Beverage **136**

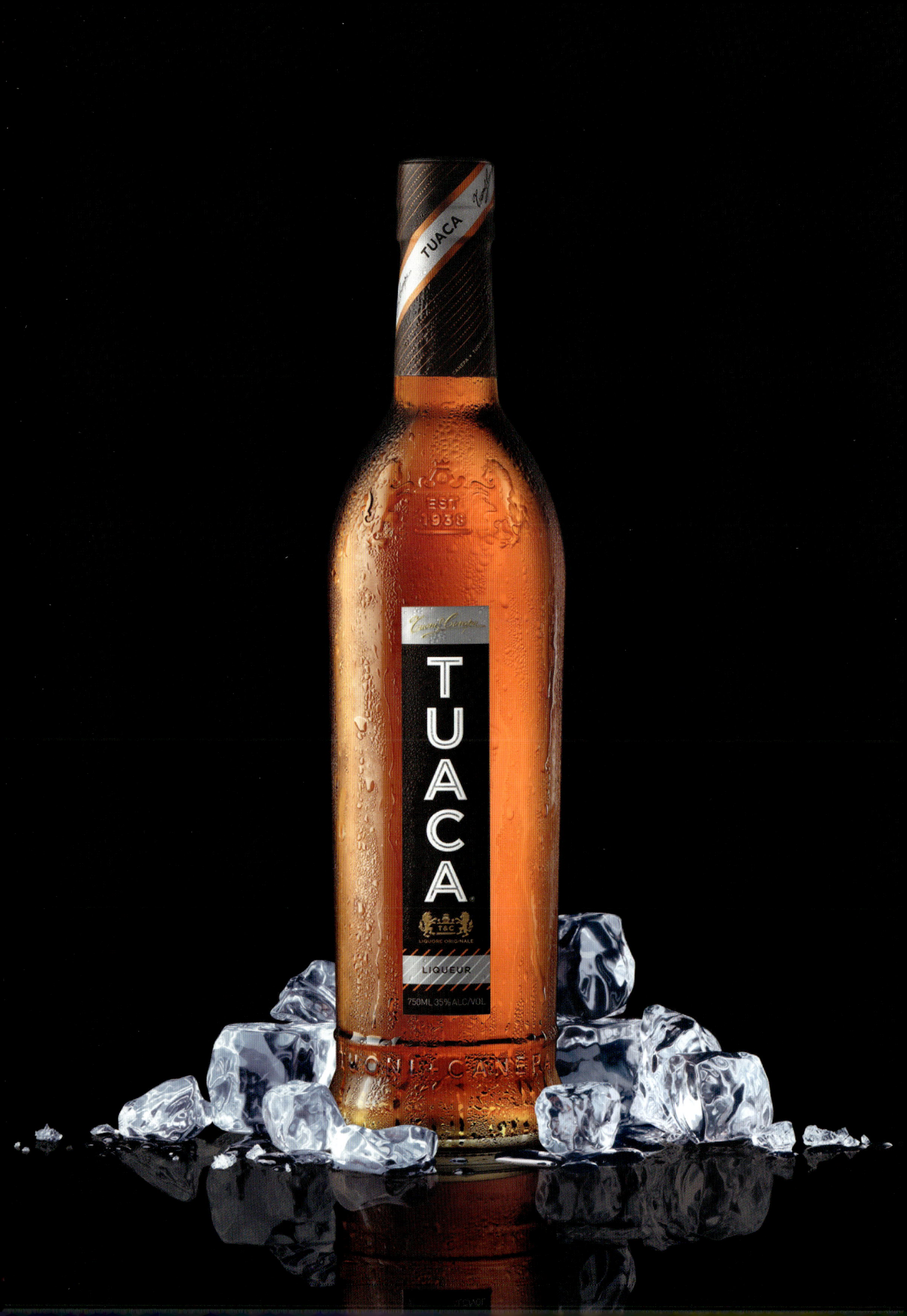
TUACA
EST
1938
TUACA
T&C
LIQUORE ORIGINALE
LIQUEUR
750ML 35% ALC/VOL

Assignment: Andrews Distributing, a major North Texas beverage distributor, wanted to increase sales by introducing their customers to a wider variety of beers. They asked RBMM to develop a creative approach capable of expansion.

Approach: RBMM began with interviews of key customers and stakeholders that led to an initial presentation of several directions. Andrews ultimately chose a flexible system, featuring different beer flavors and textures, as represented by multiple logos.

Results: The LoveBeer program was launched at a 250-person beverage trade conference, showcasing thirty-five new beer brands. Interest proved so great that Andrews is now introducing the program statewide as a retail promotion.

Designer: Brandon DeLoach | **Design Firm:** RBMM | **Art Director:** Brandon DeLoach | **Creative Director:** Jeff Barfoot
Writer: Brittany Sarrett | **Client:** Andrews Distributing

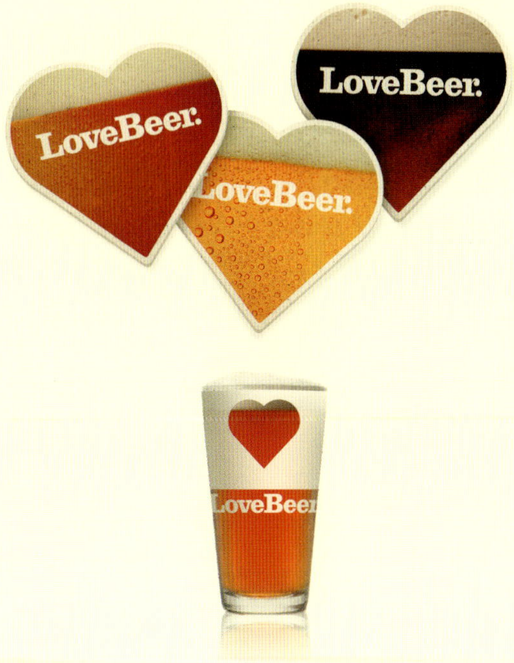

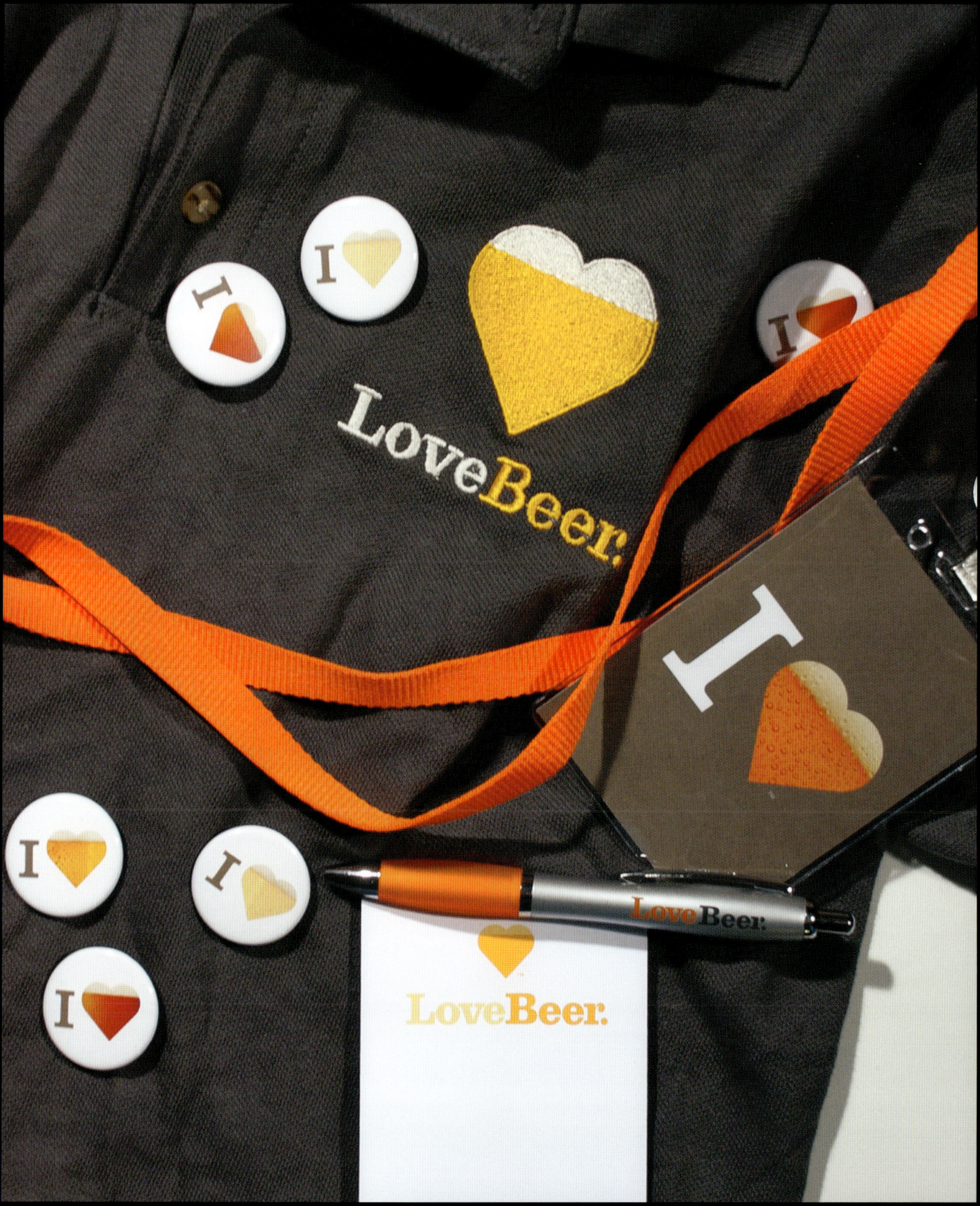
LoveBeer.
I
LoveBeer.
LoveBeer.

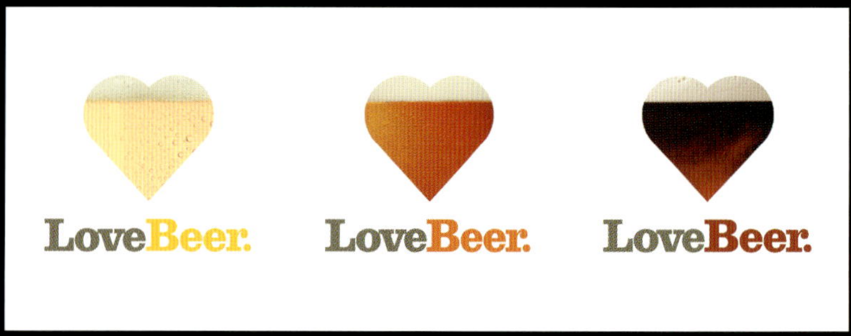
LoveBeer.
LoveBeer.
LoveBeer.

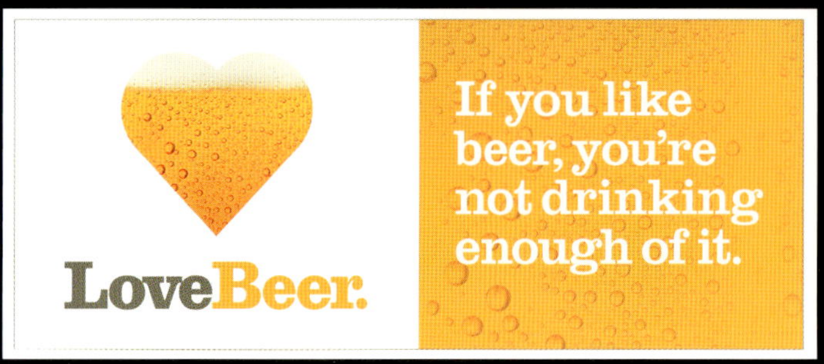
LoveBeer.
If you like beer, you're not drinking enough of it.

Assignment: This is a Swallow Nest product brand based in the USA. We developed this brand image from the raw bird's nest. We wanted an image of a privileged class, and a modern and young class of everyday drink.

Approach: We use a golden, elegant element to enhance the image of the product, so that it becomes one that people want to buy as a gift and for themselves as a healthy supplement. For the brand new beverage, the target clients are young people. They like more energetic, fresh, and trendy products. These are the elements we added to the brand for the refreshment of the bottle products.

Results: The result is excellent. The target client likes the privileged feeling of the products. The brand new bottle is especially good at selling the daily drink.

Designer: Lai Wai Kwan Gideon | **Design Firm:** Ameba Design Ltd. | **Art Director:** Lai Wai Kwan Gideon
Creative Director: Lai Wai Kwan Gideon | **Client:** Golden Nest Inc.

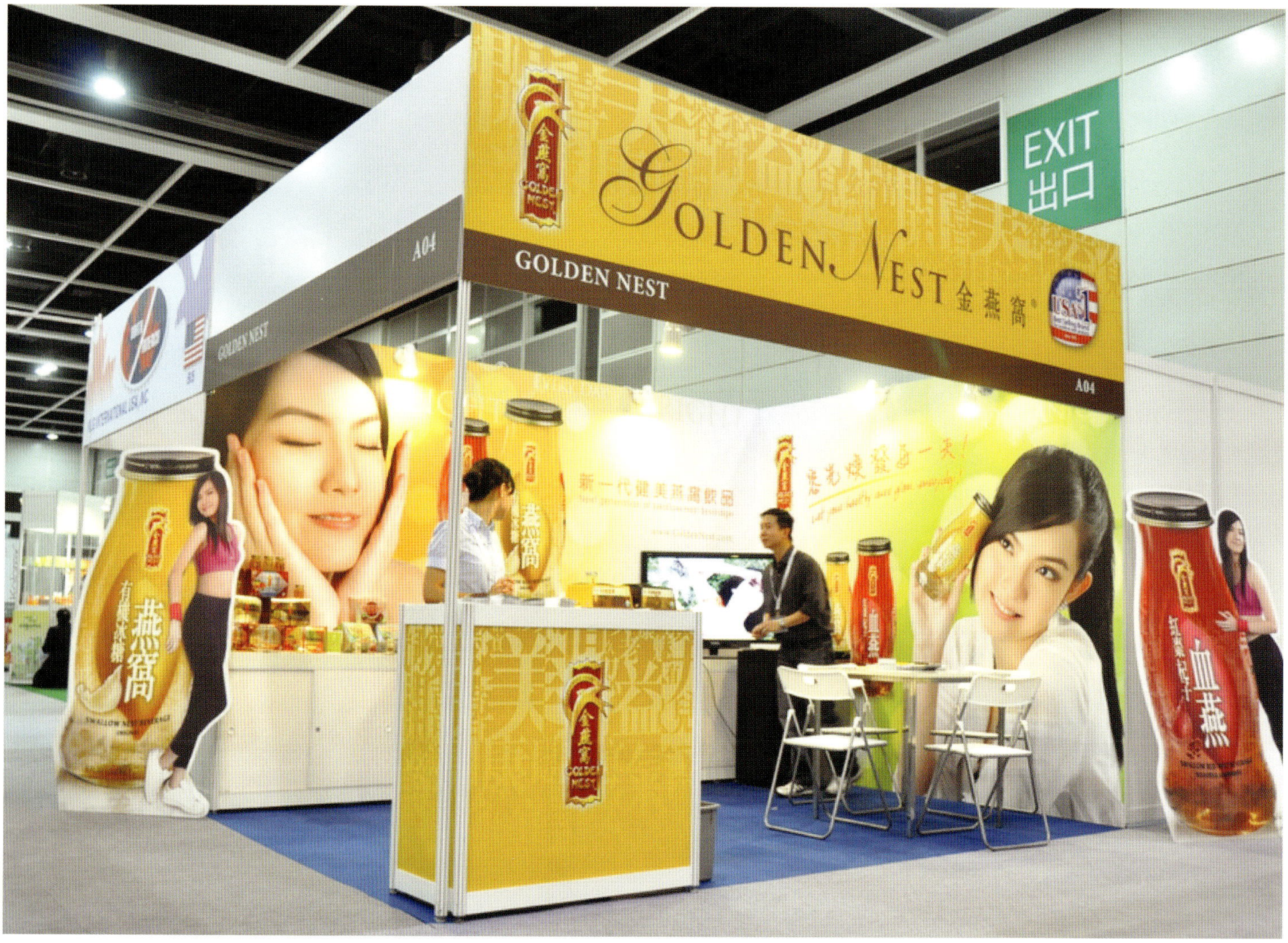
GOLDEN NEST 金燕窩
GOLDEN NEST
A04
EXIT
出口
燕窩
血燕

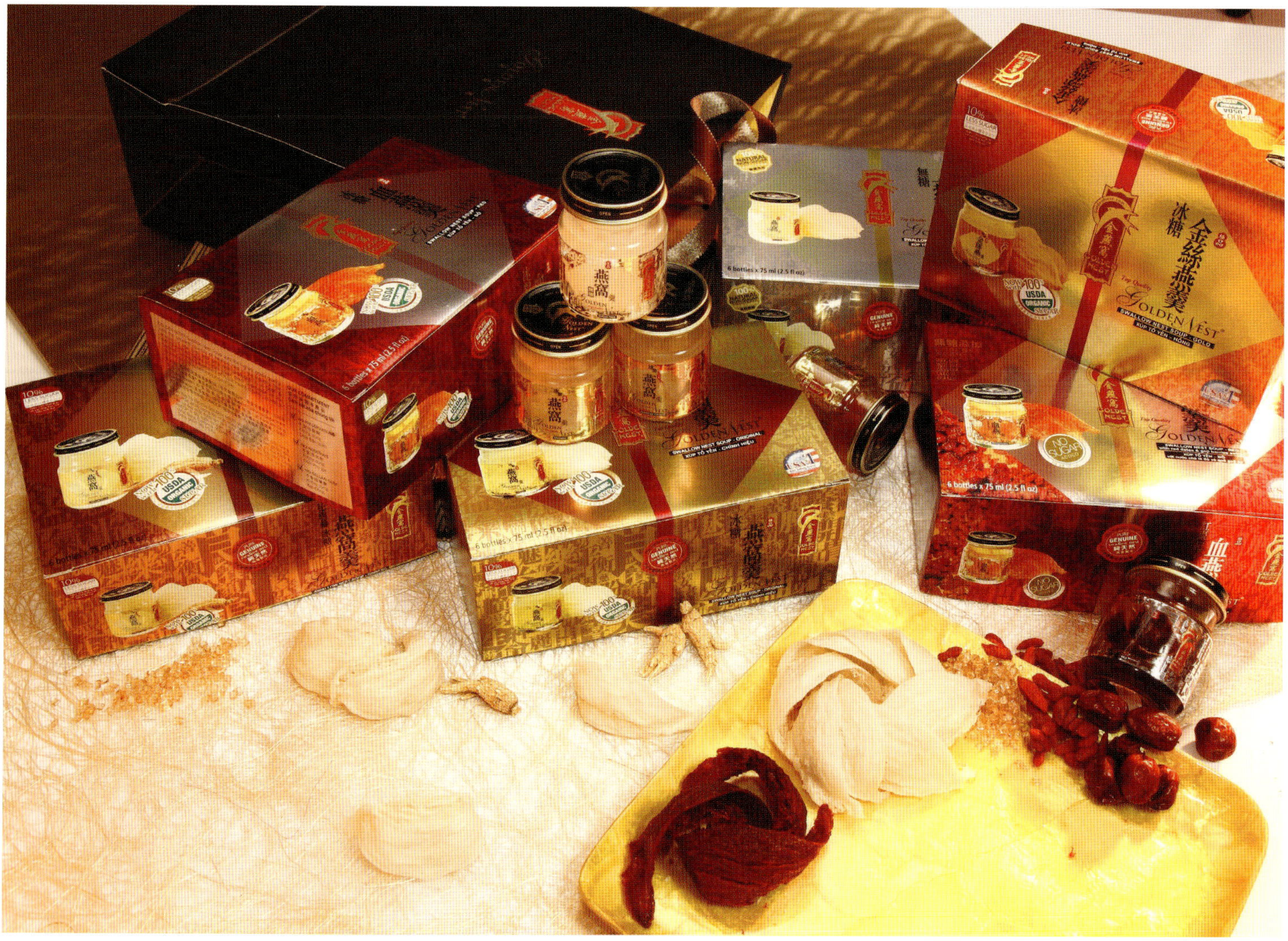

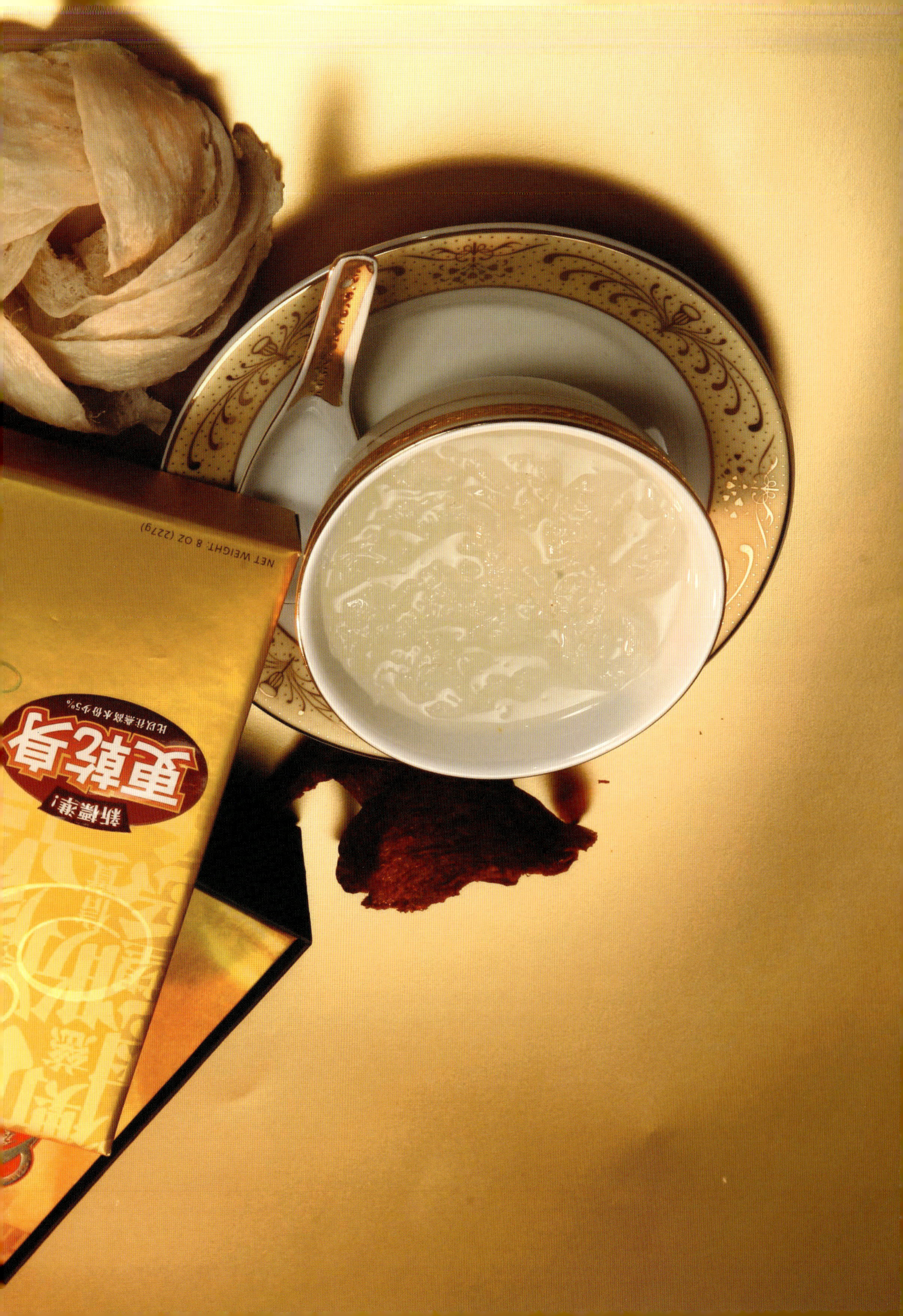
NET WEIGHT: 8 OZ (227g)
新標準!
更乾身

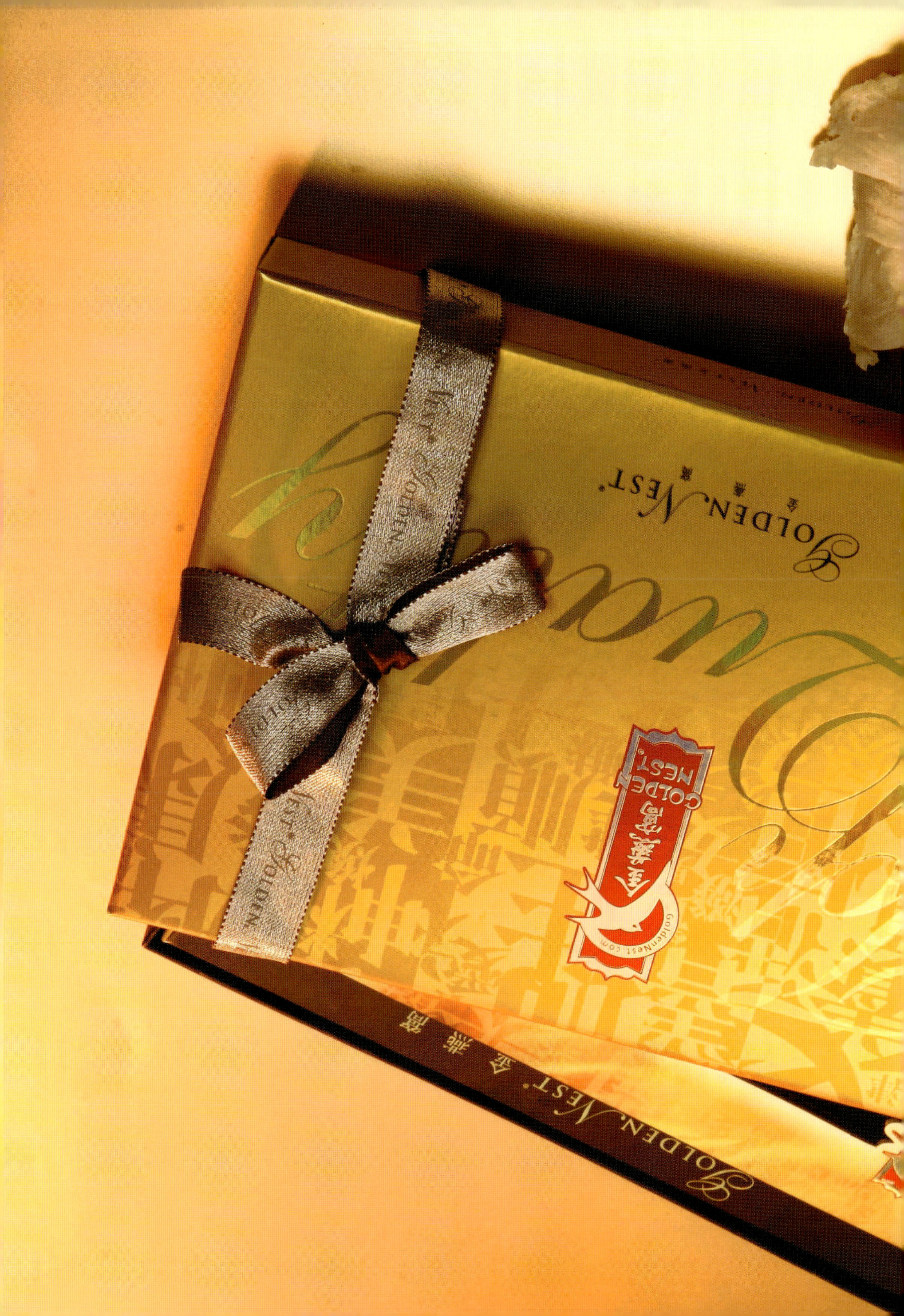
GOLDEN NEST
GOLDEN NEST
GOLDEN NEST

Assignment: Design an identity for a new brand of premium, farmed, whole fresh salmon. The product is sold wholesale through a distribution network and aimed directly at discerning chefs at high-quality white tablecloth restaurants.

Approach: Based on the strategic concept of the "Craft Salmon," we set out to evoke a feeling of quality and trust. With the passion and care of the farmers being central to the superior quality of the product, it was essential that the identity project a strong feeling of expertise and craftsmanship.

Results: Since launching Skuna Bay, it has had more than a hundred listings in the Southwest's premier restaurants, and more than fifty listings after just a month in the Chicago market.

Design Firm: DDB Canada | **Art Director:** Tim Hoffpauir | **Creative Director:** James Bateman | **Writer:** Geoff Vreeken
Photographer: André Pinces | **Client:** Grieg Seafood

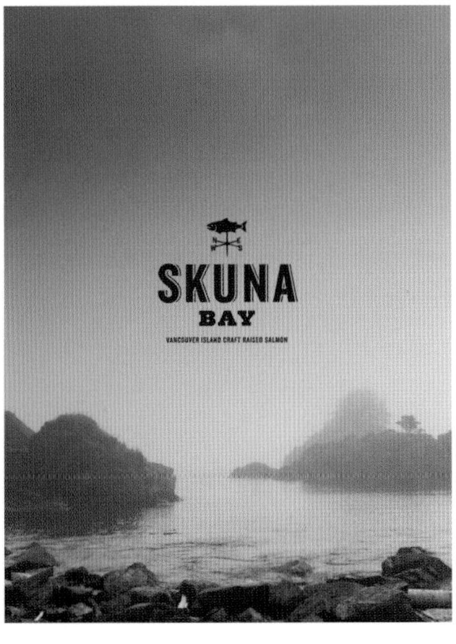

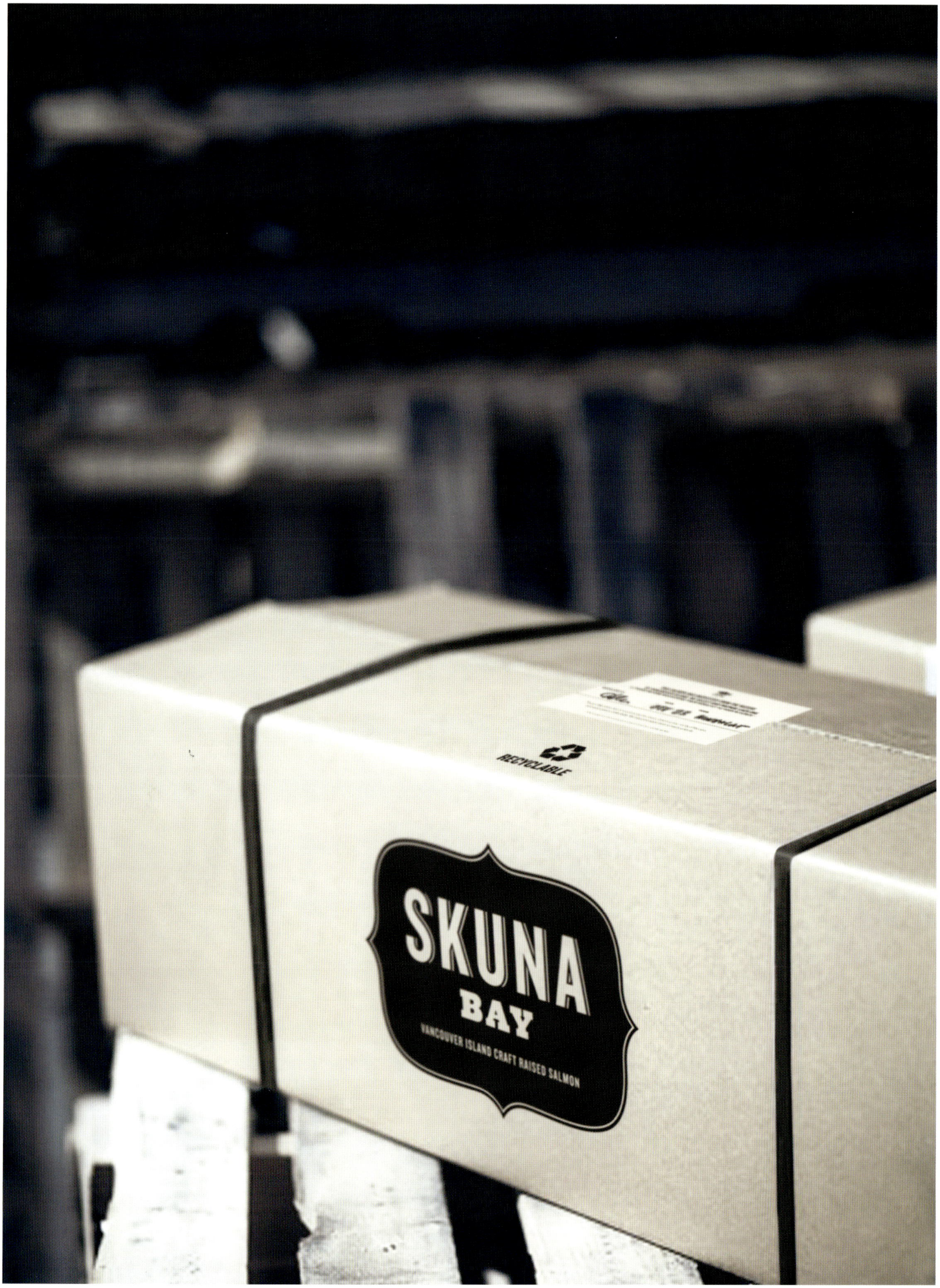
RECYCLABLE
SKUNA
BAY
VANCOUVER ISLAND CRAFT RAISED SALMON

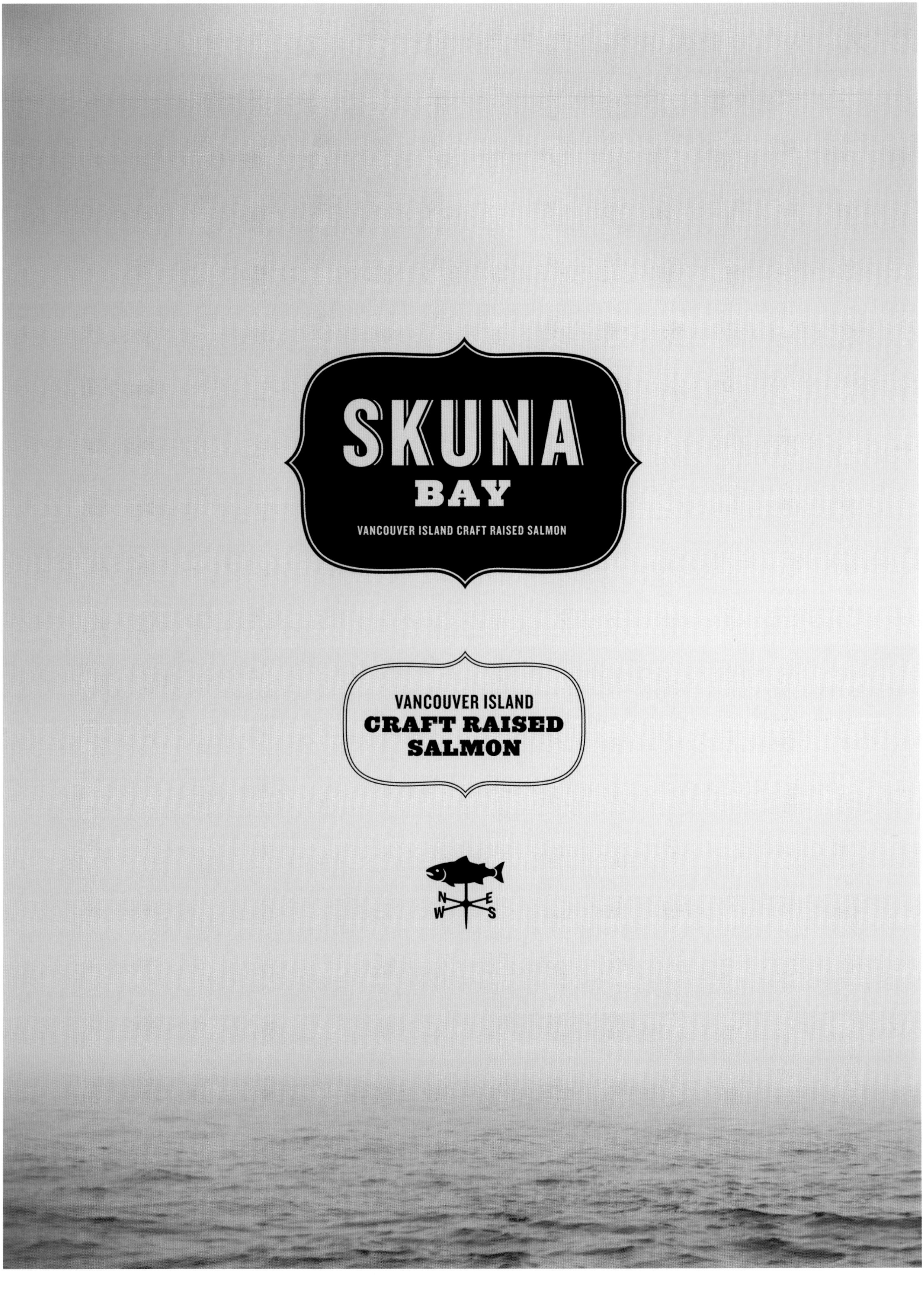
SKUNA
BAY
VANCOUVER ISLAND CRAFT RAISED SALMON
VANCOUVER ISLAND
CRAFT RAISED
SALMON
N
E
W
S

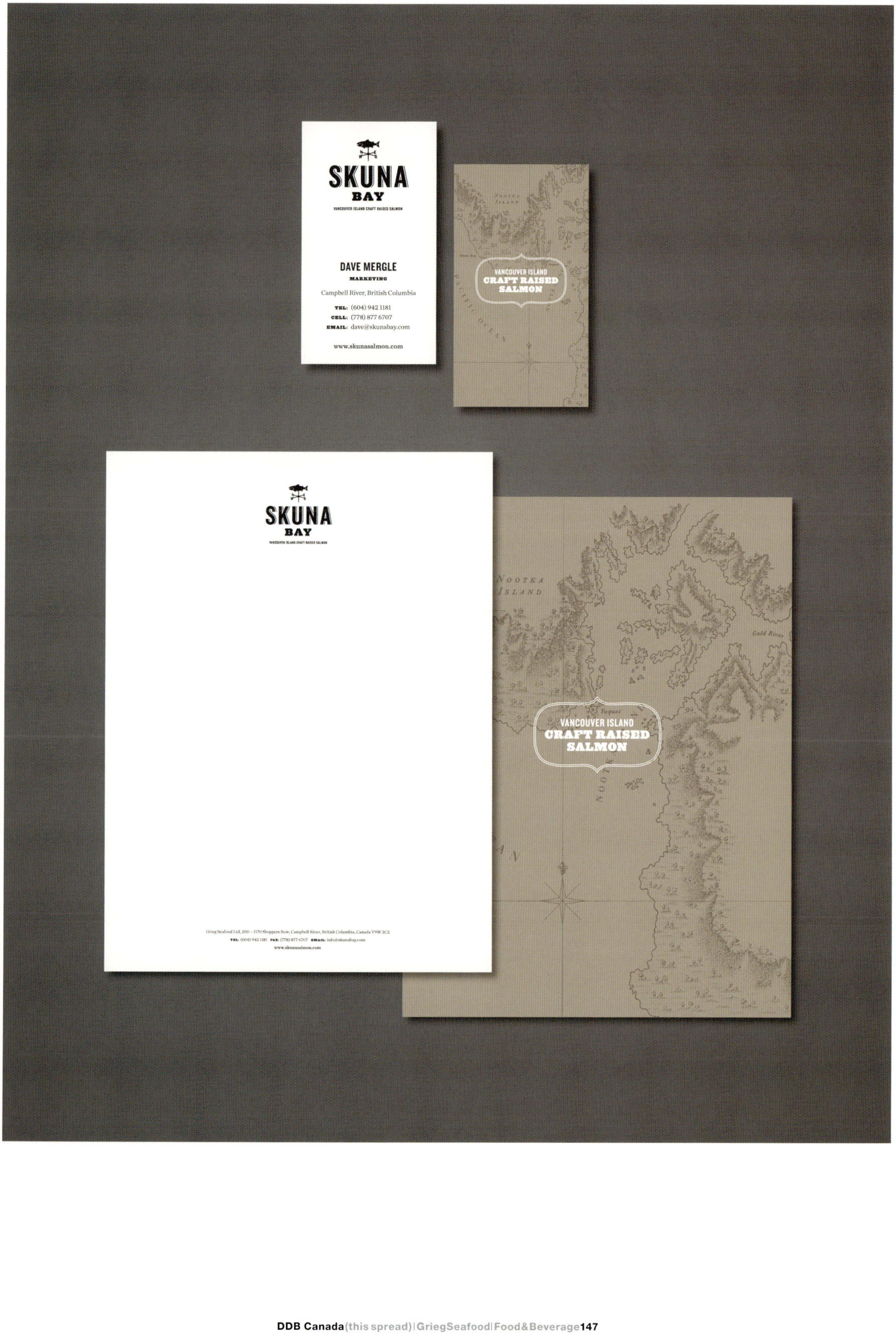
SKUNA
BAY
VANCOUVER ISLAND CRAFT RAISED SALMON
DAVE MERGLE
MARKETING
Campbell River, British Columbia
TEL: (604) 942 1181
CELL: (778) 877 6707
EMAIL: dave@skunabay.com
www.skunasalmon.com
VANCOUVER ISLAND
CRAFT RAISED
SALMON
SKUNA
BAY
VANCOUVER ISLAND CRAFT RAISED SALMON
Grieg Seafood Ltd, 200 – 1170 Shoppers Row, Campbell River, British Columbia, Canada V9W 2C2
TEL: (604) 942 1181 FAX: (778) 877 6707 EMAIL: info@skunabay.com
www.skunasalmon.com
NOOTKA
ISLAND
Gold River
VANCOUVER ISLAND
CRAFT RAISED
SALMON

Assignment: To create a brand image for retailer Urban Archaeology, a company that specializes in re-creating the style of fixtures from the late 19th and early 20th centuries for use in today's homes.

Approach: Our approach helps the company establish a distinct voice through the use of playful typography combined with still life photos.

Results: The client has been very happy with the results and with the increased store traffic after each advertising placement.

Designers: Lynda Decker, Kevin Lamb, Natalie Marshall | **Design Firm:** Decker Design, Inc. | **Art Director:** Lynda Decker
Writer: Judith Stockman | **Retoucher:** Natalie Marshall | **Photographer:** Ken Skalski | **Clients:** Judith Stockman, Urban Archaeology

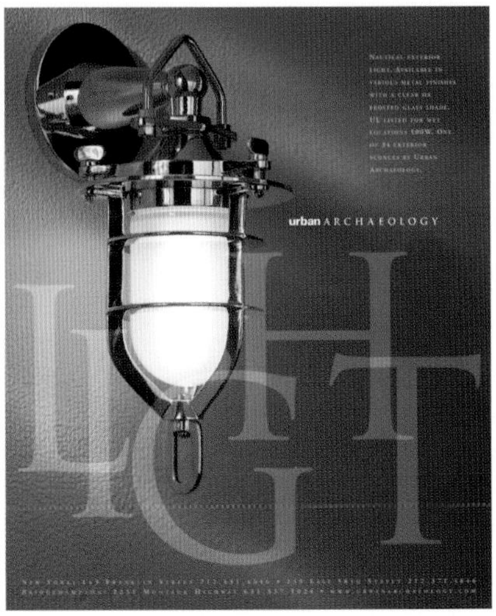

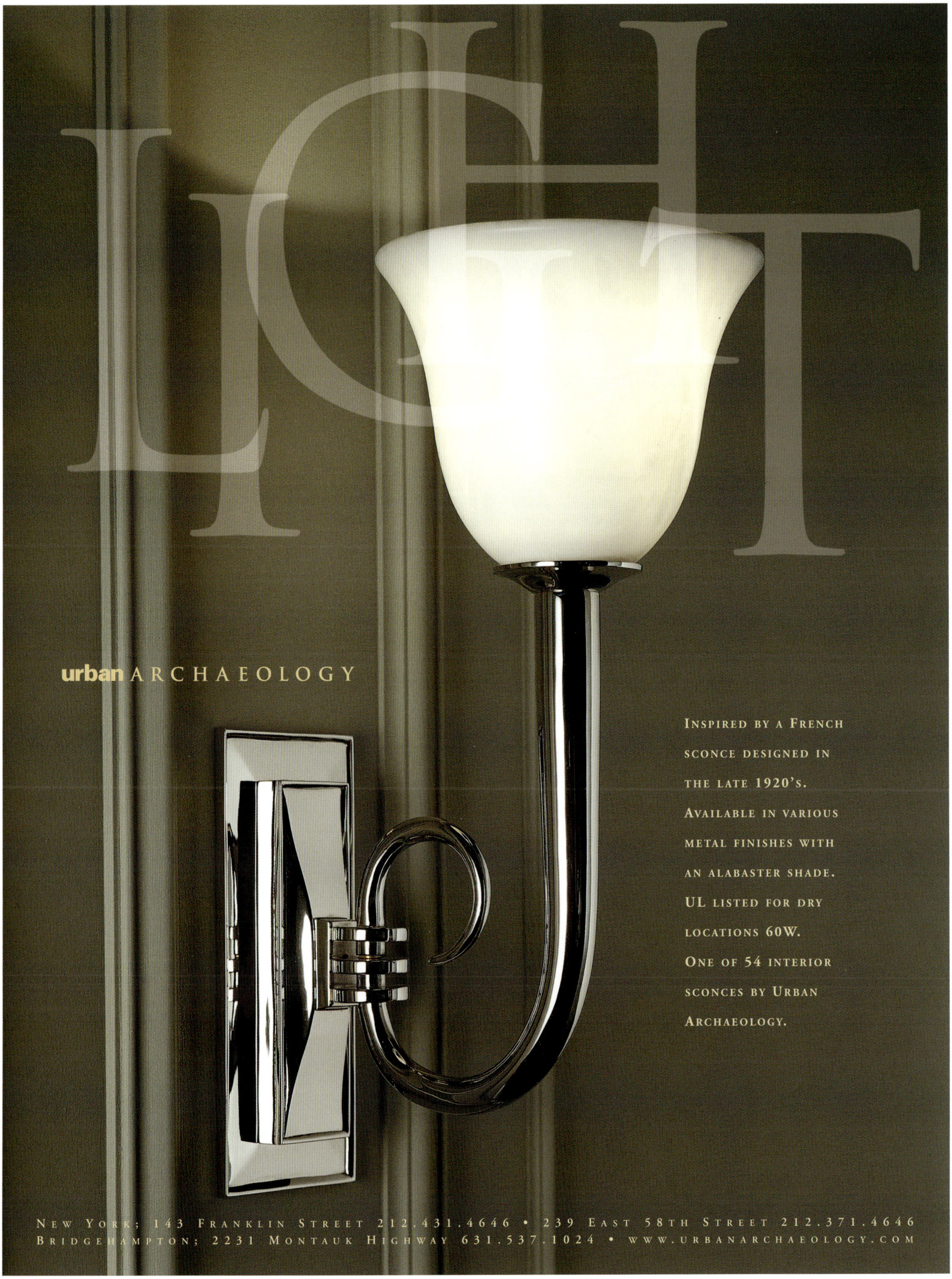
LIGHT
urban ARCHAEOLOGY
Inspired by a French sconce designed in the late 1920's. Available in various metal finishes with an alabaster shade. UL listed for dry locations 60W. One of 54 interior sconces by Urban Archaeology.
New York; 143 Franklin Street 212.431.4646 • 239 East 58th Street 212.371.4646
Bridgehampton; 2231 Montauk Highway 631.537.1024 • www.urbanarchaeology.com

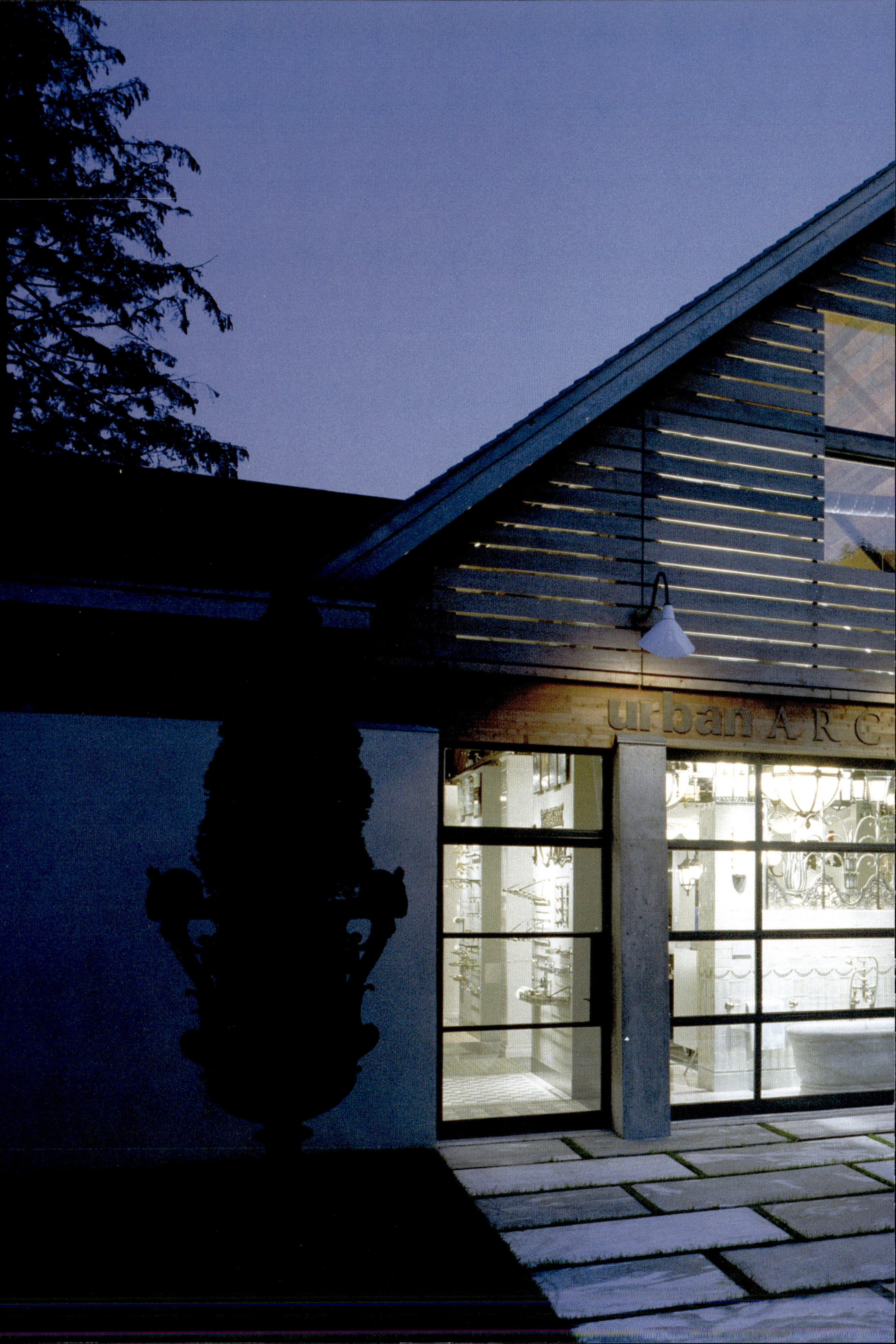
urban A R C

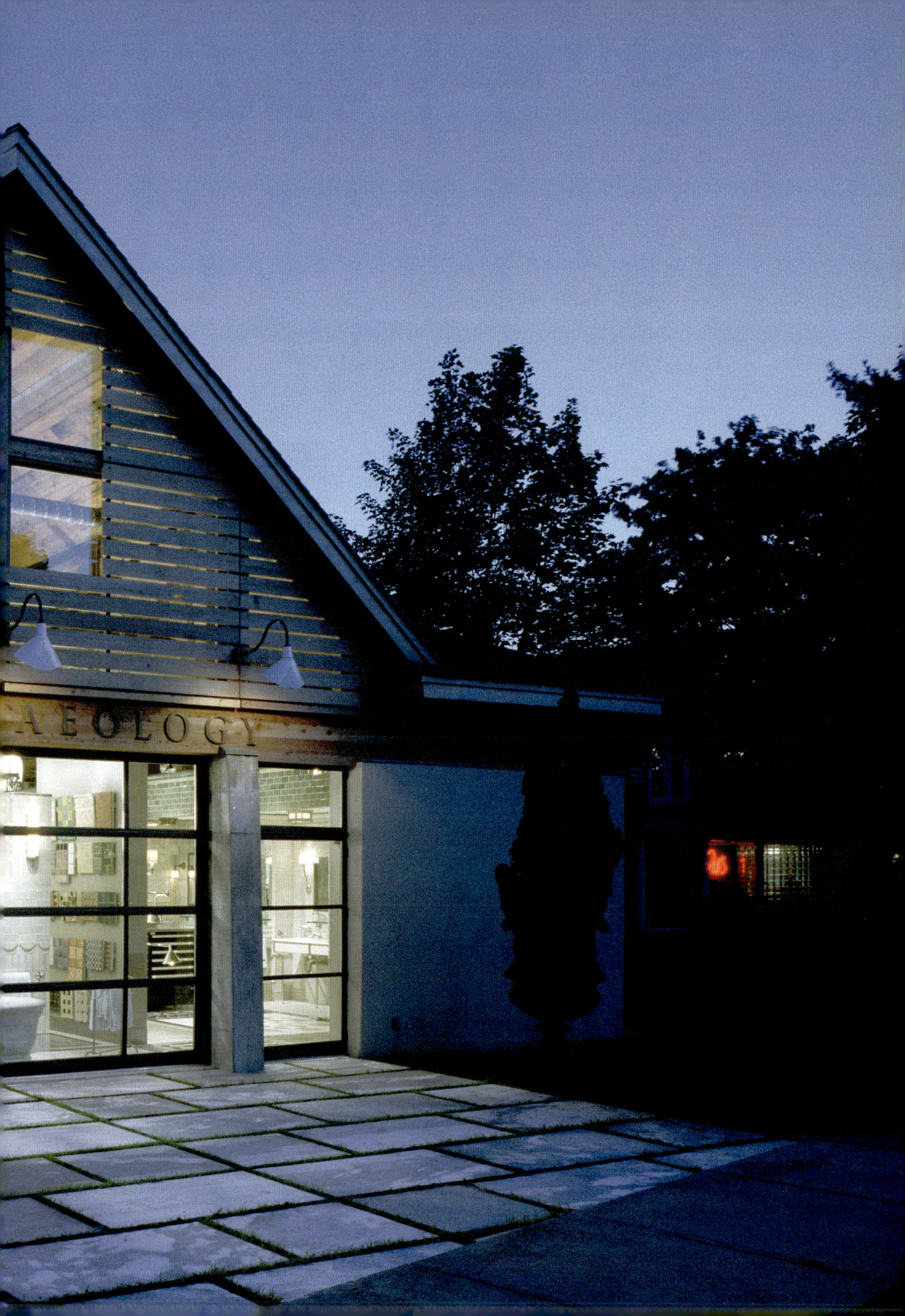
AEOLOGY

Assignment: Gasser Chair Company is a heritage-rich, leading American manufacturer of seating solutions for the hospitality and casino industries. Our mission was to reposition the brand.

Approach: Our discovery phase led to a key single insight: chairs are not just for sitting; they are an integral component of the customer experience. Rather that selling hardware, we developed a brand platform title, Gasser Dazzles, to emphasize how their chairs make a room come to life. The beginning of the process demanded a new identity that would properly align with the new vision. To start, we actually went back to the beginning—the heritage of the Gasser logo, a blue square, taking typographical and design cues from their region. After applying the classic principles of the golden section rectangle and divine proportion, the refined Gasser system was poised to represent the careful juxtaposition of engineering and art in one form. The Gasser grid was implemented to allow the maximum legibility of product and identity. The grid is executed to deliver content in a .pdf document format to digitally and traditionally printed materials. With the stage set, the performers were ready to take their place. Highly engaging photography of acrobats become metaphors attesting to the beauty, strength, and performance of Gasser chairs.

Results: From measured web traffic, sales queries, and positive industry feedback to an impressive year-over-year sales increase, the Gasser Dazzles campaign has been a success.

Designers: Andrew Yanez, Ben Bologna | **Design Firm:** Concussion, LLP | **Creative Director:** Derek Johnson | **Writer:** David Allen
Photographer: Mark Laita | **Client:** Gasser Chair Company

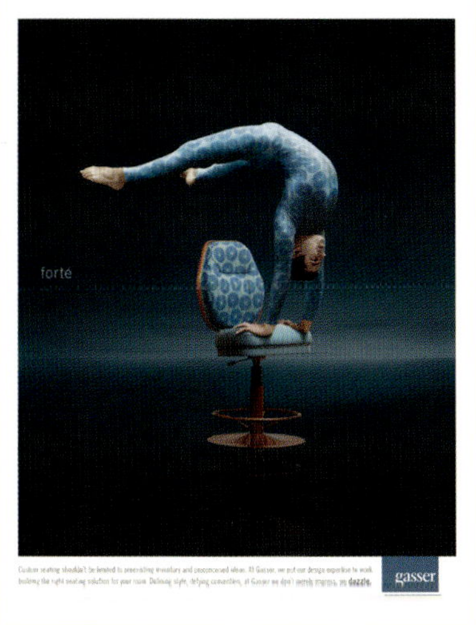

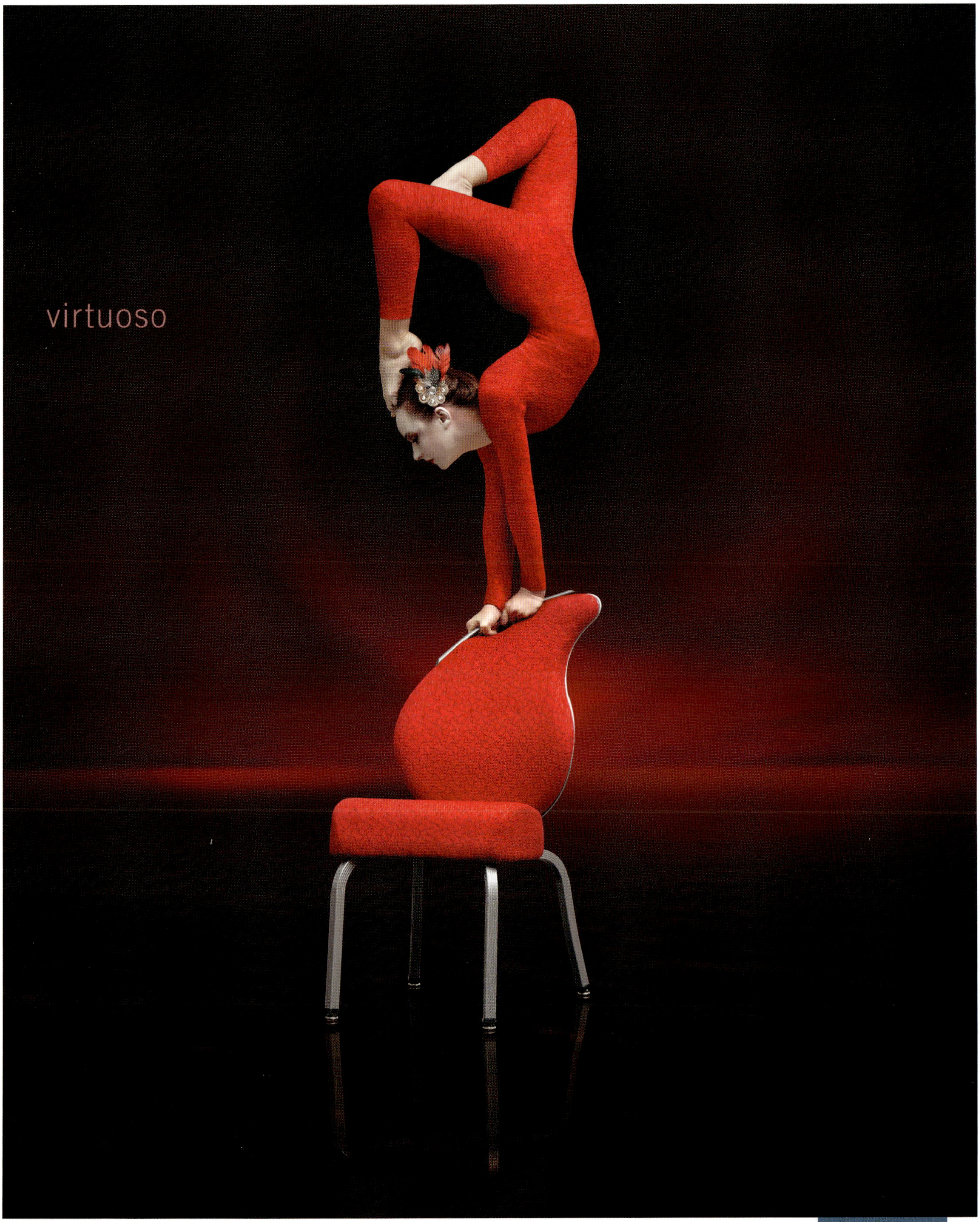

ehind the highly refined silhouette beats the heart of a gladiator. That's the genius of Gasser. We combine critically acclaimed esign with a 65-year tradition of custom craftsmanship. Because at Gasser we don't merely impress, we **dazzle.**

gasser

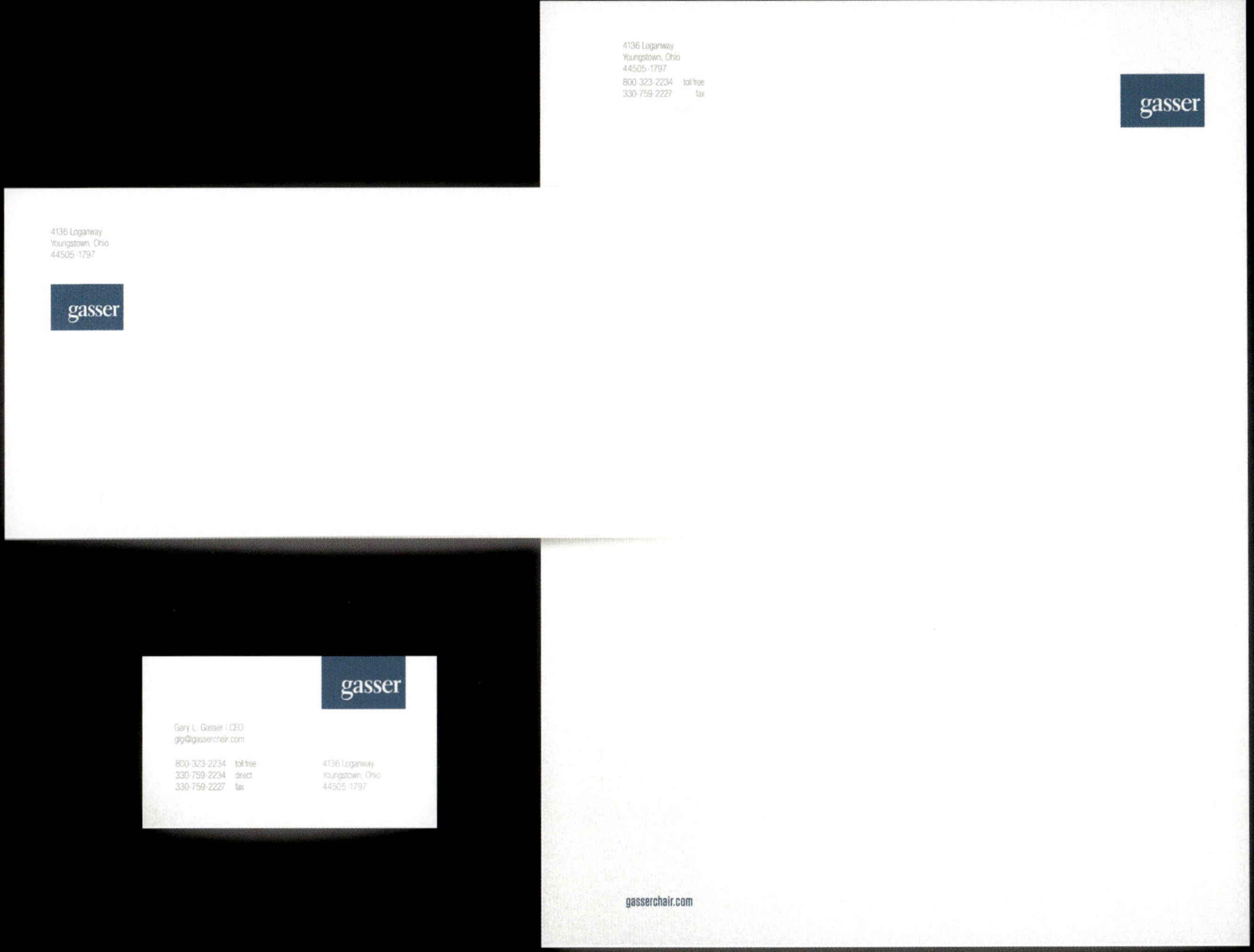

4136 Loganway
Youngstown, Ohio
44505-1797
800-323-2234 toll free
330-759-2227 fax
gasser
4136 Loganway
Youngstown, Ohio
44505-1797
gasser
gasser
Gary L. Gasser | CEO
glg@gasserchair.com
800-323-2234 toll free
330-759-2234 direct
330-759-2227 fax
4136 Loganway
Youngstown, Ohio
44505-1797
gasserchair.com

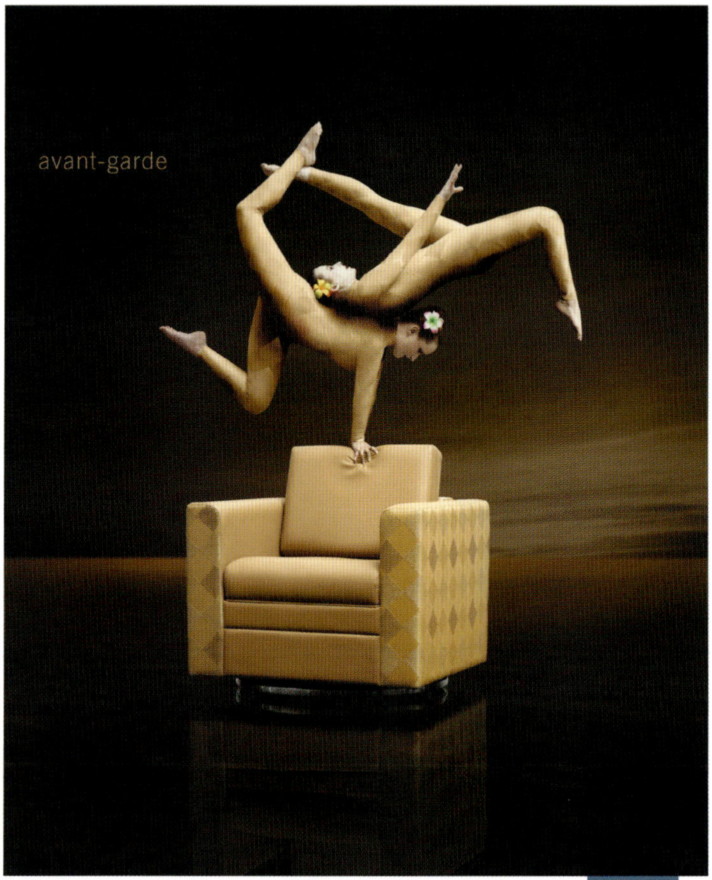

Throw out preconceived notions and you can chart new territory, one where the art of design and the law of physics converge. Fashion forward meets time-honored craftsmanship, at Gasser we don't merely impress, we **dazzle.**

gasser

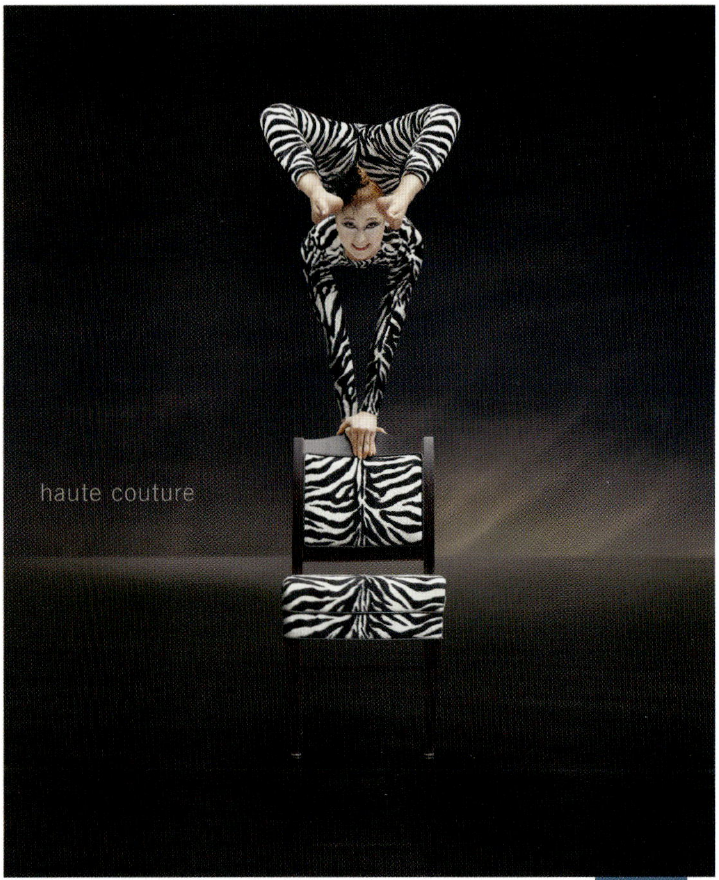

View the possibilities as limitless, and limitations disappear. Yes, high fashion and designer fabrics can coexist with Old World craftsmanship. Cutting-edge design without cutting corners, at Gasser we don't merely impress, we **dazzle.**

gasser

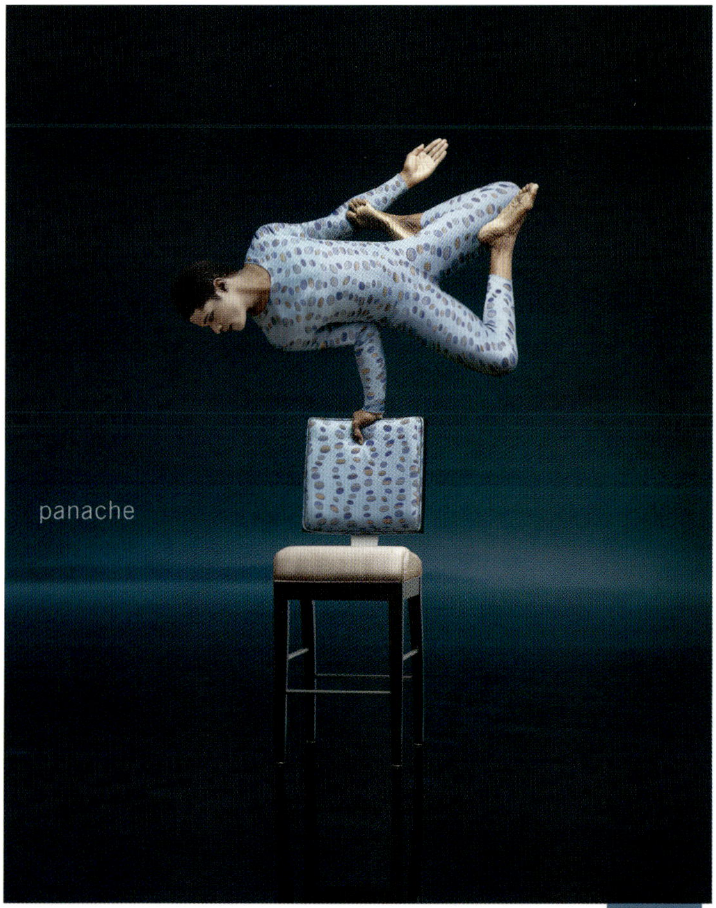

Gasser chairs occupy that lofty perch where fashion sense and common sense intersect. Incorporating a stylish flair for design with a fanatical devotion to detail, Gasser chairs don't merely impress, they **dazzle.**

gasser

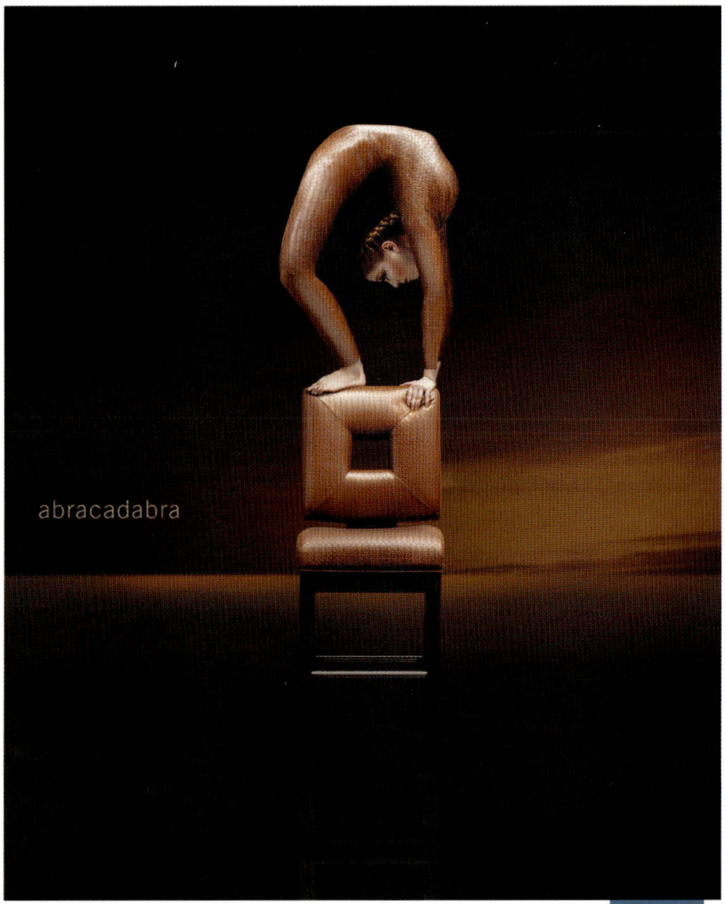

The magic of a Gasser chair is not only how it performs, it's how we perform. For over 65 years, Gasser has bent over backwards to create amazing customer experiences. Performance without proviso, at Gasser we don't merely impress, we **dazzle.**

gasser

Assignment: The project goal is to create a quirky and fun brand that is synonymous with the ideas and experience of travels and journeys, of the process of discovery, of that innocent dream-like feeling. The vision of the hotel owner has always been grounded by the history and surroundings of his property. Since each floor is designed by a different designer, the floors all look and feel very different. Our challenge is to achieve a cohesive voice and unity through the branding and identity—a voice that will also augment the ideals and creativity of the project and still preserve the honesty of "wanderlust."

Approach: Little India has always been a sort of a eye-opener and cultural revelation to travelers, providing that wanderlust effect. We want to stay true to that experience. The building, being previously an elementary school in the early 1900s, inspired us to add that child-like innocence to the branding—folding a paper plane or assembling a plane kit, the dream of traveling the world one day. Various forms of ephemerals and keepsakes experienced during a journey were carefully studied, considered, and deployed onto the collateral set: a bus ticket for rate cards, an air ticket for a brochure inserted into an air-ticket wallet, and a multi-functional notebook named ITINERARY. Various VISA stamps are ink-stamped onto the ITINERARY, depending on the various activities the guests partake in—checking in, assignment of room number, assigning the Wi-Fi password, payment, etc. The notebooks are useful guidebooks with area maps, train/bus maps, listings of shops and restaurants to check out, as well as blank pages for notes.

Results: The design of the hotel, its branding and identity materials (like the Itinerary, rate cards, and establishment cards, the check-in experience, the restaurant, and the hotel environment) have totaled up to an experience that has made Wanderlust Hotel the *it* place in Singapore. Wanderlust Hotel is also a recommended place to stay at on the Singapore government-run tourism website YOURSINGAPORE.COM. The deployment of ITINERARY has completely changed the way a guest checks into the hotel and has tremendously elevated the Wanderlust experience. It improved the check-in work flow, converting a laborious and dreaded process into something fun and a talking point; sentiments shared by both the guests and the hotel reception staff.

"I am extremely happy about how Foreign Policy has helped translate our vision into something so quirky, happy, and fun, hitting the nail right on the head, and yet a very honest portrayal of the vibe we are looking for in this hotel. We have gotten many, many good press because of this, it's a job very well done." —Loh Lik Peng, owner of Wanderlust Hotel

Not only that, but because of the successful branding, the hotel has become something of a benchmark that competitors watch and learn from. It has become somewhat of an inspiration, since we could observe several other establishments seemingly trying hard on their brand and identity. Boutique design hotels have become suddenly the hip thing in Singapore—either you want to start one, work at one, or have been to one—it makes you feel you are "in."

Designer: Yah-Leng Yu | **Design Firm:** Foreign Policy Design Group | **Creative Director:** Yah-Leng Yu | **Client:** Unlisted Collection

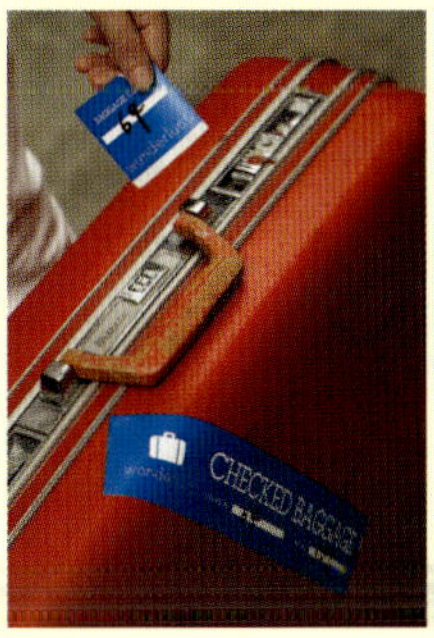

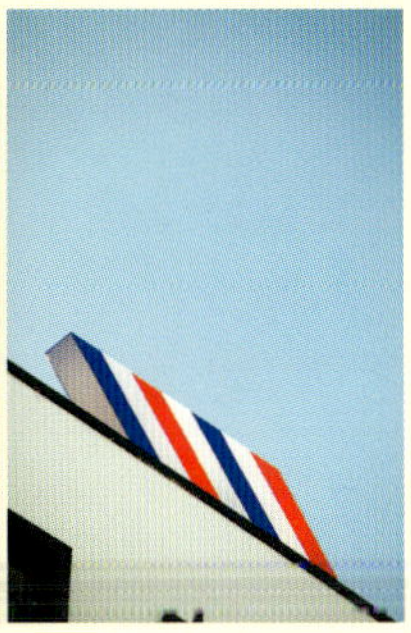

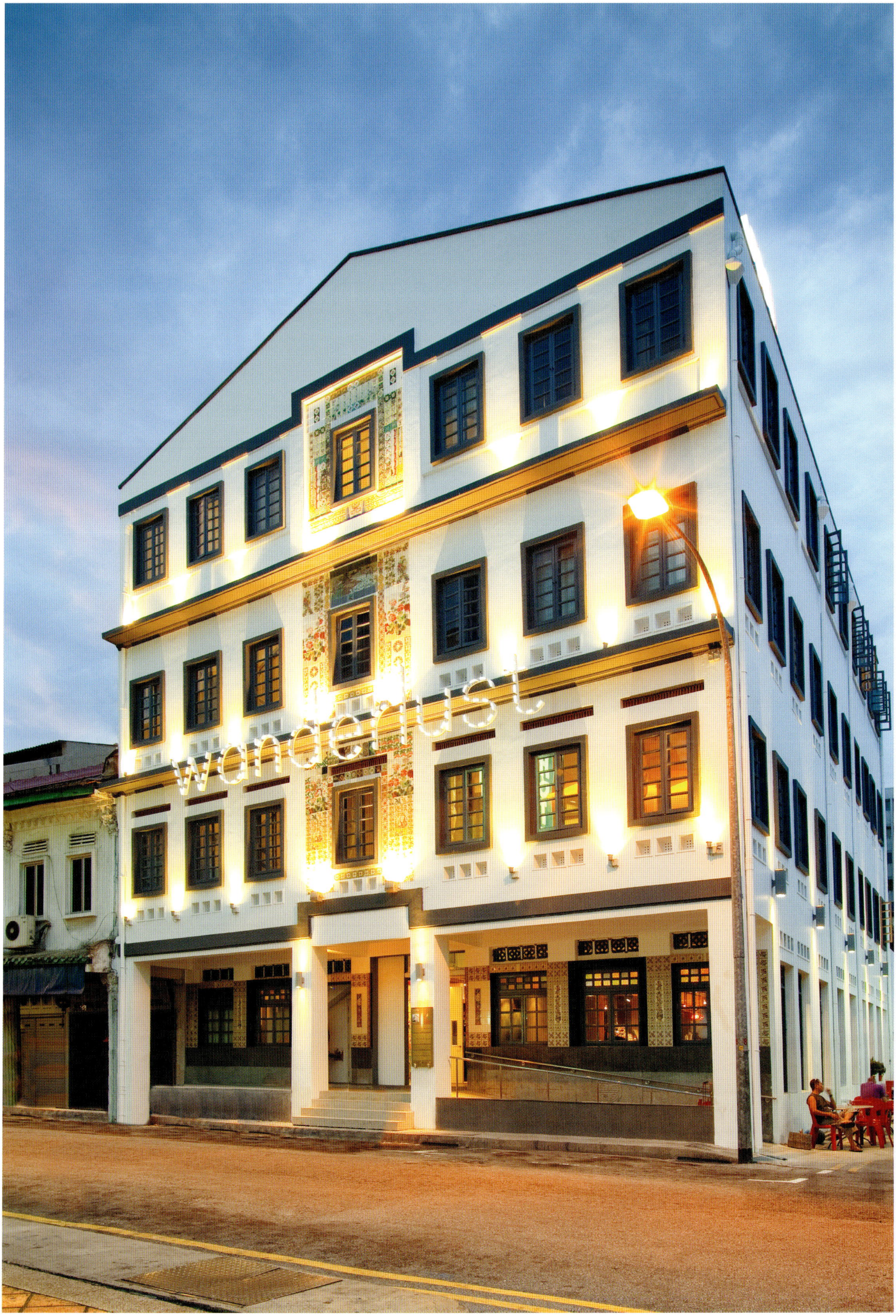

Foreign Policy Design Group (this spread)

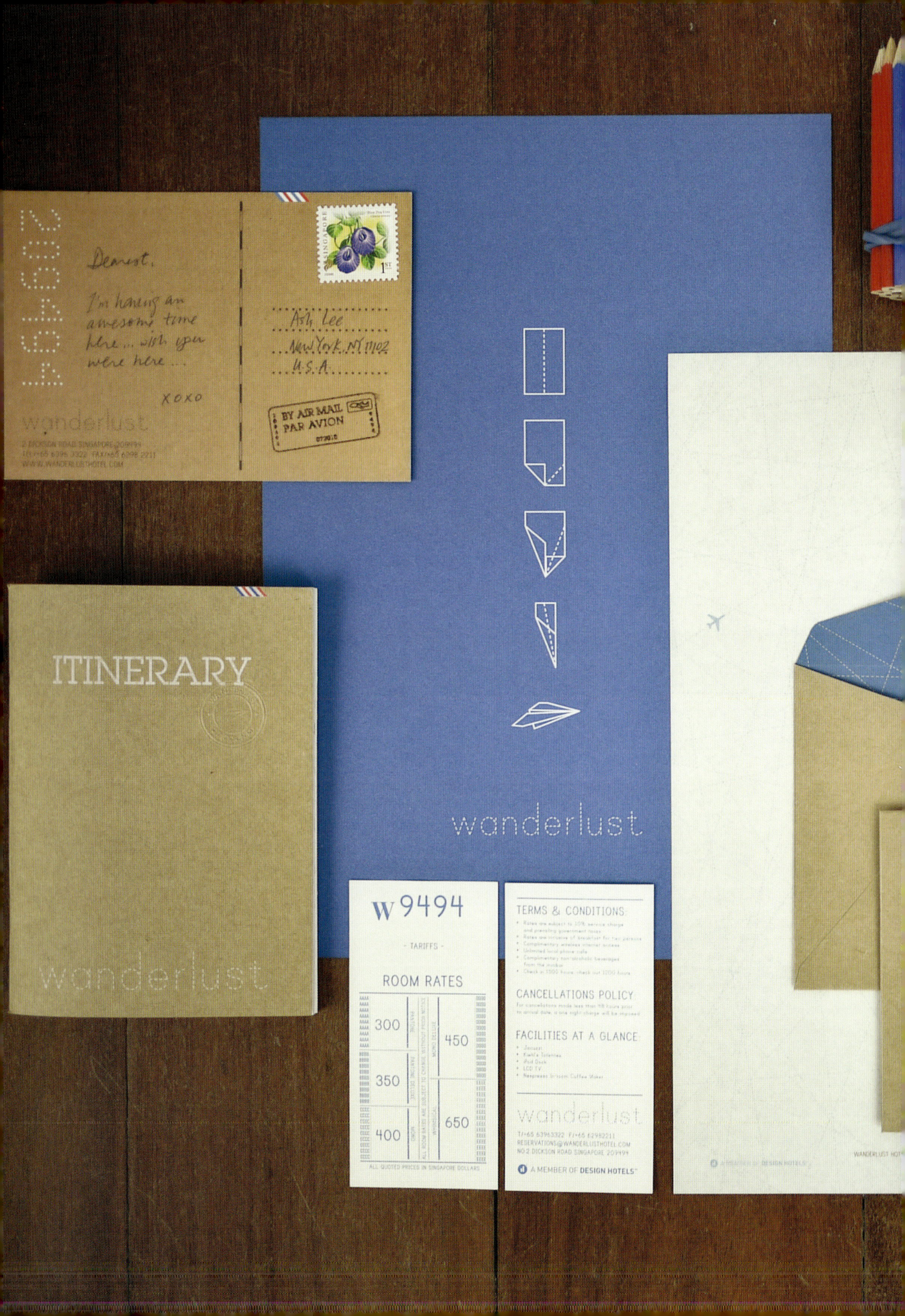
209494
Dearest,
I'm having an awesome time here... wish you were here...
xoxo
wanderlust
2 DICKSON ROAD SINGAPORE 209494
TEL/+65 6396 3322 FAX/+65 6298 2211
WWW.WANDERLUSTHOTEL.COM
Ash Lee
New York NY 11102
U.S.A.
BY AIR MAIL
PAR AVION
SINGAPORE
1st
ITINERARY
wanderlust
wanderlust
W 9494
- TARIFFS -
ROOM RATES
300
350
400
450
650
ALL QUOTED PRICES IN SINGAPORE DOLLARS
TERMS & CONDITIONS
CANCELLATIONS POLICY
FACILITIES AT A GLANCE
wanderlust
T/+65 63963322 F/+65 62982211
RESERVATIONS@WANDERLUSTHOTEL.COM
NO 2 DICKSON ROAD SINGAPORE 209494
A MEMBER OF DESIGN HOTELS™

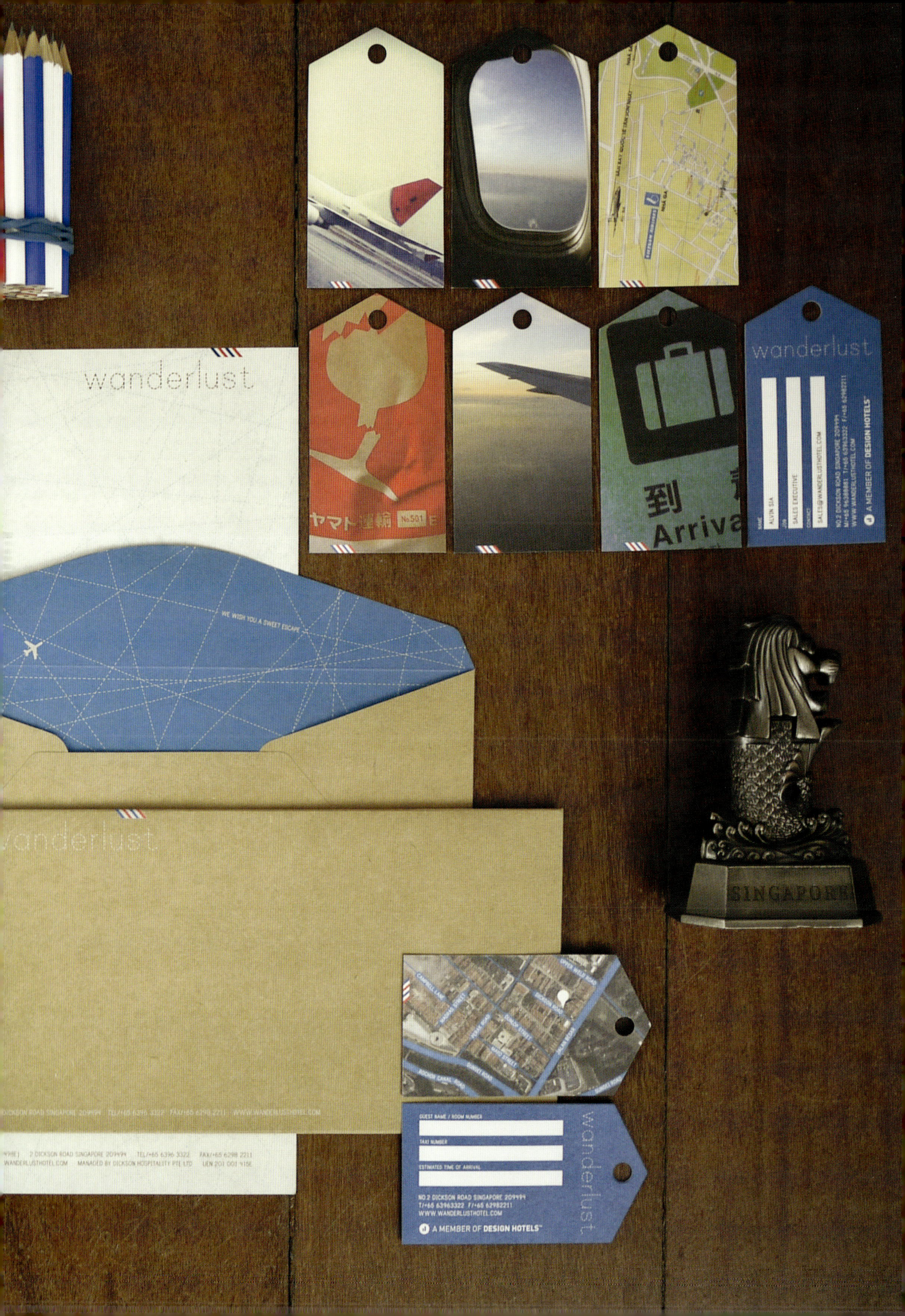
wanderlust
wanderlust
ヤマト運輸
No.501
到
Arriva
wanderlust
NAME
ALVIN SIA
JOB
SALES EXECUTIVE
CONTACT
SALES@WANDERLUSTHOTEL.COM
A MEMBER OF DESIGN HOTELS™
WE WISH YOU A SWEET ESCAPE
wanderlust
SINGAPORE
GUEST NAME / ROOM NUMBER
TAXI NUMBER
ESTIMATED TIME OF ARRIVAL
NO.2 DICKSON ROAD SINGAPORE 209494
T/+65 63963322 F/+65 62982211
WWW.WANDERLUSTHOTEL.COM
A MEMBER OF DESIGN HOTELS™
wanderlust

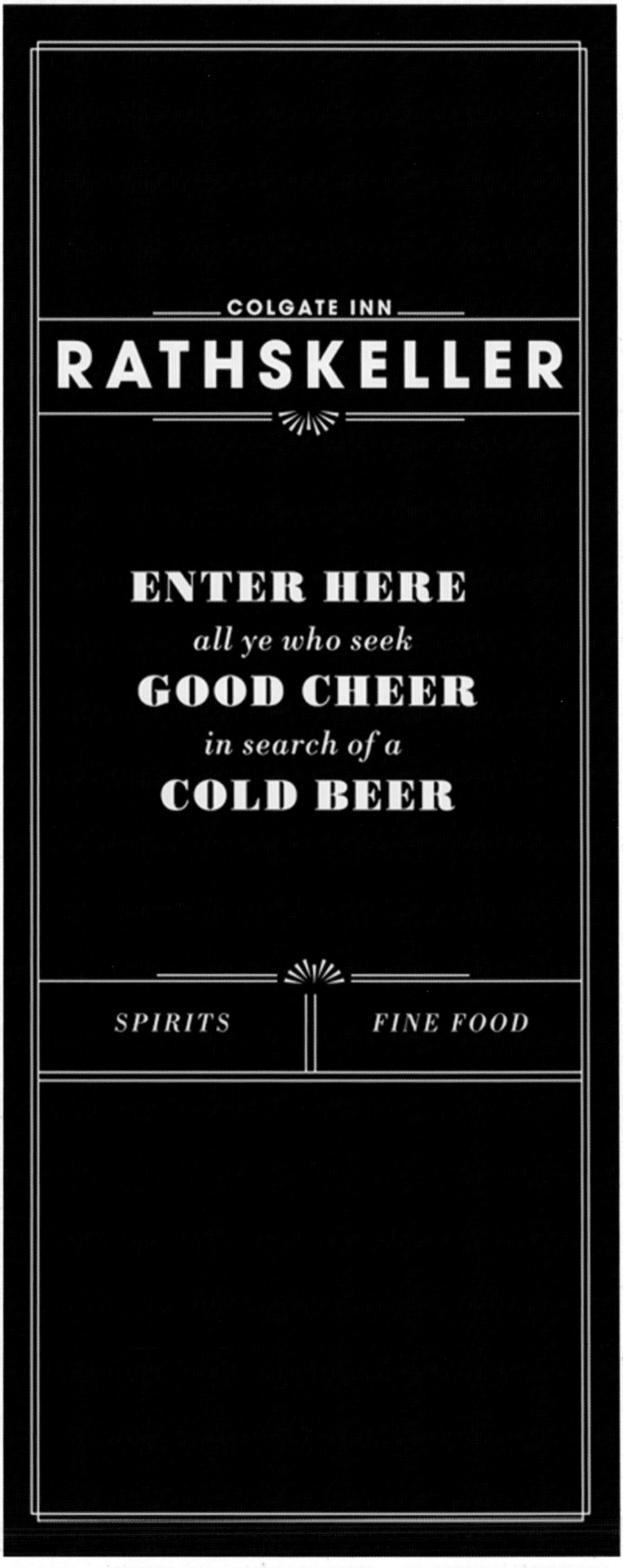
COLGATE INN
RATHSKELLER
ENTER HERE
all ye who seek
GOOD CHEER
in search of a
COLD BEER
SPIRITS
FINE FOOD

Assignment: EBD was asked to provide a solution for a brand that was collegiate but still versatile enough for the Inn to be recognized as a destination for travelers through upstate New York. Additionally, EBD was asked to incorporate Colgate University's burgundy color into the branding.

Approach: We had continuous communication and collaboration with interior designer Thom Felicia Studio, numerous University staff board members, and the Inn management team to ensure all visions were aligned. We focused on developing a design that was time-period appropriate to fit with the building and the charm of a small country inn, while featuring typography that is fresh but colonial in reference. Backs of door hangers, the sides of the signs, and insides of menus weave in the University's burgundy color.

Results: The guests are very impressed and the University is thrilled by the improvements to the Inn. According to the client, "Ellen did a masterful job navigating the diversity of opinions and priorities. The final outcome is something all stakeholders embrace. ... Their creative solution reflects the appropriate time period of the building, unifies the Inn's interior design, and embraces the charm of a small country inn."

Designer: Ellen Bruss Design | **Design Firms:** Ellen Bruss Design, LLC | **Creative Director:** Ellen Bruss | **Client:** Colgate University

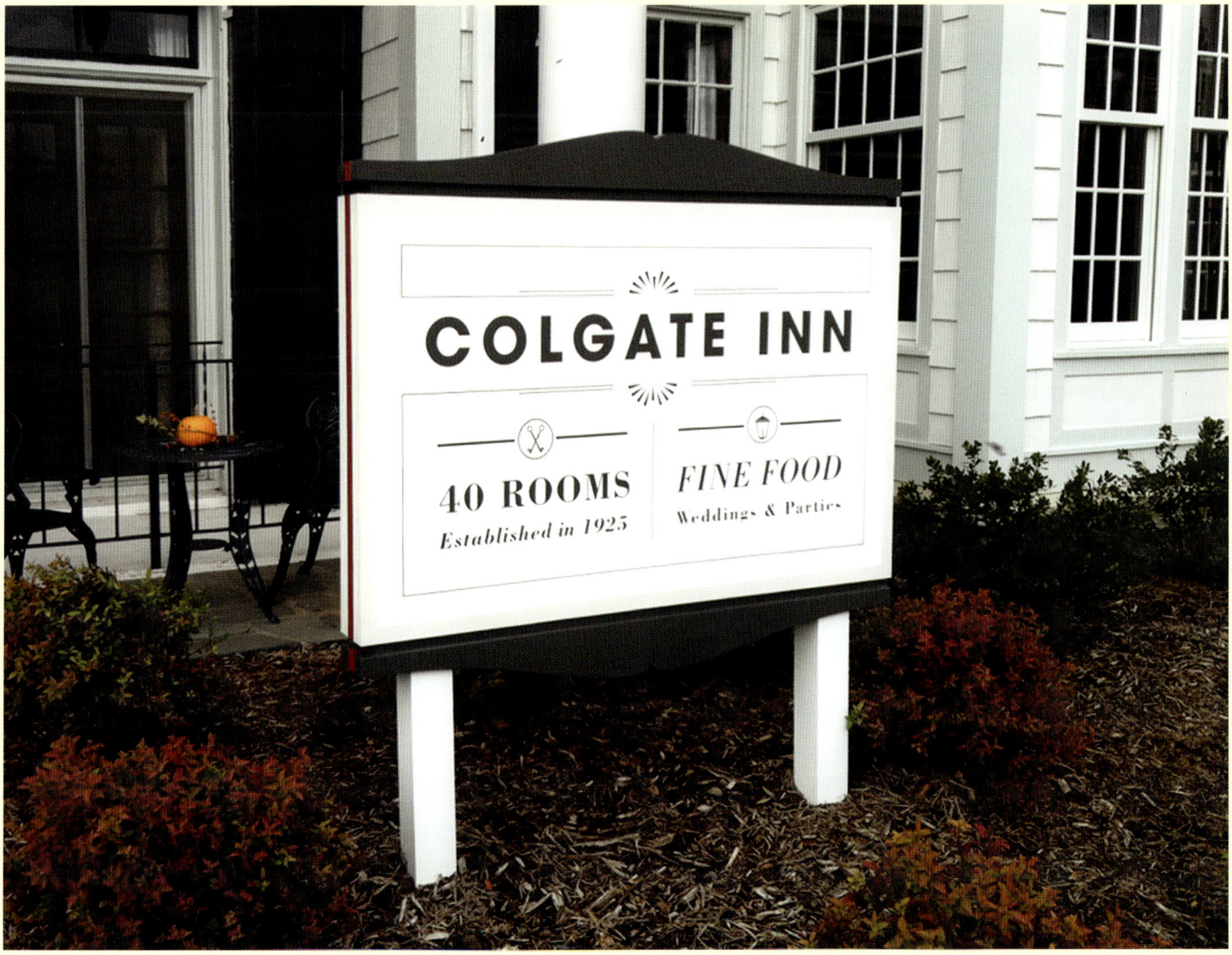

Ellen Bruss Design, LLC (this spread) | Colgate University | Hotel

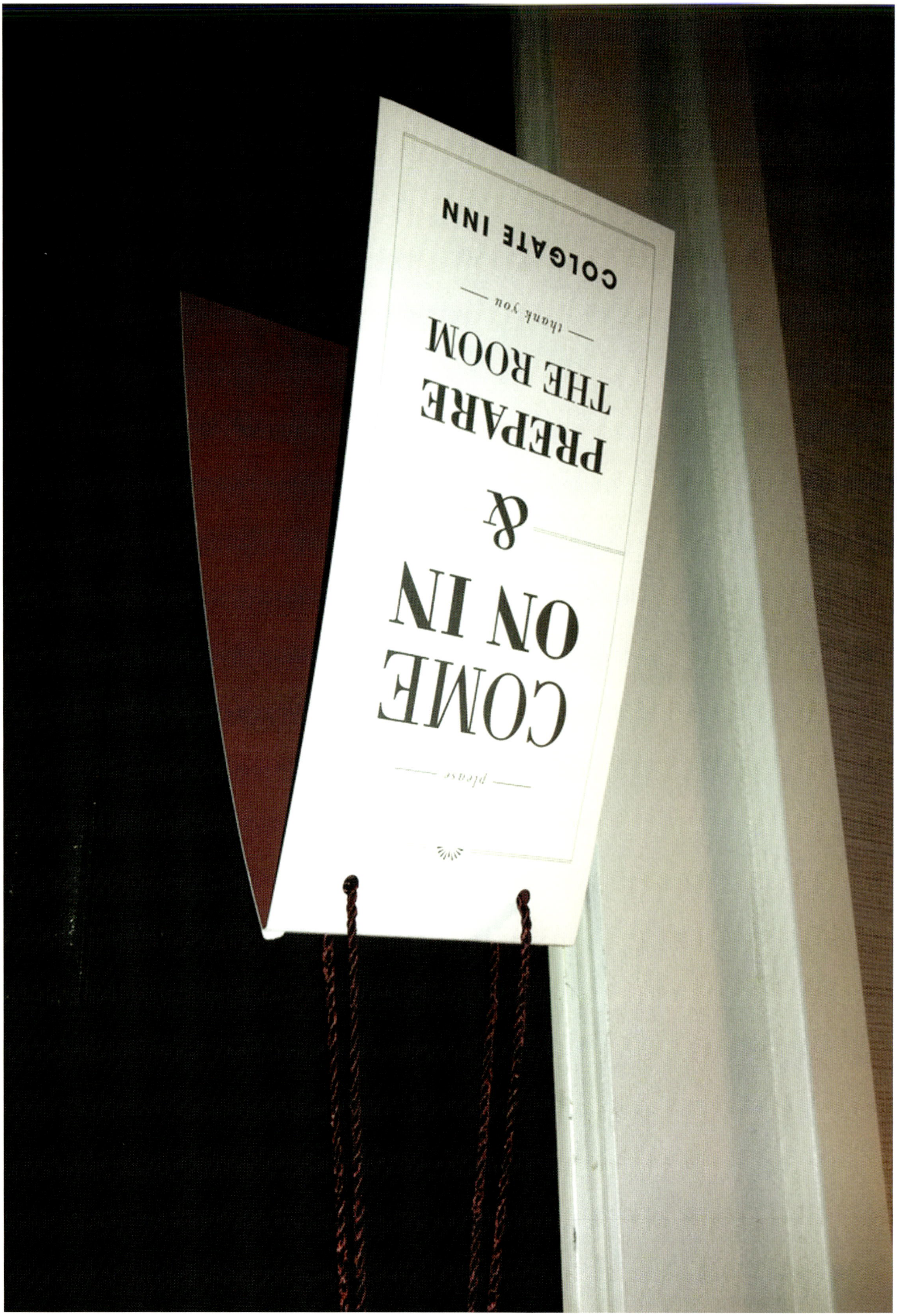
COLGATE INN
thank you
PREPARE
THE ROOM
&
COME
ON IN
please

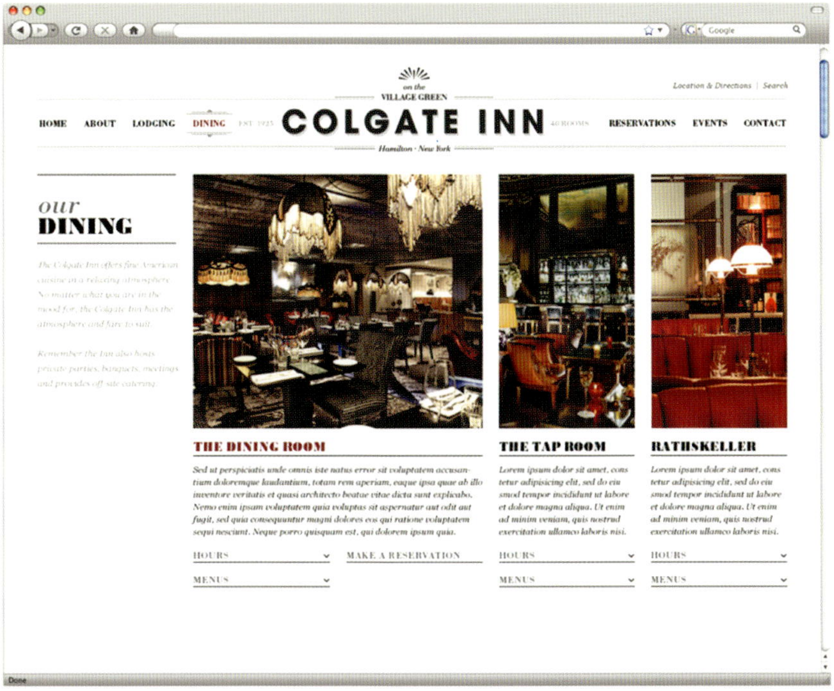
on the
VILLAGE GREEN
Location & Directions | Search
HOME
ABOUT
LODGING
DINING
COLGATE INN
RESERVATIONS
EVENTS
CONTACT
Hamilton · New York
our
DINING
THE DINING ROOM
Sed ut perspiciatis unde omnis iste natus error sit voluptatem accusantium doloremque laudantium, totam rem aperiam, eaque ipsa quae ab illo inventore veritatis et quasi architecto beatae vitae dicta sunt explicabo. Nemo enim ipsam voluptatem quia voluptas sit aspernatur aut odit aut fugit, sed quia consequuntur magni dolores eos qui ratione voluptatem sequi nesciunt. Neque porro quisquam est, qui dolorem ipsum quia.
HOURS
MAKE A RESERVATION
MENUS
THE TAP ROOM
Lorem ipsum dolor sit amet, cons tetur adipisicing elit, sed do eiu smod tempor incididunt ut labore et dolore magna aliqua. Ut enim ad minim veniam, quis nostrud exercitation ullamco laboris nisi.
HOURS
MENUS
RATHSKELLER
Lorem ipsum dolor sit amet, cons tetur adipisicing elit, sed do eiu smod tempor incididunt ut labore et dolore magna aliqua. Ut enim ad minim veniam, quis nostrud exercitation ullamco laboris nisi.
HOURS
MENUS

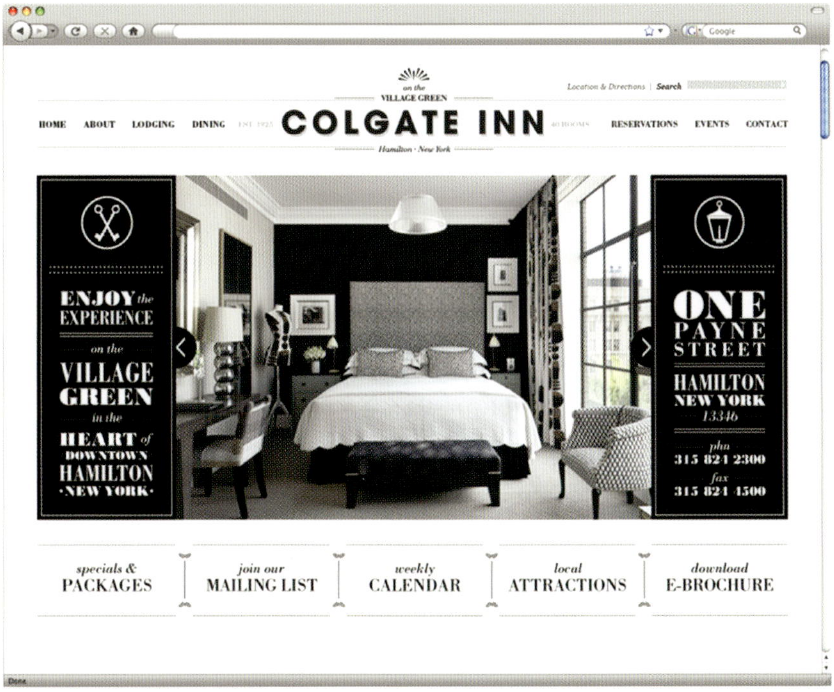
on the
VILLAGE GREEN
Location & Directions | Search
HOME
ABOUT
LODGING
DINING
COLGATE INN
RESERVATIONS
EVENTS
CONTACT
Hamilton · New York
ENJOY the EXPERIENCE
on the
VILLAGE GREEN
in the
HEART of DOWNTOWN HAMILTON
·NEW YORK·
ONE PAYNE STREET
HAMILTON NEW YORK 13346
phn
315 824 2300
fax
315 824 4500
specials & PACKAGES
join our MAILING LIST
weekly CALENDAR
local ATTRACTIONS
download E-BROCHURE

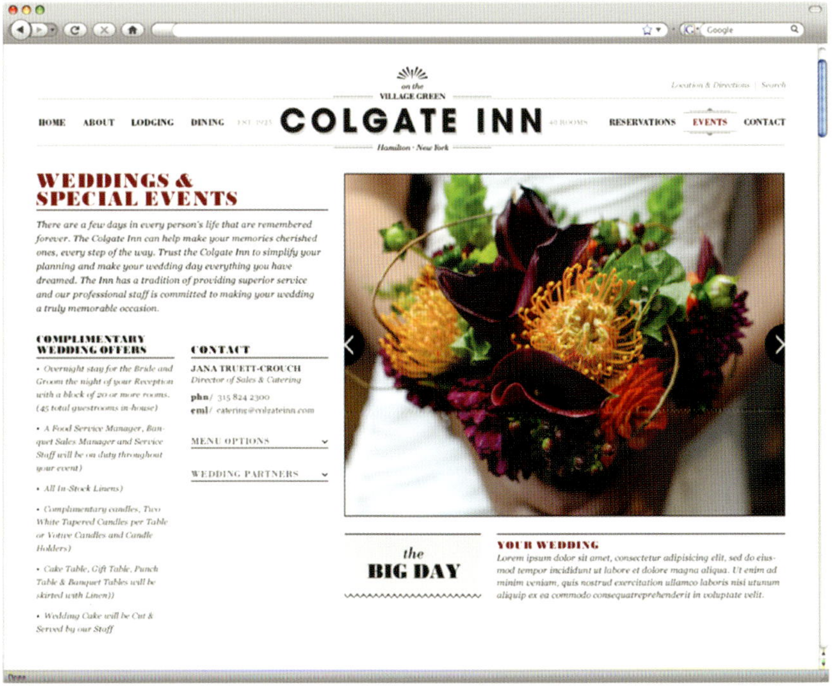
on the
VILLAGE GREEN
HOME
ABOUT
LODGING
DINING
COLGATE INN
RESERVATIONS
EVENTS
CONTACT
Hamilton · New York
WEDDINGS & SPECIAL EVENTS
There are a few days in every person's life that are remembered forever. The Colgate Inn can help make your memories cherished ones, every step of the way. Trust the Colgate Inn to simplify your planning and make your wedding day everything you have dreamed. The Inn has a tradition of providing superior service and our professional staff is committed to making your wedding a truly memorable occasion.
COMPLIMENTARY WEDDING OFFERS
CONTACT
JANA TRUETT-CROUCH
Director of Sales & Catering
phn/ 315 824 2300
MENU OPTIONS
WEDDING PARTNERS
the BIG DAY
YOUR WEDDING
Lorem ipsum dolor sit amet, consectetur adipisicing elit, sed do eiusmod tempor incididunt ut labore et dolore magna aliqua. Ut enim ad minim veniam, quis nostrud exercitation ullamco laboris nisi utunum aliquip ex ea commodo consequatreprehenderit in voluptate velit.

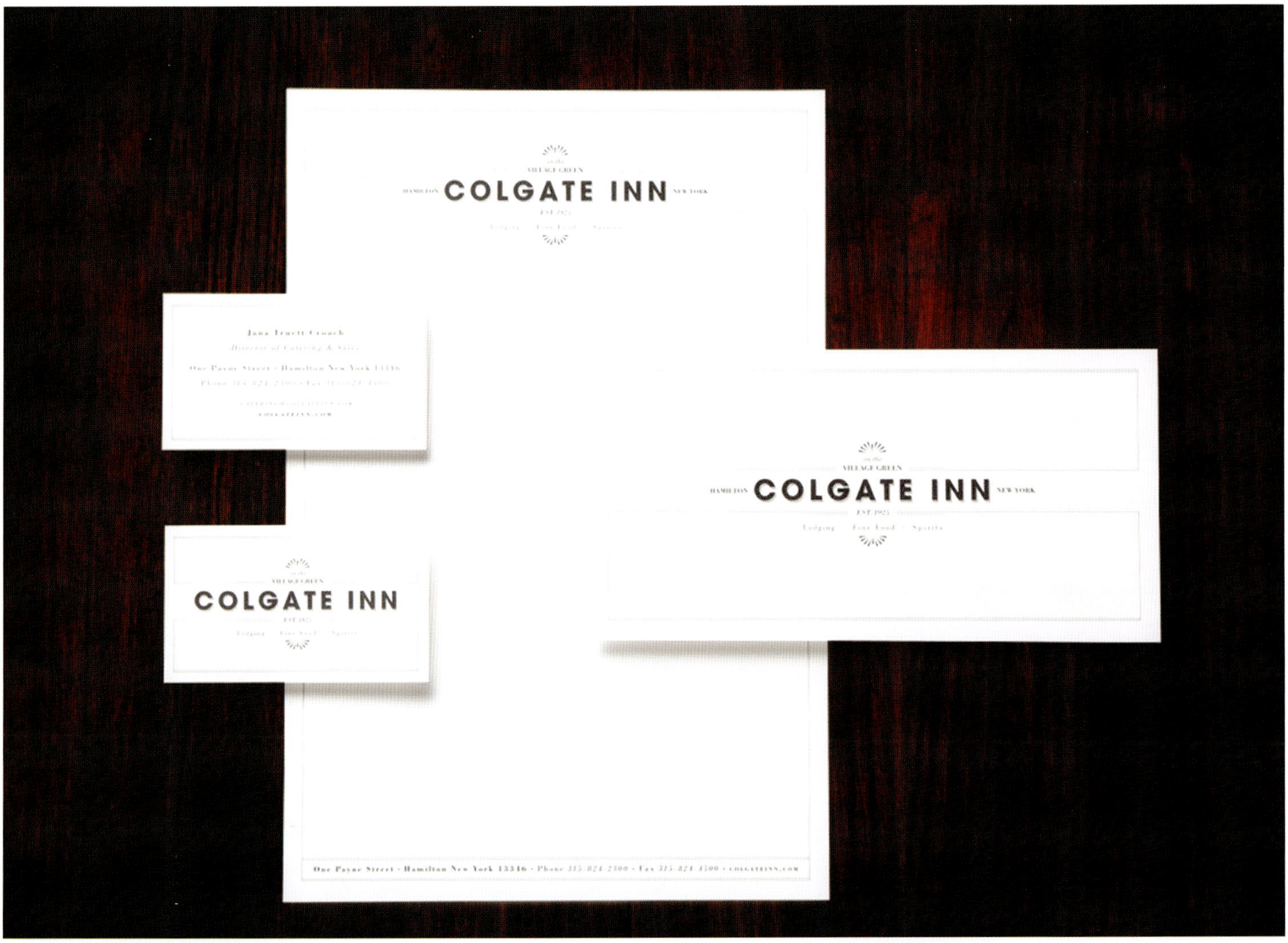
COLGATE INN
HAMILTON
NEW YORK
COLGATE INN
HAMILTON
NEW YORK
COLGATE INN
One Payne Street · Hamilton New York 13346

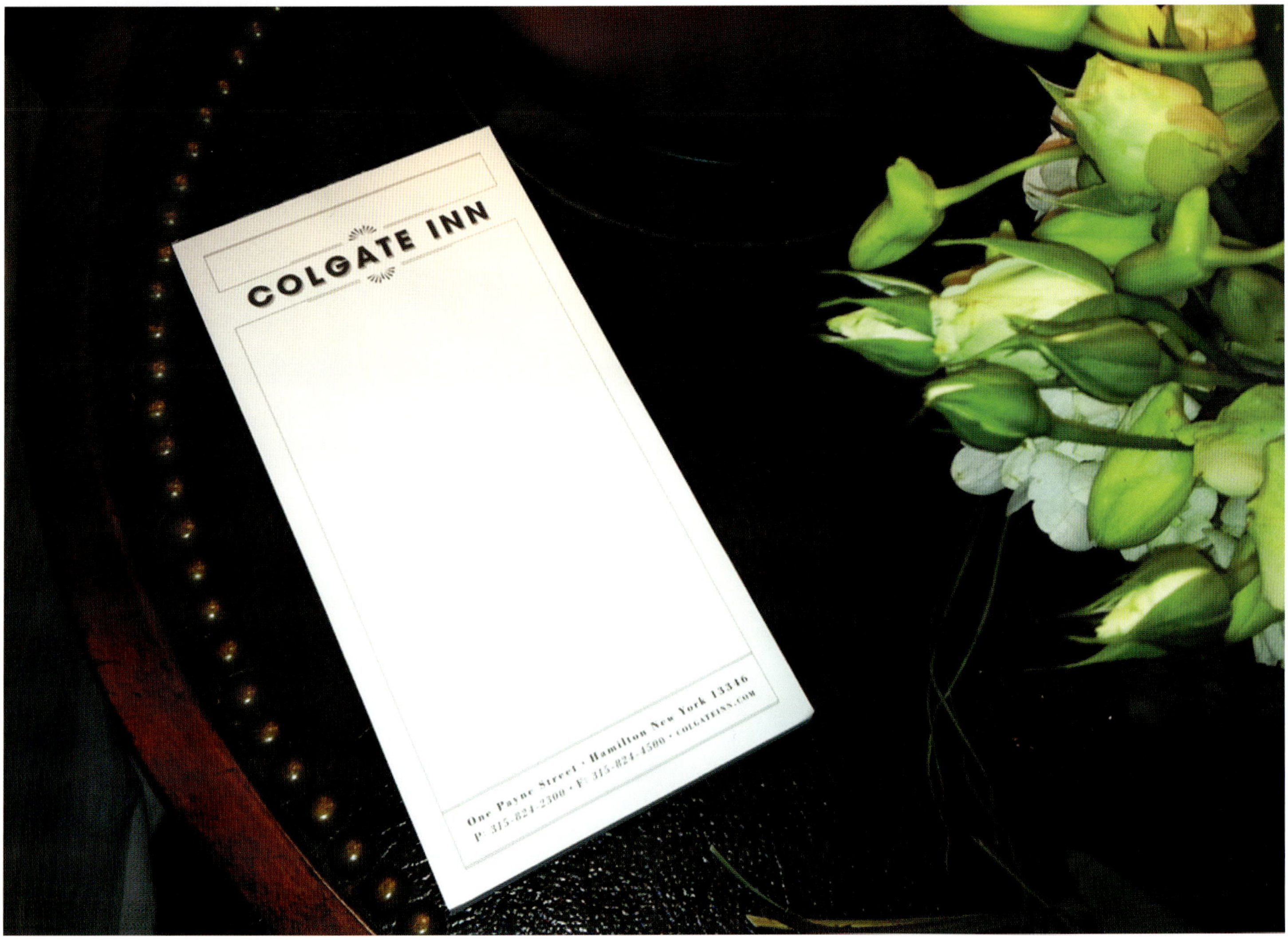
COLGATE INN
One Payne Street · Hamilton New York 13346
P: 315-824-2300 · F: 315-824-4500 · COLGATEINN.COM

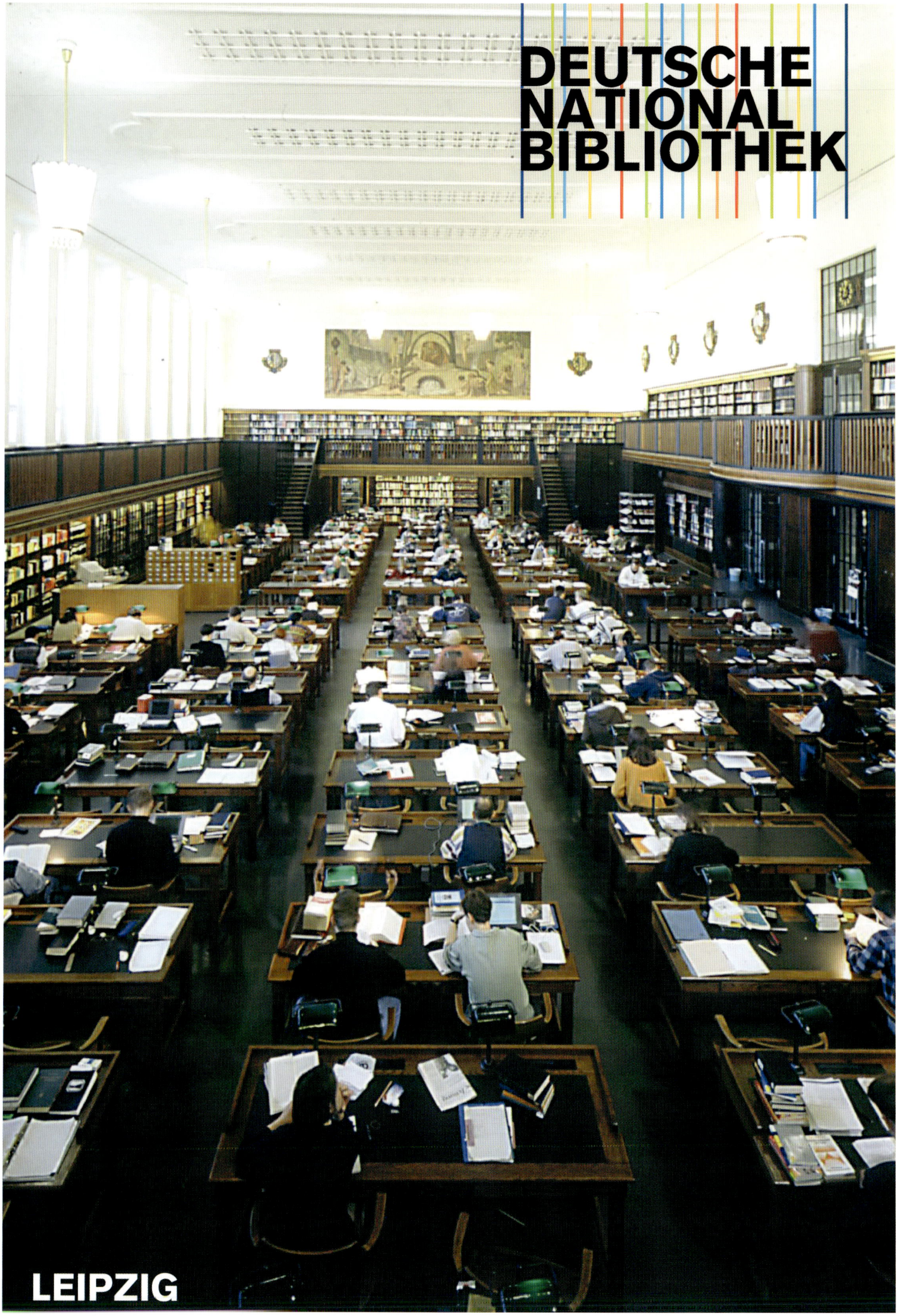
DEUTSCHE
NATIONAL
BIBLIOTHEK
LEIPZIG

Assignment: The assignment was for a new corporate design for the German National Library, which serves as the national authority for collecting and lending books, and as a museum for books and music, including a collection of correspondence and books of writers in exile.

Approach: Showing the back of books in different colors, as well as lines as metaphor for code, reflects that collecting and owning books is the main task of the German National Library.

Results: An attractive, versatile, colorful corporate design for all types of media.

Designer: Patrick Koch | **Design Firm:** Claus Koch | **Art Directors:** Patrick Koch, Claus Koch | **Creative Directors:** Claus Koch, Patrick Koch
Illustrator: Patrick Koch | **Typographer:** Patrick Koch | **Client:** German National Library

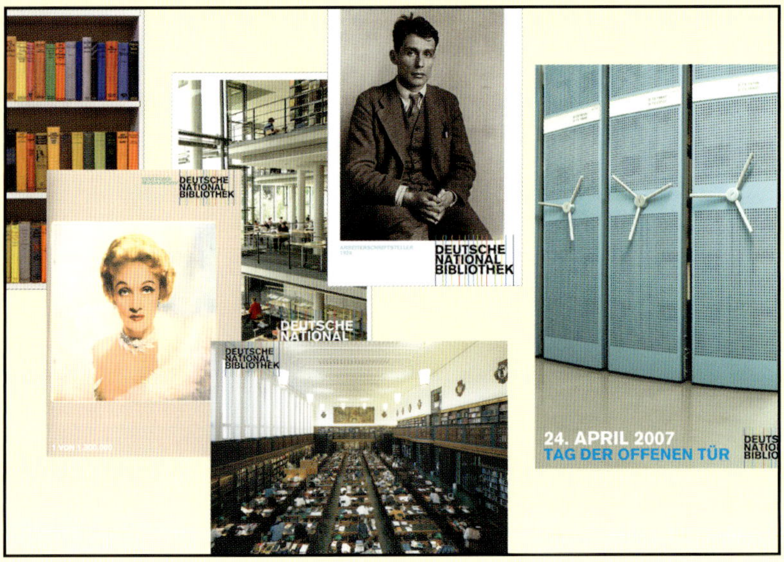

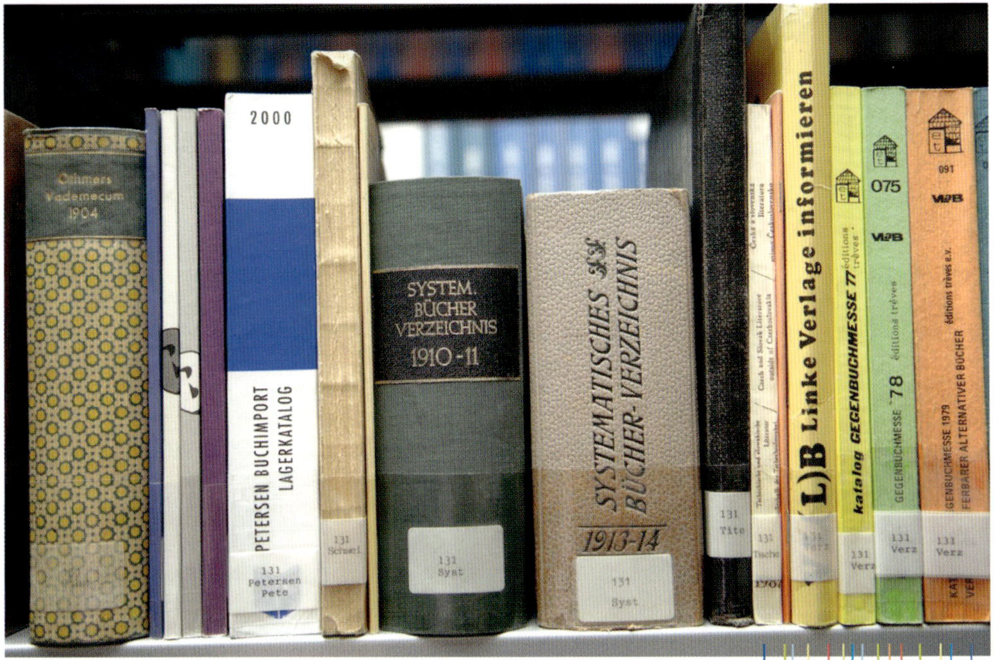

17 VON 22.000.000

DEUTSCHE NATIONAL BIBLIOTHEK

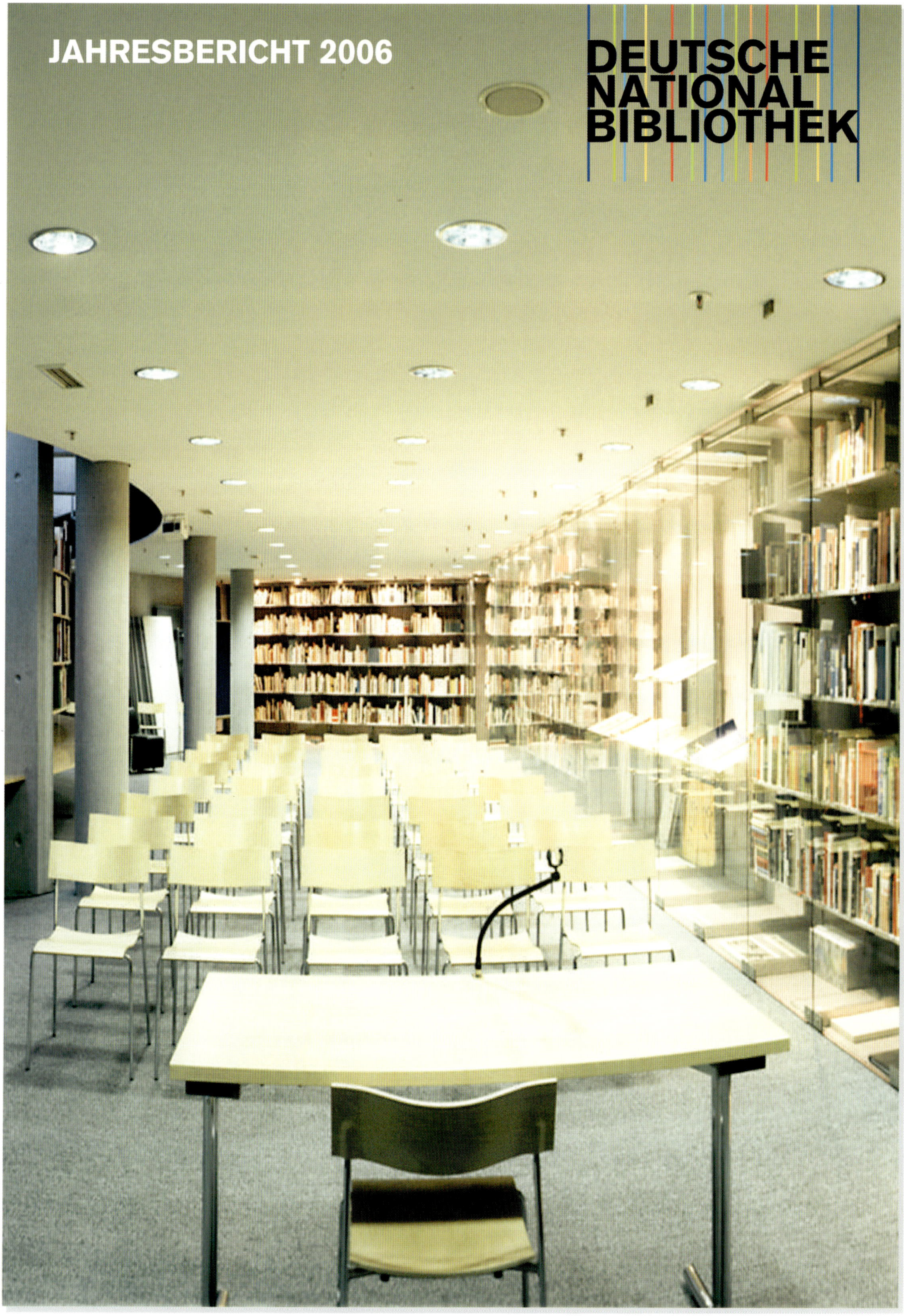
JAHRESBERICHT 2006
DEUTSCHE
NATIONAL
BIBLIOTHEK

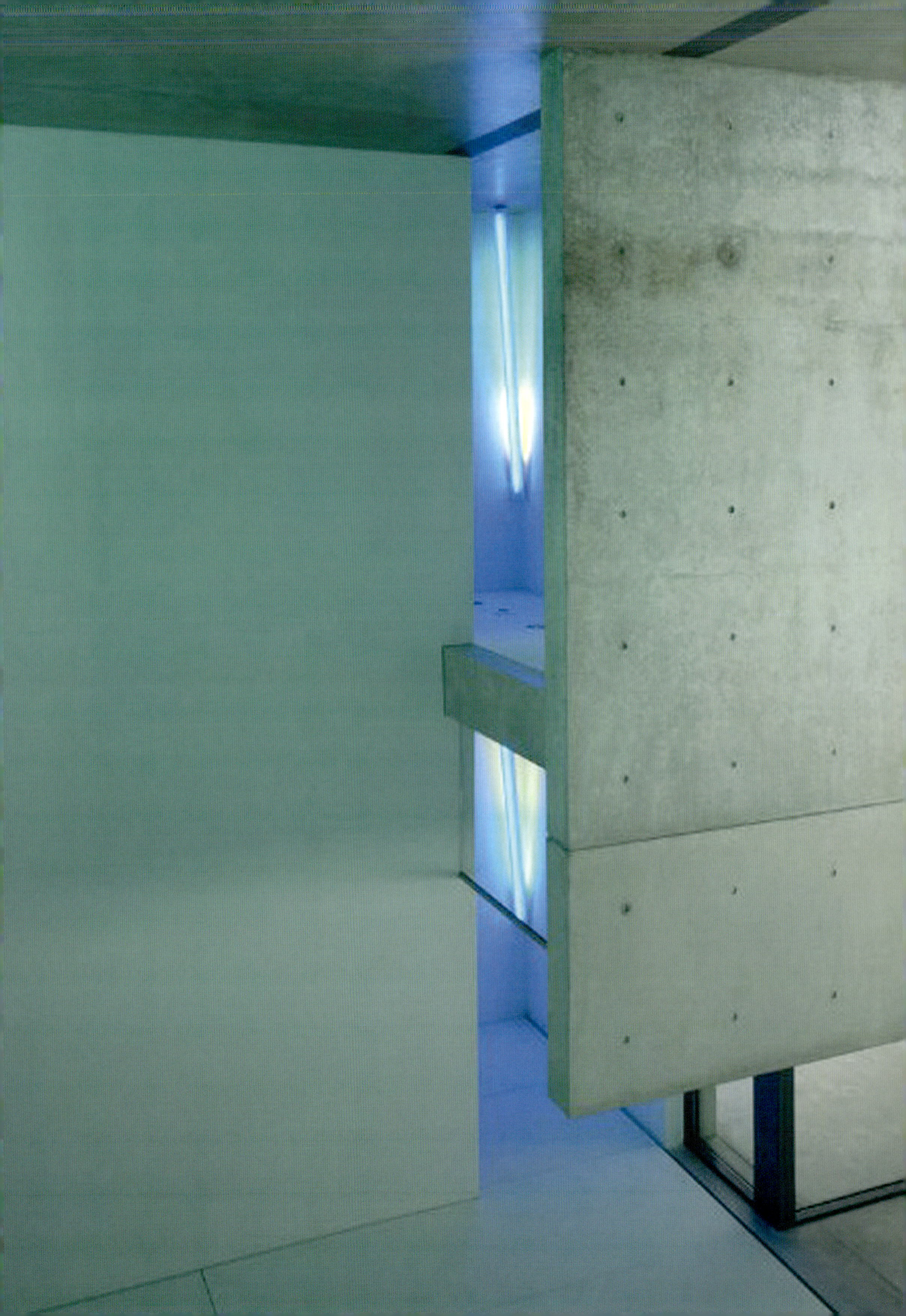

Assignment: Web and printed catalogues for an exhibition of Dan Flavin's light sculpture installations at the Pulitzer Foundation for the Arts. The Pulitzer always frames their exhibitions in the context of Tadao Ando's elegantly minimalist architecture—a departure from most exhibition catalogues, which show the work without any context.

Approach: Flavin's works filled the Pulitzer with volumes of light so present that it was like swimming in perfume. Capturing that ineffable essence was the goal for both web and print materials, with color-saturated images that shifted hue and intensity from page to page, click to click.

Results: This is one of a series of successful partnerships between TOKY and the Pulitzer. Tyler Green, of the well-respected art blog Modern Art Notes, said, "No one does single-shows-in-space websites better than the Pulitzer (witness: Dan Flavin, Water) and I wouldn't miss a one of 'em."

Designers: Jay David, Eric Thoelke | **Design Firm:** TOKY Branding + Design | **Creative Director:** Eric Thoelke | **Photographer:** Robert Pettus
Web Producer: Melissa Allen | **Lead Developer:** David Knape | **Developer:** Tyler Craft | **Client:** The Pulitzer Foundation for the Arts

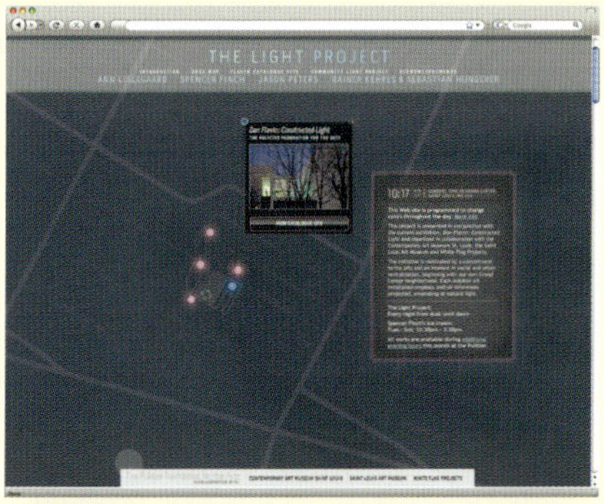

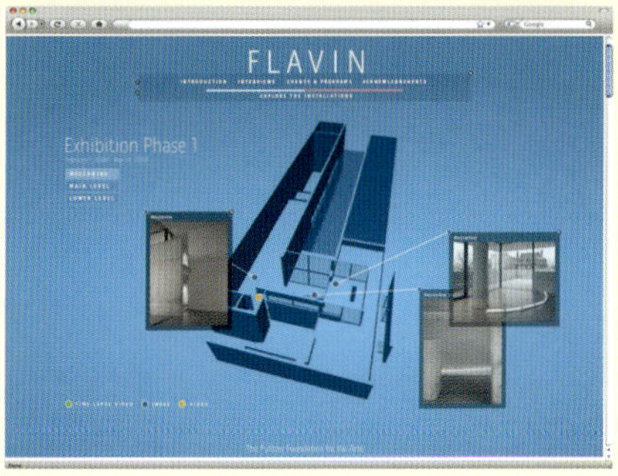

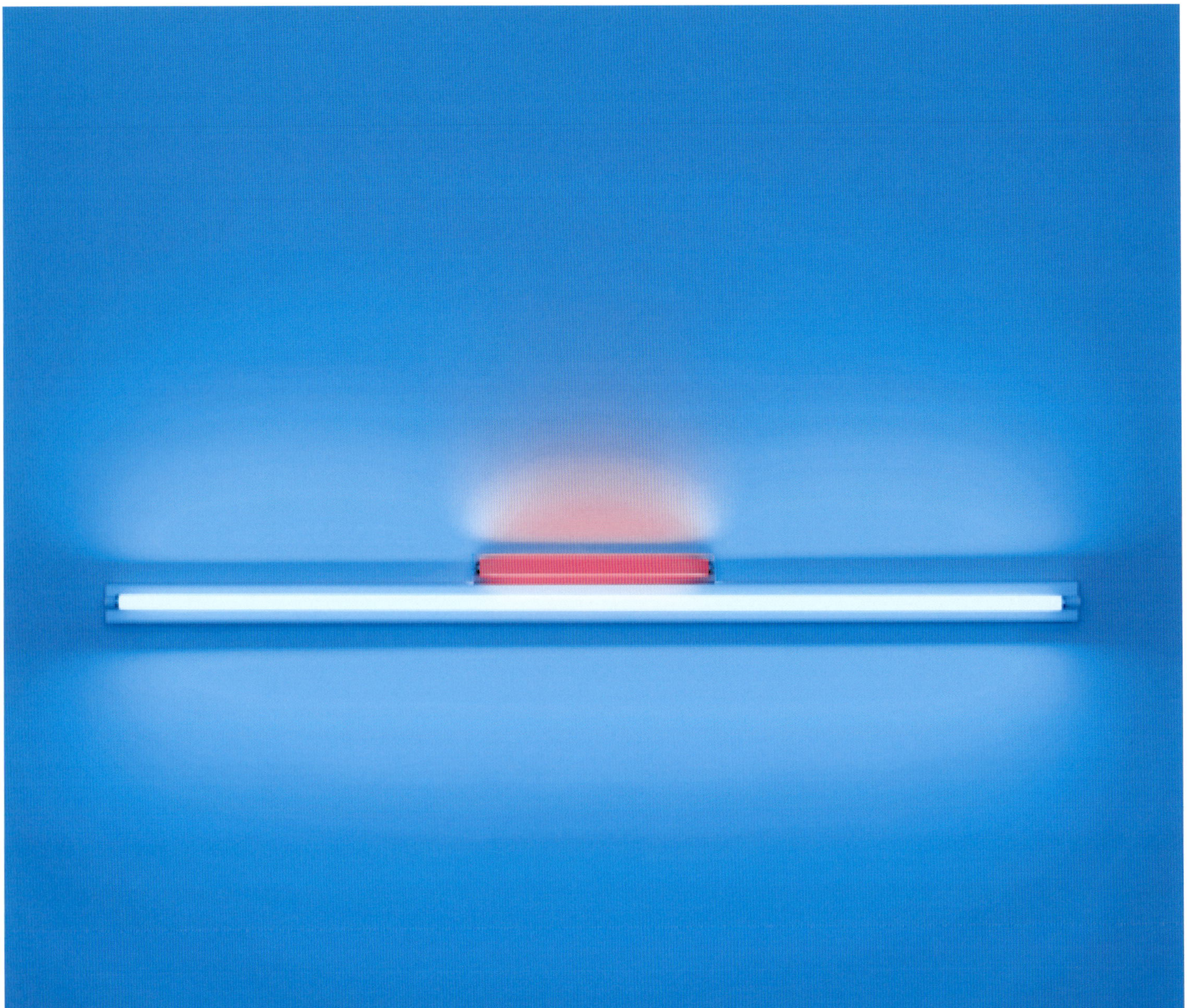
FLAVIN
CONSTRUCTEDLIGHT
OPENS FEBRUARY 1 08
PULITZER
The Pulitzer Foundation for the Arts
FEBRUARY 1, 2008 – OCTOBER 4, 2008
pulitzerarts.org | 3716 Washington Boulevard St. Louis, MO 63108

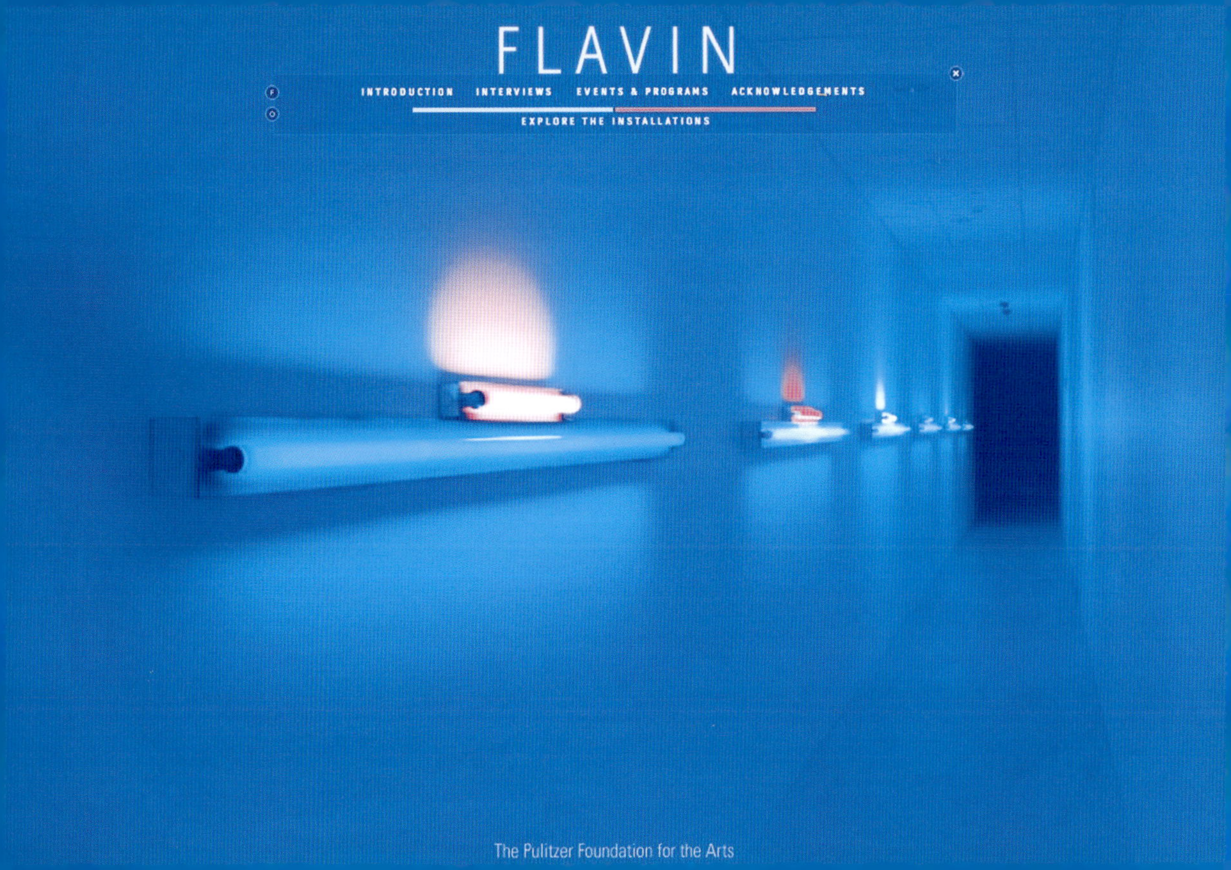
FLAVIN
INTRODUCTION
INTERVIEWS
EVENTS & PROGRAMS
ACKNOWLEDGEMENTS
EXPLORE THE INSTALLATIONS
The Pulitzer Foundation for the Arts

Assignment: The Lincoln Children's Museum sought to raise $5 million to improve and expand its exhibits. This integrated branding campaign was targeted to raise awareness among the general public about the expansion and to generate donations.

Approach: The concept was simple. We used vibrantly colorful play tools to announce that Lincoln needed to build a better children's museum, conveyed through an integrated campaign of posters, outdoor, brochure, and landing page. The brochure deepened the message by adding incomplete photos of children at play, which had to be filled in with stickers.

Results: The fund-raising campaign reached its monetary goal ahead of schedule, and the creative campaign will continue to encourage ongoing donations.

Designer: James Strange | **Design Firm:** Bailey Lauerman | **Art Director:** James Strange | **Creative Director:** Raleigh Drennon
Writer: Raleigh Drennon | **Photographer:** Kabloom Studios | **Client:** Lincoln Children's Museum

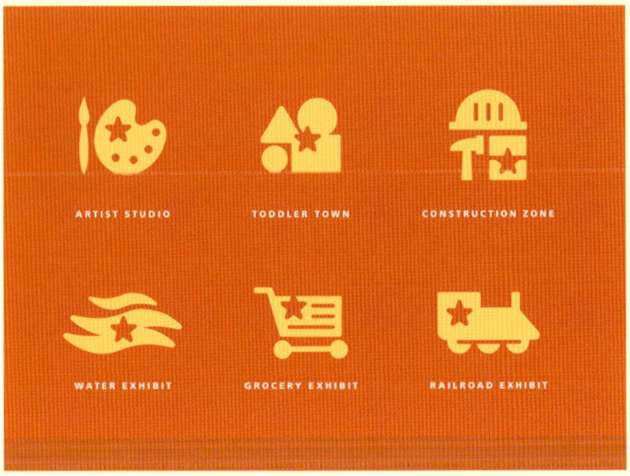

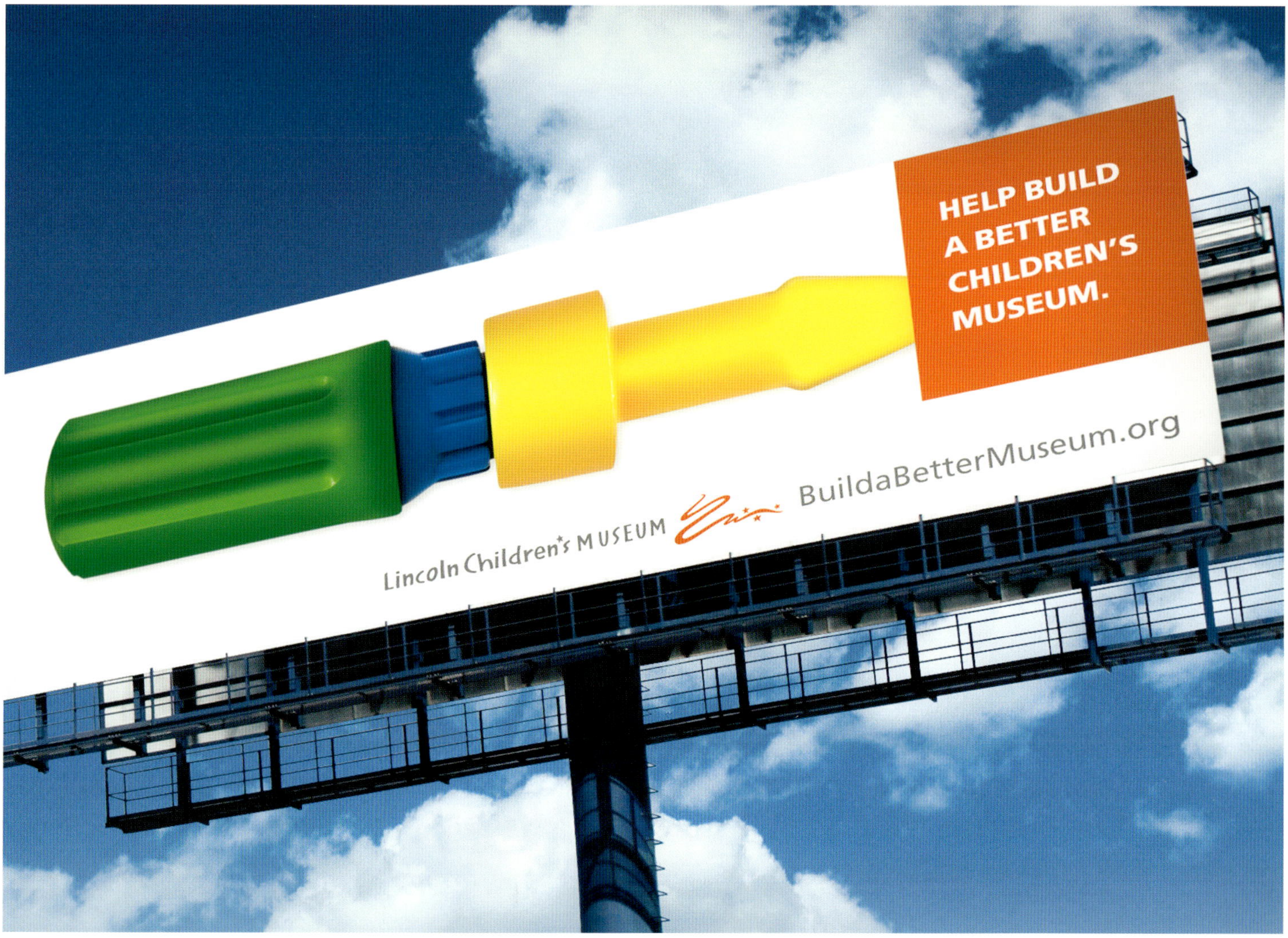
HELP BUILD A BETTER CHILDREN'S MUSEUM.
BuildaBetterMuseum.org
Lincoln Children's MUSEUM

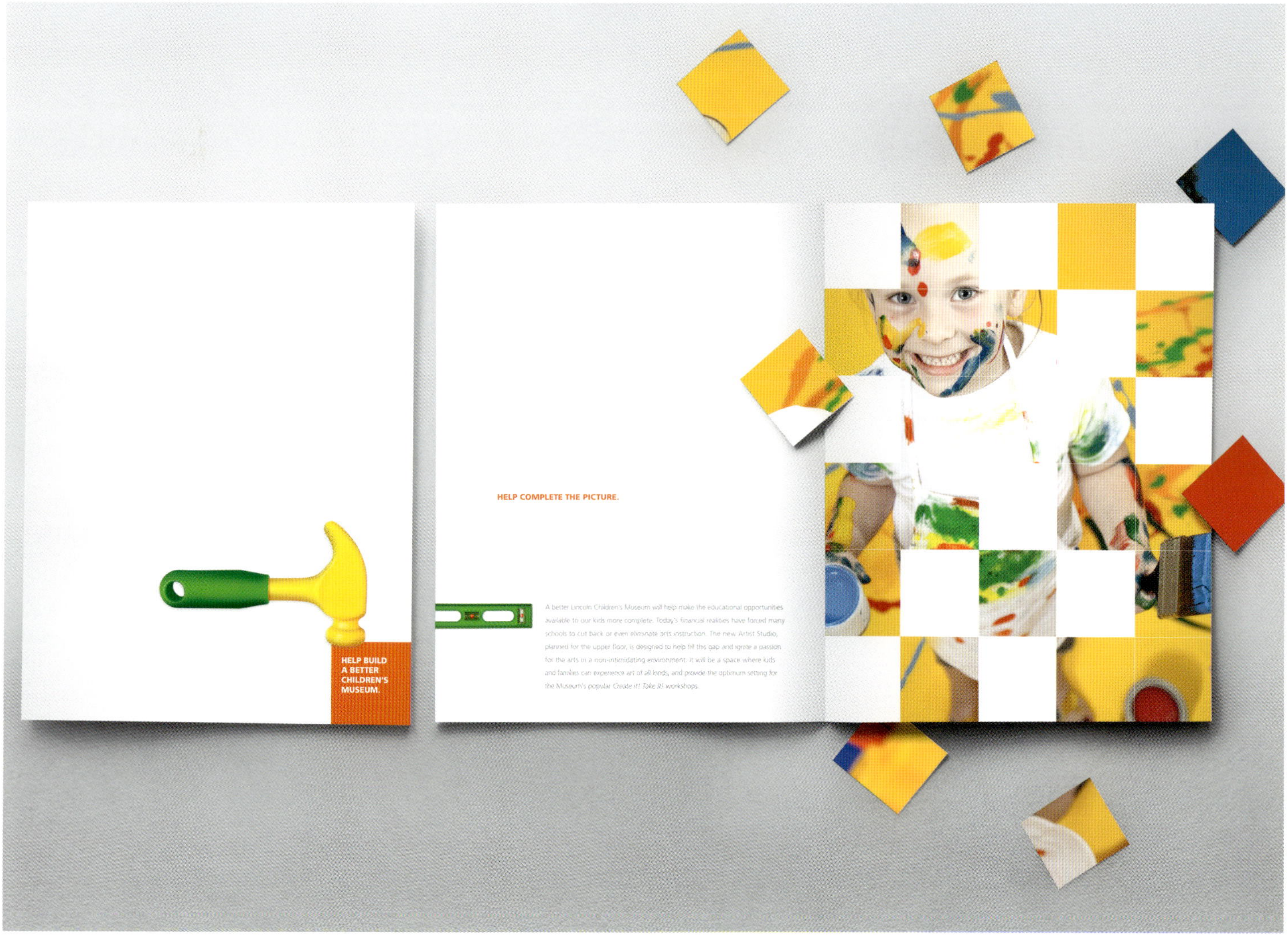
HELP BUILD A BETTER CHILDREN'S MUSEUM.
HELP COMPLETE THE PICTURE.
A better Lincoln Children's Museum will help make the educational opportunities available to our kids more complete. Today's financial realities have forced many schools to cut back or even eliminate arts instruction. The new Artist Studio, planned for the upper floor, is designed to help fill this gap and ignite a passion for the arts in a non-intimidating environment. It will be a space where kids and families can experience art of all kinds, and provide the optimum setting for the Museum's popular Create it! Take it! workshops.

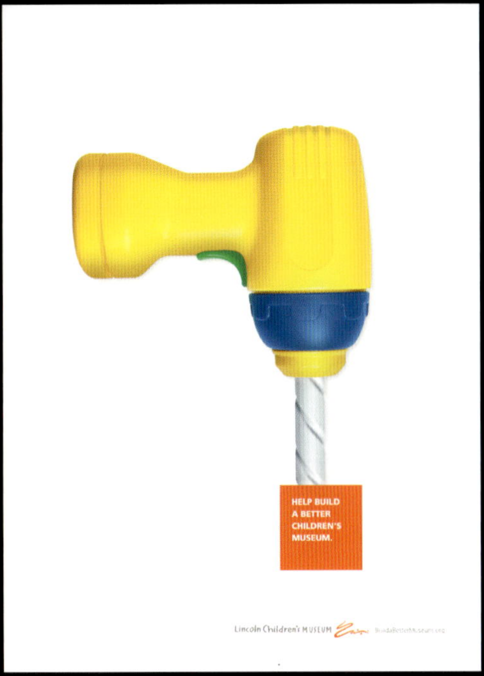
HELP BUILD
A BETTER
CHILDREN'S
MUSEUM.
Lincoln Children's MUSEUM

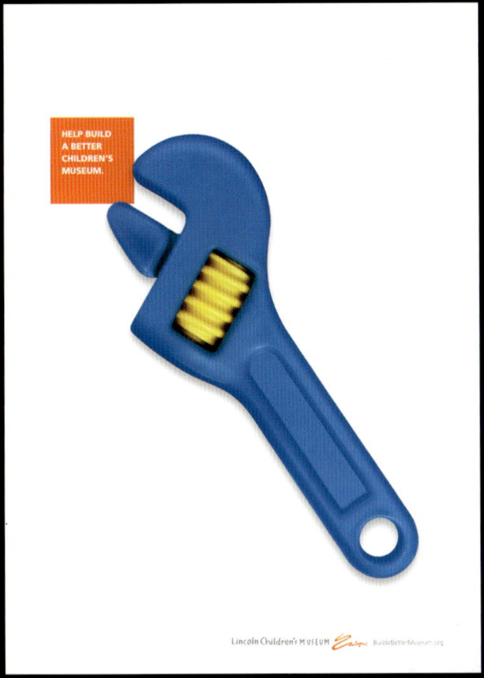
HELP BUILD
A BETTER
CHILDREN'S
MUSEUM.
Lincoln Children's MUSEUM

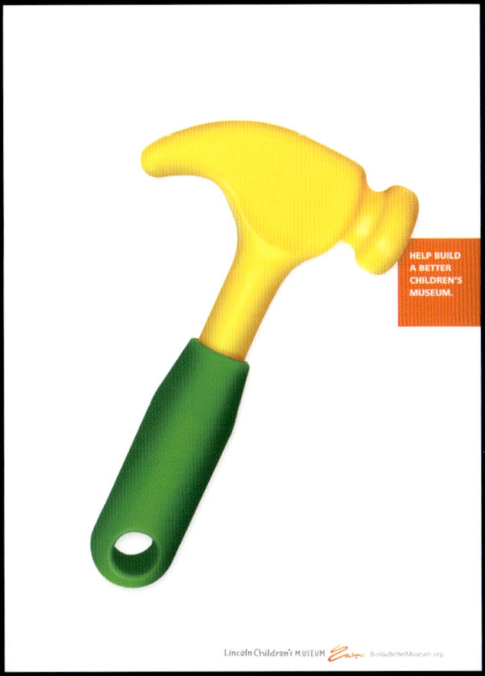
HELP BUILD
A BETTER
CHILDREN'S
MUSEUM.
Lincoln Children's MUSEUM

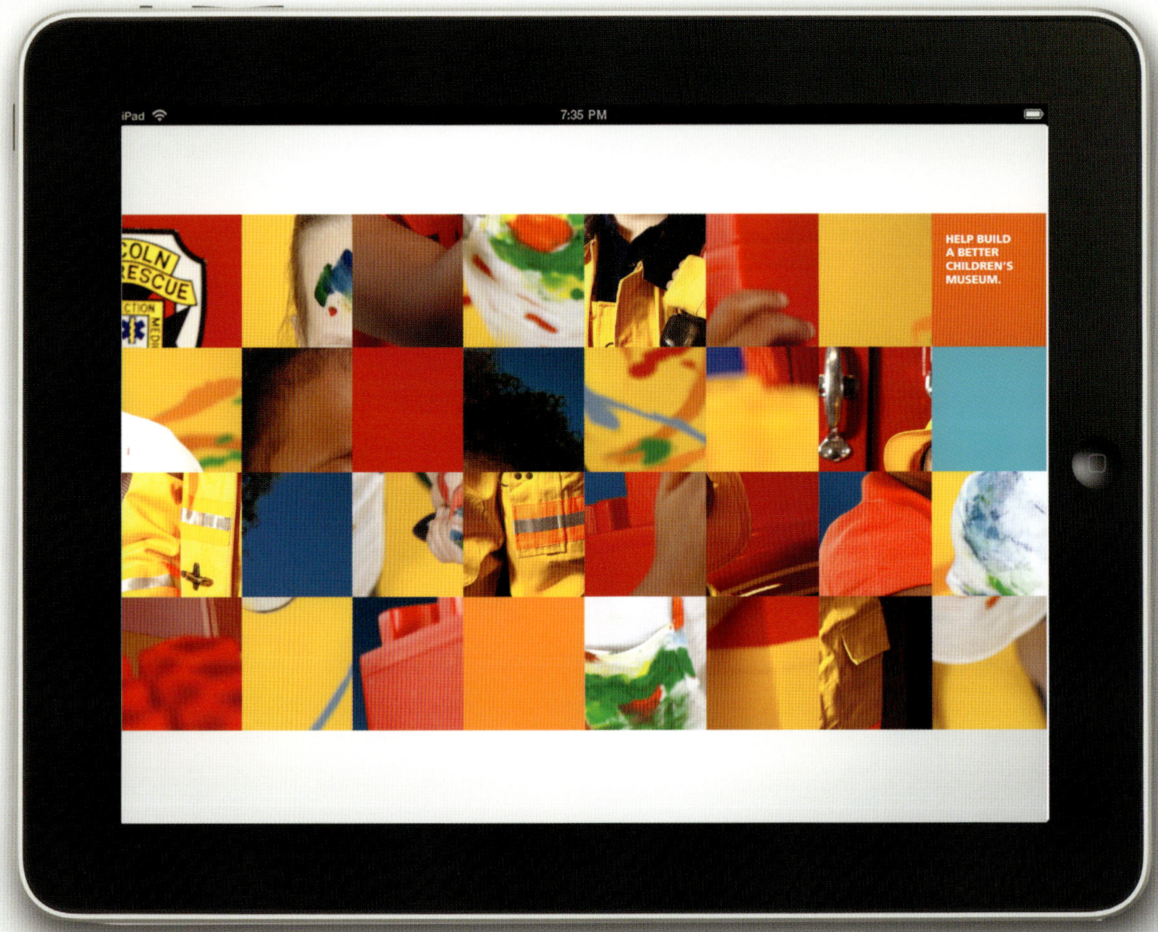
iPad
7:35 PM
HELP BUILD A BETTER CHILDREN'S MUSEUM.

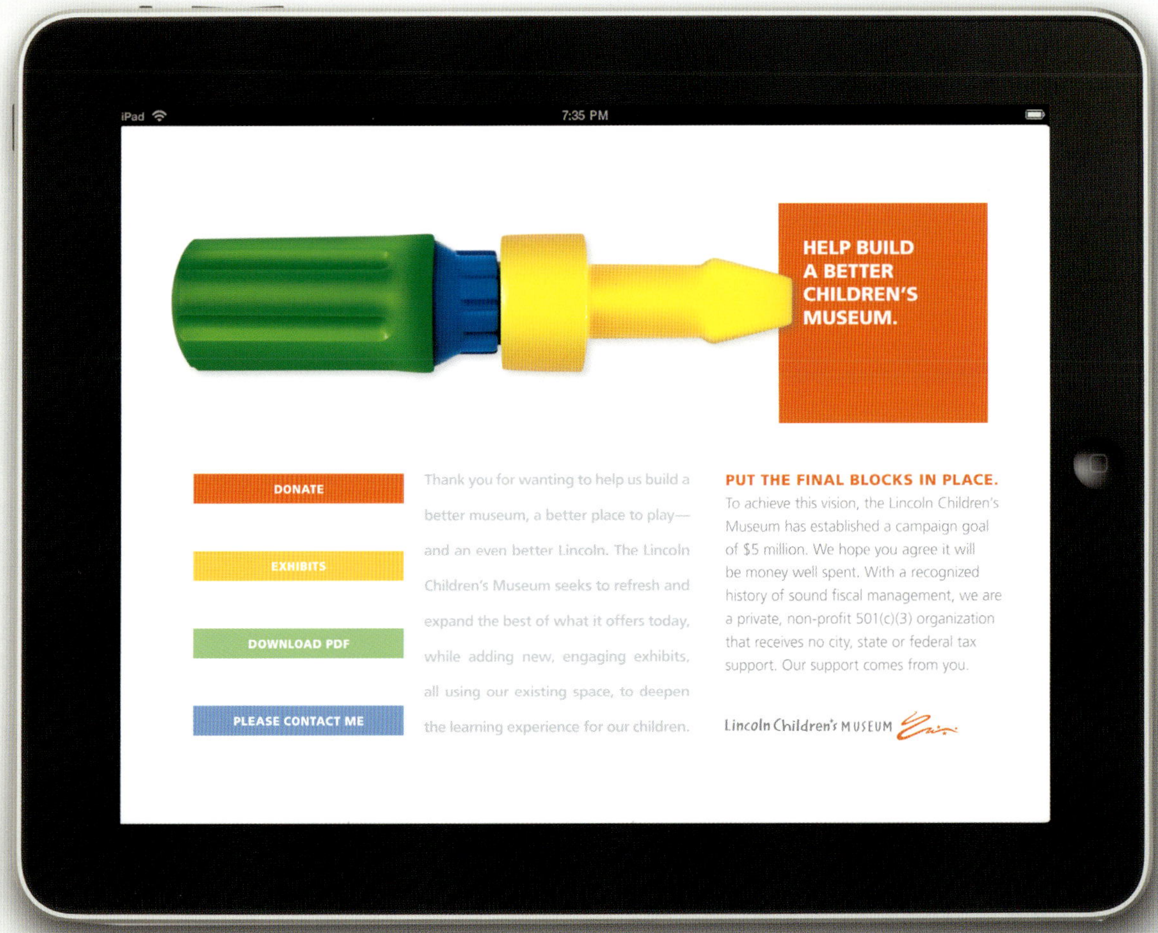
iPad
7:35 PM
HELP BUILD A BETTER CHILDREN'S MUSEUM.
DONATE
EXHIBITS
DOWNLOAD PDF
PLEASE CONTACT ME
Thank you for wanting to help us build a better museum, a better place to play—and an even better Lincoln. The Lincoln Children's Museum seeks to refresh and expand the best of what it offers today, while adding new, engaging exhibits, all using our existing space, to deepen the learning experience for our children.
PUT THE FINAL BLOCKS IN PLACE.
To achieve this vision, the Lincoln Children's Museum has established a campaign goal of $5 million. We hope you agree it will be money well spent. With a recognized history of sound fiscal management, we are a private, non-profit 501(c)(3) organization that receives no city, state or federal tax support. Our support comes from you.
Lincoln Children's MUSEUM

Assignment: The Auckland Museum holds the world's largest Maori and Pacific collection. It is a natural history as well as a war memorial museum. Museums now compete for audiences with many other types of experiences that didn't exist in the past—shopping malls, movies, digital games, as well as a myriad of other forms of entertainment, art galleries, sports, and the great outdoors. The challenge was to develop a campaign identity and communications platform that both aligned the team internally and repositioned and reconnected the museum with its external audiences.

Approach: The solution came from a fundamental questioning of what a museum is. This process highlighted the need to rethink the role of the organization and how it connected with people, both within its building and beyond it. AM was developed as the campaign mark in conjunction with a brand voice that could operate in different modes. AM is an acronym for Auckland Museum. I AM is an introduction. I AM is an affirmation. It could make statements—I AM not what you think. It could pose questions—Who AM I? It could describe the role of the institution—I AM yesterday, I AM today, I AM tomorrow. A pattern language was developed as part of the identity, referencing both the visual traditions of Maori and Pacific carving and the neoclassical architecture of the building itself. A typographic language combined different typefaces with visual elements relating to the logo mark. A simple color palette of black and white was adopted, giving a high degree of flexibility to accommodate the requirements of exhibition and event communications. A photographic portraiture approach was developed, putting the people of Auckland at the center of communication. The core identity elements were applied and extended across a broad range of internal and external communications, including brand books, collateral, exhibition and event campaigns, education programs, signage, print, online and radio and television advertising.

Results: Disney's delight with and support of the Dream Portraits effort is evident as we move into our fourth year of the campaign. While we do measure and monitor the impressions and brand metrics of the portraits, we do not yet have data for the latest effort.

Approach: The identity has spurred a change in behavior within the Museum, as well as the way its external audience is reacting to the institution. Demonstrated by increasing visitor numbers, the Museum's audiences now perceive the brand as an open platform with which they can interact. This shift from being passive spectators to active participants in the creation of content has shown itself in recent campaigns in which New Zealanders have demonstrated their willingness to participate in the creation of museum content. The involvement in the recent I AM Cheryl look-alike competition, based around one of New Zealand's most famous television characters, resulted in one of the most visited exhibitions in the Museum's history.

Designers: Dean Poole, Toby Curnow, Shabnam Shiwan, Tony Proffit, Jinki Cambronero, Aaron Edwards, Sam Fieulaine
Design Firm: Alt Group | **Creative Director:** Dean Poole | **Photographer:** Toaki Okano | **Client:** Auckland Museum

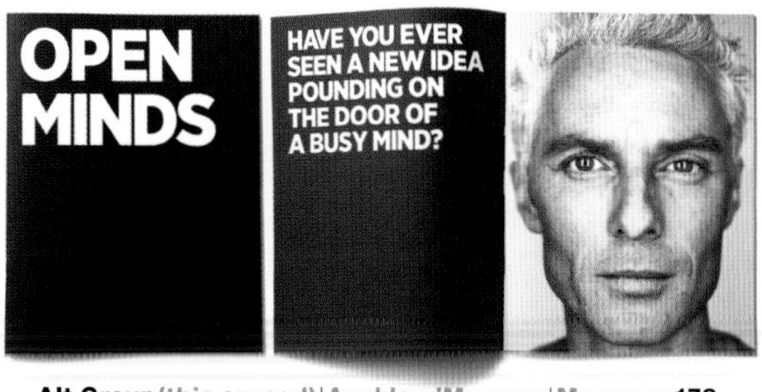

Alt Group(this spread)|AucklandMuseum|Museums**178**

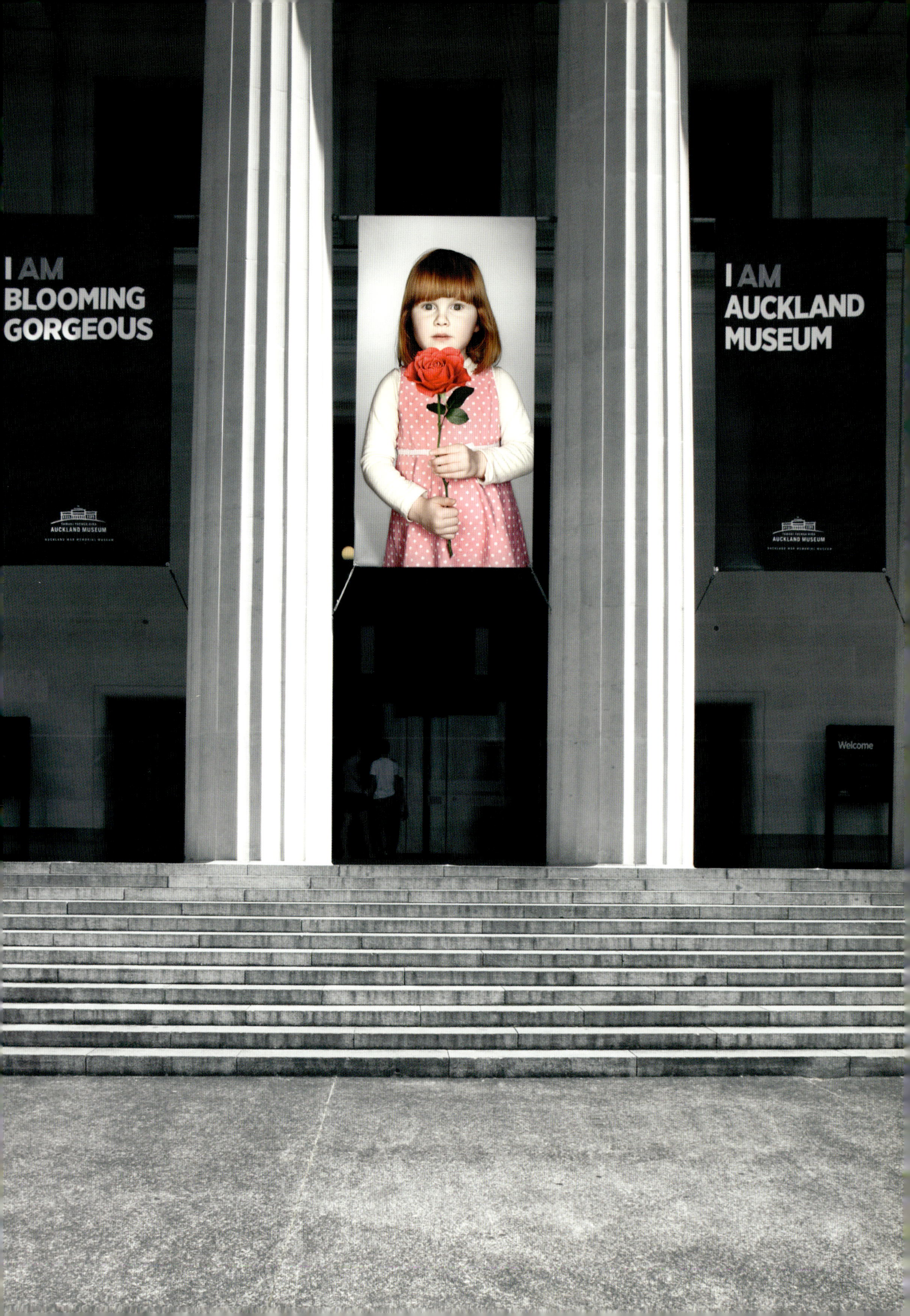
I AM
BLOOMING
GORGEOUS
I AM
AUCKLAND
MUSEUM
Welcome

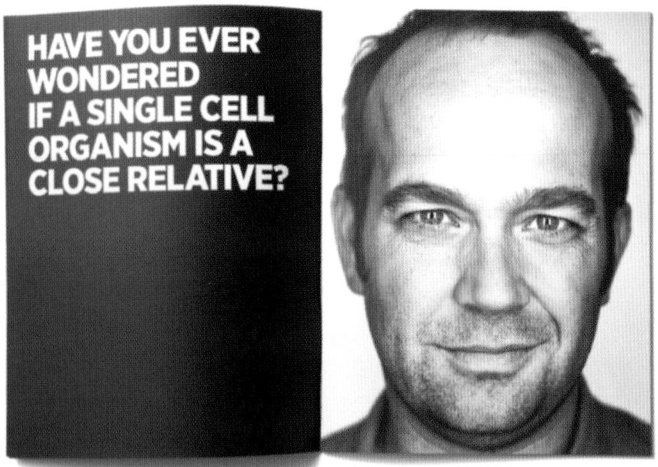
HAVE YOU EVER WONDERED IF A SINGLE CELL ORGANISM IS A CLOSE RELATIVE?

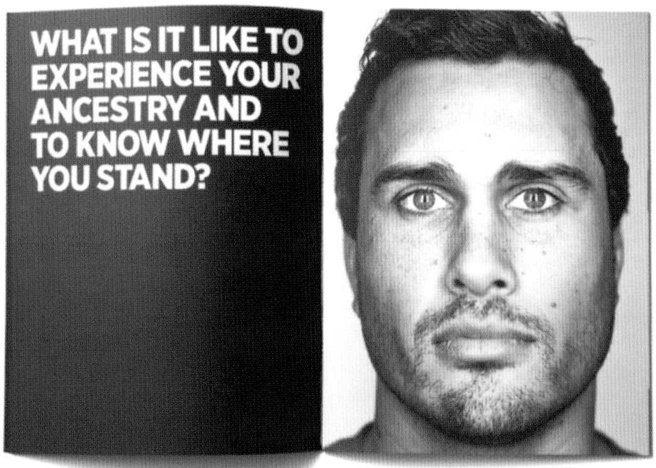
WHAT IS IT LIKE TO EXPERIENCE YOUR ANCESTRY AND TO KNOW WHERE YOU STAND?

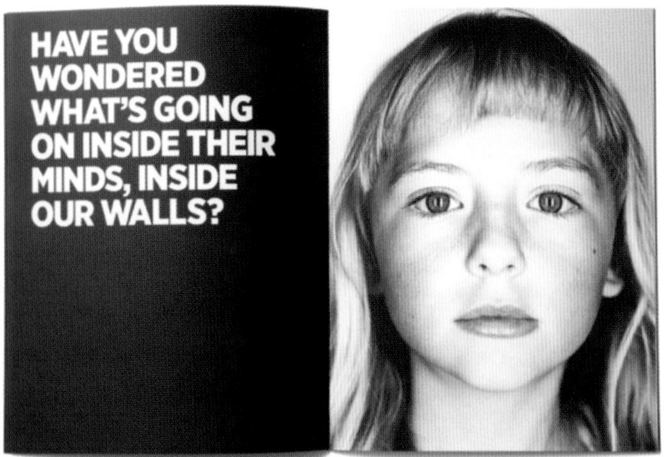
HAVE YOU WONDERED WHAT'S GOING ON INSIDE THEIR MINDS, INSIDE OUR WALLS?

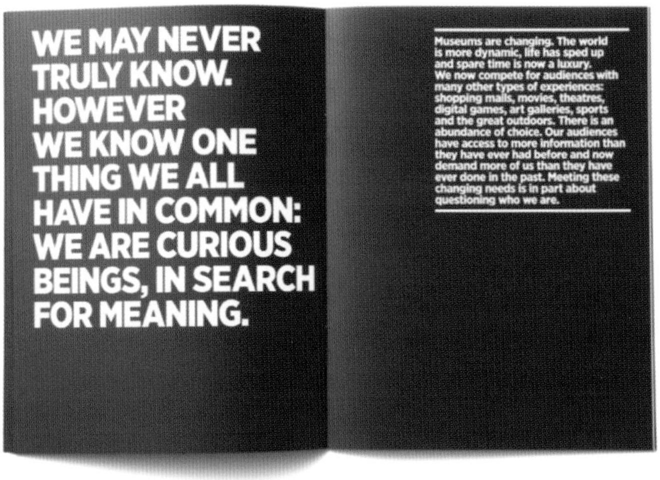
WE MAY NEVER TRULY KNOW. HOWEVER WE KNOW ONE THING WE ALL HAVE IN COMMON: WE ARE CURIOUS BEINGS, IN SEARCH FOR MEANING.
Museums are changing. The world is more dynamic, life has sped up and spare time is now a luxury. We now compete for audiences with many other types of experiences: shopping malls, movies, theatres, digital games, art galleries, sports and the great outdoors. There is an abundance of choice. Our audiences have access to more information than they have ever had before and now demand more of us than they have ever done in the past. Meeting these changing needs is in part about questioning who we are.

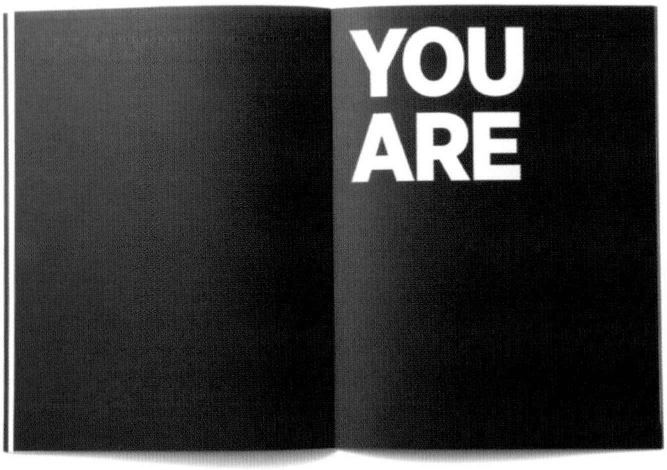
YOU ARE

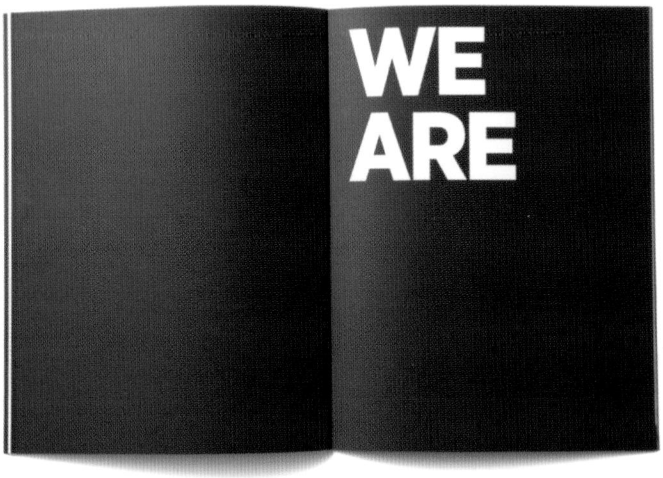
WE ARE

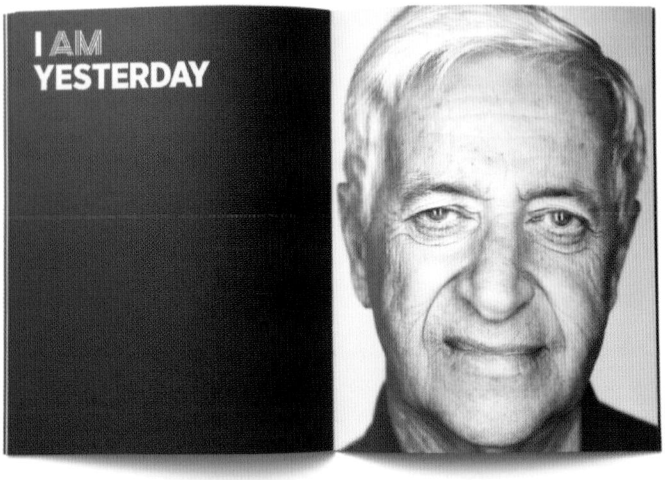
I AM YESTERDAY

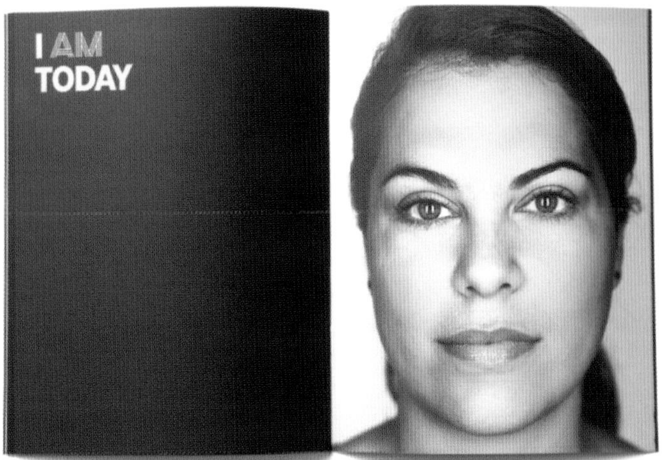
I AM TODAY

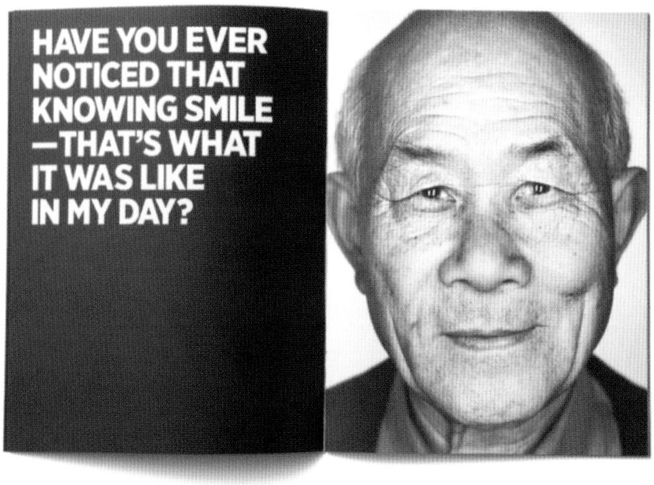
HAVE YOU EVER NOTICED THAT KNOWING SMILE —THAT'S WHAT IT WAS LIKE IN MY DAY?

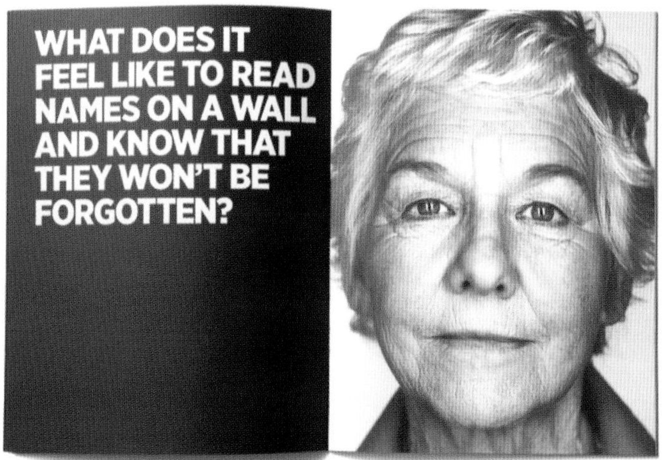
WHAT DOES IT FEEL LIKE TO READ NAMES ON A WALL AND KNOW THAT THEY WON'T BE FORGOTTEN?

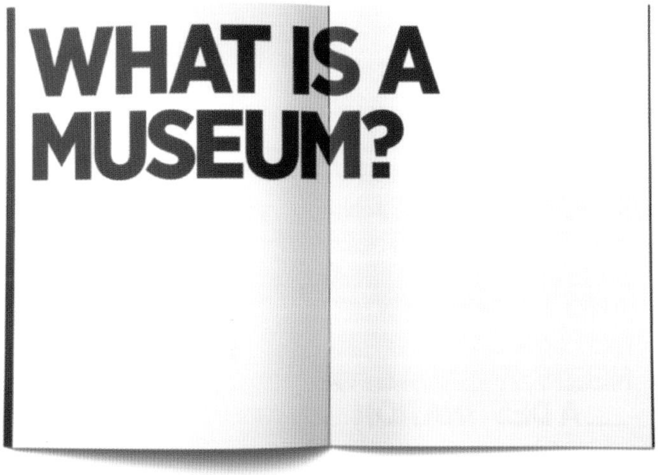
WHAT IS A MUSEUM?

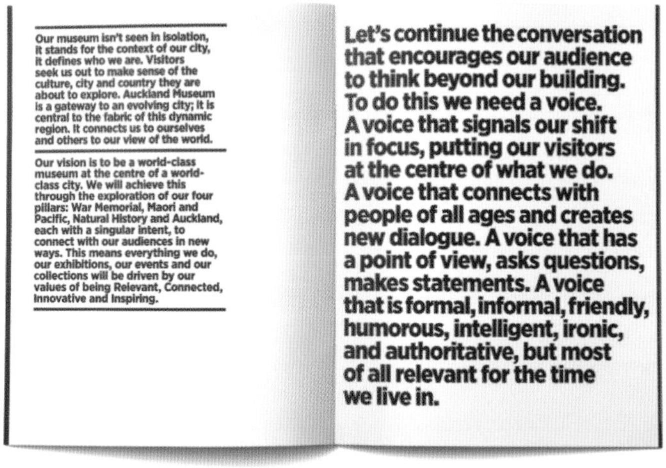
Our museum isn't seen in isolation, it stands for the context of our city, it defines who we are. Visitors seek us out to make sense of the culture, city and country they are about to explore. Auckland Museum is a gateway to an evolving city; it is central to the fabric of this dynamic region. It connects us to ourselves and others to our view of the world.
Our vision is to be a world-class museum at the centre of a world-class city. We will achieve this through the exploration of our four pillars: War Memorial, Maori and Pacific, Natural History and Auckland, each with a singular intent, to connect with our audiences in new ways. This means everything we do, our exhibitions, our events and our collections will be driven by our values of being Relevant, Connected, Innovative and Inspiring.
Let's continue the conversation that encourages our audience to think beyond our building. To do this we need a voice. A voice that signals our shift in focus, putting our visitors at the centre of what we do. A voice that connects with people of all ages and creates new dialogue. A voice that has a point of view, asks questions, makes statements. A voice that is formal, informal, friendly, humorous, intelligent, ironic, and authoritative, but most of all relevant for the time we live in.

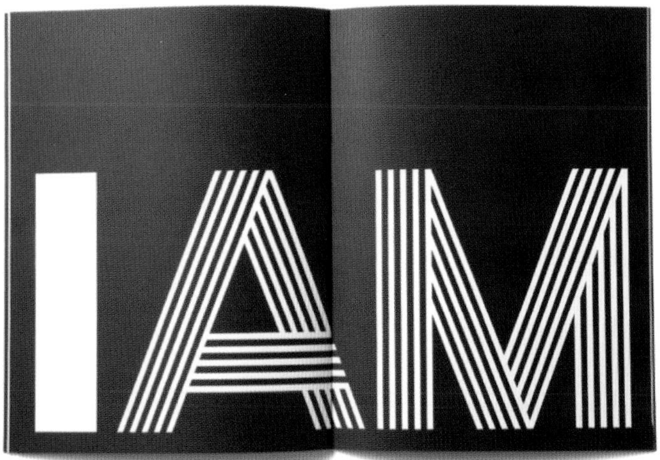
I AM

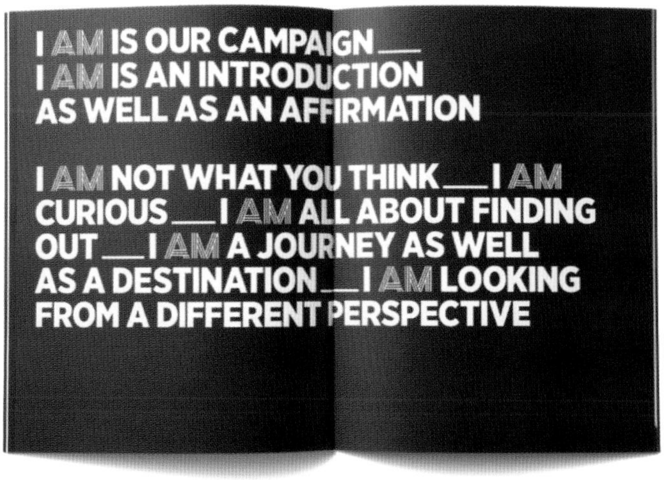
I AM IS OUR CAMPAIGN __ I AM IS AN INTRODUCTION AS WELL AS AN AFFIRMATION
I AM NOT WHAT YOU THINK __ I AM CURIOUS __ I AM ALL ABOUT FINDING OUT __ I AM A JOURNEY AS WELL AS A DESTINATION __ I AM LOOKING FROM A DIFFERENT PERSPECTIVE

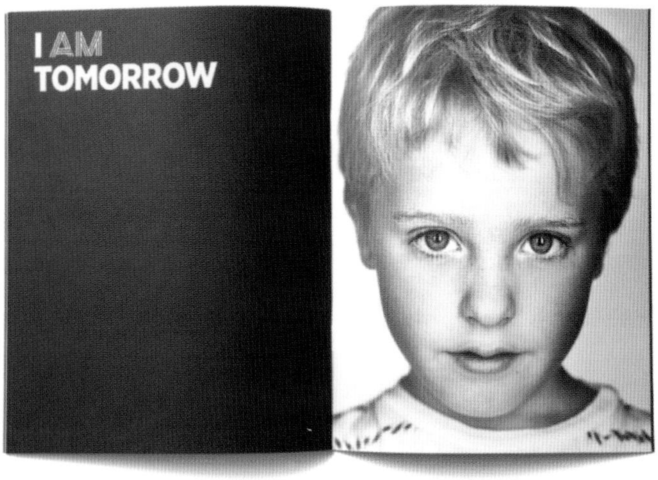
I AM TOMORROW

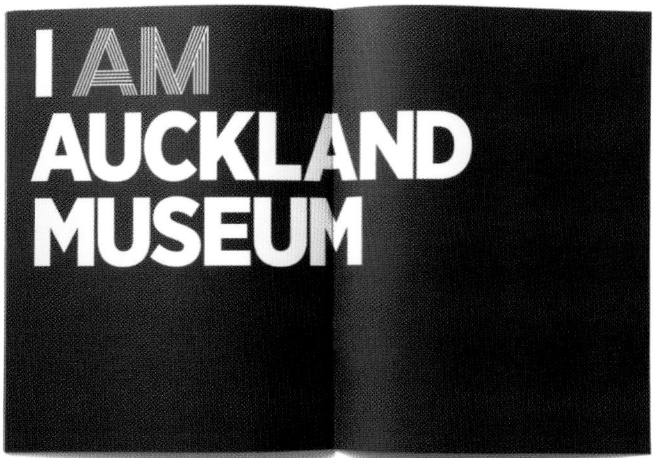
I AM AUCKLAND MUSEUM

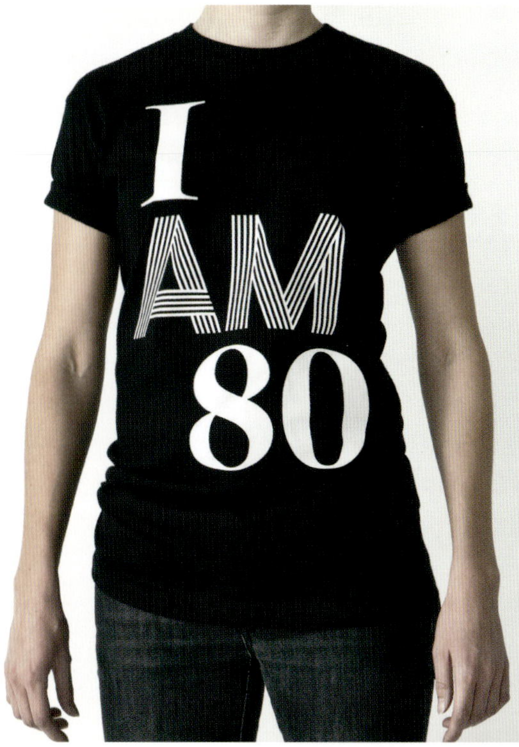
I
AM
80

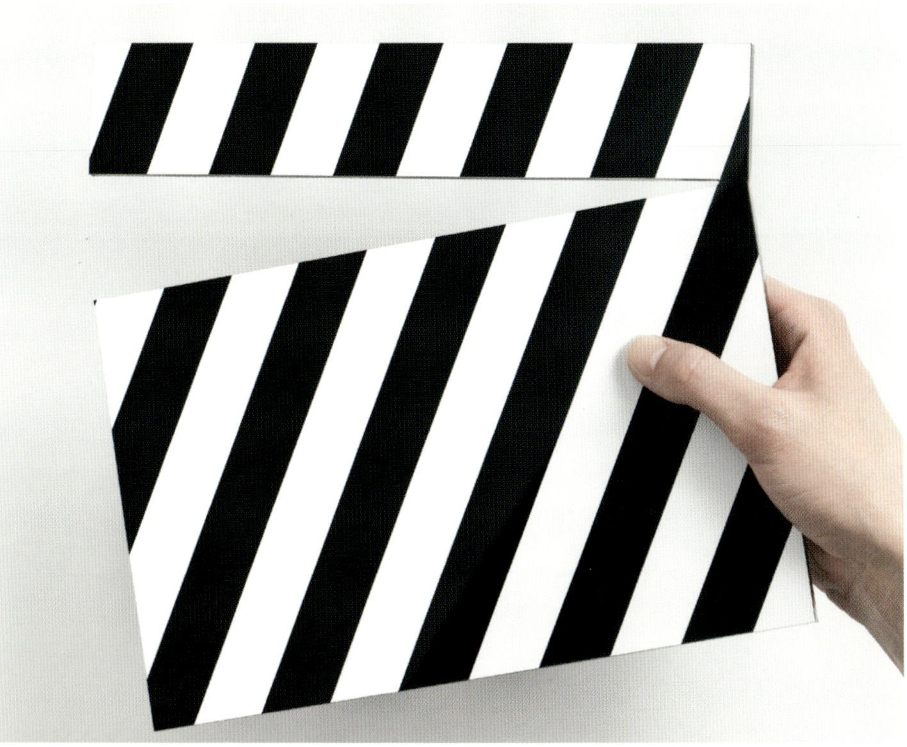

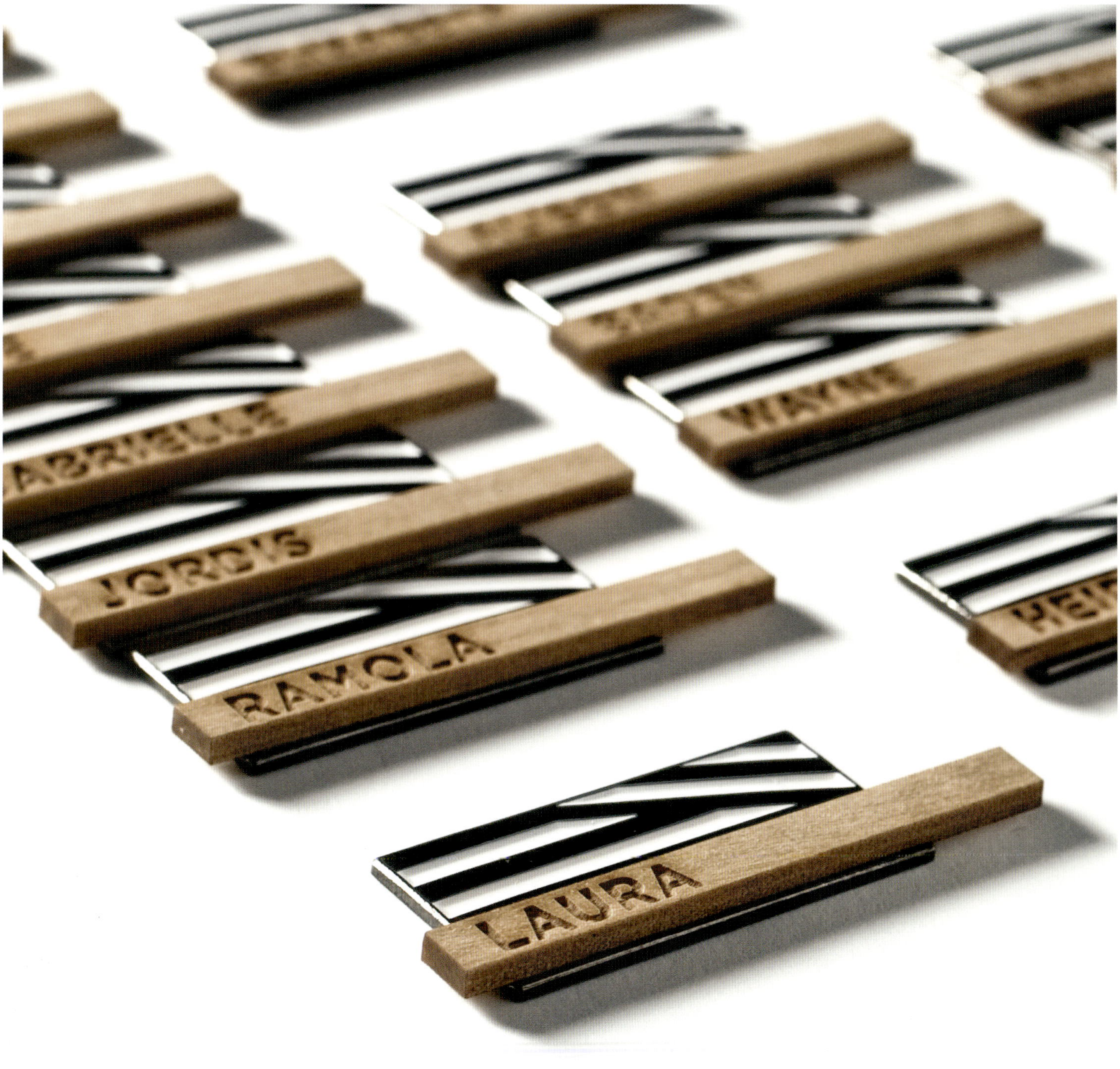
WAYNE
JORDIS
RAMOLA
LAURA

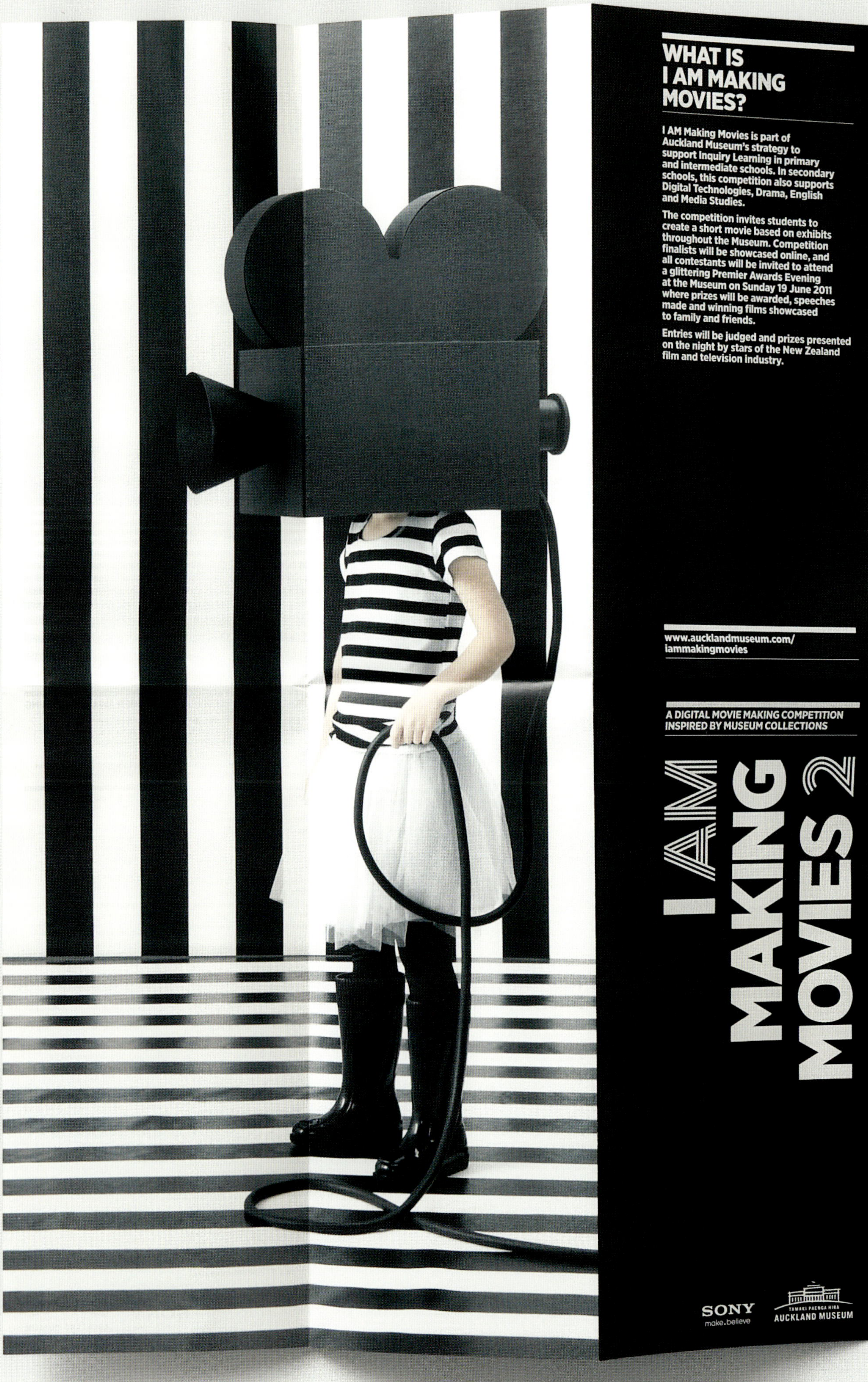
WHAT IS
I AM MAKING
MOVIES?
I AM Making Movies is part of Auckland Museum's strategy to support Inquiry Learning in primary and intermediate schools. In secondary schools, this competition also supports Digital Technologies, Drama, English and Media Studies.
The competition invites students to create a short movie based on exhibits throughout the Museum. Competition finalists will be showcased online, and all contestants will be invited to attend a glittering Premier Awards Evening at the Museum on Sunday 19 June 2011 where prizes will be awarded, speeches made and winning films showcased to family and friends.
Entries will be judged and prizes presented on the night by stars of the New Zealand film and television industry.
www.aucklandmuseum.com/
iammakingmovies
A DIGITAL MOVIE MAKING COMPETITION
INSPIRED BY MUSEUM COLLECTIONS
I AM
MAKING
MOVIES 2
SONY
make.believe
TAMAKI PAENGA HIRA
AUCKLAND MUSEUM

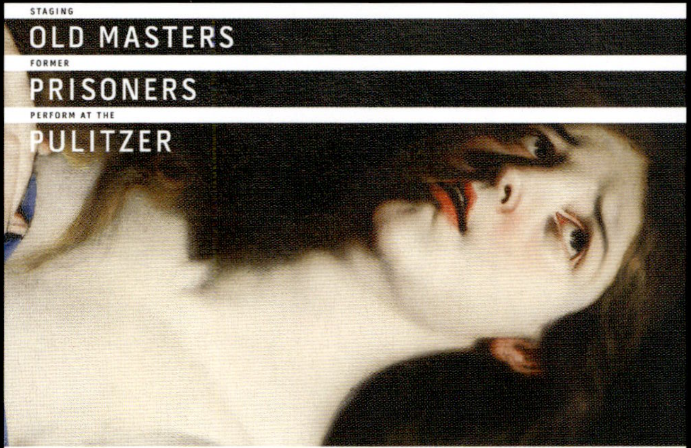
STAGING
OLD MASTERS
FORMER
PRISONERS
PERFORM AT THE
PULITZER

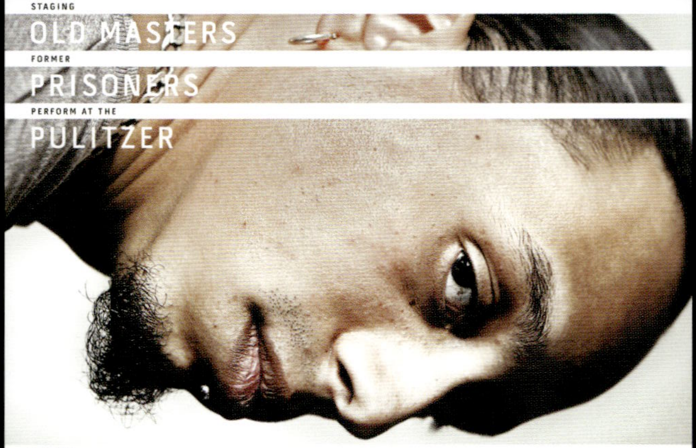
STAGING
OLD MASTERS
FORMER
PRISONERS
PERFORM AT THE
PULITZER

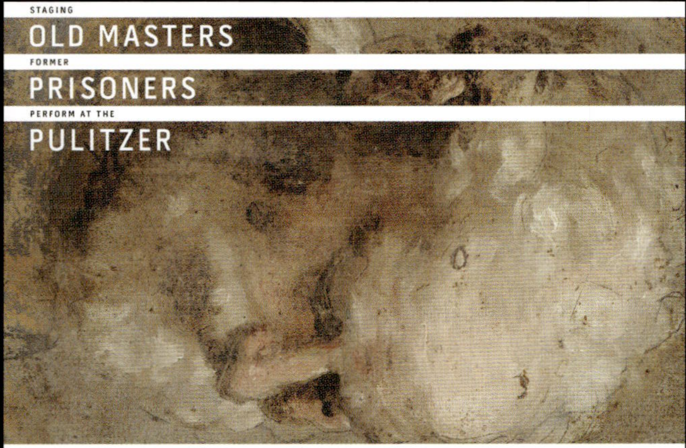
STAGING
OLD MASTERS
FORMER
PRISONERS
PERFORM AT THE
PULITZER

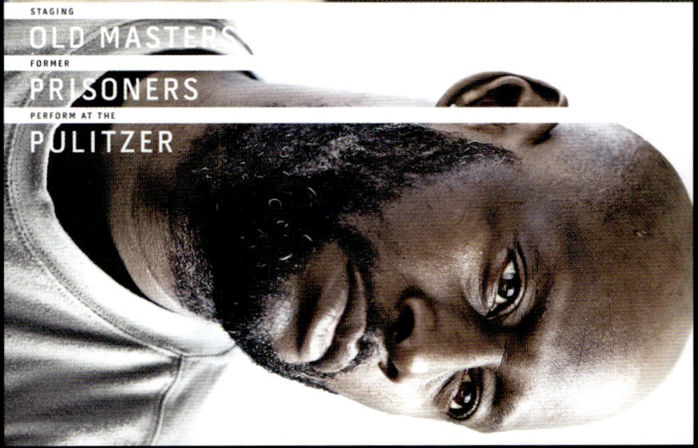
STAGING
OLD MASTERS
FORMER
PRISONERS
PERFORM AT THE
PULITZER

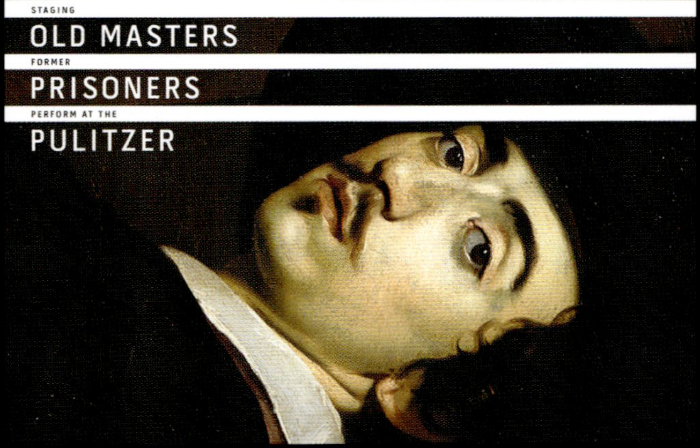
STAGING
OLD MASTERS
FORMER
PRISONERS
PERFORM AT THE
PULITZER

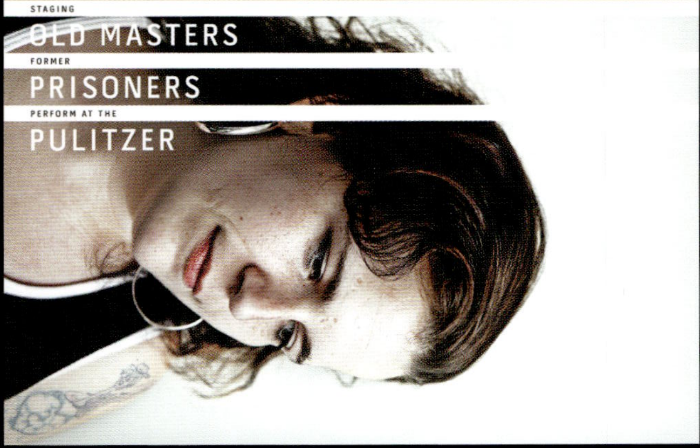
STAGING
OLD MASTERS
FORMER
PRISONERS
PERFORM AT THE
PULITZER

Assignment: The Pulitzer Foundation for the Arts collaborated with Prison Performing Arts and Washington University in St. Louis to create a unique theatrical event: "Staging Old Masters: Former Prisoners Perform at the Pulitzer." Ex-convicts, all graduates of a workforce outreach program, were taught about the artists and subjects of Old Masters paintings. Each selected one or more paintings that moved them, and then created a personal performance—music, spoken word, acting—that presented the parallels between their life and their subjects.

Approach: TOKY created posters, mailers, and ads for the performance series, juxtaposing the convict interpreters with the artwork they had selected. TOKY's Geoff Story, one of our print team creative directors, was the photographer.

Results: The performance series lasted five weeks, and was extended due to its popularity and critical acclaim.

Designers: Katy Fischer | **Design Firm:** TOKY Branding + Design | **Creative Director:** Eric Thoelke
Photographer: Geoff Story | **Client:** The Pulitzer Foundation for the Arts

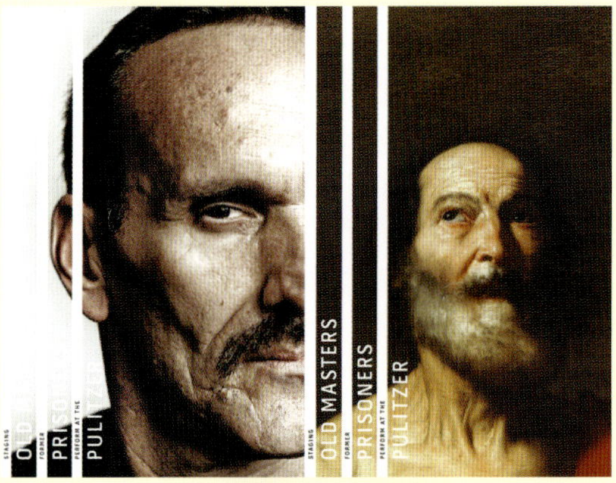

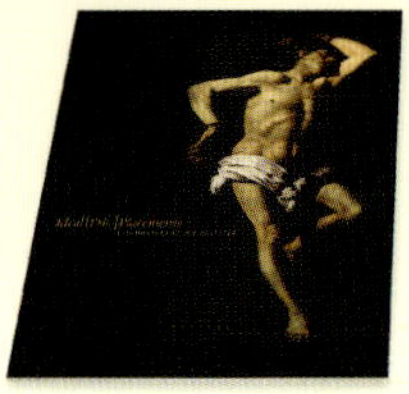

Assignment: "Universalmuseum Joanneum" is the new name for the organization that operates twenty-three of the major museums and collections in the province of Styria, Austria. Besides synergies in management and procurement, the aim of this association is to concentrate all marketing, exhibition production, and publishing activities. That called for a unified graphical language that nevertheless allows for a certain autonomy in the appearance of each department.

Approach: The concept revolves around the motif of the flag as an abstract sign of recognition (one of the oldest forms of visual communication), as an expression of hospitality and relevance, and as a sign of life. Three color fields are put together in a certain ratio that follows a "universal harmony formula," which can be found in nature as well as in art history (the Fibonacci sequence, the golden section). An individual color combination has been chosen to translate the respective field of research and collection of each department into a "color short story," such as "iron–silver–blood red" for the Armory, or "lava–earth brown–aqua" for the Geology Department. All colors together form a global palette of forty-six colors, from which, again, over 90,000 additional color triads can be composed. These are used for all parent applications (e.g., in visitor services, marketing, and administration). The corporate design is an open visual system that can compete with the manifold contents of the affiliated museums. The playful and flexible way of its application across the various tasks goes far beyond a traditional identity program.

Results: Provided with a simple set of rules, the corporate typeface, plus template files for all major print and web applications, the in-house design team of the museum today easily manages to maintain the graphic identity—without the need to refer to any elaborate design manual.

Design Firm: Lichtwitz Leinfellner visuelle Kultur KG | **Art Directors:** Kriso Leinfellner, Stefanie Lichtwitz, Harald Niessner, Katharina Untertrifaller
Creative Directors: Kriso Leinfellner, Stefanie Lichtwitz, Harald Niessner | **Client:** Universalmuseum Joanneum

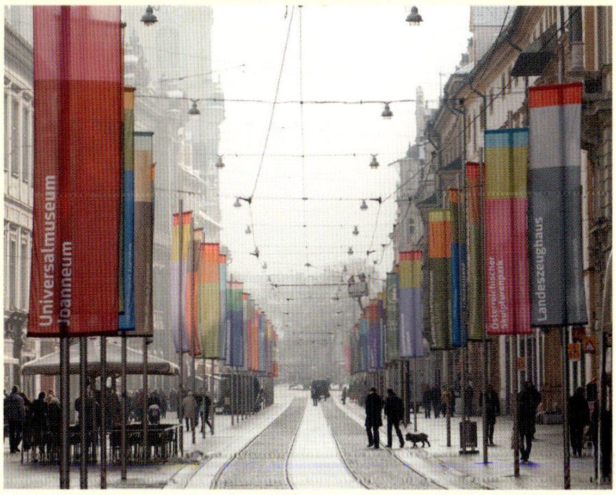

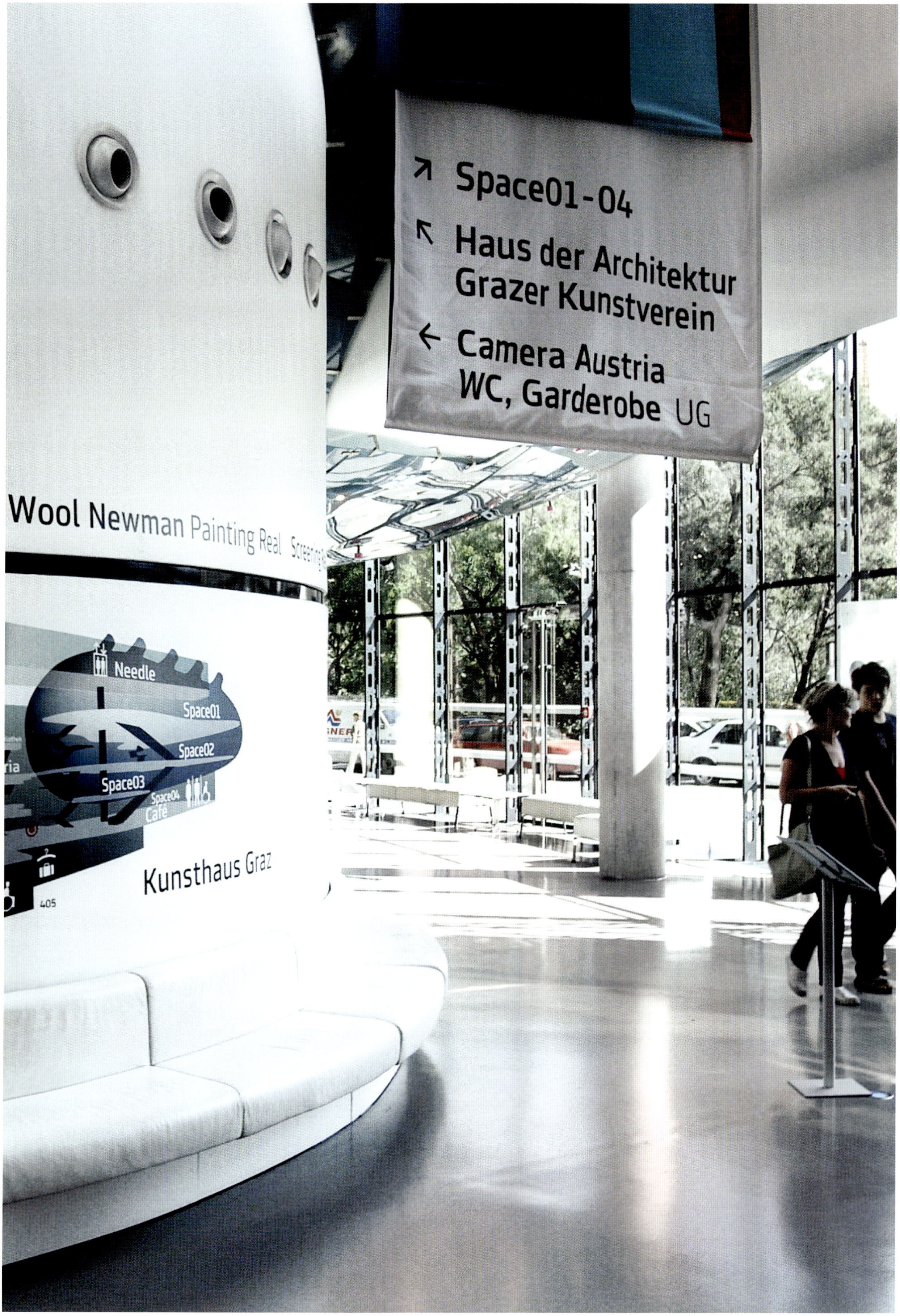
Space01-04
Haus der Architektur
Grazer Kunstverein
Camera Austria
WC, Garderobe UG
Wool Newman Painting Real
Needle
Space01
Space02
Space03
Space04
Café
Kunsthaus Graz
405

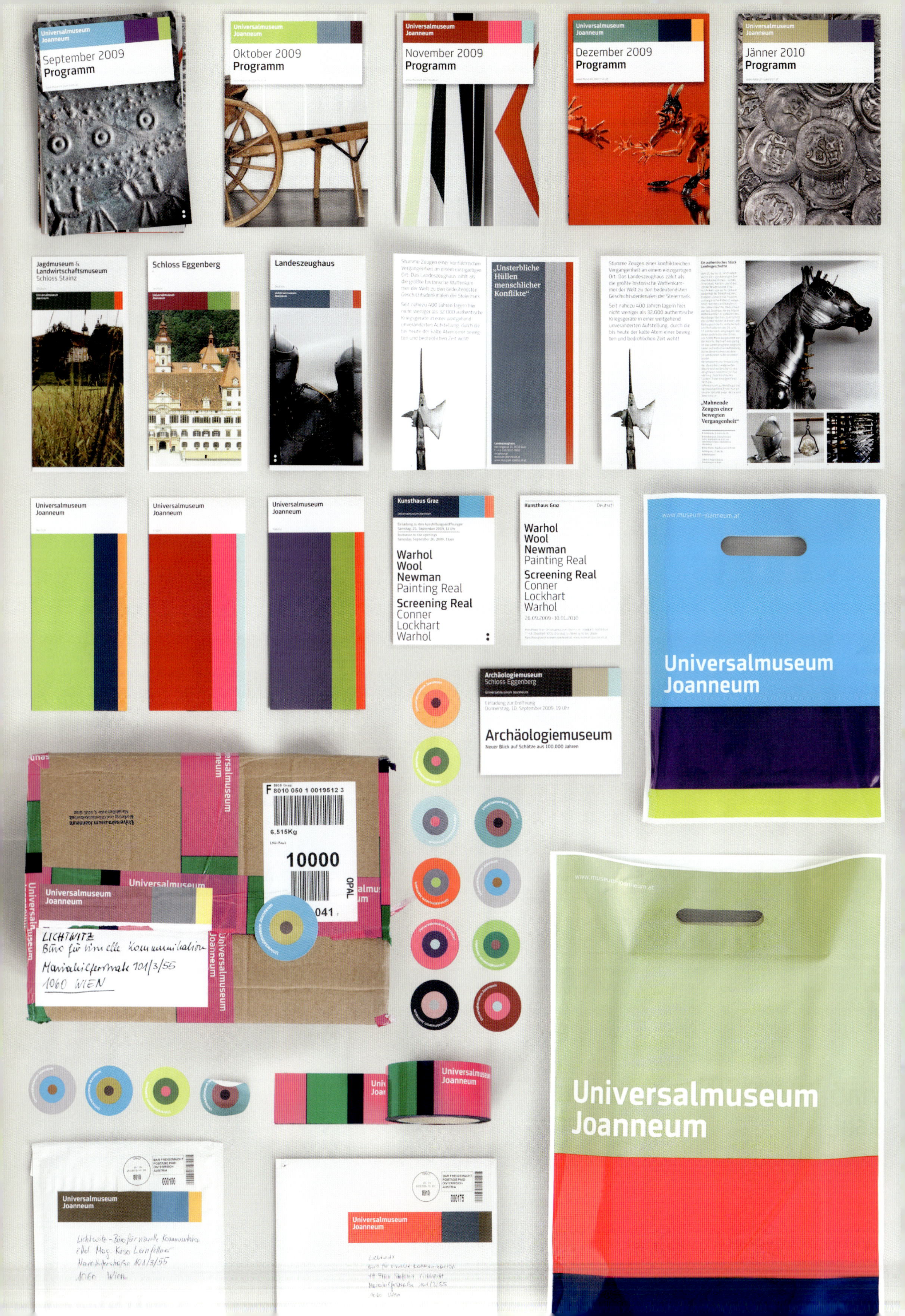

Universalmuseum Joanneum
September 2009
Programm
Oktober 2009
Programm
November 2009
Programm
Dezember 2009
Programm
Jänner 2010
Programm
Jagdmuseum & Landwirtschaftsmuseum
Schloss Stainz
Schloss Eggenberg
Landeszeughaus
„Unsterbliche Hüllen menschlicher Konflikte"
„Mahnende Zeugen einer bewegten Vergangenheit"
Kunsthaus Graz
Warhol
Wool
Newman
Painting Real
Screening Real
Conner
Lockhart
Warhol
26.09.2009–10.01.2010
Archäologiemuseum
Schloss Eggenberg
Neuer Blick auf Schätze aus 100.000 Jahren
www.museum-joanneum.at
10000
OPAL
6,515Kg
LICHTWITZ
Büro für visuelle Kommunikation
Mariahilferstraße 101/3/55
1060 WIEN

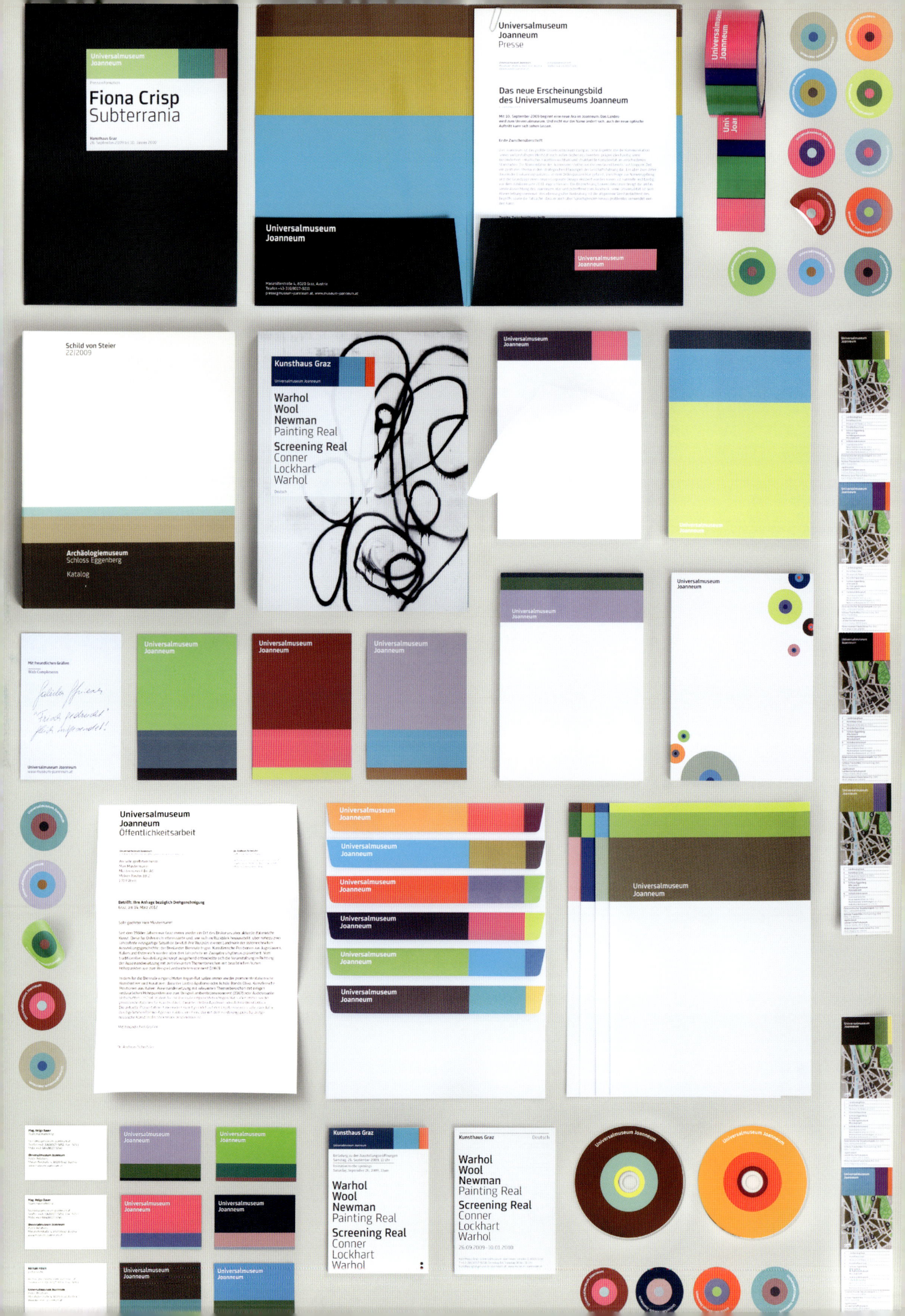

Universalmuseum Joanneum
Fiona Crisp
Subterrania
Universalmuseum Joanneum
Presse
Das neue Erscheinungsbild des Universalmuseums Joanneum
Schild von Steier
22|2009
Archäologiemuseum
Schloss Eggenberg
Katalog
Kunsthaus Graz
Warhol
Wool
Newman
Painting Real
Screening Real
Conner
Lockhart
Warhol
Universalmuseum Joanneum
Öffentlichkeitsarbeit
Kunsthaus Graz
Warhol
Wool
Newman
Painting Real
Screening Real
Conner
Lockhart
Warhol
Kunsthaus Graz
Deutsch
Warhol
Wool
Newman
Painting Real
Screening Real
Conner
Lockhart
Warhol
26.09.2009 - 10.01.2010
Universalmuseum Joanneum

Eisen
C 30 R 91
M 0 G 112
Y 10 B 115
K 55

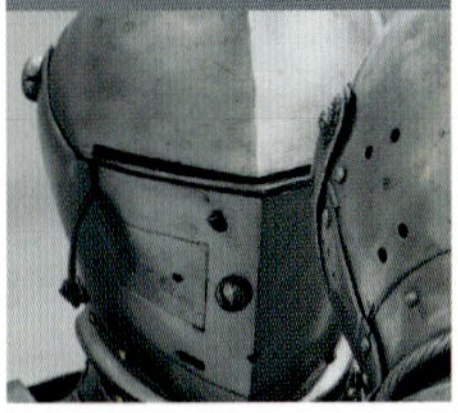

Silber
C 10 R 166
M 5 G 171
Y 6 B 174
K 30

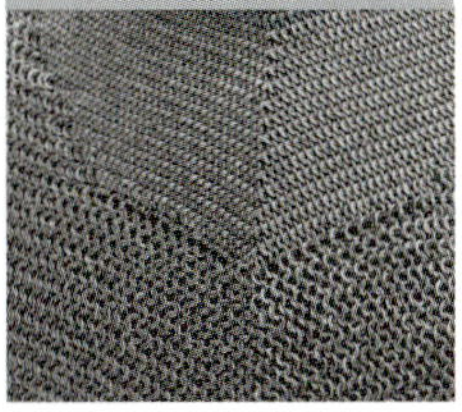

Akutrot
C 0 R 210
M 100 G 0
Y 100 B 27
K 0

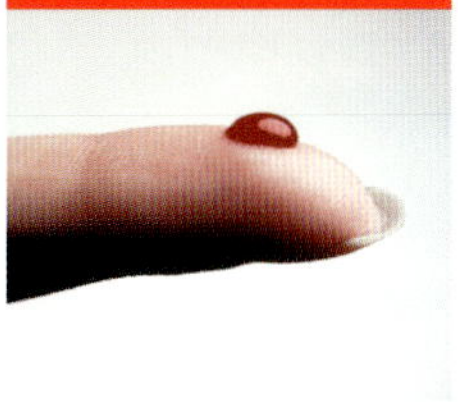

→

Landeszeughaus
Universalmuseum Joanneum

Landeszeughaus
Universalmuseum Joanneum

Museum im Palais
Universalmuseum Joanneum

Volkskundemuseum
Universalmuseum Joanneum

Schloss Trautenfels
Universalmuseum Joanneum

Künstlerhaus
Universalmuseum Joanneum

Schloss Eggenberg
Universalmuseum Joanneum

Alte Galerie
Schloss Eggenberg
Universalmuseum Joanneum

Archäologiemuseum
Schloss Eggenberg
Universalmuseum Joanneum

Münzkabinett
Schloss Eggenberg
Universalmuseum Joanneum

Römermuseum
Flavia Solva
Universalmuseum Joanneum

Jagdmuseum
Schloss Stainz
Universalmuseum Joanneum

Landwirtschaftsmuseum
Schloss Stainz
Universalmuseum Joanneum

Naturkundemuseum
Joanneumsviertel
Universalmuseum Joanneum

Botanik
Joanneumsviertel
Universalmuseum Joanneum

Geologie & Paläontologie
Joanneumsviertel
Universalmuseum Joanneum

Zoologie
Joanneumsviertel
Universalmuseum Joanneum

Mineralogie
Joanneumsviertel
Universalmuseum Joanneum

Multimediale Sammlungen
Joanneumsviertel
Universalmuseum Joanneum

Neue Galerie
Joanneumsviertel
Universalmuseum Joanneum

Kunsthaus Graz
Universalmuseum Joanneum

Österreichischer Skulpturenpark
Universalmuseum Joanneum

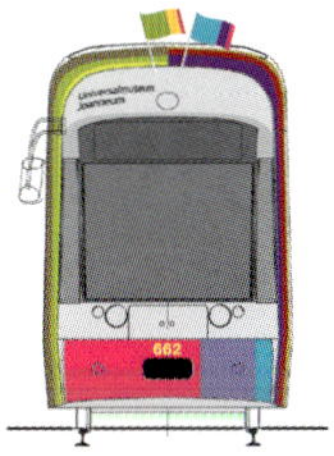

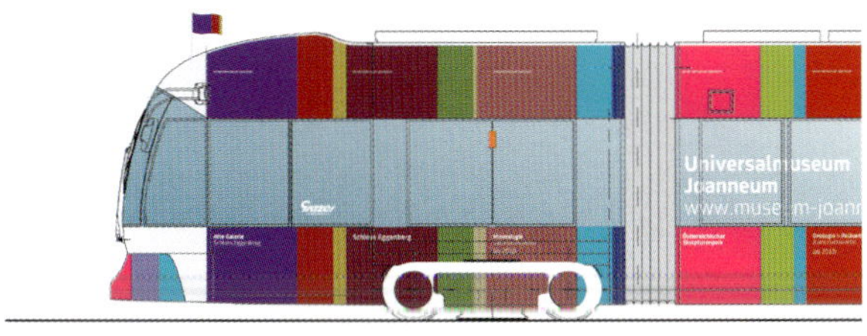

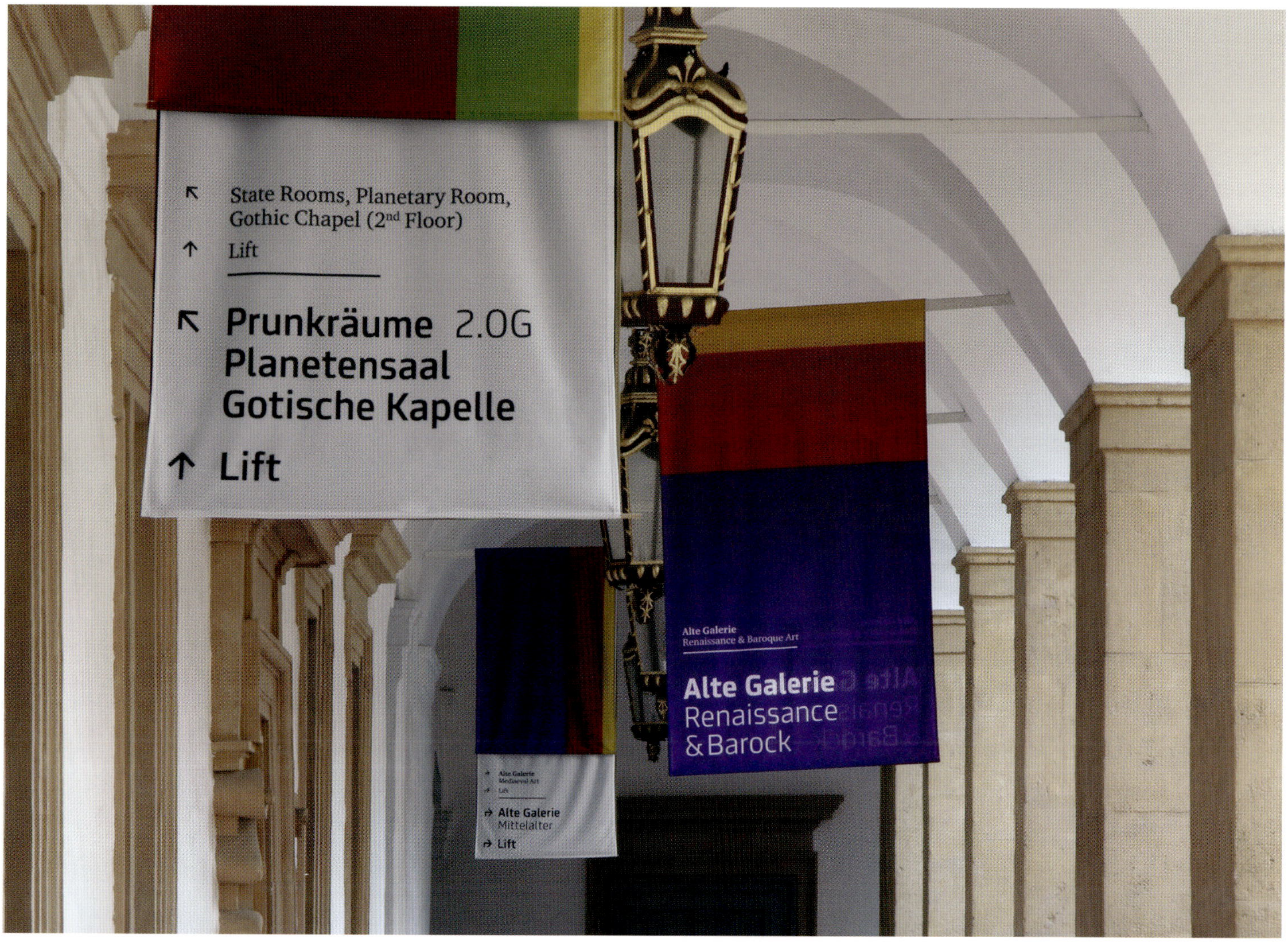
State Rooms, Planetary Room, Gothic Chapel (2nd Floor)
Lift
Prunkräume 2.OG
Planetensaal
Gotische Kapelle
Lift
Alte Galerie
Renaissance & Baroque Art
Alte Galerie
Renaissance
& Barock
Alte Galerie
Mittelalter
Lift

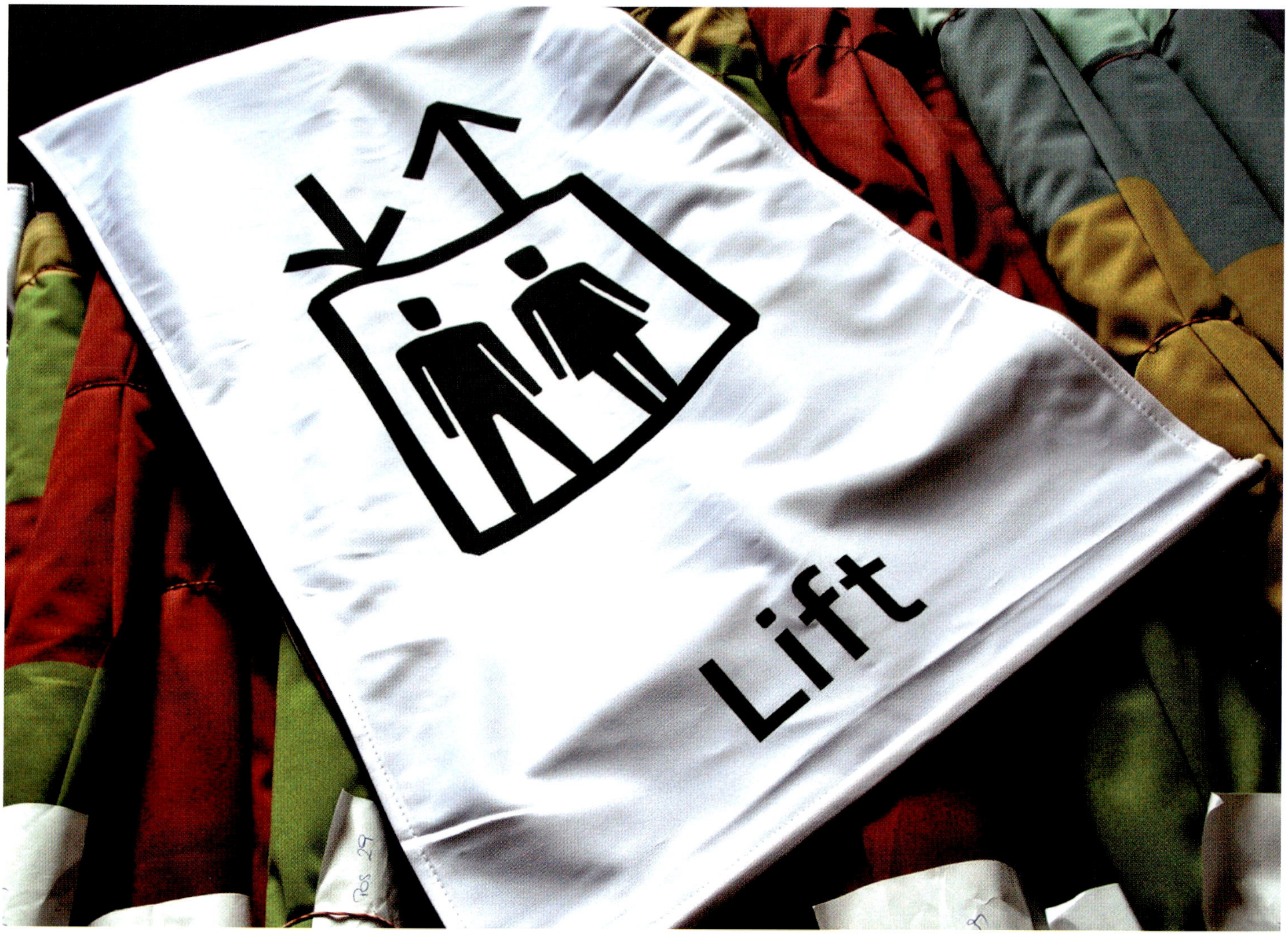
Lift

Approach: The strategy behind the Drug Policy Alliance rebrand is built upon two core concepts; inspire and connect. The simple and direct statement of "We are the Drug Policy Alliance" was developed to build on the recognition of their name and act as a rallying cry for internal and external supporters. The visual program is enhanced with bold typography, saturated color, and authentic photography, capturing real supporters as they engage in real events. All communicative decisions are evaluated on their ability to connect with and inspire their community. In addition, some brand elements are intended to be flexible, such as the "We are the Drug Policy Alliance" statement transforming into "I am the Drug Policy Alliance" when worn on a t-shirt. Employees also have the opportunity to author personal statements to be placed on the back of their business card about what motivates their work and why they have joined this alliance. By bringing voice to individuals, the collective whole was better amplified.

Results: The Drug Policy Alliance's new brand accurately captures the spirit of the organization and embraces the movement it leads. Its online presence was invigorated and after launch it experienced a 50 percent growth of their online subscriber list, which is now over 225,000 people—the highest in their history. More online subscribers has translated into more online donors and more than doubled its online donation targets for the year. The offline fundraising has seen a major bump since the launch of the new brand as well. The organization has seen an increase of 12.5 percent in direct mail donations since the redesigned packages started reaching supporters. The flexibility of the new identity, which encourages statements like, "I Am the Drug Policy Alliance," gave DPA supporters a new way to step out on their sometimes contentious issues and self identify with the brand and their cause.

They created a promotional video featuring their most prominent supporters, including George Soros and Sting, where they proclaim, "I Am the Drug Policy Alliance." Everyone in the video is a strong supporter of the organization, and the new identity gave them a proud way to declare their support openly and publicly in a way they had never done before. The promotional video was picked up by bloggers at the Huffington Post, Alternet, Boing Boing, and Big Hollywood. As a result, Fox News got a hold of the video and used it to criticize Sting and the whole organization for their views. The attention was a windfall for DPA. Fox aired the video—including important statements of their values—in three separate segments, including one where DPA's executive director debated Bill O'Reilly. The combined value of these spots was nearly half a million dollars in free publicity for the Drug Policy Alliance. The video itself has been viewed more than 25,000 times on YouTube.

Designers: David Feinstein, Nick Seay, Meghan Still | **Design Firm:** Beveridge Seay Inc. | **Client:** Drug Policy Alliance

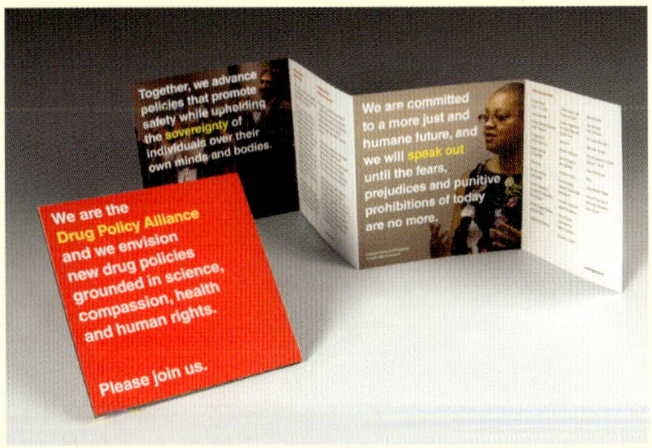

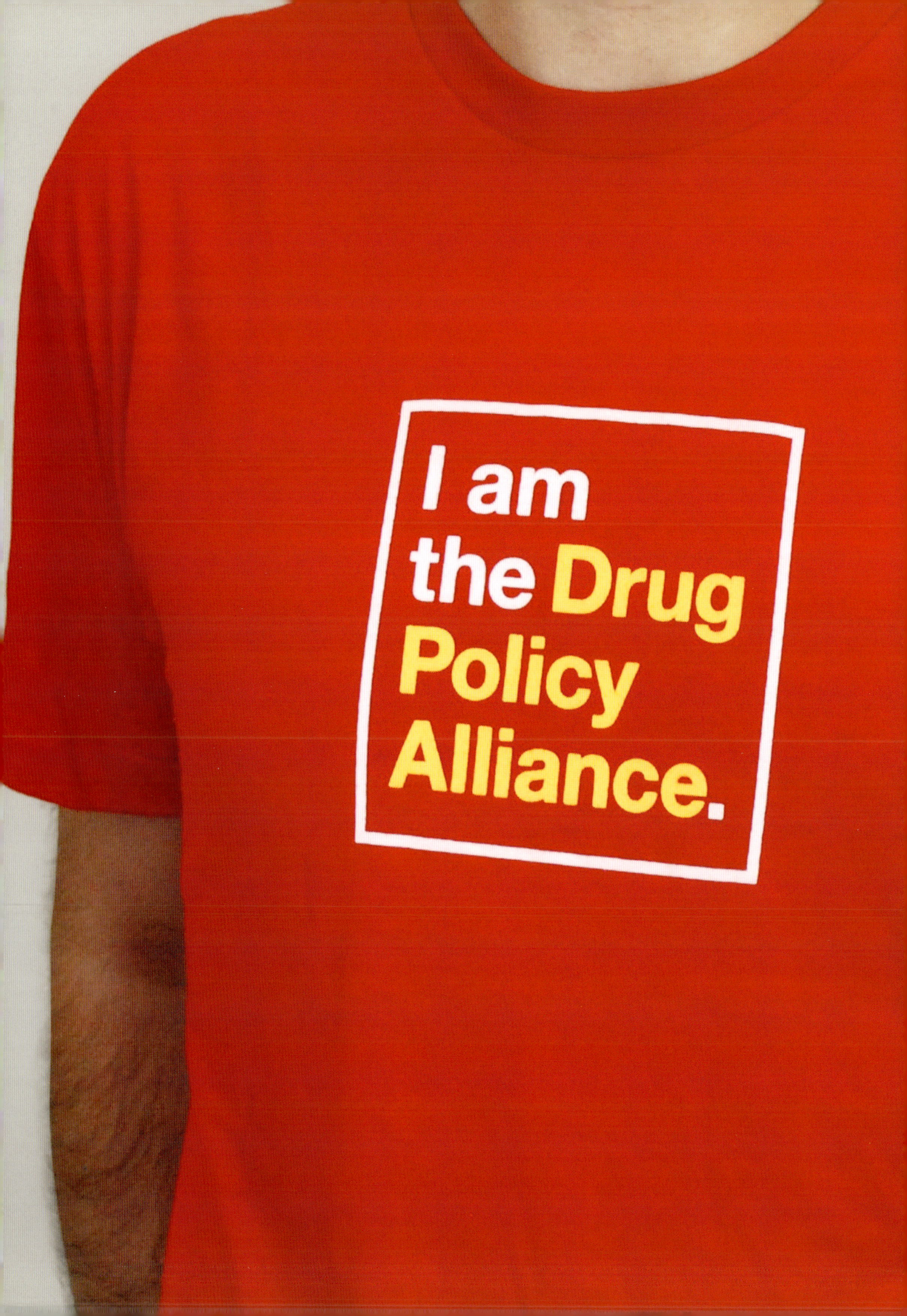
I am the Drug Policy Alliance.

We are
the Drug
Policy
Alliance.

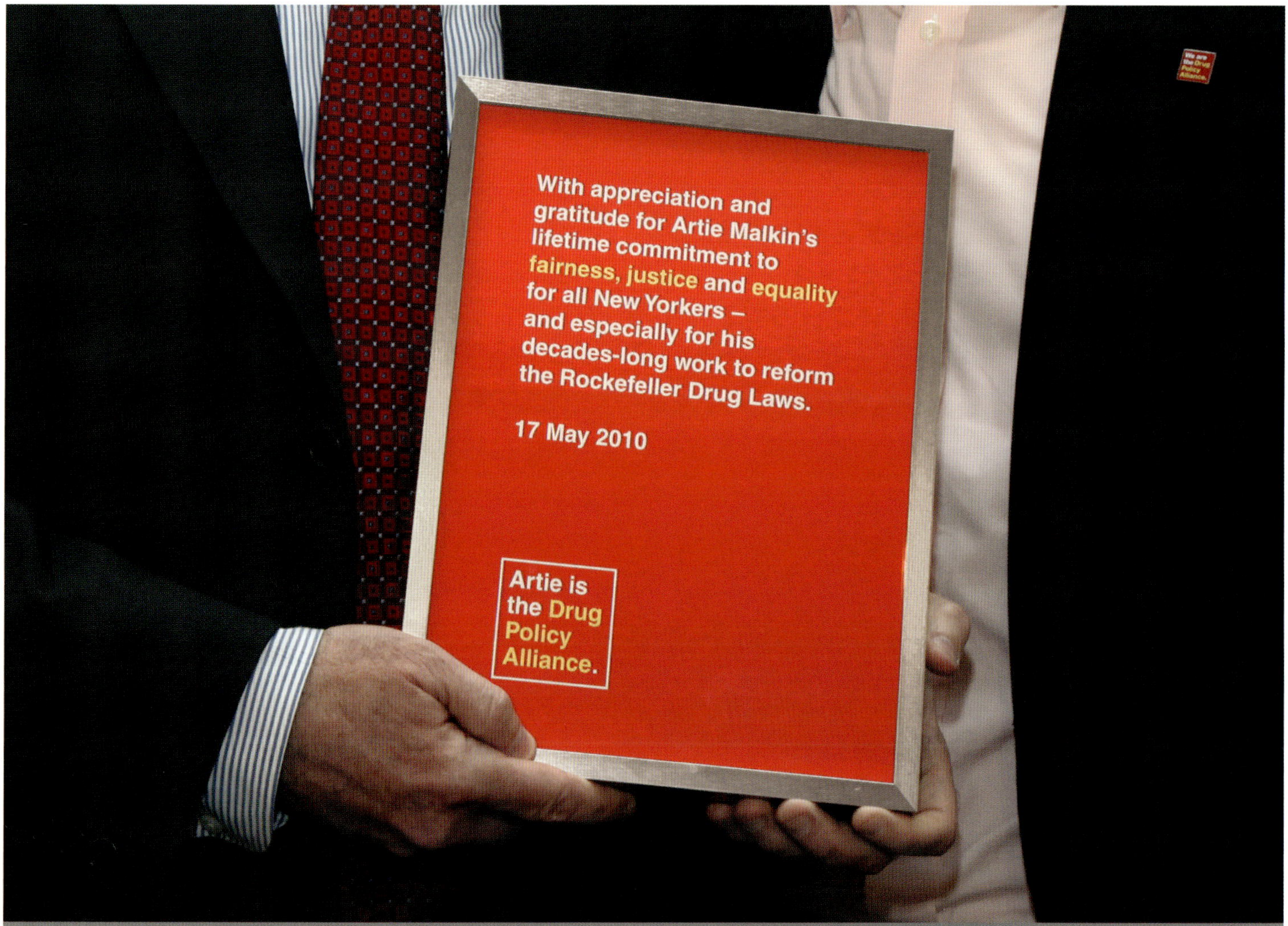

With appreciation and gratitude for Artie Malkin's lifetime commitment to fairness, justice and equality for all New Yorkers – and especially for his decades-long work to reform the Rockefeller Drug Laws.
17 May 2010
Artie is the Drug Policy Alliance.

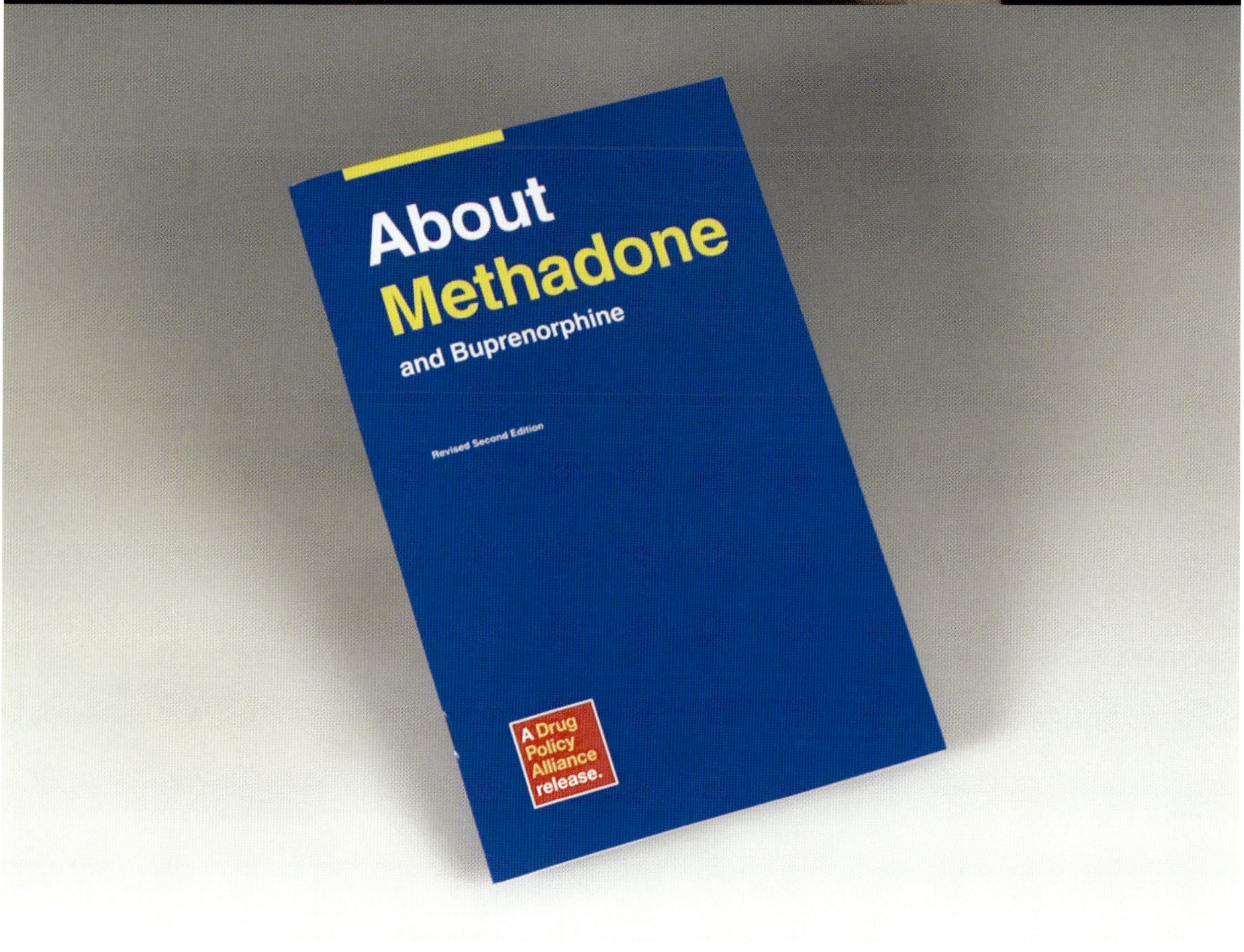

About
Methadone
and Buprenorphine
Revised Second Edition
A Drug Policy Alliance release.

Assignment: Ce-M-M- is a biomedical research institute that bridges the gap between basic research and practical medical needs, with its goal to assist in preparing the predictive, preventive, and personalized medicine of the future. The company's visual identity should be progressive yet sober, playful yet trustworthy.

Approach: In the logotype, the initials of the company are arranged like a fictitious chemical formula, ending with an open bond to reflect the willingness to establish a connection. Human silhouettes made from protein sequences serve as a secondary design element.

Design Firm: Lichtwitz Leinfellner visuelle Kultur KG | **Art Directors:** Kriso Leinfellner, Stefanie Lichtwitz, Harald Niessner, Katharina Untertrifaller
Creative Directors: Kriso Leinfellner, Stefanie Lichtwitz, Harald Niessner | **Client:** CeMM

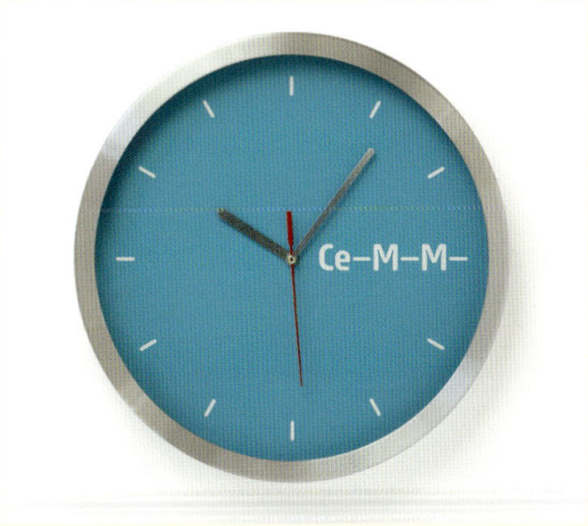

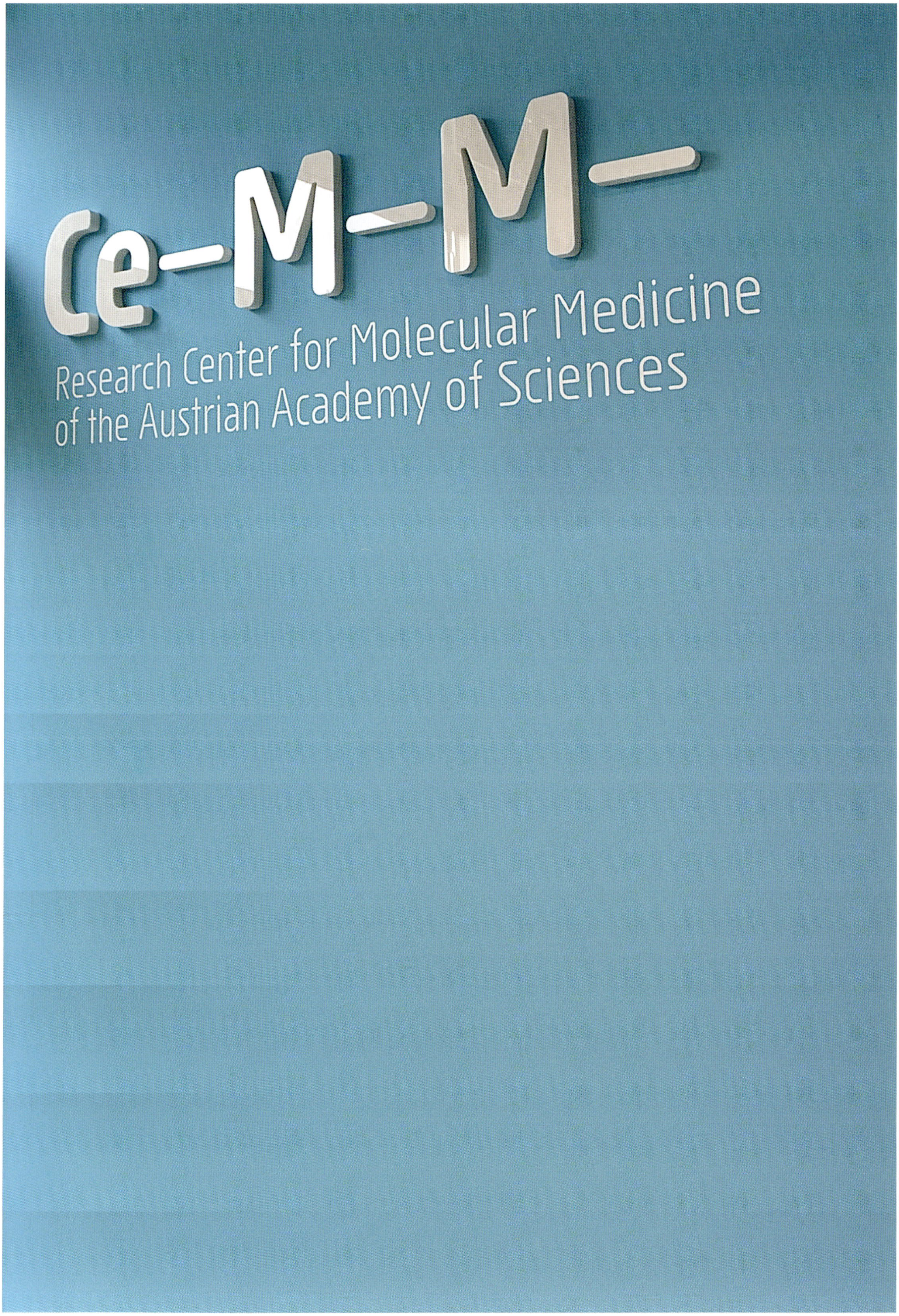
Ce-M-M-
Research Center for Molecular Medicine
of the Austrian Academy of Sciences

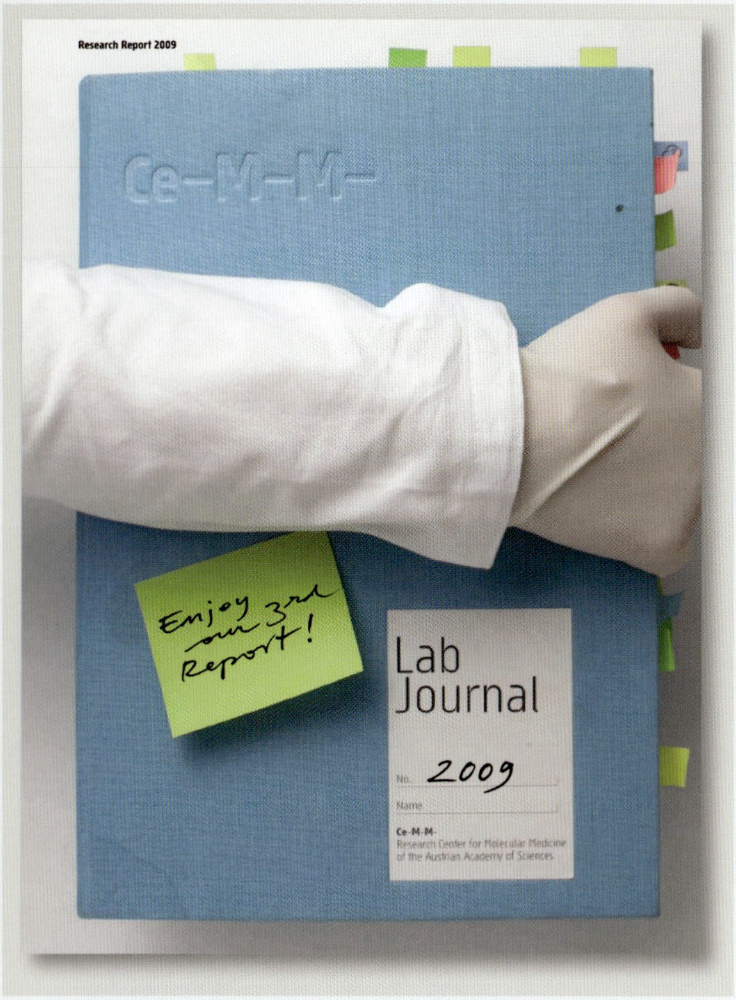
Research Report 2009
Ce-M-M-
Enjoy our 3rd Report!
Lab Journal
No. 2009
Name
Ce-M-M-
Research Center for Molecular Medicine of the Austrian Academy of Sciences

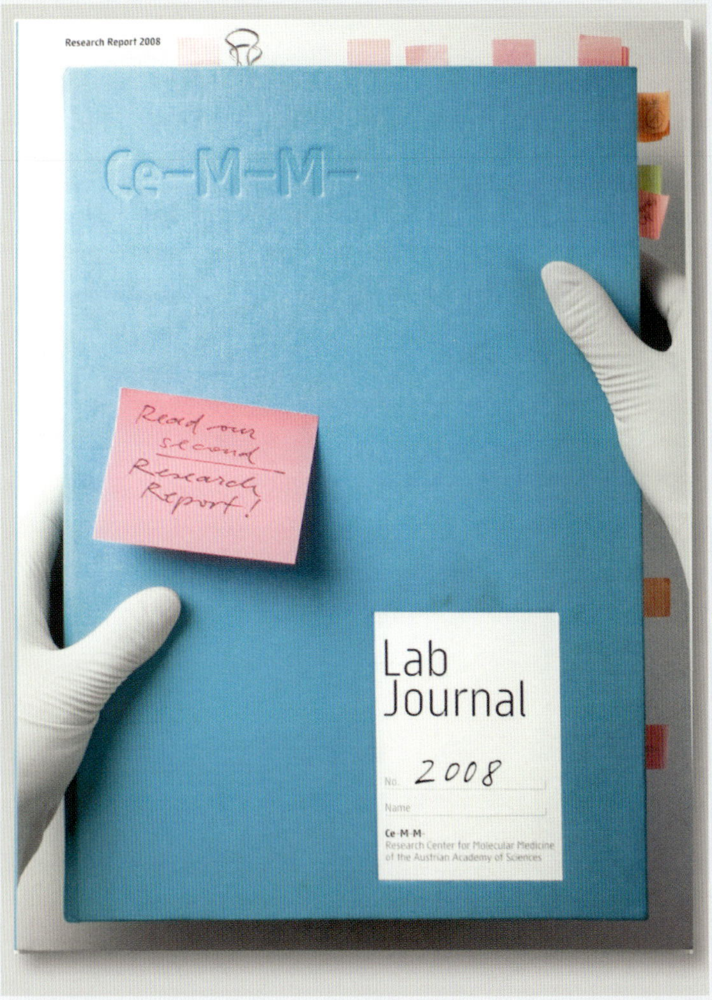
Research Report 2008
Ce-M-M-
Read our second Research Report!
Lab Journal
No. 2008
Name
Ce-M-M-
Research Center for Molecular Medicine of the Austrian Academy of Sciences

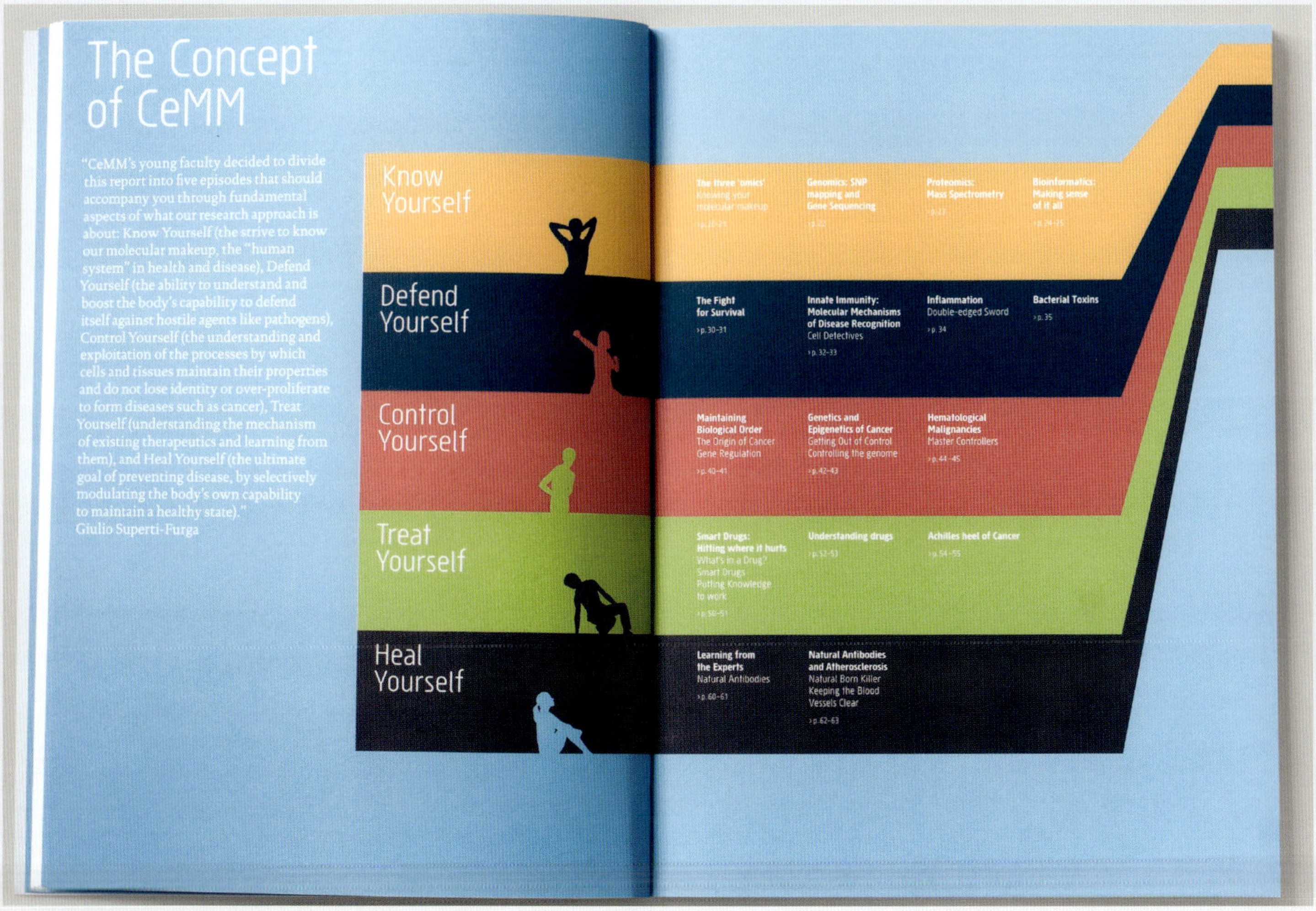
The Concept of CeMM
"CeMM's young faculty decided to divide this report into five episodes that should accompany you through fundamental aspects of what our research approach is about: Know Yourself (the strive to know our molecular makeup, the "human system" in health and disease), Defend Yourself (the ability to understand and boost the body's capability to defend itself against hostile agents like pathogens), Control Yourself (the understanding and exploitation of the processes by which cells and tissues maintain their properties and do not lose identity or over-proliferate to form diseases such as cancer), Treat Yourself (understanding the mechanism of existing therapeutics and learning from them), and Heal Yourself (the ultimate goal of preventing disease, by selectively modulating the body's own capability to maintain a healthy state)."
Giulio Superti-Furga
Know Yourself
Defend Yourself
Control Yourself
Treat Yourself
Heal Yourself
The Fight for Survival
Innate Immunity: Molecular Mechanisms of Disease Recognition
Cell Detectives
Inflammation
Double-edged Sword
Bacterial Toxins
Maintaining Biological Order
The Origin of Cancer
Gene Regulation
Genetics and Epigenetics of Cancer
Getting Out of Control
Controlling the genome
Hematological Malignancies
Master Controllers
Smart Drugs: Hitting where it hurts
What's in a Drug?
Smart Drugs
Putting Knowledge to work
Understanding drugs
Achilles heel of Cancer
Learning from the Experts
Natural Antibodies
Natural Antibodies and Atherosclerosis
Natural Born Killer
Keeping the Blood Vessels Clear

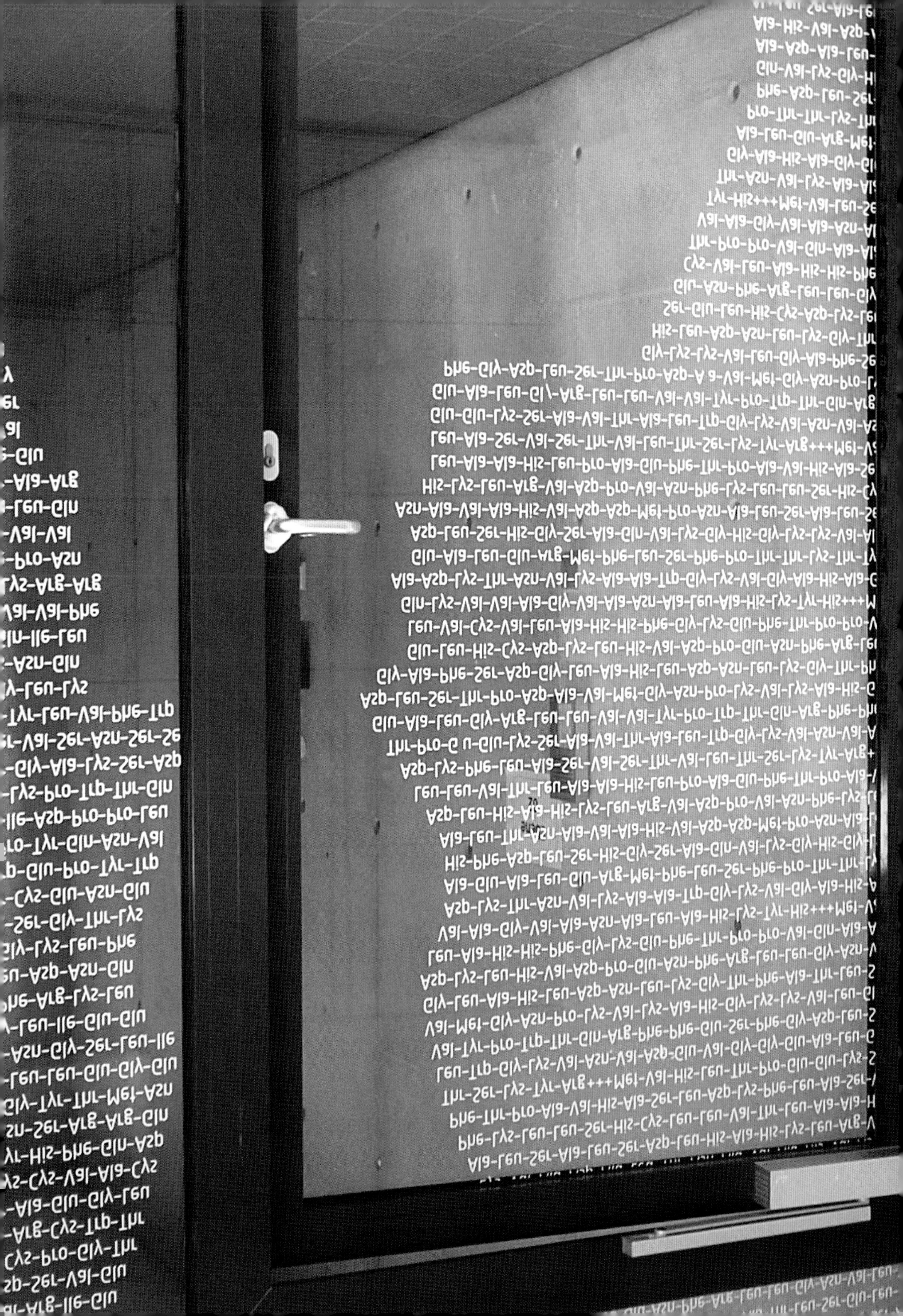

Assignment: Our assignment was to redesign a line of hydroponic nutrients packages to give them more personality and infuse them with the owner's sense of humor.

Approach: Most of the nutrients are formulated to care for serious heirloom-quality plants. Their main customers appreciate humor and follow the owner and his larger-than-life personality. Our design direction was influenced by old vegetable crate labels and vintage food packaging, while Marc Burkhardt's illustrations convey humor and personality.

Results: The client loved the finished product.

Designers: DJ Stout, Julie Savasky, Stu Taylor, Christen Humphreys | **Design Firm:** Pentagram | **Art Director:** DJ Stout
Illustrator: Marc Burckhardt | **Client:** Advanced Nutrients

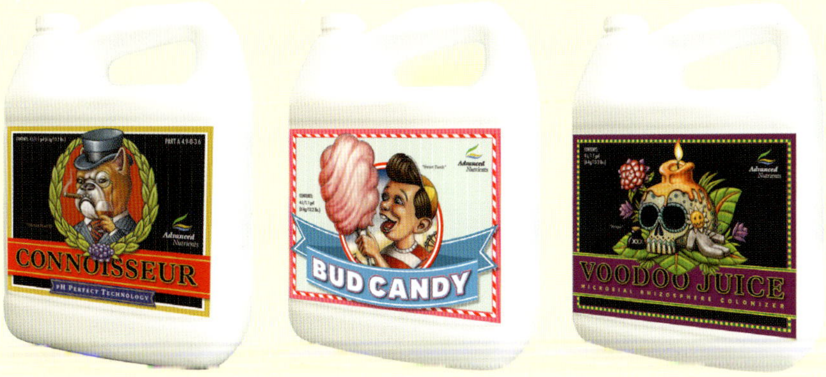

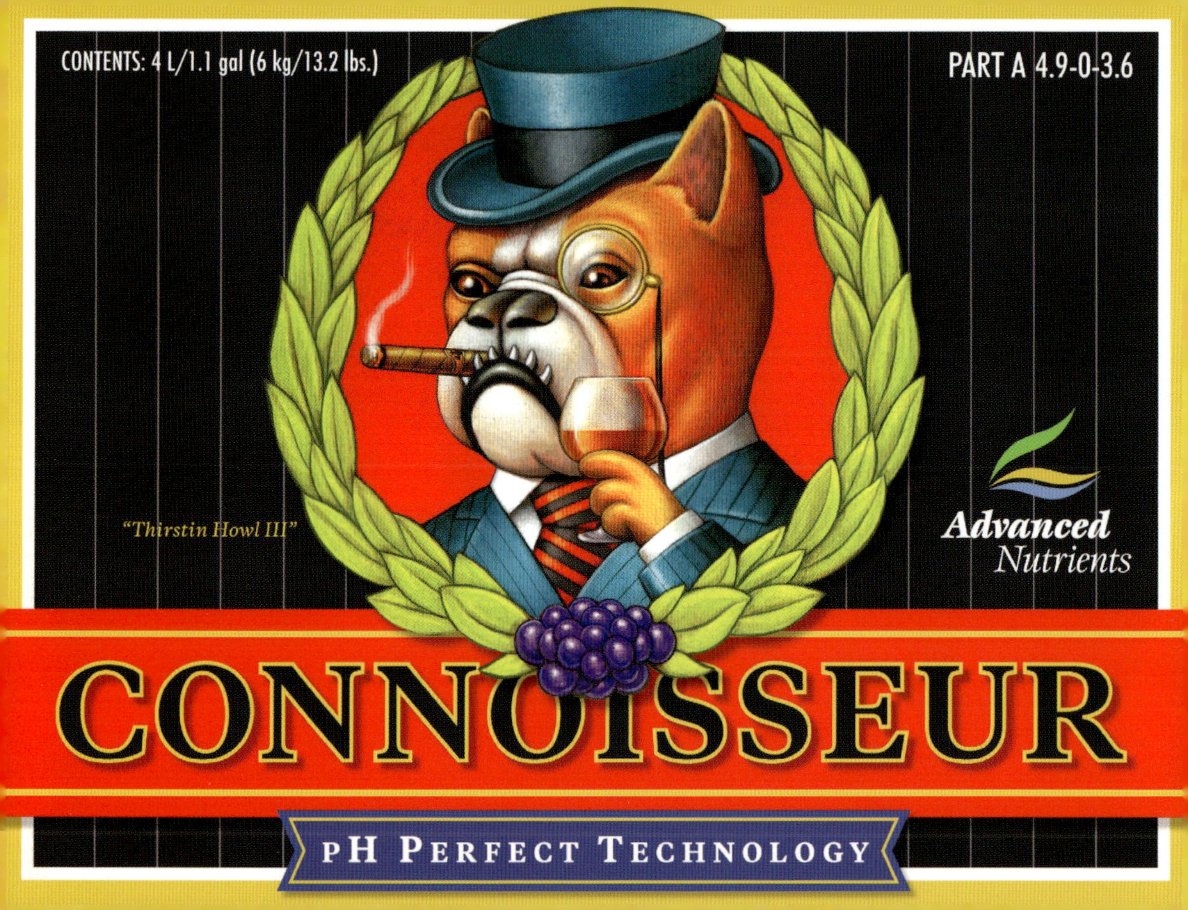
CONTENTS: 4 L/1.1 gal (6 kg/13.2 lbs.)
PART A 4.9-0-3.6
"Thirstin Howl III"
Advanced
Nutrients
CONNOISSEUR
pH PERFECT TECHNOLOGY

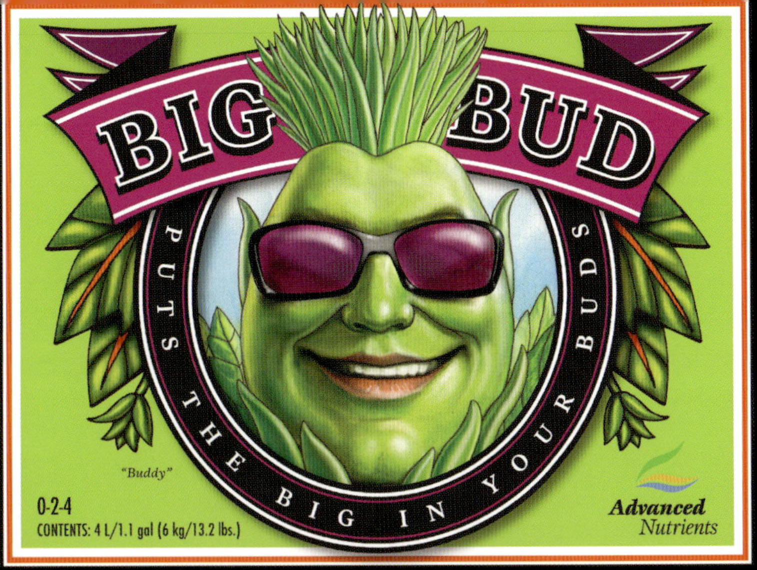
BIG BUD
PUTS THE BIG IN YOUR BUDS
"Buddy"
0-2-4
CONTENTS: 4 L/1.1 gal (6 kg/13.2 lbs.)
Advanced Nutrients

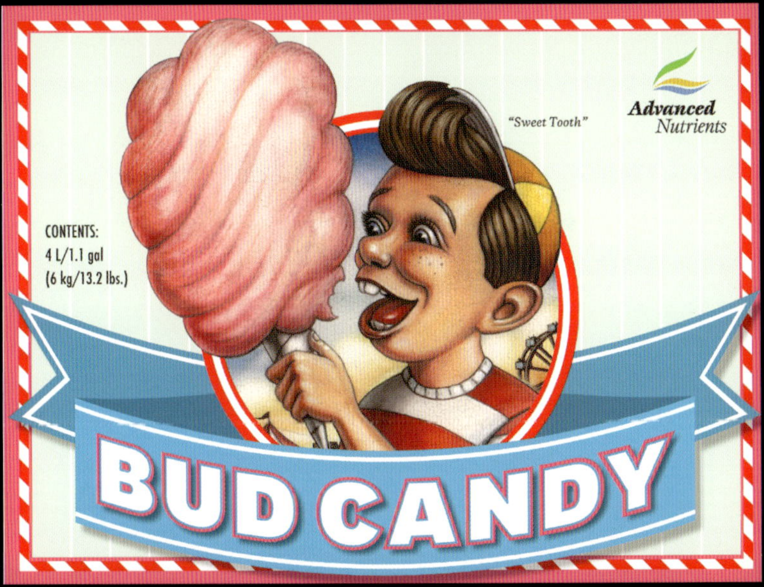
"Sweet Tooth"
Advanced Nutrients
CONTENTS:
4 L/1.1 gal
(6 kg/13.2 lbs.)
BUD CANDY

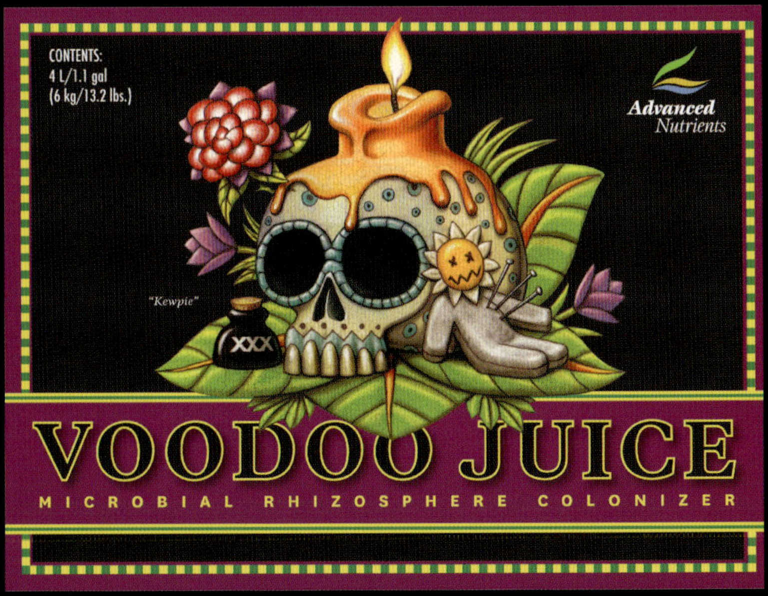
CONTENTS:
4 L/1.1 gal
(6 kg/13.2 lbs.)
Advanced Nutrients
"Kewpie"
XXX
VOODOO JUICE
MICROBIAL RHIZOSPHERE COLONIZER

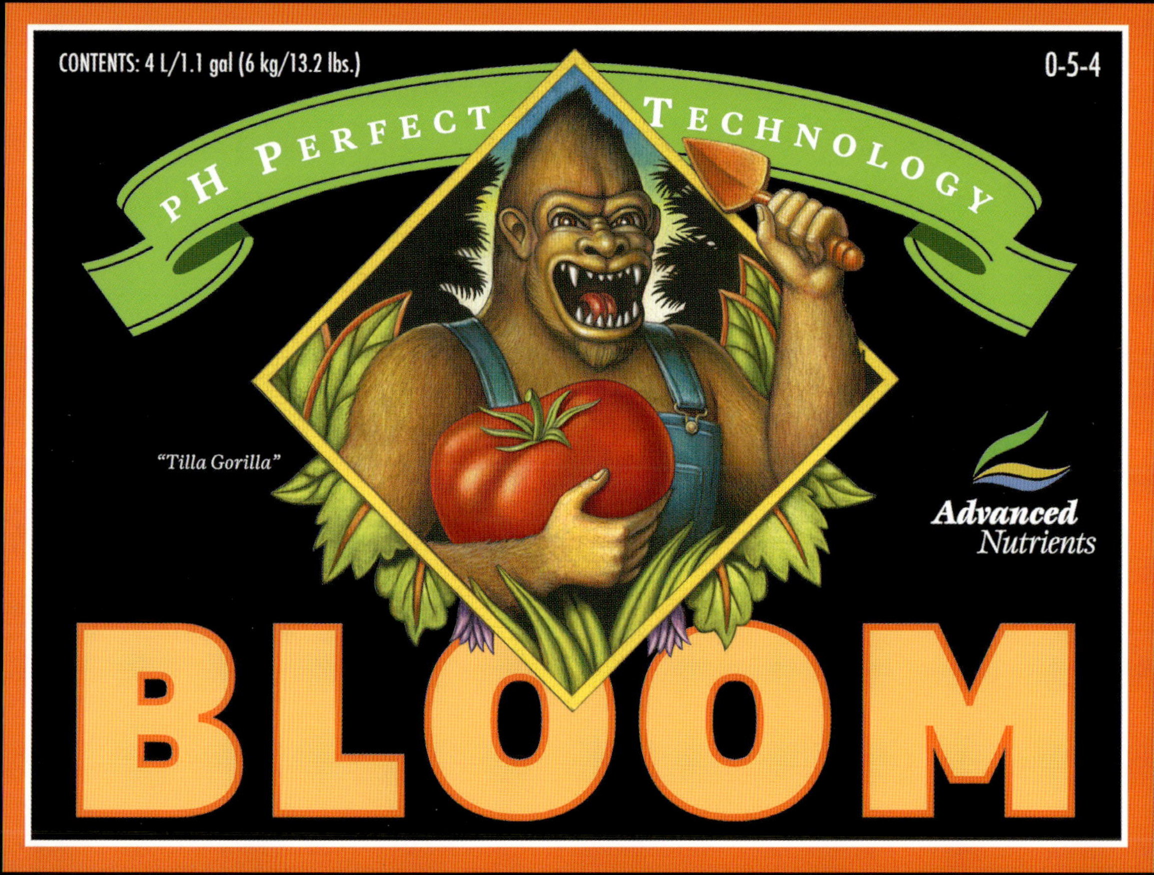

CONTENTS: 4 L/1.1 gal (6 kg/13.2 lbs.)
0-5-4
pH PERFECT TECHNOLOGY
"Tilla Gorilla"
Advanced Nutrients
BLOOM

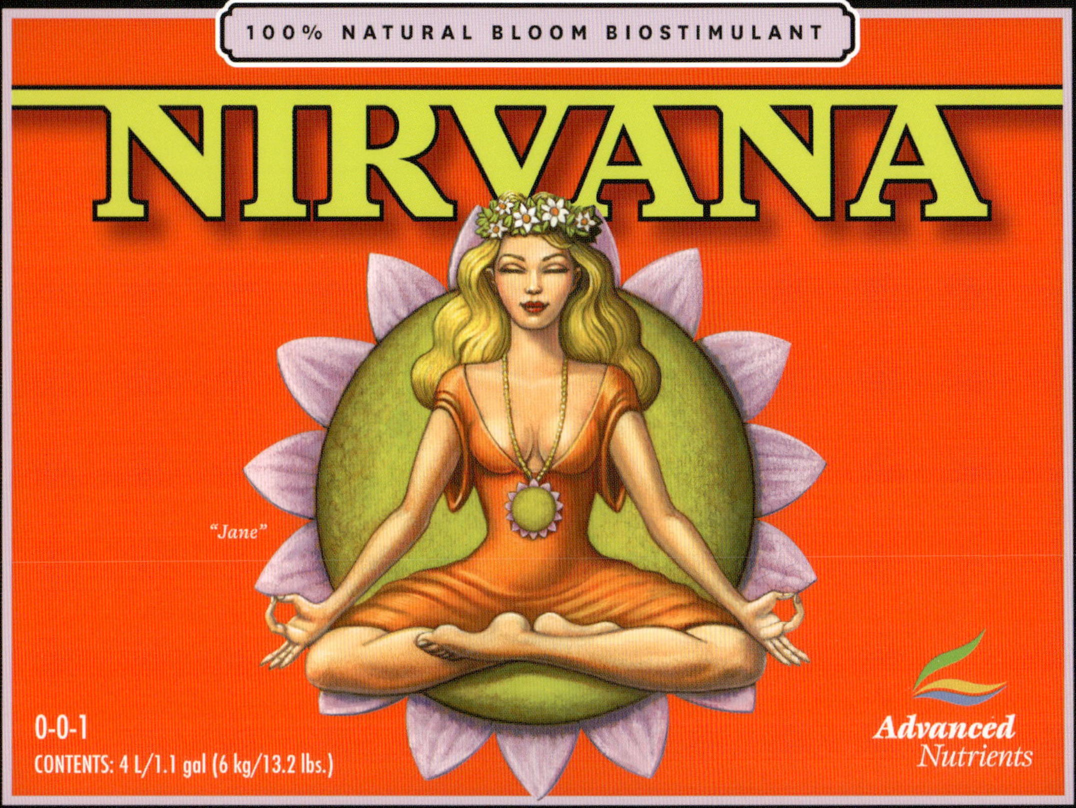
100% NATURAL BLOOM BIOSTIMULANT
NIRVANA
"Jane"
0-0-1
CONTENTS: 4 L/1.1 gal (6 kg/13.2 lbs.)
Advanced
Nutrients

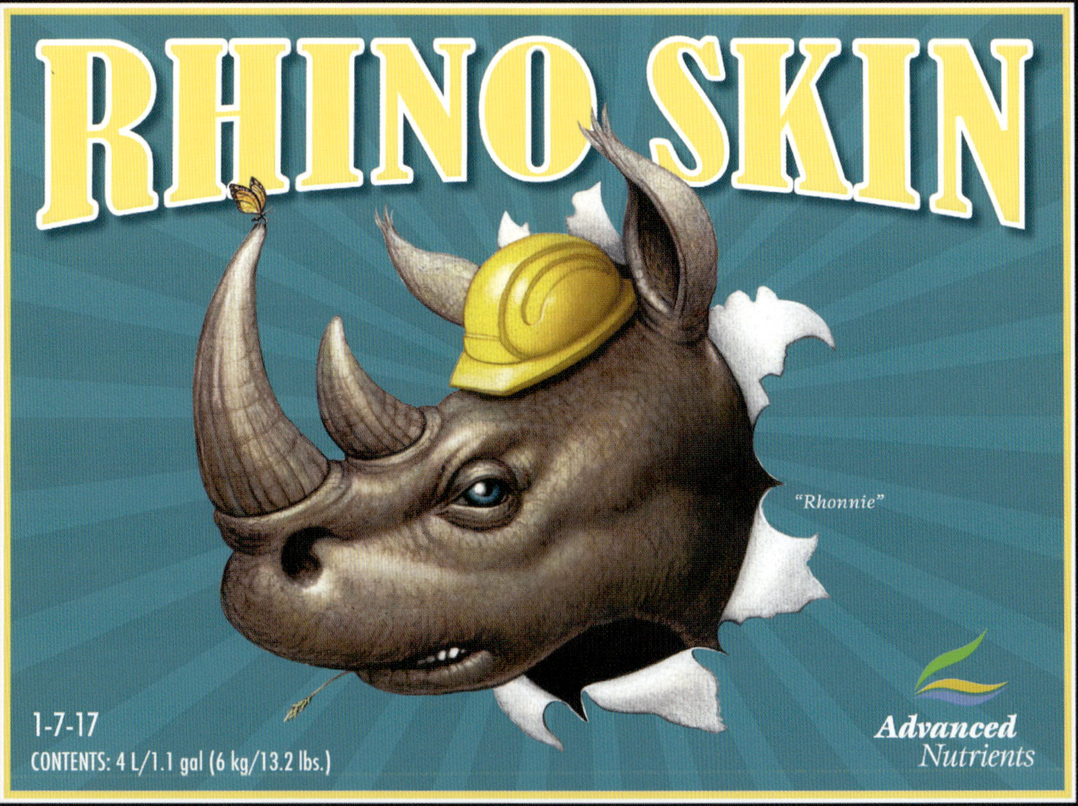
RHINO SKIN
"Rhonnie"
1-7-17
CONTENTS: 4 L/1.1 gal (6 kg/13.2 lbs.)
Advanced
Nutrients

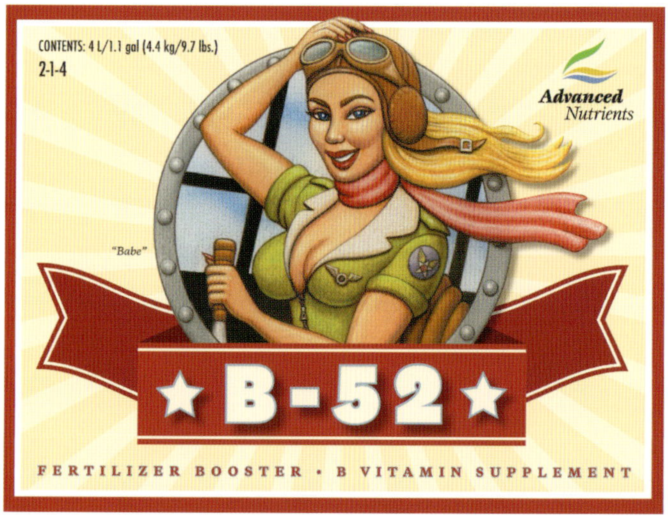
CONTENTS: 4 L/1.1 gal (4.4 kg/9.7 lbs.)
2-1-4
Advanced Nutrients
"Babe"
B-52
FERTILIZER BOOSTER • B VITAMIN SUPPLEMENT
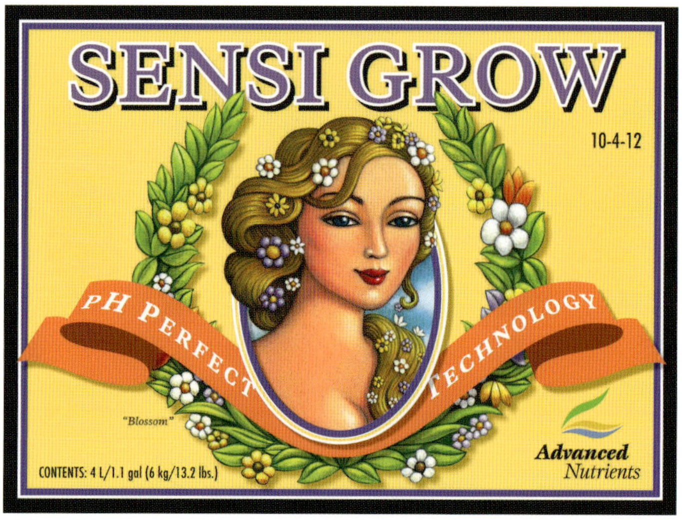
SENSI GROW
10-4-12
pH PERFECT TECHNOLOGY
"Blossom"
Advanced Nutrients
CONTENTS: 4 L/1.1 gal (6 kg/13.2 lbs.)
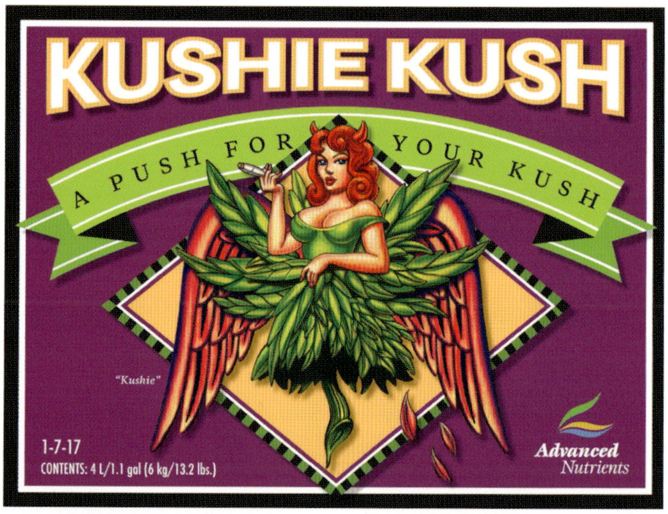
KUSHIE KUSH
A PUSH FOR YOUR KUSH
"Kushie"
1-7-17
CONTENTS: 4 L/1.1 gal (6 kg/13.2 lbs.)
Advanced Nutrients
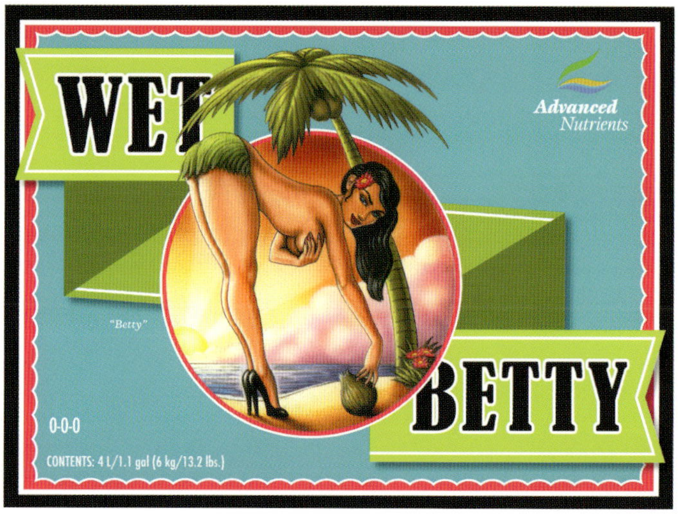
WET
BETTY
Advanced Nutrients
"Betty"
0-0-0
CONTENTS: 4 L/1.1 gal (6 kg/13.2 lbs.)
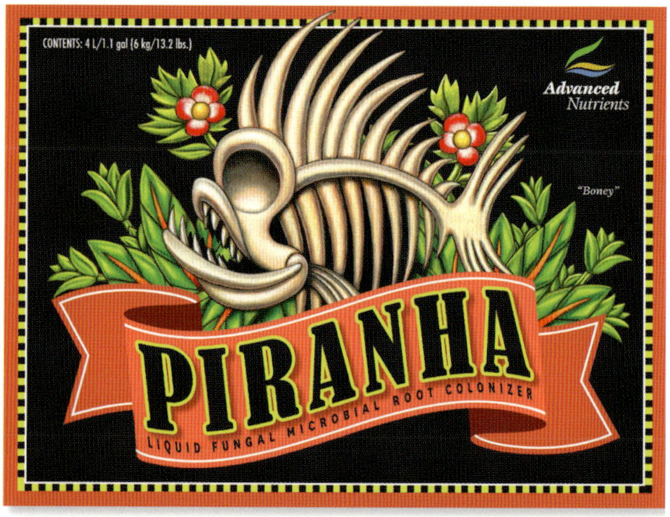
CONTENTS: 4 L/1.1 gal (6 kg/13.2 lbs.)
Advanced Nutrients
"Boney"
PIRANHA
LIQUID FUNGAL MICROBIAL ROOT COLONIZER
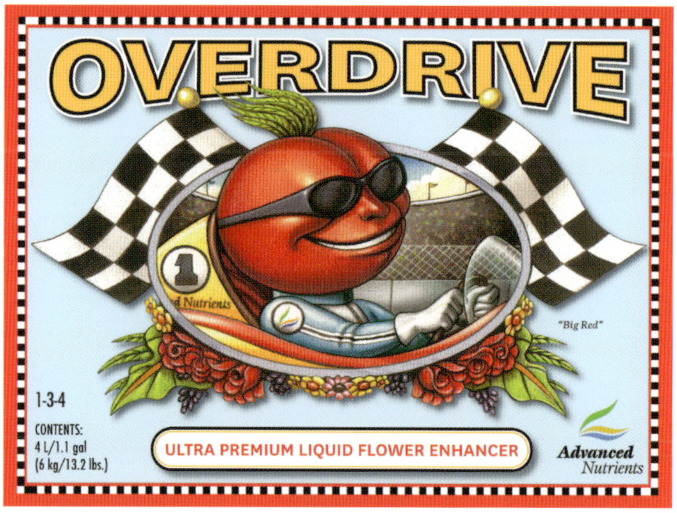
OVERDRIVE
"Big Red"
1-3-4
CONTENTS: 4 L/1.1 gal (6 kg/13.2 lbs.)
ULTRA PREMIUM LIQUID FLOWER ENHANCER
Advanced Nutrients
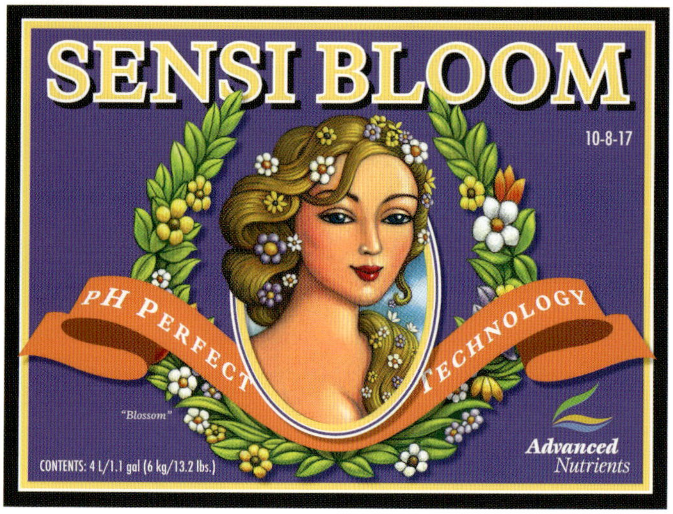
SENSI BLOOM
10-8-17
pH PERFECT TECHNOLOGY
"Blossom"
CONTENTS: 4 L/1.1 gal (6 kg/13.2 lbs.)
Advanced Nutrients
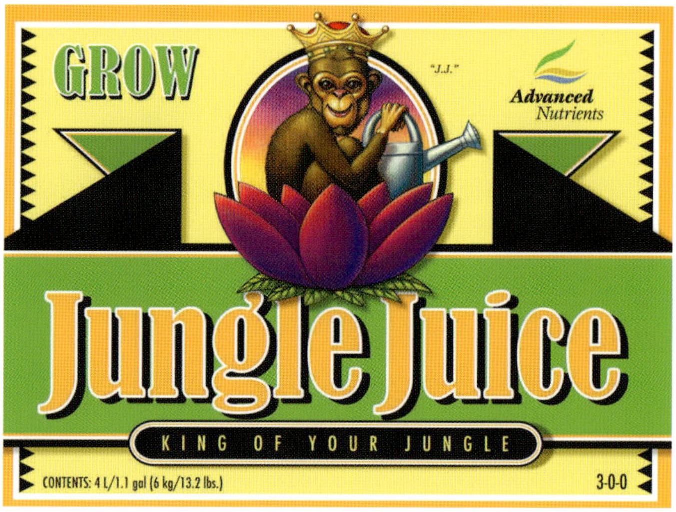
GROW
"J.J."
Advanced Nutrients
Jungle Juice
KING OF YOUR JUNGLE
CONTENTS: 4 L/1.1 gal (6 kg/13.2 lbs.)
3-0-0

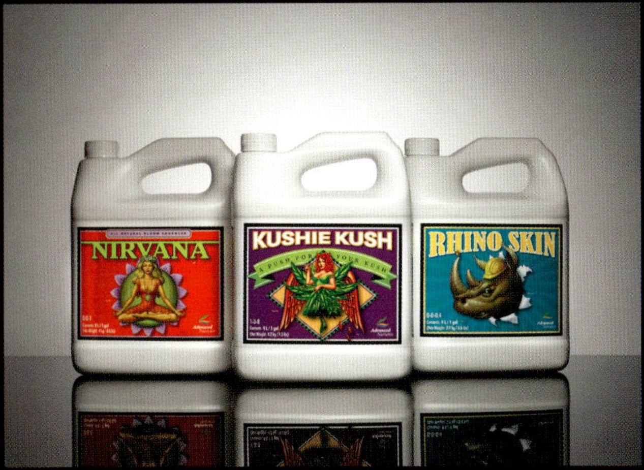
NIRVANA
KUSHIE KUSH
A PUSH FOR YOUR KUSH
RHINO SKIN

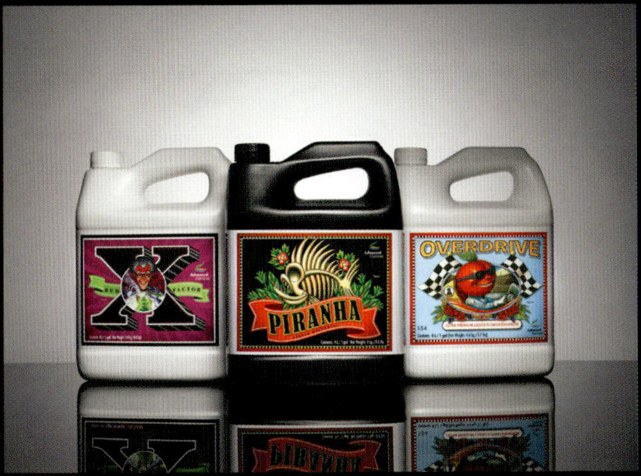
X
PIRANHA
OVERDRIVE

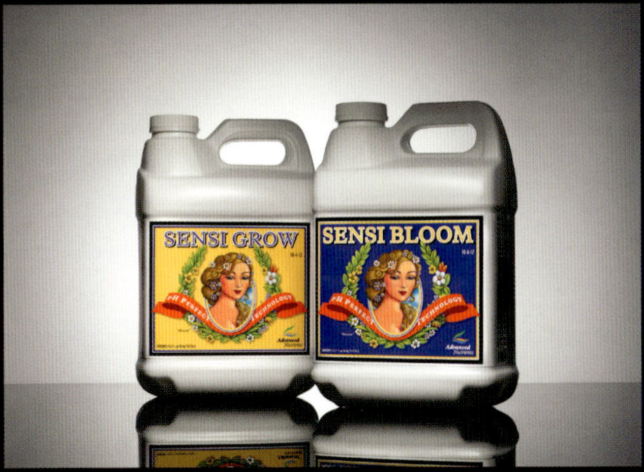
SENSI GROW
SENSI BLOOM
pH PERFECT TECHNOLOGY

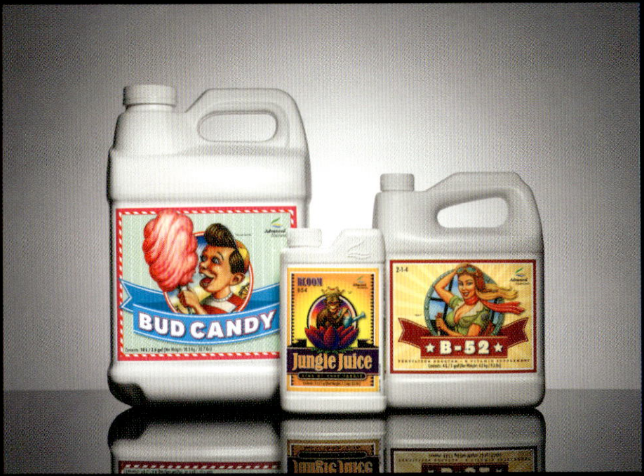
BUD CANDY
BLOOM
Jungle Juice
B-52

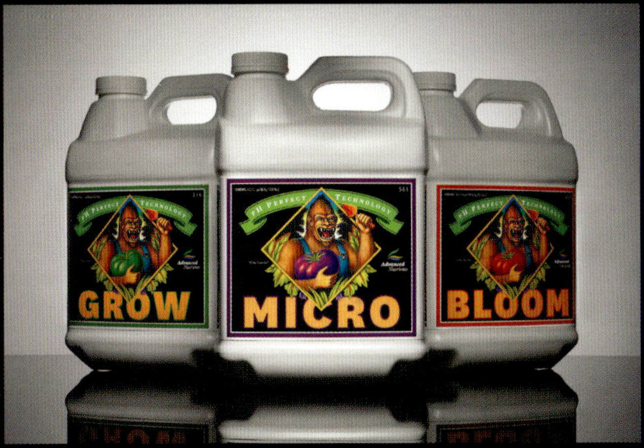
pH PERFECT TECHNOLOGY
GROW
MICRO
BLOOM

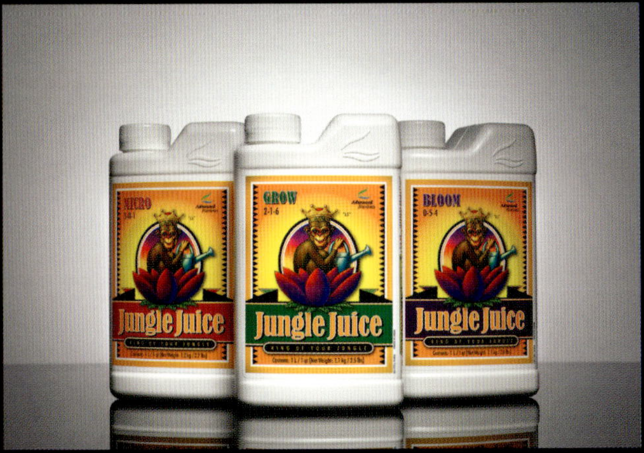
MICRO
Jungle Juice
GROW
2-1-6
Jungle Juice
BLOOM
Jungle Juice

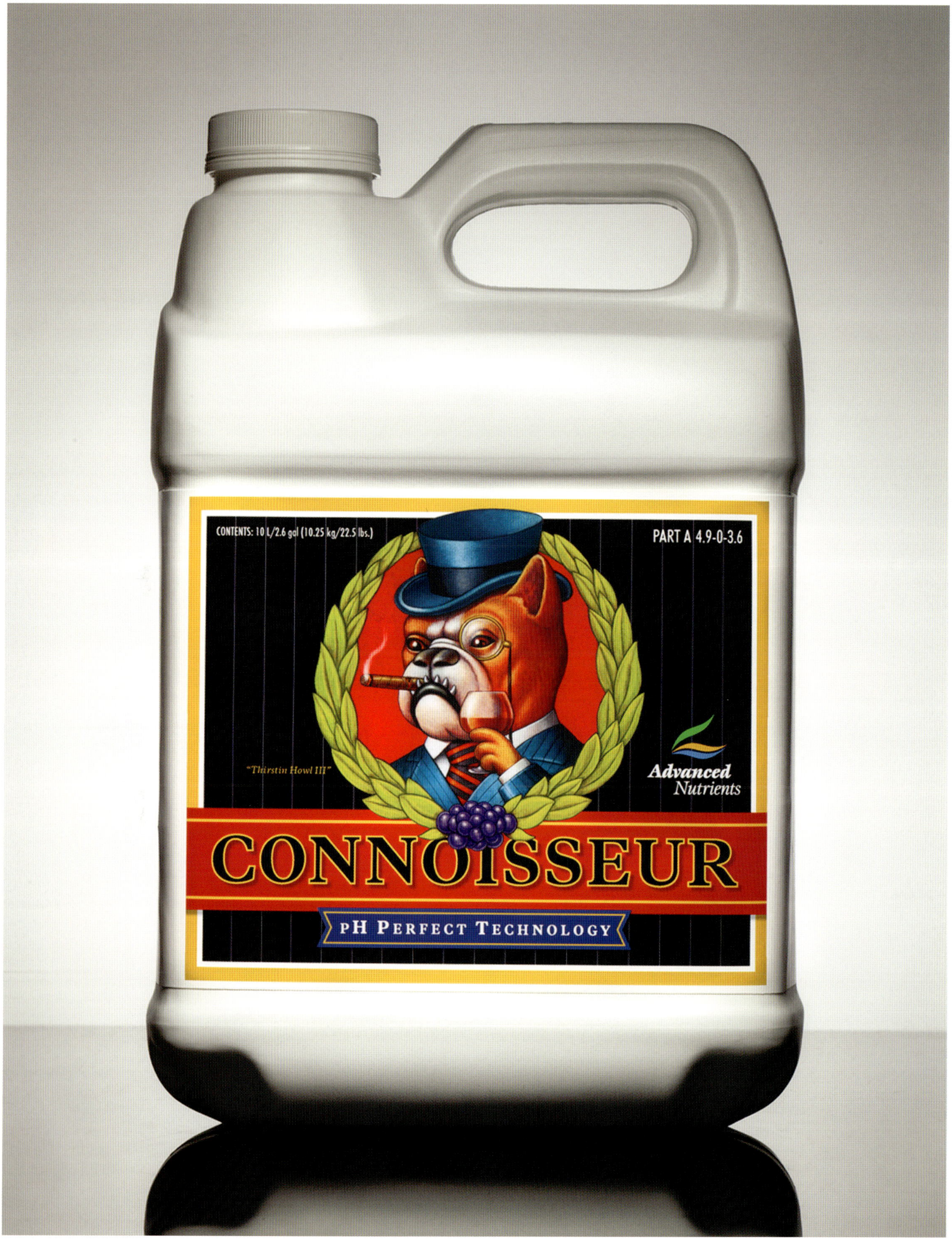

Pentagram (this spread) | AdvancedNutrients | Products 207

Assignment: Cheer has been a leading detergent brand in the US since its launch sixty years ago. Well-established as the brand made for colored clothes, its relevance in the marketplace has faded in recent years. The loyal Cheer consumer is the same woman who bought into the brand at its conception. With these consumers aging rapidly, Cheer saw the opportunity to reinvent itself by embracing its passion for color and appealing to a new consumer, one that is most receptive to preserving colorful clothes. No other brand in the category is speaking to Millennials, the untapped target doing laundry for themselves and their families for the first time. Millennials are wildly different. Cheer was determined to turn their ever-changing, eye-popping, digitized Gen-Y lifestyle into a brand they love.

Approach: A dive head-first into the Gen-Y world led Cheer to completely redefine its brand image. No longer is Cheer average and expected. Now, Cheer is alive, vibrant, viral, expressive, and digitized. Cheer now exists as a living, breathing, kinetic design system that connects with Millennials in surprising and unexpected ways. This system manifests itself through an updated brand mark, ever-changing patterns, a custom pixilated typeface and an arresting midnight blue package that practically jumps off shelf. The brand that loves color now is able to make a meaningful connection with the right consumer—the colorful Millennial.

Results: Millennials are beginning to fall in love with Cheer due to their mutual love for all things bold and expressive. As product appears on the shelf, people can't keep their hands off of it.

Designers: Jay Hoffman, Lesley Amann | **Clients:** P&G/Cheer

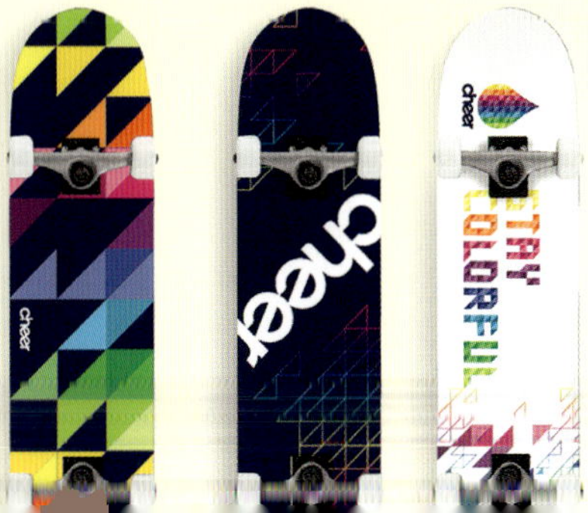

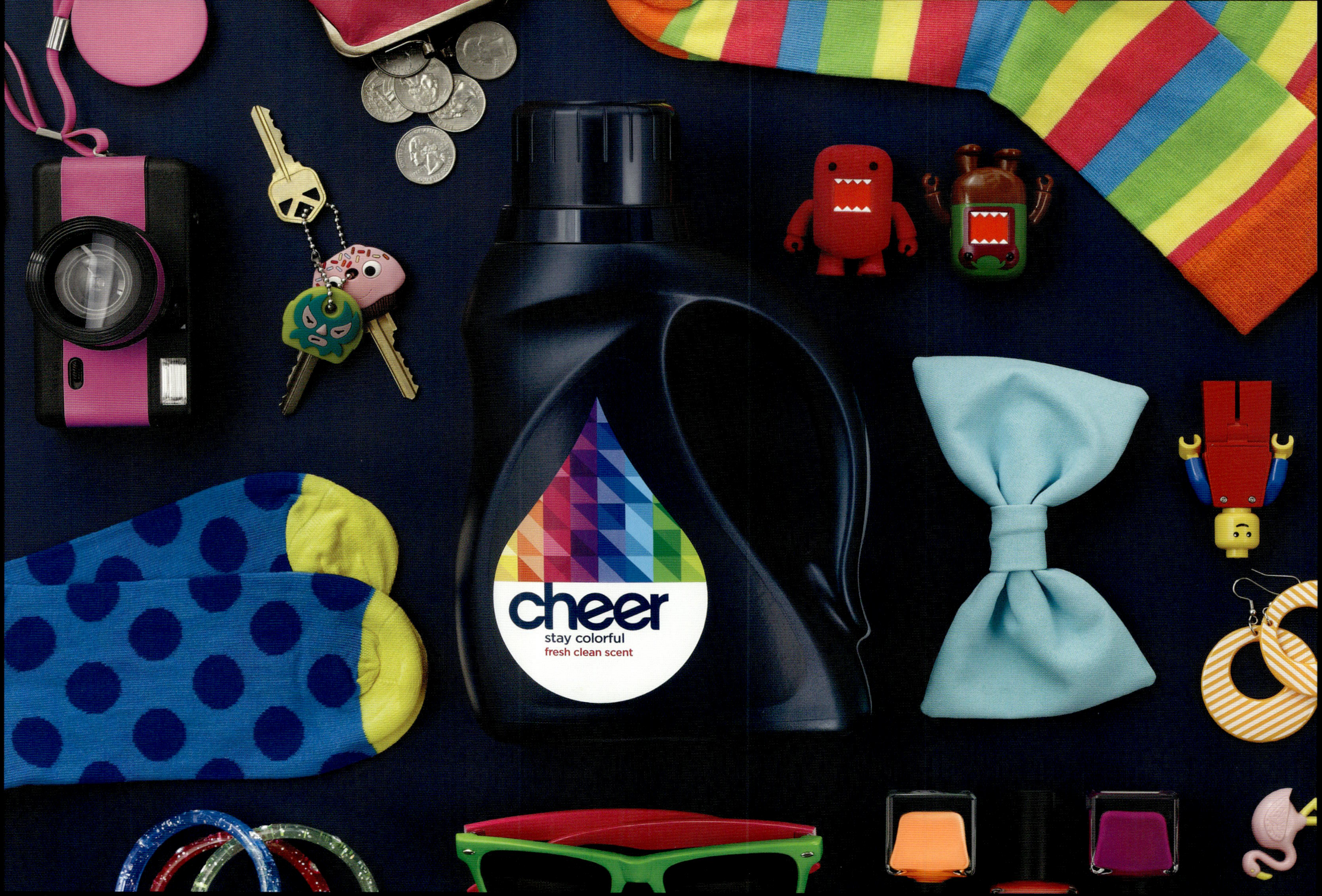
cheer
stay colorful
fresh clean scent

STOP TRAFFIC

COLORIFIC

ALL NIGHT LONG

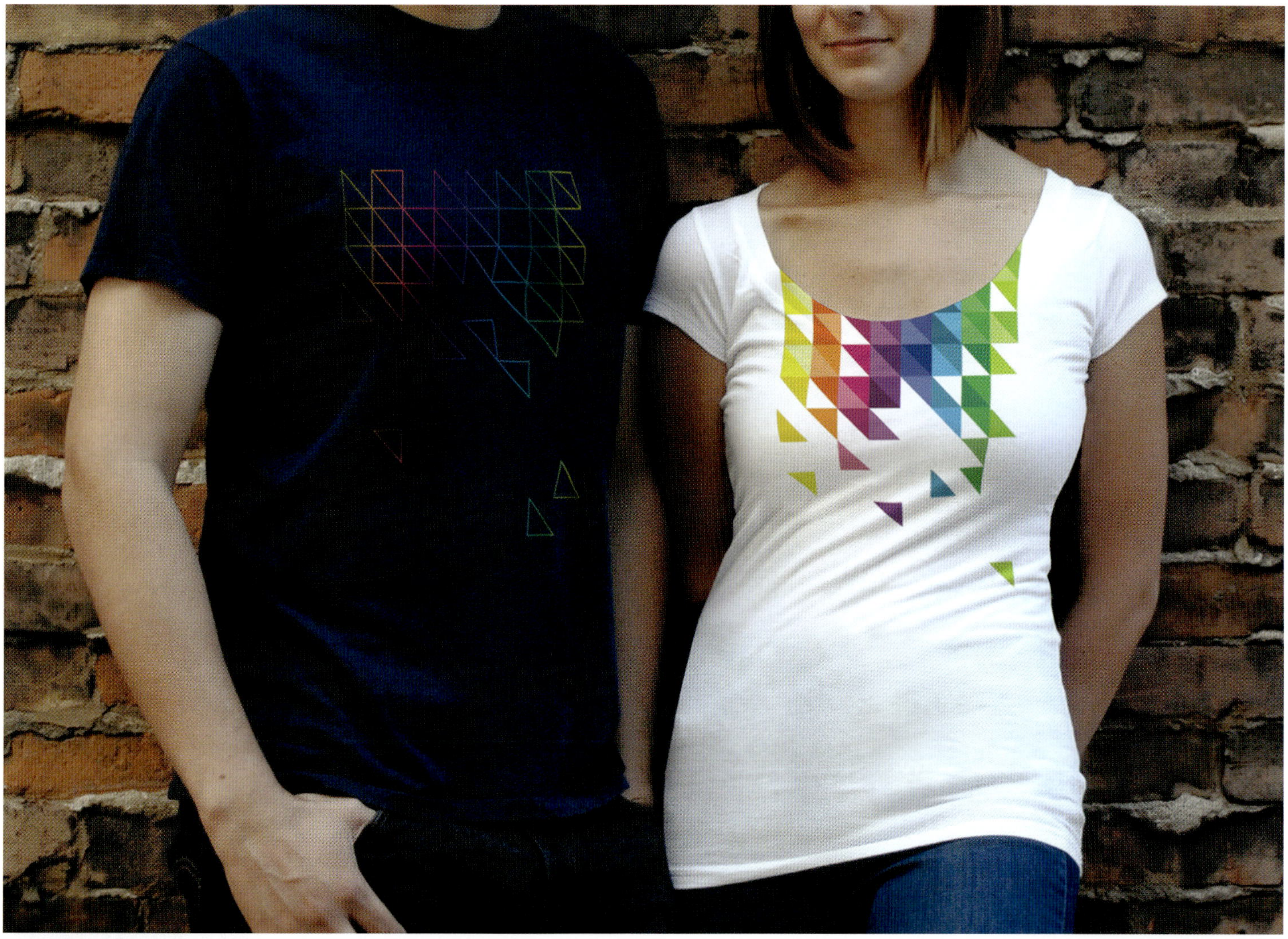

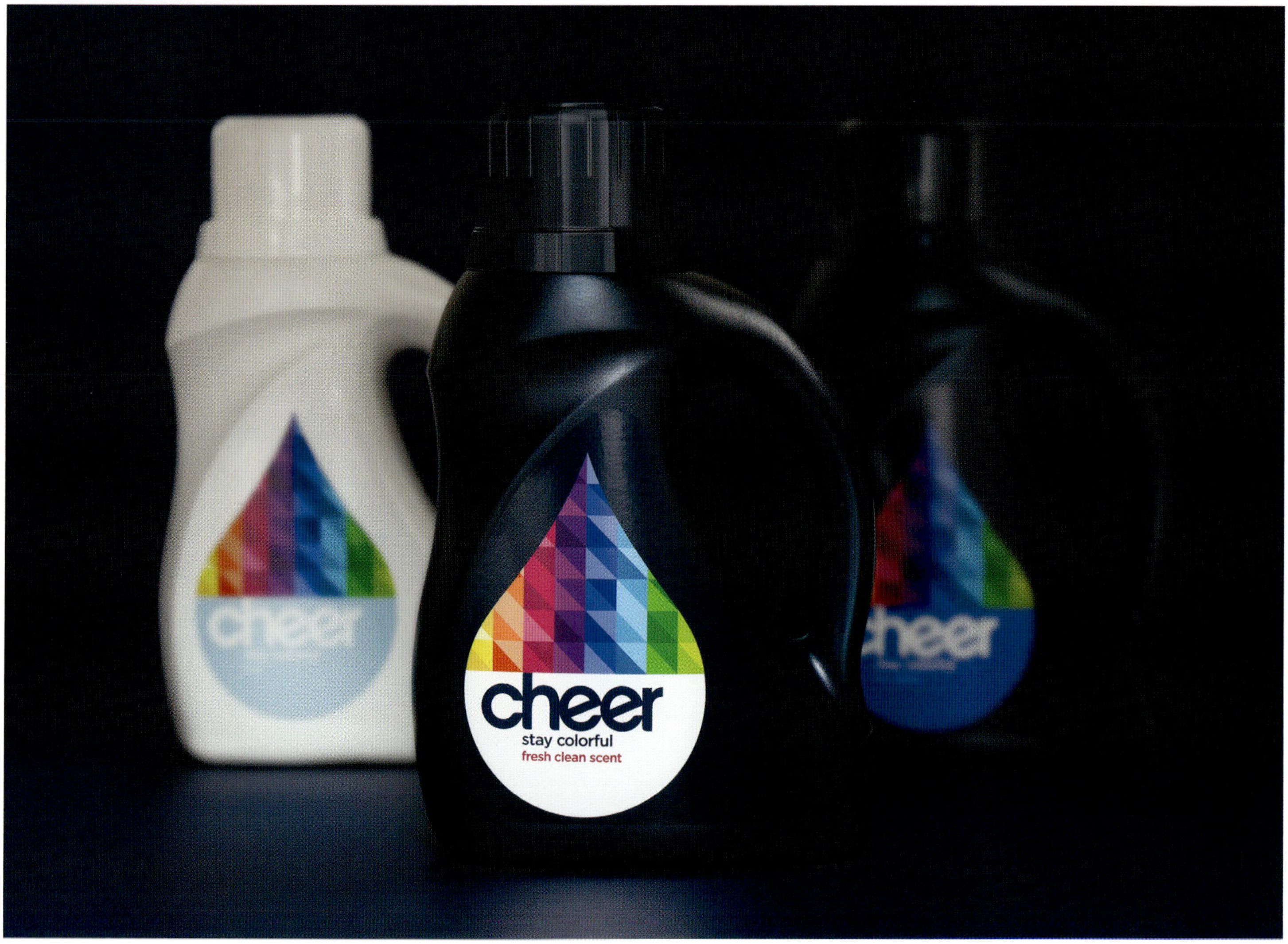

(this spread) | Cheer | Products

Assignment: The brand Betero was created to represent simplicity, geometry, local features, and a certain softness, which allows a very friendly approach to the target group. Betero makes notebooks for drawing, writing, art, or creation—sewn and handmade, in various sizes and designs—with special paper and features that make it unique in the market. Notebooks Betero are specially designed to be unique pieces for a personal collection, and the brand and corporate image stand for quality and warranty.

Approach: The name "Betero" was chosen to become a generic name, which is a result of combining several words like sketchbook, notebook, and bookshelf (in Spanish). For this name we chose a font that represents strength, safety, and quality, and rounded features that give a touch of confidence and warmth. The letter B is accompanied by a feature, which is an open book when it is flipped. The result is used as the isotype of the brand. The color black was chosen in 90% to lower the aggressiveness of the color. Beige color accompanies the idea of using materials and paper that are environmentally friendly and chlorine free. The alternative colors to the brand are red, blue, green, and orange. These represent the variety of uses and personalities that can use a "Betero." Inside the notebooks, we use shapes that represent some familiar features to Ecuador, geometric shapes and perpendicular angles between them, as the location of our territory.

Results: Betero's corporate image has achieved rapid positioning and excellent remembrance results. People use the name "Betero" instead of "book or notebook" and feel comfortable with the simplicity of the brand. This allowed them to use the product with objectivity and give it infinite types of uses. People use these products carefully and store them as part of their personal collection or as plans, projects, discussions, or creations.

Designers: Juan Francisco Martínez, Johanna Valdivieso | **Design Firm:** Johanna Valdivieso | **Art Director:** Johanna Valdivieso
Creative Directors: Juan Francisco Martínez, Johanna Valdivieso | **Writers:** Juan Francisco Martínez, Johanna Valdivieso
Client: Betero Notebooks

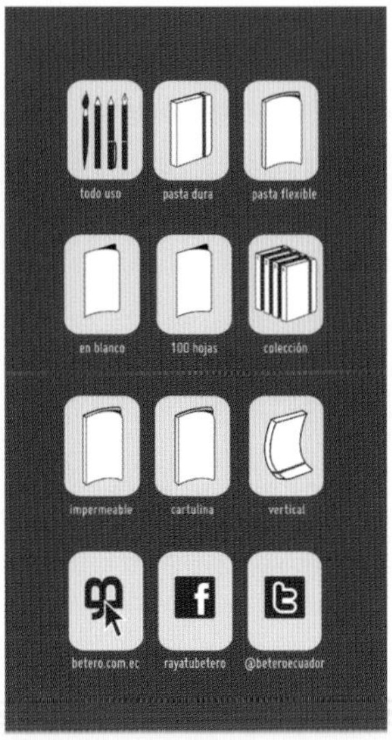

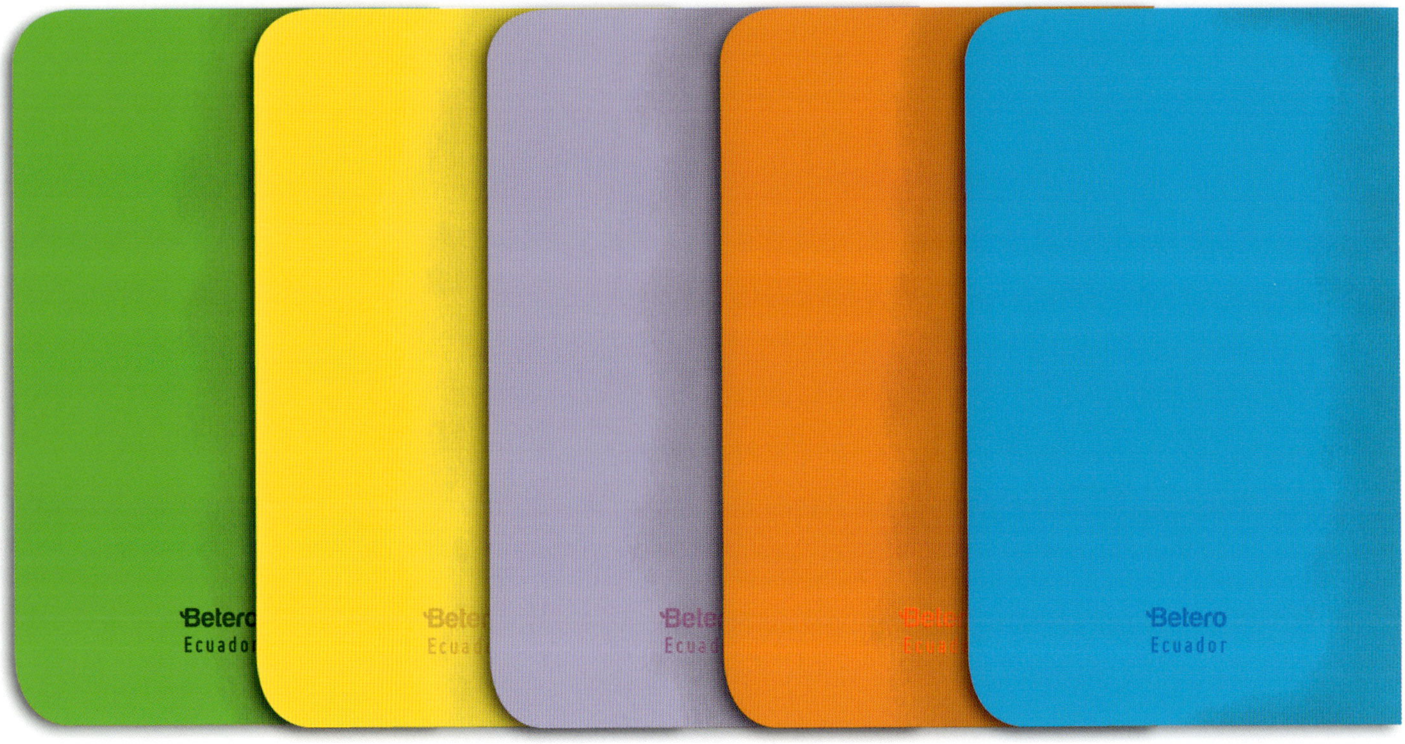

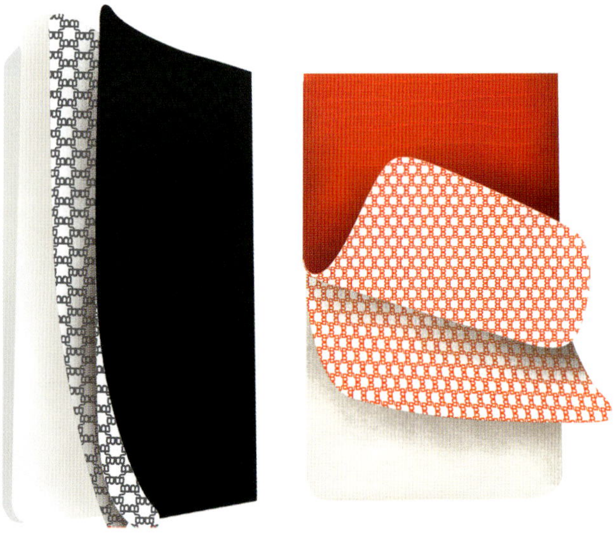

Johanna Valdivieso (this spread) | Beteronotebooks | Products

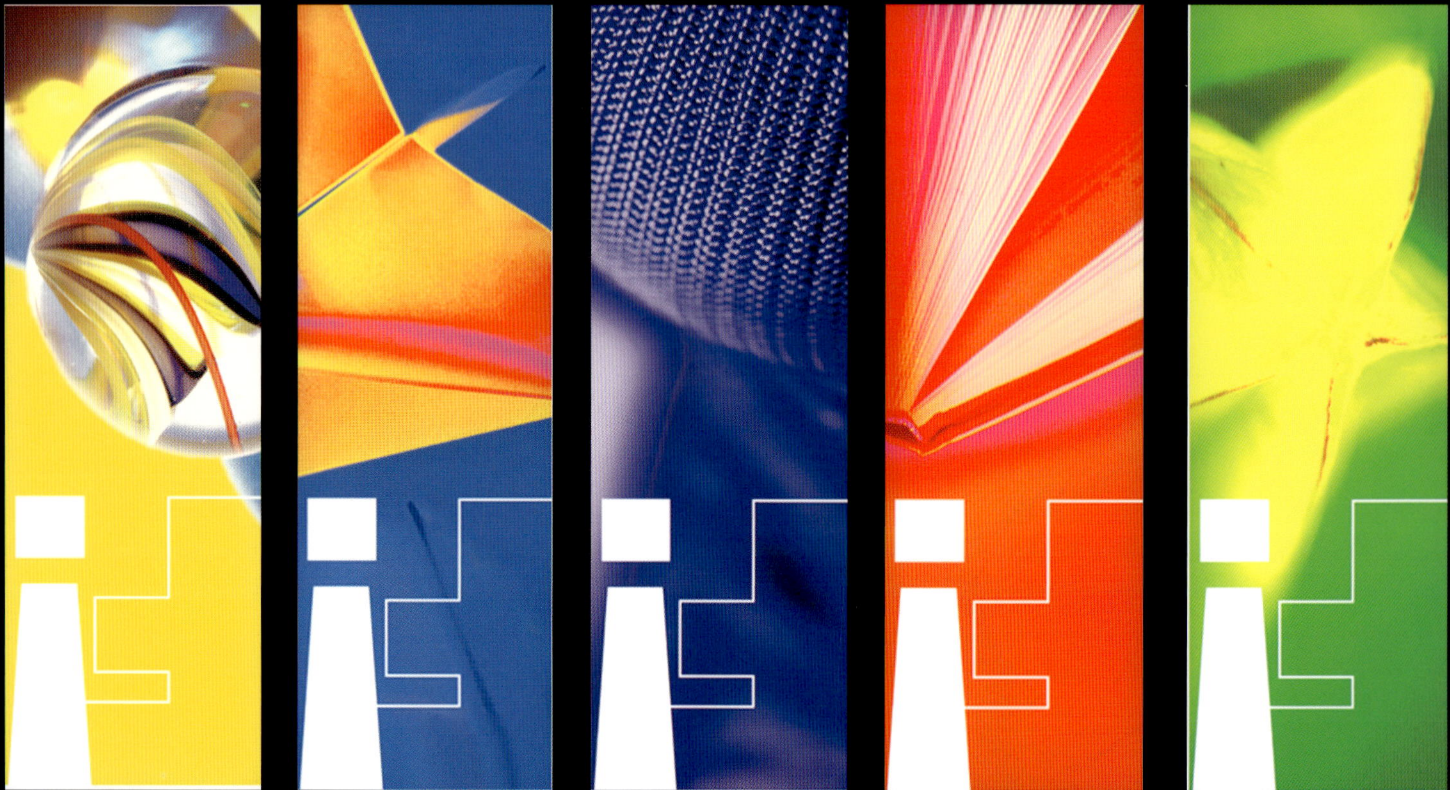

Assignment: Friedin Promotional Group sought to differentiate their offering from the ordinary "trinkets and trash" that the promotional industry is know for. Michael Friedin sought to position himself as a provider of custom artifacts that tied into a company's strategic advertising program.

Approach: Decker Design's approach began with considering ways to emphasize the custom aspect of Friedin's business. We arrived at the concept of using images to represent objects in the service of promotion. Then we decided to create a colorful palette of images that could be mixed and matched in a paperware program to create a unique experience for the recipient. Further customization of the images came about by eliminating channels of color and then unifying them as a program by masking them within a bold "F."

Results: The client loved the result! He garnered much attention from his audience (advertising agencies and client marketers) and successfully repositioned his business as a creative partner to his clients.

Designer: Lynda Decker | **Design Firm:** Decker Design, Inc. | **Art Director:** Lynda Decker | **Creative Director:** Lynda Decker | **Writer:** Pookie Foster
Photographer: David Arky | **Client:** Friedin Promotional Group

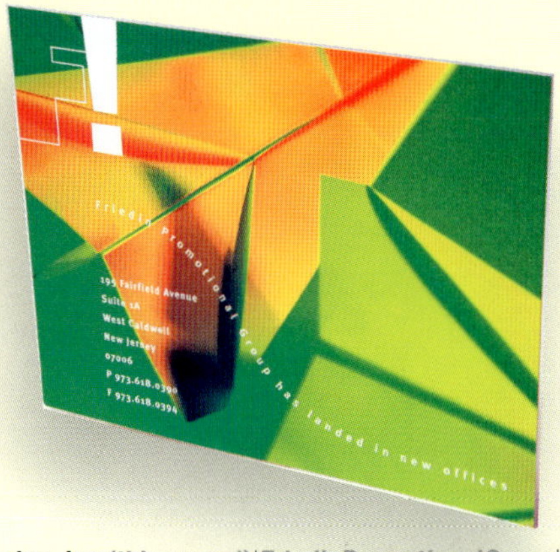

Assignment: Constantly dismissed for the same reason it is loved, Landor was tasked with bringing the packaging up to date for a new generation of nostril deprived youngsters, while not confusing the father figures that are still with us.

Approach: The solution pays homage to the heritage of a nearly 75-year-old company, while celebrating the iconic buoy bottle. Old Spice is certain to remain one of the best holiday gifts for generations of men to come.

Results: Your grandfather used to use it. We preserved the icon so you can use it.

Designers: Joe Napier, Jeff Maurer | **Design Firm:** Landor Associates | **Creative Director:** Gerhard Koenderink | **Client:** Procter & Gamble

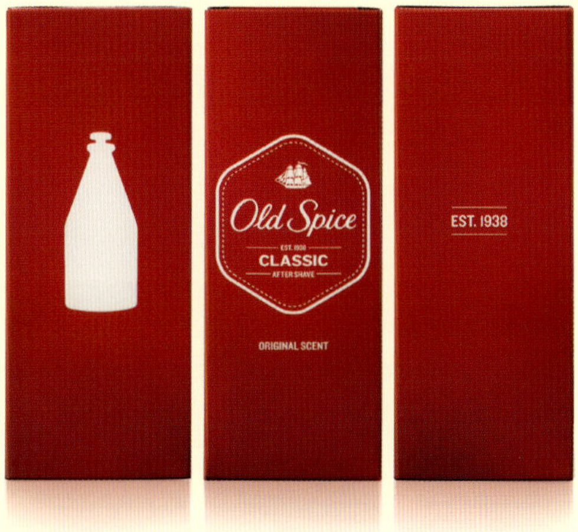

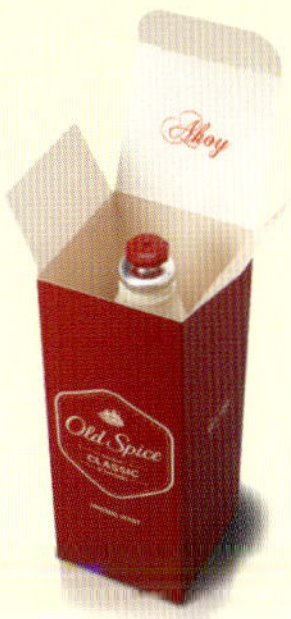

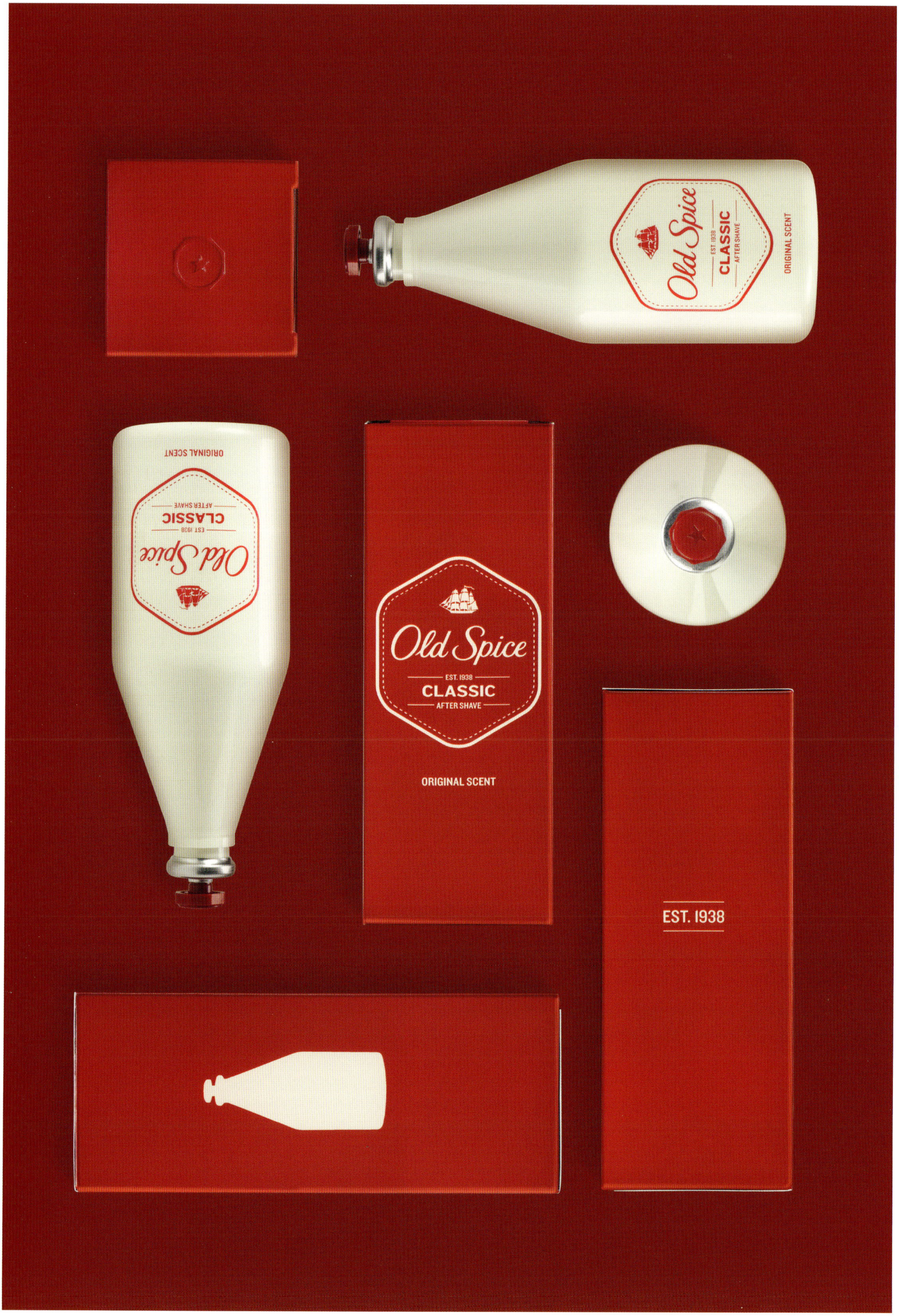
Old Spice
EST. 1938
CLASSIC
AFTER SHAVE
ORIGINAL SCENT
EST. 1938

Assignment: In order to develop a strong relationship with our clients we needed a special business gift that spoke best about who we are and what we are able to do. So, we've created this unique gift for every new client.

Approach: The "DESIGN BUSINESS BOTTLE" was made to capture the essence of our business in connection with the client's business, and that's why we designed a bottle with two necks: one for us, and one for the client. After all, aren't we all going to drink from this business? And the story is like this: we thought, "Let's make a gift for every contract we sign ... let's make a good wine bottle," and we did. The bottle has two necks covered by two glasses: one side reading "OUR BUSINESS" and the other, "YOUR BUSINESS," because, as a client, you put a little bit of your business into our business, and in the end you will enjoy the sweet wine inside.

Results: The bottle was a bigger success than we'd anticipated. The clients went nuts about the idea and we had a lot of requests for the bottle from large multinational companies.

Designer: Irinel Ionescu | **Design Firm:** AMPRO DESIGN CONSULTANTS | **Art Director:** Oliwer Iovanovici
Creative Director: Irinel Ionescu | **Illustrator:** Alin Patru | **Client:** AMPRO DESIGN CONSULTANTS

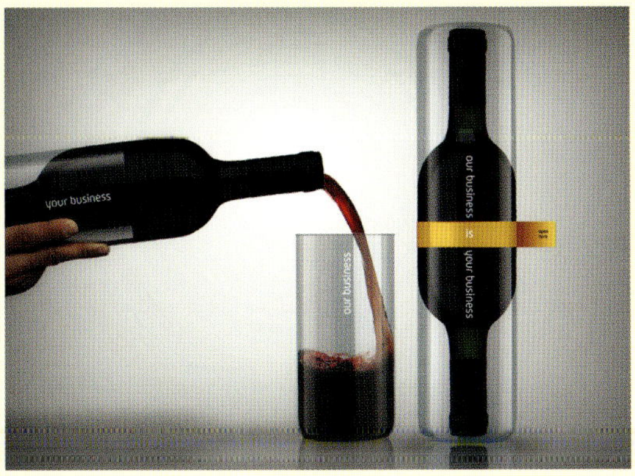

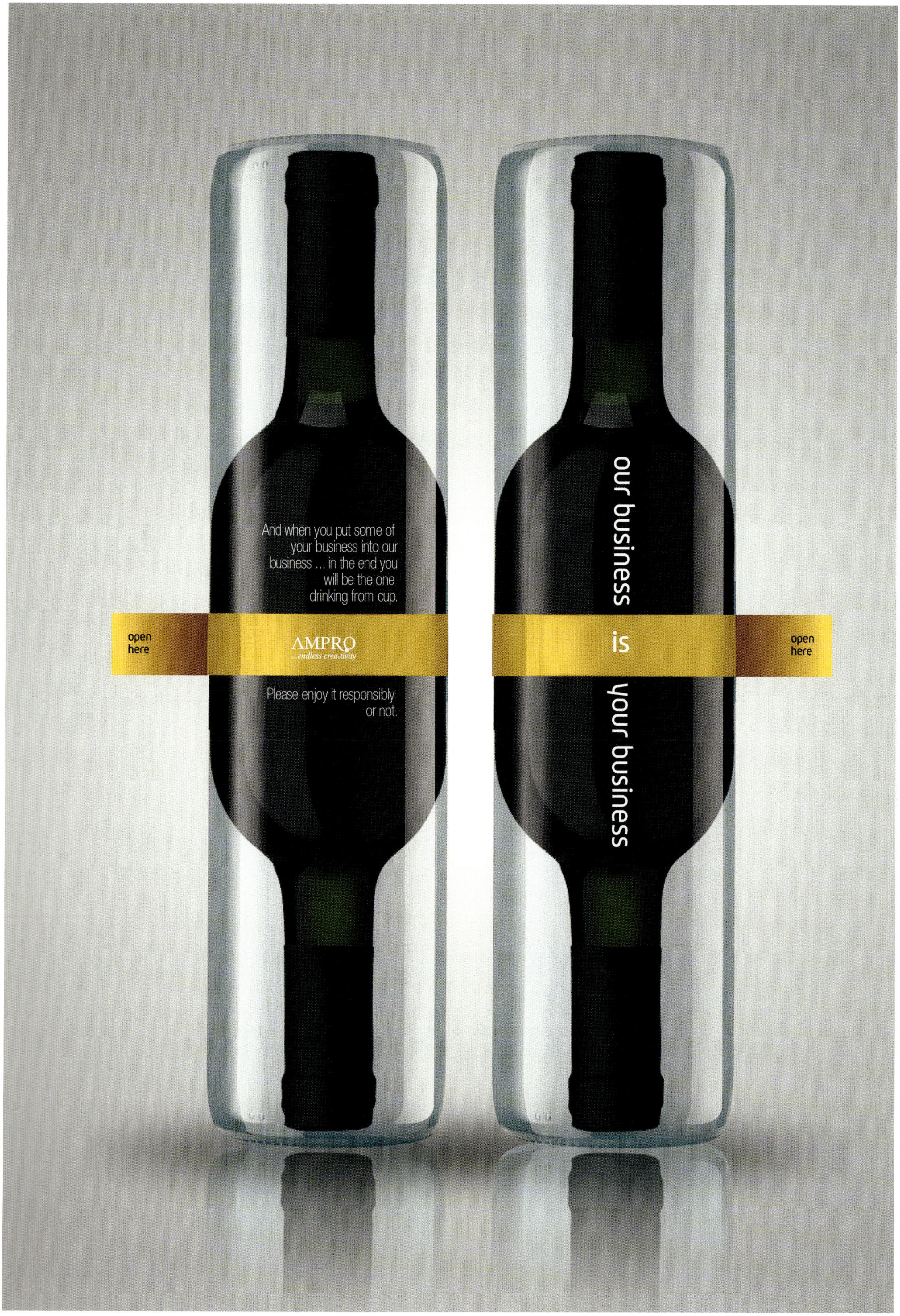

And when you put some of your business into our business ... in the end you will be the one drinking from cup.
open here
AMPRO
...endless creativity
Please enjoy it responsibly or not.
our business
is
your business
open here

Assignment: "Fabric of a New Society." The Co-operative Group has invested in a total regeneration of the land around its Manchester, UK, headquarters. The promise is to create a completely mixed-use area of regeneration in an underused area of the city. The Co-operative Group briefed us to create a visual identity system and naming strategy for the redevelopment. The city of Manchester was the site of a revolution in the textile industry, and was where Rutherford first split the atom. Importantly, this is also where the Co-operative Group grew from a small collective into one of the UK's most successful and respected companies. The visual identity had to be a symbol of the city and its people, a bold expression of the nature of the regeneration of the site. With layers of architecture and history intertwined, it had to express the diversity of activities that the area will support.

Approach: At the heart of the identity is a strong, recognizable wordmark, NOMA, an abbreviation of North Manchester comparable to Tribeca or SoHo. NOMA breaks the norms of property development naming in the UK, combining Manchester's heritage and modernity.

Results: NOMA launched to public and commercial acclaim at MIPIM in Cannes from May 8th to 11th, 2011, and continues to gather notoriety and local affection as the site is developing and building its reputation consummately. The identity, with its interwoven and overlayed elements, is a perfect expression of the strategy "Fabric of a New Society."

Designer: Tom Ledwidge | **Design Firm:** Landor Associates | **Creative Director:** Peter Knapp | **Client:** Co-operative Group

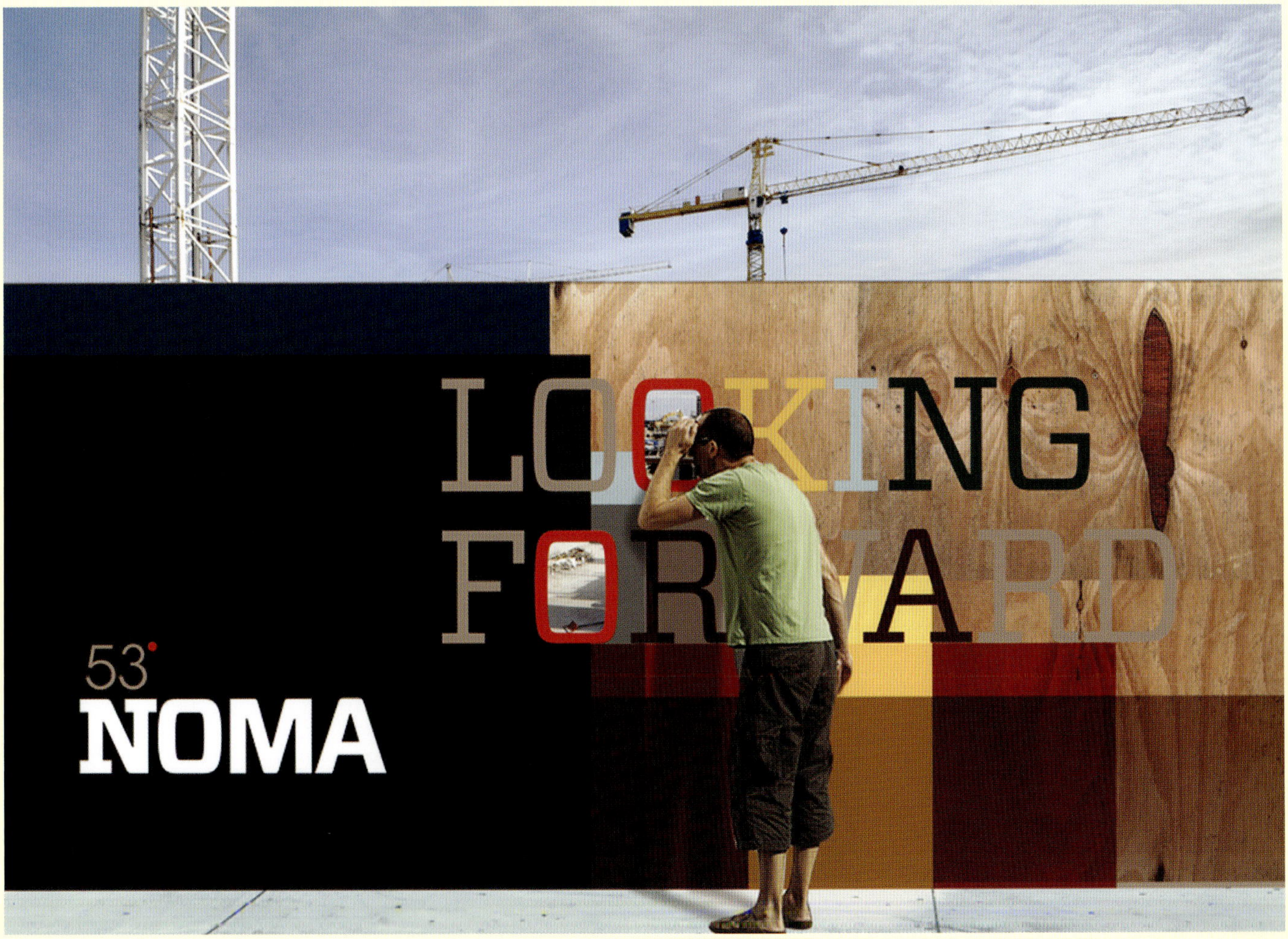

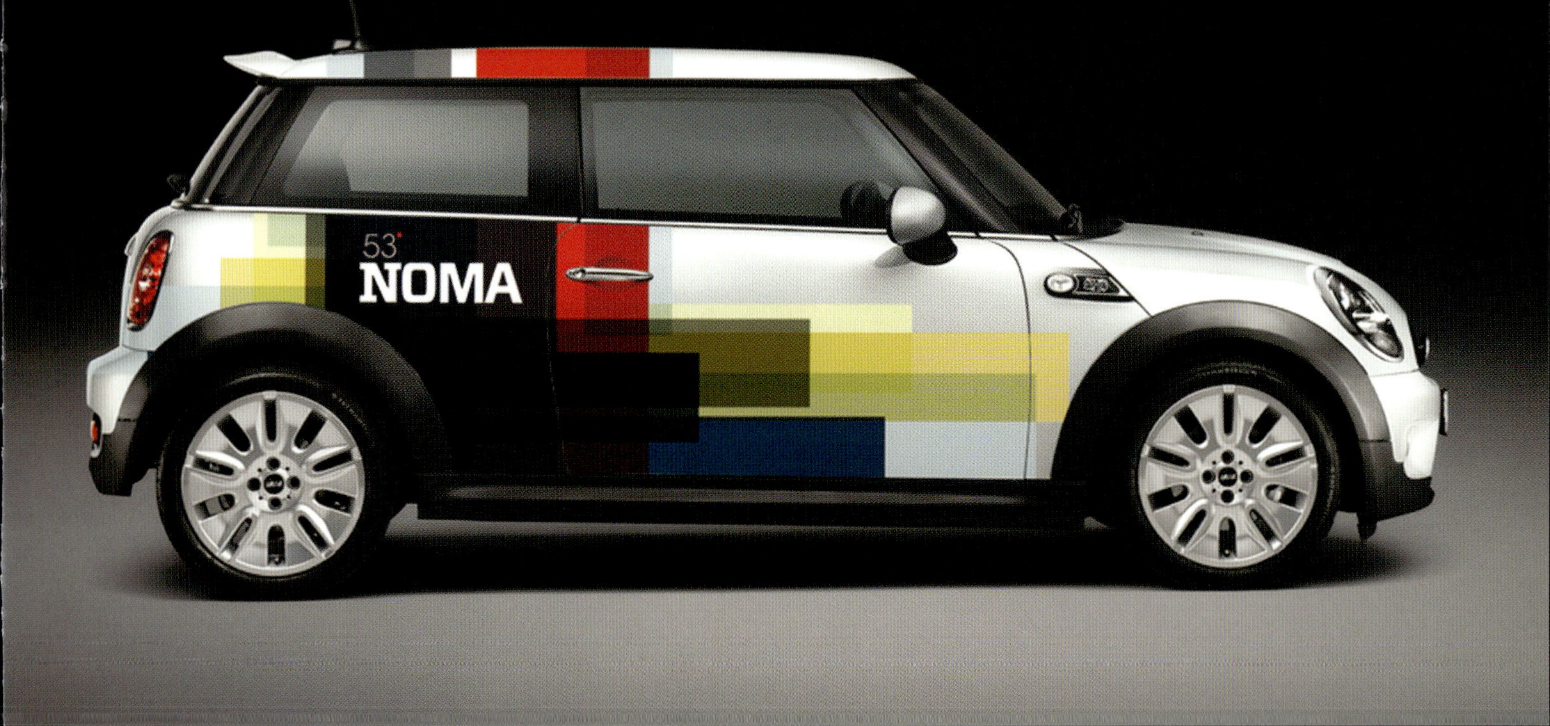
53°
NOMA

Assignment: Melbourne is a dynamic, progressive city, internationally recognized for its diversity, innovation, sustainability, and livability. The City of Melbourne Council supports the city's world-class offerings, represents it nationally and internationally, and ensures it remains a preeminent Australian center for culture, arts, dining, entertainment, education, and shopping. Since implementing its previous identity fifteen years ago, Melbourne has experienced significant change. As a result, the Council had accumulated a range of isolated logos for various services, which had become increasingly difficult and costly to manage. The fragmentation of Melbourne's identity meant equity was driven away from the core brand, and the Council realized that it needed a long-term solution.

Results: The city of Melbourne's Lord Mayor, Robert Doyle, said, "The City of Melbourne adopted its current brand in the early '90s. Both the world and the city have changed. The "M" design will become an icon for Melbourne, synonymous with the modern, vibrant, cool city Melbourne is today and will continue to be in the future. The new identity will deliver more impact, be stronger, more flexible and reduce confusion as to who is delivering services. It will build greater long-term identification. ... The new brand is strong and leading-edge, and will be instantly recognized as belonging to the City of Melbourne."

Chief Executive, Dr. Kathy Alexander, said the City of Melbourne now has a new corporate identity to reflect its global leadership position, unify its range of services, and take the new Council into the future. "The new brand identity will mean increased time efficiencies for the organization by adapting readily to in-house designs and existing graphic imagery, and allow us to build our corporate identity. It is important to consolidate our branding, as there are now a large number of logos in the marketplace that reflect the work carried out by the City of Melbourne. We are conscious of the need to act responsibly with the ratepayer's funds, and we are rolling out the new brand progressively as things need to be replaced. It is a brand for the organization, businesses, residents, and visitors. We are creating a singular identity that will be easier and more cost-effective to manage. By speaking with one voice, under one brand, we will present a united front with all our individual programs contributing to the City of Melbourne's reputation for excellence in leadership, innovation, and community service."

Designers: Jason Little, Sam Pemberton, Jefton Sungkar | **Design Firm:** Landor Associates | **Art Director:** Jason Little
Creative Director: Jason Little | **Client:** City of Melbourne

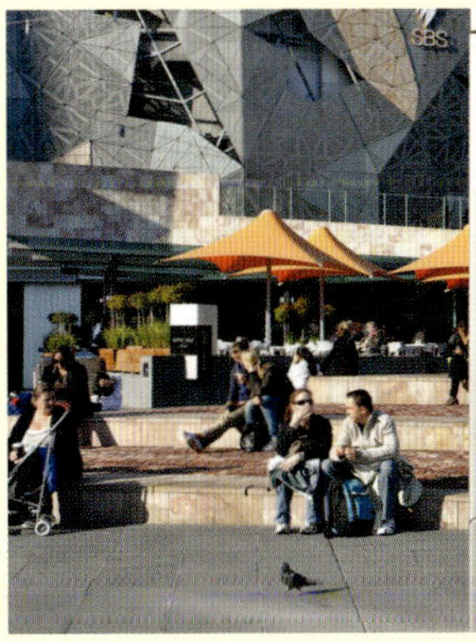

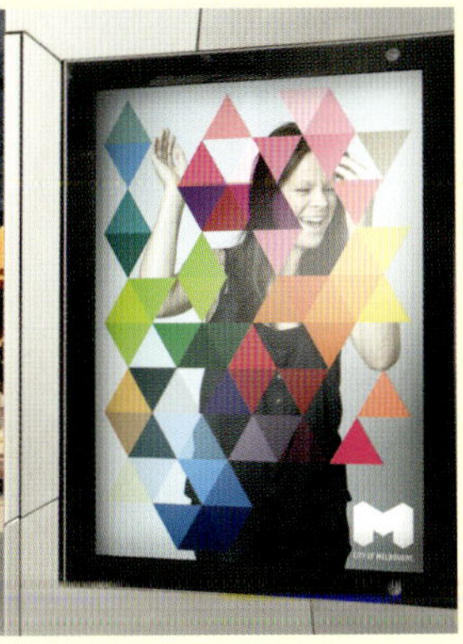

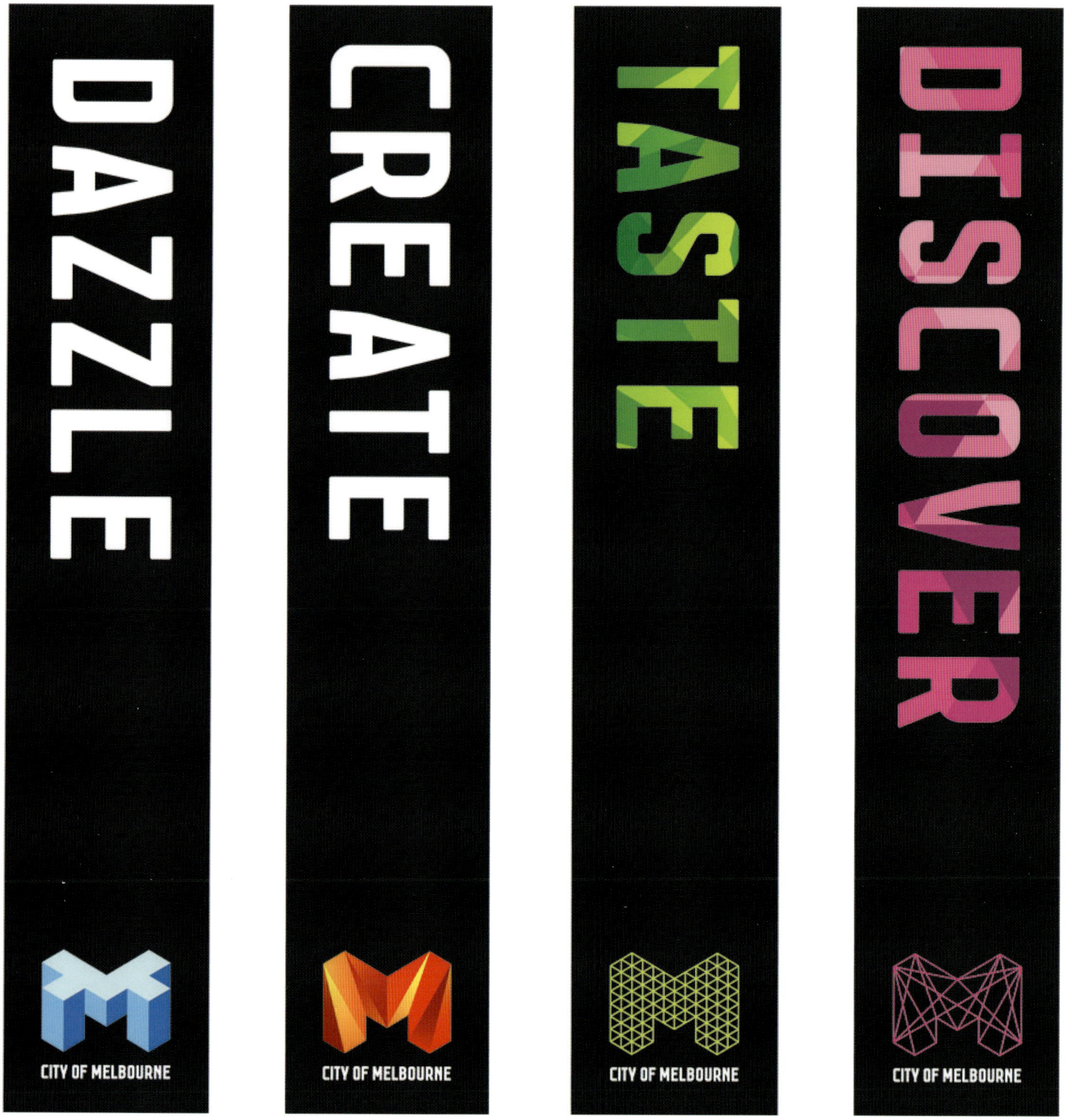

Landor Associates (this spread) | City of Melbourne | Real estate

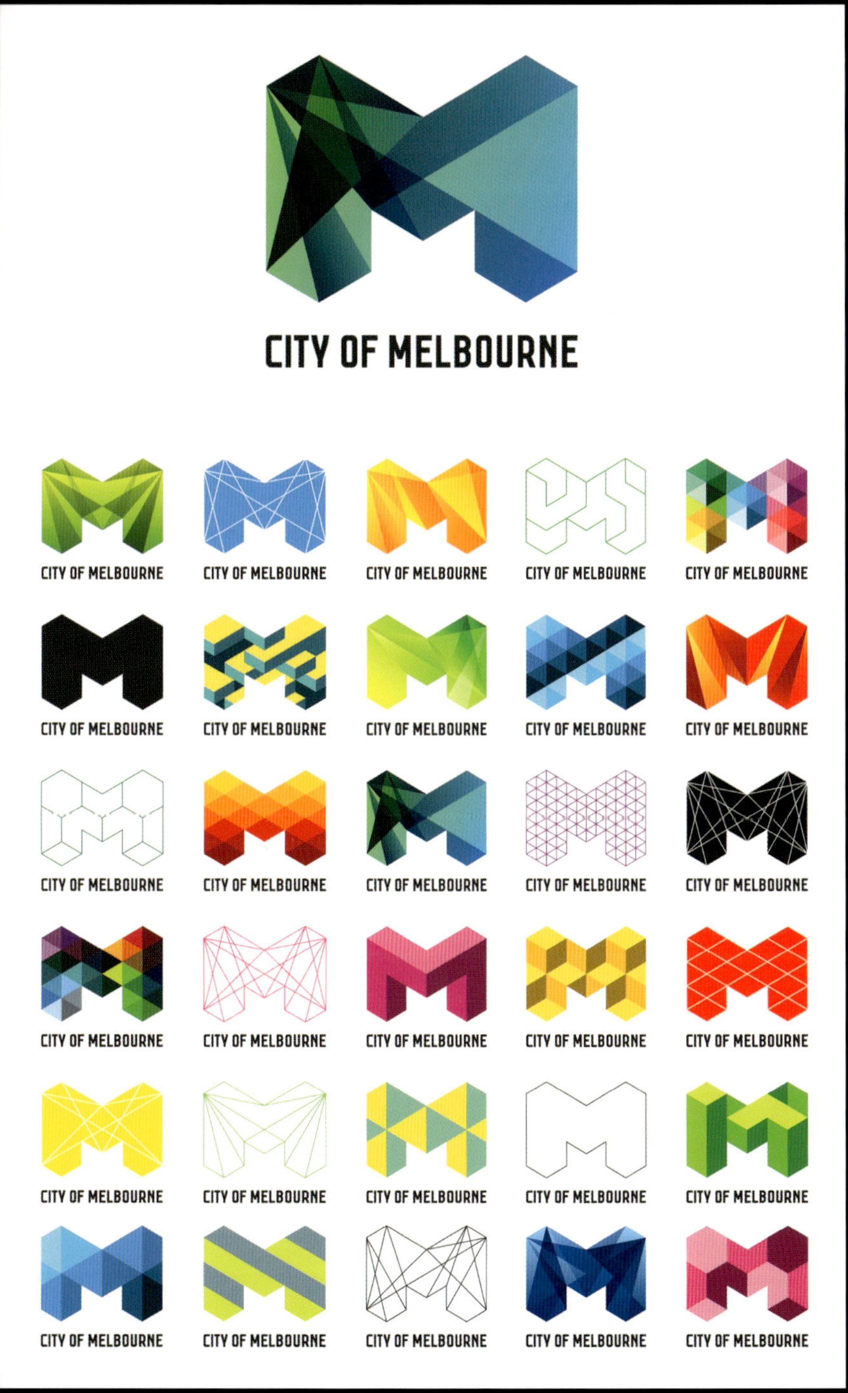
CITY OF MELBOURNE

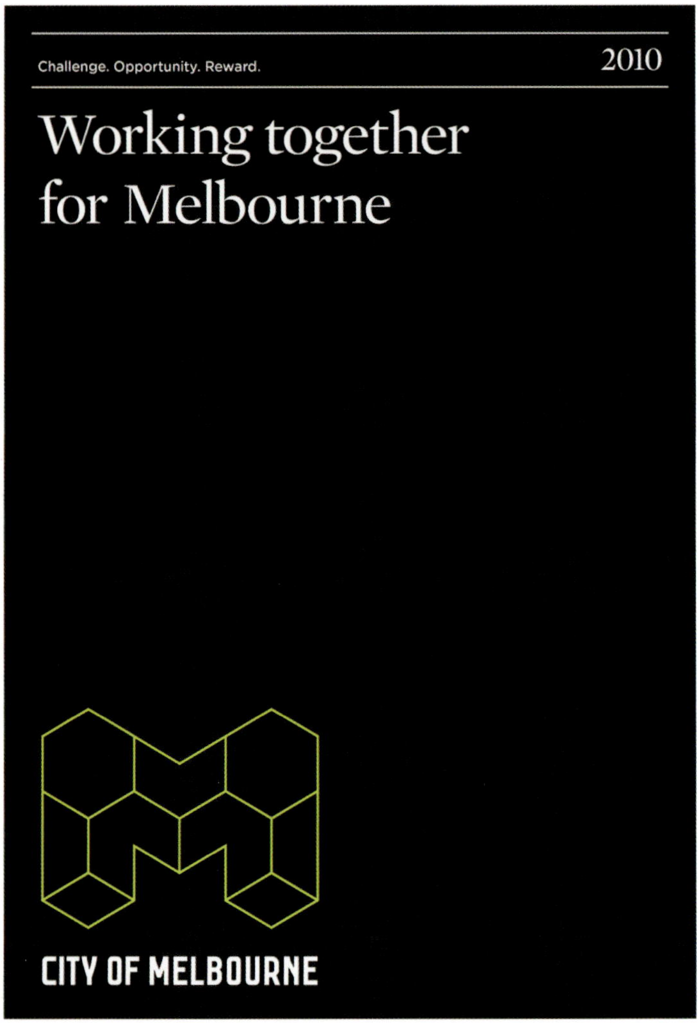
Challenge. Opportunity. Reward.
2010
Working together for Melbourne
CITY OF MELBOURNE

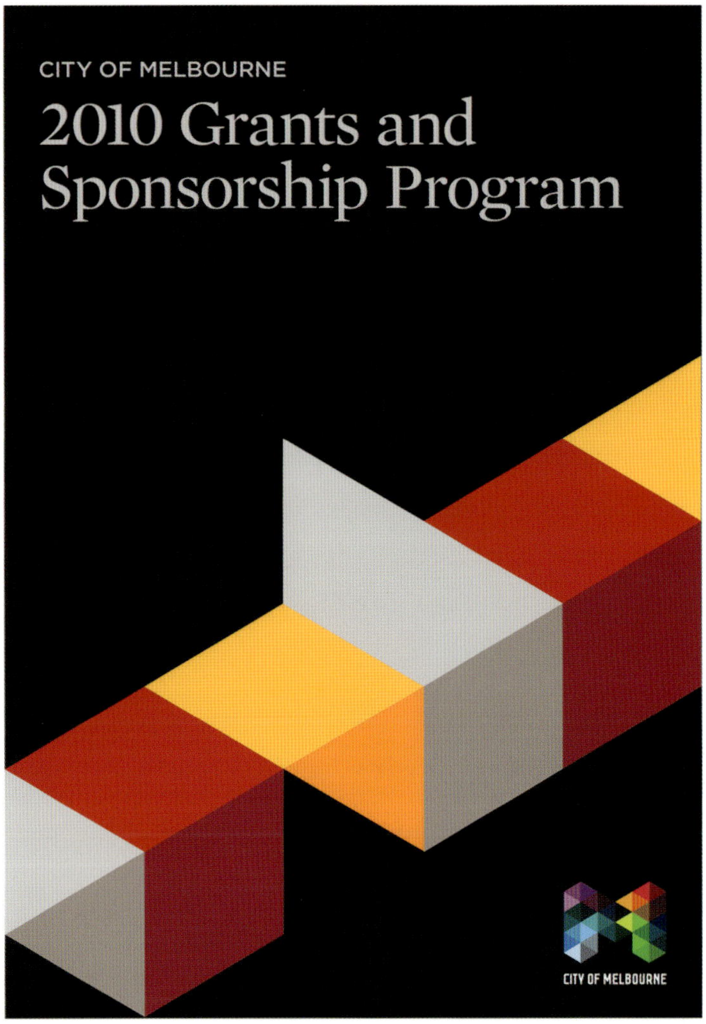
CITY OF MELBOURNE
2010 Grants and Sponsorship Program
CITY OF MELBOURNE

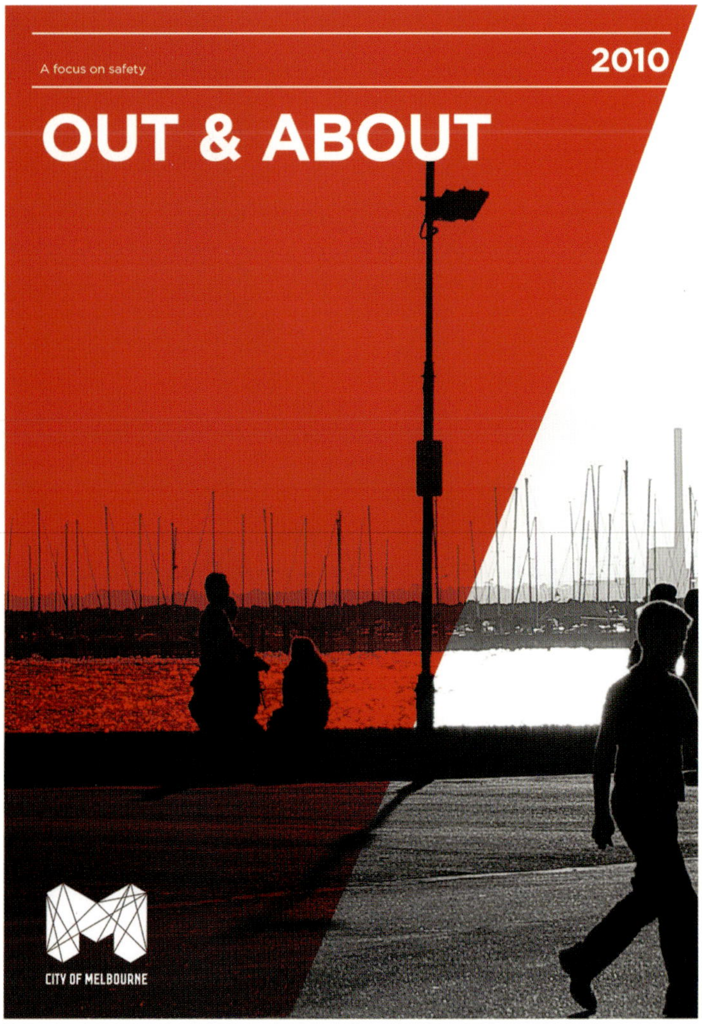
A focus on safety
2010
OUT & ABOUT
CITY OF MELBOURNE

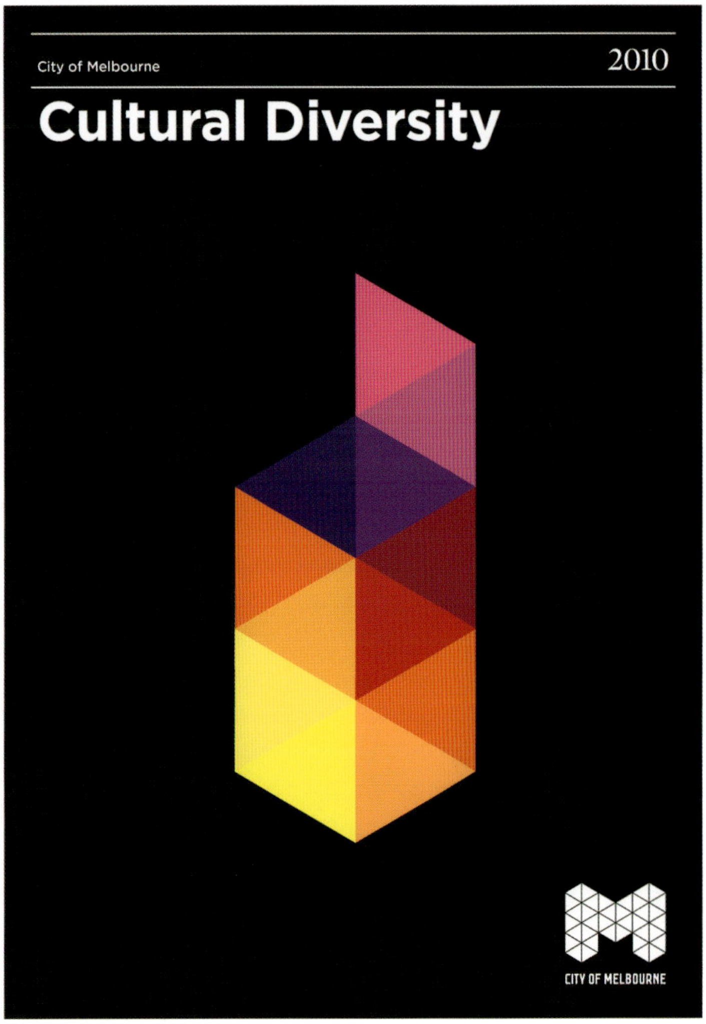
City of Melbourne
2010
Cultural Diversity
CITY OF MELBOURNE

Assignment: The goal was to create a name, brand, and visual vocabulary for a start-up restaurant in the highly competitive gourmet cupcake market that could function as effectively on a national stage as it could locally. Our vision was to create an identity that resonated with the consumer and that reinforced the perception of the restaurant's signature product.

Approach: We began with developing potential names, and conducted one-on-one and group testing with consumers in the target demographic. We conducted extensive identity research in the local and national markets for similar businesses. With the name determined, we moved on to develop a color palette and a logo that visually reinforced the essence of the Jones Bros. Cupcakes restaurant experience. Ancillary brand icons, interior and exterior signage, packaging, menus, business cards, digital billboard advertising, wall and window graphics, and a website completed the initial brand system.

Results: The result is a flexible and robust branding tool kit. Every element reinforces the other elements of this brand system, yet each can stand on its own merit. The branding has garnered praise for Jones Bros. Cupcakes from major design publications and recent national TV exposure, such as on the Food Network's *Cupcake Wars*. Jones Bros. has quickly become an Omaha must-see destination. Its success has contributed to its expansion plans. Most importantly, the owners of Jones Bros. Cupcakes have repeatedly acknowledged their belief that the branding and its execution have been instrumental in their initial and ongoing success.

Design Firm: Webster | **Art Directors:** Sean Heisler, Loucinda Hamling | **Creative Director:** Dave Webster | **Client:** Jones Bros. Cupcakes

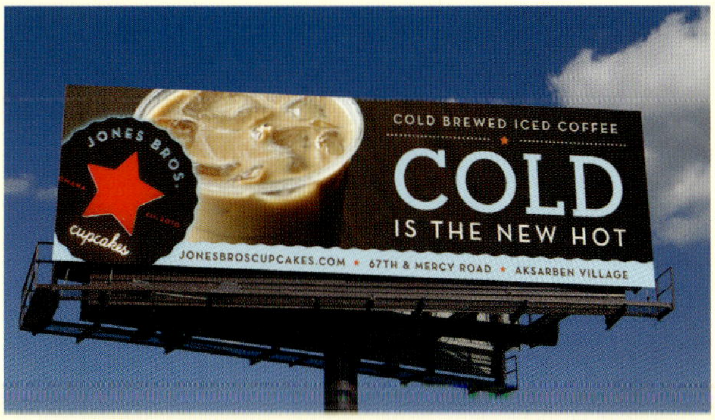

Webster(this spread) | JonesBroscupcake | Restaurants**226**

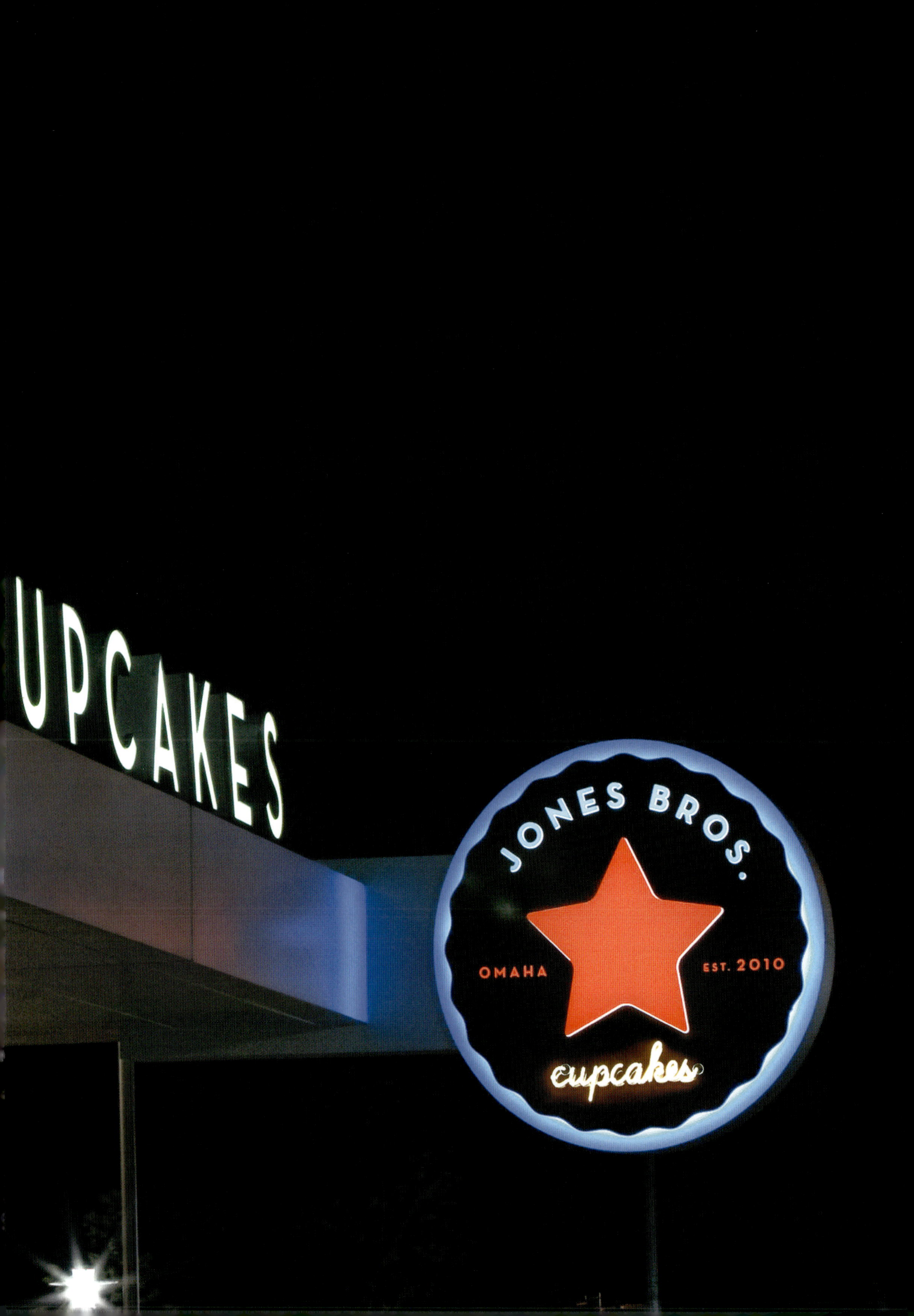
UPCAKES
JONES BROS.
OMAHA
EST. 2010
cupcakes

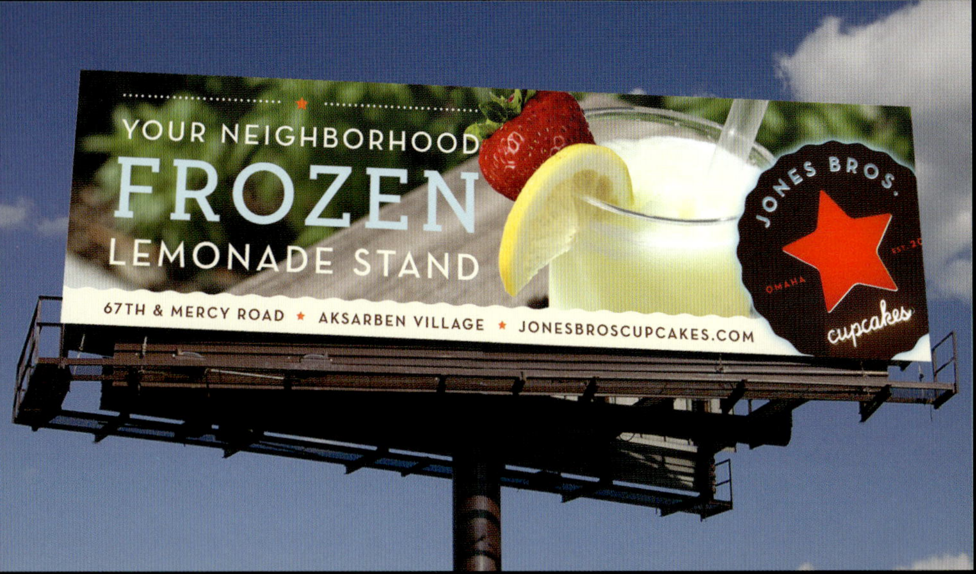
YOUR NEIGHBORHOOD
FROZEN
LEMONADE STAND
67TH & MERCY ROAD ★ AKSARBEN VILLAGE ★ JONESBROSCUPCAKES.COM
JONES BROS.
OMAHA
cupcakes

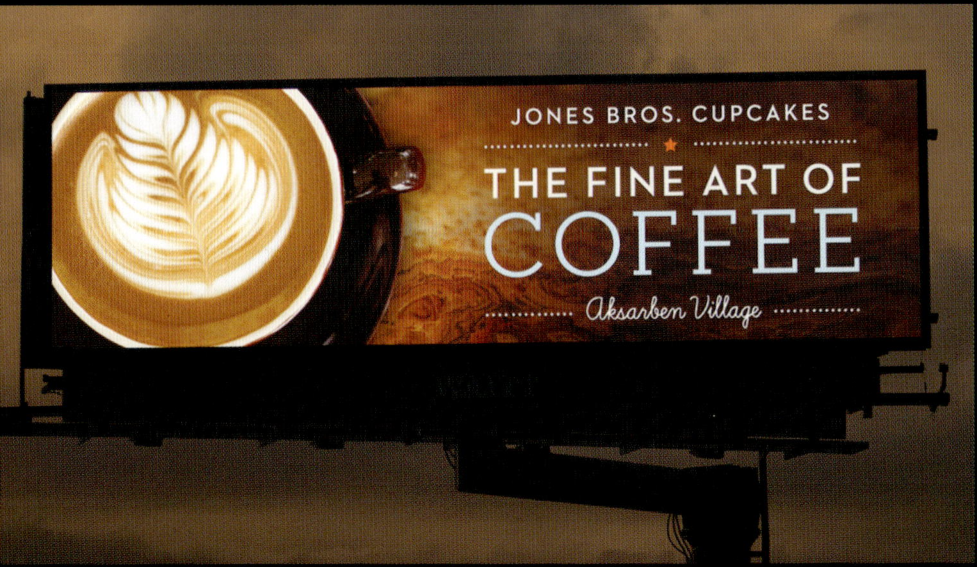
JONES BROS. CUPCAKES
THE FINE ART OF
COFFEE
Aksarben Village

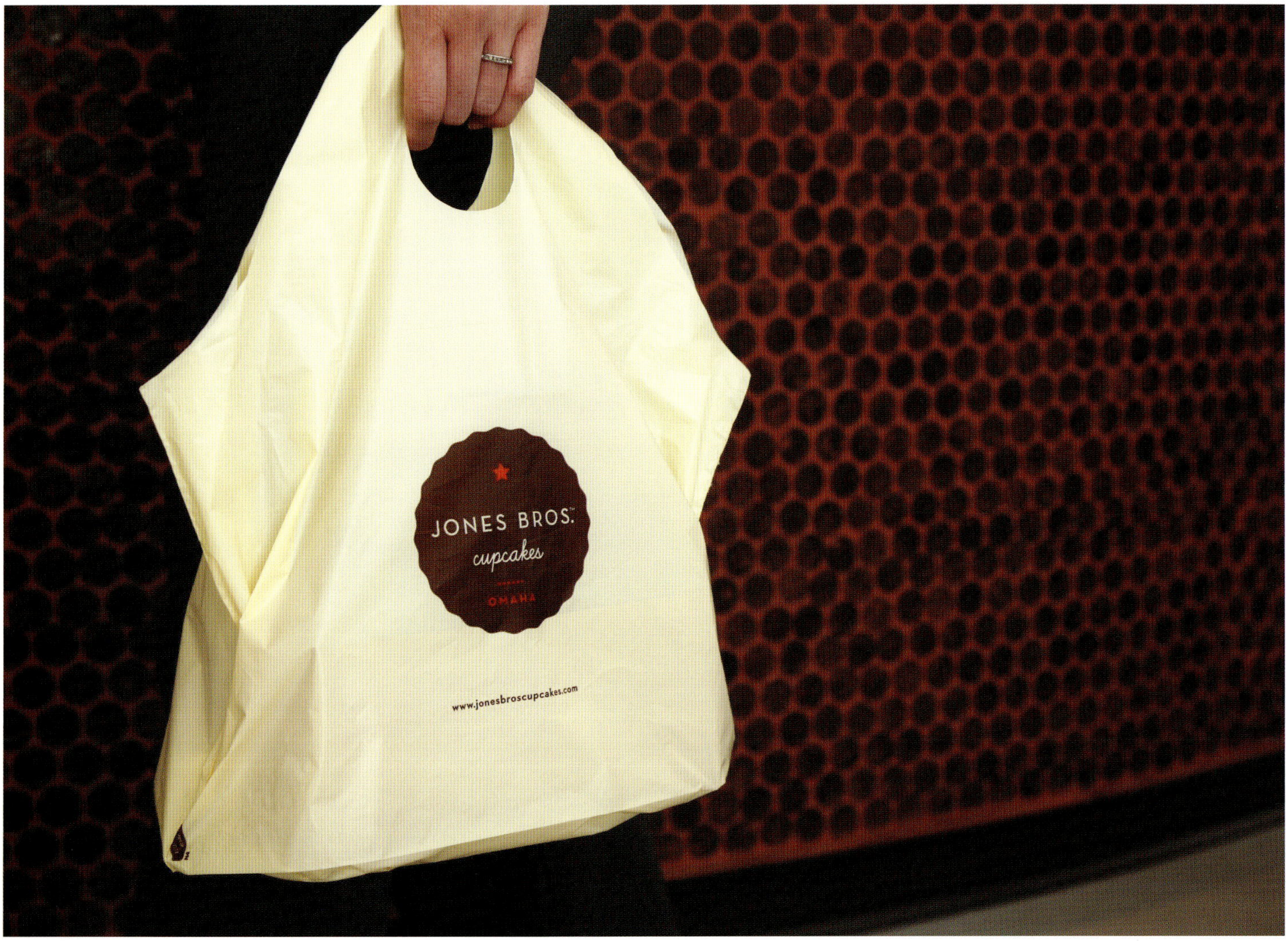
JONES BROS.™
cupcakes
OMAHA
www.jonesbroscupcakes.com

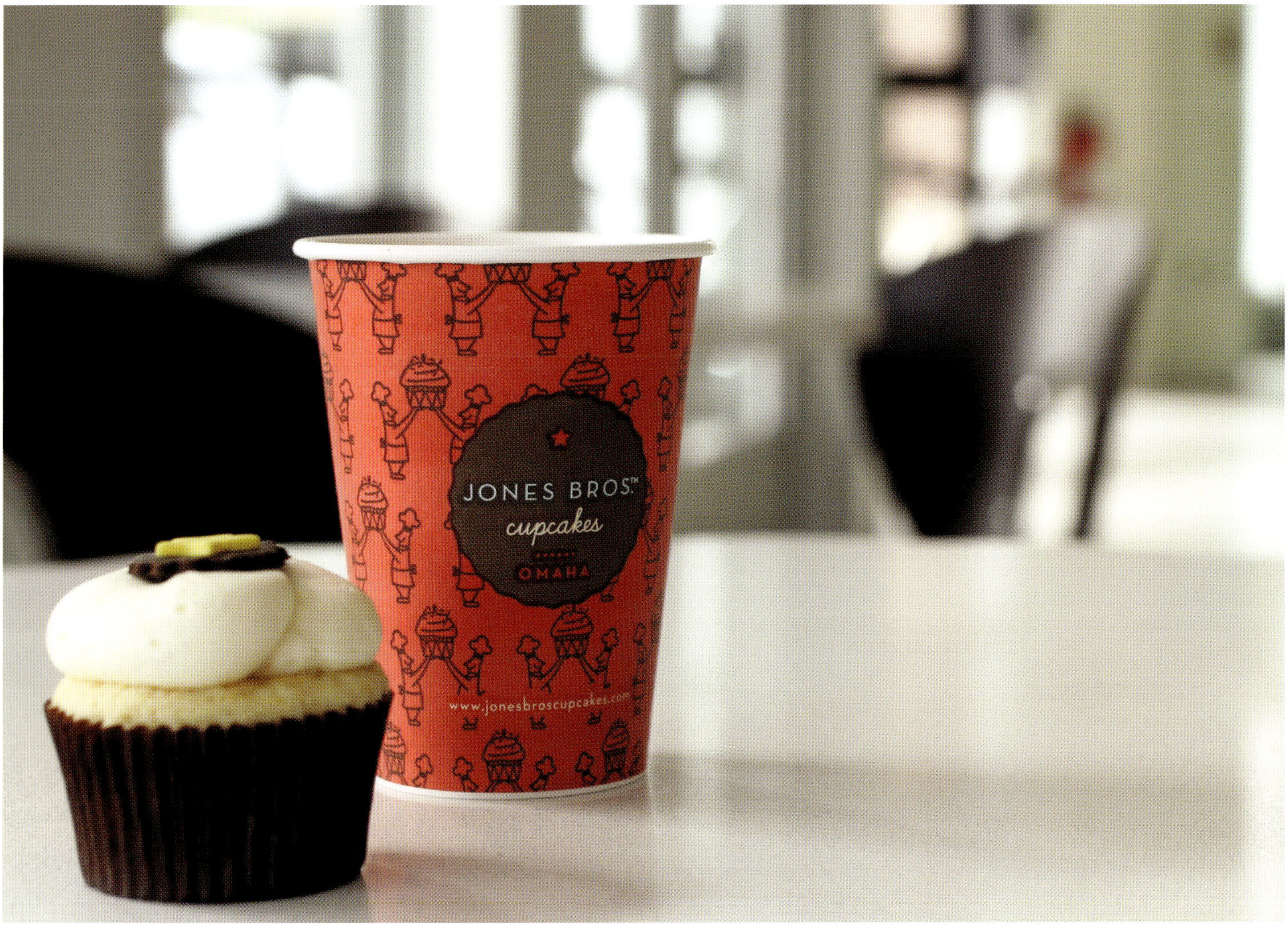
JONES BROS.™
cupcakes
OMAHA
www.jonesbroscupcakes.com

Assignment: The Arrogant Butcher was the first venture into downtown Phoenix for Fox Restaurant Concepts. The client wanted the restaurant to feel as if it had been around for generations, although it is located in the newest development in the city. From the initial naming of the restaurant to the identity and grand opening events, we were tasked with creating a restaurant that would draw people to downtown Phoenix and showcase the best attributes of Fox Restaurant Concepts.

Approach: We began by presenting hundreds of name options and spent time making sure the identity, image, and attitude of The Arrogant Butcher were right. When the look and feel had been established, we translated them into menus, signage, uniforms, ads, social media, and collateral. Along with designing the large mural, we also hand-painted it when the client couldn't find a vendor to complete the work in time for the grand opening.

Results: The visibility and popularity of the restaurant has been exceptional. The design work has been featured in many trade reviews and publications. The Arrogant Butcher commonly hosts large events and has become a destination for locals and travelers alike. The client was pleased with the final result and suggested that we enter the work into the James Beard Awards. We have had an ongoing relationship with Fox Restaurant Concepts and continue to help them strengthen their brands.

Designers: Stewart West, John Johnson, Jason Johnson | **Design Firm:** TunnelBravo | **Art Director:** Jason Johnson
Creative Directors: Stewart West, John Johnson | **Writers:** Stewart West, John Johnson, Jason Johnson | **Client:** Fox Restaurant Concepts

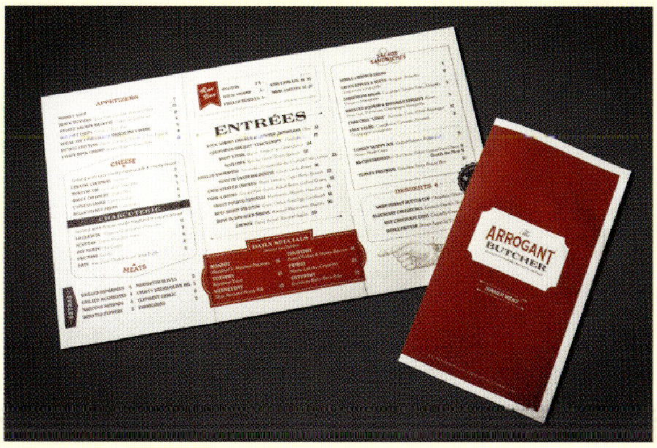

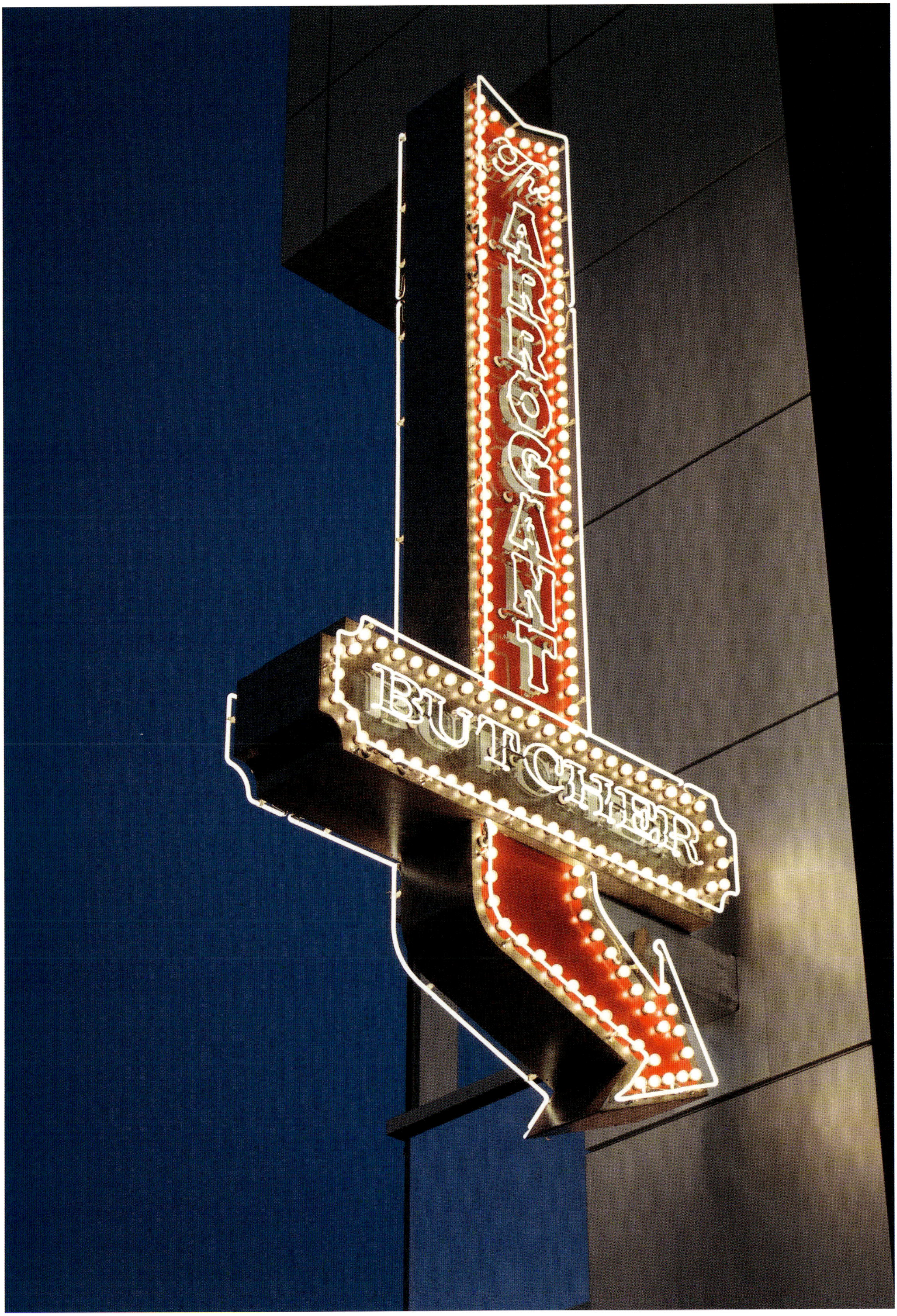
The
ARROGANT
BUTCHER

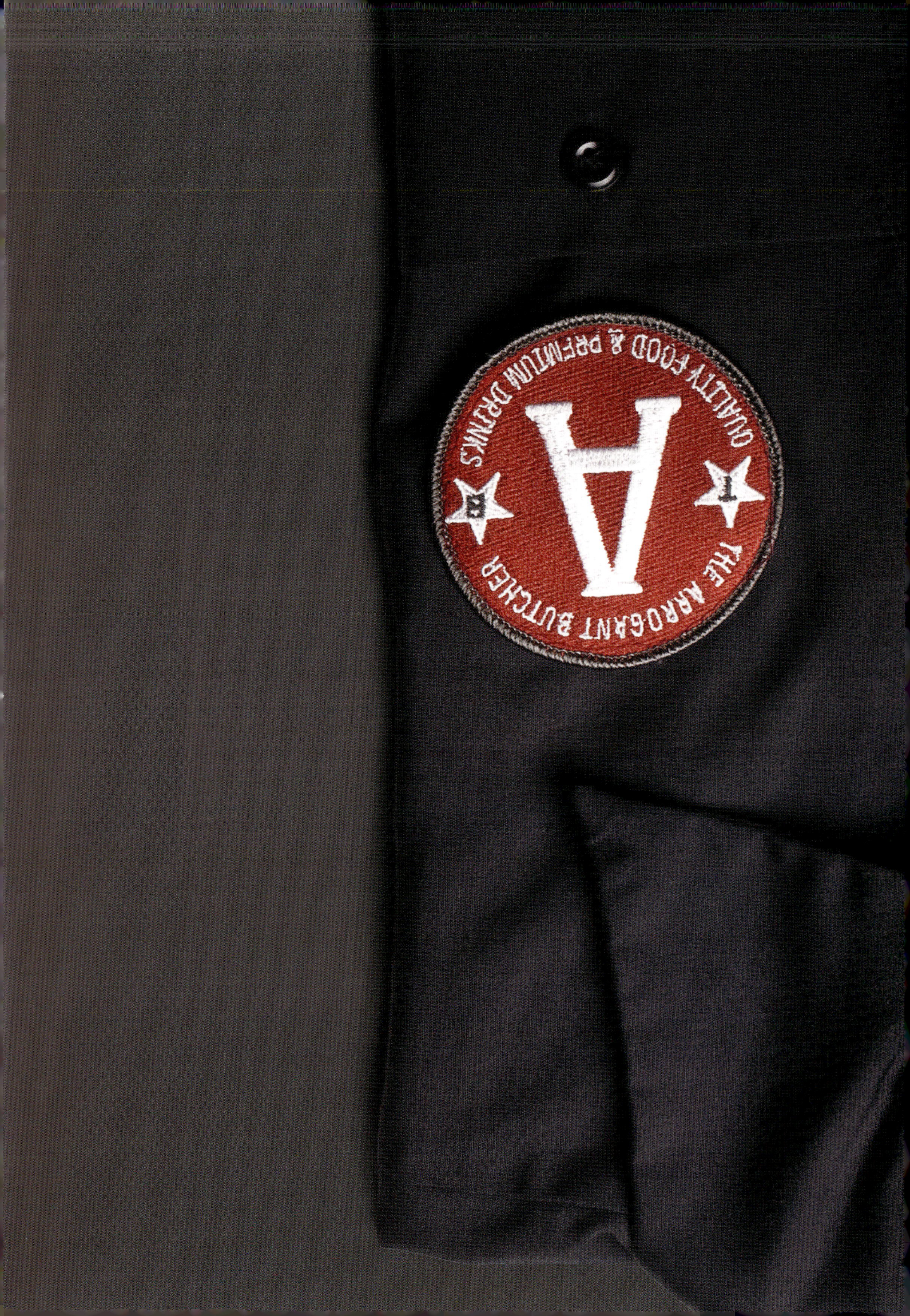
THE ARROGANT BUTCHER
QUALITY FOOD & PREMIUM DRINKS

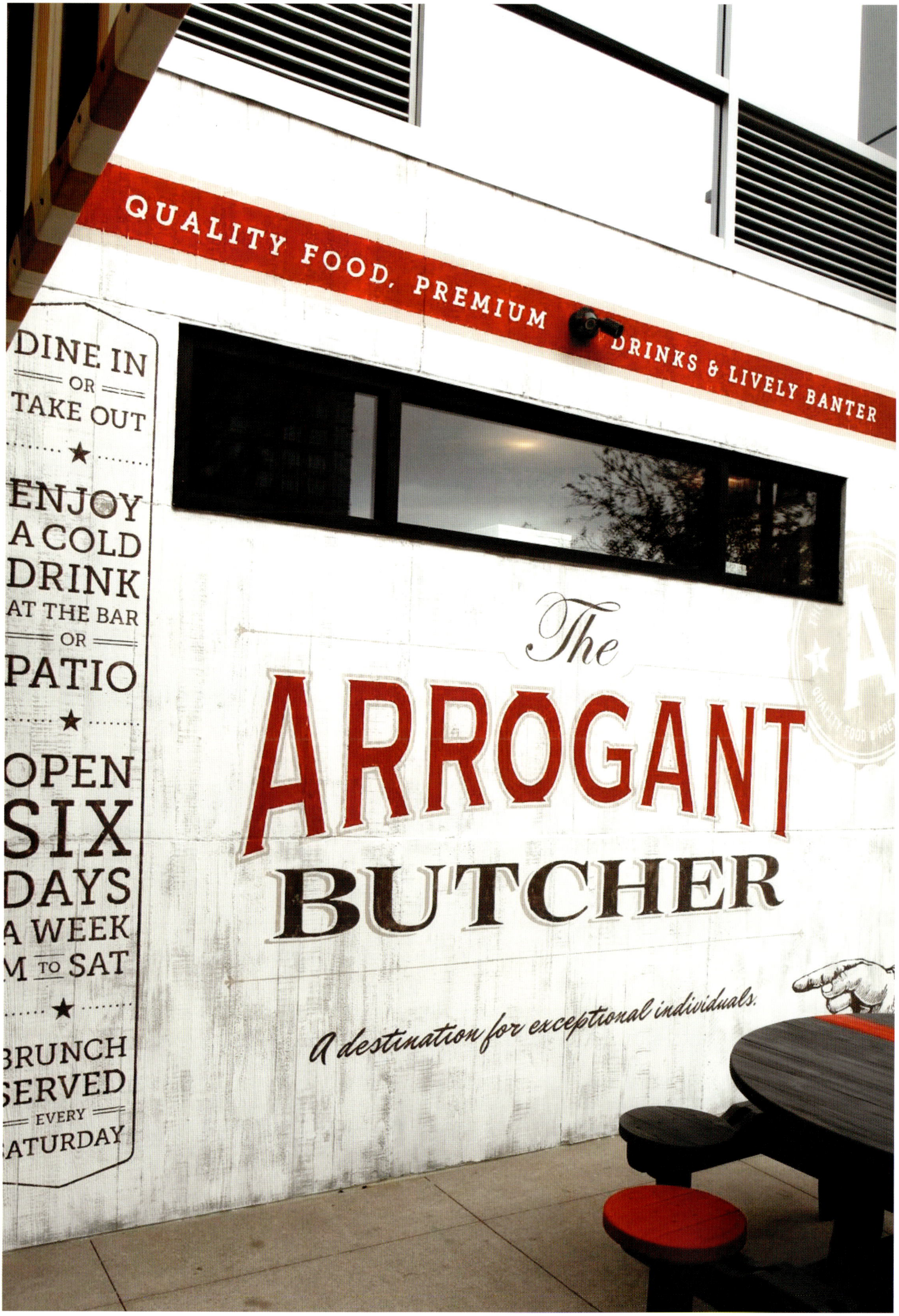
QUALITY FOOD, PREMIUM DRINKS & LIVELY BANTER
DINE IN
OR
TAKE OUT
ENJOY
A COLD
DRINK
AT THE BAR
OR
PATIO
OPEN
SIX
DAYS
A WEEK
M TO SAT
BRUNCH
SERVED
EVERY
ATURDAY
The
ARROGANT
BUTCHER
A destination for exceptional individuals.

Assignment: Develop an identity for a rock & roll fried chicken joint located on the very hip and Austin-like Congress Avenue.

Approach: The design of the restaurant uses old wooden crates in its architecture, so we used patterns of old scrap wood, used in makeshift chicken coops, in the design of the website, menus, and other graphics. The restaurant is named after the owner's grandmother, who was hot, so our old school neon sign is a tribute to her in a 1940s pin-up style.

Results: The place is doing great and the sign was called an "instant Austin landmark" by the Austin newspaper.

Designer: Barrett Fry | **Design Firm:** Pentagram | **Art Director:** DJ Stout | **Client:** Lucy's Fried Chicken

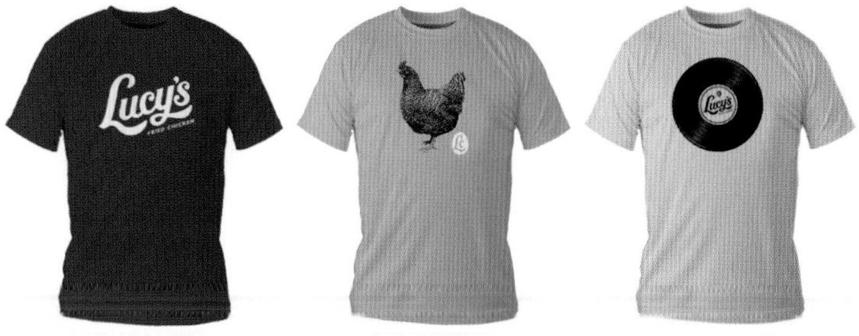

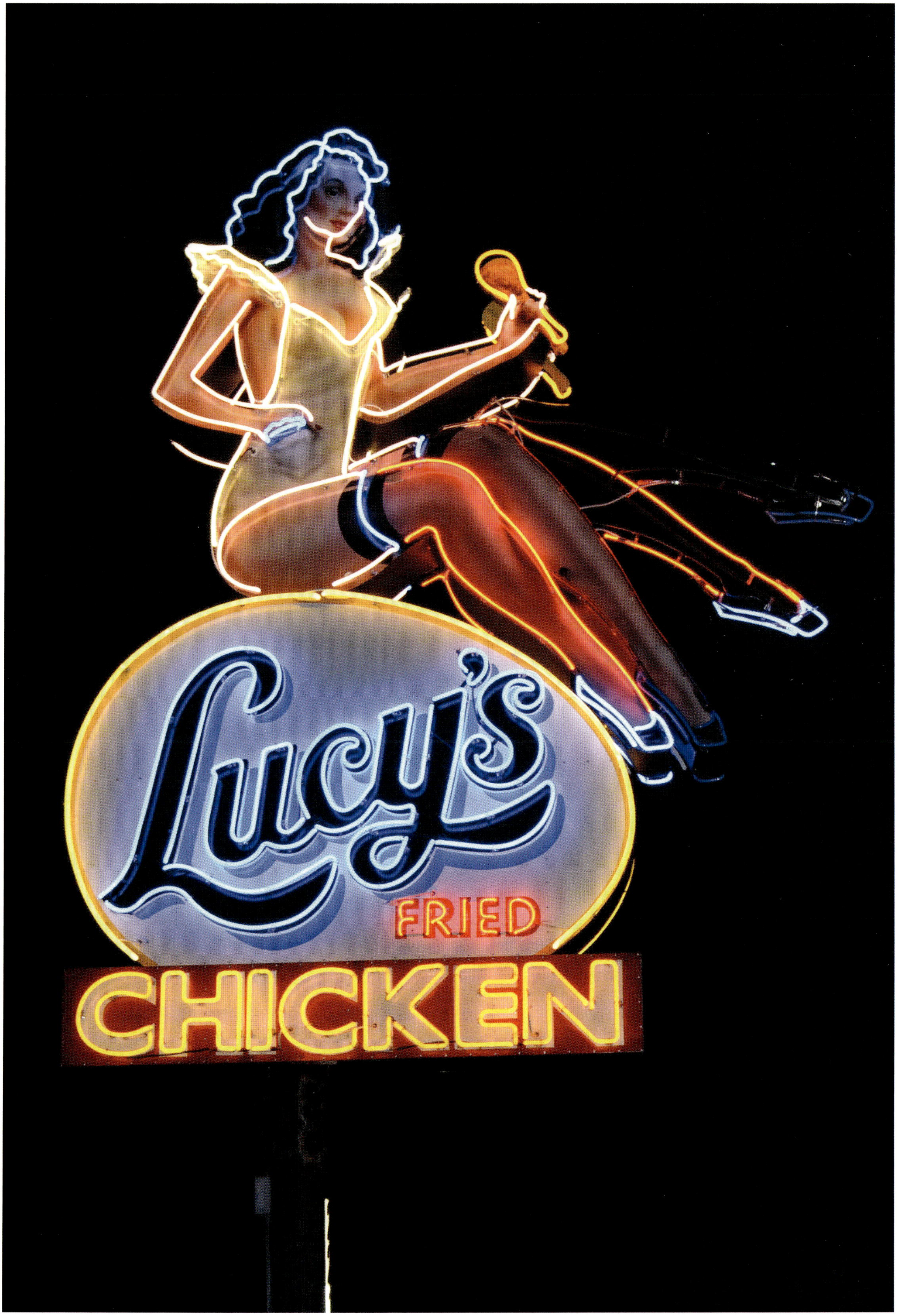

Pentagram (this spread) | Lucy's Fried Chicken |

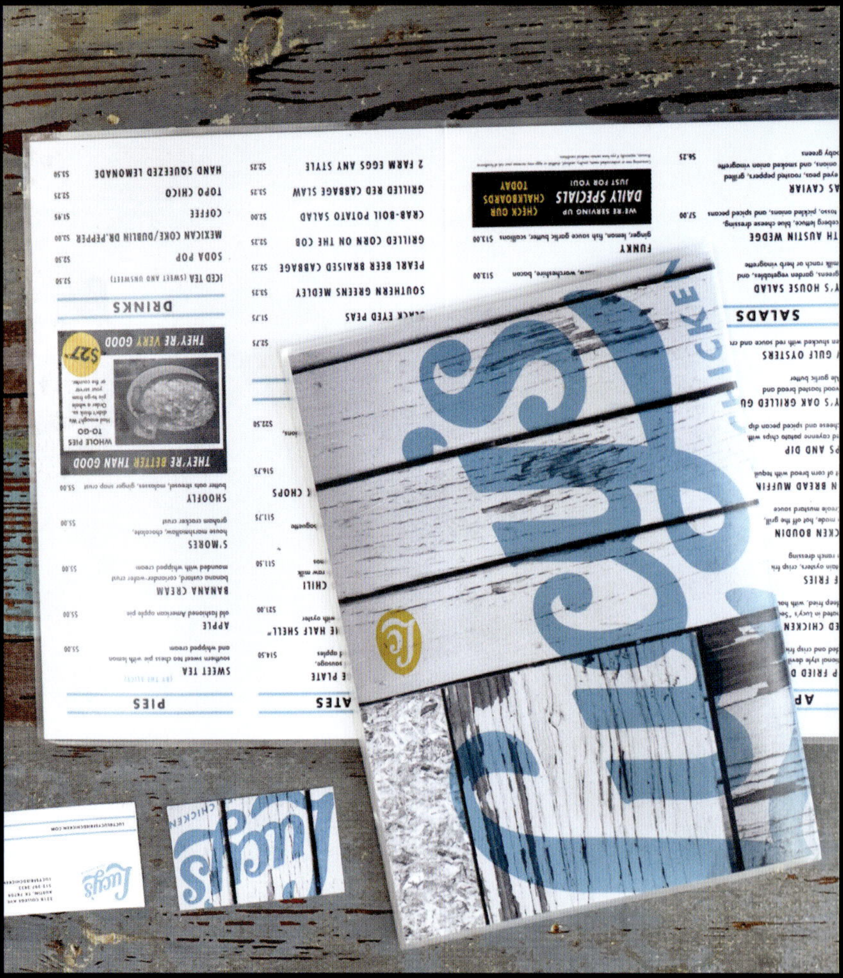

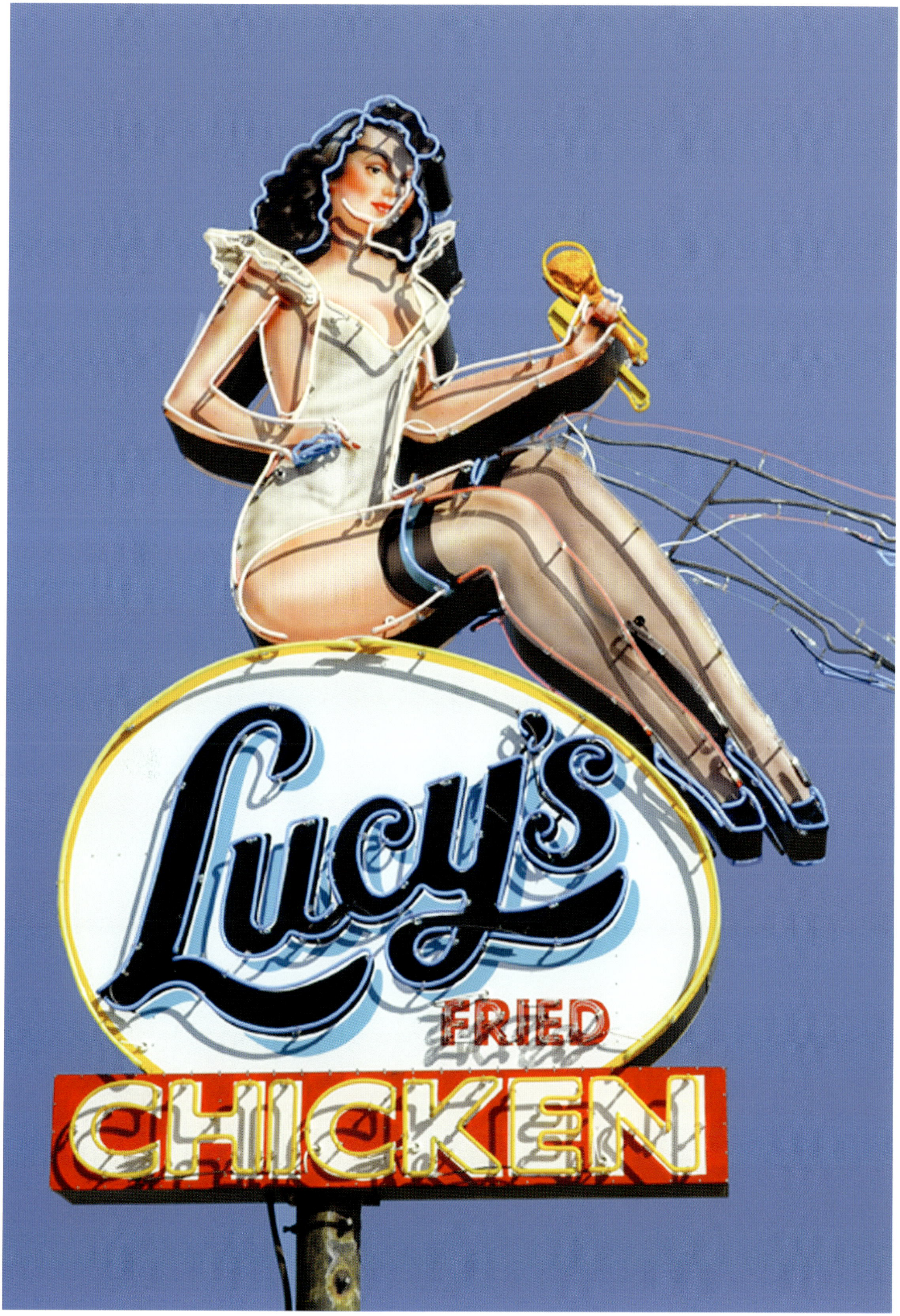

Pentagram (this spread) | Lucy's Fried Chicken | Restaurants

Assignment: Amaryllis, Inc., is a premiere floral and event design studio that was in need of a rebrand that reflects the high level of personal service, focus on detail, and unique solutions that set them apart. Whether orchestrating an intricate event or delivering a beautiful arrangement, everything they do is done with individual care and is reflected in their motto: There is nothing standard about anything we do! Amaryllis has been in business since 1989 and their identity was showing its age with the focus on a script "A" and disinterested typography that was obviously created by the quick-print shop that produced their business and note cards.

Approach: The script "A" had become such a recognizable symbol for the company, that the clients were very attached to it, and because we recognized it did have equity, we focused on keeping it part of the system. A series of hand-drawn "A" letter forms began where we explored very slight modifications to more drastic departures. The result ended up being a cleaned up version of the original, yet we were satisfied that we had been diligent in developing the best mark for the client. The rest of the identity system was designed to set itself apart from the competition with an emphasis on full flood photography, a system of labels, and a variety of paper stocks and printing methods. We sought to convey the special attention to detail and highly customized nature of Amaryllis' floral and event design by highlighting the variety of components in the stationery and sales kits presented to clients.

Results: Being a highly visual business, it's ironic that the majority of the floral and event design companies have very dull and unimaginative identities. The success of Amaryllis' new look was immediately apparent by the number of compliments not only from their potential clients, but also from their peers and competition. One visit to their website, clearly shows them to be in a league above their competitors.

Designer: Kaleena Porter | **Design Firm:** The General Design Co. | **Art Director:** Soung Wiser
Creative Directors: Soung Wiser, Scott Livingston | **Client:** Amaryllis Floral + Event Design

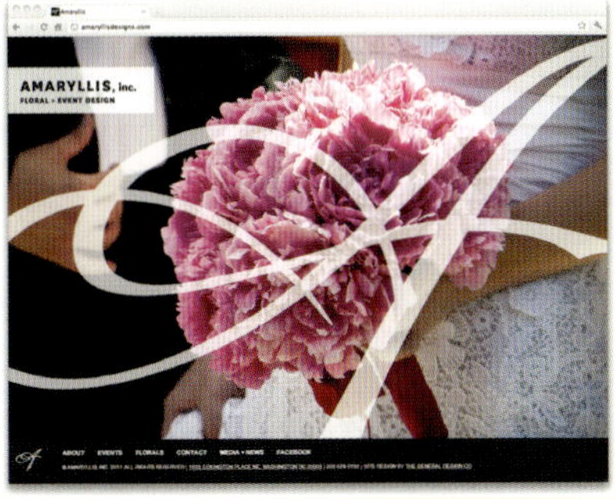

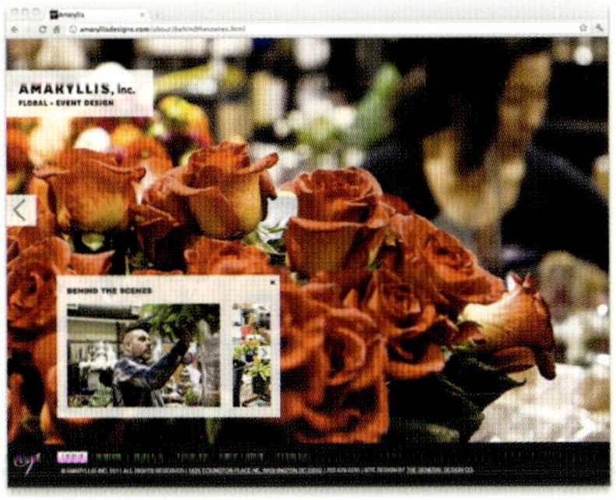

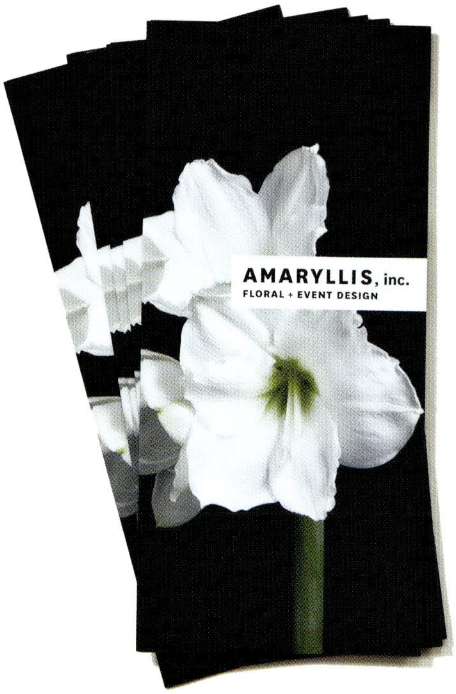
AMARYLLIS, inc.
FLORAL + EVENT DESIGN

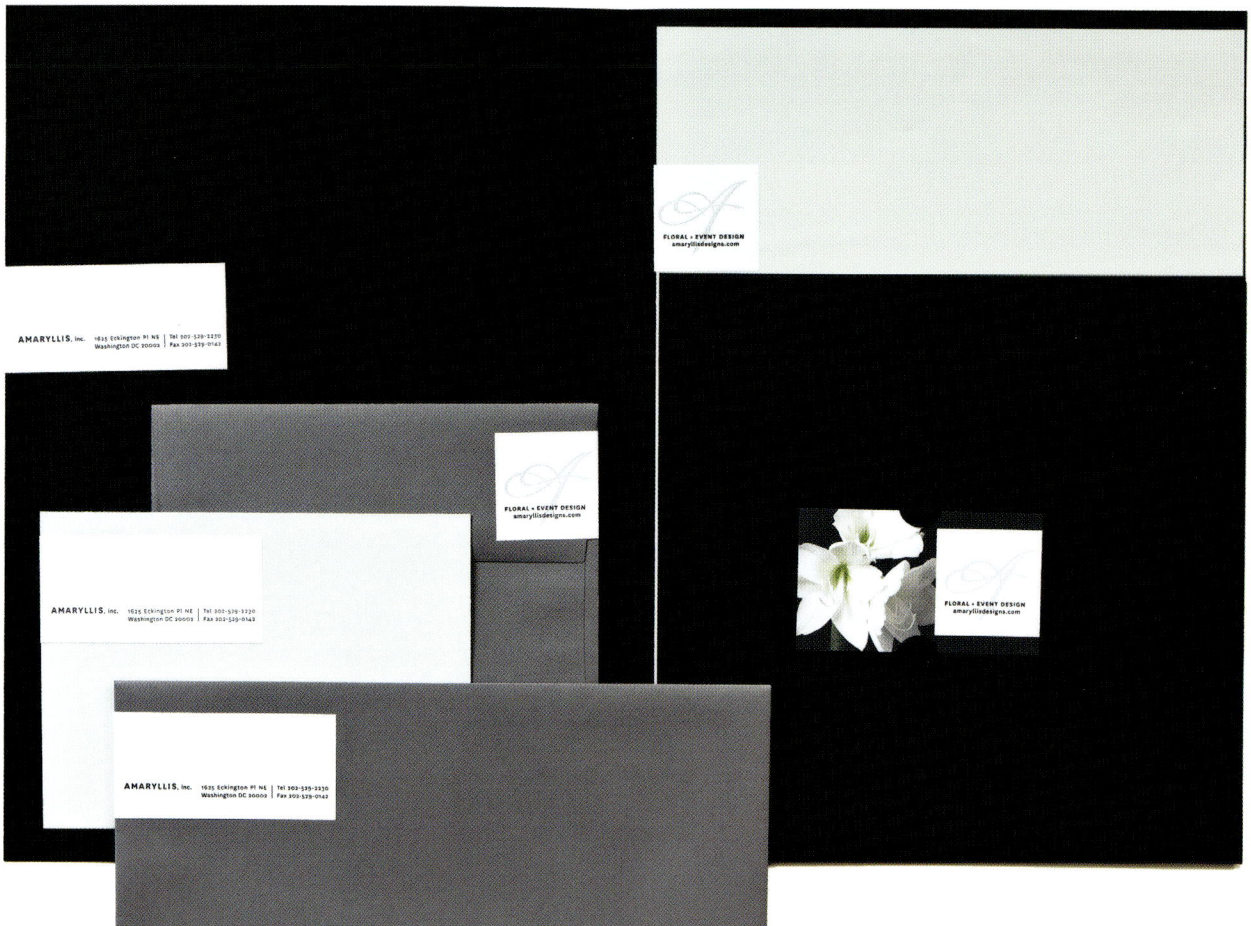

Assignment: The poster-leaflets communicate the App FImobile with its new features and the possibility to download for Apple iOS iPhone and Google Android.

Approach: The heritage of Apple and Google are nearly the same: They both started as little garage companies and then developed further with the start of mobile communication.

Results: The design with pure typography, with a focus on icons, metaphorical pictures and graphics evoke the interest of the target group. It was a must-have for design and communication enthusiasts focusing on simplicity.

Designers: Christoph Beier, Silke Nehring | **Design Firm:** beierarbeit | **Creative Director:** Christoph Beier | **Client:** Finanz Informatik

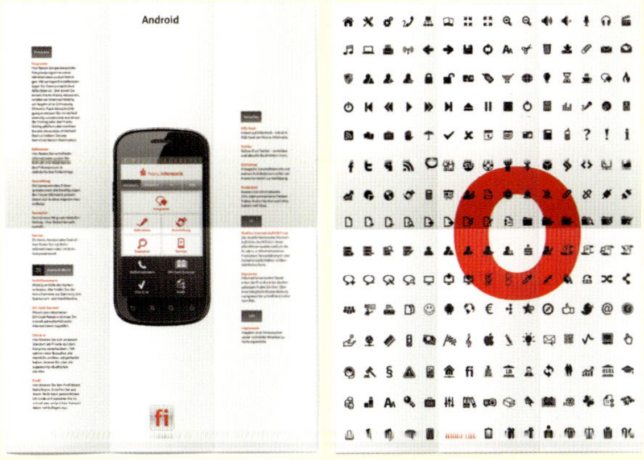

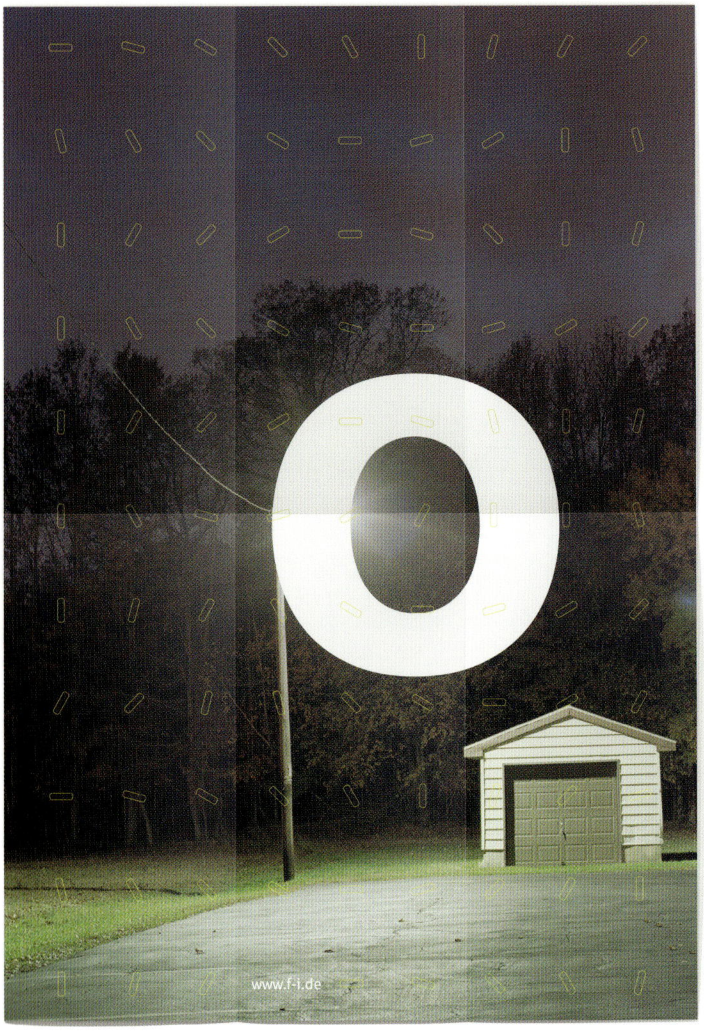
o
www.f-i.de

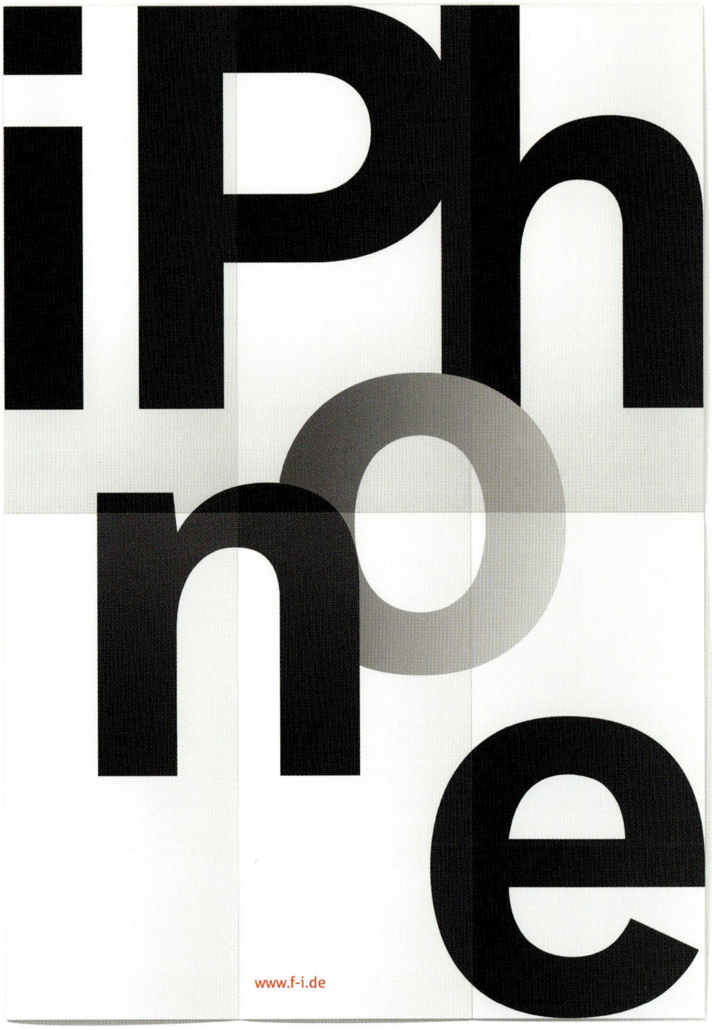
iPhone
www.f-i.de

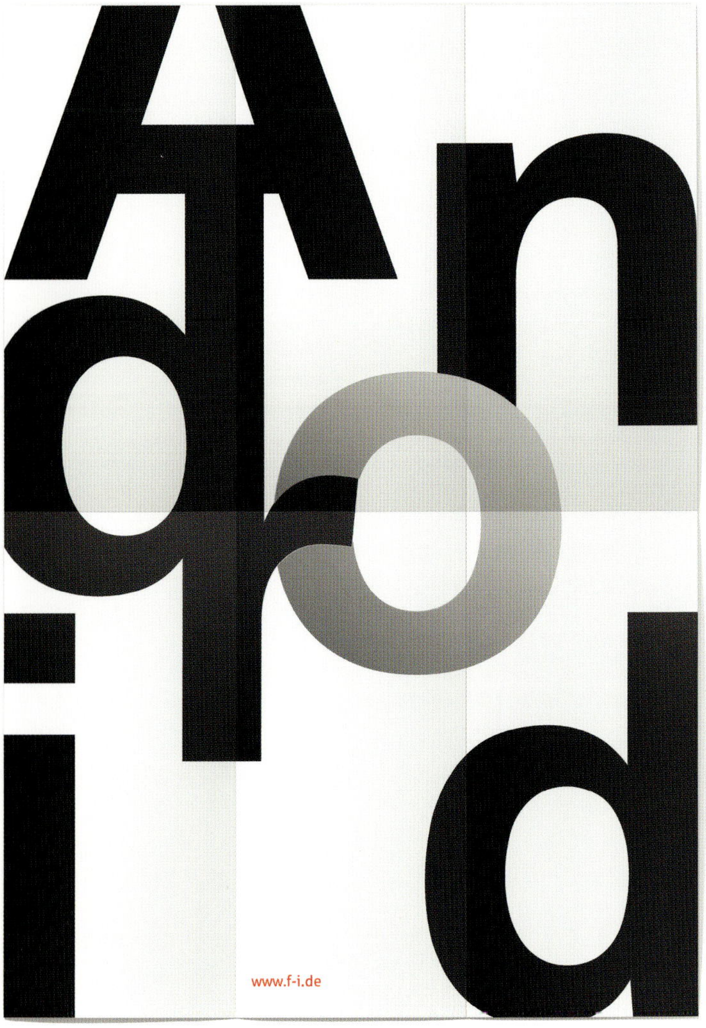
Android
www.f-i.de

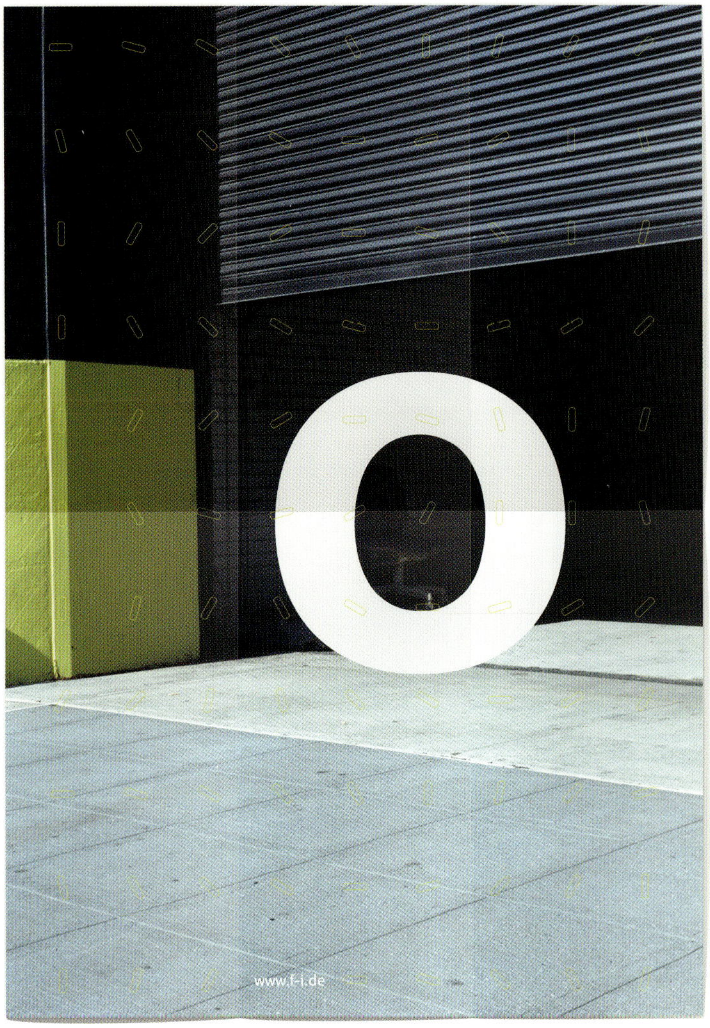
o
www.f-i.de

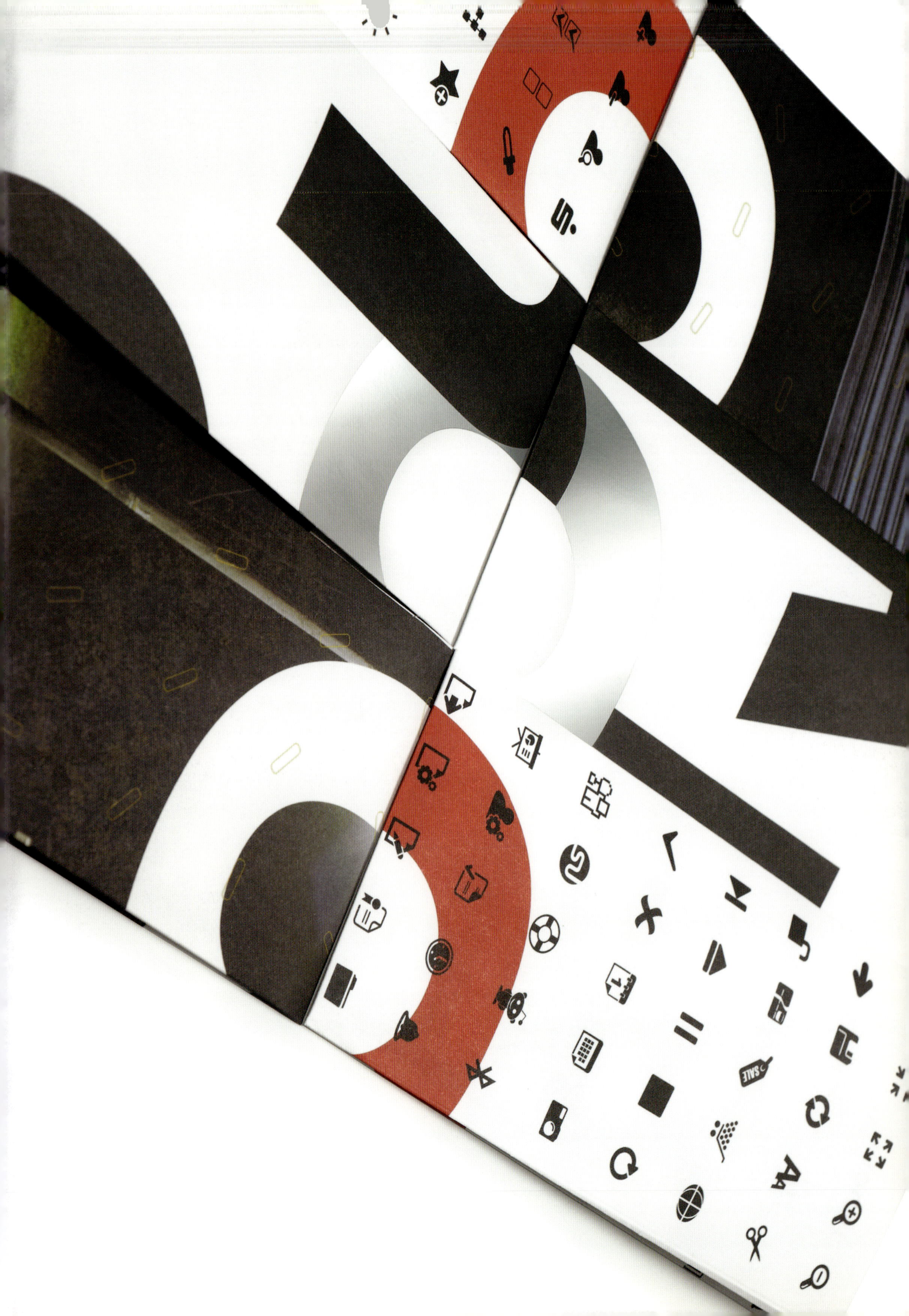
SALE

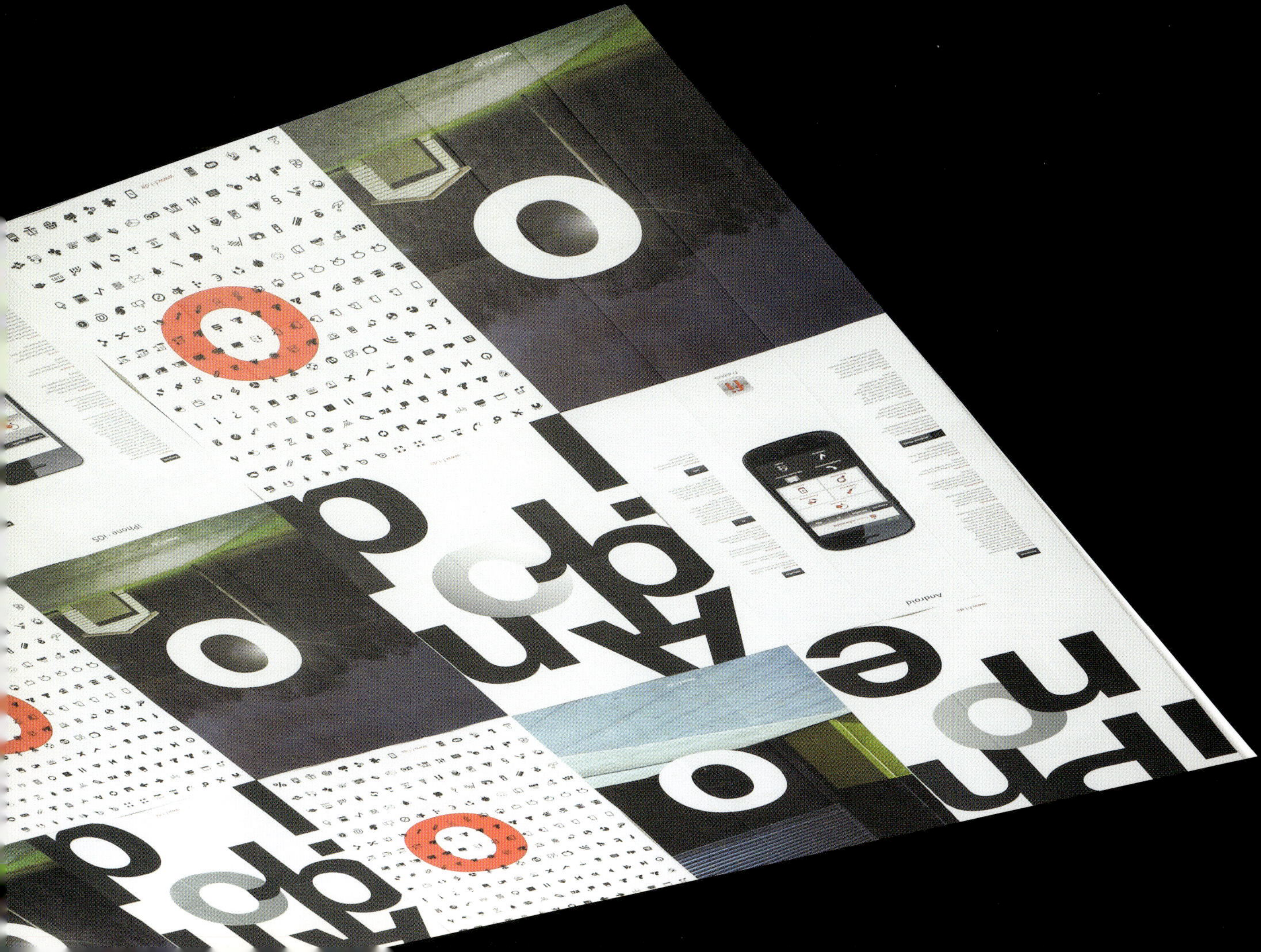
Android
iPhone iOS

Assignment: Omaha's Henry Doorly Zoo is a world-class zoo with impressive exhibits, strong conservation and education missions, and a heritage rich in tradition. The previous identity featured two lions meant to symbolize the Henry Doorly family and the bronze statue at the entrance to the Zoo. Our goal was to update the Zoo's identity to one more fitting of its prominence in the global zoo community, while still recognizing the importance of the Zoo's mission and heritage.

Approach: We developed an identity that features four quadrants: the Desert Dome, two penguins, two lions, and a leaf in hand. The Desert Dome symbolizes the world-class exhibits found at the Zoo, the lion silhouettes serve as a tribute to the heritage of the Zoo and the old logo, the penguins symbolize the education mission by showing a parent penguin interacting with and nourishing a baby penguin, and the leaf in hand symbolizes the conservation mission. Penguins are the most popular animals at the Zoo, and the aquarium is the largest aquarium within a zoo in the United States. The leaf represents world conservation efforts, specifically, plant species brought back from near extinction by zoo botanists. Vibrant colors contrasted against a black-and-white type block create a modern, yet timeless feeling.

Results: The identity was embraced by leadership at the Zoo, as well as by the community, and led to new environmental design and an ongoing advertising campaign, and an overall update of all applications throughout the Zoo. The new identity has received numerous industry awards.

Design Firm: Webster | **Art Director:** Sean Heisler | **Creative Director:** Dave Webster | **Client:** Omaha's Henry Doorly Zoo

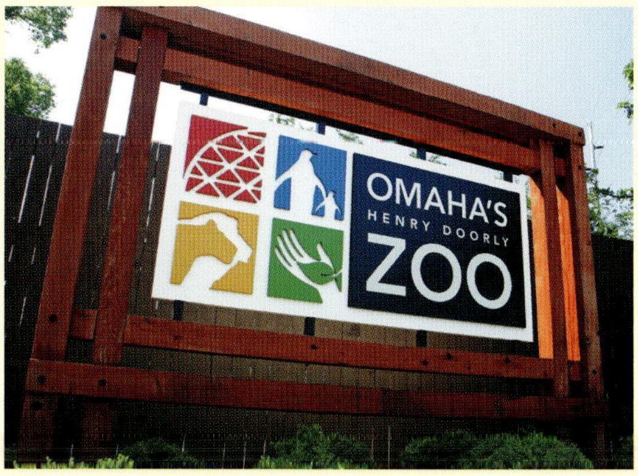

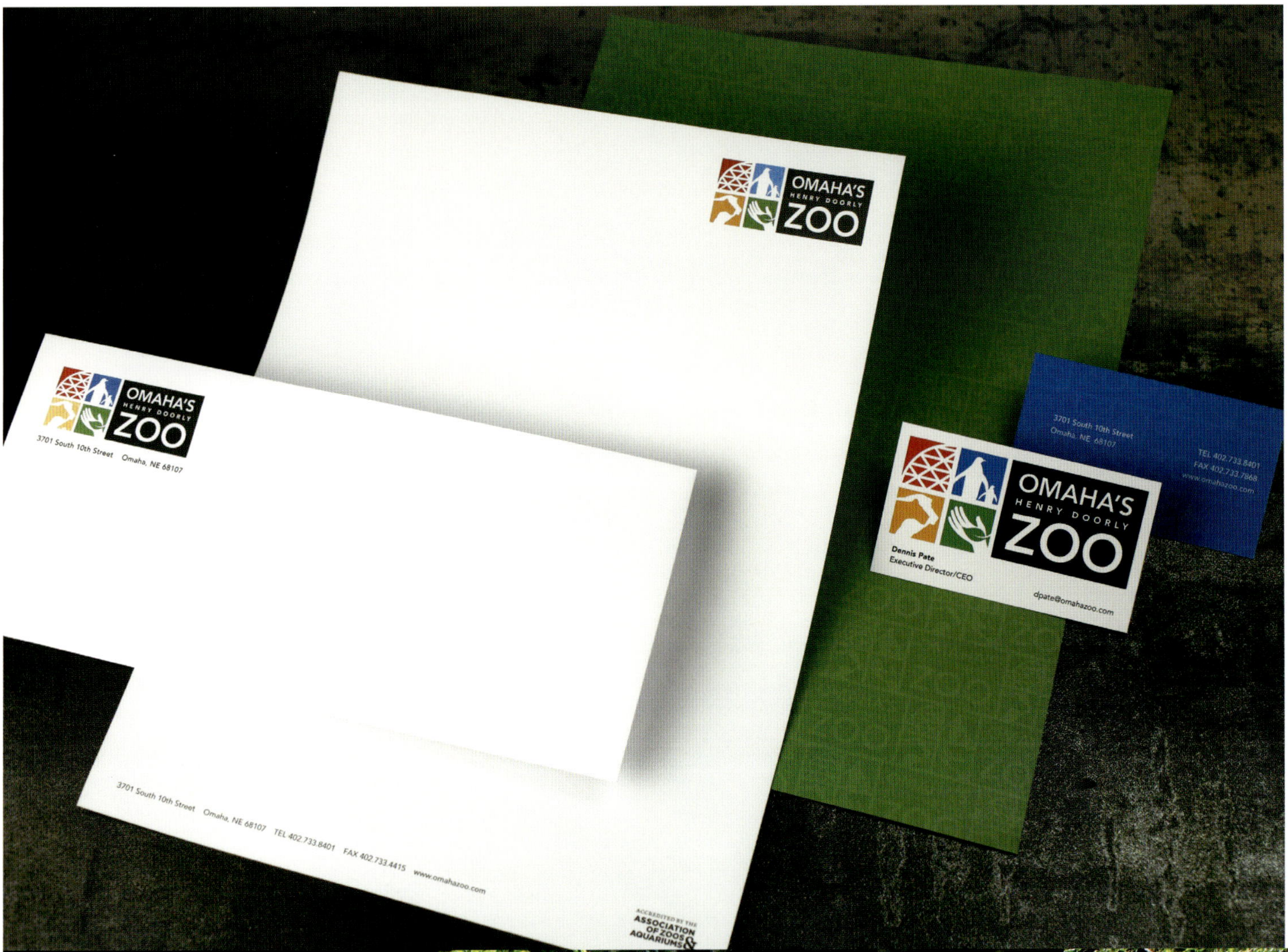
OMAHA'S
HENRY DOORLY
ZOO
3701 South 10th Street Omaha, NE 68107
3701 South 10th Street Omaha, NE 68107 TEL 402.733.8401 FAX 402.733.4415 www.omahazoo.com
ACCREDITED BY THE ASSOCIATION OF ZOOS & AQUARIUMS
Dennis Pate
Executive Director/CEO
dpate@omahazoo.com
3701 South 10th Street
Omaha, NE 68107
TEL 402.733.8401
FAX 402.733.7868
www.omahazoo.com

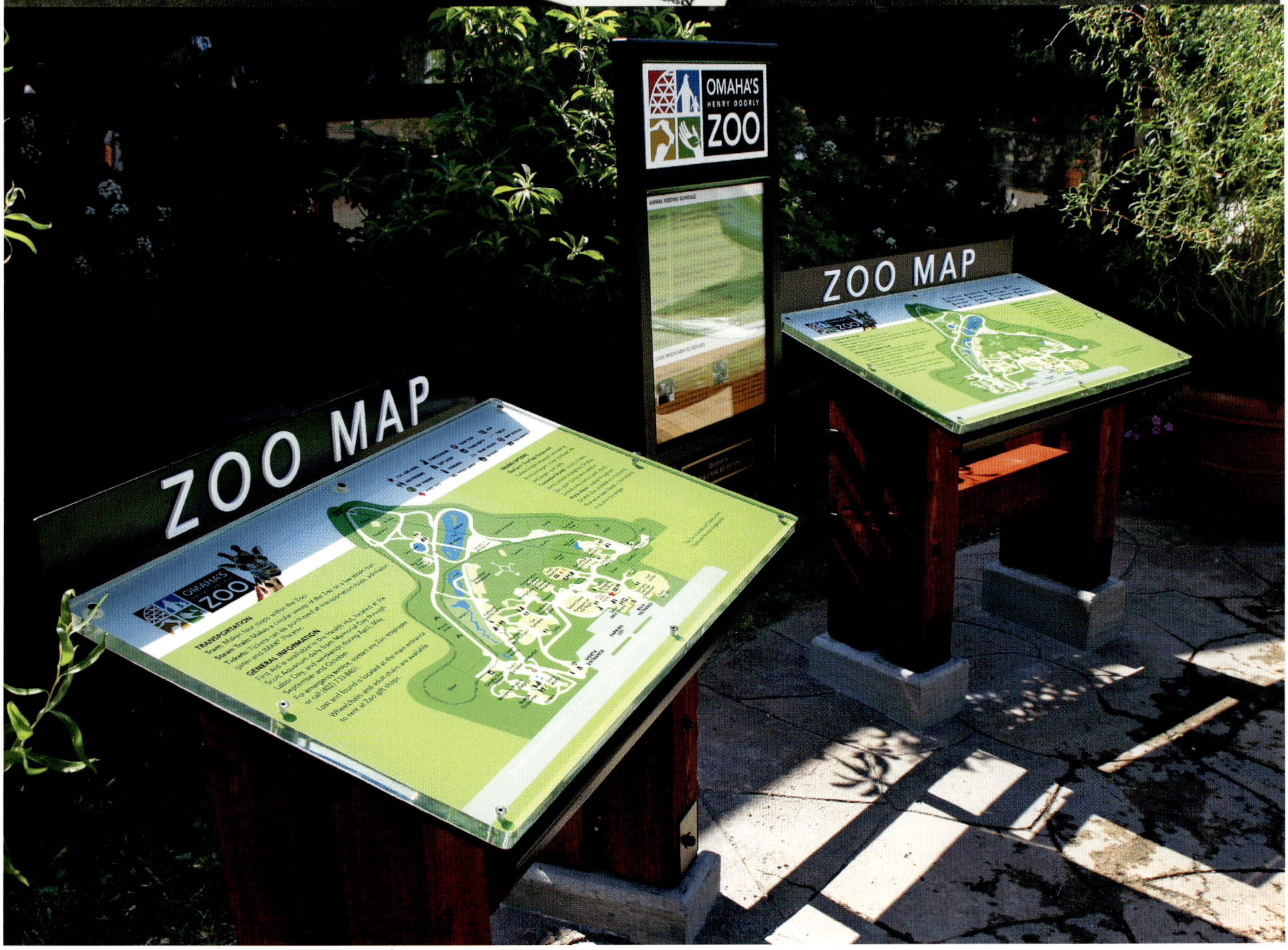
OMAHA'S
HENRY DOORLY
ZOO
ZOO MAP
ZOO MAP

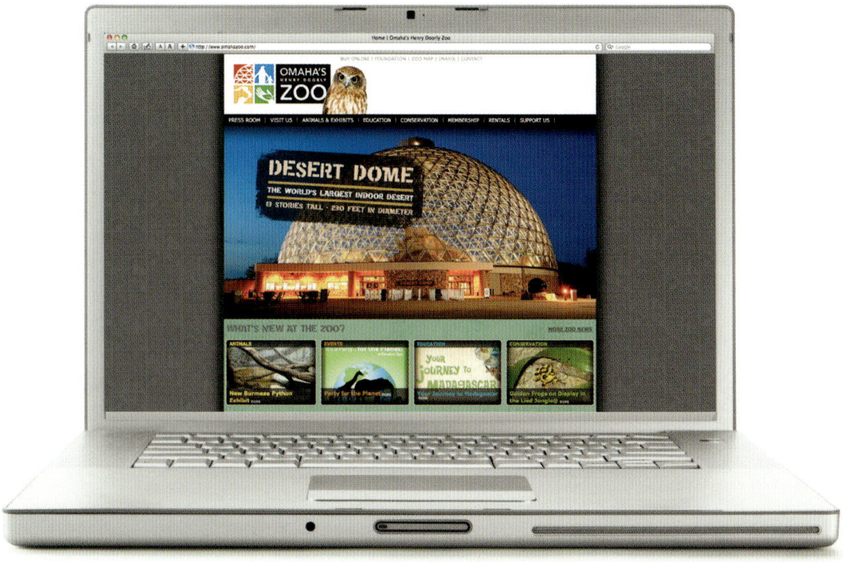
OMAHA'S
HENRY DOORLY
ZOO
PRESS ROOM | VISIT US | ANIMALS & EXHIBITS | EDUCATION | CONSERVATION | MEMBERSHIP | RENTALS | SUPPORT US
DESERT DOME
THE WORLD'S LARGEST INDOOR DESERT
13 STORIES TALL · 230 FEET IN DIAMETER
WHAT'S NEW AT THE ZOO?
New Burmese Python Exhibit
Party for the Planet
Your Journey to Madagascar
Golden Frogs on Display in the Lied Jungle

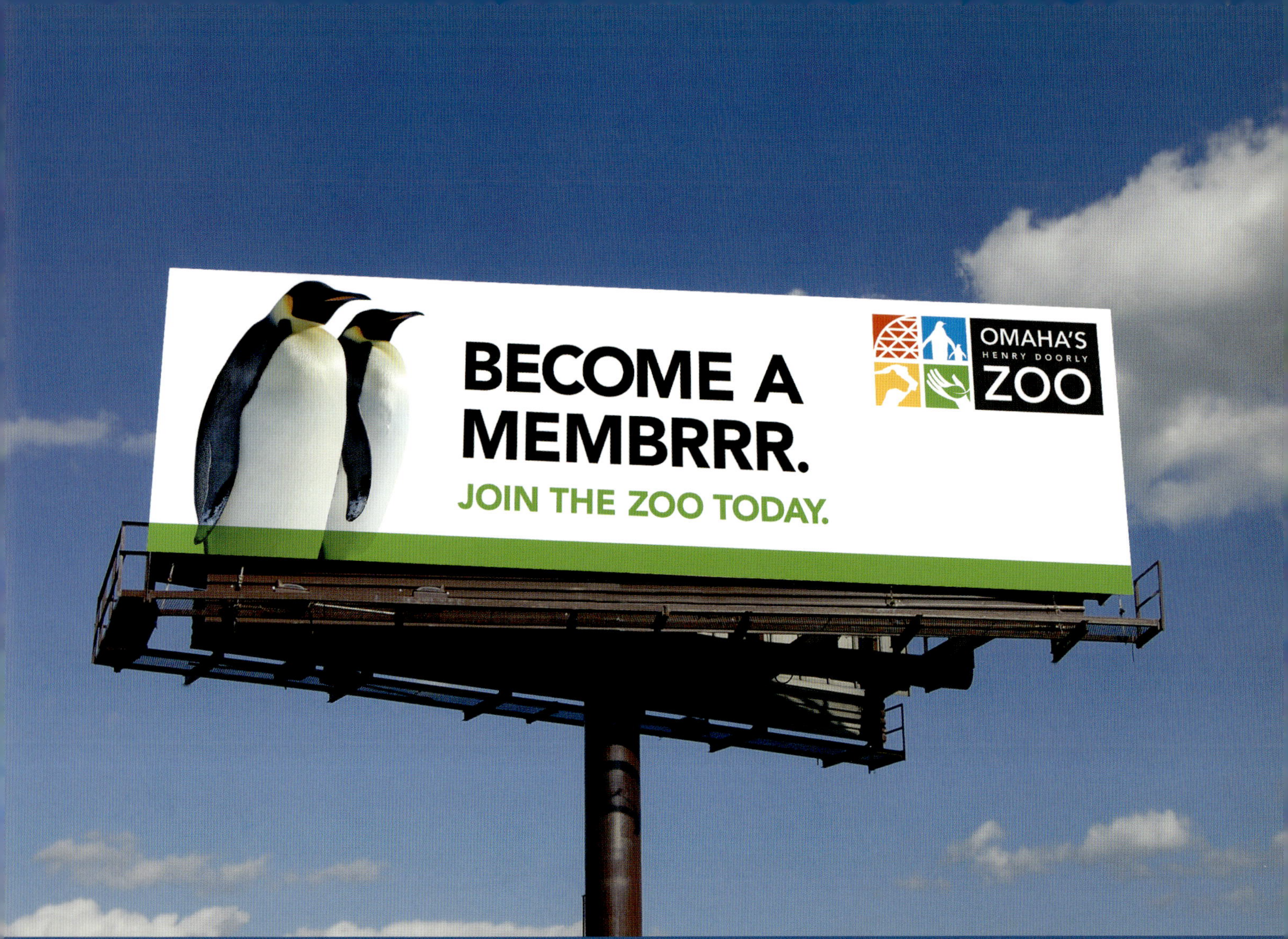
BECOME A MEMBRRR.
JOIN THE ZOO TODAY.
OMAHA'S HENRY DOORLY ZOO

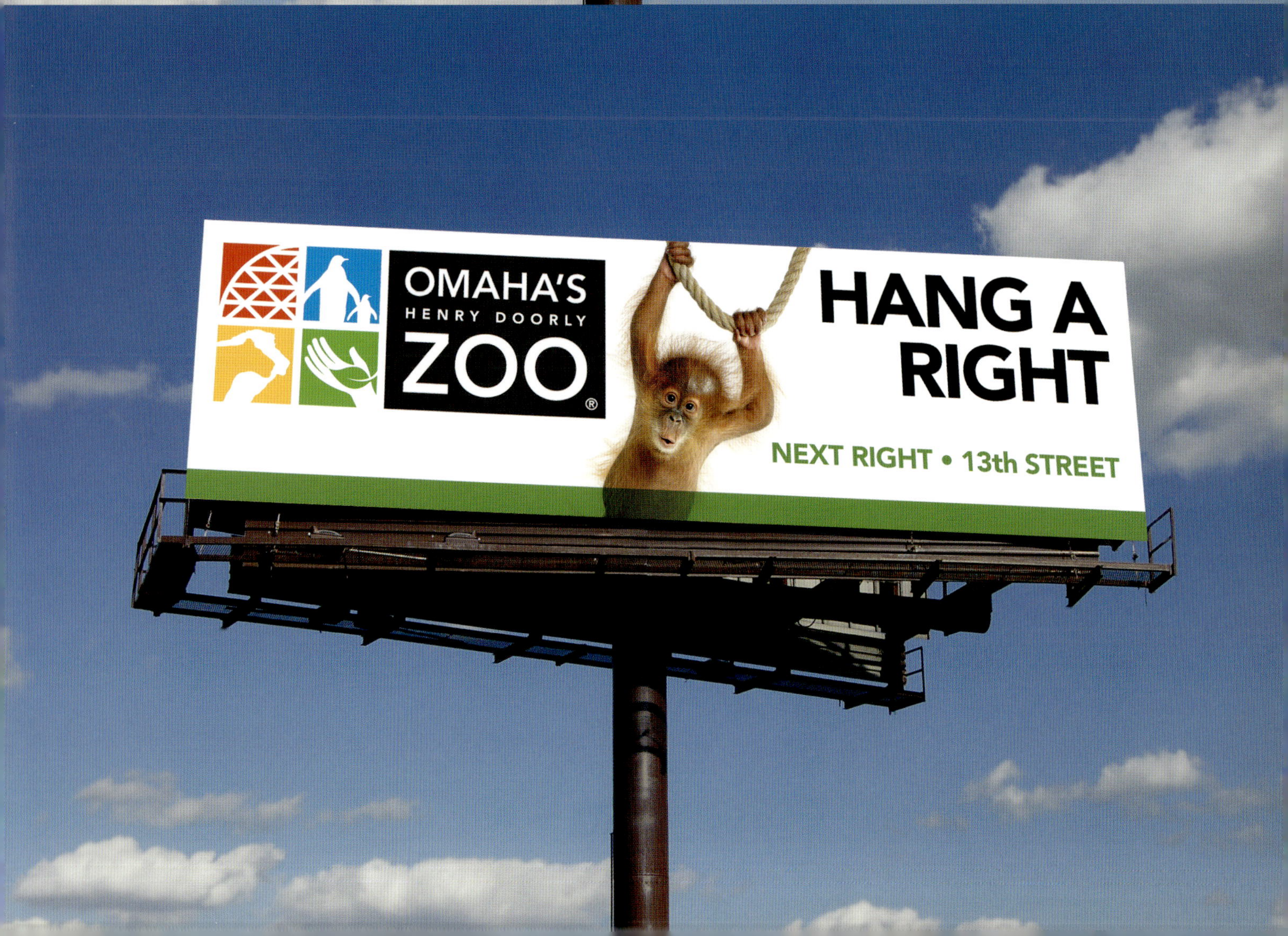
OMAHA'S HENRY DOORLY ZOO
HANG A RIGHT
NEXT RIGHT • 13th STREET

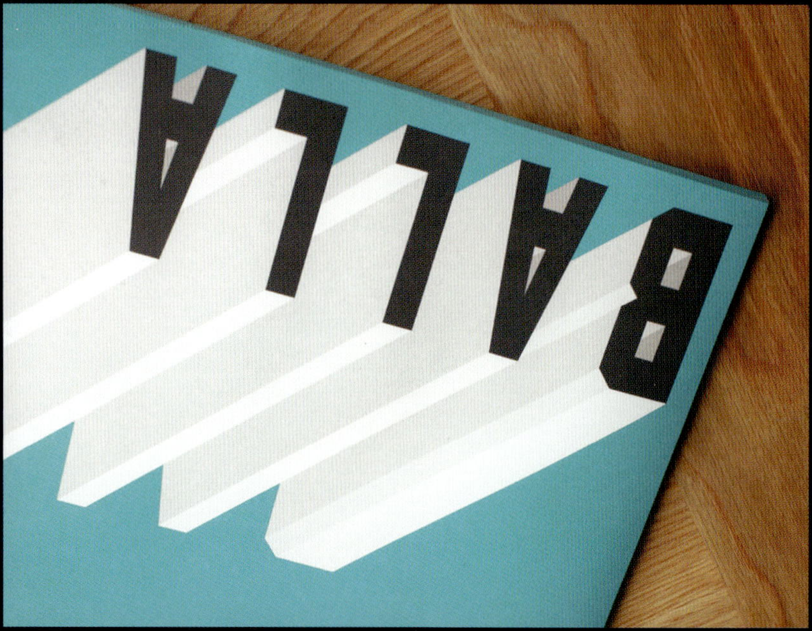
BALLA

Major Taylor Cycling Accessories

Artmusic Australia

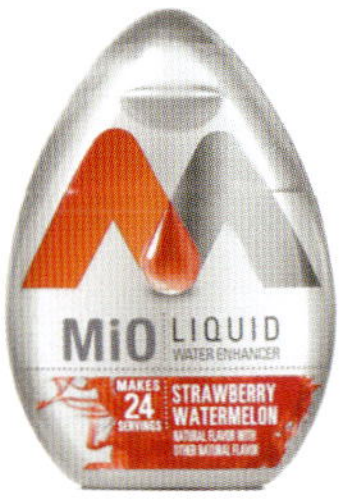

Kraft Foods

Float Water Therapy

Broken Hill City Council

Brewery Ommegang

Procter & Gamble

City of Lakes Nordic Ski Foundation

Graze Market

Marcelo Aguiar

Winners Directory

PLATINUM

Alt Group www.altgroup.net
16 Mackelvie Street
Grey Lynn, Auckland 1021,
New Zealand
Tel 64 9 3603910

Cue designcue.com
520 Nicollet Mall, Suite 500
Minneapolis, MN 55402, United States
Tel 612-465-0030

Firewood Inc.
821 Sansome Street
San Francisco, CA 94111
Tel 415-391-8800

Pentagram www.pentagram.com
1508 West 5th Street
Austin, Texas 78703, United States
Tel 512-476-3076 | Fax 512-476-5725

Peopledesign peopledesign.com
648 Monroe NW, Suite 212
Grand Rapids, MI 49503, United States
Tel 616-459-4444

STUDIO INTERNATIONAL
www.studio-international.com
Buconjiceva 43
10 000 Zagreb, Croatia
Tel 3851 3760 171

The General Design Co.
www.generaldesignco.com
1624 Q St. NW
Washington DC 20009, United States
Tel 202-640-1842

WAX www.wax.ca
320 333 24th Ave. SW
Calgary AB T2S 3E6, Canada
Tel 403-262-9323

GOLD

Ameba Design www.amebadesign.com
Unit 402, China Aerospace Centre
143 Hoi Bun Road
Kwun Tong, Kowloon Hong Kong
Tel 852-2389-6981 | Fax 852-2763-9800

AMPRO DESIGN CONSULTANTS www.ampro.ro
Banat Street 19, District 1
Regina Elisabeta 44, scara 2, et 1, ap 12, District 5
Bucharest 10933, Romania
Tel 0040 213121046 | Fax 0040 213121031

ANIMA DESIGN STUDIO
Olmedo OE5-56 y Benalcázar, Dep. 4 Quito
Pinchincha, Ecuador
Tel (593-2) 295 6625

Bailey Lauerman
1248 O Street, Suite 900
Lincoln, NE 68508, United States
Tel 402-475-2800

beierarbeit GmbH http://beierarbeit.de
Kiskerstrasse 4
33615 Bielefeld, Westfalen, Germany
Tel +49 521 7871030 | Fax +49 521 97799446

Beveridge Seay, Inc.
2000 P Street NW, Suite 700
Washington DC 20036, United States
Tel 202-822-3800

CH Design
30 Danforth Street
Portland, ME 04101
207-772-9801

Claus Koch GmbH
An der Alster 1
Hamburg 20099, Germany
Tel 0049 40 44189691

Concrete Design Communications
www.concrete.ca
2 Silver Avenue, 2nd floor
Toronto, Ontario M6R 3A2, Canada
Tel 416-534-9960 | Fax 416-534-2184

Concussion LLP
707 W Vickery Blvd., Suite 103
Fort Worth, TX 76104, United States
Tel 817-336-6824

Decker Design
14 West 23rd Street, 3rd Floor
New York, NY 10010, United States
Tel 212-633-8588

DNA Design dna.co.nz/
Level 2, 262 Thorndon Quay
PO Box 3056
Thorndon, Wellington 6140, New Zealand
Tel +64 (0)4 499 0828 | Fax +64 (0)4 499 0888

Duffy & Partners www.duffy.com
710 South 2nd St., Suite 602
Minneapolis, MN 55401
Phone 612-548-2333
Fax 612-548-2334

Ellen Bruss Design
2500 Walnut St., No. 401
Denver, CO 80205, United States
Tel 303-830-8323

El Paso, Galeria de Comunicacion
www.elpasocomunicacion.com
Sagunto, 13
28010 Madrid, Spain
Tel 34 91 594 2248 | Fax 34 91 447 8016

Estúdio Sem Dublê semduble.com
Rua Senador Xavier da Silva, 488, sala 1106B,
Centro Cívico
Curitiba, Paraná
80530980
Brazil
55-41-32038927

Foreign Policy Design Group
VBOX 888426
Singapore 919191, Singapore
Tel 65.8126894

Frost* Design frostdesign.com.au
1/15 Foster Street,
Surry Hills, NSW 2010
Sydney, Australia
+61 2 9280 4233

Gee + Chung Design
www.geechungdesign.com
38 Bryant Street, Suite 100
San Francisco, CA 94105, United States
Tel 415-543-1192

Graphics & Designing Inc.
G&D Alchemic House
3-3-1 Shirokanedai, Minato-ku
Tokyo 108-0071, Japan
Tel +81 33 4490 651

Higher
Golubeva st 22-1, apt. 434
Minsk 220116, Belarus
Tel 3.75173E+11

Ivity Brand Corp. www.ivity-corp.com
Rua D. Luis 1, no 19, 30
1200-149 Lisboa Portugal
Tel +351 21 396 7142

karacters design group / DDB Canada
www.karacters.com
1600-777 Hornby Street
Vancouver, BC V6Z 2T3, Canada
Tel 604-640-4327 | Fax 604-608-4452

Landor Associates landor.com
1001 Front Street
San Francisco, CA 94111, United States
Tel 415-365-3713

Landor Associates Sydney landor.com/Sydney
11/15 Blue Street
North Sydney NSW 2060, Australia
Tel (02) 8908 8700

Leynivopnid leynivopnid.is
Solvallagata 66
+354 840 0220
Reykjavik 101, Iceland

Ig2boutique Ig2boutique.com
3575, boul. St. Laurent, Bureau 900
Montréal (Québec) H2X 2T7, Canada
Tel 514-281-8901

Lichtwitz Leinfellner visuelle Kultur KG
www.lichtwitz-leinfellner.com
Mariahilfer Strasse 101/3/55
1060 Vienna, Austria
Tel +43-1-236 7 632 | Fax +43-1-595-272727

Mark Oliver, Inc. markoliverinc.com
1984 Old Mission Drive, Suite A-15
Solvang, CA 93463, United States
Tel 805-686-5166

Mindsalt www.mindsalt.net
1205 E Washington Street, Suite 108
Louisville, KY 40206, United States
Tel 502-562-2338

Poulin + Morris Inc. poulinmorris.com
46 White Street, 2nd Floor
New York, NY 10013, United States
Tel 212-675-1332

RBMM rbmm.com
7007 Twin Hills, Suite 200
Dallas, TX 75231-5184, United States
Tel 214-987-6500 | Fax 214-987-3662

Shepherd www.shepherdagency.com
500 Bishopgate Lane
Jacksonville, FL 32204, United States
Tel 904-359-0981

Simon & Goetz Design GmbH & Co. KG
www.simongoetz.de
Bleichstrasse 64-66
60313 Frankfurt am Main, Germany
Tel +49 (0) 69 968855-0 | Fax +49 (0) 69 968855-44

Skillet Design and Marketing skilletcreative.com
One Main Street
Union Station, South Pie
Burlington, VT 05401
802-735-0727

SVIDesign www.svidesign.com
124 Westbourne Studios
242 Acklam Road
London W10 5JJ, United Kingdom
Tel +44 (0)20 7524 7808

The White Room Inc. Design/Art Direction
www.thewhiteroom.ca
191 First Avenue
Toronto, ON M4M 1X3, Canada
Tel 416-901-7736

TODA toda.com
20 Jay Street, Suite 828
Brooklyn, NY 11201, United States
Tel 718-797-2302 | Fax 718-797-2307

TOKY Branding + Design
3001 Locust St.
St. Louis, MO 63103, United States
Tel 314-534-2000

TunnelBravo www.tunnelbravo.com
225 East Germann, Suite 260
Gilbert, AZ 85297, United States
Tel 480-649-1400 | Fax 480-649-1400

Webster Design Associates
www.websterdesign.com
5060 Dodge Street, Suite 2000
Omaha, NE 68132, United States
Tel 402-551-0503

DESIGNERS

DESIGN FIRMS

ART DIRECTORS

CREATIVE DIRECTORS

PHOTOGRAPHERS

ILLUSTRATORS

CLIENTS

COPYWRITERS

Graphis Titles

Poster Annual 2013

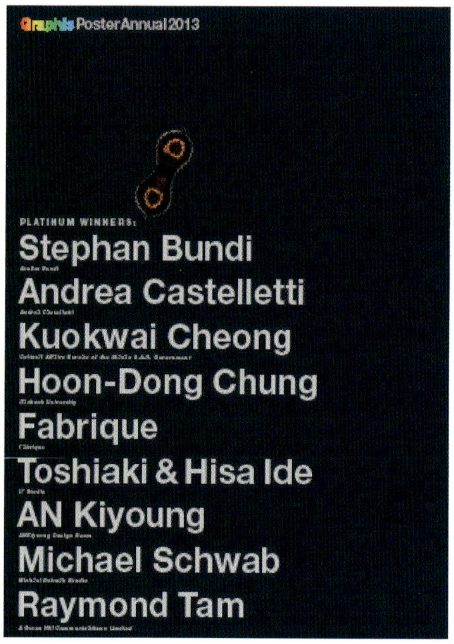

2013
Hardcover: 240 pages
200-plus color illustrations
Trim: 8.5 x 11.75"
ISBN: 1-931241-29-8
US $120

Graphis Poster 2013 is the definitive showcase of the 100 best Posters of the year chosen from numerous international entries. The collection features 9 Platinum and 91 Gold award-winning Posters from Italy, South Africa, Switzerland, Korea, The Netherlands, Japan and the United States, amongst many others. Graphis also features an interview with **Rick Valicenti**, the founder and Design Director of Thirst in Chicago — a firm devoted to "art, function and real human presence."

Advertising Annual 2013

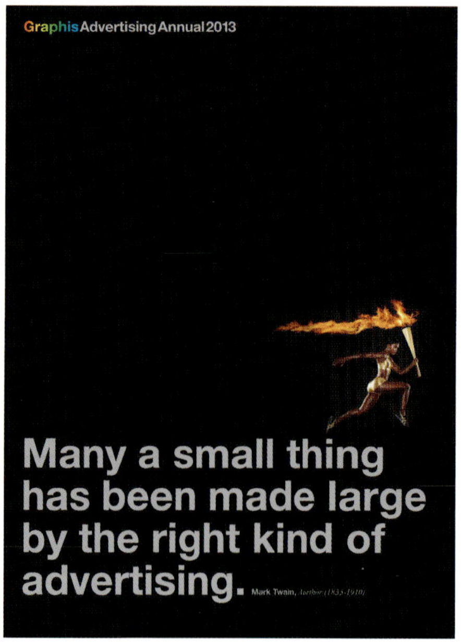

2013
Hardcover: 256 pages
200-plus color images
Trim: 7 x 11 3/4"
ISBN: 1-932026-79-5
US $120

Graphis Advertising 2013 presents some of the top campaigns of the year selected from hundreds of entries. Featured are seasoned works from accomplished advertising agencies, such as **Goodby, Silverstein & Partners**, **Bailey Lauerman**, **BVK**, **DeVito/Verdi**, **HOOK**, and **Saatchi & Saatchi**. Each spread presents the work with a case study description written by each agency. These campaigns provide insight into the agency's creative process and how they met the needs of their clients.

Design Annual 2013

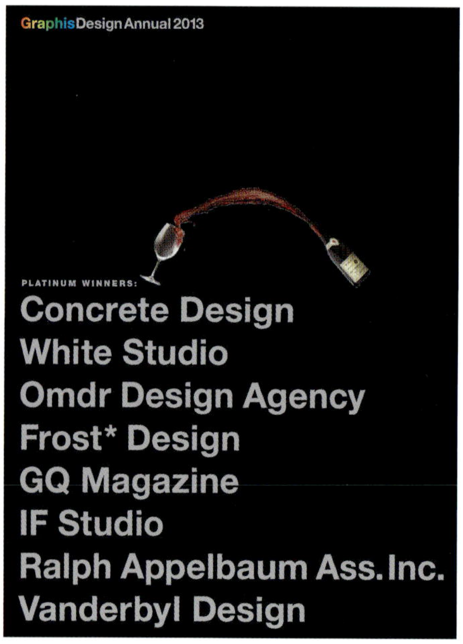

2013
Hardcover: 256 pages
200-plus color images
Trim: 8.5 x 11.75"
ISBN: 1-932026-77-1
US $120

Graphis Design 2013 features the most compelling design work of the year selected from hundreds of international entries. This volume includes Platinum award – winning entries from **Alt Group**, **GQ Magazine**, **Turner Duckworth**, **Strømme Throndsen Design** and **White Studio**. All published entries are presented on a spread with a case study description written by each designer or design firm.

Branding 6

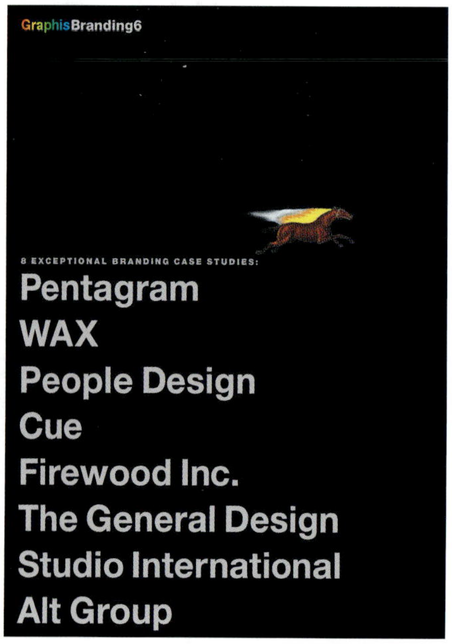

2013
Hardcover: 256 pages
200-plus color images
Trim: 8.5 x 11.75"
ISBN: 1-932026-78-8
US $120

This book presents interviews, company profiles and visual histories of some of the biggest names in design and retail today, including: Q&A with **Pentagram**, **WAX**, **People design**, **Cue**, **Firewood**, **The General Design Co.**, **Studio International**, and **Alt Group**. All that, plus hundreds of images from the year's Graphis Gold Award-winning branding campaigns. This is a must-have for anyone interested in successful, creative branding – designers, businesses, students and fans alike.

Photography Annual 2013

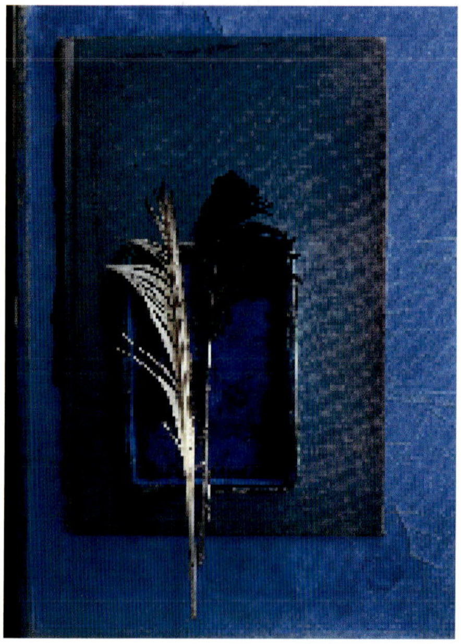

2013
Hardcover: 256 pages
200-plus color images
Trim: 8.5 x 11.75"
ISBN:1-931241-80-1
US $120

Photography2013 is a moving collection of the years best photographs. Shot by some of the world's most respected photographers and selected from an international pool of entries, these beautifully reproduced images are organized by category for easy referencing. This year's book includes an interview with photographer **Bill Diadato**, discussing his background and the inspiration behind his work.

Masters of the 20th Century

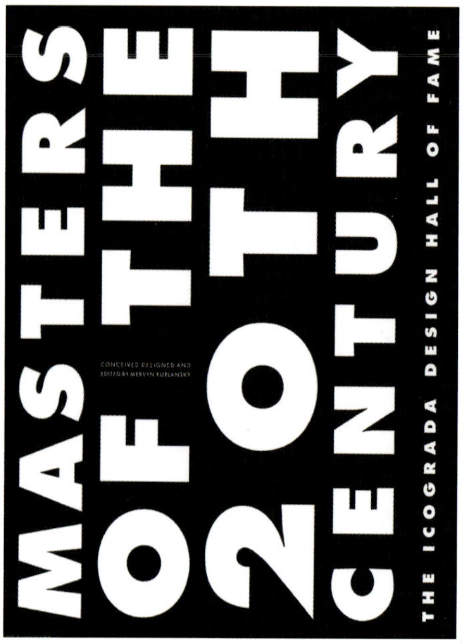

2012
Hardcover: 360 pages
200-plus color illustrations
Trim: 10 x 12"
ISBN: 1-888001-85-2
US $70

This is a huge volume that features the work and biographies of more than 100 top designers worldwide. Designed and edited by **Mervyn Kurlansky**, with distinct profiles of **Pierre Bernard**, **Wolfgang Weingart** and many others. A testament to exceptional talents and proof that they'll be remembered for generations to come, this book comes complete with a companion CD-ROM containing hundreds of additional images. Forewards by **Steven Heller** and **Marion Wesel-Henrion**.

Available at www.graphis.com